THE
WRONG
REALITY

THE WRONG REALITY

The Essential Truth
About Ourselves and Our World

By John Bapty Oates

The Wrong Reality: The Essential Truth About Ourselves and Our World
ISBN-10: 0-9551503-2-9
ISBN-13: 978-0-9551503-2-6
Published by CheckPoint Press

CHECKPOINT PRESS, DOOAGH, ACHILL ISLAND, CO. MAYO,
REPUBLIC OF IRELAND
TEL: 098 43779
EMAIL: EDITOR@CHECKPOINTPRESS.COM

WEBSITE: WWW.CHECKPOINTPRESS.COM

Text layout and cover design by CheckPoint Press

This book is listed in the National Library UK, and the US Library of Congress

A Special Acknowledgement

A very special thanks goes to my wife
Marguerite, for her loving care and
support throughout these many years
of writing, sustaining a precious and
everlasting bond between us

About the Author

John Bapty Oates began free and independent thinking at age 4 in 1929, essentially questioning why the human race, being capable of high intelligence, did not conduct itself or its affairs intelligently.

He has been conditioned to the minimum by reading and formal education; now concluding that this is no disadvantage—but is helpful to the discovery of our fundamental truth, or humantruth as he calls it.

He maintains a website; www.humantruth.org

ABOUT THE BOOK

This challenging book examines the state of the human mind and our world today, carrying essential thought further than ever before and making the profound discovery that what we regard as 'our mind' is in effect two minds; the conscious and the postconscious ('unconscious' describes a *state* of mind).

The brain mutation that made us human gave our existing conscious mind much increased capacity yet allowed it to remain motivated chiefly by instinct.

As a result the human race, despite high intelligence, has mainly applied itself to pursuing and developing the unintelligent competitive drives of instinct; responding to market forces - political and other pressures - continually causing man's inhumanity to man.

But mutation provided a large surplus mental capacity that was sidelined and ignored by the conscious. This uncommitted, powerful reasoning capability formed itself into the postconscious mind; the source of conscience - with freedom and independence to follow its own unconstrained course.

The function of a free conglomeration of neurons, axons, dendrites, synapses etc., can only be the ultimate discovery of truth. No other function makes sense. Clearly then, the objective of our chief faculty, the postconscious, is truth, and such an intelligent species as ourselves needs to be guided by that truth (ie to be supraconscious), recognising it as the basis of complete agreement and cooperation, to be realised in a new world community.

Instead, guided by instinct, we have subjected ourselves to the Machine and its amoral Wrong Reality, with some good but also many immoral, crazy, painful and devastating consequences.

This book tells the story of our tragic march towards Machine-based societies and points the way to surely the only enduring solution; our collective advancement to supraconsciousness, and to a truly humane, or 'humantrue' society.

THE WRONG REALITY

FOREWORD

Books are generally part of the norm. As a rule they are written by authors who occupy a certain place in the 'real' world. The writing is designed to interest or entertain the public. People have developed certain expectations of books; they like those which offer to help and strengthen the self, to make it more contented and successful in the world, to reconcile the existing self to its present reality. Publishers are aware of those expectations and usually publish only those books that promise to interest and entertain a wide enough public as to bring in a profit. That is the present 'way of the world'. This book envisages a very much better world, and a very different, humantrue way of life.

I think it is fair to say as a rule that books do not greatly change their readers. Most of us enjoy reading books that broadly harmonise with our own outlook, even though they may present a world different from ours in detail. We do study some books dealing with certain special subjects for the sake of the facts or insights they contain, which we in turn wish to learn. We read, with detached interest, views and opinions which go to one extreme on our left so-to-speak, and another extreme to our right; while we ourselves keep treading our old familiar middle path, little changed. In other words, we regard books as adjuncts of ourselves, or as objects that are subject to our whim, to be accepted or rejected, liked or disliked, noticed or unnoticed by us, at will.

We don't expect a book to be more closely representative of us than our own selves, showing that there is another, truer, potential self that we do not yet recognise. We don't expect a book to penetrate further into ourselves than we wish; to question our cherished beliefs; to undermine our defences and to move us well away from our old familiar path. This book does, or aims to do, all these things.

I am approaching you not as you presently are but as you truly, potentially are, and hope that you will approach my efforts not determined to maintain your present self, but willing to seek and find your true self. I hope you will not let your present self turn you away from this book, but that you will allow the book to challenge your 'higher' mind; that you will listen to your own thoughts that then emerge.

Should you choose to ignore these words, that choice will be made by your conscious self, but it is likely that your 'higher' mind, i.e. your postconscious, will take them in despite that self. The function of the postconscious is truth. Its true conclusions are available to consciousness, but not its deepest reasoning that goes to form those true conclusions. Since it is the same, or potentially the same mind in everybody, any well-developed postconscious that reveals its truth shall be revealing the actual or potential truth within any other postconscious. That is what this book is trying to do. It goes against convention, but present convention is false. Above all else we need human-truth.

J.B.O.

HISTORY - writing of the first edition of this book was completed in 1990 against the background concerns of that time. World events have moved on, of course, and this new 2008 edition reflects some of the changes. Nuclear power was abandoned and Capitalist/Communist confrontation has largely disappeared, mainly due to public protest. Awareness of the global warming threat has dramatically increased, as has scientific understanding of the origins of this planet and of the formation of life.

On the other hand wars have continued, despite public protest, and the old confrontation has been replaced by that between Democracy and Islam. To combat the threats of climate change it is proposed to reintroduce nuclear power.

In these and many other respects this short passage of time makes no big difference, for the characteristics of our existing wrong reality and this book's purpose to expose them, and change them, remain the same.

J.B.O. 2008

TABLE OF CONTENTS

PART I: EVOLUTION OF THINKING BEINGS

PART II: AUTOMATION OF THE HUMAN MIND

PART III: LIBERATION OF THE HUMAN MIND

PART IV: REVELATION

PART V: INTERPRETATION

PART VI: ILLUMINATION

PART VII: REALISATION OF HUMANTRUE SOCIETY

PART VIII: FURTHER ILLUMINATION

LIST OF DIAGRAMS BY CHAPTER

Chapter 2

Figure 1: The Simple Cell

Figure 2: Cellular Organism

Figure 3: Multi-cellular Organism Figure 4a:

Figure 4a: The Dawn of Consciousness

Figure 4b: Early Consciousness

Figure 4c: Average Consciousness

Figure 5: Perfected Dolphin Brain

Figure 6: Apefolk Brain

Chapter 3

Figure 7: The Human Mutation - Logical Outcome

Chapter 4

Figure 8: Present Human State - Immature Mutation

Chapter 8

Figure 9: Typical Unfulfilled Human Mind

Chapter 12

Figure 10: Ultimate Human Mutation

Chapter 13

Figure 11: The Fulfilled Human Mind

Chapter 42

Photo: Chinese Boxer Rebellion

Photo: WWI Dogfight

Photo: The Jarrow Crusade

Photo: Vladimir Lenin

Photo: Mahatma Gandhi

Photo: Mussolini & Hitler

Photo: Nazi Death Camp

Figure 11a: The Moral Guide

Under the international 'fair rules' copyright doctrine as per *The Chicago Manual of Style* 15th Ed. 4.75-4.84, gratitude is respectfully extended to all those whose writings or opinions are referenced in this work. Apologies are respectfully offered if any references have been omitted either in error or due to absent sources.

The images in Chapter 42 are courtesy of CheckPoint Press archive.

PREFACE

The objective of this book is to help in bringing about a benign, peaceful, happy - i.e. humantrue - society. This will be a worldwide society whose basic values and practices are in accord with the fundamental understanding, thinking and feeling of every individual. These values and practices will be constantly and universally upheld because they have been fully and willingly agreed. This society will ensure that the minds of its children are fully opened so that they share in this common, and true, understanding, thinking and feeling from the beginning.

In a humantrue society there will be a great sense of trust in all mankind and a feeling of total security. There will be no locking of doors to protect property. Children shall go out to play without fear. We will have the comforting knowledge that everyone in the world shares the same basic concerns. We shall be free of anxiety, because the reason for our living will be the well-being of each other.

A great feature of humantrue society will be co-operation. We shall conduct our affairs according to true reason. We shall be enabled to understand and follow our moral code, which requires that we co-operate rather than compete, and to show the utmost kindness and compassion to each other. By way of reason, co-operation ensures that the species survives with the minimum of pain, hurt and damage, either to itself or to its environment.

We shall give and share. This is the intelligent thing to do and the one way of ensuring that all people are equally provided for. A humantrue society will be unable to do otherwise, because this is a true principle, and our intelligence makes us perfectly capable of carrying the principle out.

A humantrue society will be united. Based upon intelligent agreement, we and our framework of life shall treat everybody as equal, with no artificial differences. This makes sense, because our chief faculty is our mind; the function of the intellectual mind is truth, and essential truth is one and the same for everyone. Responsibility for a humantrue society can be entrusted to no other than each and every individual. This is the only way of ensuring that society is humantrue. By dividing 'power' amongst all individuals it loses its separate influence and reduces to nothing, whereas the strength of responsibility increases with wide sharing. Life in a humantrue society will be simple. It will be entirely understandable to every responsible individual member. There will be nothing of more consequence than the gentle, loving, constructive everyday concerns of the individual. There will be general concern to put the minimum strain upon Earth. The practical processes of living will engage our minds only as far as is required to carry them out thoroughly; otherwise our intellects will flower in every possible abstract way; through music for example.

That is how life on Earth should, and could, be. It is not how human life currently is. We are, or seem to be far from achieving such a society. This is not because it is an impossible dream, but because we have not yet made the effort to break the bonds of conditioning and to realise our intellectual potential.

Without doubt we are a race of superior intelligence, yet it does not strike us that the basic practices of our society are far from intelligent. Consider some of these practices and our consequent behaviour (fully explored in Part IV.) Our subjection to a competitive money economy for example, which employs most of us (but unemploys many of us) in its interests rather than being employed by us in the human interest. Under this demonstrably false economy, or management, many people waste enormous effort and time in simply handling, calculating and multiplying money and measuring everything in terms of money. As another example of unintelligent practice, take the fact that we continually progress, materially, technologically and politically. We accept material progress as an inevitable fact of life, hardly stopping to consider the opposite view - that it is undesirable, unjustified, and that we accept it merely out of habit. Finally, look at our practice of submitting to the institutions of a system dedicated to ruthless pursuit of the instinctive competitive drives (finance, commerce, industry), but also to other institutions of the same system (law, police; the military) which curb some of the inevitable inhumanities of that pursuit, and are supposed to protect us when it goes recklessly out of control.

Some of the extremely traumatic recent events in our history are at last beginning to bring home to us our own shortcomings. War is a feature of amoral, competitive, divided, authoritative society; a phenomenon resulting from small differences escalating to huge conflicts because society lacks benign self-control. Within the last seventy-five years many, many millions of humans have died in two world wars and countless smaller ones, in the course of which human behaviour has descended to unbelievably callous, merciless and bloodthirsty levels. During the same period millions more have died of cruel oppression; also from starvation, neglect, and disease because society has failed to look after them.

These enormous figures are easy to quote dispassionately, but just imagine the suffering and heartbreak surrounding each death.

Occurring in a period of only sixty years, and still going on, is brutality of a more disturbing kind behind closed doors; by ruthless torture often ending in execution. One way of persuading oneself of the need for fundamental radical change is to remember that human individuals just like ourselves gassed the Jews in Hitler's concentration camps, enslaved and slaughtered peasants and politicians alike in Stalin's regime of terror, degraded, terrorised, maimed Cambodian civilians on the orders of Pol Pot, and then, in Yugoslavia and Rwanda, were murdering, raping and displacing whole peoples because of cultural and religious differences.

The fact is that mankind is unpredictable, dangerous and uncontrollable, and shall remain so unless and until we become what this book shows we ought by nature to be - supraconscious. The whole purpose of this book is to make clear the full significance of this word, and to show without doubt that it is our true nature to be supraconscious.

It is when ruthless leaders come to believe they cannot control or neutralise people in any other way that they order, and we perform, unspeakable atrocities. These horrors result from the accepted amoral norms being taken to extremes. In certain circumstances all humans are capable of this terrible behaviour. For all the complexities of our applied intelligence, our intellect is yet unfulfilled. Though we believe ourselves to be, or try to be gentle, compassionate and peaceable, too many of us, too often, show the characteristics of sophisticated predators.

Our present false habits and standards, chained to existing society's amoral rules and instinctive practices (competitive money orientation, political dishonesty, self-interest, racial and other forms of discrimination) contain the potential for exploding into these extremes of horrendously violent and inhuman behaviour. That is the false picture we have always had before us. This book sets out along the road to the altogether happier, humantrue outlook already briefly described. The book reveals humanity's true potential for supraconscious awareness. If we fulfil that potential we shall bring about a world where anything other than gentle, compassionate and peaceable behaviour shall be impossible.

A humantrue world would be right and good for us, but it is a prospect so remote from present reality as to need great initial mental effort to envisage.

There is no doubt that we are capable of that vision however, and once we see it and determine to make it our reality, we shall achieve a humantrue world relatively easily. The question is, are we willing to make the initial effort?

———————————

You, I, and all human individuals throughout the world have brains of enormous capacity. There may be about one hundred thousand million neurons in the human cerebral cortex. Of these, about ten thousand million comprise the covering cortex, the neocortex, separated into six layers with a huge potential number of correlating dendrites, axons, and synapses. Some other animals, such as whales and dolphins, have actually or comparatively larger brains but not this same layered neocortex. It is this that gives us our infinitely superior, and in my view, optimum reasoning power.

Were we truly represented by our faculty of higher intelligence, unique on Earth, we would surely now be living in peace and contentment. But our instinctive impulses are much more representative of us than this faculty of knowing and reasoning, or intellect.

It is the animal character of humanity, using its brain as calculator, which has aided and abetted our astonishingly rapid, yet essentially retrogressive development, from individual rivalry to world war, for example, and from local pecking orders to the wealth and poverty of nations.

Yet we each have the ability to be morally aware of right and wrong, good and bad principles, and our reasoning capacity gives us the responsibility for applying those principles in our world.

It is with our active assistance, and despite our mental capacity, that our world functions on wrong and bad principles. Society is a permanent battleground, with competitive aims and interests locked in continual combat. The inner intelligence of the mind looks on like a horrified, protesting spectator, wondering why life cannot be altogether benign and pleasant. It is the nature of high intelligence to answer all questions and solve all problems - to make life in its own image, so to speak. This thoughtful process must result in continual improvement of society towards perfection - unless it is prevented. Since existing human society is progressing otherwise, it is clear that in our case the process has been prevented.

THE AUTOMATON

We do try to improve our society, with some success, but this is a fringe activity, not that to which our energies are mainly applied. Humanity is not making intelligent progress towards answering and solving its questions and problems, is not building a growing body of agreed truth that shall be our infallible guide. This is the process that is being prevented, for the reason that we are not guided by our intelligence. We are driven, body and mind, by an automaton.

The automaton is a self-acting influence, the mainspring of our society. It embodies the principle of competitive conflict, an instinctive driving force. This is the principle on which our world society is founded, its chief motivation; the first and foremost influence over our development so far, and the basic cause of our problems. The stressful state of human society is not primarily due to the present conflicting characteristics of its individuals, but is inherent in the automaton that developed those characteristics, which has imposed this conflict on us, yet with our help.

The bulk of history has been made by the application of our minds and bodies to the automatic drives. We have pursued a growing complexity of competitive aims and material interests, and these have become the norm. The whole interconnected system of practices and institutions that dictate, represent, and control our activities needs a name - let it be called the MACHINE.

HUMANS IN HARNESS

We are harnessed to the automaton, whose influence permeates every inch of the fabric of our lives. And we serve the Machine whose institutions, representing every conceivable aim and interest of those automatic drives, have taken over the exploitation and control of our resources and activities. The Machine includes institutions that we suppose to be working in the interests of our own protection and well-being. But whilst serving even these institutions we remain harnessed to the automaton, in whose interests we are acting contrary to our well-being.

Even though we become aware of our true interests and opposed to the Machine, it is extremely difficult to throw off our harness and escape from servitude. The Machine provides most of the necessities of life, to obtain which we have to serve it, or conform to its practices. The Machine has weaved most of the fabric of society, and provides the framework of our community. It also controls the means of widespread communication, by which we are not so much humanly united as wired-in to a network that connects our automatic selves together.

Were we to become wholly and fully true to ourselves we would have to be isolated individuals, but such personal independence is hardly practicable because of humanity's overwhelming dependence on the Machine. As things stand, if we are to provide for ourselves, join in community, and attach some meaning to our lives, we are obliged largely to conform to the norm. We do not find it easy to express our true inner thoughts to others, or even to ourselves, because those thoughts are abnormal in the eyes of automatic reality.

In this book that you are now reading - an attempt to express wholly true reasoning - every word and every construction of meaning has to fight against enormous pressure from the Machine to crush it down into conformity. If this writing is to have any hope of breaking the iron grip of that normal conformity, it must make automatic reason wither and die from exposure to truth. If that makes it so unfamiliar, abnormal or intense as to be hard to read, so be it. Maybe the conclusion to be drawn is that writing which is easy to read may not convey truth, and true breakthrough requires much hard work on the part of both reader and writer.

BRAIN FIXATION

We are born into this world with some instinctive inherited intelligence, but no ready-made complete processes of true reason. The human baby is expert at recognising its mother, for example, but not at judging whether she is right or wrong. Several years must elapse before every component of our faculty of intellect reaches full potential, and we become fully capable of reasoning for ourselves. In the interim we are exposed to direct experience of the world as it appears to be, or to indirect experience by way of TV programmes, comics and books. We are also exposed to the influence of parents, peers and teachers. Before our minds are fully fledged and potentially able to work out the truth of it all, we have been subject to about fifteen years of brain-fixation. Despite the crazily unreasonable picture which human life presents, if anybody reaches this stage with determination to discover truth, almost nobody sustains it.

We are also born with temperament, a series of emotional capacities each varying between strong and weak, mostly evolved as the accompaniment to instinct for coping with life in the natural world. In the process of growing up we have to learn how to adjust these emotions and adapt them, first to the Machine, then to the human community.

Normally our realistic characters are formed in three ways. 1: By our fixed mental conditioning and circumstances in existing reality. 2: By our reasoned and emotional reactions to the concepts and facts of our reality - whether we accept or reject, like or dislike them. 3: By the balance or imbalance resulting from 1 and 2 - whether we react destructively against reality; whether we passively accept and make the best we can of the here and now; or whether we act constructively to gain for ourselves an advantageous position in the Machine.

What constitutes our willing brain fixation is either that we have allowed our minds to be so conditioned that we cannot perceive any but these three ways, or, that seeing another possible way, we deny it. Whether our character is formed by the first, second or third way, or by a combination of all three, practically all of us accept the underlying facts of existing reality. Many people protest against the inhuman effects, but almost nobody questions the fundamental principles of the Machine.

For example, we think law and order depends on strong government and do not consider an alternative view - that government may well cause lawlessness by relieving people of responsibility for their society. We consider that the competitive money economy reflects the facets of human nature, and do not normally think to the contrary - that apparent human nature has largely been formed by the characteristics of the money economy.

HUMANITY V. THE MACHINE

The Machine is our motivation, and the framework of our society. It depends on us to keep it accelerating along, which we do because we believe there is no alternative. But this is our public activity. Privately we observe different standards. So although our public activity supports the amoral and immoral affairs of the Machine, we are unwilling publicly to admit this because it contravenes our private morality. Yet at the same time we believe it naïve to expect that our private morality could possibly govern our public activities, so we pretend that we want to be moral but are continually frustrated by events which we also pretend are beyond our control. We pay lip service to humane standards whilst at the same time methodically betraying them. For example, humans talk endlessly about peace, but forever make war. We increase efforts to fight escalating crime, but steadily move ever further away from understanding and removing its causes. The divorce rate increases as our general failure to co-operate, tolerate and agree seeps more deeply into our personal lives. Were we making true progress, war, crime, policing and divorce would be steadily declining.

We keep these double standards by dividing ourselves into two; a public, hard outer shell of self, and a private, soft inner awareness. We are able to sustain our outer shells by the fact that the hard reality to which they belong constantly confirms the belief that we have no alternative. Also, our outer shells employ the denial factor, refusing to respond to the still, small voice of conscience. And so we demand Machine satisfactions to make up for the loss of true fulfilment. We defend our automatic selves, and these satisfactions, on the grounds that they are the most that we can expect or hope for. It is the hard outlook of our outer shells that we mostly act upon. When it comes to a choice between morals and lawful gain of money for instance, the great majority choose money. From this viewpoint the virtual eclipse of our true awareness can be justified, because the soft inner shell can be seen as a weakness, having to take a back seat in the tough, real world. Under the surface, our lives are really a struggle between our humanity and the Machine, and the Machine always comes out on top. We are hardly aware of this fact because, on the surface, we are all working for the Machine, on its side in the struggle. To move out of this wrong reality and into the right one, we need to wake up to the fact that our true humanity is fighting a losing battle. Whoever we are, we need to realise that each and every one of us belongs on the human side. The Machine is the common enemy on the other side. It can be defeated if we become united.

The subjects touched upon so far shall be returned to later, more fully and from different angles. This is the beginning of an exploration, and I hope you will reserve critical judgement until it is completed.

THE WRONG REALITY

Part I
EVOLUTION OF
THINKING BEINGS

Chapter 1

FORMATION OF LIFE

In tackling the subject of evolution, and the formation of life, my object is not to impart knowledge but to draw conclusions from knowledge that most of us already possess or can easily discover, conclusions which are not normally drawn. I want to show that humanity's present nature and state is not inevitable and was not preordained by evolution; that our evolution was a means of producing intellect in human form, and that intellect is itself a means the achievement of whose ends requires a human nature and state very different from that which presently exists here on Earth.

It appears to be generally accepted, and has been made clear to me by Peter Russell (The Awakening Earth, publisher Routledge & Keegan Paul), that a Big Bang originated this universe, about fifteen billion years ago. Approximately one-hundredth of a second after this event nothing existed but pure energy at a temperature of 100,000,000,000degC. At that precise time there were none of the elementary particles of matter - electrons, protons, etc.- because nothing of that sort can exist at such high temperatures. The terms here used to describe time, heat and the character of matter are those invented by humanity as relevant to our particular experience of the subsequent universe.

The foregoing information is part of current scientific theory. It is acceptable not only because it is the result of advanced scientific thinking based on long research but also because it is reasonable. In the search for the true meaning and purpose of life, without the benefit of modern scientific research, humanity has resorted to the imagination and supported its chosen beliefs with contrived reason. While these beliefs could not be proven, neither could they be disproved. Now that we have well-founded theories about the creation and evolution of life, a major obstacle has been cleared from the way of reason towards truth.

It is necessary to comment on the meaning of truth. This word is hard to define because we presently use it to mean many different things. Those meanings that I ascribe to it are given in Part III, Chapter 13, and Part V, Chapter 32. In the meantime I suggest that you keep an open mind as to the significance of this word.

Humanity's search for truth has been concentrated very much more on the discovery of scientific fact than on reasoning with the knowledge we already have. Consequently we are on the verge of total scientific understanding, yet wallowing in increasing social chaos because we do not understand ourselves or our reality. The relevance of our ability to describe the creation of this universe to within one-hundredth of a second of the Big Bang (even though we do not know what occurred before that precise time), and its subsequent history, is that it should eradicate all previous fanciful explanations of the creation of ourselves and our world, and bring us, so to speak, down to earth. But this is not the case. We still prefer searching for answers to finding them. Automated man worships science. Scientists have travelled far along the road of knowledge but appear to have missed the way of true reason, and seem to be raising up other fantasies to pose as human truth.

The significance of our relationship with the universe, and the meaning and purpose of life, is fully explored in Chapters 36 and 37. Right now I think it useful to point out that however mysterious things seem when partially hidden from our understanding, when fully exposed they are revealed as matter-of-fact. It is reasonable to deduce that any thing, once it is fully explained, shall take its logical place in the train of causes and effects of all things. This applies to abstracts as well as to actual things. No material thing except pure energy could survive the Big Bang, but abstracts could survive it, parts of the truth in which, as I believe and shall suggest later, all ultimate meaning is to be found. To fulfil truth is the purpose underlying all the matter-of-fact processes of the universe. Our present concern - evolution - we can reasonably presume to be the result of another abstract, which not only survived the Big Bang but caused it to occur rather than allow energy to cancel itself out. This is the influence, to express energy in all conceivable ways, which has resulted in the existing universe. It has ultimately produced human life, not as an end in itself but as a means to an end. And humanity does not need to make yet more new discoveries to learn the essential truth. That truth is not mysterious and unknowable. All that we need to know is already knowable. We have but to open our minds to optimum reason.

To continue with generally accepted scientific theory, three minutes after the Big Bang the temperature of the rapidly expanding universe was 900,000,000degC, and neutrons and protons began combining to form stable atomic nuclei. About 700,000 years later the temperature had dropped to about 4000degC, and electrons and nuclei were combining to form simple, stable atoms, mostly hydrogen and helium. Below 4000degC gravitation draws atoms together, and the more they group together the more gravitational pull they exert. This process, continuing for some thousands of millions of years, eventually produced huge clouds of hydrogen and helium gas, whose internal condensation formed stars. During this time the universe had become very cold overall, but collapsing stars generated such heat that some of them exploded. Within these supernovae new and heavier elements of matter were formed and spread throughout the universe. Eventually much of this matter condensed into new stars, some of which exploded in turn. In this way all the stars, suns and planets were formed, including Earth and everything on Earth, and including our sun, a mass of hydrogen burning at 4000degC, and giving off the necessary energy to sustain our life.

It was once thought that the creation of life was a supernatural event; then that the conditions in which it could occur were very rare. Now it appears that the vital components are easily made and put together, given the right physical and chemical conditions, and that all kinds of suitable conditions are, or were, to be found. Our planet Earth came into being about 4500 million years ago, and the seas that soon formed did provide such suitable conditions for molecules to combine into macromolecules which in turn, about 1000 million years later, combined into simple cells.

It is not the aim of this book to retail the evolution of life in detail so much as to explore its significance in relation to the development of intelligence. Significant factors are that there seems to be a strong universal intention to create life; that there appears, at least on Earth, to be a planetary determination to progress and protect life; and that the progress of life inevitably brings about the advance of intelligence. To me, this suggests a purpose; not the purpose of a supreme power (which would hardly need to be so dependent on physics, or expected to have to wait so long for results), but the purpose of a weak force that can be achieved only with the help of intelligence. This question also is pursued further in Part V, Chapter 36, and Part VI, Chapter 37.

The biosphere's determination to progress and protect life is suggested by James Lovelock in his book GAIA (Oxford University Press), and is also dealt with by Russell. To begin with our atmosphere was probably methane, and the early simple cells were bacteria and algae. These cells lived by photosynthesis, producing oxygen as a by-product. Oxygen was poisonous to these bacteria and algae, then the only representatives of life on Earth's crust, but for a long time it was absorbed by the oxidising of minerals such as iron, thus keeping these organisms safe. Eventually, when all the available minerals were oxidised, life was threatened with extinction, not only from poisoning by the rising amount of oxygen in the atmosphere, but also from destruction by ultra-violet light, which had previously been vital to the creation of life. However, the extra oxygen rose to the upper atmosphere where it was converted into an ozone layer that shielded Earth from much of the ultra-violet light. By the time oxygen had accumulated in the lower atmosphere, some bacteria had developed which could tolerate it. Certain of these bacteria continued to use photosynthesis and became plants. Others developed the ability to use oxygen, giving them such effective flexibility that they went on to become animals.

Such events could be said to be a matter of chance, but Lovelock's Gaia hypothesis suggests that the biosphere of Earth is a self-regulating entity with the capacity to keep the planet healthy by controlling the chemical and physical environment. Also that the physical and chemical condition of the surface of the Earth, of the atmosphere, and of the oceans has been and continues to be made fit for life by the presence of life itself. This might be regarded as a fantastic notion, but surely it is no more remarkable than the development of human intellect.

The Gaia hypothesis is reinforced by ensuing events, explained in detail by James Lovelock, partly summarised very neatly by Peter Russell, and further summarised as follows. Throughout the history of life on Earth, the surface temperature of the planet has kept to an average between 15 and 35degC, despite drastic atmospheric changes and a 30% increase in heat from the sun. The level of salt in the oceans has remained consistently below 4%; if it had risen above 6%, even for a few minutes, life in the oceans would have ended. Ever since an oxygen atmosphere was established, the oxygen content has remained at a level of 21%; a few per cent less and many life-forms would be unable to survive (perhaps we would be unable to think, for example); a few per cent more and everything combustible would eventually burn. The presence of ammonia in the atmosphere is precisely regulated so as to keep a level of acidity in rain and soil that is optimum for life. The process of methylation recycles iodine, which is vital to the production of hormones that regulate the metabolic rate, and removes toxic substances such as mercury and arsenic from the local environment by converting them into gaseous forms. The ozone layer, already mentioned, shields us from annihilation by ultra-violet radiation.

The early development of life on planet Earth proceeded in this way: given a generally hospitable environment under the care and protection of Gaia, simple cells united with others to become sexually reproductive, further uniting to become viable organs, then complex organisms of internally co-operative multifunctional cells. As these organisms became more complex, so did the nervous systems required to facilitate their internal functions and external activities, also the central brain required to co-ordinate them. The forms these organisms took and the habits and characteristics they acquired were partly determined by their environment, and partly by the fact that they were in competition for the food supply.

Considering the elemental building blocks of life, when chemicals came together to form macromolecules, and chains and groups of these, Russell says 'what requires to be explained is why this occurred'. It seems to me that we also have to ask the questions - why did the simple cells not remain as they were, merely content to adjust their numbers to the food supply? Why does life progress? Why do life-forms compete; is it because a compulsion to progress brings them into competition, or because the presence of competition compels them to progress? Why is there evolution of any kind, and for what reason do individual life-forms maintain and reproduce themselves? Why does Gaia sustain the biosphere with such care? I give my answers to these questions in Parts V and VI.

We humans are presently fascinated by facts. They attract us because they simply have to be accepted, whereas whole reason is a struggle because it requires more than facts. The physics and chemistry of the universe, and life, is interesting but does not yield the answers to those questions just raised. Those answers shall be found at the very end of the most significant evolutionary development, the subject of the next chapter - the advance of intelligence.

Chapter 2

ADVANCE OF INTELLIGENCE

This chapter, and the book as a whole, relies much less on conclusions drawn from established fact and more on deductive reasoning than is normal; less on that which actually exists and is accepted, more on that which ought to exist and be understood. My thinking process has never been held to a reality that is the subjective concept of consciousness contained by that reality, but an objective, outside view of reality, including a view of consciousness. In order to understand my view of evolving intelligence, the reader should be prepared, where necessary, to accept new meanings of words, such as conscious and unconscious.

Through integration of macromolecules the first life-form came into being on Earth - the single-cell creature:

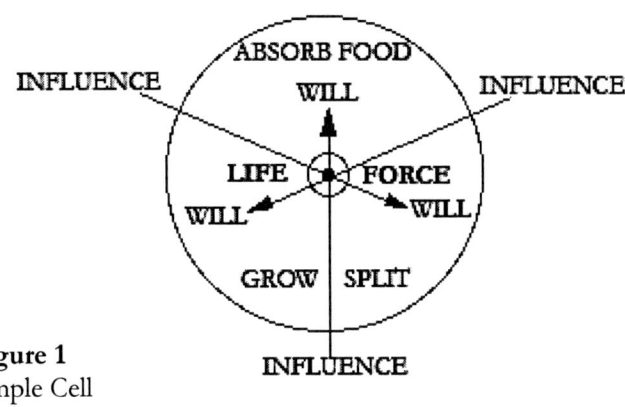

Figure 1
Simple Cell

This bacterial life-form comprises three functions of such direct sequence that it can only be described as a single, relatively simple unit (complicated though it is, in fact, having several DNA molecules, thousands upon thousands of RNA and protein molecules, and many millions of smaller organic molecules) whose purpose and structure is almost exactly described by its activity. The three functions are these: (1) the cell absorbs food and converts it, by photosynthesis, into energy in order that it may absorb more food, and convert it into more energy, and so on. (2) The cell grows and, (3) in due time, with the help of its DNA, splits into two replicas of itself, thus doubling its single activity. The purpose that such single cells at first appear to be fulfilling is that of expressing energy to the optimum.

This term' expressing energy' keeps recurring in the following pages and requires some explanation. By 'expression', in this context, I mean 'to use inventively - to pursue the possible applications of energy to the limits of complex ingenuity'. As I hope to make clear, this means exploring the true possibilities until the advance of intelligence has reached the point where a form of energy, human life, has acquired the means of expressing truth - intellect.

Putting aside the question of what persuaded molecules to integrate and what gave purpose to single cells, we can imagine that once such a cell is built and programmed it and its progeny could go on indefinitely, like a perfect engine. It has no central nervous system but evidently does not need one. Absorbing food is automatic; the cell's DNA might cause it to grow and split automatically, and the whole be kept going by self-generated energy. Eventually the single-cell population would reach the point where it had out-grown its food supply, when many cells would starve to death but the rest would carry on as before, unchanging.

But this is not an ordinary cause-and-effect system. There was no purely chemical or physical cause why these cells came into being and began converting matter into energy. The same influence that caused their creation continues as the force that gives them to live. They are not ordinary systems because they represent life, impelled by this will to live. This will comes to them direct from life-force, impelling them not merely to continue unchanged but to take every opportunity to progress and improve their techniques of expressing energy. The same life-force would also be exerting itself to defend and protect its creation, both internally and in the biosphere (Gaia).

The fact that life-forms have changed and proliferated enormously points to a greater aim, beyond the purpose simply to express energy. That purpose could have been achieved by these simple cells adjusting their numbers and habits to the available food supply, with comparatively little change and in a non-competitive way. History suggests that the greater aim, to be achieved by optimum competitive expression of energy, is to develop ever more advanced and complex life-forms.

Many of the bacteria and algae continued in simple cell form, reproducing by identical splitting, or dying and being replaced by free-floating DNA meeting suitable conditions in order continually to produce new cells. Genetic errors in reproduction, and random combinations of genes in the production of new cells, resulted in the emergence of cells with new characteristics, many of which survived. Over a period of about two thousand million years this process of change enabled life to adapt to the introduction of oxygen to the atmosphere, for instance. Today, the influenza virus can change rapidly enough to produce, each year, a new strain capable of defeating anti-bodies that were developed as rapidly the previous year to combat the old strain.

A more dramatic cause of change, which created complicated life-forms, was the integration of cells. Two or more cells joined together, forming one cell with a nucleus, a combination which increased the prospects for successful survival. This was a first step towards achieving increased efficiency by the internal co-operation of different cells and functions. Such integrated cells had the advantage that the nucleus could develop independently and, under protection from its external casing, free of direct interference from the world outside.

Advancing change was facilitated by the means of reproduction. As cells became more elaborate the effects of error and randomness in the distribution of genes became more far-reaching. Eventually, by way of natural selection, the creatures that progressed furthest and succeeded best were those which assumed female and male genders and reproduced sexually. Each offered its genes for random selection by the embryo, to which the female gave form and the male the spark of life, which then grew independently as to fundamentals but dependent on one or both parents for nourishment and guidance. Sexual reproduction foreshortened the processes of change by the cross-fertilisation of ever more intricate genetic variations.

Life's early evolution, up to the development of complete cells with a nucleus, took place in the seas over a period of of about 2300 million years. Some 1000 million years later, photosynthesising multicellular organisms - plants - had inhabited dry land, and animals followed 50 million years later. We are particularly concerned with the free-moving, intelligent higher life-forms, especially the most advanced, the human species, and features of the evolutionary process which gave us our characteristics.

The foregoing scientific information was obtained from the work of other people and their writings, particularly the books already acknowledged - James Lovelock's *Gaia* and Peter Russell's *The Awakening Earth*. Whilst acknowledging these two authors for their knowledge of science, however, I do not go along with their other reasoning, that concerned with moral rather than factual truth.

The original photosynthesising types of simple cell must have multiplied until the point was reached where all available elements which they required, once freely and abundantly present in the sea, had already been converted into energy, and newly released elements were being immediately consumed. I have already suggested that an influence to express energy is responsible for the universe and for the creation of life. It might have been expected that when life in the sea reached this balance, the photosynthesising cells producing oxygen (followed by other cells which were able to utilise that oxygen) would stabilise their numbers to coincide with the rate at which needed elements were newly released into the sea. This would be the optimum expression of energy, as things stood. But I also suggest (in Part V, Chapter 32) another influence whose objective is to advance life until it becomes aware of truth, and to which this balance of activity, in the sea, was unacceptable stagnation.

Under this second influence (which I had not intended to insist upon, since it cannot be proved, but which becomes more convincing the further my thoughts progress), certain cells, unable to accept stalemate and feeling the urge to progress, turned to the only alternative food supply - other living cells. This would seem to go contrary to the first influence (to express energy) since by one cell eating another two energy converters would be reduced to one. But the second influence, by complicating life-forms in pursuance of its objective, also served the first influence in that life was thus impelled and enabled to extend its activity onto the land and into the air.

Still confined to the sea, simple life-forms became more complicated. As food became scarcer, they had to develop means of locomotion to find it, also the ability to convert what they could get into the forms they needed to sustain themselves. As competition for this food increased, their movements and senses had to be more and more efficient if they were to survive. When cells began eating each other, survival came to depend upon being well equipped for attack and defence - skilled in competitive conflict. Measures had to be taken to attempt the protection of offspring. To illustrate once more that the object of all this activity does not seem to be purely to express energy by living, but to encourage the creation of optimum intelligence, consider a food chain in the sea. The millions of one species at the bottom of the chain feed on inorganic matter, whilst all the rest depend on this species, and each other, for food. Apart from the supreme predators, each species has to vastly over-reproduce just to maintain numbers and survive, a seemingly pointless exercise until its objective is perceived. Suppose that every living member of this chain were to be evaluated with respect to mass and energy and totalled one million units. Then suppose that all but the lowest species were eliminated and, after a period of adjustment to life without predators, all members of that harmless species were evaluated too. It seems certain that, subject to availability of food to sustain them just at this level, they must total more than a million units. This also assumes that it was predation that kept their numbers to the previous lower level. I recognise that the populations of victims and predators normally fluctuate in inverse proportion. Victims would tend to total more because of energy retained which would have been dissipated by the various predators consuming each other, i.e. finding, killing and reproducing the same food. In terms of the mass and energy of living matter, all the predators would appear to be unnecessary, until it is noted that amongst species at the tops of food chains, and practically invulnerable to all predators except mankind, are Earth's top intelligences - whales and dolphins, for example, and humans.

The more advanced cells, with complicated nuclei, joined together into colonies, and colonies into organisms, the better to survive against competition (united we stand, divided we fall). Different colonies, in their own interests, performed locomotive, defensive or combative functions, or became direction finders and distributors for the organism, in its overall interest. All these cellular functions, the frameworks that held them together and the casings that protected them, required to be fed. There had to be many means of taking food, breaking it down into the numerous elements that the many different cells required, and providing this food, together with oxygen, to all parts as appropriate. There also had to be a nervous system, to help the organism's various functions to co-operate by passing messages to and fro.

In some sense it could be argued that all this is irrelevant; that the human race now exists, with intelligence enough to decide its future by concentrating on the future, never mind the past. But for reasons that shall become clear it is necessary to show our evolution so far to have been a sequence of random responses to growing influences. The situation it has brought us to is not a suitable springboard for further progress. Now is the time for deeply thoughtful reconsideration. Were we the ignorant children of an all-wise universe, it would be difficult for that universe to justify its long-drawn-out production of ourselves and, having brought us into being, to explain why it has not caused our rapid enlightenment. I believe, on the contrary, that we are hoped-for pioneers of enlightenment in a largely ignorant universe, but still following the processes of random evolution, unaware that we have reached our utmost potential already.

It is again necessary to ask why - why did simple cells form nuclei and progress to such levels of complication? I have suggested before that two influences are involved, one to express energy, the other to pursue truth. Life was created and evolves under the former influence, to express energy by all possible means, and it was this that led creatures to depend on eating each other. By doing so they walked into the competitive trap. The essence of life is to succeed in living and reproducing - to survive. Once in the competitive trap, to survive means to advance, progress. To fall back, or merely stand still when competitors are advancing, is to fail. This raises a question that it is my object to answer. The first influence's purpose (to express energy) is to serve the second influence (to perfect intelligence). What happens, and what should happen, when that purpose has been served?

Success goes to those creatures best equipped for attack and defence, and this determines progress. Predators have the advantage that their food has to some extent been processed already by the creatures they eat. Life-force has been built into their every cell from the start, and is now the impulse of their nervous system. Not just the original influence to survive passively (i.e. to express energy but to progress only as far as their present limitations permit, as in the case of green plants) but the purposeful influences both to survive and advance, which only free-moving oxygen-burning creatures are capable of fulfilling. These influences, in the form of will, strongly compel all creatures to explore and progress in such ways as require ever higher intelligence. But a further question is this. When intelligence is perfected, can it overcome the will to go on competing? This is the question that humanity now faces.

The question is 'Can intelligence, once perfected, overcome the instinctive will to go on competing?', and in answering it we have to bear in mind those two influences which are involved - (1) To express energy and thus not only create life but also develop its forms and functions in every possible way, and (2) to advance the faculty of intelligence until it becomes capable of comprehending truth. This question is important in leading us to perceive (and the aim of this book is to help the reader so to perceive) that while the animal's purpose is to fulfil itself by following instinct, the true human purpose is to fulfil truth by following intellect.

Free-moving multi-cellular creatures continued to be impelled by the force of will, derived from the two influences defined above, but also now had a nervous system, a simple kind of intelligence for transforming vital need into effective action. As these creatures became more complicated, so their nervous systems became more intricate, making it necessary to set up a central co-ordination of this system, the brain, so that functions could be performed in efficient sequence. Logically, the brain should also contain the force that impels the whole organism, the will. But the whole creature is a collection of individual cells, each with its own function, with knowledge of that function alone and the will to perform it. Yet each cell has also a sense of corporate purpose for the common interest; this was what brought it to join a colony and brought the colony to join an organism. Each cell gives up a degree of independence, restricting its activity and its reproduction to the common interest, repelling invading bacteria and viruses and helping to keep the whole body healthy. In return the parent body feeds the cells and mobilises aid when they come under attack or suffer injury.

So all the organism's many cells contribute a portion of their influence and independence to its will, to the combined strength of the organism's independence and influence to which they all submit in return for its patronage. Such creatures have passed through a period of random change in the vital pursuit of competitive success. They have developed means of sustaining and reproducing themselves that secure their survival. Having now a brain, with a strong will in command, they are in a position to experiment with further changes. But random change might well endanger survival. There is a need to establish the success already achieved and to make it secure. The very determination of an organism's will to have its functions continue performing exactly in the manner which had already proved successful caused it to impose upon itself a pattern of behaviour which it then became the predominant will of the organism strictly to observe. This pattern of behaviour is known as instinct.

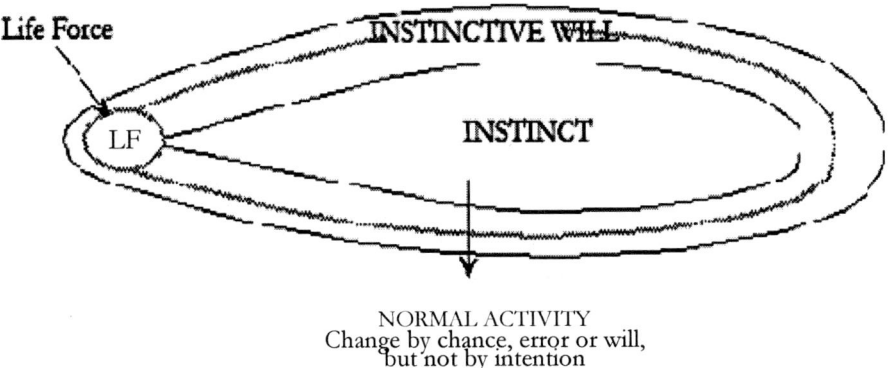

NORMAL ACTIVITY
Change by chance, error or will,
but not by intention

Figure 2
Symbolising Brain of Cellular Organism

Instinct is a governing programme, embodying means of impelling and inhibiting a creature's behaviour in the related interests of its many cells, itself, and its species. It is easy enough to comprehend that animal life is dependently subject to instinct but not so easy to understand why. It is vital that we do understand this, because our present problems are the result of our misunderstanding of that which impels us. Our instincts were genetically laid down - strongly imprinted over a very long time. Many are essential, and some harmless. But many others are dangerous, and although these ought to be outmoded our society remains such that we constantly revert to them. Perhaps these undesirable instincts can never be erased, only overlaid. We have to learn how to make them so completely redundant that we never again need them and can never again call them up.

Figure 2 represents the central, controlling nucleus of the multi-cellular creature - the brain - the being's essence, or self. The creature is identifiable, to an outside observer, as a set of physical characteristics, and by its familiar pattern of behaviour that is animated by feelings conveyed by its nervous system. Its self is aware but is not yet capable of self-awareness. Nor is this self independent or autonomous. It is a series of strict and entirely predictable responses to instinctive instructions, powered by the original life-force will to survive and reproduce, which encapsulate the creature and operate through its instinct. This may be changed only by genetic mutation brought about by accident or chance, capitalised by will, but not by intention.

However, although locked into a fixed programme of behaviour that forbade any other avenue of change, most of these creatures followed a path which enabled them to change dramatically. Before they had any means of foreseeing or planning the future, they progressed to advantage. One reason is this; that whilst one part of instinctive will is to obey the letter of instinct, and so prohibit change, the other part is to reflect the spirit of instinct which is to try and change for the better. Another reason is that instinct dictates the behaviour of the organism as an individual whole, but the individual cells that make up the organism have no instinct. Simply obeying instructions from the organism's brain, they co-operate to ensure that the organism functions successfully because their welfare is synonymous with the well-being of the whole. But simple cells also respond to the spirit of instinctive will, and are free to experiment with mutations which can be adopted, or rejected like a disease or cancer, by the ordinary process of natural selection, without in any way compromising the security of overall instinct.

Before the formation of its instinct the situation of the multi-cellular organism was very subtle. Its needs were those of its component single cells and cell colonies; it had no independent needs. Its will was partly that of its cells and partly that which they gave it to protect their interests, so that it had force of will before it had acquired its own individual interests. These interests, as well as those of its component cells, were catered for by its completed instinct that became the vehicle of its individual will.

It has to be considered how instinct came to be established. There being nothing capable of working it out or applying it, instinct must have created itself. In principle it is related to the universal cycle of 'explosion and implosion', birth and death. Instinct is a programme made up of extreme impulsions and inhibitions, established by progressive selection as an average between extremes, which constitutes a continual expression of energy, and is proved by experience to secure successful survival. The programme of action and reaction is imposed by way of emotions that have been brought forward from experience resulting from past behaviour, and made into anticipatory feelings that guide present behaviour.

For example, hunger is a pain accompanied by anticipated pleasure, and these are relieved or fulfilled by eating; sexuality is a desire accompanied by anticipated pleasure, and these are fulfilled by the sexual act. Animals neither eat because they know their bodies need food nor copulate because that is necessary to securing the future of their species. They obey the impulsions and inhibitions of instinct, a kind of knowledge automatically calculated from past experience as a series of emotional "do's" and "don'ts", which is quite unaware of the future and unable to predict or prepare for it, and which is supposed to be locked away from a creature's voluntary interference and to prohibit any contrary behaviour.

Whilst a creature was developing, the will, random mutations, and progressive selection played their parts. The objective was survival success, and by the time this objective had been achieved every feature of the creature's behaviour was secured by its instinct to ensure that its success would be maintained. The creature's 'self-will' became increasingly identified with the centralised brain containing the letter of instinct; resistant to and impatient of the body's independent experimental mutations, which were faster than error or chance but still too slow and uncertain. There was a growing sense of mounting competition, an awareness of the vital need to progress faster if only to keep abreast, a sense that the brain should not be dominated by instinct but should have its own means of modifying and manipulating instinct and, consequently, a more direct influence on progressive mutation.

So fixed instinct became representative of stagnation and the danger of extinction. But it would be equally dangerous to throw open instinct to random change, tossing away the security which had taken so much time and effort to build. There had to be some means of voluntarily experimenting with possible changes without disturbing the status quo. This means was the preconscious, whose gradual development is shown in Figure 3, stages A, B, and C.

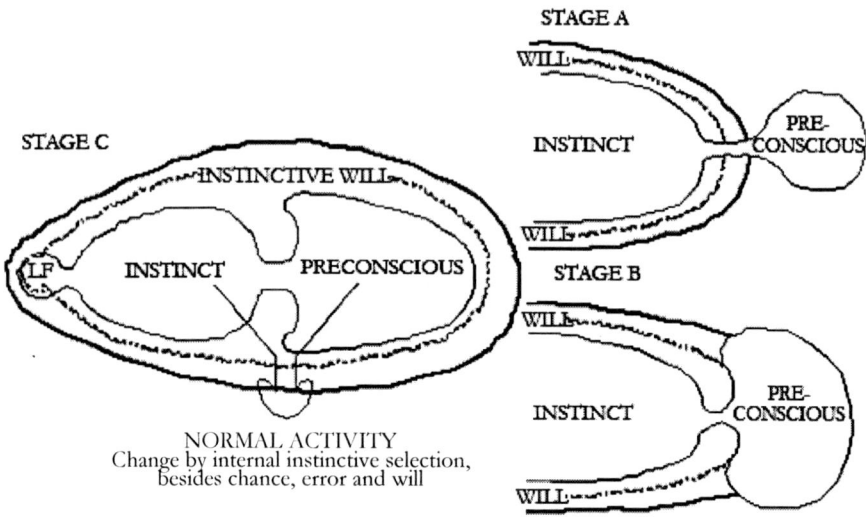

NORMAL ACTIVITY
Change by internal instinctive selection,
besides chance, error and will

Figure 3
Symbolising Brain Transition From Cellular to Multi-Cellular Organism

The preconscious would have begun as a small extension of the cells which contained and administered instinct, formed outside the encapsulation of instinctive will (Stage A). This allowed a small degree of anticipation, a crude kind of thought, free of instinct but without danger, once Stage C was reached, because instinctive will was again firmly in control of the brain and of the creature's every activity, with no new move being possible without its permission. So this preconscious faculty served life-force will, but its relative freedom allowed it sometimes to by-pass a slight inhibition and lean towards a simple advantageous change. The will could then give this proposal independent trials. If the change proved a failure it would be dismissed, but if it proved advantageous it would be adopted as part of instinct in place of previous practice, and the old inhibition that would have forbidden this change would be rejected and a new inhibition brought in to secure it. Multi-cellular organisms had abilities and characteristics arrived at by natural selection. Preconsciousness allowed them to speed up the acquisition of new habits that had survival value. For example, in a creature whose instinct was always to move forwards, the preconscious might sense the possibility of going backwards also and, one day, might cause this to happen. Such a break in habit would be painful at first, but it would be incorporated with instinct when found to be advantageous. Chance or random experiment could have produced the same result, but that is uncertain and could have taken very much longer. Such changes in the habits of organisms that were to become advanced life-forms, as they diversified, sometimes required complex physiological changes. It seems to me inconceivable that such changes could have occurred without the aid of the preconscious faculty, which implies that this faculty must have developed very early in the evolution of such organisms.

It took very roughly 1300 million years (the figures here quoted are approximate - when dealing with such huge time spans accuracy is hardly significant) for the first form of life created, the simple cell, to develop into the complicated single cell with nucleus; about 500 million further years for simple multicellular organisms to develop; and another 400 million years or so for complex multicellular organisms such as molluscs to emerge. This was progress by means of mutations due to chance, error, will, then preconsciousness. This progress required the development of the nervous system, and its gradual acceleration was facilitated by the advancing efficacy of that system. Viewed differently, Earth history could be said to be that of the development of intelligence, of which physical life is but the incidental vehicle. The potential perfection of intelligence was achieved when humanity appeared. From then on perhaps there was no need for life to progress further. Maybe if that potential were released all life would settle down to a state of stable continuation. In the present interim, with our intelligence far from being perfected, it is certain that, on the contrary, advanced life-forms on Earth are gradually declining and under threat of extinction.

It appears that after about 2950 million years of life on Earth, and another 150 million years in which plants colonised dry land - that is to say about 400 million years ago - the approximate situation of our ancestral complex multi-cellular organisms, as they began developing into animals (prior to colonising dry land over the next 50 million years), was this. They had some form of nervous system and a rudimentary brain. Overall they were impelled by life-force, represented by will, and subject to competitive conflict, which combined to cause progress. Physiologically they had come to be represented by instinct that contained and guarded all the characteristic habits randomly acquired and naturally selected. Now they also had a preconscious faculty that enabled them to bring about beneficial changes of instinctive habit by a rudimentary kind of self-determination which could be described as *intention*.

Physiologically, complex multicellular organisms were represented by their bodily form, similarly evolved by mutations and natural selection, capitalised on by will. The pattern of a creature's physical organs and functions was recorded, guarded and passed on by genes. There was competitive pressure on these patterns to change also, for a dramatic change of habit often required a new or re-shaped organ. The genes had always been vehicles of mutation, by way of chance or error altering or omitting instructions or re-arranging their sequence at the time of regeneration. Until now mutations had been subject to simple natural selection. If a certain mutation was of immediate benefit to the creature inheriting it, in that it survived better than its fellows, that creature would be preferred and its descendants would come to predominate the species. Mutations of no immediate benefit would not be preferred, and those that were a hindrance would quickly die out. This meant that no dramatic changes which were vital to survival were likely to occur, for if such a change required to be built in stages, some stages, being of no apparent benefit, would not be preferred, and even if none of the stages actually died out, no single creature would inherit them all in sequence in order to develop the mutation in full. To expect a complex mutation to occur in one regeneration, complete in every respect and therefore immediately effective, is like expecting not only that the concept of time and all the separate parts of a watch should come into existence at once but also that those parts, thrown together at random (after any number of millions of attempts), would fall into place as a complete working watch, which its owner straight away used to tell the time.

The fact is that extremely complex organs *were* developed and perfected. It is obvious that this took some time, although it has now been discovered that evolution occurred in jerks; quite big changes have been accomplished in as little as a thousand years. I have already suggested that a major essential element of mutation is the intervention of will, the impulsion to live felt by every cell in an organism combined into the whole will of the organism progressively to improve its method of living. There seems to be another possible explanation of evolution that combines strength of will and subconscious intention in another way. Take the example of the stick insect. It is extremely unlikely that it emerged from one single complete mutation. It is equally unlikely that each separate feature was formed by chance at different times. But suppose that the original creature, at the pre-stick-insect stage, was so desirous of becoming identified with the safe and secure twigs it lived on, so escaping the notice of predators, that the cell-aligning, twig-forming influence was somehow passed from the tree to the insect genes, the latter possibly having already ingested materials suitable for its reconstruction in twig-form by eating parts of the tree.

I am certain that no amount of time or blind strength of will could produce a pair of eyes, with all the systems to go with them. This required the preconscious faculty, once it had become fairly well developed (Stage C, Figure 3), to give the overall will some concept of sight and its value. This would be passed to cells at the front end of the creature, directing and urging their effort towards realising that concept, however vague it might be at first. The more progress was made the more clear the concept would become, so that directions could be made ever more precise and coordinated, and progress would accelerate.

Concerning the creation of eyesight, it can be appreciated that cells at the front end of a creature which let in light have a potential direction-finding value, so that if they occurred by chance mutation they would give an immediate advantage, but only if there were means of interpretation which enabled the creature to use this potential. Without these means the light-cells would have no advantage and would not be preferred, so the means of interpretation must come first. But such means, without anything to interpret, even if they could have been constructed by chance, would have no immediate value for survival.

Yet such embryo faculties could have a value that was evident to the preconscious. It is possible that creature Z might build up an internal means of picturing shapes and directions from knowledge of creature X, its preferred prey. This means would convey information about X's shape through sensors in Z's mouth and throat, and about X's orientation by feelings conveyed through Z's hairs, feelers and legs, spread out in every direction. It is possible to ascribe this development to the process of chance natural selection, but to co-ordinate it and hold it together required strength of purpose given by the developing preconscious.

I understand that the nuclei of the common cells of our bodies, such as those of the skin, contain all the genetic instructions required for the building of our whole organism. Also that the genes of many animals, including humans, contain a small separate element that is common to all. This suggests to me that they all derive from a remote common ancestor. If a nucleus derived from one animal is inserted into the ovum of a similar animal (in some cases a different animal), a complete reproduction of the former will grow from it. This is because the ovum contains all the chemical compounds needed to activate all parts of the genetic chain of the nucleus, in correct sequence, and because the ovum is situated in the appropriate place - the womb. This reproduction begins as a process of cell division, and presumably goes on to a procedure whereby the different chemical compounds are conducted to appropriate parts of the embryo, where they will begin activating specific instructions in common cells to begin construction of particular organs in their correct positions. As the embryo grows and matures many more evolved procedures are triggered which pull the whole together as a working creature.

By imagining evolution going into reverse we can see how this process was gradually built up, but also that each complex organ, like the eye, must have had a beginning. For instance, we have some primitive marine creature to thank for our eyes. They have been much modified by subsequent evolution, but the original eyes and their genetic pattern must have been devised by that primitive creature alone. Perhaps it happened in this way. Sensing the need of a means of seeing - a new faculty - it procured and deposited at its front end a new chemical compound, new in the sense that this creature had never used it before so that none of its existing cells could be activated by it or live in or on it. Maybe a series of cells were newly created in this chemical soup and, after many abortive experiments, like cancers, certain cell types would emerge which were in tune with the creature's sense of desire for sight, and which the creature's will would then protect, nourish, and its genes regenerate. And these new cells, in turn, would serve the will by activating new growth, always aimed in a purposeful direction whose ultimate achievement would be the construction of a pair of eyes.

When these subtle actions, reactions and interactions of energy, through genes, nuclei, cells and chemical compounds, are considered, together with the fact that the impelling life-force will and controlling instinct had extended and connected itself to all organs by way of the nervous system, it can be appreciated that there was relentless pressure and enormous potential for progressive change. We tend to be fascinated by all these processes. Yet when it becomes known, evolution appears as a series of mechanically logical steps. This is made clear by microscopic photography of muscular cells pulling the head-features of an embryo into position, and a computer simulation of the simple contraction and severance of cells producing the beginnings of the lens and retina of the eye. Again, the sorts of questions that ought to exercise our thought are 'why does all this happen?' - 'to what end?'

The answers to these questions are to be found in, and by, the end-product of all life's development on Earth - the human mind. Today we use, or misuse, our eyes though we might have no idea how or why they were developed. We can learn how our eyes developed by understanding that life's microparticles and microprocesses can be influenced by the will, producing macro-changes. We can also learn precisely how our eyesight now works by studying its entire mechanism in greatest detail. But this leaves unanswered the question why, and to what end, which is the ultimate aim of this book to answer. This aim includes a vital human objective; to show that just as some primitive subconscious creature sensed the needed value of sight, so do we sense the need to discover truth; and just as it was able actually to achieve its vague intention, so we, with our far superior faculties, are able to achieve *our* dream of a better world.

The centre of self gradually moved from instinct into the preconscious, but it was a slight shift because the preconscious faculty was still tied closely to instinct, the capacity of its cells and interconnections necessarily pitched at a certain low level, which disallowed any calculation not in the direct interest of instinct. This faculty grew larger the further creatures developed, and was progressively encapsulated by instinctive will. It took over many functions of the body, as an extension of instinct, functions whose actions, to our subsequent consciousness, mostly take place subconsciously. Perhaps the preconscious could be described as looking outwards from a platform of instinctive intelligence, but quite without ability to view the self from outside, or to look critically at instinct, or in any way to break instinctive bonds, only to extend them.

We are now concerned with the most advanced animal life-forms, those which had developed the senses of sight, smell, hearing and touch, and which had utilised these to secure successful survival by way of an efficient array of instincts. Where nothing seriously threatened this success it would appear that instinctive will completely encapsulated the preconscious (Stage C, Figure 3) as would seem to be the case with the crocodile for example, sealing it off from further mutation so that it continued unchanged, maybe for many millions of years. But where serious threats to survival did arise, such animals (dodo's for instance), unable to adapt by way of some appropriate mutation of form or habit, became extinct.

It seems to me that if any creature is to go beyond the Stage C preconscious state it must have developed all the vital senses. From the viewpoint of the influence to express energy, a fully developed preconsciously instinctive animal that survives without any further change, such as the crocodile might be, is a success whilst those who die out are failures. From the viewpoint of the influence to grasp all life's opportunities to advance, however, the crocodile too is a failure. From the latter point of view, fixed preconsciousness is stagnation, like instinct, a state which could have been achieved by single cells continuing unchanged, without need of life progressing further. The fact seems to be that most animals did progress to the next stage of brain development.

Consciousness

In the following I continue with my deductions from basic knowledge of the past and observation of the present with the object of showing that vital reform is our voluntary responsibility. The conscious faculty appears to have started in the same way as the preconscious - as a dramatic extension of the brain in response to some threat to survival. The animal concerned already possessed all the vital senses given by a brain and nervous system which, though they had served it well in the past, were encapsulated by instinctive will. A separate faculty was needed, with a will of its own, a faculty which did not contradict instinct and understood it, but was not rigidly bound by it.

The early conscious faculty independently observed the outside world, as far as its capacity allowed, and occasionally made decisions which overrode or redirected the animal's tried and proved instinctive inhibitions and drives yet were shown to be in its best interests. This animal, for example, might consciously realise that it need no longer run away from another species of animal which it had long instinctively feared and, by standing up to its enemy, defeat it. As another example, take a small bird with a 2cm long beak, trying to reach grubs that commonly live in 4cm deep cavities. The purely instinctive bird (if such were possible) would give up, but one day, perhaps after many thousands of years, a freak bird would be born with a 4cm long beak and, succeeding much better, would eventually represent the species. The preconscious bird would concentrate its will on beak growth and, perhaps after a thousand years or so, might also achieve a 4cm long beak. The conscious bird could achieve the objective within one generation, and without physiological change, by simple reasoning - by teaching itself to dig out the grubs with a thorn or splinter of wood that effectively extended its beak to the required length.

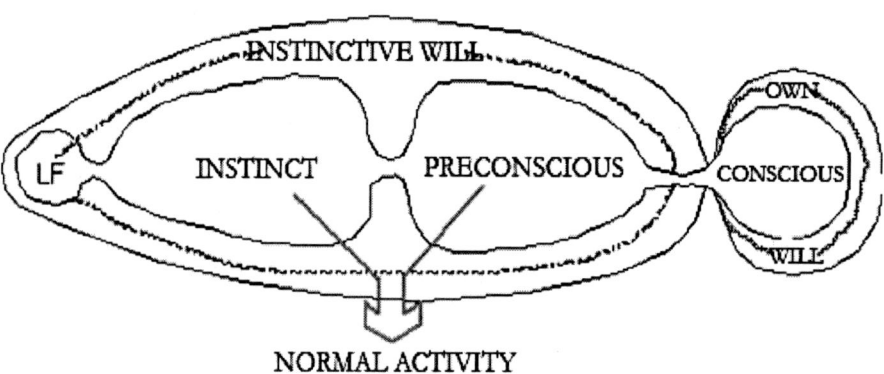

Figure 4a
The Dawn of Consciousness

As the conscious faculty went on growing, the 'self' of the animal began to pass from the preconscious to the conscious and it might appear, for the first time, to have gained freedom from its instinctive bonds.

This was the only way forward for an animal otherwise rigidly restricted by instinct, yet it seems to present dangers by going contrary to the life-force purpose, represented by instinct. But whilst the conscious was relatively independent and self-willed, instinct, to the same degree, was independent of consciousness, and instinct unconsciously controlled most bodily functions; also, subconsciously, most physical activity. True, consciousness could override some instinct and itself cause physical activity, but instinct promoted its own interests by subjecting the conscious to emotions and fears that were hard or impossible to override.

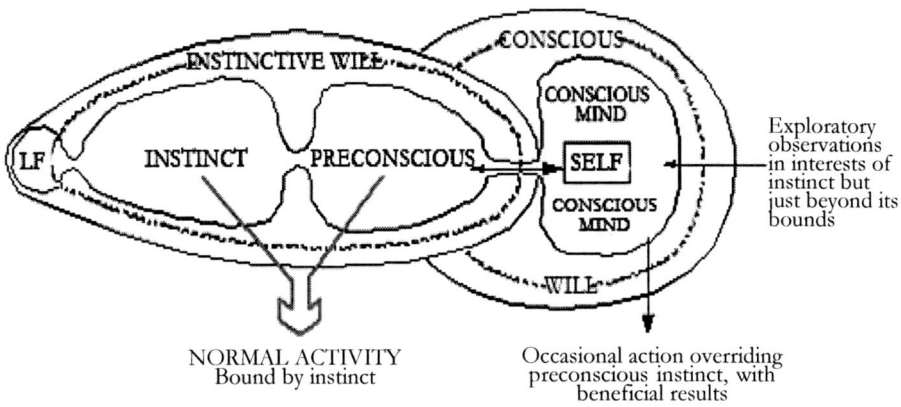

Figure 4b
Early Consciousness

Furthermore the animal, though conscious, was as yet unaware of any but its own 'reasons' for existing. When early consciousness looked inward, as far as it was able, it did not see itself; it saw the animal's instinctive preconsciousness. When it looked outward it saw an interesting world, but the mainspring of its interest was the whole animal's instinct. Yet consciousness was the true beginning of thought, in that it had the potential for evaluating the animal's interests and giving preference to certain of them in order to perfect its way of life.

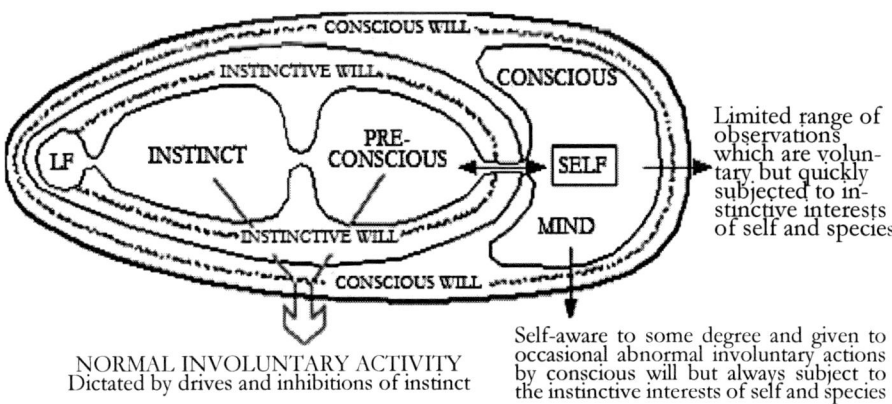

Figure 4c
Average Consciousness

Consciousness, then, is the innate knowledge of instinct made available to the 'self' and an enlarged knowledge of the world made available to instinct - the opening of awareness to a share in the understanding and responsibility of instinct, previously locked away and imposed by remote control for the sake of security. The fundamental reason for consciousness being developed, whatever actually caused it, was the survival need of a creature to develop further. Thereafter, consciousness grew not only for practical purposes but for reasons of its own, and this seems to me to mark a partial and potential shift from the influence to express energy to that which persuades life to grasp all opportunities for progressive change - the influence for truth.

This next stage in the development of the conscious (Figure 4C) shows it to be much enlarged, and conscious will enveloping the whole animal, i.e. its brain. In this way the animal's progress into the future would be steered by its most advanced faculty, but the bulk of its activity would remain the established responsibility of instinct, encapsulated by *its* will. There would be exchanges of influence between preconscious instinct and consciousness, and mutations or changes of habit could still occur randomly, or by intention of the former, or by strongly willed intention of the latter. The animal's self was now firmly in its conscious, vaguely seeing as well as feeling itself to be its range of habits and emotions and the centre of its observed world but quite unable to see, or to be critically aware of, its true conscious self.

At this stage the conscious faculty was capable of deeper reason than that embraced by standard instinct, and it introduced subtle variations in behaviour patterns that seemed immediately to benefit the animal concerned, for instance the chimpanzee's ability to deceive. Happiness is a state of fulfilment of purpose and faculties and this now depends on consciousness, as well as preconscious instinct, being fulfilled. The wolf species is an example of consciousness disciplining some instincts and enhancing others for the sake of happy survival in the most adverse arctic conditions. The wolf pack is led by a female and breeding is strictly limited in order to match numbers to a usually scarce supply of food. This, together with almost self-sacrificing care, affection and disciplined comradeship, makes the wolf a most satisfactory animal in that it seems to have achieved a balance between harsh circumstances and self-generated compensations. Yet because it is a delicate balance, not to be disturbed without risk, the wolf resists change.

Wolves must have developed their consciousness out of dire necessity and, having succeeded, have taken it no further. The chimpanzees, having reached a similar stage of consciousness, are a very different case. Living in the lush jungles of Central Africa, they appear to have achieved survival success very easily, leaving time to spare. They developed curiosity, helped by the dexterity of their hands, which in turn encouraged mental adroitness and led to further curiosity. This combination is a fast and most effective means of mental enhancement, and it is judged to have been an ape of this kind that engendered the pre-human species. Curiosity is the turning of spare time and energy to observing and investigating without necessity, for its own sake. This led chimps and then pre-humans to changes of habit which then became instinctive or learned features of life and survival, changes which had not derived from strict necessity but from intelligence, becoming *developed* needs rather than original or basic needs.

The effect that the conscious had on different species of animal depended upon its capacity, and the extent to which its capacity grew depended upon the degree to which it was stimulated. In the building of instinct, in some animals the combative element had come to dominate character - the predators - and others took passive roles - the victims - but all the successful ones learned to moderate their characteristics and adapt for survival. Similar influences affected the nature of conscious growth, but consciousness continued growing in various directions which were not always helpful to survival but which did encourage further mental progress.

Some seventy million years ago it seems that Earth was well populated by advanced animals and mostly covered with vigorous plant life. As a logical outcome of the practice of animals eating each other, very large predators once existed which were capable of killing any other animal. Perhaps in time such predators had made themselves extinct, because of over-killing or for other reasons, and a balance had been established between predators and prey. Another logical outcome of animals eating plants would be enormous creatures with huge appetites, not vulnerable to any predator. Such animals did exist - dinosaurs and the like - and might likewise have become extinct through over-eating, also from trampling the vegetation. In the event the dinosaurs fell victim to a major mass extinction, probably caused by a huge meteorite colliding with Earth, raising worldwide dust clouds that created a prolonged winter that they failed to survive. No doubt there is a link between this event and the presence in the sea, some ten million years later, of even larger animals, whales, which had returned to the sea from dry land.

The human is evidently the only species of life on Earth yet to achieve a brain capacity capable of independent optimum knowing and reasoning, or intellect. There is some dispute about this because certain small-toothed whales (odintocetes) - dolphins and porpoises - have brains as large or much larger than ours. However, as S.H. Ridgway points out in Research on Dolphins by H.M. Bryden and Richard Harrison (Clarendon Press Oxford 1986), the integrative and analytical capabilities of brains are a matter of quality rather than quantity; of level rather than volume. Yet when brain weight is compared with body weight or length, it appears that the greater the size of an animal the larger the quantity of brain cells required (although there are variations in brain size in whale species of similar weight). This would explain the large brain size of the non-intellectual elephant, compared with the human. The large brain is not necessarily an advanced brain, but may be required solely for the motor, auditory, visual and somatosensory functions of large animals. Of course, huge numbers of extra cells are required for the intellectual faculty of the relatively small human species, and when brain weights are compared with the weight of the spinal chord, fishes show less brain than chord, cats a ratio of 4 or 5 to 1, apes 8 to 1, Tursops (a genus of dolphin) 40 to 1, and mankind 50 to 1. Various other relationships such as brain size to maternal metabolic turnover (Martin 1981) appear to confirm these comparisons.

As well as relative size, the comparative construction of cortexes suggests the level of intelligence. However, to judge whether any other animal has also reached the human level of potential intellect, we need only to judge its circumstantial behaviour. It seems to me that all creatures but one require and use their every brain cell because their brains are geared to natural instinctive reality. The exception is the human species with a brain, as we shall see, of large capacity whose potential we have not yet realised. I judge dolphins to have risen no higher than the conscious level (to use my own system of comparison) on the grounds that if they possessed the faculty of intellect would not they, if only indirectly, by their observed behaviour, have demonstrated it to us by now? Had they been as intelligent, or more so than we, whales at any rate, because of the way we have treated them, would surely have attempted to communicate with us. By communicate I mean more than benign fellow-feeling (of which dogs and horses are also capable); I refer to intellectual exchange. The power of intellect allows a choice to be made from all possible modes of behaviour, as we know well. Whale and dolphin behaviour indicates to me that they have little choice and cannot themselves conceive of any fundamentally different way to behave.

Whales and dolphins are animals that once lived on land but returned to the sea about sixty million years ago. They had to overcome the tremendous problems this entailed, but since becoming biologically adapted to their aquatic environment they have had a long time to perfect this way of life. They have had the relative ease of almost weightless movement, with wide-ranging freedom to explore the open seas, little or nothing to fear from predators, and unaffected by catastrophes which caused regular mass extinctions on land. Knowing where to find food at different times and over large distances requires intelligence and skill but, when the food is plentiful and there is no fierce competition, does not require the aggressive drives of instinct. It seems to me that these animals were so easily successful that they were able to concentrate on developing the benign instincts - the rewards and satisfactions of care and compassion - and to allow the aggressive drives to fade away. Dolphins are in some danger from predators, but I imagine that in their element, like us in ours, they are so skilled and superior in intelligence as to be at minimum risk and not to feel threatened. The human threat, to whales in particular, is so comparatively recent that perhaps they have not had time consciously to adjust to it in order to make any kind of response.

Almost certainly dolphins have the largest conscious capacity of any species of animal, including the human. When these animals returned to the sea they already had a fairly well developed (if relatively primitive) brain that had evolved to suit their life on land. They not only had to adapt its existing systems to changed functions but also to create new systems to serve entirely new functions appropriate to the aquatic environment, so their brains developed in a different way from the brains of land animals (see Fig.5). They had to perfect capacities for pulmonary breathing, thermal insulation, procreation and birth in water, and techniques of swimming, communication, hunting and deep diving, with all the intricate biological complications that these things involve. All this could only have been accomplished by an almost entirely unsuitable land instinct giving up its responsibility for survival to a rapidly-grown, very large conscious faculty, which established its own alternative to the old preconscious instinct, i.e. a new conscious relationship with an equally new subconsciously automatic pattern of behaviour. It seems to me that all these must have been voluntary mutations brought about by conscious intention of the conscious will. The dolphin brain appears to have taken 40 million years to perfect, but since the species has succeeded, its original transformation to a reasonably viable aquatic animal must have been abnormally rapid in terms of evolution. It was faced with the sudden need to adapt or replace a pattern of instinct and nervous system which, together with their associated bodily functions, were largely redundant. This must have been done almost immediately as to fundamentals, then perfected without basic change.

It is presumed that, as land animals, the dolphin's ancestors were already high in the competitive life-hierarchy and, psychologically, did not have to rise in the hierarchy to gain their new position. This voluntary mutation could be accomplished only by a massive increase in the number of cells in the conscious faculty and by co-operative behaviour of that mass of cells within this, the only faculty capable of working for the species' survival.

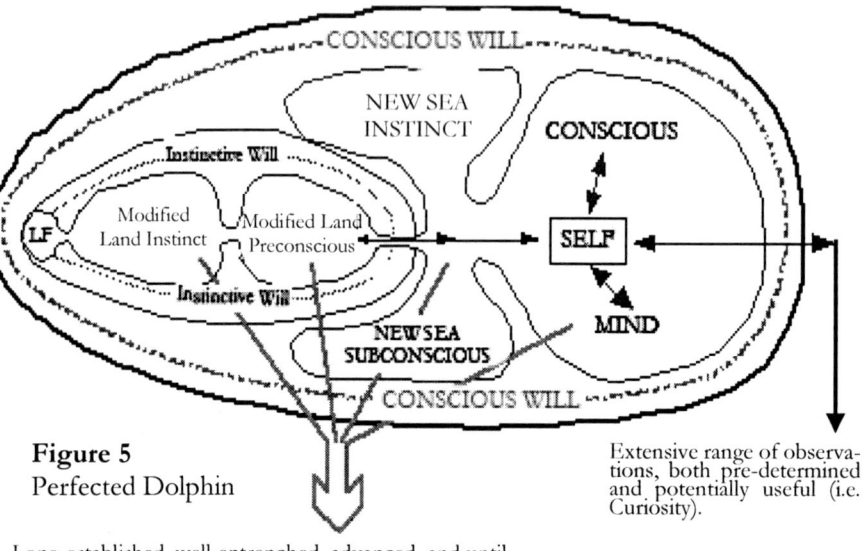

Figure 5
Perfected Dolphin

Long-established, well-entrenched, advanced, and until very recently very successful co-ordination of instinctive, preconscious, subconscious and conscious faculties, governing all motor functions

Extensive range of observations, both pre-determined and potentially useful (i.e. Curiosity).

Also play, and exercises of emotion and intelligence comparable to musical performance.

This oneness of dolphin brain development, where there was co-operation within the whole conscious faculty instead of interplay between different levels (as in the human case,) seems to be confirmed by the monotonous, almost undifferentiated structure of the dolphin neocortex. That the species has continued successfully, when this lack of interplay seems to make further changes practically impossible, must be because life in the sea is stable compared with life on land and does not require continual significant change. This seems to be confirmed by the fact that the dolphin brain, whose neocortex is as convoluted as that of the human brain, but half its thickness, has not changed for twenty million years. In my view this means not only that dolphins have not achieved intellectual capacity but they are not advancing towards it either, nor likely to do so.

Our feeling that dolphin intelligence is on a par with our own seems due to their long history of friendliness towards, and interests in, man. This feeling has recently come to include whales as we have learned more about them. We know that these two kinds of creature demonstrate good humour and tenderness in their relationships, and we have heard the haunting underwater song by which they communicate over great distances. Protest against the killing of whales is widespread and our feeling for them is enhanced by the mystery of life under the oceans. It is well to realise that dolphins and small whales are themselves practised predators. I think we should also admit that if they were as intelligent as we the fact would be much more evident. The intellectual faculty cannot be contained by, so as to be solely devoted to, practical and emotional matters of survival. It must spill out into extraordinary expression that there is no mistaking - in art, music, or the expounding of ideas. Otherwise the faculty will be utilised by instinct, as is the case with ourselves, to further competitive drives, fulfil ambition, express aggression. None of these things is clearly evident in the behaviour of dolphins and whales.

We might think that the behaviour of captive dolphins in marinas exhibits a human level of intelligence. They can be taught to carry out quite difficult tasks, or perform clever tricks that do undoubtedly require good intelligence. But remember that horses, monkeys, dogs, parrots and even fleas can be similarly taught. These performances depend upon a close human presence, like the strong-willed hypnotist taking the initiative with submissive subjects, and/or upon some kind of reward system. To test whether it is an accurate indication of intellect, put yourself in the dolphin's position. Surely the most gentle of humans would object strongly to being captured and denied freedom by aliens, however 'friendly', and put on display. Would any but the mentally deficient human then condescend to do tricks? And what would we think of our captors who, believing us to be as intelligent as they supposed themselves to be, nevertheless subjected us to these indignities?

It does not seem to strike us that the gentle and caring characteristics of dolphins and whales, which attract us to them, reflect our repressed inner selves. It is not such gentleness but the high-handed way we patronise dolphins, and the cruelly commercial way in which we still treat whales (in some areas), which represents the public human character. It could be said that dolphins and whales are sensibly in optimum harmony with their environment because they have not achieved our intellectual level, whilst we are destructively oppressive because we have. In this light it might then be claimed that it is we who are backward and they who have actually fulfilled the potential of our intellectual level. But again, if they had would they be willing to take part in circus trickery? In fact it is we humans who are of the highest order of intellectual and therefore moral potential and, erroneously thinking that they are too, we have even less justification for capturing, displaying and breeding dolphins. In truth we can only explain our attitude by admitting that we are yet far from fulfilling that potential.

I have brought this matter up because to question whether dolphins or whales possess high intelligence leads us to question the nature of high intelligence. In attempting to judge the intelligence-level of dolphins from evidence of their behaviour, we may be led to judge whether our own behaviour is a true reflection or a betrayal of our own intellectual capacity.

By understanding the moral virtues which limited consciousness can aspire to, as exemplified by the dolphin, we shall come nearer to understanding the responsibilities of unlimited intellect.

There is no doubt in my mind that human intellect as a whole is yet in its infancy. Even so, an outside observer of this planet could be left in no doubt, from the evidence of our unreasonable, self-destructive and bizarre behaviour, that although we have not fulfilled intellect (this concept is explored fully in Part III) we clearly possess its powers. Dolphins are biologically highly complex but, I repeat, there is nothing in their behaviour to suggest mental achievement beyond advanced instinctive consciousness. The reason must be that they never had to face a challenge that their conscious faculty could not meet - they were never threatened with such catastrophe that if they did not acquire an additional mental level, with the ability to look critically at themselves and their ways in order to change them, they would die out.

Apefolk

To return to the land animals of about three million years ago: the self was situated in a relatively small conscious faculty - see Fig. 4C - and behaviour was almost entirely dictated by instinct, periodically enhanced by explorations of consciousness. These explorations were carried furthest by apes, such as chimpanzees, by way of curiosity aided by the beginnings of manual dexterity. One particular ape advanced in curiosity much the furthest, breaking instinctive bonds and enlarging its conscious faculty beyond the point of no return, a point where control of its being passed from an instinctive body, aided by the conscious self, to the conscious self leading the instinctive body. These advanced apes were our predecessors, whom I shall call the apefolk.

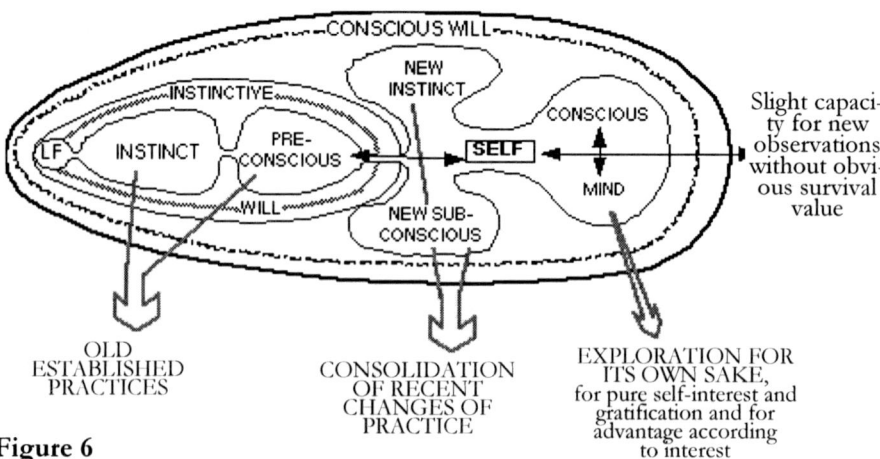

Figure 6
Apefolk Brain

(Note to the reader: In this Chapter, and elsewhere, the author's information is as much based upon deeply reasoned deduction as strictly factual. It is not intended to build knowledge but to broaden and stimulate fully correlated thinking)

As the apefolk learned from new observations, and calculated certain alternative ways of achieving instinctive aims, occasionally taking the risk of breaking old taboos, they slowly progressed by trial and error. To begin with, their brains would be as shown in Figure 4C, but towards the end of their era, after about three million years, I imagine the picture to be more like Figure 6.

Life-forms had always advanced cautiously with one foot, leaving the other firmly planted in instinct. The apefolk seemed sometimes to jump recklessly forward with both feet. But they were not leaping into darkness because life-force impulsion was still the guiding force of their life, and although it was their consciousness that actually decided to make the jump, the source of that decision, and the experience on which it was calculated, was predominantly instinctive.

Consciousness in some sense freed itself from instinct, yet it was still anchored to the same basic exclusive interest that was served by instinct - self-survival. The conscious will pursued this interest exclusively because it was not so equipped as to be aware of any other. Obeying evolved instinct to the letter had once been vital to securing survival. But instinct had imperfections, and consciousness was able to improve on it, purposely rather than by chance, the better to serve self-interest. Previously, subconscious instinct had curbed the new conscious faculty by subjecting it to emotions - attractions and fears too strong to be overcome. Now the fulfilment of advanced consciousness became an emotional necessity, as well as the fulfilment of instinct, making the overcoming of some fears and the breakdown of some inhibitions not only possible but essential to the satisfaction of the self, whose interest was now open to conscious as well as instinctive interpretation.

Apefolk began to eat the flesh of other animals to supplement their usual diet of fruit and nuts, and to raise themselves permanently on two legs the better to carry things and constantly to observe their surroundings on the grassy plains. These are examples of changes in habit which were not attributable to chance but to the intention of will, and of changes of form which are the body's helpful response to such intention. These new patterns of behaviour were not necessarily better in terms of immediate survival, for the apefolk could have remained apes (species of which still continue to be successful), unless these changes were forced on them by increasing competition - perhaps from overcrowding due to constriction of their habitat during an ice-age. But to the apefolk they must have seemed changes for the better because they answered that newly felt need not only to break new ground but also to take some part in making decisions. Although they were still very much governed by instinct, consciousness gave them a new sense of freedom as they overcame some instinctive inhibitions. And, of course, such progress also appealed to them because it obeys the influence exerted on all life to pursue change to the optimum.

Apefolk must have had a range of inherent instincts similar to those of the dolphins, but were venturing into unknown territory where the struggle for survival was much more intense than in the sea. Now being faced with fierce competition from animals better equipped with the means of attack and defence, yet knowing themselves to be of superior intelligence, they adopted the offensive drives of instinct rather than its passive defences as the chief hallmarks of their character, using that intelligence as their main and very effective weapon. During most of their relatively short history the apefolk came to occupy a unique position amongst Earth's animals, being not the strongest or most fearsome of creatures yet successful competitors, resourceful and adaptable, and representing the penultimate stage in the struggle of blind evolution towards its goal of self-awareness.

It is difficult for us, with our higher level of intelligence, to imagine how the apefolk saw the world from the fastness of consciousness, and how far they managed to progress. They appear to have had no language as we know it, nor capacity for critical self-awareness such as stimulates language - the need to convey to the self and to others meanings different from those which are already instinctively understood. In a vague way they could survey their own instinctive subconsciousness but from the same side of the fence, so to speak, which enabled them to see some better ways of applying the interests of instinct, but not to envisage alternative interests. They had only instinctive morality, yet could impose on instinct new practices which served better than the old. When apefolk became habitually upright, it was not only to observe their surroundings better but also to free their hands and aid co-ordination by bringing their manual activity within range of their level gaze. Their skulls slowly grew in size and changed shape to accommodate the developing brain. My judgement of the apefolk is based on the assumption that they remained locked in consciousness and only recently became extinct; that though descended from them (or from one species of them), we humans are the result of a profound mutation which, whilst leaving us little changed on the outside, made us into another species of altogether different mind.

The apefolk were a developing species, striving to succeed in a highly competitive situation. Of necessity this would mean adopting the mainstays of raw instinctive success, the pecking order and survival of the fittest, as between individuals in a group and between groups. Normally, when animals reach the limit of their scope they do not settle but keep pressing on aggressively. It is likely that they never learned to limit their killing so as to conserve the food supply, nor to limit their numbers by somehow restricting breeding. This would be because they were unwilling to have their conscious freedom restricted by seemingly unnecessary new inhibitions, and that, in turn, would be because their adaptable versatility enabled them to move on and spread out to pastures new and to thrive on a wide variety of diet.

It is probable that the apefolk learned to use simple weapons like sticks, which they would sharpen, and stones, which they would split to obtain sharp edges, but not to use tools otherwise. They eventually used fire for cooking meat and for comfort and safety at night; also for frightening predators such as lions away from a kill in order to take the meat for themselves. It is likely that they would get this fire from natural sources and keep it burning always, carrying it with them as they moved from place to place, being unable to make it themselves. It is doubtful whether they took to clothing themselves much, or built permanent shelters, but they did live in caves, where available. It is uncertain that they ever took to the water, although recently suggested that they must have done so. They would be able to dig for roots, insects and small animals with sticks, but not to make traps. Although having no language, they must have had a fairly comprehensive range of signs and signals to communicate with each other - facial expressions, hand signals, marks on the ground or on rocks and tree trunks.

By human standards the apefolk made slow and limited progress, yet they advanced much further than any other land animal. As I have said already, consciousness was a forward leap in evolution. Why was it so slow to develop, and why, no matter how large its capacity (e.g. in elephants, whales and dolphins), does it remain limited? I have already hinted at the answer when suggesting that although consciousness leaped forward, instinct was the source of the decision to leap. The conscious faculty is an extension of the preconscious,which is an extension of instinct that, in turn, grew out of life-force. These extensions raised the capacity of intelligence, each advancing to a new frontier, but they all shared the same system of comparative judgement - the same slowly-evolving nerve system in the brain. Thus they were subject to a fixed set of values and concepts, laid down long ago. It was the fundamental instinctive responsibility of intelligence to see that these were never contravened. It is obvious that instinct would take a lot of persuading that a new departure, suggested by the conscious, was an improvement on an old habit and did not contravene basic values and concepts, and this explains the apefolks' slow progress. No decision would have to be made about random mutations, of course, but these were unlikely to occur in a complex and already successful species, and if they did occur they would be adopted or rejected by natural selection. Instinctive caution prevailed because the conscious faculty failed to overtake instinct, for the reason that it lacked the facilities to conduct independent reasoning and record it in its own memory. This in turn explains why no animal but ourselves is capable of self-reflection, which would be utterly unacceptable to instinct in any case.

As regards their competitive struggle against the rest of nature the apefolk were successful enough. I don't think it was external opposition that initiated their destruction but that they were the cause of their own downfall. Because of their exceptional capabilities they were able to obey instinct by pursuing its drives, but to excess, compensated for by denying, to the same but opposite degree, instinctive inhibitions. This could not be forbidden by instinct because at first it seemed to be successful. But it was out of phase with the balance of nature, contrary to that evolved system which has its own laws, in which every creature normally has its dependent place guaranteed by obedience to its own instinct, and in which change, if it is to be feasible, is usually minor and gradual, or, in the case of dramatic change, is in response to a creature getting out of balance and is immediately beneficial. In the balance of nature every creature achieves optimum tolerance of its circumstances and maximum resistance to dangers. Reckless change may well bring benefits on one side, but leave the creature exposed and vulnerable on the other.

Indiscriminate hunting would not matter whilst there was plenty of free space, but these primitive apefolk could not venture too far north, and eventually there must have been overcrowding. This would mean shortage of food, fighting between groups over kills, for territory and for water, and domination by the fittest. This is not uncommon in nature, but a balance normally obtains whereby conflict has settled down within reasonable limits so that it serves rather than threatens survival. The apefolk, because of their large conscious capacity, would carry their conflicts to damaging extremes and would yet be a long way from finding a tolerable balance.

Another drive, as strong as that of the male to compete for advantage, is the sexual urge. When the living is easy, with no pressure to restrict mating in some way and so keep numbers in check, animals may become promiscuous, particularly in warm climates where there is little seasonal limitation on birth. The current behaviour of baboons in South Africa serves as an example, indicating that the transition from instinct to intellect necessarily proceeds by way of unpleasant behaviour. The state of heightened tension in which the apefolk now lived, due to squabbling and fighting within the group and the threat of attack from outside, might have the same effect. If the females would not or could not submit to them, the males may have resorted to rape, or homosexuality, or the females may have resorted to prostitution in return for male protection. The result may have been the spread of a terrible disease such as AIDS - a virus normally kept at bay but then moving in to take advantage of an unnatural situation, just as it is amongst humans today.

Whatever may have been the case, I think it likely that the apefolk became neurotic and brutal, fearful and obnoxious to all other animals and candidates for self-destruction. But such behaviour goes against nature, and the consciousness of the apefolk themselves must have cried out for reimposition of the benign and inhibiting instincts which they were ignoring, and for the return of their species to a balanced state. This would be expressed as a strong conscious will for significant change, which eventually could have brought about an extremely dramatic mutation.

The physical evidence implies that, in terms of technology, pre-humans developed hardly at all between the making of the first flint cutting tools and the appearance of the true human species some two or three million years later. There may well have been significant development of a different kind, of which there would be no surviving physical evidence - the slow development of thought. As well as 'doers', the physical/instinctive majority who made the flint spear-heads and were content that the traditional and on the whole successful strategies should not change, there must have been individuals who were vaguely dissatisfied and 'dreamed dreams'. As far as the serious business of survival was concerned, these 'thinkers' would be discounted or regarded as eccentric or mad, just as they are today, but their thoughts, however vague, would have a generally disturbing effect.

It seems likely that one apefolk mother, somewhere in Central Africa between forty and one hundred thousand years ago (estimates vary), could have conceived the genetic pattern for a new extension of the brain. The urge for this mutation must have been gathering strength in pre-human consciousness for some time, and maybe it was another new and unexpected threat of catastrophe that triggered it off, or some challenge connected with the end of the last ice age. Whether or not this was so, the event set the seal on the apefolks' fate and marked the beginning of a new, human species.

Chapter 3

BIRTH OF INTELLECT

However it may have occurred, this new brain growth added another dimension to the primate brain's neocortex - the unique human integrative and analytical function which I call the postconscious. This was a growth of intelligence, a further extension of the apefolk mental system, but not just another appended mass of cells to give new dimensions to instinct, as the preconscious and conscious faculties had been. This was an added level, a complete mind in its own right, able critically to observe the motivation and behaviour of the self with which it was associated, and to judge that self with integrity. This level was the superior of instinct, capable of taking full responsibility for the self. In order to do so, instead of merely observing that which was of direct instinctive interest, and a little beyond out of curiosity, it had to observe everything possible, firstly because there was no telling what foreknowledge the humans would require to succeed in these their new extra-instinctive activities, and secondly because everything is grist to the mill of total understanding, and it would be only by total understanding that the postconscious could ascertain what was best for the human species.

It seems to me that ten thousand million new neurones were created, or a new genetic programme was set up allowing and preparing for their creation or activation and interconnection as, or if and when, required (making the whole cortex up to one hundred thousand million actual or possible neurones, and a possible number of interconnections now estimated at ten to the power of several millions) to give this enormous extra observing, reasoning and memorising capacity. While the postconscious was fully aware of everything going on in the conscious, its own workings were screened off from the latter, unconscious, and only its conclusions offered to the conscious self. This faculty must have developed remarkably quickly, because it would not be reliably effective until it became a complete system and there was an urgent and vital need for it. In the first human child it must have appeared as a tumour, growing to such an extent that the brain pressed downwards within the fixed-dimension skull to the point where it compressed the throat and windpipe. Whereas it is assumed that the apefolk were able to breathe and swallow at the same time, as monkeys can, the first human could now only do these things alternately, and this led to the formation of the larynx which enabled us to articulate speech. This transformation evidently still takes place in human babies at the age of about six months.

It is said that the human neocortex makes up 80% of total brain size, compared with 70% in the case of the chimpanzee. This 10% growth in the neocortex may represent the explosive mutation that produced the postconscious faculty although it does not appear to be a large enough cause to produce so significant an effect. The diagram in Figure 7 below is not meant to indicate so large an increase in brain size as it suggests, but to show the dramatic increase in reasoning capacity caused by this mutation. It was not the huge number of additional cells alone that gave us this added capacity but the fact that they made up a separate, higher faculty that afforded optimum reasoning potential. So we can explain the apparent fact that the brain of Neanderthal man was larger than the human brain if we assume that the former lacked the latter's six cortical layers.

Figure 7
The Human Mutation -
Logical Outcome

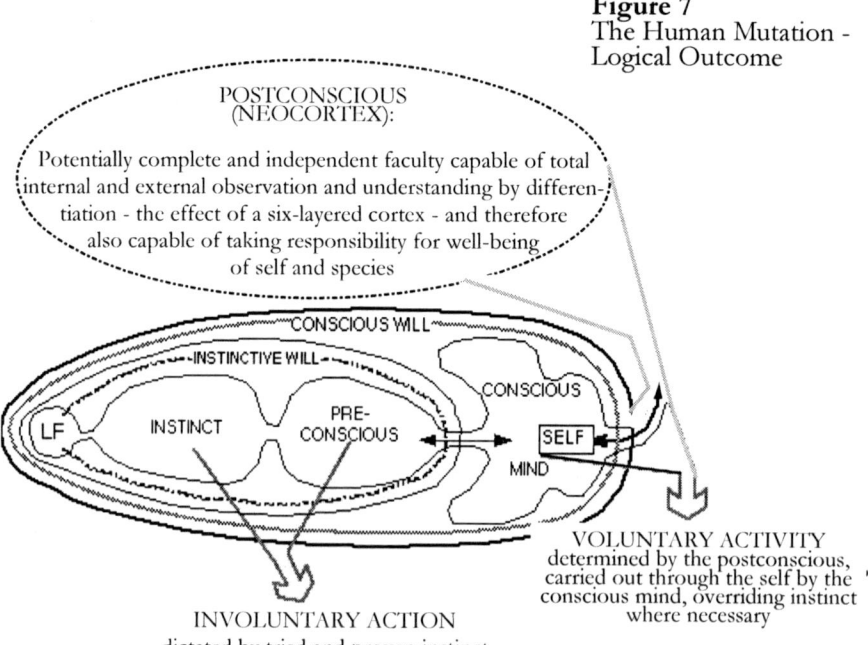

POSTCONSCIOUS
(NEOCORTEX):
Potentially complete and independent faculty capable of total internal and external observation and understanding by differentiation - the effect of a six-layered cortex - and therefore also capable of taking responsibility for well-being of self and species

CONSCIOUS WILL
INSTINCTIVE WILL
CONSCIOUS
LF   INSTINCT   PRE-CONSCIOUS   SELF
MIND

VOLUNTARY ACTIVITY
determined by the postconscious, carried out through the self by the conscious mind, overriding instinct where necessary

INVOLUNTARY ACTION
dictated by tried and proven instinct

I do not insist on this theory of the emergence of the human species by sudden mutation but it is the most likely that I have been able to deduce and it nicely explains subsequent developments.

The postconscious has its own memory, entirely separate from the old system of comparative judgement that obeyed a fixed set of instinctive 'do's' and 'don'ts'. It had to be so because the apefolk's troubles came from using their higher intelligence to pursue the drives of instinct too far. It was now logical that responsibility for life should be taken away from blueprints evolved out of the past and given to patterns arising from reason. The faculty grew to its full capacity, presumably somehow knowing to stop growing when the evidently optimum figure of 10 to the power of 11 cortex cells had been reached (the restricted capacity of the cranium is unlikely to have limited further growth, for that would mean that its limits exactly coinciding with this optimum figure.) Presumably the postconscious started work on its most urgent task, that of formulating an alternative motivation and code of behaviour and pressing it on the self in place of instinctive consciousness. A hundred thousand years later it is still at work but, for reasons that I shall try to explain, it has made little progress.

The most significant feature of developing life has been its rising level of intelligence. Yet, although instinct, the preconscious, and consciousness have produced complex animals, these can hardly be said to be vital developments, since primitive life would have flourished without them. The human mutation has resulted in the most complex developments of all, changing the face of Earth, yet we are less happy and contented than the apes we sprang from. That mutation was the birth of intellect, the significance of which we do not appreciate because we have not fulfilled its true potential. We have developed many skills to a high degree, such as language - a greater stimulator of mental development than manual dexterity - and the many arts and means of communication, but we have failed to do that which is best for us and our world. Human intellect has not grown to maturity, but is still a child.

THE WRONG REALITY

Part II
AUTOMATION
OF THE HUMAN MIND

Chapter 4

THE CONSCIOUS ASSERTION

The postconscious set about its task, that of shifting responsibility of the human species for itself from instinctive consciousness, by which the apefolk were destroying themselves, to consciousness of true reason. But long before it could make any real progress the old established conscious will asserted itself, taking over the whole new brain capacity for its own use. But this massive increase in reasoning ability was far more than instinct required. So the conscious took over for its direct utilisation about 40% of the postconscious and this continued for a long time (see Fig.8) but eventually this too proved unwieldy. The conscious solved the problem by simply *attaching** that 40% extra capacity to its existing mind, to whose practices and principles it was partly subjected, making it the utilised postconscious. (*It could not be *added* because it was differently constructed). The remaining 60% was pushed aside and closed off, thus facilitating the free and independent postconscious and potential supraconsciousness (see Fig.10, Chapter 12).

The apefolk, subject to threat, had felt the urge to mutate. Perhaps the influence on all life to advance towards the ultimate took the opportunity to make this a brain mutation. Perhaps it was the only mutation which now had any possible chance of succeeding.

Under the utilised postconscious, the first humans were in a peculiar situation in which individuals were enabled to believe they were being morally right when in fact, they were doing moral wrong - such as religionists who kill in the name of a creed that forbids killing. At any rate, potential intellect now existed on Earth, even if it was immediately subdued so as not to be fulfilled from that time to the present, about 4000 generations later, making this an immature human mutation.

It is often difficult to decide whether the mechanisms of a conscious organism determine its intelligent self, or vice versa. In my view the forefront of the brain is always straining at the leash, the true potential self always trying to lead the way towards the optimum, but otherwise intelligence and its mechanisms are virtually one and the same - each the other's creation. The human mechanism of higher intelligence, with all its vast potential, remains the prisoner of consciousness, yet the self is capable of changing all that.

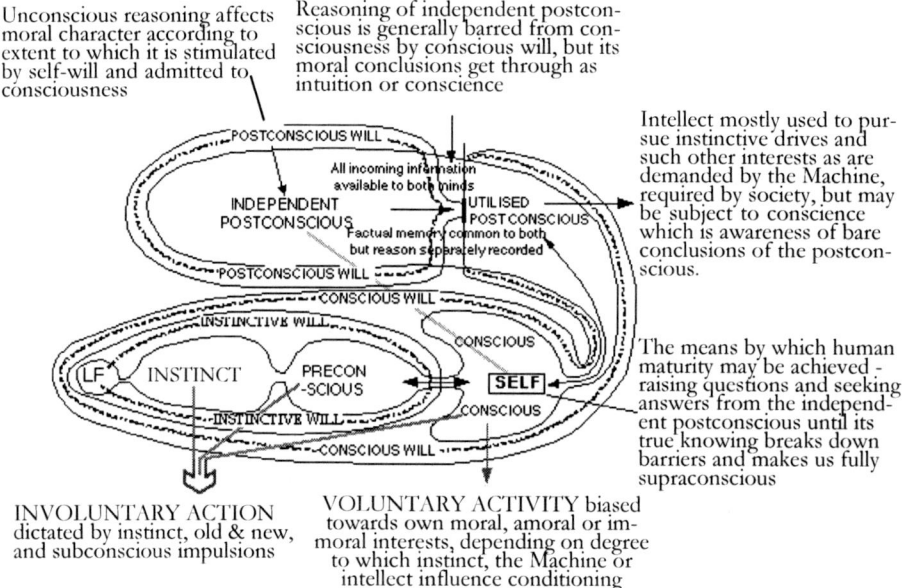

Unconscious reasoning affects moral character according to extent to which it is stimulated by self-will and admitted to consciousness

Reasoning of independent postconscious is generally barred from consciousness by conscious will, but its moral conclusions get through as intuition or conscience

Intellect mostly used to pursue instinctive drives and such other interests as are demanded by the Machine, required by society, but may be subject to conscience which is awareness of bare conclusions of the postconscious.

The means by which human maturity may be achieved - raising questions and seeking answers from the independent postconscious until its true knowing breaks down barriers and makes us fully supraconscious

INVOLUNTARY ACTION dictated by instinct, old & new, and subconscious impulsions

VOLUNTARY ACTIVITY biased towards own moral, amoral or immoral interests, depending on degree to which instinct, the Machine or intellect influence conditioning

Figure 8
Transitional Human State - Immature Mutation

Consciousness contains the self and receives from the world outside that information which preconscious instinct has not already dealt with and which it is conditioned to notice or judges to require notice. The conscious self is the arbitrary centre of being. It is capable of making out-of-the-ordinary decisions, but to arrive at these decisions it applies the utilised part of the postconscious faculty. This utilised part of the postconscious was partially programmed by the conscious mind and is exposed to the influence of conscious will. The independent postconscious is separate, its strength coming not only from its own will, but also from the power of its true knowing. It is free to reason truly within itself, as is its pure function, but the output of its reason is normally prevented, and its truth has no power unless recognised. Consciousness blocks the output of reason from the postconscious, refusing to recognise its truth and denying it entry to the conscious mind, because postconscious truth goes directly contrary to the great weight of false automatic reality.

Although the postconscious is divided, with its utilised part now partially associated with the falsely contrived reasoning of the conscious mind, fundamentally it functions as one. All information coming in to the brain via the senses is made available to both its postconscious and conscious parts. The two parts share the same factual memory but their interpretation of that information, their reasoning, is recorded separately - that which is true going to the postconscious memory and part-truths, which the utlised postconscious has been associated with, going to the falsely contrived conscious memory. That the true morality of the postconscious and the immorality of the conscious can influence people to a widely differing degree, and that individual conscious minds can represent a variety of different falsely contrived fabrications, explains why individual minds, having the same information available to them, can form very different conclusions and contradictory opinions and beliefs.

Only the more superficial workings of the utilised postconscious were available to conscious awareness. The independent postconscious, when we permit, makes us aware only of the conclusions resulting from its reasoning; it does not admit us to the reasoning process itself. We tried to impose our will on the utilised postconscious to reason as our conscious selves require. Alternatively, however, we can apply our will to encouraging the independent postconscious to reason to the optimum, thus so reinforcing the power of its knowing that its findings overcome normal resistance, reach our conscious awareness and redouble our effort of will to encourage the process further.

Even if we do not use our will in this way, and are aware only of the output of conscious reason aided by the utilised postconscious, our independent postconscious has observed and memorised everything, including the fact that its counterpart is being falsely programmed and used and is laying down false memories. Our independent postconscious knows everything knowable about ourselves and our experiences of the world. It is capable of reasoning the truth from this knowledge, and will have made some progress in this regard in every mind. So the postconscious generally knows far more than the conscious self specifically knows, and reasons much further than we understand, or are even aware of. Yet each independent postconscious is capable of fulfilling that knowing and understanding and imparting it to us, if we will allow.

It is important to realise that presently we humans are our conscious selves. We cannot properly be called self-reflective because whereas the postconscious is capable of looking at our whole being, including itself, we normally take serious notice only of the conscious and that part of the postconscious that we once utilised and dominated with our conscious will but that has now been returned to the postconscious proper. The human conscious self retains the power to take whichever direction it chooses. It can be wilfully instinctive, consciously disciplined in the values and ways of existing reality, or open to the moral guidance of the independent postconscious. It is normal for individuals to be strongly subject to the first two of these influences, and influenced to a much lesser and ineffectual degree by the third.

I have suggested already that postconscious memory is available to both its independent parts. But memory is not just a storage facility for facts. It is a record of all that we have observed and reasoned, and is continually being reviewed and revised. And the postconscious is able to reflect on itself, so it is able to put a true valuation on its records - in the case of incoming information, the degree to which it is true or false, how far its reasoning has been advanced, or doctored, and how honestly or dishonestly its 'facts' have been established. To the purely instinctive creature, its memory is not only all that it can recall but also all that it can act upon. The modern human has potential choice between instinctive/conscious and postconscious memories, and between different versions of them. The instinctive/conscious self usually chooses its own preferred version, already prejudiced in its favour, in order to react spontaneously in what it conceives to be its best interests according to the facts and concepts of its personal versions of reality. This, again, accounts for the wide differences in human opinion and belief and comes from the same source that created wide social variations, compared with the almost identical characteristics of individual animals of one species. We are much more intelligent than the apefolk, who were superior animals, but we have, near the threshold of consciousness, many of their instincts which should no longer be necessary to us - competitive spirit, desire to kill, fear of wild animals, fear of the dark, etc.

This subject may be difficult to take in. I think the mind tends to resist examining itself, but this examination need not be as difficult as it seems if the process is built up in stages of reasoning. And it is very necessary understanding, for it helps to clear away the mystery presently obscuring the normal human mind. The next five short chapters investigate the causes of the mind developing as it has, and the following Part III considers how we can encourage it to develop as it ought.

Chapter 5

PRIMITIVE PERFECTION

It can well be imagined that the first humans were better equipped to survive than the apefolk in whose midst they appeared. It can also be imagined that no love was lost between them. The more intelligent humans would come to despise their primitive brothers, keeping themselves apart and growing as a separate and distinct species. The apefolk would be envious, resentful and afraid of these interlopers, but as they far outnumbered the humans they were able to drive them out of Central Africa, apparently to the north. The apefolk already occupied territories to the north - the more temperate parts which were still quite favourable to their survival - but although they had been relatively successful against the rest of the animal world, it is likely that owing to their wasteful habits their population had reached a maximum long ago and might now be declining because of fighting amongst themselves and disease.

The humans would be much more adept with hand and eye than the apefolk. To defend themselves they must have quickly become expert in fashioning and wielding better weapons, which would also make them superior hunters so that they survived more successfully wherever they went and increased in numbers. I calculate that out of one mated pair from the original mother's offspring, an increase of 50% every fifty years (not out of the way in the circumstances perhaps) would produce a quarter of a million humans in two thousand years. Thereafter, as long as their success and rich opportunity continued, the increase would be much more dramatic. Humans became ever more successful as they learned more skills - the making of fire, trapping and herding animals, catching fish, erecting shelters and making clothes.

During this period humans became more erect and lost much of their body hair. They and the apefolk would keep their distance, but it was inevitable that in due course they came into conflict over game, watering places and territory, especially the best land that the apefolk occupied. As time went on the number of skirmishes must have increased, so that soon there was virtually a state of war between them. The humans were still outnumbered but they had much better weapons, and the best weapon of all - their high intelligence. I do not think that humans would eat the apefolk they killed because they were too sensitive of their close relationship, nor that they would molest the females of that species because they despised them, but I imagine the apefolk would have no such scruples. To take baboons as an example once again, where they have come into close contact with humans in South Africa and have been fed attractive junk foods, they have turned to stealing with violence and have been hunted down and shot. For these reasons it seems to me likely that the humans deliberately turned on the apefolk with the intention of exterminating them. They hated the apefolk and wanted to rid themselves of their presence, but they also must have felt an instinctive desire to get rid of their main competitor.

I am inclined to believe that as many apefolk died of some such terrible disease as AIDS as were hunted down and killed. If they were so unfortunate as to be riddled with it, this would be added reason why they should be hated and exterminated. This might also have a bearing on our ancient sexual taboos. However it was, they were overcome, their territories taken over by humans, perhaps the last of them retreating into the Himalayas, and known as Yeti. Humans now separated roughly into three divisions, First, Second and Third. The First were the most aggressive against the apefolk perhaps, becoming the most competitive and ambitious, occupying the more fertile territory, establishing the Machine and forming the patterns of civilisation, in such countries as Egypt, China, India, Greece, Italy, South America, Spain. Then there was the Second division of humans who were driven, or retreated, into the wetter, colder, more northerly lands. Toughened by the harsh conditions, they eventually overtook the rest and set in motion the accelerating expansion of the Machine which has engulfed the whole world, resulting in the facts and concepts of today's reality. These two divisions will be dealt with in the next chapter.

Finally there was the Third and more passive grouping of humans, who occupied the less accessible plains and jungles, such as the Red Indians of North America, the Aborigines of Australia, but particularly the Bushmen and Baka people of Africa and the Incas of Peru. The significance of these large and once flourishing communities is the lesson they offer. Whilst we share with them the same ancestor and the same mental capacity, their philosophy is, or was, very different from ours. This implies that the modern human nature and state is not inevitable; that happiness and satisfaction may be attained by following the true reasoning of intellect by way of the simple answers and solutions that lead to that goal. It also indicates that the alternative way of energetic application of intellect to ruthless pursuit of instinctive drives by way of every possible complex discovery and technological achievement clearly does not bring happiness and satisfaction.

The Bushmen probably came down from the north to occupy Africa some 22,000 years ago. If they had to fight and kill off the apefolk who were already there, it can only be assumed that this action so horrified as to determine them against such behaviour thereafter, unless absolutely necessary, for it was not subsequently characteristic of them until they fought and lost the battle with their recent invaders. This question does not arise, of course, if it was the case that some unknown catastrophe, which the humans were able to survive, wiped out the apefolk. The Bushmen flourished until those recent invaders, 'civilised' humans invading Africa from north and south, steadily killed off or neutralised them, not without difficulty but evidently without the slightest compunction or regret, until, earlier in this century, only a few of them were to be found living in the traditional way, in the inhospitable Kalahari desert.

The African Bushmen found a perfect balance between duty and hardship, joy and relaxation, to which their expectations were exactly adjusted so that they were fulfilled, happy and contented (within the limits of their awareness.) They were territorial, but the very thought of hurting any of their own species was so distasteful that each group kept strictly within its agreed borders. Nevertheless, they killed unwanted babies, to which the mothers always agreed, however reluctantly, because of the strict necessity for keeping down numbers. They had religion, a deep belief in powerful 'spirits' that had strong influences and effects. Of course, it was not these 'spirits' but their own ancient belief and collective will that caused these effects and by which each individual, by self-subjection, was strongly influenced.

They were skilled hunters, with bow and poisoned arrow, trappers of small animals and birds, gatherers of fruits, nuts, and roots that they grubbed out with special sticks. They were great cave and rock-wall painters of animals and hunting scenes. They were musicians, carrying their instruments about with them and gaining comfort and inspiration from music and dancing in the cool evenings. They were story-tellers, with a great tradition. And they were healers, with wide knowledge of medical concoctions. They did nothing that was not needful or sympathetic to their unchanging existence alongside nature. Everything they did they endowed with feeling for its deepest significance, applied to it the utmost skill, concentration and energy, and endeavoured to bring to it joy and satisfaction.

They practiced equality, a society without leaders and authority, run by cooperation and shared responsibility, with no pecking order. They had very few possessions - only the absolute essentials - went practically naked, and built shelters that they occupied between walkabouts. They were gentle, always expressing regret at the killing of animals they required for meat, and would show communal sympathy with their sick, trying to comfort and cure them by the laying on of hands and invoking of spirits, their kind of faith healing.

The good example of the Bushmen might have been lost to us had not Laurens van der Post given an eye-witness account of them in his book 'Bushmen of the Kalahari' and on film. These people sustained their society for a very long time, and would have gone on doing so but for the invasion of 'civilisation'. The same can be said for the Incas of Peru, whose true morality was betrayed by superstition, then trodden in the dust by the blood and gold-thirsty Catholic Conquistadors.

There is yet more we can learn from the simple wisdom of the good Bushmen (and women). They achieved their satisfactory state and balanced society despite the fact that their brains were arranged as shown in Figure 8 (Chapter 4), just as ours are. They, however, applied themselves to the full range of instincts, putting the benign foremost as becomes the dominant species, and used their power of intellect to achieve satisfactory fulfilment in harmony with nature. They did not look for change for its own sake but were content with what they had, primitive as it might appear to civilised eyes, because it was a happy balance.

The Incas are included in the 'Third division' of human societies because although they developed a highly organised system of living it was not to the same pattern as the 'First division' civilisations. This appears to have been a benevolent society, not founded on the competitive drives; an economy that was not based on money. It may not always have been so, for the Incas had leaders, and formal religion, and went in for ceremonial splendour. But, partly because they were non-aggressive and trusting and partly because they believed their fate to be the fulfilment of a dreadful celestial prophecy, they allowed a handful of Spaniards to either massacre or enslave them. On the other hand, paradoxically, the Bushmen fought fiercely and to the death against their invaders. Perhaps that merely illustrates a basic difference in the concept of freedom between a 'wild' nomadic community and a static, organised and domesticated community.

I suppose it is possible for the conscious mind to draw contradictory conclusions from examples such as these. All that should concern us is that we draw true conclusions. It seems to me that the Bushmen maintained their unchanging ways because those ways appealed to the intelligence as good and fair, and for that reason had been agreed. The Bushmen also maintained their unchanging ways because those ways were successful, but it is important to consider what this means. The Bushman society was successful because it was not a structure superimposed on the people - it *was* the people, representing the principles to which each person had agreed in the common interest. This was not like our present society - a separate organisation exploiting the differing abilities of people in order to supply their various demands as consumers, while at the same time trying to control them as a conglomerate whole. This was the nearest human approach yet to the ideal society, in which each and every individual took responsibility for the whole - each gave effort and received benefit equally, willingly and cheerfully, and then, with responsible consideration, did their own personally fulfilling thing.

Chapter 6

MACHINE FOUNDATION

J ust as the activities of an individual creature are predictable if the characteristics of its species are known, so it is necessary to recognise the principles on which the framework of our society - the Machine - is built in order to understand the present chief characteristics of the human species.

The Machine was founded on the automaton, whose influence became a fundamental characteristic of humanity at the time when conscious will took over part of the postconscious faculty. The natural purpose of instinct is to play a balanced part in securing survival. Humans were impelled by this automatic influence to pursue the instinctive competitive drives far beyond that natural purpose to secure survival so that, instead of being means to that end, these drives became ends in themselves. Nature divides its creatures into groups. Some groups may be ruled by leaders, others by the pecking order, but these rules apply only because they have proved beneficial to survival of the group, or species. If a rule does not bring benefit it will die out through the process of natural selection. Humans henceforth followed a course of unnatural, and unwise, selection. Having burst the bonds of instinct, they succumbed to an alliance between the liberated positive forces of instinct and the applied power of super-intelligence. They divided from each other, became different from each other, and took competition to the extreme of fighting each other to the death. This behaviour constitutes a threat to contentment and ultimately to survival, going contrary both to the tried and proved balance of nature and to the responsibility of intellect.

All the early humans, faced with a superior number of enemy apefolk, perhaps also with an epidemic disease, or possibly with some other threat of catastrophe, must have united in large groups, each obedient to a single leader, the better to cope effectively with the common danger and apply their common determination to achieving survival. Once they had overcome these extraordinary threats they were left with the ordinary challenges of survival and, in theory, the opportunity to choose what kind of life they would lead. But their leaders now held power (a new phenomenon that took a feature of instinct - the natural supremacy of the strongest - and converted it into the established institution of permanently conferred dominance,) and their choice, having tasted power, would be to hold onto it and keep the status quo. So the First division of humans maintained the leadership structure, and this obliged them to confirm and incorporate other instinctively originated principles into an artificial civilisation - the early Machine - in the more conducive climates of Egypt, Greece, China, India and the like. The Second division of humans, rebellious perhaps, moved north and, for some thousands of years, remained comparatively primitive as the struggle to solve the problems of sheer survival in colder climates absorbed all their energy. The Third, and wiser division of humans reacted against Machine principles, as we have seen (Chapter 5). We are presently concerned with the First division, the spearhead of human advance towards modern times.

The obligations which acceptance of leadership placed on humanity derive from the fact that leadership is associated with competition rather than co-operation, and that once it had served its original extraordinary purpose there was no real need of it. The truth was that survival could best be secured by small, partly self-sufficient but co-operative groups held together and served by the common code of the species. But supreme leaders, viewing the situation from a position of power, could not or would not concede this truth, and nobody else was in a position to make them concede it. So the structure of society did not change, and to justify itself leadership invented new purposes and needs and imposed them on peoples.

The purpose of leaders in nature, such as the leaders of wolf packs living under exacting conditions, is to carry out a function vitally necessary to survival, the achievement of which is their reward. In easy conditions, human leaders pursued the unnecessary purpose of dominant control and acquired a need to enjoy privileged reward, which amounted to ambition to profitably extend their domination as far as possible. This meant that leaders used the high intelligence of humankind to prosecute group warfare, the strongest of them eventually triumphing and setting themselves up as dominators of great kingdoms and empires - self-interested sovereign powers, competing with each other.

Government by supreme leaders is one of the false foundation stones of the Machine; false because it makes itself necessary by disallowing true human autonomy. As dominions became larger and leaders could no longer exercise direct control, systems of remote control became necessary. One of these was the institution of law and law enforcement, which was not only a means of authority imposing its will on 'the people' and refusing to allow them freedom to take their affairs into their own hands, but also of obliging people to do certain clearly desirable things which, given freedom to follow their intelligence, they would have done voluntarily in any case. But since the system tended to foster ignorance, it could appear to be necessary because of its apparently beneficial features. For example, it is possible that if the apefolk did suffer from AIDS, this terrible disease may have been transmitted to humans, whose sexual habits were probably free at that time. The ordinary individual would be unlikely to connect the disease with the actual cause of its spreading, but the leader, taking a wider view because of his position, might make that connection. It would then be made a matter of law that sexual intercourse be confined to the partners in marriage, for life, with severe punishment for transgressors, perhaps death, originally, for them and their issue, which was not mere retribution for breaking the law but designed to stamp out the disease by eliminating sufferers and carriers.

Kings now required a hierarchy of officials to administer and enforce the law and command their armies. The division between this minority and the subjugated majority reintroduced the natural pecking order as the rule of inequality. Inequality of status and reward brought about the rule of possession, the practice of defending the acquisition of some thing by 'putting one's name on it' so to speak, and having that title protected by law. The concept of possession in turn gave birth to the idea of barter, by which things were given a 'possession-value', and changed hands only in exchange for some other thing whose value was judged to be equal. But barter was cumbersome, and soon coins that betokened that value were exchanged and re-exchanged for goods, chattels and land. The introduction of money also facilitated taxation, which was tribute as a substitute for slavery. This tribute was to pay for the maintenance of authority and defence of the realm, and was made necessary only by the unnecessary existence of kings and their hierarchies lording it over their warlike kingdoms in competition with other kingdoms.

Leadership had now been transposed into dominant authority that created and then tried to ignore its own problems; which did not serve humanity but was served by it. Generally speaking, humans worked for the high elevation of the institutions supposed to represent them, and in return most were given low status and commensurately low levels of sustenance. To reinforce acceptance of the situation, it was morally justified by religion whose leaders occupied places in the privileged hierarchy. Religion taught good morality, up to a point, but also taught obedience to an authoritative system that did not reflect that goodness, and whilst it was good in parts, no doubt, the situation as a whole was not humanly justifiable and did not encourage true morality in anyone.

Those monuments which are held to reflect the glory of humankind are pyramids, palaces, castles, temples and churches, built by enslaved or employed workmen for the glorification of secular and religious establishments, that were and are actually irrelevant to the true potential of humanity. All other advances in the free exercise of intellect, such as music, literature and other arts, if they are to be assessed truly, are to be viewed in the same light. While they may be about reality and have arisen from its progress, they should not be taken to imply that human civilisation has meaningfully advanced. They are small successes relative to our great failure - marvellous but irrelevant examples of the scope of intellect that should illustrate how much good we could have done compared with the little good we have done.

The original First division civilisations flourished for thousands of years then began to stagnate. About fifteen hundred years ago the Second division humans, more primitive but also more energetic, began asserting themselves. By trading and conquest they outstripped or overran the old civilisations and all but wiped out or enslaved the Third division humans and seized their lands. The powerhouse of human 'progress' then became centred in Europe, later to shift to North America, and now moving again, probably to the Far East. The money economy led the way and people followed as the demand for willing labour resulted in the practice of incentive employment - enticing effort from workers rather than driving them to it. Soon the power of accumulated money - capital - became dominant and determined what could and would be done. Capital went hand-in-hand with human inventiveness to launch the industrial revolution.

Invention, however, was no longer a matter of human ingenuity rising to answer vital necessity, but the application of the human mind to science and technology, and its application, in turn, to competition in money economics and profitability in the market place. The competitive money economy now took over the real reins of authority from human governors, yet at the same time, as more and more people gained a financial stake in it in the shape of jobs, property or capital, the way was cleared for political representation of the people - a way made automatically viable by the fact that people were now bound to the Machine by apparent but misplaced self-interest as well as dependence and conditioning.

The money economy is not devoted to the clear and simple humanitarian objective to provide absolutely all the real needs of all the people. On the contrary, it is devoted to producing goods and services that can be sold to consumers at a profit, employing those humans whose labour it needs for that amount of money which shall induce them to do the work. People whom the Machine needs are paid well, moderately or poorly according to its valuation of their worth, and those it does not need are paid very little money, or none at all. Similarly, some nations benefit highly from the Machine and others poorly, according to whether their prosperity or poverty is in the interests of its profitability. So the world is divided into nations with an international pecking order, and the people of each nation are subject to their own internal pecking order. There are differences of language, custom, skin colour, ideology and religion between nations, and differences of status, education, privilege and money income between each nation's people. Humans are not working for the common good and happiness of a united human race but for the Machine, and the Machine is working for itself.

———————————

This chapter has been a potted history of the Machine, from its foundation through the automation of humanity to the present day (a critical analysis of practices and institutions of the Machine is given in Part IV). It has also been a short indictment of the Machine, seeing it as a tide that has swept us blindly in the wrong direction. Our existing complex and highly disturbing reality is the consequence of making permanent the temporary solutions to an emergency - long ago adopting the competitive drives and setting up authoritative leadership - so that they became the basic principles of our society. The following two chapters show how the consequent pattern of our lives has conditioned us and formed our character.

Chapter 7

AUTOMATIC CONDITIONING

As you read this, almost certainly you shall be judging it with a mind that is conditioned to some degree. This is not an insult but a statement of fact, for practically everybody is conditioned to the extent that they accept without question the fundamental concepts of existing automatic reality (see Preface). It is a convention, to which even the most compassionate, just and self-sacrificing of humans usually conform, that we must deal with the world as it stands in the inescapable here and now. It is most important that you the reader of this book, if it is to mean anything to you and if humanity at large is ever to change itself and its world for the better, recognise this convention as a fallacy. The conditioning of the great majority of minds so obscures the whole human truth that they fail to recognise it. As a result, however true these minds are to the conventions, they are rendered incapable of judging truly. This failure and incapability is not seen as such by the individual, of course, unless and until that conditioning is cleared away. Only the individual can clear it away and discover human truth - it is our personal responsibility.

Human minds are universally and extensively conditioned, chiefly by the Machine. Therefore that this chapter about conditioning is preceded by only a brief analysis of the Machine may appear strange. If the Machine largely shapes human thinking, then a penetrating account of how it works would surely also tell us a great deal about how the mind works. But by our conditioning we are attuned to automatic reality, and incapable of unbiased critical judgement, as pointed out already. Fully conditioned minds accept the world as it is - a chaotic mixture of good and bad, love and hate, violence and gentleness, honesty and dishonesty, terror and tranquillity. Criticism of the here and now, or radical thinking, is considered naïve. If the automated mind understands humanly true principles, it is in the same sense that fairy tales are understood. They are not fully understood as having vital human relevance and are judged impracticable. Only when our minds have removed their conditioning can we become fully aware and thus fully able critically and truly to judge the Machine, and this awareness shall surely bring a resolve to change reality accordingly.

(Note: I would remind you of the comment, made early in chapter 1, on the meaning of truth - that it is hard to define, that the meanings I ascribe to it are given in chapters Chapters 13 and 32, and suggesting that in the meantime you keep an open mind. In the paragraph preceding this note I mention humanly true principles. By this I mean such truth as is readily knowable and relevant to human wellbeing and from now on I shall refer to this as humantruth, the subject of Chapter 13.)

Up to a point we are all conditioned by instincts. Our automatic human conditioning began when power was given to leaders. Followers, the majority, were gradually given to believe that what they were expected, or forced to do by order of their leaders, was vital and unavoidable activity, rightly to be expected of them. This early orientation of the human mind, by the wilful manipulation of intellect, has persisted and influenced all our subsequent thinking. From that time to this, with exceptions already mentioned, we have been trapped in a cage of submission to direction from outside ourselves, a cage whose main bars are those that we willingly hold in place. Such has been the strength of this basic conditioning that while real authority has now passed from leaders to the automaton and the money economy, and has been modified in many ways, we are more than ever submissive to the Machine, whose material advantages increase in inverse proportion to its moral degradations.

We are brought into this reality at birth, and become able to think about it at age 4 or 5 when our minds are at their purest, being yet little formed. We have been given certain vague prejudices and emotional attitudes, but I believe that at this stage, provided our minds have been stimulated sufficiently, we are yet independent enough to determine the basic attitude of our thinking. Our brains are arranged as shown in Figure 8, and we have about ten years before us during which, one way or another, our minds will develop their character. We are faced with a reality which our independent postconscious knows to be contrary to truth, or illogical to reason, but which our conscious mind, supported by the utilised part of the postconscious, is likely to believe ultimately cannot be escaped. Which of these do we listen to; where do we position the self? In extreme cases, where childhood reality was so horrific that it could not be fully admitted to consciousness, a person would invent one or more alternative personalities into which to escape. I think that in every case humans contrive to split the self into two co-existing parts, which we try to make complementary though they are essentially contradictory - a hard outer shell which is adjusted to Machine reality by conscious will, and a soft inner core which reflects the benign instinctive emotions and, to varying extent, the conclusions of the independent postconscious.

During our formative years we are exposed to all the influences of the Machine, from aggressive indoctrination at one extreme to moral exhortation at the other. We play at soldiers and watch war and gangster films; play at shops and learn the value of money; sing hymns, take part in nativity plays, and so have the false imagery of god implanted in our minds. We experience the conflict of the world, feel it in ourselves as we too divide into an inner core and outer shell, and see it in our parents as they strive with each other and are torn in the struggle between trying to give us true guidance and affection and having to cope with the Machine which preoccupies their thoughts and absorbs their energy, falsifying and wasting them.

Consequently we are very soon inured to, if not made aware of, automatic life's fundamental contradictions. Humanity's inner-core morality is represented in the outer world by religion, but religions have compromised that morality in order to establish a platform that the Machine tolerates - the church - no doubt forced to the false conclusion that an adulterated message is better than none. Education is an instituted function which has the task of developing young minds, and it is surely obvious that the only way of doing this is to enable the mind to become fully and truly aware. But education is an institution of the Machine dedicated to preparing our outer shells - to acquainting humanity with, adjusting it to and preparing it for, its automatic past, present and future.

So we are conditioned according to instinct and the pattern of existing reality from the very start. The Machine permeates every inch of the fabric of life, and since we are inescapably part of that fabric, it also permeates our minds, especially through its competitive economy. This economy presents an immediate moral dilemma. If we think about it honestly we see clearly that it is immoral. It thrives on inequality and indiscriminately allows extremes of poverty and plenty to exist side-by-side. But we are all dependent on it for our livelihood so that by merely living we support it and contribute to its mastery of us. Yet we have a moral obligation to provide for our families, an obligation which we normally fulfil by going along with the money economy to our best advantage, an obligation which we will find great difficulty in fulfilling if we reject or drop out of the money economy on larger moral grounds.

By being automated we are not made the same. In fact one of the main attractions of the existing reality is that it is full of variety. But automated individuals have all taken the same course of accepting the Machine with all its contradictions. This puts them in competition, obliged to take opposing, conflicting parts. They may also take very different, if illogical, moral standpoints. Politics is an institution of this reality that endorses the Machine and accepts as inescapable fact that the competitive money economy is the ultimate governor, but it is also a forum in which true moral concerns, if they can prevail in competitive debate to the point of compromise, often succeed in modifying (but not fundamentally changing) automatic policy.

We remain conditioned primarily because we are unaware of being conditioned. We remain unaware because we do not allow the true thinking of our independent postconscious to penetrate our consciousness. We close ourselves off from awareness in this way for two main reasons. Firstly we are impressed by the overwhelming existence of the Machine reflected in the way the busy world behaves all round us, confirmed by almost every meeting, conversation, newspaper, book, TV and radio programme, debate and political speech. Also we are oppressed by the obligation to obey Machine law rather than conscience, the need to be constantly alert to protect ourselves in all ways, the fact of our dependence on an inhuman system which narrows us down to concentrating on its interests, efficiently doing its work, and conforming to its standards, for the sake of survival and in hope of reward.

Secondly, we remain conditioned because it is abnormal to look for truth; it goes against the grain to try and break down well-known reality - however bad it may be, we prefer the devil we know. Our normal reaction to the burdens, impositions and horrors of this life is not to prevent them but to find compensations. We tell ourselves we have but a short time to live, so we should find satisfaction in the situation as it exists. We try to see its beauty and turn a blind eye to its ugliness. We may feel we have not justified our personal existence unless we have succeeded in 'being someone' and 'getting somewhere.' We may feel that the most we, or anyone, can do is simply to accept the here and now but try to relieve its sufferings and cheer it up. We may be prepared to sacrifice the true ideal to the welfare of immediate family, to a local sense of community and the pleasure of friendship. We may feel it is better to resign ourselves to making the best of a bad job rather than argue the toss. People who are conditioned in these ways find some sort of security, even comfort, in confining themselves to this limited understanding, acceptance and expectation. And, by the automatic law of supply and demand, this is what they are given by the Machine in the form of information, material goods, services and entertainment. Thus is the conditioned process reinforced and perpetuated.

In consequence of all these things the human self learns not to listen to its independent postconscious, because whatever this better part of the mind thinks or rather knows to be true the lesser conscious part thinks otherwise. Humanity presently takes as the basis of human life, and always has taken, that which the Machine dictates according to its own automatic scale of false and inappropriate forces and values.

Just consider - if we lived in an ideal state, a humantrue reality, we would likewise be held to it by the fact that it everywhere existed, but additionally by the fact that it was in tune with our deepest true awareness. It would be easier for us to change to a humantrue reality than it is to maintain this existing false one, once we had made up our minds to do it. But herein lies our greatest difficulty, that of determining to overcome our conditioning and make up our minds truly.

Chapter 8

FORMATION OF CHARACTER

I hope we agree that to understand and realise humantruth is vital. Automatic conditioning is a serious obstacle to that understanding. Given time and determined effort, however, it can be surmounted. But conditioning has the physical/mental effect of forming a specific character by constructing the conscious mind in a particular way. When determination of conscious will is concentrated on upholding and defending that character, then its conditioning is unlikely ever to be broken down, because the individual is mostly unaware of it.

The reason for our unawareness is that our thinking - that which appears true to us - is formed by our particular construction of mind, a construction of which we do not allow ourselves to be critically doubtful if our determination to defend it is strong. In our confused and contradictory society a strong character can appear to be an asset, and is generally admired, but the fact that such personal bias is common means that many people, especially as they get older, seem wilfully beyond the possibility of finding true awareness.

As everybody knows, all kinds of different characters exist, but each has been formed, however differently, for similar reasons: we are given the strong desire to live; we see no alternative but to make a place for ourselves in the Machine; we are subject to all-round pressures of conditioning; and our intelligence gives us cause somehow to justify our existence to ourselves, to others, or to some group consensus. This does involve a pursuit of truth, but only up a limited point - the pursuit is not taken to the ultimate humantruth. The problem is that humantruth is made up of many parts and is wholly true only when all its parts are present. But each part, or small selection of parts, is true in itself and can cover a false situation with a cloak of apparent truth provided that the other parts are steadfastly ignored. A sense of the whole truth can persuade people to dedicate themselves to an ideal and, rarely, to the profound search for that whole truth, a search which does not allow the mind to be made up until it is completed, nor the character fully formed until the humantruth is realised. But idealists are presently in the minority. The majority of humans are realists, and since existing reality is false they cannot truly justify their consenting support of it except to say, 'you have to do the best you can in the here and now'. They might even repeat that supine quotation from Candide - 'all's for the best in the best of all possible worlds.'

The upshot of what I have said so far - a central problem of humanity which this whole book addresses - is firstly that our evolved reality is hostile to our intellectual potential and requires us to function well below our true level. Secondly, that we have become so adjusted to this reality as to render ourselves evidently incapable of achieving our intellectual potential. And by becoming so thoroughly automated as to be thus unable, as well as unwilling, to function at a higher level, we give our higher minds little or no encouragement independently to fulfil themselves despite their imprisonment.

As very young children our minds are clean sheets which, as we grow up, we fill in and try to balance by processes of reason. But general reality does not make reasonable sense, so this has to be contrived reason by which we attempt to make sense of reality. Our early experiences are largely imposed on us, the backwash of automatic instinctive drives. Our reactions and subsequent actions also derive from our own instincts, ancient and modern, from inherited emotional tendencies, and from our own attempts to reason whether we should go along with the norm or turn against it. That children display a certain innate aggressiveness could be a throwback to the early humans' violent extermination of the apefolk, a hitherto unnatural tendency towards killing one's own kind reflected in numerous subsequent wars. Similarly the attitude of our male/female relationships, though now changing, must have been inherited from our early survival struggles when the male functions of hunting, defending and fighting were put first and the female role took second place together with all other activities behind the front line of struggle.

We are given to judging other peoples' moral characters by certain set standards, but the formation of human character is presently a balancing act with very different personal circumstances, capacities and feelings. Sometimes it is an impossible act and the resultant imbalance becomes intolerable, with dramatic consequences. It is important to realise that whatever any of us does - however wrong, bad or inexcusable it may appear to others - it is right and good, or understandable, or unavoidable for us; the result of a decision which was the only one we could make in our circumstances; a matter of logic. Any behaviour can be traced back to a cause that explains it. In a world of baby battering, torture, mugging, terrorism and war this is a comforting thought, for it recognises that these horrors are not inbuilt human characteristics, but the superimposed effects of unreasonable causes. We all have moral values, but some of us are pressed by the amoral and immoral Machine to break them. The accepted standard of morality is that of the privileged middle class, unaware of its own contribution to immorality. Part of our reality is that if we were to choose a purely moral course we would not survive. In order to succeed in the Machine some degree of amorality or immorality is essential.

It is true that with determination virtue can triumph in certain cases, and circumstances cannot always entirely be blamed for our shortcomings. But the way to look at it is that present reality does not work for the encouragement and strengthening of morality, but against it. Very often our circumstances are such that we do not have the strength or resources to rise above them. We are drawn along by the attractions of the Machine, as well as pushed along at its direction, and are not united by our common true humanity. This lack of unity prevents us gravitating to a common morality. Existing reality being competitive and divided, humans are separated into different places, circumstances and ranks. We all feel compelled to fill roles in the monetary system of supply and demand, according to competitive laws of cause and effect - to submerge the potential character of the inner core under an assumed character imposed on the superficial outer shell of self by position in this automatic reality. So practically all individuals think of themselves as moral, but their morals have been bent already to suit their personal situation.

For example, a soldier in his private life may be gentle and peaceable, but in war becomes a ruthless killer. The first is his private character for which he is answerable; the second is his public character or outer shell, his duty to the Machine for which it is responsible, not he. A priest, in both his private life and official capacity, may be and is expected to be gentle and peaceable too, yet he will bless the soldier before battle. The priest evades his moral compunction - to oppose the battle and persuade the soldier to lay down his arms - with the devious argument that he himself is not breaking his vows, whilst the soldier has taken a different oath and is further justified by the fact that he is defending the 'true' faith. The kindly economist, who would rather die than see his wife and children harmed or deprived, can calmly justify the deprivation or starvation of millions by putting it down to 'inevitable' market forces. All these characters would claim to be moral. The dedicated protestor cum terrorist with a genuine cause has as good a claim to morality as they, because he or she, to put right a great wrong and relieve the suffering of many others, will risk or suffer death by causing a much lesser wrong. Yet the terrorist is almost universally condemned whilst the others are not, because he or she is outside the Machine and they are within it.

Why is it that these amazing contradictions are accepted as normal and credible? It is because their setting is an equally contradictory reality, and both have characterised our civilisation since its beginning. We were not born with such differences; they have been built into us since - incorporated into the individual construction of the conscious mind that we call self. We are born with the same instincts, and with differences of temperament, but, given ideal circumstances, we could control and keep these within acceptable limits, for our high intelligence tells us broadly what is right and good, what is wrong and bad. But we are not born into ideal circumstances; we are born into a reality that harnesses us to the Machine. Required to adopt its fundamental concepts and aims, which go contrary to our moral values, most of us comply for the sake of survival, believing we have no alternative. This may affect us temperamentally, our moral objections giving us difficulties that cause emotional distress. To avoid distress, many of us isolate or adulterate our morals in order to make them compatible with our activities. Some of us, who want to be highly effective and successful units in the Machine, capitulate altogether to its amoral or immoral values, hardening our hearts against human moral niceties and giving ourselves up to the instinctive drives and the aggressive parts of temperament. I repeat, a high degree of moral sensitivity is a disadvantage in this automatic reality.

There are many divergent interests in the money economy, many opposing sides in the competitive conflict, and many different departments of the Machine. Humans are selected to serve those departments according to suitability, having learned to prepare themselves through education and by deliberately adjusting their characters, as far as they are able, to achieve suitability. Machine efficiency brings automatic security and reward, and those who achieve it spontaneously, because they are exactly conditioned, can, in their human incompleteness, nevertheless be contented and acceptable to themselves and to automatic society. Generally speaking the highest status and reward goes to the most integrated with the Machine, i.e. to the most automated.

An alternative, truly human, society would be adjusted to human morality and accord with it, by which all people would be united. In this existing reality humans adopt or capitulate to automatic amorality, or immorality, by which they are disunited. This is my recurrent theme, fully dealt with in Part VII. The foregoing explains why there are so many different human characters, but not how the mind is made to stoop to them, and maintain them. This is a biological process, already described in Part 1, Chapter 3. The conscious combined with the utilised part of the postconscious - i.e. the conscious mind - is subject to the conscious will, which loosely confines its thinking and recording to matters which are of actual or likely concern to the individual's chosen version of reality. The self then selects from this the memories and processes of reason which are of especial significance to its precise position in reality and gives them superior signal strength, so building, out of these limited correlations, a 'mind within a mind' - a personal construction of even more limited, and therefore false, thought. Most of us presently think with this personal construction whose calculations, actually the products of incomplete reasoning and external and internal conditioning, appear to us as true thoughts.

The following Figure 9 attempts to demonstrate how the normal mind presently works. Its greatest part is the independent postconscious, and I believe this to be the large brain area that, according to physiological examination, has no apparent function. It appears to have no function because it has no direct connection with, and is not used by, consciousness. Were it to be removed, and indeed a large part of the utilised postconscious also, the automatic performance of the individual would not noticeably be affected. The independent postconscious is kept alive by the universal influence for truth, which recognises it as vital to the fulfilment of intelligence, which is its flame of hope; otherwise it would die out. An alternative explanation as to why the independent postconscious remains alive, though neither used nor to any great extent heeded by consciousness, is that it is the true representative of the human being. As such it is even more subject to the life-force impulsion to go on living than the conscious mind and body. Though largely neglected throughout our history, it will not die out as long as hope remains.

The influence of the independent postconscious on the human individual is indirect; we can admit it or shut it out, encourage or discourage its development, which is by way of forming atoms of thought into molecules, globules, then constructions - a process whose ultimate end is to become one completely true construction. The utilised postconscious develops in the same way but under direction of the conscious will, and certain of its limited constructions and globules of thought are given preference by the conscious self in order to form the self's peculiar thinking and reasoning, and to determine its actions and reactions. How do these mind constructions work? Well, to begin with they are created by, and then perpetuate acceptance of, a false and contradictory reality that requires this deception. Because of our belief in the existing automatic reality, we invent or allow to be imposed upon us a personal language which describes our reality to us and us to it.

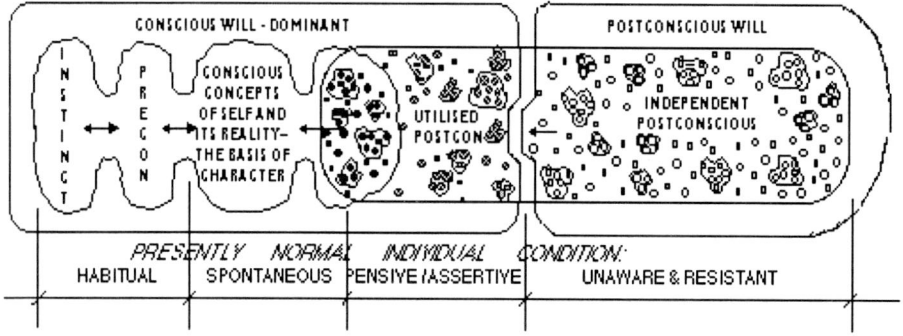

KEY: (Relating the Self to Postconscious Mental Activity)

- • = Isolated Atoms of Thought

- o = Molecules of Associated Thought

- ● = Black, ConsciouslyPreferred as Bias of Individual Thought and Action

- ◌ = Grey, Recognisably Supportive of Individual Bias

- O = White, Excluded from Consciousness because Critical of Individual Bias, or Unsympathetic, but Occasionally breaking through as Inspiration or Conversion

- 🐾 = Globules of Correlated Thought or Reason which, when Enlarged and Interconnected, become Constructions. In the Independent Postconscious, Truth is Arrived at when ALL Thought is Complete and Interconnected.

Figure 9: Typical Unfulfilled Automated Human Mind,
Demonstrating how Character is Formed

We need this limited language in order to cope with reality. More than language, it is a kind of window on the world which shows us only what we require to see. It is the preferred thought of the conscious mind (incorporating part of the utilised postconscious,) to which all incoming data is chiefly referred for comment, opinion and decision. It eliminates worries that do not directly concern us, so that if well provided for we can be happy though millions elsewhere may be starving. It enables us to so concentrate on a special skill, such as medicine or law, that we make few errors, yet fails to make us aware of alternative views of more profound significance. It facilitates a prescribed interpretation of all things, such as a particular religious or ideological outlook that gathers false strength from its refusal to examine itself critically. This personal language, related to a limited construction of thought, allows the mind to fix its purpose unswervingly upon some duty or objective, making that duty or objective an end that justifies any means of achievement by overruling all moral objections. It enables the conscious mind to be trained in such a way as to function principally as a memory bank, with its process of recalling bare knowledge little hindered by critical interference from the much more vital pure reasoning processes of the independent postconscious mind whose function is the discovery of optimum truth.

As a result of forming our characters in these ways we cut them short of their true human potential so that they fail to work together for the common good. We mould them to a selection from the many and variously limited functions of the Machine. These functions can only be described as good according to limited automatic values; according to their success in achieving their own limited objectives. They cannot be described as wholly good, or as good in terms of the true interests of humanity at large. So the 'good' character, member of a prosperous and dominant nation, admired for being his own man, courageous, honourable, loyal to his own social circle, can, to the rest of the world and by being true to this character, become a 'bad' politician, general or tycoon. The big American businessman who boosts the wealth of his nation is good in the USA, but bad in the Third World. The individual who puts optimum interest and energy into one worthy objective may turn with maximum aggression against anybody who threatens it. Institutions presently seen as virtuous might not really be so, for only those activities that genuinely contribute to the good of the whole may be regarded as truly virtuous. Instituted charity, for example, is ineffective because it is a limited reaction to the Machine which falls short of the ideal - it is a small humane hand offering help here and there whilst the large automatic hand is causing neglect - and it helps to perpetuate an uncaring society by trying to fill the gaps which a good society would not leave unfilled.

A vast amount could be, and has already been, written about the presently possible variations of human character and behaviour. It is now generally accepted that the effects of childhood vary from one emotional extreme to the other because the temperament and character of parents, and of the genes passed on by parents, so vary; that our relationship with our parents is the salient factor in the development of our character, and we tend to believe that our consequent characteristics are inevitable. Adolf Hitler might be quoted as a dramatic example. The second world war and the cruel extermination of millions of Jews might be attributed to the suspicion that this one man's step-father was the result of a 'disgraceful' adultery between a domestic servant and a son of the Jewish family which employed her, and to the fact that this step-father treated the young Adolf like a dog. Nevertheless, it is most important to realise that the effects of such early experience are not irrevocable, and that such traumatic early events do not necessarily lead to such dramatic consequences, for the postconscious mind - true representative of the self, unaffected by emotion and dedicated to truth - can and should take responsibility for any and every individual. This is a fundamental truth of the supraconscious philosophy.

Bad parents are those who are themselves victims of harsh experience, probably beginning with their own ill-treatment in childhood - links in a chain of suffering continually forged because of the failure of human intellect to fulfil itself above all. Whether this chain continues unbroken depends upon how the mind reacts to circumstances. Whether accumulated feelngs of hate are overcome and dissipate themselves through time, or erupt in violent revenge, depends on the opportunities open to the individual concerned. Presumably Hitler neither had time nor space intellectually to come to terms with his past. But he was given power enough for the perpetration of ghastly deeds that his gut-feelings dictated, whilst his reason was so twisted as to obscure from his awareness his own inhuman immorality. Otherwise he too must have recoiled in horror. But the independent postconscious remains true in every case and can prevail against false emotions and twisted conscious reason, if only it is enabled by awareness and allowed by will. If and when this awareness generally prevails in the world, it shall eradicate not only the circumstances that produce bad parents but also the opportunities for unreasonable and violent emotions to have broad and serious effect will also be eradicated.

In this present reality, generally speaking, it is still considered a weakness publicly to doubt, question or criticise the fundamental norm on moral grounds. This is because the fundamental norm is an automatic reality, and for that reason all the Machine's top executives are automated to a degree. Yet our society is the scene of a battle between our essential humanity and the Machine. Therefore it might be expected that our elected representatives would be strongly on the human side in this battle, but this is not so. As often as not those at the top of the political hierarchy are equally unshakeable automated personalities, hopeful of influencing but bent on asserting automatic policy. We who elect them have many different characters, hold all kinds of contrary opinions, and thus disagree. Consequently, even though the Machine fails to sustain so many of us and clearly does not represent our true human qualities, we normally support the automated hierarchy because it is established, solid and seemingly invincible; because there appears no clear and coherent moral alternative, and because human thinking is confined to the conscious mind and dominated by conscious will. We are accustomed to believing that differences of character and opinion are inevitable, so that complete agreement is impossible. It is of the utmost importance to overcome this attitude because we must be united if we are to assert ourselves over the Machine, and we cannot unite as long as we disagree. A particular example of this general problem is the fate of many marriages in the UK at present - divorce for one out of every three couples.

We should work towards agreement and cooperation. This is not a matter of becoming the same but of essentially harmonising. Consider this example:

Three characters (X), (Y) and (Z) are each incomplete and apart. By each becoming (XYZ) they do not lose (unless individuality is regarded as a matter of deliberately being as different as possible) because their characters and relationships are now richer. Marriages of (X)(X), (Y)(Y) or (Z)(Z) seem ideal but are potentially unstable because all the partners are incomplete and liable, due to their separate and different roles, to change differently and grow apart. But marriage that grows into (XYZ)(XYZ) has enough in common that it should be permanently stable. Of course dissimilar people are attracted and join together for natural reasons. When (X) and (Y) marry they need to change themselves and each other, for intelligent reasons, to become (XY)(XY) at least. Otherwise there is disharmony, a symptom of disagreement over essentials which might seem to be cured by (X) divorcing (Y) and going off with another (X) but which does nothing to prevent the fundamental disease but merely maintains separate groups of (X), (Y), (Z) and untold other characters who, even of they can sustain agreement among themselves, remain pledged to disagreement with every other group.

This book is the record of a long search for truth. You may find fault with parts of its reasoning and I would point out that no group of words can itself comprise a wholly true expression. Its truth depends upon relationship with all thinking of the mind from which it came, and its truth in relation to this book depends upon the relationship between every other group of words which this book contains. Even so you may disagree with my findings, and you may be quite certain that you are right, just as I am. But let us both stop to realise that we cannot both be right. How can we be equally sure that we have not approached the truth by way of a conditioning that gives us a special perspective, true to its complete self but not wholly true?

Chapter 9

GROWTH OF AWARENESS

We have seen how the disciplines that enabled humans to overcome threatened catastrophe founded the Machine and dictated the progress of the mainstream of human life. Some groups (the Third division, Chapter 5) were able to relax those disciplines and gravitate to a well-organised but simple and contented life, as closely as possible in harmony with nature. These groups, while nearer the truth than we, did not achieve intellectual fulfilment; they reached a state which, good as it was, depended upon tacit agreement to progress thought no further, whilst the mainstream (Second division), although heading in an anti-human direction, stimulated its thinking to a degree which has prompted a growth of awareness and actually brought the human race much closer to the possibility of such fulfilment.

The Machine weighs heavily against human enlightenment, but our awareness nevertheless grows in many respects. Automatic progress is advancing at a fast and accelerating rate, however, and human awareness, generally under pressure to keep abreast of this progress, is not succeeding in penetrating the Machine to its false foundations. It is noticeable that many, or most, people think very little good of the human world in general. They may approve and cling to parts of it, but on the whole they deplore it. This is not surprising, for the world's shortcomings are everywhere in evidence, and any analysis of the human world must come up with the same opinion. What should be surprising is that whilst history will show this to have been the common opinion of the world, so far no determined collective effort has been made to change ourselves and our world fundamentally for the better. But this we can understand when we know the power of conditioning which makes automated minds believe that no change is possible.

People often ask what does the future hold, as if it were not in their hands - anybody's hands, high or low. Then what does decide our future, and why don't we? A similar question is also commonly asked - what is the world coming to? It has probably been asked since civilisation began, but nowadays we generally believe we know the answer - the world is coming to disaster, unless something is done.

Clearly it is not our true power of intelligence that runs our affairs and decides our future but the Machine, which has cared for us so little, and so badly, as to bring us to this present deplorable, and dangerous situation. So we ourselves must take responsibility for avoiding disaster and then fulfilling ourselves truly. But how do we set about it? The first thing to do this book has already done - to discover how our society was founded and how it has evolved and deposited us in the wrong reality. The next thing is to become aware that the chief obstacle to our changing the world is our customary placement and conditioning of 'self' - that we refer everything to the judgement of ill-formed characters and opinions. Of course, reform must take full account of the individual. That opinions need to be changed does not mean that change is to be enforced, but that truth puts responsibility on every individual intelligence to get his or her opinion right, and thus agreed.

Immersed as we are in the Machine, it takes effort to get a clear objective view of our lives. Any process of living must involve labour, care, and some anxiety. We need to wake up to the fact that human life is overburdened with worries, fears and tensions, large and small, which are not to do with the necessities or true satisfactions of life but are automatic impositions. Our way out of this situation is by the common truth reaching into our minds. When we strive with each other on the Machine's terms we behave like an animal in a trap - the more it struggles the more it is hurt and the faster it is held. Our Machine society represents both the trap and the victim: we the automated people made its strong spring and sharp jaws; we put it in position, and set it, and then ourselves fell into it. It is we, therefore, who must release it.

If our awareness is to grow into an effective force for good, we must be able to see the complete picture of worldwide humanity. This requires that our intelligence cultivates total, , if usually unconscious, awareness of it all at once and all the time. At present we look at the picture in disconnected fragments, and our attitude and understanding fluctuates according to which fragment has our attention.

We are informed by the Machine, voluminously. In the here and now, whether thinkers are listened to by other thinkers is more a matter of who they are than the whole truth of what they have to say. Whether automatically conditioned minds take in any particular piece of reasoned information depends upon its realism - whether the information comes from the Machine, or from automatic reality, not on whether it comes from the true intellect. Enlightenment is piecemeal. There are books on many subjects, but none attempting to get it all together. Political leaders may occasionally take a truly moral stand rather than the automatic attitude, on this or that issue but never on all, or most, issues. The Machine is paramount. Machine-rich nations are unwilling to give up their advantages. They continue doing things for money-economic reasons rather than moral reasons because that is the automatic way and because their people do not want to be poor. Machine-poor nations have no such advantages, and their moral argument against the rich is linked to their wish to gain riches for themselves. All aspire to true morality, but their circumstances in the Machine determine how much of it they can and will afford.

I have said already that when the interests of humanity and the Machine clash, the latter always wins. Nevertheless, where it makes no difference to the money-economy our true humanity is coming much more to the fore, even in the attitude of authority. The values and standards of the family and close community are, in some respects, impinging on the Machine. In some places maternity hospitals and their approaches to childbirth are much more sensible, caring and kindly that they used to be, for example. In many countries there are welfare or social security systems that go some way to prevent extreme poverty or disadvantage. Even in such countries where, according to the money economy, these systems can no longer be afforded they have to be kept up because the moral case for them is now so powerful. On the other hand the money economy decides who shall be prosperous and who shall suffer the comparative poverty of social security handouts, by determining the level of unemployment.

I am getting old. It is a mark of the elderly that they dislike change, but perhaps this is a reaction to youths' liking for it. I abhor the progress of science and technology for its own sake, not only for fear of the consequences for life in general but also because of the lifestyle it brings in its wake, oriented to the Machine rather that to the true fulfilment of humanity. It is a very strong trick of instinct that prevents the young knowing and anticipating what it is to be old. No doubt this trick is essential to automatic reality, in that it keeps Machine-serving life blindly optimistic. But it is not a good thing that the only outlet for the future hopes of enthusiastic youth offered by the Machine is rapid advance into the unknown. Nor is it a good thing that humans do not learn to know better until they are old, if they learn at all, and that the world is then in the hands of the younger generation who will not listen. People would not be divided in this way, by age or any other thing, if we each in our own way were contributing to the same concepts and facts of life, so that we all shared that optimism, rather than have it burn in youth by a trick of instinct, and turn to pessimism in old age.

THE WRONG REALITY

Part III
LIBERATION
OF THE HUMAN MIND

Chapter 10

POTENTIAL

Animals are controlled involuntarily by instinct, for their own good. Humans need to control their affairs voluntarily, by the reasoning of intellect. We are presently in between the two states; neither one nor the other; out of control. We are dictated to by the automaton as animals are directed by instinct, but our free intellects protest against much that results. This is the chief potential of intellect that we have failed to achieve - the potential, by fulfilling this our greatest feature, to govern ourselves as befits us. It is the reasoning of intellect that gives us true human morality - humantruth - which, being the product of our supreme faculty should be our governing guide.

Another potential of the human mind is our contentment and satisfaction. The behaviour of matter is pre-ordained by the characteristics of energy. The ordered behaviour of atoms and molecules is a sort of contentment, given zest by the semi-random behaviour of sub-atomic particles. The alternative, from matter's viewpoint, is unhappy disorder. Similarly, the contentment and satisfaction of animals lies in the fulfilment, by instinct and in every respect, of the definite functions for which they have been fitted by evolution. This is given zest by such as birds singing, by curiosity, and by the ever-present possibility of progressive change. In our case the fulfilment of intellect would bring satisfaction derived from social activities designed for human contentment by humans, with the added zest of its abstract expression, in music, pictorial art, literature for instance, which might become the greater part of that contentment and satisfaction. The alternative is extinction.

We have seen how human minds are imprisoned in the Machine by conditioning. Such conditioning has to be removed if we are to fulfil our potential. The catch is that we have to achieve the reasoning potential of intellect, truth, in order to remove our conditioning. This is done by realising that it is our outer shell that is conditioned and that our inner core is the true self in embryo. It is by the independent intellectual development of the inner self that it shall grow to discredit, defeat and take over from our conditioned outer shell.

Chapter 11

INTELLATION

How do we achieve the intellectual potential of reasoning in order independently to develop the inner self? Presumably by thinking. But humans have been thinking for many centuries, without breaking down automatic conditioning and discovering truth. The reason can be seen by reference to Figure 9, Chapter 8 - Typical Unfulfilled Automated Human Mind, Demonstrating How Character is Formed. Our thinking has always been that of limited constructions of mind biased towards specific versions of reality and different departments of automatic interest. The verb 'to think' describes a consciously wilful process of personally prejudiced calculation adjusted to a selection from the facts and concepts of reality within the Machine. A different word is needed to describe the much more pure and thorough mental process which true understanding requires.

The word I have chosen is intellation, an explanation of which is made easier if you refer to Figure 8, Chapter 4 - Present Human State - Immature Mutation. To intellate is to correlate every item of knowledge with every other item, and subject all to every conceivable path and interconnection of reason. To begin this process we must start transferring power from our conscious will to strengthen the independent postconscious mind's equivalent of will - its force of reasoning and power of knowing. This is simply done by strongly, deeply and sincerely wishing to know the truth about everything. It is then necessary to relax our wilful control of the output of the independent postconscious and allow and encourage it to enter our consciousness. Finally we must listen to the true guidance of the independent postconscious and prefer it to the directions of the combined conscious/utilised-postconscious, so that our voluntary activity is influenced ever more by the former and ever less by the latter.

The mind of the presently normal individual is made up by the self's subjection to, and manipulation of, the combined conscious/utilised-postconscious faculty. This limited faculty works to a prejudiced pattern, carefully recording and committing to immediate memory only that information which suits predetermined patterns of incomplete reason and conditioning, so as readily to be recalled in support of the conscious self's preferred pattern of prejudice. All other information, with incomplete constructions of reason, is committed to more remote memory that can be recalled by the person but is not immediately connected to his or her spontaneous character.

The mind of an intellating person is not made up by his or her consciousness. Consciousness is aware of the questions and problems; it is also aware that it has been given to know, or does not know, the answers and solutions. If it does not know them, it exerts its will towards knowing, and waits. The postconscious does not work to any preconceived pattern. It is a faculty whose function is truth, and that is its sole activity. The independent postconscious of the intellating individual is constantly seeking, also waiting, for information that will make a connection that will bridge a gap in a train of reason, contributing to the vital objective - the eventual completion of a whole pattern of truth.

To put it another way, intellation is wanting and fully intending to know the truth. It is a matter of our conscious selves questioning the postconscious again and again until it finds answers that we know to be true. For the postconscious this is a matter of considering every item of essential knowledge, relating each of these to all other items by links of reason whose signal strengths are determined according to their preferential degree of true value. The links of reason are formed into patterns that continue seeking essential knowledge and exploring vital reason until they are truly balanced. These patterns are then interrelated until they form one whole complex pattern of perfectly balanced knowing and reasoning, or intellect, which is truth. This is fulfilment of the whole cerebral cortex, leading the way to being human to the optimum.

The process of intellation should not need to be taught because it is a logical process - the natural way for free, unhindered postconscious minds to work. Teaching is necessary because our reality is humanly unnatural. Our minds are not free, as we have seen, and to begin intellating requires a voluntary decision to rise above existing reality. To continue the process cannot be straightforward, as it would be, relatively, were we living in an ideal reality. This is not only because our existing reality is built of much inessential knowledge and false links and patterns of reason, from which the truth is to be disentangled, but also because the task is further confused by our personal conditioning and prejudiced constructions of mind.

Another obstacle to intellation is that postconscious reasoning is unconscious to the self, and brought to our awareness only with effort, unless it breaks through as inspiration. Existing reality, on the other hand, and all the clamorous affairs of the Machine, is glaringly obvious to consciousness, and presses on us overwhelmingly. Furthermore, the postconscious reasons rapidly in a complex signal-system of its own which it then translates into a simplified, coagulated form suited to the more ponderous understanding of consciousness, i.e. language, which serves as a medium of communication with other conscious selves. The other selves then pass the message along for re-translation by their own postconscious faculty back into its own signalling-system.

I believe, and indeed can show from experience, that for the most part intellation goes on at night, during sleep, in all minds to some degree. In my case, when the process was in full flow, revelations were poured into a receptive consciousness each morning and written down. These revelations came as certain knowledge the truth of which I had no doubt and of which, until that moment, the conscious self was unaware, yet they may have been in process of formation for years, the result of much determined effort in the past. In the case of an unsympathetic consciousness, such revelations shall be more retarded because unstimulated, and may be felt as the pricking of conscience but are otherwise unadmitted, shrouded, put to the back of the mind and kept from disturbing the self's preferred character. It is logical that our sleeping time should be given to this cogitation, because we are exposed to such volumes of input all day. Dreams are awareness of items that will not be put away or cannot be slotted in, which come to awareness between sleeping and waking. Decisions, whether arrived at during day or night, are mostly made on the basis of prejudiced character or biased mind construction, or simply automatic precedent. Minds which are determined on truth will decide on the basis of true knowing and reasoning or, if possible, not at all. For this reason indecision is a surer indication of intellation than decisiveness.

The relationship between consciousness C and the postconscious PC is an intricate interchange. We are directly aware with C and only C, but it is the indirect, unconscious awareness of PC, even where we try to be open to its utilised part alone and closed to its greater independent part, which gives our reality its depth and breadth. Yet although C relies on the PC for its advanced nature, C still holds the whip hand because it intervenes between PC and the preconscious and instinctive controls of the body, so that PC is entirely dependent on C for life.

In this existing reality humans do not normally intellate - they think. Intellation is the necessary beginning of the completion of humanity's mutation - the realisation of our intellectual potential. It requires that we abnegate our present selves, on our own assurance that the individual shall be contented and secure only when bound to truth by his or her intellect, which then becomes the common intellect and the agreed communal bond of truth.

Chapter 12

SUPRACONSCIOUSNESS

It was said in the previous chapter that by intellating we fulfil the whole cerebral cortex, and the result, inevitably, is truth. As a first step to supraconsciousness we have to be prepared to accept that this is so. Ask yourself whether the hugely advanced mental capacity, given to us by mutation, has proved of any benefit. The fact that part of it was taken over by instinctive consciousness and the rest, the postconscious, dominated, marginalised and ignored, has denied us the full potential benefit, supraconsciousness, but it has had certain value.

Clearly, the dominance of the conscious mind has enabled us to prosper, after its fashion, but the conscious, even with its added capacity given by mutation, is very much a lesser mind, with limited reasoning power. It persists in reaching false conclusions. That is why the world is in chaotic conflict. This cannot be right for a species possessing a supreme faculty whose function is truth. A human mind that reaches false conclusions is not working properly or fully, or freely. To say otherwise is tantamount to claiming that the purpose and function of an engine is to break down. Neither a human mind nor any thinking apparatus can reason reliably if part of its function is to reason falsely. Truth is indispensable to reason, for reason that is not reliable is worthless, and dangerous. But in the existing world at large many different theories are relied upon, many different opinions and beliefs held, various practices followed, nearly all of which are incomplete and false.

Having accepted that our purpose is the fulfilment of truth, the next step towards supraconsciousness is to abnegate self and become bound by truth. The self does not then regard itself and its personal reality as being its greatest concern. It realises that a whole reality which is unitedly cared for by all selves is far better than that which results from each self caring mainly for itself. Experience of the world right up to the present moment demonstrates the painful results of the latter, and we have probably always inwardly known that the former is right.

To be truly human, the individual must be bound by truth. Since truth is fulfilment of the postconscious, the humantrue individual has to be closely identified with the postconscious. This requires that the self be re-positioned within the postconscious, whose innermost workings must remain unconscious to the self but to whose reasoned conclusions the self must be most immediately subject. The self is now subject to the postconscious, strengthened by the latter's will, and has a superior relationship to the old conscious mind which, in turn, has a superior relationship to the new subconscious instinct established under this new arrangement as well as to the old preconscious instinct. This new relationship between the postconscious mind and the self is true supraconsciousness see Figure 10:

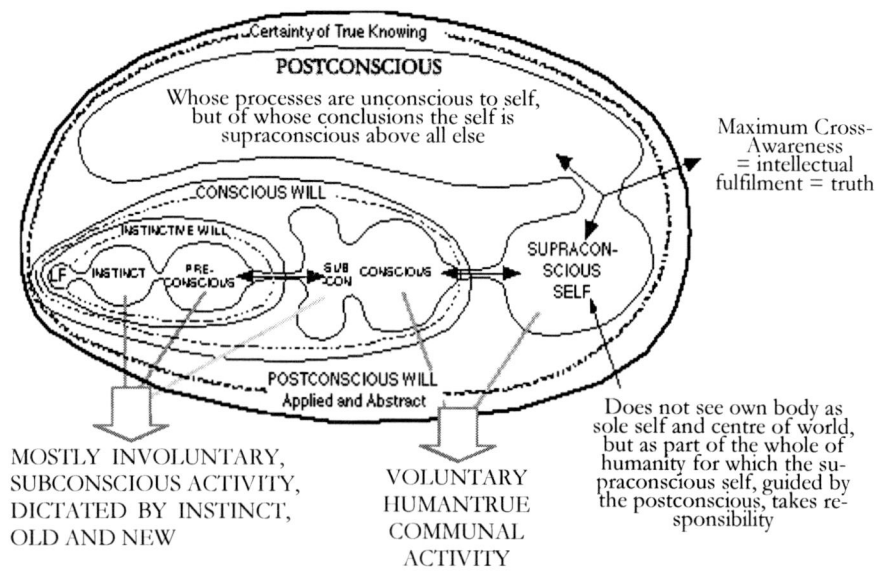

Figure 10
Ultimate Human Mutation - The Supraconscious State

Utter awareness of truth carries absolute responsibility to abide by that truth. The self that puts itself in the position of supraconsciousness voluntarily undertakes that responsibility, but it has the disadvantage of still existing in a false reality. So though it wishes to shoulder that responsibility in all things, whilst that self's mind exists in automatic reality it is obliged, for the sake of survival, to conform superficially to that reality. Individuals who are supraconscious cannot deny truth and are bound to work towards an ideal reality. Until that ideal is realised and whilst it is being prepared for, such individuals can only accept and carry that responsibility in their minds. If compelled to be false in the here and now they are aware of being, for the present, inescapably so. But when supraconsciousness has prevailed and the ideal society exists, there shall be no necessity to be false. The ideal shall then be responsibly and unswervingly maintained because supraconscious minds can not conceivably betray it, and practical reality shall then fully reflect both our truth and our responsible will.

There are many pressures opposed to the ideal, of course, chief of which is the conviction that the ideal could not work - it would break down because of the innate faults and crude appetites of human beings. But those faults and appetites derive from instinct and necessarily belong in an automatic reality founded on instinct. It is important to realise that just as animals are interlocked with their compulsive instinct for survival, supraconscious humanity would be inseparable from truth, and that would work for their survival which, I repeat, the Machine threatens. Another obstacle is inertia, the sheer disinclination to make the great effort undoubtedly required, which can be overcome only by the awakening of a contrary desire and determination. Yet another great pressure opposed to the ideal comes from the fact that our present satisfactions are widely adapted to Machine delights. It seems that individuals can visualise reality changing but not themselves. So automatic progress is usually welcomed because it offers prospect of yet more similar delights, whilst moral reforms are rejected because they seem to represent self-sacrifice. The answer to this is to raise the level of awareness of other and better satisfactions that the ideal would bring.

Supraconsciousness has to be self-taught, because being human today is subject to a natural priority of attention given to the relationship between instinct or gut-feeling and actual reality. The postconscious speaks to our conscious selves from the other side, in another way relating to an ideal reality that does not yet exist. It is like a new music that our ears are not attuned to, so that we do not understand it, and which we resist because it is unfamiliar. Intellation and supraconsciousness is listening to this music and absorbing the new understanding it brings.

Consider again the position of the soldier, priest, economist or terrorist, mentioned in Chapter 8. Their duties were given to them by the Machine and their motivation comes from humanity's automatically evolved history. As a result of them becoming supraconscious, true morality would be their motivation. The soldier could no longer believe in his profession; the priest must become a radical reformer; the economist must put morality before market forces; and the terrorist must turn away from violence, realising that only good means can be justified by good ends and that local inhumanities will never be eradicated until our whole reality is humantrue.

Chapter 13

HUMANTRUTH

This word humantruth has been coined to distinguish that truth which is knowable, and highly relevant to our daily lives, from the whole truth that I believe to be understandable to the human mind but which may never reach our understanding, and which, though it is of great interest, is not presently relevant.

I have already said that truth is the fulfilment of the postconscious mind, the function of intellect, and therefore the fulfilment of being human. Supraconsciousness binds us to the truth, and more important than the amount we know is that all of our understanding should be true and our reality seen in relation to that. There is much uncertainty and confusion about the meaning of truth and it is frequently claimed to be unknowable, or non-existent. This is my definition of it (in the year 1990):

There are seven meanings of truth

1. All that presently exists and all that has existed in the past, comprising the whole truth whether or not known.

2. All possibility.

3. That which is unquestionably so.

4. Utterly complete reasoning of all that is knowable.

5. The conclusions towards which all strands of pure reason unerringly tend.

6. A state of being that is dissatisfied with anything less than truth, that is devoted to pure reason and accepts responsibility for conducting its physical existence accordingly.

7. The source of right, honest and good morality on which that state of being is founded (see end of Chapter 32 - Roots of Religion for further explanation).

We do not know all truth, of course, but we are not so far away from understanding its essentials that we can't make certain true deductions. We do have at hand all the information we require to reason our way to knowing what I call humantruth, which is defined in this way: Humantruth is all knowledge of ourselves, and of our planet Earth, reasoned according to the optimum well-being of both. This is the same truth for us all because we are all of the same species, we live in the same world, our postconscious minds are similar, and each and every intellect, being given the same essential facts, can arrive at but one honestly reasoned conclusion.

It is sometimes claimed that truth is a conceptual relationship between the observer and the observed, which can change as the viewpoint of the former and the position of the latter changes. This is a simplistic view which chooses to ignore that it is vital for each member of a species to observe that truth which is relevant to all, at the same time recognising that all viewpoints and positions are actual or possible, and the whole truth includes them. It is a view applicable to animals, because they are instinctively limited to one concept and incapable of comprehending truth, but that does not make it a true view for us to adopt, whether in relation to them or to ourselves. It is true that disagreement amongst humans occurs because we each claim that we know what is true. This does not mean there is no knowable truth common to us all, only that it has not yet been discerned. Whatever any person perceives, all others can perceive also. The truth about that which exists but which nobody perceives is that nobody can yet perceive it. Although we don't perceive it, however, it still exists, and it is part of our truth to acknowledge this. I believe that truth certainly does exist, in all the seven meanings above, and that the human intellect is potentially capable of understanding the first three meanings, though we may never fully achieve that understanding. We are by our nature designed to acknowledge, and already capable of embracing, the fourth, fifth, sixth and seventh meanings.

In important matters we cannot afford to have random differences. Where we have different emotional attitudes towards certain unimportant things, our truth is that we do feel differently about them, not that these things themselves are different. Where we have different emotional attitudes towards important things they should give way to the responsible attitude of true reason. The truth about the present fact that humanity cannot perceive, or realise, the same vital truths is not that those truths do not exist but that humanity is not yet willing to make the effort to cover all perceptions and thereby reach agreement.

As an example of an unimportant difference: one person views an object as beautiful, another as ugly. The truth about this situation is that the two minds are differently conditioned; that the object is one and the same; and that beauty is not an absolute quality.

As an example of an important difference: one person regards homicide as justified when it is the means of securing a good end, and the other that truly good ends forbid the use of bad means. The second is the true moral view, for it seriously takes as binding that no human shall kill another, according to which homicide can never be justified under any circumstances (excepting mercy killing in extremis and by consent). The conclusion to be drawn is that a society whose good name requires immoral acts is itself immoral, and we require to change it, not to change our morality to suit it.

Truth, then, is not a shield of limited fact that may be used to defend personal bias. It is all propositions which, when subjected to all possible doubt, questioning and criticism, and correlated with all knowledge and reasoning, emerge with undeniable signal strength to form total conviction. Humantruth is the product of all propositions relevant to human wellbeing correlated with all available knowledge.

The following illustrates how individual observance of humantruth shall bring about its realisation in the world. The individual feels pain and seeks to avoid or alleviate it. But the individual is aware that all others also feel pain, so is impelled by supraconsciousness to seek the avoidance or alleviation of their pain also. The humantrue individual views pleasure, satisfaction, contentment and fulfilment in the same communal way. When all individuals thus make themselves responsible for all, they shall increase happiness by the fact of its being contributed to by all, and by the knowledge that it is shared by all.

All human brains are potentially similar organs for pursuing one and the same process. They appear to have the same capacity (10 to the power of 11 cells), but to vary in concentration and efficiency. How much such variations may be due to inherited characteristics, such as differences in the level of energy made available to the brain, and how much to differences of experience and stimulation in upbringing, is uncertain. What is certain, in my view, is that any single mind is capable of judging and understanding the essential truth about human society, as it is and as it should be. Therefore, in this sense, the potential mind of humanity is far superior to the actual facts and concepts of reality that presently dominate it. In this regard any individual mind that accepts its responsibilities is equal to any other, and the same relevant information is available to all. Two minds that achieve their essential scope shall reach agreement on the same body of humantruth. Therefore if all minds intellate, if only to a minimum degree necessary, and become supraconscious, then the whole human race shall be essentially in agreement.

The power of intellect must subject itself to voluntary control through collective agreement because it is capable of pursuing disagreement to the extremes of destructive conflict. Disagreement is appropriate only to instinct because animals are incapable of voluntary agreement and need a degree of controlled conflict within the species to survive. So agreement is as vital to the stability and survival of humanity as disagreement is to the balance of nature. To agree must be the voluntary intention of fulfilled intellect, and to its true reason an undeniably good intention is as supraconsciously compelling as instinct is to the animal.

Free intellect can give us both the ultimate meaning of life and the means of its optimum fulfilment, by way of supraconsciousness of humantruth. When we have achieved that state, our minds, which form the common humantrue character of ourselves and our society, will be as shown in the following Figure 11 - the truly logical completion of Figure 9 - Automated Human Mind

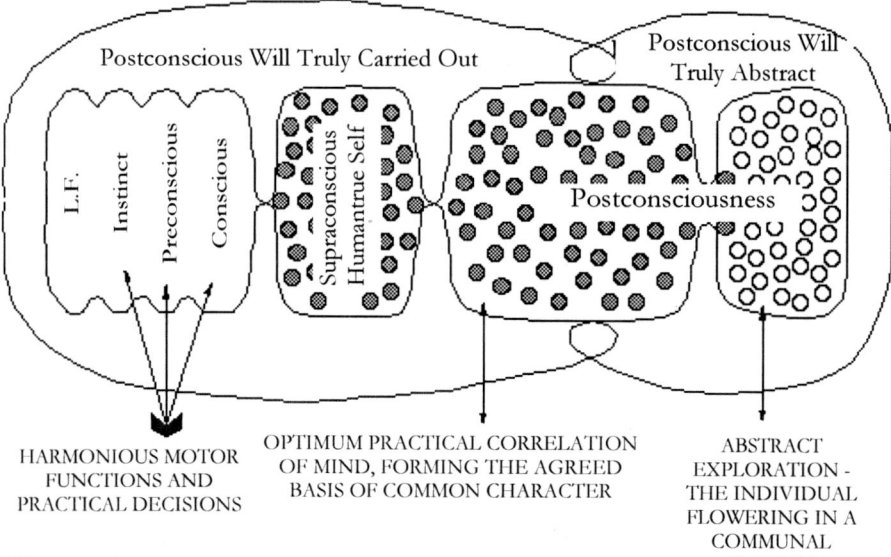

Figure 11
The Fulfilled Human Mind - Our Mutation Reaches Maturity

Chapter 14

NEW AWARENESS

I have tried to present to you a brief essential history of humanity which demonstrates that we are in the wrong reality. This truth is hard to discover, but once perceived it gives a new awareness of the world. However, throughout my thinking life, faced with constant pressure to conform to the norm, I have been assailed with doubts. Could almost everybody else be right, and had I, after all, got it wrong? In due course the full force of reason would re-assert itself and reinforce my conviction that I had not got it wrong. You may be troubled by similar doubts, based on the thought that the vast majority can't be wrong and reinforced by the feeling that you do not really want to be convinced otherwise, so as to be marked out as eccentric.

If it were the case that the Machine is indomitable and that the circumstances of human life were always to remain as they presently are, then it could be said to be beneficial that our minds are conditioned and our thinking restricted. The less that people think about the rights and wrongs of it all - the more they concentrate on their own automatic interests - the better they are enabled to endure, and survive. With so much to recognise that goes contrary to reason and compassion, so much to remember that is unpleasantly disturbing, so much to fear in a world of many terrible possibilities, the open mind can seem to be a curse. The most humantruly wise person will be the least prepared for coping with the world as it is.

If you achieve the state of total awareness which realises humantruth you must also suffer in this way, but only as long as you are in a minority. When the majority are with you it shall be another matter. Unless you lead the way by opening your mind, however, there can never be a humantrue majority. And in the meantime, true awareness carries the hope of beneficial worldwide change, whereas the existing automated human race, conditioned though it is, still suffers, or is made miserable by the knowledge of worldwide suffering about which it can do nothing.

Some may consider themselves to be familiar enough with human nature to know that the humantrue ideal couldn't work. This is to judge with conditioned mind and unopened eyes a whole race of people of similarly limited awareness. You may be satisfied with life as it is, subject to certain reservations such as that war and deprivation should be abolished. This is to believe that we can dictate policy to the Machine when, on all major matters, it dictates to us. The Machine does not work for human good, but just because the vast majority accept its principles and automatically follow where it leads does not mean they are incapable of supporting and sustaining the humantrue ideal. And it is foolish to imagine that the Machine can ever be so controlled by us as to keep only those of its parts we like or can tolerate, and cut out those parts we abhor.

Change to a humantrue society shall be achieved by a humanity changed by the new awareness of supraconsciousness. Until we have all reached that intellectual potential we cannot say whether we are satisfied with reality, or necessarily resigned to it, or judge whether marginal changes can be made which shall satisfy us. Once we achieved that potential we could not possibly tolerate existing reality and would be well aware that once the ideal were attained its maintenance would be a common human responsibility which we could not fail to uphold. Intellect is the fountain of true morality, and it is our true nature to fulfil both. Such fulfilment gives us knowledge of what we can humantruly do before actually doing it, and assures us that we shall faithfully sustain it because to do otherwise shall then be unthinkable to us.

Remember, your construction of mind and character was probably made to fit a personal reality that was carved out of a world reality that is false to your humanity. If you still find that hard to accept, think of this. Here we are, an intelligence on a tiny planet in space, supposedly getting close to knowing precisely how we came to be, even to within 100th of a second of the Big Bang, yet so ignorant and primitive that we give the conduct of our world to principles other than our own, so that we are virtually in a state of perpetual armed conflict, in fear of one another, and in awe of that which controls us.

It is not a question of whether or not you agree with me, but a question of truth. Is all this that my mind has told me true? As far as it goes I am convinced that it is, however mighty the opposition to it may be, for, to quote the sixth meaning of truth given in the previous chapter, these are the conclusions towards which all strands of my utmost reason, which I believe to be pure reason, unerringly tend. If we resist the truth, it is not the real us which does so. If we do not accept but wilfully deny it we shall fail as an intellectual species. There can be no half-measures. This book is not intended to be read, put away and forgotten by unchanged minds. It is intended to mark a turning point in human awareness, the beginning of a new supraconscious era. It is not that I am suffering from delusions of grandeur, only a conviction of humantruth, the realisation of which should not be delayed. We cannot afford to wait in the hope that solutions to our problems will turn up - we have to begin making change happen *now*.

If we accept the concept of a humantrue reality and reach for supraconsciousness, we shall have begun already to remove our conditioning, to change our character and look at everything in a new light. We shall have started to put into practice the belief that our truth must be reflected in our society. We should resist being persuaded, by the great contrary weight of existing reality, into thinking this impossible. We should no longer allow that anything guides us which we do not know to be absolutely right, and should never again allow ourselves to think according to the present norm.

The next step towards creating a humantrue reality is to reveal what is wrong with this one, which our new awareness enables us to do.

THE WRONG REALITY

Part IV
REVELATION

Chapter 15

THE WRONG REALITY

The fundamental physical reality of Earth is fixed, by and large, by its physics and chemistry, caused to behave as it has done by virtue of being a planet in a solar system that is slowing and cooling down, in a universe that seems to be in the later stages of expansion following the Big Bang.

The biological reality of Earth is that those physical conditions allowed a subsidiary activity to come into being some 3,500 million years ago - life - and may enable it to continue for as many years into the future. The biological reality of life-forms, so far, is that they are compelled to seek continual survival by adapting to their environment as best they can, and they are urged to progress towards an optimum. This implies a purpose, and the evidence indicates that this purpose is to achieve intellect. Except for reminding you that the fulfilment of intellect is truth, I will leave my own theory as to the objective of true realisation to Part V, Chapter 32, Roots of Religion.

Life is a gathering of forces and substances into a self-acting entity whose properties are different from and independent of those of its component forces and substances, though not of its fundamental influences. Inanimate growth, such as that of crystals, follows a pattern inherent in its constituents, and has no other purpose but to grow accordingly. Life, once animated, develops its own pattern as it advances. Herein lies one indication of its higher purpose. I repeat - why should not life grow in simple form and multiply until it can go no further, then necessarily stop spreading and sustain itself in that position? Why, when their original food supply became scarce, did Earth life-forms diversify and turn to the apparently pointless habit of feeding on each other? The answer is that competitive struggle demands constant improvement in efficiency, which involves increasing complexity, which requires ever higher intelligence. In practical terms nothing is achieved by this. Life could be served just as well by a few types of bacteria and amoeba covering the world, the consumption and production of oxygen and carbon dioxide balancing each other. Intelligence, on the other hand, is achieved by great and continual effort, and its only discernable purpose is the eventual realisation of truth. If this is the purpose of life, it must have come from some source.

I have already suggested that the source of the purpose of life was an influence to express energy to the ultimate, serving an overall influence for the realisation of truth. The former influence explains the proliferation of life-forms on Earth, and the latter explains the concept of Gaia. The existence of Gaia, itself an influence on the biosphere to maintain conditions suitable for life, can only be due to an influential purpose to have life progress to the optimum. That Gaia allowed the oxygenation of the atmosphere 3,000 million years ago, which was a major disaster for many creatures then living, yet has maintained it at a level of around 21% for the past 1,500 million years, supports the contention that Gaia is party to the influence to realise truth, for it is oxygen-burning life-forms which have dramatically advanced in intelligence.

The spearhead of that advance in intelligence is the human species. We have the most advanced neocortex on Earth, but we have not fulfilled its unique integrative and analytical functions so as to become truly intellectual - ie supraconscious. We have passed beyond adapting to our environment and now manipulate it, because we have failed to adapt to the most fundamental change of all which took place in ourselves when we became human - the acquirement of a postconscious faculty - a failure which now threatens not only our own species but Earth as a whole, and even the universe. We have not yet realised our right reality. Human destructiveness would be, and no doubt has been or is being paralleled, on every other life-supporting planet by every other creature that also acquired potential intellect but remained driven by instinct and therefore locked into the wrong reality.

In subsequent chapters of this Part, we look at instituted practices of the Machine that are familiarly accepted by our automated minds but quite unacceptable to fulfilled intellect. Take just one example - the use of pesticides, which was for some years indiscriminate though it is now controlled in many places. Rachel Carson (Silent Spring, Penguin Books) brought it to our attention that pesticide residues are present in all creatures on Earth, from penguins in Antarctica to human nursing mothers in the USA.

An overall survey of this planet would show that the human presence, whilst giving some of us new automatic interests and benefits, has produced many such detrimental results. The advent of higher intelligence, which surely ought to have enhanced the general quality of life, has, in a very short time, actually lowered it, and the process is continuing.

If we are to judge our reality, and ourselves as part of it, we have to look critically at the whole, taking nothing for granted. When we examine human history we tend to look on its events as having been inevitable, taking account of the circumstances at the time. We look on the present as a logical extension of the immediate past, according to circumstances inherited from the further past. In doing so we do take for granted those facts and concepts that came to pass and now exist. Instead, we should consider that which we ought to have striven for in the past, and achieved so that it now existed as our reality. Only by judging in this way can we correctly condemn that which is false and determine how to change it. Because of the way in which all things interact, I believe we shall find that every part of the existing wrong reality is to some extent false, and that total change is needed.

We should look at ourselves just as we look at other creatures. We see that in almost all respects they fulfil their attributes according to their circumstances. This cannot be said of us because our chief attribute enables us to make our circumstances as we wish them to be. We also see that other creatures seldom do anything detrimental to their survival success. The same is not true of ourselves, despite the fact that our numbers are still rapidly increasing, because we are laying up troubles that threaten our survival. We are no fools, neither is any of us born 'bad' or 'evil' (see Part V), but we are made fools of by our automatic wrong reality so that we do 'bad' and 'evil' things - in other words we individually act in our own apparent, automated interests but against our real interests as an intelligent race. Our competitive society has caused many bad qualities to be required for success and many good qualities to be associated with failure. Individuals who are successful in a bad or useless context may claim righteousness because they display good qualities in other contexts. If we mean to judge truly, we must honestly examine every facet of reality.

We spend a great deal of time in recalling past history and very little in planning the future. The former is easier because it is a matter of fact; the latter more difficult because it is obscure and controversial. Our irrevocable past is presently allowed to shape our unstoppable future. We may cry over our past wrong-doing and the suffering that came of it, but we seldom fully recognise our present recklessness so as to foresee the suffering it will cause. Nor do we even allow present suffering to change our current ways, and if we learn at all it is normally years after the event and usually too late. So our history influences us more to continue as we are than to learn fundamentally better ways. Yet it was not our true inner selves that made history. It was a sequence of events - the Machine directing, leaders reacting, and our outer shells obeying and following, labouring and enduring. We do not believe we can escape the present because it doesn't signify change. But we can responsibly question the past and see it as irrelevant. We can then effectively remove its influence by ignoring it, clearly criticise the present wrong reality by standing back and viewing it supraconsciously, and so proceed to plan a humantrue future.

There is no doubt that many of the people of the world have materially gained from the advance of the money economy but it is equally certain that all have suffered by it. The happiness of the human race as a whole could have been increased intellectually, with comparatively little material progress. The Machine cannot make humanity happy because the more it progresses the less we can become humantruly fulfilled and the more we are likely to feel the lack of such fulfilment, whatever the material gains.

AUTOMATIC DRIVES

Chapter 16

COMPETITION

As I said before, our reality is a battle between the Machine and our humanity which is the equivalent of instinct versus high intelligence, or intellect. Competitiveness is an instinctive drive - an impulsion, like hunger, which is necessary to animals for the survival of species. It includes one species attacking another for food, and defence against such attack. It also includes the practice of members of the same species dividing into groups and fighting (but rarely killing) within and between these groups for food, mates and territory.

Thinking of life as that of animals rather than plants, it is necessary for humans to defend themselves against, and sometimes to attack, kill and eat other animals. But it is not the true nature of intelligent humans to fight and kill each other, nor to strive against each other for advantage. The reason is that as a maxim, survival of the fittest is not appropriate to the human intelligence. Evidence of this is that we aspire, by way of medicine etc., to having all humans survive to old age, fit or unfit, and we try to ensure, up to a point through various welfare schemes, that people do not die of starvation or neglect. But we have long been divided into national and cultural groups and harnessed to conflicting functions of the money economy, and this holds us to competitive ways despite our true nature.

So we behave competitively because it is our established way, to which we instinctively respond. Our structure is moulded round instinctive competition so that our personal lifestyle, if not our very survival, presently depends on it. We have first to compete in educational examinations, then for jobs, for a place to live, for possessions and promotion. Much of our work is for industries that have to compete for contracts and against which workers' interests have to compete in setting the levels of wages to be paid. But the fact that competitiveness is so firmly established is not the only reason why we generally accept it. We commonly believe that progress is not only inevitable but desirable, and that competition encourages progress. We believe competition keeps down prices by increasing efficiency. We are adjusted to it, to the point where we rely quite largely on the excitements of competitive sports, games, and struggles depicted in books and films for much of our satisfaction. For these reasons we normally oppose radical reform, feeling that it would rob us of these satisfactions and put nothing in their place.

It is necessary to put aside the norm and keep a clear and open mind in order to see the effects of competitiveness on our society. It is a reason underlying the establishment of such undesirable values as possession, status and rank, for it is the principle and practice of competition that has helped to create inequalities and equated them with degrees of advantage. It creates insecurity and the need to seek security by defence against the threats which competition itself causes. Because it is a feature of the Machine that we serve but not of the morality that automated people can only pretend to, it leads to secrecy, deception, and it provides both reason and excuse for selfishness and treachery. Worst of all, competitiveness calls up and breeds aggressiveness, results in conflict, culminating in international war. The present day climax of competition is the threat of nuclear and germ war.

The fact that conflict, weapons, war, violence and inhumanity are common words of our basic vocabulary and concepts that occur in our daily news and entertainment is the measure of our familiar acceptance of the unacceptable.

It is true, of course, that it was by following the competitive urge that we gained our intellectual potential. But if we are to fulfil that potential, we have first to seek then to follow truth, in the light of which we shall see that competition is now unnecessary to us, because it is supportable only by instinct, not by reason.

Chapter 17

THE MONEY ECONOMY

Free Enterprise and Trade.

The money economy (the way we are presently managed) is the chief vehicle of competition. It began long ago with the practice of barter, which grew alongside the concept of possession. This concept of possession recognised title to ownership of things, thus reducing the need to constantly defend possession of them, and barter was a means of obtaining things by exchange, without having to fight to possess them. There is a view, amongst those who are disenchanted with the money economy, that if we returned to barter all would be well. But barter is the ancient father of modern economics - which in turn has inherited its characteristics. Barter itself was fathered by the principle of competition, for it is not a means of providing for the needs of all; nor is it a matter of parting with something only in exchange for something else of equal value, (which is bad enough), but of seeking to exchange to advantage, which is worse.

The practice of bartering, or buying and selling, is so ancient that we seem unable to imagine an alternative. It is possible to see it as workable in principle if accompanied by goodwill, but whilst true human kindness would be willing to give, the principle of barter is that you do not give without return. The practice of barter has become part of human nature, but in that it serves the impulses of competitive self-interest and fails to share equally, it is unworthy of intellect, and so not our true nature.

Barter might work temporarily, between peoples possessing different things of need to each other and in equal measure. But from the beginning of civilisation competitive human groups fought for possession of territory, and territories were not equal in size or productivity and might have to support many or few people. So some people were rich in resources and could afford to demand the highest exchange value in barter, so becoming richer. Others were poor and unable to afford to supplement their resources by barter, so becoming poorer. Thus, whilst barter reduced the tendency to fight for survival between individuals, and equal territories, it increased the pressure for war between unequal territories. Also, by fostering competitive possessiveness and creating the quality of richness, barter encouraged acts of conquest out of greed for greater riches. All of this that applies to barter applies equally to its successor, the money economy.

The money-economy takes the grounds for decision-making away from human reason. It is a constraint, but upon good as well as bad behaviour. It contains no moral excuse, and the balance it achieves is not for the general good, like the balance of nature, but is between a privileged minority, which may express itself wilfully in all kinds of instinctive and intellectual ways, and a majority, whose expression is restricted and stunted. But those freedoms that the Machine does give to humanity are given on the Machine's terms. No humans are able openly to oppose automatic reality. The minority are free only to exploit the automatic systems. For instance, the farmer is not really free to decide how to farm - the money economy and attendant technology virtually determine his choice of decisions. But he does take those decisions, whilst the farm workers, representing the majority, do what he tells them to do - through him they serve the Machine. They do exert a certain restricted influence in that they make demands on the Machine's supplies, but they have no power of decision.

Money determines both demand and supply, for example in the field of housing. There is no question but that everybody needs good shelter, and all desire that it should be well built, situated and arranged. We are fully capable of building every house accordingly, varying the size only to suit the size of family. But our houses vary enormously, from mansions to hovels, for no good and intelligent human reason, but for money-economy reasons. Those with the most money are able to demand the supply of houses that carry their desires to extremes of luxury. As a consequence, those with the least money gravitate to the lowest extremes of poor housing - to slums and shantytowns. We take this to be logical, because we think in money-economy terms, but there is no human logic in it.

However, in the more 'advanced' societies, we would like to think that humane considerations prevent the extremes of wealth or poverty being reached. The chaotic inhumanity of unchecked competition is acknowledged, but paradoxically it is the main tool of competition, the implacably amoral money economy, which is also used by governing authority - humanitarian, moral or democratic as we might suppose that authority to be - in the attempt to control the worst extremes of competition, by such as taxation and systems of social security. There is a growing movement critical of our present economic systems, but it will get nowhere unless and until it realises that to rectify any one feature of the present social system requires that its whole economy, i.e. management, be changed.

Money economics is not a true human science - if it is a science at all - because, like the whole of our automatic society, it is a mixture of incompatibles; at best it is an attempt of moral intelligence to take a meaningful part in an unintelligent game with its own unchallenged, amoral, hard and fast rules. The money economy is supposed to be the responsibility of intellect but it is beyond human intelligence to predict or control, not only because it is so firmly established, independently of intellect, but because it appeals to human wilful instinct. We should have but one moral standard - that of supraconscious humantruth - but we have three. We might automatically calculate that a project is economically viable, or intellectually judge that it is morally indefensible, but as a compromise decide that it is politically acceptable. Even where we succeed in a measure of control over economic extremes, e.g. by the Monopolies Commission (which is a compromise only halfway to intelligent because it sees competition as healthy in that it keeps down prices, as opposed to market domination by one manufacturing concern which results in higher prices), we are not thus controlling the money economy, only partially restraining its overall control of us.

The money economy relies heavily on incentives. The appeal of its material rewards to our instincts incites us to do whatever the Machine requires of us, to the point where we are unwilling to do any work without reward. This gives rise to the view that incentives are a good thing, for without them we would be willing to do nothing, and stagnate. The truth is that without the Machine we would revert to doing that which was necessary, but voluntarily and intelligently. Money incentives cause unnecessary production and give other reasons for activity than the need for that activity and its products. This brings us once again to the inescapable conclusion, which reason must repeatedly reach, that society is not run by humanity in our interests - it runs automatically in its own competitive interests.

The money economy has pursued its own interests by making us units in a consumer society, whose combined function is to dispose of its products so as to make its continuing seem necessary. It has given meaning and purpose to our automated lives by creating the power of money, a power which is conveyed to us as we earn it and released by us when we spend it. Money has also cultivated pride of possession, another source of power to be got from the Machine and from the envy of an automated society which values above most things the ownership of money, goods and chattels.

A major division in our world society is that between rich and poor in terms of money, and between privileged and underprivileged in terms of possession and status. Those on one side of this divide have a very different view of the Machine from those on the other, but both views perpetuate this reality because almost all humans are presently automated. If the poor revolt, it is not against the Machine but for a bigger share of its rewards, and the rich resist because they do not want to lose their advantages. When the average family income is £12000 per year, the family living on £7000 feels relatively neglected, and the individual who is paid £100,000 or more per year for skilled intelligence is being rewarded for his or her least human qualities. This is not the way for an intellectual race to conduct itself - this is the behaviour of a sophisticated animal.

Economics changes the environment, raising its tempo and stripping it of natural beauty in order to bind us to both producing and buying the products and services of the Machine, and thus robbing us of pleasures and contentments of the old environment to which we were instinctively adjusted, or the intellectual fulfilment of a new environment for which we are truly and wholly fitted. We must expect that our growing pressure on Earth requires some technical development, but the way in which our society is developing into a super-Machine is fraught with the pitfalls of unbridled instinct and does not fulfil intellect. Money economics is a mathematical discipline that has, in theory, infinite possibilities but the world, and even the universe, is finite. The competition between nations means that economic development is held back in one place while it forges ahead in another but overall, unless we overcome it, it shall go ever more quickly forward.

It is an incredible fact that we do not see the ultra-stupidity of the competitive money economy, even in the face of its crushing neglect of about a quarter of all humanity and the unequally graded fortunes of the rest from poverty to prosperity. One reason is that the system is served by experts whom we suppose to know what they are about but who are conditioned to money thinking, employed by the system to think that way, and watched and relied upon by other experts who are geared to the identical system. Their findings have to accord with the aims and values of all institutions of the money economy, whose gears are meshed together in the same way.

These experts are on the rich and privileged side of the human divide, their experience, life-style and mental outlook different from the underprivileged on the other side. I have pointed out already that the Machine is perpetuated by the fact that people on both sides are automated. Automatic reality has three more tricks to keep it dominant and unchallenged. One is that practically all humans are so preoccupied with either keeping their privileges or trying to make ends meet that few feel free to intellate so as to become critically aware. Another trick is that those in authority are those who have been prepared for it by appropriate conditioning, and are the most highly rewarded, so they automatically support the money economy. The rest who are least successful or rewarded are subject to responsible authority, and their dissatisfaction is made to look like irresponsible ignorance. The third trick is that being preoccupied with and prejudiced towards the outlook of their own side, neither side sees the other's viewpoint. In particular the privileged lack conscientious sympathy for the deprivations of the other side.

It is commonly thought that we have to have money economics and free enterprise and trade - that's what makes the world go round. This is simply because we have always had them, cannot imagine life without them, presently depend on them, and will not see beyond them. Even communism, which supposedly abhors free enterprise, still uses money, and still trades. All countries progress according to present economic circumstances and in more or less the same way, whatever their politics. Ask yourself if these things are necessary. Do they work for the general human good? Is the whole money economy inescapable? Is it a system designed fairly to distribute the world's produce, to see that the needs of all humans are met? - if so, it is patently a failure. Or is it merely a means of ensuring that as we are able and willing to give our labour, so shall we receive our reasonable wants? - if so, it cannot be said to work. Is it, then, a means of controlling human greed, by subjecting it to the rigid law of money exchange? But who is to say that this economy does not of itself create and encourage greed, by making it profitable to manufacture things, to arouse desire and demand for them by advertising, and to make their supply available through commerce and trade - things which would not be desired if they, and the economic valuation of them and their possession, did not exist? Or is it just a method of maintaining the natural pecking order? - if so it is unworthy of an intellectual race.

Free enterprise and trade are necessary features of the money economy. These are activities of human individuals and groups motivated by desire for its profits, not by concern for the general human good. When these activities decline - when there is economic recession - human suffering follows, to be relieved by economic recovery. This does not mean that flourishing free enterprise and trade is a good thing, but that human well-being depends on chance - on the random processes of a mathematical system, rather than on the intelligent care of a humantrue system. The competitive money economy is supposed to be efficient whilst publicly owned industries are said to be inefficient, and this is no doubt so, in money terms. But consider the gross inefficiency of trade, in real terms. With some exceptions, such as certain restrictions on the arms trade in the UK, we will manufacture and sell anything to anyone willing to buy, whatever it is and wherever they are. Goods are transported the length and breadth of a country, often similar goods in opposite directions, or across the world between different countries, for the sake of money profit and without regard to the waste of road, rail and sea transport, of the metal and energy which goes into making the trucks, wagons and ships, or the fuel to drive them.

On top of all this largely unnecessary activity is an equally wasteful, pointless discipline imposed by the money economy. This insists that every transaction of making, buying, selling, transporting and servicing must be accounted for. The processes of money-accountancy are extremely complex, all-embracing, and are taken very seriously by the Machine, yet they are entirely irrelevant to the fundamental organisation necessary to a humantrue society. Were they to be eliminated it would still be necessary to calculate needs, and supplies to meet those needs, but that is all. Think of all those things that are familiar and obligatory parts of our automatic reality but which have no essential part to play in good human relations. Payslips, tax returns, customs and excise laws, bank statements, bills, receipts, cheques, quotations, check-outs, tenders, dividends, share certificates, interest rates, balance sheets, price lists, credit cards, auctions, debt collectors, capital gains, insurance premiums, liquidations, assets, budgets. Think of the huge amount of wasted effort and resources all these represent; how many millions of people are employed, and computers used, to deal with them, and how much private time everybody is compelled or incited to devote to them.

Let me take an example which demonstrates how free trade, by converting desire into demand and then supplying that demand, can obey the laws of the money economy by providing a food which is unnecessary, to say the least, whilst failing to provide adequate supplies of other foods which are vitally needed. In the fifteenth century Western traders discovered an irresistibly attractive and therefore highly saleable product - sugar. Up to that time human intake of pure bulk sugar had been limited to occasional consumption of honey. Otherwise our healthy needs were provided by the natural sugar that our bodies can efficiently extract from a wide variety of foods from almonds to ripe fruit, and from barley to leeks. The new product was first extracted from sugar cane in the West Indies, using Negro slave labour. Nowadays it is also extracted from sugar beet in Europe. It is refined mostly to pure white sucrose, consumption of which has steadily increased.

William Duffy, in his book Sugar Blues (published by Warner Books), points out that sugar is now introduced into many things to make them more saleable - not only foods like bread and tinned beans, or drinks like Cola and beer, but also into tobacco and medicines - and maintains that it is not only unnecessary but, in the large quantities commonly taken, extremely harmful. Sugar is like a drug - most people, in the West anyway, partaking of their quick 'fix' every two or three hours each day. It is held to be unwholesome, contributing to mental diseases, diabetes, cancer, coronaries - "a poison more lethal than opium", especially to those unable to handle it. Sugar has always been a successful industry of profit to the Machine, which is why the case against it is officially denied and therefore yet little understood by people in general.

Money is not a token to facilitate proper production and distribution of needs - it is a tool of the competitive economy. It is also itself a commodity which, like all other commodities, is unequally and unfairly distributed, and which can be traded for profit, especially between countries. As an economic tool, when given into our hands it compels us to make it work for the Machine. The individual puts small amounts of money to work simply by spending. Large amounts may be used to take possession of means of production and distribution, of land and industrial processes, and to employ intellect, skill and labour - manipulating these facilities in its own interests and for its own purposes, rather than for those of humanity. Furthermore money may be accumulated, as capital that has such power over us as to render our true humanity relatively powerless. It takes away our responsibility and gives it to the Machine, leaving us to do first that which it entices or obliges us to do, or forces on us, and only then to do whatever human good it permits and enables us to do. An example is the industrialist who spends his whole life making vast profits from the sweated labour of others and in his will sets up a charity for the benefit of old retired workers who are suffering the consequences.

We have a certain number of people in the world, representing a certain volume of need, and of labour. We have at our disposal certain resources of energy and material. Logically our concern and activity should be devoted to putting all these assets together so as to sustain ourselves and maintain the biosphere as happily and satisfactorily as we possibly can. The indictment of the Machine and its money economy, in the service of whose highly complex affairs most of us are engaged, is that it does not sustain and maintain the world in this way - quite the contrary.

The money economy has created huge but largely unnecessary facilities and activities that engulf and choke true human potential. Big industrial complexes, commercial groups or financial cartels require big factories, huge machines, heavy transport, big fuel consumption, complex roads and harbours, big sales. They engender service industries, sophisticated accountancy, computerised banking, market research, blanket advertising, prestige building, heavy selling, big worries, dominating powers. In financial terms their products may be cheap, but in human terms they are far, far too expensive. Our labour and intellectual effort is not being applied to our well-being by way of a humane economy but merely to a rapidly accelerating, ritual and mindless consumption of resources.

Our society embodies established practices protected by laws, including; administration of law; a system of education; a pattern of rules applied to possession of property and money, its exchange and taxation; a form of governing control over the public. Within these laws, rules and controls our present society provides; road, rail and air transport facilities; postal, telephone, printed, radio, television and computer communications systems; food, clothing, shelter, power, heat and water supplies, and waste disposal. The existence of such comprehensive facilities does not indicate a good society, especially when they are not made fully available to a large proportion of the population. The character of a social system depends on the concepts of reality it obeys. Our world society, harnessed as it is to the Machine and its competitive money economy, has a bad character. This is borne out by the fact that we are divided into competitive nations, each of which devotes a large proportion of its resources to maintaining its own independent military force.

Many of the ills of our society are put down to the inevitable effects of market forces, but these forces are not held accountable for the suffering they cause. They are backed by established custom and have the powerful protection of economic law. Yet many of us are becoming more and more concerned to stamp out the evident ills of our society. This brings us ever nearer to realising the need to remove the economic law that helps to cause them and replace it with human wisdom and compassion. But, so far, we have mostly turned to other institutions of the Machine for temporary cures. In the North, rather than forsake the extravagant habits and diet which the Machine concocts for us, we turn to health-service medicines to counter the ill effects, and tranquillisers to shield our emotions from nerve-racking automatic affairs. Similarly, rather than face the knowable dangers of economic growth and progress, we put our hope and trust in science and technology to discover or invent ways of averting those dangers.

As individuals we are, or count ourselves to be, privately humane and honest, but the Machine makes collective, public cheats and liars of us all. The competitive money economy is the major dictator of our character, whether as passive demanders or active suppliers. As suppliers, the more scrupulous of us might ensure that our products and services are good but will not hesitate to use deceitful ways of selling them. The less scrupulous will use the same deceit to sell bad products and services. Both will see their activity as legitimate, though that which both supply, good or bad, may be humanly inessential.

We view these shameful practices shamelessly because they are so commonplace as to be beyond our sense of shame. Advertising is often a blatant ploy to trick us, but is widely practiced and tolerated. The world of finance is essentially an exercise in bloodsucking, but its human leeches do not hang their heads, and we respect its institutions of banking, insurance and stock broking. Mature automated men or women might say these were exaggerated charges, but the charges are truly made against the Machine, not against its human adherents who would be expected to deny that they are engaged in trickery or bloodsucking because it is common practice, known as 'business'. This way of gaining wealth, power and privilege is not only condoned by our society - it is applauded. Yet it is a kind of stealing; taking unjustly from others and exploiting them.

Here in the rich North we all take a share in the processes of the money economy and believe that with intelligent application they bring human benefit. In the poor South the majority have no opportunity to take a share yet still believe the process holds their hopes of benefiting in the future, not realising that their poverty is necessary to Northern prosperity. If they in the South are to enjoy economic expansion it will be at the expense of recession in the North. A competitive money economy needs winners and losers, without which it loses its peculiar meaning and impetus.

The competitive money economy depends for its automatic success on creating a consumer society whose major preoccupation is demanding, supplying and using everything the Machine produces. Such a system has its good points. It is exciting because it is energetic and ever progressively changing. The supplier has to sweetheart the consumer to capture demand. This brings a kind of freedom that is better than dictatorship in that humans with power have to watch their step with the public, up to a point. But it makes all subject to the automaton, tied to its objectives and products, squandering the Earth's resources, failing to fulfil unlimited human resources, and relying on the conflict of inequality.

That the money economy does not truly cater for human needs but ignores those needs when they do not serve its own purposes is demonstrated by the situation in the UK in 1987. The economy was in recession, not for human but economic reasons, as a consequence of which four million men and women were out of work. This means they were no longer paid a wage but given at most half the value of their wage in social security benefits. Their needs, or the real needs of the whole community, had not changed. They had done nothing knowingly to cause this recession. A recession is not like a natural calamity, such as a bad harvest or plague, the burden of which is inescapable. It is an unnecessary calamity which we endure or tolerate simply because we accept and do not question the competitive money economy. Those thrown out of work may be buying their homes on mortgages, in which case they would probably be evicted. Those still working for the Machine do not help the others, not because they do not sympathise but because to do so goes contrary to the self-interested norm, which allows us no idea of individually taking responsibility for the whole community as we should. We simply accept that life must be a continual round of booms, recessions, tax returns, wage claims and all kinds of other monetary manipulations and burdens that are irrelevant to our real concerns and potentials.

Money economics is a particularly difficult subject of criticism, partly because it has always been a target of ill-considered protest, partly because it has strong instinctive emotional appeal, and partly because it is so deeply ingrained in our thinking. Protest is usually complaint against the 'haves' on the part of the 'have-nots'; understandable but ineffective because the objective of the latter is to reverse their fortunes, not fundamentally to change the whole system. How firmly the money economy is established is demonstrated by our common acceptance of comparative terms such as wealth and poverty, profit and loss, payment and receipt, creditor and debtor, which would have no meaning in a humantrue society.

This chapter, like the book as a whole, is intended to serve as a programme or stimulus of intellation and discussion. The subject of economics is to be dealt with more fully in publications to follow. The chapters of this book are offered for their radical angles and viewpoints, as springboards for new intellation rather than catalogues of cut and dried information. The important thing is to have a truly reasoned mental foundation, in the light of which all further knowledge can be separated from its automatic connections and brought into true relationship. If we swallow knowledge complete with these automatic connections we shall remain automatically hooked to the Machine. On the other hand, if we take in knowledge, including that which is opposed to the Machine in one or another specific sphere, not wishing to be prejudiced but without a truly reasoned mental foundation, the result will be confusion. The individual's task is to construct this mental foundation, and I am trying to help by easing and shortening what might otherwise be a longer and more difficult process.

Chapter 18

AUTOPROGRESSION

The notion that we must progress is ingrained in our present character. The cause of this is that our minds must naturally progress towards total understanding because of their energy and curiosity. But this is not true human reason. Since we are harnessed to the Machine, our thinking is and has long been applied to technology or diverted by the money economy to the interests of the Machine. As a result we have come to think of progress in material and financial terms, and individually apply our minds and energies to the automaton; hence the term autoprogression. As individuals we submit to this existing reality, trusting that by instinctively orienting ourselves to its rules - by 'doing our own thing' on its terms, and pursuing its objectives in our own automatic interests - we may find a sort of happiness and satisfaction. This is usually not so much a sin of commission as omission, since the great majority of us believe the present to be the only possible reality, offering our only opportunity of happiness, and fail to envisage the humantrue alternative.

Early in our history, when we were struggling to prevail against the restrictions of natural reality, such progress brought benefits. The application of intellect to skilled techniques of basic survival gave to the African Bushmen a happy way of life that did not upset the natural balance but brought them to an optimum level of satisfaction within it, according to the intellectual level they had reached. When the intellectual level rose elsewhere, in the minds of other groups, it did not show them the wisdom of savouring their new understanding whilst otherwise remaining unchanged - they immediately began to apply it to autoprogression which, once it had taken hold of their minds without being questioned, could not be stopped. The

Bushmen had reached a point in their development which, with common and innate understanding, they determined not to progress beyond. This was not the only point of development appropriate to that decision, and was probably partially dictated, later on in central Africa, by the harsh limitations of their environment. The fact is - a fact which their unspoken understanding must have embraced - that further material progress would be of no real value to them, for the advantages would not outweigh the disadvantages. This does not mean that there are no benefits from intellectual progress alone. From the evidence of their cave painting, music and story telling, the Bushmen did progress and benefit in this way.

Where civilisation autoprogressed it fulfilled certain needs but created its own additional needs, the further fulfilment of which brought added burdens and dangers. For example, invention of the wheel lightened the labour of transporting goods but at the same time increased it by opening up the unnecessary trading of goods for money, and heightened human conflict by its application to weapons of war. Useful items such as the wheel were not and still are not made available according to real need but for money-profit and other automatic advantage. Autoprogression serves the Machine's competitive concept of reality by always aiming to reduce money-costs in order to increase production. Where it succeeds, humans consume ever more resources, whether as food, or material goods, or as weapons of war, in many ways contrary to their well-being and dangerous to their prospective survival. Where autoprogression fails the Machine withdraws, and fewer resources are made available for human consumption, causing deprivation to the point of starvation. It is against the nature of the money economy to strike and sustain a balance between the two extremes.

So autoprogression is essential to the Machine and, since the Machine depends upon our willing effort, autoprogression must also appeal to us. This means that its achievements and goods must be attractive to us, and since it is we who accomplish the achievements, and manufacture and consume the goods, it is in our automated interest to make the whole process attractive. There are none but ourselves to use the Machine's services, nor to produce and consume these things. Rather than contemplate the drastic step of giving up the whole procedure, however, realising that it is not only unnecessary but also a great burden laid on us, we try to increase the artificial advantages of autoprogression to a point where they seem to outweigh the disadvantages. Very few of us fully succeed in this, but most hope to do so. For many of us the hoped-for automatic rewards are what we chiefly live for, to be realised only if we continue to go forward in this way - to autoprogress. Our material and technological standards are continually raised, and our expectations rise with them, so that we resist any subsequent attempts to lower them. Even when the burdens of automatic life are unrelieved by rewards, or we are personally bored by materialistic existence, our spirits may be lifted by the spearheads of autoprogression - the space shuttle, computer technology, planned Mars landings, or genetic engineering. Or we might simply live for football or darts, the fortunes of our chosen teams, or for the success of our nation's athletes in the Olympic Games.

In parts of the world, such as here in Britain, we enjoy much higher standards of living than we used to, and could say we have the Machine to thank for it. Yes, there is more comfort, less hardship and drudgery than there was, but for us every new advantage has brought built-in disadvantage, because the chief reason for autoprogress is not the balanced benefit of humanity. In the past our level of expectation was much lower so that it took much less to make us happy, particularly as we were not aware that any other condition was possible for us. Now our material expectations are much higher, and the Machine is capable of meeting them. But our minds have also been stimulated to a higher level of moral-awareness, which our autoculture does not reflect and which, in the process of providing material rewards, the Machine betrays. If we had planned our social advance according to true human reason and for the good of the entire race the result would have been utterly and wholesomely different. As it is, imbalance is the norm. Whilst we in the North receive more than our share of material things, and are in that sense happier, others elsewhere in the world receive much less, yet carry more than their fair share of the burden of providing for us and, in this worldly sense at least, are less happy. Even so we, in our affluence, suffer unrest, insecurity, fear, uncertainty and anxiety, because of inequalities and disagreements inherent in our society which lead to crime, violence, instability, and tensions arising from threats of impending disasters of all kinds.

All this that makes up our existing reality is the end result of a system that is all right in its own terms, all wrong in human terms. It does not serve us, so we should not serve it. Our present world is the result of our exploitation of ourselves and Earth, by instinct with the aid of intellect - the result of autoprogression or, if you prefer, civilisation. Are we really capable of pretending that our extremely bad record is good - so good as to warrant extension of this reckless exploitation into space? How can anybody dream of humanity leading the way to a 'galactic super organism' when we find difficulty in successfully running a local council? Our space projects are really dreams of escape, but the burden we want to escape from is self-imposed by our conscious selves on our minds, and would be carried with us wherever we were to go. We are products of Earth that have not yet found our proper place *here*.

The nature of autoprogression is that it proceeds to make things happen, by our agency as a sort of side effect of the work we do. Our personal aim is to gain satisfaction, prestige and reward. As we work, we allow ourselves to be persuaded that the product, being of vital interest to the money economy, must be of value to humanity. This stills our consciences, allowing us to concentrate on the job in hand and preventing us from projecting our concerns effectively into the future. The microchip, for example, simply happened in this way. It is something which every industry has to use to speed production in some way, or lose in the general competitive race, but whose introduction was not planned and whose effect on humanity was hardly considered and so not foreseen. I shall return to the microchip in the next chapter (on employment). Right now, let us consider two other examples of autoprogression.

Human evolution. By automatically pursuing the science of biology we have learned how to modify the genes in a cell, opening the door to the creation of completely new species. Since this existing reality is wrong, any new species we tailor to fit it shall also be wrong. In view of the fact that we hardly realise this is the wrong reality, much less know what would be the right reality for us, we cannot know what would be an ideal species to create. Besides, genes are nature's tools for securely fitting all life-forms into their reality in a balanced way. Our job is to make what changes are needful in world reality, by intention. We, and all other creatures, shall then genetically adjust, as we have always done, in a much more satisfactory and natural way than is likely if blinkered science intervenes.

Computers. This is a particularly vital subject because the aim is to develop computers that think, when that capacity of mind is our own chief attribute that we have not yet fulfilled. This development is proceeding so fast that its ultimate aim has been brought rapidly forward from the realms of fantasy into impending reality. Not so long ago it was publicly announced that the race was on to make fifth generation computers with capacity far beyond anything existing. Now it is anticipated that sixth generation computers will be achieved in the 1990's. But the target is UIM's - ultra intelligent machines - the first generation of which will be able to process information (whatever that may truly mean) better than the human brain. Second generation UIM's will (it is confidently predicted) have capabilities way beyond human intellectual abilities, and third and fourth generations will follow with exponentially rising levels of intelligence.

Do we want thinking machines with capacity way beyond ours? As I have said already, we have yet nowhere near fulfilled our intellect. Until we have done so we are in no position to decide to create UIM's. Admittedly existing computers are already better at calculating and reproducing information than the average human brain. We already submit to fellow humans who are above average in this respect - the experts. Clearly the human race shall be obliged to bow down to the almighty expertise of its fourth generation UIM's if and when they super-compete internationally and maybe on an inter-galactic scale one day. This is why the Machine wants them, because our morality is a nuisance to it; once it had them it would by-pass us, and then we would never be able to fulfil our own intellect effectively, for we could not argue with their supposed, officially acknowledged superior intelligence. Not only would many of us become physically superfluous, as is already happening, but all of us would be made mentally redundant.

The point about human intellect is that its most immediate truth, of the utmost significance to us, is humantruth - wholly appropriate to our life on Earth but hardly likely to appeal to an ultra-intelligent Machine. Our intellect is the supreme achievement of universal evolution. Our bodies are agents of the influence to express energy, but our minds are creations so to speak, of the influence for truth. Our fulfilled minds shall turn us against the Machine and towards truth. UIM's are the product of intellect abjectly applied to instinct, serving the Machine. Their human inventors produce them without any clear idea of what will result - for egoistic, romantic, ambitious or purely practical and financial reasons rather than humantrue reasons. If these UIM's were really to surpass human intellect they would be designed independently to correlate more knowledge than we can absorb, but also with more complete processes of reason in which case they too most turn against the Machine which gave birth to them. Obviously the designers of UIM's have no intention of allowing this to happen. These super-computers will be programmed according to automatic concepts, and so shall be merely extensions of the automatic thinking of existing reality - calculating according to the conflicting elements of the competitive norm. In other words they shall be incapable of thinking truly, of intellating, and shall thus be infinitely inferior to human intellect, being externally programmed and incapable of free intellation and self-determination. The whole UIM project is based on misunderstanding of intellect, a true understanding of which would not have occasioned the idea to arise, and would now cancel it as undesirable and futile. Our intellect is capable of comprehending truth from the viewpoint of life, which represents the ultimate meaning and purpose of the universe - of existence. The material existence of the universe, like the human body, is merely the vehicle of that truth. No amount of extra thinking capacity to absorb endless universal facts can surpass the human intellect as an instrument of truth - only mislead it, further confuse the issues, and more firmly establish the Machine.

Consider some further examples of autoprogression. In the van of modern industrial practice is precision engineering to accuracies of the order of 10 to the power of minus 6 millimetres, presently used, apparently, to produce musical compact discs and improved microchips. Science and technology has brought this civilisation to the threshold of space-colonisation. Many humans are now linked to highly complex communication systems that are spreading and growing in power and complexity all the time. It is doubtful whether anyone can give good reason for these developments, in human terms. Autoprogression is the reason for them happening, which intellect cannot justify. They contain their own justification, confirmed by their automatic evolution - that energy shall express itself in any and every possible way. That this is so, and that these things are not practiced in the human interest, can be judged from the apparent fact that here in the rich North it takes fifty times more energy (chiefly derived from oil) to produce our processed food than we get from eating it.

What we are doing, by this accelerating evolution, is no different in character from that which evolution has always done - blindly going where opportunity leads, without purpose of our own. Amazingly, most humans are not fully aware that these staggering things are happening, and the fact is that we can achieve a perfectly satisfactory standard of living without them. Highly precise engineering was developed for money economy reasons and to meet automatic standards, not to fulfil the most pressing human needs. It will become vital to our living standards only if and when it is so widely practiced that we come to depend on it, unable to function without it. As for the colonisation of space, if there is ever to be good reason for it that reason doesn't exist now. And complex communications are of little use if that to be communicated has no real humantrue purpose or value.

Whilst autoprogression, which lacks true human purpose, is bad, this is not to say that all products of human ingenuity are so. The solar cell, for example, is a simple, direct and harmless way of tapping the source of all Earth's available energy - the sun. That we have not fully exploited the solar cell, despite its advantages and all our scientific and technological resources, is another indication that we are not in control of our destiny, pursuing human interests, but are harnessed to the Machine, serving its interests. Instead, we are replacing the dirty and dangerous method of burning coal with the possibly potentially more dirty and dangerous method of nuclear fission. A primary reason for this is military, for a by-product of nuclear reactors is plutonium, an effective component of nuclear weapons. These weapons still threaten the world with explosive destruction and carcinogenic radiation. The very main reason for being against nuclear power is the chief automatic military reason *for* developing it.

There is an argument in favour of autoprogression that many important discoveries are made by accident, in the course of other research and development; also that useful products emerge as 'spin-offs' from the invention of special materials and techniques required for quite different purposes. This may be so, but returns us to the question of advantage and disadvantage. This case in favour of autoprogression is that by satisfying our curiosity, with no known benefit in sight, we challenge ourselves to develop new technologies that sometimes happen to prove useful. My case is that such effort to discover diverts attention from real necessity; leads us into activities like space exploration, which, seen in this light, are disadvantageous; and that the so-called advantages, like heat-proof porcelain from the development of rockets, may be of interest to the Machine, and of use to sophisticated cooks, but do not provide vitally needed solutions to the real problems facing humanity.

I do not subscribe to the argument that unless it is to satisfy curiosity or gain personal advantage humans have no cause for endeavour and will stagnate. This is the argument of our instinct, not our potential intellect. What better true cause can we have for trying a new thing than the knowledge that it is vitally needed, and what better reason for doing what we do than that it is for the good of the whole race, and of the whole Earth? It could be argued that without the tools, disciplines and techniques of automatic research we could not have come to understand the concept of Gaia, for instance. This has two answers. One is that the discovery of Gaia *was* an act of imagination on the part of James Lovelock, contrary to the normal pressure and direction of scientific research. The other answer is that without our history of autoprogressive science and technology, which characterises the modern Machine, we would not *need* to understand Gaia because we would not be threatening it. Were we a humantrue society, Gaia would simply be continuing to look after us, and all other life, without our knowing help, or ignorant hindrance.

Perhaps we should consider a possible danger, arising from our restriction, exploitation and destruction of instinctive natural life - that the surviving species of all kinds may react with an upsurge in their own intelligence levels, resulting in counter-measures against us of rapidly increasing and deadly effectiveness. Perhaps the diseases that plague us are not only due to our unhealthy habits. It may be that cancers and viruses are the spearhead of this counter-attack, since viruses and bacteria, being the simplest life-forms, are able to change most quickly. It is possible that even Gaia may turn against us in the interests of life on Earth as a whole, by ceasing to compensate for the results of our activities such as the rising level of carbon dioxide in the atmosphere, and thus allowing us to become extinct by way of our own recklessness. Remember that our civilisation and, more especially, our industrialisation *have* occurred very quickly in planetary terms. Also remember that we may not notice moves against us, since we are not looking for them and do not have comprehensive records which go back far enough.

Chapter 19

EMPLOYMENT

Animals, wild creatures totally governed by instinct, busy themselves with providing for themselves, but they are not said to work, much less to be employed. We were once the same. The effort we made to live was part of living. We were free to live, or die. We instinctively and urgently wanted to live, and reproduce so as to continue life, and from that the effort to do so naturally followed. This effort became known as *work* when that freedom was lost to us and we were forced unwillingly to labour for masters, indirectly of our own needs and harder and longer than those needs once required.

Then, when the majority were no longer forced to work for a minority of humans, we all, in our various ranks, became obliged to work for the competitive money economy of the Machine. This is known as *employment*, work for money, the sole means of purchasing survival. We can not now live without money, which is obtainable only from the Machine; therefore we are obliged to go cap-in-hand to the Machine for employment. The Machine is responsible for deciding what work shall be done, for it holds the purse-strings and, according to profitability, determines how much money we shall be paid for that work. We are responsible for securing the Machine's employment of us, doing its work to its satisfaction, and living according to what the amount of money it pays can buy back from it.

Inwardly, we are all free to decide whether or not to conform in our minds to this automatic system. Outwardly, what freedoms we have are automated, and severely limited. We are 'free' obediently to submit to the Machine's education, or otherwise apply ourselves to gaining its approval and privileged employment, and to live in a style that this economic level makes appropriate. We are 'free', having accepted a lower level of employment and a more cramped economic style of life, to unite with fellow workers to bargain for 'fair' wages and conditions using the threat of withdrawing our labour. We are 'free' to decline employment and face starvation or, in the case of the rich nations, to live on the lowest possible income paid by welfare or charitable institutions to the unemployed. We can develop ways of supporting and enriching life independently of the Machine and its money economy, but we can do this only on the margins of reality while still being basically Machine-dependent.

We are *not* free to decide overall what work shall be done; to do work that the Machine disallows, however humanly vital; to survive or prosper when unwilling to do the work which the Machine allocates or allows, in the way it requires; to live as or where we wish, or live at all, without the Machine's money; to demand work which the Machine is not willing to provide. We are free to prosper by limiting our ambition to self-interest, but since our work is mostly imposed on us, or enticed out of us, we are not free to feel the enthusiastic goodwill which goes with good labour voluntarily contributed to the common cause. There is all the difference in the world between giving our effort in that spirit of willing responsibility and toiling unwillingly in our own defence or purely for selfish gain. We are carried along by the autoprogressive, money economy tide, our reality a day-to-day practical and political adjustment to its waves. Some of us resist and hold back against the tide, but mostly the economically strong push forward, pressing back the weak. We have not yet acquired that enlightenment which would give us the collective will to swim against the tide and to break its power over us.

Our deeply ingrained concept of employment, which translates the combined effort for the well being of whole humanity into the separated individual's need for a specific Machine job, is as ridiculous as our concept of reality. And the practice of one human employing others for profit is morally akin to slavery, a creator of inequality. It is our present reality, almost unquestioned, that we need employment to survive, and the Machine is the only employer. So we work for the competitive money economy, keep its lores and look to it for survival of our species, when its objective is not whole human survival; it is not interested in humanity at all as a morally aware intellectual race, only in autoprogression of itself by human agency.

Consequently, humanity generally depends for its continuing life on employment, which accrues to its detriment and possibly to its eventual destruction. The Machine cannot of itself *do* anything. It directs but must rely on humans to act. Mostly we do anything that the Machine requires us to do, whatever it may be and whatever the circumstances. We don uniforms, gain degrees, take office, accept rank, make and use weapons, bulldoze rainforest, build nuclear power stations, compete with each other, cheat one another, argue with one another, crush one another - all for automatic reasons.

Just as the concept of employment is an economic phenomenon, so is the occurrence of unemployment. It is the logical accompaniment of competitive inequality, a necessary casualty of money-economic recession, the low point of cyclic automatic activity as it oscillates between rest and the full generation of energy, naturally, like winter as opposed to summer, but with the difference that whilst we cannot control the seasons, we can and should control our own economy, or management. Each time a cycle touches bottom enough determination and energy has been gathered to begin striving towards the top once more. This activity characterises instinctive life, which has no motivation but the impulsion of energy to act and react, reflected in the explosive birth of a life-form, then of its seed, its implosion to death, and the explosive re-birth of its seed.

When there is unemployment we cry out for jobs. It is the cry of the mentally blind, mesmerised by automation into believing they are unable to take responsibility for their own affairs into their own hands. We are asking employment of the very automatic economy that has carelessly caused our unemployment. That we do not prevent unemployment is because we have no control over money-economic recessions. This in turn is because recessions are part of an instinctive cycle that we aid and abet, and to ask instinct to contradict itself is asking the impossible. We shall get rid of unemployment only when we have thrown out the concept of employment; when we have subjected our instinct to the full wisdom of our intellect, so giving human life its true motivation.

Unemployment is part of the myth of the money economy that insists, when in recession, that there is no work for many of us when there is work in plenty. The reason behind this is that, according to the current rule, we may not work except for money. So when there is no money to pay us we may not work. What is the *real* difference between times of full employment and massive unemployment? In terms of humantruth there is *no* real difference. The work needing to be done is the same, needful resources are the same, and our capacity for labour is the same. It is only an artificial economic difference that creates this human suffering. Let me repeat - in a humantrue society such labour would be done as was necessary to provide all needs, and needs would be simply provided. The money economy is an unnecessary and inhuman intervention that upsets this straightforward voluntary equation.

Humanity in general accepts automatic reality without question, but we do vary in our reactions to the effects of automatic policies on people. Chapter

23 deals with the political division between Right and Left. Generally speaking the former supports the authority of the Machine over the people, and the latter champions the rights of the people against the Machine. The majority of those on the Left are the least rewarded, least privileged and most vulnerable, the manual workers, whose rights are represented by the trade union movement, a movement whose influence has been very much reduced in recent years. This movement has opposed employers, but not the Machine. It has accepted that its members are employed by the money economy, and that its job is to make their employment secure and to raise their rewards and privileges to the highest possible level. This has relieved or re-distributed but not eliminated poverty; it has changed but strengthened the Machine by spreading the practice of consumerism; and it has had no good effect on the cycles of periodic prosperity and recession, except that in periods of recession the wages of union members may not be reduced out of hand and workers either continue on full pay or are made redundant and receive very much lower welfare payments. By no means all workers now belong to unions, however, and in the case of non-members wages are again at the mercy of market forces.

What I am trying to demonstrate is that humanity cannot be benefited effectively by automatic means, only by ridding itself of the Machine. The Machine is a system for serving the automaton by way of many institutions, of which the trade union movement is one. In times of comparatively full employment all our work is devoted to the Machine, whereas we should be devoting ourselves to overthrowing the Machine. As it happens, some unemployed people have found that by rejecting normal automatic standards they have converted their state of unemployment from one of deprivation to one of new opportunity for understanding themselves and their world. They have discovered something better than working for the Machine. This is but a short step from realising that the Machine is unnecessary and that only it prevents us all voluntarily working for humanity.

The institution of employment, then, is a strong factor in our failure to realise humantruth. It has the effect of continually reinforcing our automatic conditioning, often for reasons that seem good. All who are employed are busy fulfilling some function of the Machine, more or less. By this means most are also fulfilling a family responsibility. To be humanly, companionably satisfactory is to be content with one's lot. To be satisfactory in automatic terms is to fulfil one's function to the best of one's ability. Those who go against automatic reality appear, in this light, to be recklessly trying to upset the applecart, failing in their private responsibilities by publicly opposing the Machine.

Automatic functions are separated and competitive, not co-operative. Each tends to deal with its own matters within its own strictly limited boundaries. All vie with each other for resources, priorities and profits. So they tend to occupy fully the conscious minds of the humans engaged in them. If all these functions were for one common human purpose they would have to take criticism of the Machine seriously, for they clearly do not work for human good. But they all do work for their own different, specific, competitive, automated purposes, which make sense only to minds that remain submerged in the automatic chaos.

The individual whose reasoning questions this reality might be heard, but in the end those who listen have to return to their automatic functions, and if they are to give these functions their full attention, as they must do for Machine-success, then they do not normally allow such critical comments to penetrate beyond the periphery of their minds. What is required, and what this book aims for, is abnormal human effort to break this deadlock.

Chapter 20

INSTITUTION

Competitively divided and conflicting functions of the Machine, as well as contradictory automatic concepts, make it necessary for automated humans to limit and adapt their characters accordingly, as we have seen, in order to come to terms with existing reality and make the self a viable entity in it. Our society long ago found it necessary to separate these divided aims and interests into *institutions,* each within its own demarcation lines. By this means, though the aims and interests of automatic society contradict one another, and in combination are contrary to whole human interest, each institution on its own can provide those individuals loyally serving it with specific reasons for doing so, within the authoritative framework and reasoning of the Machine. This has the effect of keeping human individuals confined to their chosen divided, competitive, subservient characters, preventing or discouraging them from correlating their awareness and so rising towards supraconsciousness.

The institution has its own specific aims, and its own rigid and limited set of rules. It has its own narrow, highly specialised conscience. It does not have a human conscience. Those who serve it are required to second their consciences to its rules; that is a condition of their employment. The more loyally and efficiently they serve its aims and interests the more highly they are placed in its ranks of power, privilege and reward. Therefore, the higher men and women ascend an instituted hierarchy the further their applied intellects are likely to depart from supraconscious humantruth. Since humans in authority are those at the highest levels of such hierarchies, including all the communications media, it follows that the thinking that has greatest influence on humanity is automatic thinking.

Present human society - the Machine - is a framework composed of many such institutions, each with its own 'truths'. Although they mostly represent the predominant automatic drives, some incorporate reactionary human interests, and leanings towards more moral influences. But our society has always been powered by the competitive money economy, and all institutions wield that power to some degree. However, whilst the whole situation, from the viewpoint of humantruth, is fundamentally amoral or immoral, it does incorporate its own, if very limited, moral code - its own version of true and honest conduct - which merely seeks to prevent institutions or humans from too grossly interfering with, or too conspicuously injuring one another. So far all more truly moral movements, in order to be effective, have sought the power of institution. By doing so they have taken their place in the here-and-now, their truth adulterated by the aims and interests of automatic reality, failing to rise to awareness of humantrue morality.

It is humantruth alone that makes total sense to human intellectual reason. Institutions make sense only to themselves in their context, and to humans conditioned to believe in them. Yet it is extremely difficult for human intellect clearly to demonstrate that they are nonsense, for two reasons. Firstly, institutions actually exist as part of an overwhelmingly accepted reality, and are party to the all-pervasive money economy. Secondly, they are separate even so, with their own especial reason for being. Consequently they cannot be opposed, singly or collectively, on one broad and true front because each presents one of many different narrow fronts. On their own ground, on their own terms, they cannot be faulted because they are fulfilling their declared function and logically fit into their automatic background. Broad overall criticism of that background, even though showing it to be a nonsense, can be dismissed out of hand as naive because it goes contrary to existing reality and can be seen as indicating inability to cope with that reality. True criticism can not be accepted by institutions because they depend and rest upon the grand illusion and their part in it. Truth can be admitted only by human individuals who are willing to prefer their own true reason to the facts and concepts of existing reality and its conditioning of their minds.

As an example of the institution contradicting wholly humantrue reasoning by upholding its own limited version of truth, take a typical commercial enterprise, manufacturing cosmetics. On the grounds that it employs people and contributes to economic prosperity, this industry can justify making a needless product, wasting irreplaceable materials, producing toxic wastes, often cruelly experimenting on animals to make their product safe for humans, misusing labour and skill which could be devoted to needful things, and encouraging women, and men, to embellish their bodies. It can be said that we are free to decline to use cosmetics, and that they are supplied to meet demand. But demand, not abstinence, is encouraged by many means, including advertising that appeals to primitive instinct rather than intelligence. People respond, despite their intelligence, because they belong to an instinctive reality of which such response is a common part. Individuals who do not respond, such as women who will not wear cosmetics, can be made to feel deprived because there is no alternative intelligent reality for them to join.

Another example that involves institutions under fire from moral awareness is that of leaded petrol. Exhaust fumes of vehicles burning leaded petrol were found to cause brain damage, particularly in children in urban areas. The truly human reaction to this would have been to outlaw leaded petrol immediately so as to prevent all further damage. The actual decision, in Britain, was to phase out lead in petrol over a considerable period of years, because of the difficulty and cost of converting all existing engines, and redesigning all new ones, to burn unleaded petrol, and of putting the new petrol on the market. This example illustrates that the Machine does not give way to human moral concern unless there is an undeniable and serious health risk, and even then it did not abandon its principles in this case, for economic considerations took precedence. No doubt a total ban on leaded petrol would have been economically disastrous, but it would have speeded up the necessary conversion work wonderfully. Perhaps a better alternative would have been to ban leaded petrol for any but vital use. As it is leaded petrol is still being used, though unleaded is steadily taking its place, but all petrol-burning has ill-effects, and the fact remains that we continue using petrol in vast quantities, for although engines become leaner, car sales continually rise.

Chapter 21

NATIONS

Nations are the largest and most powerful institutions of our automatic reality. They were not planned by intellect as sensible institutions necessary to the humane functioning of world society. They originated in that animal necessity which seeks to establish and defend a territory large enough to support the family, group or tribe. Nations were enlarged by competitive aggressive conflict between leaders for dominance. They were given organised form by the worst instinctive features of humanity; a pecking order in which the majority were subjugated and suppressed by a self-interested and often tyrannical minority.

The borders of nations, or groups of similar nations, were originally determined by natural barriers such as mountains, rivers and seas. Within their national borders, cut off from contact with other nations, people acquired physical and cultural differences which made them strangers, easily persuaded that they were enemies of each other, like different species. At the same time the major automatic influence on the whole civilisation process gave virtually all peoples the same advancing Machine. Whilst the competitive money economy largely rules the relationships of nations, and of people within nations, the long moral struggle between humanity and the Machine has brought a kind of human unity to some degree within nations, and even a small degree of unity between certain nations (e.g. the European Community.) The need for unity is urgent, but this process has been too slow and limited. We do not have further centuries to wait, and in any case there is evidence that even this slow progress will not continue. Civil disturbances in many countries suffering economic recession have indicated a breakdown of national unity, revealing that it was falsely based and fragile.

When the natural barriers between nations were overcome by technological advances in means of transport by land, sea and then air, the result was commerce, interchange by way of trade; an economic struggle of nation *against* nation, according to the rules of the competitive money economy. But this advance of civilisation did not break down human cultural barriers. In keeping with the worldwide competitive concept, peoples nurtured, inflated and defended their differences of language, habit and appearance. The majority of individuals had lost much of their sense of personal identity because of subjugation, but they could partially regain it through a sense of national identity, under their national flag. This explains the phenomenon of men willingly fighting for a governing authority that cruelly oppresses them. It represents human development in an opposite direction to that which is truly proper to an intellectual race.

Human individuals may be beginning to see that they, morally and intellectually, must take responsibility for humanity, regardless of nation. But the preference for the national interest works against this, and is a habit hard to overcome. This habit consists of not only patriotic loyalty but also fear of the consequences of disloyalty, summed up by the maxim 'if you are not with us, you are against us' - fear of ostracism, loss of privilege, or painful reprisals. For instance the German people, despite private misgivings, fought for Hitler's cause because he made it Germany's cause, a cause which the great majority of other peoples, once the nature and threat of it was realised, everywhere abhorred. Patriotism is fortified by the human wish to identify the self with something stronger than self, in the name of which one can willingly and voluntarily act without regard to the still small voice of conscience.

The fundamental reason why separate nations still persist is that they fill the roles of chief opponents in the general worldwide competition. The money economy needs them just as it needs supply and demand, profit and loss, rich and poor, and the Machine needs them as major protagonists in this conflict. Autonomous, sovereign nations subject to this automatic system make acceptable the unacceptable - the existence side-by-side of very prosperous and very poor nations. Both are isolated, with no protective higher authority to appeal to, so that the poorest have no recognised claim on the richest but appear to have only themselves to blame, and the richest have no obligation to share their good fortune. Should it come to war between them the whole world, subject to the same system, may press for peace on humanitarian grounds, but, until more recently through the United Nations Organisation, has had little or no moral authority or power to insist on it.

Just as in personal terms intellation is a matter of supraconsciously following true reason, often against instinctive and economic self-interest, so in collective terms it is a matter of caring for the well-being of all humanity, against the preferment of national interests. The fact of the existence of separate nations is of significance and service only to the competitive Machine. National divisions are a prime cause of man's inhumanity to man. The existence of nations is of no value or assistance to the cause of humanity as a whole.

Chapter 22

LEADERSHIP, AUTHORITY AND GOVERNMENT

The concept of leadership is not unique to humans; it is quite common in nature. Migrating geese follow leaders. Wolf packs obediently submit to the authority of a leader, once it has been tested and accepted, as a vital part of their instinctive pattern of survival. Humans similarly submit to authoritative leadership, originally also for survival but no longer necessarily so because humanity is now subject to many conflicting motives, in very confusing, competitive circumstances.

It is likely that amongst the apefolk the most important of individuals would be the best male hunters, and probable that hunting skill was the qualification for leadership of the early humans in their struggles to survive catastrophes. These leaders would be given power of authority in order that, in the face of threat, they would carry out the vital function of directing and co-ordinating effort. But when such threats passed their authority and power remained, for they would not be willing to give it up. That they were not willing to relinquish power was not only for egoistic reasons but also because their function, though no longer necessary, was already firmly established as an integral part of the emerging Machine. The then existing order had become so dependent on governing leadership that without this leadership it would collapse, as experience has shown. Being a competitive order, the power of authority of leaders was needed to control its conflicts, which meant keeping humans harnessed to the automaton, including leaders, contrary to their true interests and intelligence.

Yet, knowing no better, humans became automatically, emotionally attached to this the competitive order, accepting its reasons why they should submit to authority and remain separated into nations, and why their survival success should depend upon the competitive success of their nation, represented by its leader. So from the moment that the Machine was founded human life became an artificial game. It was never our habit to seek and follow the true guidance of our minds, but simply to conform to governing events, or react to them with emotion supported by incomplete reason. This is why true reasoning, which must overcome this contrary emotion, is now so hard and unpopular a practice. Given this sort of reality, in which true reason has no place, it can be seen as logical that our society requires, and has always required, the dominance of one body of opinion over many conflicting opinions, one governing authority to cut through a confused lack of consensus and make decisions.

Fundamentally, human individuals share more or less the same inner sense of true morality. As I have said already, human life is a battle between this and automatic reality. It is a battle that never ends within us but which, we outwardly but mistakenly concede, humanity cannot win. It is our outer shell that is attached to existing reality and accepts that leading authority is appropriate to it. But neither our reality nor its government truly represents us, nor do we represent our true selves. Our reality is ludicrous and becoming ever more obnoxious. The born-again, fundamentalist Christian revival in the USA is equally ludicrous, but understandable, for it is an extremely simple emotional reaction against the horrors of modern society (but not against the basic values of the Machine). It champions the Christian religion as the only institution of the Machine that pretends to simple good morality. It is an extreme social reaction which does not seek change of the social framework, the basic cause of chaos, but attacks the opposite of its own morality, the extremes of immorality which it identifies as drug and alcohol abuse, atheism, homosexuality, socialism, radical opinion, and the like. It uses television to spread its hysteria and appeal for money. With that money and the voting-power of millions it is putting pressure on government to identify with its extreme views. Were it to succeed, the resultant repressive, totalitarian regime would oppose the advancement of liberated awareness, which, slow and relatively ineffective as it has been, is nevertheless the only genuine hope of realising a morally good, i.e. humantrue, society.

In Chapter 10, Potential, I described leaders as unnecessary dominators of humanity. Seen in another light they appear as submissive servants of dominant institutions. A leader was once one whose learning and skill brought him, or her, the responsibility of leadership. Then he acquired authority, which not only entitled him to lead but also to command others to follow. Now leaders are executives of commanding institutions, the foremost among followers of these institutions. Institutions are the self-supporting and often conflicting units of our highly complex society, the basic makers of decisions. A single institution would be preferable, but could not possibly represent the many contrary aims and competitive policies of a Machine-society. Supreme leaders such as presidents are arbitrators between the conflicting purposes of domineering automatic forces vested in institutions. Authoritative government is necessary only as long as the unnecessary Machine continues to exist. The supraconscious concept is quite different - that we should follow the humantruth; which is reflected in the pure reasoning of every inner mind.

The present fact is that the Machine does powerfully exist. The majority of us take our cue from leaders in authority. We listen to people who are in the public eye, at the top of the automatic hierarchy. But individuals in the public eye are not likely to be persons who understand humantruth, or, if they do, they are unlikely to express it.

By submitting to authority we not only submit to the Machine as well, for the reason that authority is bound to support the Machine; we also agree to regard as misfits, or enemies, those who oppose authority or break its laws. We can be persuaded to go to great lengths to uphold authority - e.g. by putting its values before human values, which we do when we wear military uniforms - particularly when not to do so would render us liable to punishment as criminals in the eyes of the law. These things are made so by the generally automated state and attitude of existing society. The issues appear differently to supraconscious eyes.

It is sometimes suggested that the answer to world conflict is to have one supreme world leader. This is an impractical suggestion, either for our existing automatic reality or in an ideal state. As already argued, the existing worldwide competitive money economy requires many divided nations, and the powerful authority of one leader in each nation is necessary to control, or attempt to control its conflicting institutions. Since each nation clings to its own particular and different culture, it would be very difficult to find one leader whom all people felt to be representative of all. Even if this difficulty were overcome, imagine how obviously insane the competitive system would appear in a world supposedly united under one leader which nevertheless retained the existing money economy. For the system to continue to work (insofar as it can be said to work) the supreme leader would have to arrange, deliberately, for some nations to be rich and privileged and others deprived. Clearly the concept of a world united under one leader would not be served by such disunity. Equally clearly, that concept cannot be realised by a competitive system, for such a system cannot tolerate human unity. A united, peaceful, co-operative world - the ideal state - can only be achieved and sustained by a united, peaceable, co-operative humanity, who would not then require leadership, authority, or government.

As is the case with every feature of existing reality, we are ruled, through thousands of years of conditioning, by a conventional attitude towards leaders. It is their hard outer shells, not their inner humanity or fulfilment of their intellects, which has brought them to the top of the hierarchy. We really know this, yet we follow them nevertheless because we, like it or not, are integrated into the same reality. It is our outer shells also which follow-the-leaders and by virtue of their authority can then do no wrong in terms of this reality.

It is only when our leaders go to extremes that they, and we, are called to account. For example, in the Germany of 60-70 years ago, members of the SS and warders of concentration camps did unspeakable things which, backed or impelled by authority in their reality of the time, they hardly recognised as such. It was only when they were faced with their deeds against the background of another, more humanly enlightened reality that they recognised the enormity of what they had done. Even so, if they were under orders they were exonerated - only those who gave the orders were condemned. Those were horrific acts, but if the whole human race could be brought to judgment in the light of humantruth, today, all would be found guilty of inhumanity. But all could be exonerated, including leaders, for all are under orders from the Machine.

Consider the personal situation of leaders. They have won the competitive struggle to reach the top by reinforcing their hard outer shells. Power is assigned to the tough external character of the leader, whose inner humanity is mostly submerged, under control. Leaders are expected to fulfil this traditional, realistic role. Those who attempt to take on a humanistic role usually fail, though they appeal to public inner thought and feeling, because the only way for them, or anyone, to succeed in the Machine is by taking a tough, realistic, automatic role. But leaders remain individuals, with a personal reality subject to hidden emotions, prejudices or ambitions. This private entity is isolated from others by the leader's position, and may grow independently. It is fallible, yet may wield enormous power. As a result it is possible that enlightened leaders might arise who turn us from the automaton and towards humantruth, which the Machine would not like. There are signs of this, and I believe that it must inevitably happen eventually and hopefully not too late. For the present it's more likely that most leaders remain, unwittingly, locked into the Machine, while others go to extremes of violent oppression, as in the past, to the horror of suffering humanity. If automatic reality persists, I can imagine legislatures proposing, and the Machine allowing, that governing authority be handed over to the most advanced ultra-intelligent computer on the grounds that it would be infallible and unemotional, and, having been most thoroughly programmed with all the facts and concepts of automatic reality, would be able to reach automatic decisions or forcible compromises much more quickly and dependably than any human leader, brooking no argument. This could close the door for ever on any possibility of our true humanity prevailing against the Machine.

Strong authority is thought to be necessary for the control of the irresponsible. The theory is that the majority decide what is to be done and all are obliged to conform. In fact, human affairs are so continually changing because of autoprogression that public influence can have only a loose and limited effect, whilst authority takes day-to-day decisions. And in any case these decisions are really choices between alternative options of the Machine. The irresponsible are presently seen as those who in various ways do not conform to the automatic norm, including those who try to prefer humantrue interests. Authorities are appointed by the Machine to maintain its interests, keep the conformists in harness, and discredit the non-conformists.

The hugely extensive paraphernalia of government can be considered necessary to direct and control the great and advancing complexity of automatic affairs (as long as they continue). Human beings are constantly entangled in these affairs, engaged in the struggles of a competitive consumer society, preoccupied with the complicated matter of survival in the Machine. Many people spend much of their time just trying to keep abreast of this automatic tide, and others in trying to escape from it. Consequently most of us never find time to settle, to understand how these practical matters could be mastered and simplified, giving us space for true fulfilment.

Whether we accept or reject the concept of leadership, authority and government depends on whether we accept, firstly the Machine, and secondly existing human reality. If we believe that our present automatic nature is inevitable, then we can believe and accept that it is we who have made the Machine what it is. If we believe our potential nature is to be better than we are, but that the Machine is our logical and inescapable social framework, so that our lives have to be a struggle between our true and automatic selves, then we must accept that the institutions of government are necessary. But if we believe in our true, supraconscious, morally aware potential, then we must realise that we can change to a humantrue reality, ridding ourselves of the Machine and with it the concept and practice of leadership, authority and government which shall then be unnecessary. My own picture of humantrue society is put forward in Part VII.

It is necessary here to remind you, and myself, that all this cannot reflect all the intricate crosscurrents of my own reason, nor can it be directly implanted in any other mind. What prompts this remark is the recurring realisation that I am not translating the whole content of my mind into the written word - additional concepts keep occurring to me and I become anxious that I shall not do full justice to each and every subject. But although the whole content of my mind has not been and of course could not be written down, it is the background (of reason) to all my writing, and if it is broadly true, as I believe, the words will ring true. These words can only act as stimulants to your own intellation, which, as it develops truly, shall, if my findings are true, reach similar conclusions. If my intellation is incomplete, you might go further and bring it to completion. Where my reasoning is wrong, you may well put it right. I have tried to open myself to true reason but must not claim a monopoly in truth. The aim of each individual should be to discover truth and help all to discover and realise it.

Chapter 23

POLITICS AND LAW

To begin this subject of politics and law, it is necessary to see that the Machine cannot be made subservient to humanity whilst automatic reality exists, yet also to see that nowadays especially humanity will not submit to total dictatorship of the Machine. But when we talk of democratic freedom we are looking through conditioned eyes at a relative freedom. The fact is that we are first of all subject to automatic lore, on the principles of which the Machine is founded. The law has chiefly reflected that lore but, where the latter has conflicted too obviously and painfully with human morality, politics has changed the law in the human interest. In many ways domestic life is on average less brutal than it was, but in very few respects does our reality serve our true interests. We do not normally perceive this because we are so used to being harnessed to the automaton as to believe politics to act freely in our general interests. The law is essentially much less protective of us than it is a vital protective of the innumerable practices and institutions of the Machine, in a reality where automatic interests are to be preferred.

The origin of politics was public unrest, in the days when the Machine was in its infancy, and kings, rather than the automaton - the self-acting mechanism of the competitive pecking order and money economy - appeared to be in supreme command. The ruling minority could not safely remain so without the implicit consent of the majority, and the latter were becoming ever more aware that they were unnecessarily oppressed and exploited. But it was the *nature* of kings, as it was and is the nature of the underlying automaton, to oppress and exploit its human units of labour. So conflict was inevitable, because it is in the nature of the human mind, especially when it suffers injustice, to grow in awareness. As long as kings were obstinate rebellion was the majority's only remedy. But rebellion did not suit authority; it threatened its position and ruined its affairs. Neither did rebellion suit the majority, for it brought hardship and rarely succeeded because the authorities had the power, the weaponry, and held the purse strings. Even when it did succeed, the outcome was always a new ruling minority to replace the old, with little real change.

But the rise of unrest and the growth of awareness were unstoppable. Neither the ruling minority nor the great majority could defeat the other, for there has to be a place for each in the Machine. So, short of very radical change, the only possible outcome was for the former gradually to give away its power to the latter, whilst the automaton retained, and in fact increased, its power over both. This was a continuing compromise of which politics became the instrument. *Politics, government* and the *human majority* are distinctive labels applied to separate and unequal groups of humans representing humanity at large in different and inappropriate ways, because all actually represent the conflicting principles of the automaton.

It is important to realise this - that politics is not concerned with true morality; with the real fundamental interests of humanity. The political institution has already sold out these vital human concerns to the Machine, which was founded and formed by, and continues to rule by, the automaton. Politics represents the struggle for power - an automatic invention - amongst different authorities, financial interests, ideologies, cultural groups, ambitious individuals and adventurous ideas. Each of these seeks a comparatively small part of the much greater power which existing reality exerts on us and which should not humantruly exist.

So politics does not represent true humanity but those facets of human being that are in service to the automaton, and their relationships with the Machine which serves the same master. Therefore politics is a compromise between our personal, but automated, interests and the impersonal self-interest of the Machine. Our outer shells have already compromised our inner true morality, or overruled it altogether. This is because there is no place in the Machine for purely human moral matters. It follows that truly moral objectives cannot be pursued with success politically - they would not be accepted as realistic - and it further follows that for the same reason such objectives are not easily pursued by any other normal means. As long as the present reality continues politics may not challenge the Machine, because it is party to the Machine, and therefore may not truly serve humanity.

The law is said to be the rock on which 'democratic' society rests. It does recognise certain human rights, but does so in the context of automatic reality, whilst you and I are now trying to judge this false context from outside. It should be obvious that the law does not uphold fundamental human interests. It is not a full positive guide to humantrue moral behaviour. It is an institution, of the Machine, which presumes, with realistic reason, that the automaton is our positive motivation and guide and therefore that negative inhibition is the proper function of the law, to keep the positive instinctive drives from reaching extremes. We take profitable advantage of our fellow-humans as a matter of course, not because the law directs, but usually in ways that the law does not prohibit. When we do it in unusual ways, which the law *does* prohibit, we are said to commit crime. Neither law nor politics are concerned with humantruly right practices so much as reconciled to wrong. They embrace a standard of morality that has a high tolerance of inhumanity, so that wrong practices are given wide scope and brought to a stop only when a point is reached where the dulled public conscience cannot but awaken in protest.

Politics is also an institution of the Machine, allied to governing authority and the existing concepts of reality rather than to people and their inner morality. Were this not so, politicians, honestly doing what they are supposed to do, would be bound to turn against the Machine. We the people accept this as inevitable, just as we accept automatic reality. We have scant respect for politicians but believe politics to be a game they have to play and we have to depend on. We do not expect it to have a humane bias because we innately know that we do not have control of our lives. We expect politics to be in a continual state of confused argument because experience has shown that agreed consensus is impossible in this competitive reality. The scene of this reality is set against an automatic backcloth that shows human moral aspirations as at best impractical and at worst naive. In a 'democracy' it is possible to say that affairs are ruled by majority opinion, but this is not real human opinion. It is that which the majority have selected from a number of automatic options because there are no better ones - particularly no humantrue options - to choose from. I am not saying that we do this knowingly, and it may be that we *feel* we are doing the right thing. I am saying that we would know in our heads, and so *truly* feel, what *was* right were the opportunity to make the truly right choice presented.

Automatic reality sometimes imposes moral blackmail, for instance in wartime when the individual is faced with the easy conventional choice of military service or the painful choice of pacifism. Since to kill is clearly contrary to human morality, which governments are supposed to represent, the choice of peace should not be left to courageous individuals but ought to have been made already by governments. But the Machine chooses otherwise, and the law reflects the contradictory compromise of politics by forbidding killing on an individual level, calling it murder, but permitting it at the national level, calling it patriotic duty. By the time the individual is faced with this choice, which the law takes the right to impose, war is already a fact, and a matter of life or death. By this time his or her country has declared its cause right, and its enemy's cause wrong. But the enemy has done the same, and both cannot be right. If all individuals on all sides were to choose peace there could be no war, and that would be morally right. It is clear that the true morality of the individual is not reflected in world affairs. Instead the Machine is normally able, when it wishes, to impose its amorality or immorality on humanity with the help, or without the hindrance, of politics and law.

It has been pointed out in the last chapter how we tacitly concede that humanity cannot win its battle with the Machine. We salve our consciences by making a show of humanity, but actually always bow down to automatic authority in the end. Politics facilitates both the atonement and the obeisance. In Germany it allowed Hitler to rise to power despite moral objections because the majority of the people stood to benefit in many ways. In other countries that opposed Hitler, moral objections were politically sustained once the survival of their ideologies and institutions and very lives came under threat. Hitler's new order contained nothing that clashed with the principles of automatic reality. It would have replaced free international competition with domination by one 'master race', but by removing conflict and gearing all effort to its own autoprogressive objectives, in the interests of its own version of the money economy, and by cutting out all purely human morality which got in its way, it would have served the automaton well. The objections to Naziism were the conscientious objections of intellect to the Nazis' abhorrent, excessive inhumanities. Were that intellect now truly fulfilled it would be in opposition to all immoralities, old and new, great or small, together with the dominant powers of the Machine and its human authorities which cause them and the weak compromises of national and international politics which allow them, now as then.

So-called civilised humans have always hankered vaguely after meaningful change. Although great changes have taken place we still hanker, because we have always failed to recognise the source of our dissatisfaction as the false basis of our society. The Machine offers alternative satisfactions, of course, in varying degrees - from lavish for the highly privileged, who will not do with less, to meagre for the underprivileged, who continually demand more. Politics has contrived, by way of compromise and diplomatic intrigue, to give way to each side in turn so that the imbalance remains. As a result humanity is generally reconciled and adjusted to an overall framework that depends and thrives on these conflicting aims and interests. *The whole of our history is virtually irrelevant to us because its consecutive events have either been caused by the automaton or related to these contrivances.* This does not imply that no political struggle has been well-intended and partially successful, but that politics is now more a means of evading than tackling the important questions and problems, and the Machine offers little but automatic meaning and autoprogressive change. The Norman conquest, for example, established law and order in England to replace barbarism, but it was simply a more organised form of the same old governing recipe. In China, Confucius tried to stabilise society by having all ranks respect, value and be content with their own status and that of all others - unsuccessfully, because it was an attempt to reconcile people to the unacceptable.

We have managed, by way of those struggles of humanity against the Machine which politics has taken up, to humanise society in many respects, yet the state of the world is no better, and probably worse than ever it was. This is because politics has also acceded to automatic demands that are against the interest of humanity - the humane advances have been made at the expense of further advancing the automaton. Democracy is preferable to human dictatorship, but is only one step removed since we are dictated to by the Machine. We imagine ourselves free when our differences are represented by two or more political parties locked in competitive conflict. Real freedom will have been won when there are no differences between us or the principles by which we live - when we have agreed on one and the same humantrue constitution of society. We have continual political argument because our society is a competition between different interests. The argument is broadly divided into attitudes, represented by opposing parties of Right and Left. The Right favours increased domination of humanity by the Machine, and gets its main support from persons who personally benefit from automatic reality, or hope to do so. The Left favours increased influence over the Machine by humanity, and gets its support from moralists and people who are deprived by automatic reality. At its best the struggle between Right and Left reflects that between the Machine and our true humanity. At its worst it is merely a battle between the privileged, who want to retain or add to their advantages, and the underprivileged, who want to grab the rewards for themselves.

Therefore politics is an obstacle to humantrue realisation because it debars pure reason and true morality, yet it is the only recognised forum where questions and problems can be discussed with any hope of resolution within the present framework. Our humantrue values are kept private. Publicly, automatic values apply. Individually we would not kill a rival or let a neighbour starve, but collectively we do both. Politics exists *because* we are divided and cannot agree, because we are saddled with a reality that forbids agreement. Politics *depends* and thrives on disagreement, without which there would be no further need of it, and it would disappear. Were we all agreed on policy, it would only remain to discuss practicalities, and once they were resolved no more centralised debate would be needed. That politicians do not see this is because they are preoccupied by their profession as well as conditioned by the automatic reality of which that reality is an instituted part, and are governed by its internal codes and ongoing relationships. They are held in thrall by politics in the same way as we are all mesmerised by existing reality, because its affairs are closely related to automatic events - because all this is what is actually happening in the here and now. Politicians are not so much wrong as trying to make sense out of a situation that is wrong. Politics is a discipline that obliges politicians not to persist with a good but unpopular or unprofitable measure, but to substitute a less good, or bad, but popular or profitable measure, so perpetuating the moral lassitude and lack of true perception that can make good measures unpopular.

Law is also an obstacle to humantrue realisation in that to go against the norm can easily involve breaking the law. To oppose the norm openly and so strongly as to defeat it would be difficult without breaking the law because virtually all normal practices and established institutions are integral with the Machine and so protected by law. Besides, any aggressive lawbreaking is likely to involve human suffering and bring understandable retaliation. Under the money economy, especially when power is also wielded by some rigid ideology, the avenues of change prescribed by law are closed to highly radical reform unless overwhelmingly supported by majority will, but the majority are unlikely ever to hear of such proposed reforms through conventional channels, and the prosperous who might hear are unlikely to take notice and promote them. In countries where the majority are deprived and there is strong will for simple reform, the law is likely to be loaded against the majority, and against intellectual reformers, by a rich minority. These are some of the reasons why the Machine, though essentially anti-human, prevails over us even so.

When we think of the law we probably think of crime. It is part of our adjustment to automatic reality that there is bred into us an attitude to certain activity as crime. What is criminal activity? It is the unlawful counterpart of legitimate automatic competitive conflict, or the outcome of unbearable psychological pressure or of material deprivation. It is a loose, unofficial sort of institution, an occupation often handed down from generation to generation which is essentially no more dishonest in its aim to profit from the efforts of others than legitimate business. Generally speaking it offers a degree of independent adventure, excitement, danger, profit, and the opportunity to show initiative and daring on the part of individuals to whom the Machine would normally offer nothing of the kind. Crime at any level, whether it be a matter of sheer survival, of making an adequate living, or of misappropriating millions, always has an element of violence because it goes contrary to a norm that embodies the morality we pretend to, and because desperate criminals are implacably opposed by the law and its determined enforcers who attack the symptoms rather than attempt to prevent the deep causes of crime. To succeed in crime is *necessary* to most criminals because of the combination of their conditioning and circumstances. Strong opposition may well turn some of them to violence if that is necessary to their success.

There are many kinds of crime and many causes. Some psychopathic crimes are so horrific as to be unforgivable except on the grounds that the perpetrators are so mentally diseased that they must somehow be removed from society for its safety and in their own interests. These may be cases of genetic error about which nothing can be done. Everything *could* be done to eliminate psychological damage due to bad circumstances and inhuman treatment during upbringing. Crime is sometimes put down to low cortical tone - slowness to inhibit spontaneous violence - but in this connection we must take account of the strong influence of an amoral, and often unjust and immoral society *towards* violence on the part of the underprivileged, for they are the ones with most practical need to commit crime and least reason to obey the laws of an unsympathetic Machine which excludes them.

Crime could be said to be caused by the inculcation of minds with the instinctive drives of a false and inequitable existing reality, but not with the moral inhibitions of intelligence. Contributory factors could be the impairment of brain function due to serious brain damage at birth or from subsequent head injuries, or due to the direct or inherited effects of alcohol, tobacco, bad diet including excessive sugar, lead and other toxic pollution of water and air. Lawful national inhumanities can encourage or provoke criminal activity. The indifference of authority towards the underprivileged causes vandalism. Unemployment helps to cause civil disturbance. Governmental oppressive injustice provokes terrorism and such governments employ people to become torturers. International bigotry and rivalry has brought about military confrontation, involving the possible use of nuclear and chemical weapons. Such lunatic threats create a sense of insecurity and hopelessness that must contribute to drug and alcohol addiction which, in turn, lies behind much crime.

The fundamental cause of crime is a lawful reality that does not cater for true human morality. It is a reality that does not enable, allow or encourage us to be humantrue but gives us much cause, opportunity and necessity to behave amorally and immorally. This reality produces individuals, in diverse circumstances and suffering from all kinds of mental conditioning and damage, who are allowed the right to their opinions but are made responsible for their actions according to the fixed laws of a society which neither represents, nor is responsible to, their inner values.

So crime is that activity which goes contrary to law, but viewing it without the normal bias we can see that the law is not necessarily moral. For example take two persons, one with money the other without. Both would like a radio. The first goes into a shop and buys it. The second steals it. Now what is the difference between the two cases? Only the difference that the first has money. Does this make his action more moral and himself more entitled to the radio? It does not make him more moral for he got the money by serving the amoral Machine, and he is only more entitled to the radio in an automatic, competitive, money-economic sense. In human terms the second person is at least as entitled as the first but to be a good citizen is expected to submit without demur to a social order that would condemn him or her to deprivation. Other issues are involved here, but I am asking you to consider this particular approach to crime. The crime rate has steadily increased as human awareness has advanced. It would be expected that if crime were the only actual immorality this would be otherwise. *The implication is that the Machine has no more claim to true morality than the criminal.* This should lead to the realisation that crime is endemic to automatic reality; that it will not be eradicated until the Machine is abolished, and that a humantrue framework alone will make it possible for human society to practice its natural morality.

There is a natural tendency for non-stimulated, underprivileged individuals at the bottom of the hierarchical pyramid to revert to barbarism. Excluded from the polite order that the higher reaches of society can afford, they tend to revert to the ruthless, disordered, irresponsibly low standards from which our civilisation has attempted to emerge. They appear to be free to choose more gentle social ways, but when you are at the bottom, without hope of help, that may seem so difficult as to be impossible. In an automated society only those minds are stimulated which the Machine requires intelligently to do its work - the supposed civilised with a degree of status or authority. It might be expected that these privileged humans, especially their leaders and the intelligentsia, would perceive that if the disorderly members of society are to contribute to the responsible order of things they too must have some degree of privileged status. But they do not see it this way. To do so is contrary to the competitive economic conventions of the Machine. Everywhere can be found the rich or very rich living alongside the poor or starving. Such is the power of automatic conditioning that shuts off our outer perception from the compassionate awareness of our inner conscience.

Far from understanding and seeking to prevent its causes the privileged condemn and punish barbaric behaviour, calling it crime, vandalism or civil disturbance and setting the forces of law and order against it. When oppression and deprivation becomes unbearable and people, unable to obtain redress or relief through recognised channels, turn to acts of violence as their only hope, this is called terrorism and ruthlessly dealt with. We see terrorism as despicable but fail to see as equally despicable our own indifference to circumstances so unbearable as to drive people like ourselves to these awful acts of violence. The lesson to be learned is that this competitively violent conflict is the automatic norm. We must understand that by its very nature the Machine must contain an authoritative, privileged upper strata; that in support of this automatic reality the unorthodox self-help activities of the lower orders must be classed as unlawful crimes and stamped out, and that violent actions on the part of the upper strata to win and maintain their advantages must be accepted as lawful.

A problem of law is that it is administered by humans, and of criminal law that it is enforced by humans against other humans classed as criminals. All other conflicting institutions, whether serving the automaton directly, or supposedly serving humanity, or both (like politics), are also served by humans. This masks the fact that the real struggle of our present reality is us against the unnecessary Machine, and that we should not be pitted against each other. But in cases of public disturbance where human protestors are confronted by human police, the Machine makes out that these are different kinds of people rather than similar people having different roles in automatic reality, different loyalties and mental conditioning. The same applies in the case of war, dealt with in the next chapter. In a dispute between the British government and the coal miners' union over the former's decision to close certain mines and to put many miners out of work, the miners struck in protest and picketed all mines in an attempt to force a reversal of that decision. The government brought in large police forces to break the strike and there was violent action and reaction on both sides. Police forces were formed originally because automatic society, especially the competitive money economy, produced crime. Unions were formed because automatic society produced exploitation. Both are supposed to be upholding human interests. That their differences developed into pitched battles before this case was resolved, in the law courts in the Machine's favour, demonstrates that politics, which might have been expected to resolve the dispute before it came to a head or at least to put it into true perspective, cannot successfully prefer or even reveal the true human case where it directly conflicts with the interests of the automaton and Machine.

Everything that everybody does has reason in their eyes. This reason is seldom sound because we presently exist in an unreasonable world. The worst human activities come out of the worst human circumstances. Out of the best human circumstances considerable good may come, but both bad and good human activities are tied to the facts and concepts of an existing reality that is bad overall. Bad, violent activity is humanly unacceptable but is not made good by calling it crime and making it unlawful. To make it good requires that it be made unnecessary and uncalled for. This in turn requires a good reality that removes the causes of crime and embodies circumstances out of which only good can come. Change to a good reality shall only be possible when all minds are stimulated, and when mental stimulation is synonymous with supraconsciousness.

Here let me make a remark that applies to all automatic institutions. Politics and law are unintelligent practices that we take seriously because they are integral with our inappropriate reality. Were they proposed as new ideas they would not be acceptable to intellect, because to practice politics means to be in a continual indeterminate turmoil, and the practice of law indicates that there are reasons for going against the social order as strong as those for conforming to it.

If reading this book becomes wearisome to you, consider whether it is because these words lack vital meaning or because you fail to assimilate their meaning. Remember that whether or not my work is altogether right, this level and completeness of understanding is essential if we are firstly to survive and then to find happiness. This understanding requires great perseverance but its pursuit brings growing satisfaction and its realisation would be our ultimate fulfilment. It is a matter of stretching ourselves in order to fully *be* ourselves, which we will never be if we consciously decide against making the effort. Should we achieve a humantrue society, so that this higher level of understanding is common, then it will be possible to convey its meaning with the words, allusions and connotations of simple familiar language. Current language is ill fitted for conveying that meaning because, as the historic idiom of the Machine, it is best suited to automatic conformity to the present norm.

Chapter 24

MILITARY FORCE - INTERNATIONAL ARMED CONFLICT

The truth about present worldwide human reality, that has constantly to be kept in mind, is that in many ways it is hard and often brutish. This overlying fact is borne out by the existence, in every nation, of military forces, and by the frequent occurrence of war. It is not the fundamental nature of humankind that makes this so but that of the Machine. True human nature is otherwise, an underlying fact borne out by the existence everywhere of concerned and caring family and social community life. Both hateful war and loving companionship are traditional features of the here and now. This is senseless, but to make sense of the world is not at present the normal objective of our vast intellectual powers. We take sides in the automatic competition, apply tame logic to justify our own side, then allow biased emotion to bring us into conflict.

What are military forces? They are groups of human beings who submit, voluntarily or involuntarily, to the special laws, and deploy the armaments, of organisations - institutions of the Machine - whose ultimate purpose is the killing, maiming and subduing of other human beings. Their weapons include guns, mines, fire, gas, germs, conventional and nuclear explosives, carried by tanks, aeroplanes, ships and rockets. The world's existing weaponry, in particular nuclear and chemical, is capable of destroying all human and animal life on Earth. National Governments, divided one from another, control most of the armed forces of the world; their activities are cloaked in secrecy, and the public conscience may normally exert an influence only through dubious political channels. Once war is declared it becomes the duty, enforceable by law, of every able-bodied man to become a soldier, of every soldier to kill enemy soldiers, or civilians where required, and of every member of the public to give support.

Armies are traditional. They perpetuate themselves almost without question. In times of peace they are docile but in wartime they are given priority and all effort is devoted to prosecution of the war. We accept armies as a matter of course but why is this so, and why have they come into such common and unquestioned existence? They originated right at the beginning of human history when it was necessary to co-ordinate our efforts under a leader in order to overcome any threat of catastrophe. Subsequently that leader would form an armed guard to protect his dominant authority. To this end he would make it unlawful for any but this guard to carry arms, for fear of rebellion. When neighbouring leaders threatened to invade, the public being unarmed their leader would be obliged to establish a larger, permanent force of fighting men, an army, to defend his territory. Feeling powerful and ambitious he himself might order the invasion of a weaker neighbouring country, and thus become militarily and economically stronger. In this way a worldwide international norm has been established by which the size, success, prosperity and safety of a nation partly depends upon the size and efficiency of its armed forces. Commercial success can make a nation economically strong, for modern instance Japan, but military weakness can make that nation feel vulnerable in this world reality, and will inevitably lead it to arm itself.

In the more enlightened modern age it might be asked why humans continue voluntarily to join the armed forces and serve them loyally. To begin with, these forces are closely tied in service to the governing authority - that is why they are called 'armed services' - and representative of patriotism. Many magazines are published on the subject of flags, uniforms and weapons. Numerous books and films are produced which tell of the glorious adventures of war but not of its tedium, suffering and tragedy. There is an understanding amongst TV and press reporters, who see at first hand the bestial ugliness of war, that according to the strange morality of the here and now the public are not to be exposed to these real horrors. Those who have fought in wars shield their families from its realities in the same way. Members of the armed forces are usually recruited from the younger generation, youths of eighteen attracted by the glamour, unable to get any other job or wanting to learn a trade, seeking to distinguish themselves in a demanding career - all ignorant of the true significance of their service and of its realities, either in 'peace' or war. And when war comes, the political leaders, whose sabre-rattling intransigence with 'foreigners' may have brought it about, send countless innocent young men to kill or be killed, and might do so out of similar ignorance of the reality of war, influenced, perhaps unwittingly, by the knowledge that they themselves are privileged to escape it.

As intelligent beings we should be prompted by conscience to be guided by our true minds; we should do nothing until supraconsciously certain that it is right. But this requires that we are fully aware. The young person who can join the military forces in peacetime without a qualm is incomplete, not fully awakened, just as the whole human race that perseveres with automatic reality is not fully awakened. His reason for joining is that the war organisation *exists,* and its advertised glories and advantages are *apparent,* whilst the true reasoning against the whole concept is not mentioned but banished to a much more remote field of thought. To the young, being close to danger is better than boredom. Permitted violence, spurred on by fear, is an outlet for frustration, with the added advantage of being lawful. The soldier goes beyond acceptance of amoral automatic reality; in addition he obediently submits to much more limited and rigid rules. To some extent the same applies to all in uniform. When competitive conflict shows signs of erupting in violence the human collective conscience needs to be at its most sensitive if war is to be avoided. But the response is normally a military one - a matter of the soldier's mentality, the worst extreme of automatic thinking in its robot-like obedience to prescribed rules of combat without conscientious choice, representing human sensitivity of mind at its lowest ebb. Politicians do have some choice but this aggressive road is the easiest to take because it can be backed by established military reason, whereas pacification could lead to military defeat. In the world of the Machine, right belongs to the victor.

It might be asked why, when our enlightenment is advancing and our awareness of the folly of war is increasing, we continue to maintain military institutions. It is because these and other automatic institutions powerfully exist. By their peculiarly separate constitution and motivation they perpetuate themselves by their own momentum and are not easy to remove. When there is no true reason for divided nations existing, artificial reason is manufactured from the fact that they *do* exist and are bound to defend their sovereign independence with military force. The individual's reason for accepting the military and war is that, being lumbered with this reality, he or she has to behave appropriately to the here and now. This means that we, as patriots and if called upon, must help to defend our nation against other nations, and protect its internal system of law and order against civil disobedience. Automated individuals will also go along with the strong money economy reasons for military activity. The armed services provide a considerable proportion of civilian employment, from scientists engaged in research and development of weapon systems to workers in the armaments factories. Production of arms is made financially viable by selling to other nations the weapons that are surplus to home requirements. From the automated human viewpoint war can benefit the money economy by transforming recession into prosperous full employment.

All this is undoubtedly presently so but the contrary is humantrue. This reality, with its cold and hot wars, continues *because* the normal mind accepts it. It is our humanity that is the important element of our reality, and intellectual integrity is the foremost element of our humanity. If individuals on all sides saw the truth they would also see that there was no need for nations to defend their different positions, for their peoples would then hold the truth in common. And a humantrue constitution, resulting from this recognition of what is right, would prevent wrongdoing from arising, as Part VII, will show. It is the fact of our acceptance of the Machine that requires that we maintain it. Non-acceptance would lead us to abolish it, chiefly by withholding support.

Wars occur with an automatic will and are not otherwise justifiable. They occur because every nation has an army whose use is available to its government; because sooner or later the competitive conflicts of automatic reality must come to a head; because when that happens there is no other realistic solution but war, for reasoned peaceable alternatives would reveal the basic folly of competition and could not be allowed by the Machine; because all humans in all occupations and at all levels are harnessed to automatic objectives, including military ones, and will obey the Machine when it orders them to fight. We have reduced the extremes of conflict within nations - civil war, for instance, seems to be a thing of the past in many countries - but it is yet beyond us to control war between nations. The reason is that violent release of aggressive forces is necessary to the Machine. As its minor expressions are controlled it boils up towards a major and more devastating explosion. The will of the Machine for war, supported by automated human will, is presently much stronger than the majority human conscience. This is one explanation of the ultimate failure of the United Nations Organisation. There is a human intellectual wish for unity and peace but the Machine overrules it. By their automatically constituted nature nations cannot agree, and by way of the right of veto which the UN allows them, sovereign nations are enabled to remain determinedly competitive. The concept of national defence, commonly adopted without thought, arises from this determined competitiveness whereby all nations must look to their protection because each poses a threat of attack. If that competitive threat did not exist, neither would organised military forces exist, whether ostensibly for defence or actually for attack.

Wars are ruinous of true human interests and the permanent existence of armed forces is an affront to our intelligence, yet by working the competitive system we all contribute to the causes of war. By government propaganda and media preoccupation with automatic rather than true human interests, we are generally pressed into the mould of normal reality that embraces wars as constant realistic probabilities. The military has little human conscience and war can never be morally justified, but war can be politically justified and is conventionally provided for in international law. Though we have no wish for it, once war is declared we are involved. Once we are involved there is one-way pressure to fight for our own side and most of us become enthused by patriotism. Wars do not bring out the morally-aware best in humans but the instinctive worst. A most dramatic example of humanly unnecessary automatic build-up to major war was the East/West confrontation. With the defeat of communism in Russia this particular confrontation no longer exists, but it must be remembered that Russia turned to communism in 1917 to eradicate gross inequality, and that such unfair inequality still exists both in Russia and, to varying degrees, everywhere else in the world, so that the 1917 revolution could be re-enacted anywhere. Since the causes of East/West conflict still exist, I shall repeat my comments on it that were written in 1990, when the conflict itself existed.

The East/West confrontation is unnecessary because although representing opposite extremes of human reaction to reality - the political Left and Right - this bitter conflict is due to these extremes being polarised in the opposing attitudes of Russia and America, whereas the human cause can be served only by rejecting both, and the false reality they reflect, and by peaceably following humantrue reasoning. But despite the fact that there is no real difference between the millions of people of both East and West, this confrontation exists because of the inflexible enmity of two governing authorities.

The East/West differences are supposed to be a matter of ideology, but that is not the truth of it and serves mainly as excuse. Any reasonable mind should perceive that there is a lot of moral sense in Marxism but not in Russian-style state control, and that democratic freedom is desirable but not in the form of American-style money-managed autoprogression. Both preach parts of the true human cause but neither practices the whole. The people of both sides are similar humans, with the same basic needs and interests, whom neither side truly represents. Any reasonable mind should also perceive that the way to resolve these differences is for the two sides to discuss them honestly and reach agreement in the interests of all people. This means each giving way to the other and implementing necessary changes as agreed. But the present fact is that the ruling minorities of both East and West are locked into situations that prevent them from reasoning truly. They feel bound to nourish the fabric of life that is their reality, which gave them responsibility and rewards them for doing so, and to hold it together with the forces of law and order. It seems to them that not to do so is to court disaster. That is their personal conditioning. But they are also subject to the general conditioning of automatic reality. This lays down that it is in the nature of individuals and nations to differ, to compete so as to bring their differences into conflict. In the absence of intellectual reason for such belief the argument between communism and capitalism shows instinctive causes.

So the East/West conflict persists for no intelligent reason. Were all human minds reasonable it could be resolved tomorrow, leaving no more valid excuse why all our differences cannot be resolved peaceably. But our instinctive hard outer shells are not averse to war and have the upper hand. Yet our inner consciences, aware of the danger of nuclear holocaust, are not altogether stifled. Leaders of the two sides meet for discussions about nuclear weaponry, but only with the object of eliminating this the worst symptom of their unnecessary enmity, not of eliminating that enmity itself or its 'acceptable' symptom, i.e. conventional war, by addressing its true causes. They both seek artificially to stabilise an insanely unstable situation, just as they similarly, each in their own way, try to control the internal conflicts of their own social systems by efficient enforcement of its law and order. In their selves all humans want peace, including these leaders but they, hamstrung and unrepresentative of true humanity as they are, can only achieve an insecure, lunatic East/West standoff. This is a cold war unrecognisable as true peace whereby, neither side intending but both fearing attack, both are deterred from attack by each being capable of crippling if not destroying the other.

I have already mentioned the subject of freedom and it is on this that the East/West conflict pivots. It is important to face this subject freely and clearly, for it is made an obscure question by the fact that both sides frown on individuals who do other than praise their own side and condemn the other. The West is relatively free from state interference but not free from economic control; it is responsible to the lore of the money economy and shirks its responsibility to humanity where the two are in conflict. The East is strictly state-controlled but freed from preponderant control by market forces; it puts basic responsibility before that of economics. People in the East who seek the interest of self, or of a forbidden doctrine, may be punished by the state. People in the West who do not or can not serve the Machine as it requires, or who put the common interest before self-interest, are liable to suffer the poverty of the unrewarded and to be made ineffective by lack of official support and by general indifference.

It is a matter for profound relief that the East/West confrontation - the cold war - is at an end, but we should be in no doubt that, given the present Machine-reality, a similarly desperate situation could arise again, as indeed is now the case, in 2008, with the Middle East confrontation.

Military force is a familiar feature of our existing reality whose logic shall be removed when replaced by a humantrue reality in which there can be no cause for war. The case against war is a logical part of an intellectual and compassionate human race's case against our existing, unworthy reality.

The absolute essence of this case is that all the trappings of nationhood are superfluous. We are all similar individuals. I am one such individual, writing to others, bypassing everything that has no true human meaning or value. In this relationship we have no differences. We share the same view, that the efforts of humanity need to be re-directed, in a spirit of comradeship, towards making it possible that all shall be joyfully fulfilled by life.

Chapter 25

UPBRINGING AND EDUCATION

I t has been shown already that intellation is the true activity of higher minds; that we, as a species having the power of intellect, ought to be supraconscious and find humantruth. But there is evidently little or no intellation going on in our world and we are presently firmly fixed in the conscious state. Human states of mind range between extremes - from the ignorance of unstimulated illiteracy to the excessive and specialised knowledge and limited general conscious reasoning, but little reasoning in genuine pursuit of truth, of the academic. This applies to the most advanced countries of the world, which pride themselves on extremely comprehensive institutions of education that their young attend for at least eleven years or for as much as twenty years. The institution of education is an integral part of civilised reality. Since that reality is humanly false and continues to be so, and since humanity has failed to achieve supraconsciousness and continues so to fail, it follows that our system of education is also false in that it has failed to help us accomplish our true potential.

The reason for this, of course, is that we are harnessed to the automaton, governed by the Machine, and as yet unawakened. Consequently our concept of education is to raise the young in accordance with automatic reality; to familiarise them with its past and present; to adjust to it, survive in it, and continue it into the future. For us as children the process begins with parental upbringing. Parents are individuals who themselves may differ in their various views of reality, on whom we are wholly dependent, and who treat us and influence us according to their values and circumstances, largely behind closed doors. So the early formation of each generation of human minds mirrors the inequalities of the previous generation, ranges from zero to 100%

stimulation and from one extreme to the other of knowledge, bias of reason or opinion, and emotional attitude. All parents have this in common - that they live in and have borne us into automatic reality. However much they may deplore it, almost all bring up their children according to automatic concepts.

When we enter school we carry our own peculiarities of character, the result of home conditioning, and come into contact with teachers and other children, all with different constructions of character. These are not just natural variations of temperament, but of belief, attitude, expectation, valuation, estimation, ambition, and capacity for understanding. We are joined by a hotchpotch of others in a remarkable kind of conspiracy, which all are poised to continue, as in the past, and which few have so far tumbled to. The children's differences, widened by teachers who have passed through the same experience, reflect those of their parents who are themselves made different by the parts they play in the competitive conflicts of the Machine. But we all commonly share one and the same acceptance of this existing reality, inculcated in us because our forebears believed it inescapable and made it their duty to prepare us for the inevitable. Schools cater for our different qualities, abilities and aspirations because this fits in with automatic reality, but it gives the false impression that our troubled world is the result of conflict between chaotic human nature and the attempts of responsible authority to harness and control it. In the sphere of education volatile human nature is represented by the disunity of teachers and pupils, authority is represented by the school and its curriculum, and the pattern of automatic reality by the common denominators of behaviour to which teachers and children gravitate. The whole process shackles our true intellect and innately kind and co-operative nature, and brings the instinctive drives to the fore.

As a race we may well achieve almost full understanding of physical reality yet we have hardly begun to understand the true significance of the human mind. We still confine and limit the human self to the closed sphere of consciousness, like the animals, but whilst animals are guided by a strictly appropriate instinct, we follow many conflicting automatic paths with the aid of the instinctive and calculated application of intellect. We should be intellating, and accepting the consequently true guidance of intellect, because whole correlation is necessary to true understanding of anything and until we understand everything essential we are lost. Education as it exists merely plays a part in forming our *automated* understanding of existing reality of which it is a practiced part. It fills minds with knowledge in sequence according to its own programme of essential learning, but not in a sequence that a mind's whole and true understanding requires. It expects us to *use* our minds, like computers, programmed by the Machine and used by our conscious selves for successful performance in automatic reality. Our schools and colleges divide us into occupational categories, ranging from the superfluous unemployed to the highly specialised employed, resulting in imbalanced intellects in none of which is more than a minor proportion of essential factors fully correlated.

The institution of education is allied to the Machine but the teachers it employs are thinking humans who might well feel responsible for informing and forming young minds truly. So education might be placed between two stools were its teachers awarded that freedom by its institution, but they are not. Being an established institution, education is barred from revealing the truth about present reality and standing against it. This is not only because it cannot conceive of opposing the reality that spawned it, or of biting the hand that feeds it, but also because its job is to prepare individuals for taking part in that reality - individuals who, as a normal rule, expect to profit from this preparation. So the institution of education has to compromise. It contrives to provide 'true' information but does so by concentrating only on certain parts of the whole picture and interpreting them in certain preconceived ways. These are the parts which describe our entire past experience with interpretations that give it meaning in terms of the present, i.e. the factual history of the Machine as though inevitably pre-ordained rather than as the pursuit of narrow automatic concepts, contrary to reasoned human morality, which have accumulated to form our existing reality. So education upholds fundamentally false facts and concepts of this reality, whereas intellation would surely oppose them in favour of the ideal to which most of the experiences, and perhaps all of the supposed lessons of history are irrelevant.

An uncritical early experience of automatic reality, including its education, makes it extremely difficult, but not impossible, later to become supraconscious. That few if any become so may be because they need help to break down years of conditioning as well as requiring a strong wish to be supraconscious, and such help is almost nonexistent. Our best hope of breaking through is to begin, almost before the automaton can apply the pressures of its conditioning, with a highly critical attitude to reality and a determination to accept nothing that is not clearly true. This means not receiving teaching in the normally required way of taking in what authority considers to be good and necessary for you. It means not falling into the temptation to conform for the sake of future self-interest. It means reading between the lines of that which you are given to study - even mathematical and scientific fact - and of sacrificing the automatic advantages of having such facts at your fingertips for the sake of a vital prior necessity for putting these facts into a humantrue context. It means using teaching as stimulation rather than instruction in order to keep the mind free from manipulative conditioning.

The education process measures mental maturity on a realistic time-scale, based on the time it normally takes a mind to reach a level of achievement suitable to its employment by the Machine, and a degree of understanding in tune with the automated human world. The supraconscious mind must construct *itself*, in its own time and by a very different sequence. The essential basis of its construction must be completed before it can judge the need for, critically assess, and put into true perspective much of the factual information normally absorbed during the formative years. Whole reason is hard to come by in this unreasonable reality because the formative years are not initially devoted in this way to making the mind a platform of true reason from which knowledge can then be rightly gauged. Such a process is discouraged by the fact that a humantrue mind would embody ideals which the world almost wholly ignores, and, as already pointed out, would be uncomfortably alien to the reality in which it must presently live. Conventionally educated minds are programmed like computers to get the automatic answers and solutions required by the Machine to the realistic questions and problems it poses. The automated mind accepts 'real' facts uncritically, such as the autoprogressive development of the microchip. A supraconscious mind would have foreseen the inhuman effects of the microchip and opposed its unbridled development.

As the result of its upbringing a child enters school with certain aptitudes and certain incapacities. Further educational conditioning tends to develop the aptitudes and confirm the incapacities. Individuals who were quite unable to master arithmetic in childhood often discover latent mathematical ability later in life. The normal effect of home and school or university education is that the mind is persuaded that it is unable to deviate from firmly laid tramlines - incapable of totally independent thought. Such a mind appears unable to think of anything other than what it has been given to think *about*, employing that which it has been given to think *with*. This gives the intellectually myopic individual a sense of personal reality that fits the chaos of entrenched world reality, and may furnish survival locally but threatens it worldwide. Such persons may resist the prospect of true awareness because it looks like ruining their otherwise secure position, promising to be a long and difficult process that would disturb the realistic concentration they require for local automatic success.

The slogan of the present system of education is - EDUCATION IS TO PREPARE US FOR LIFE. This requires to be changed to - EDUCATION IS TO LEARN THE FOLLY OF THIS LIFE AND PREPARE FOR A BETTER ONE. If it is thought too difficult a thing to do, consider that people already study extremely difficult subjects of far less importance (I predict that one day, if we survive, it shall be unthinkable that we were once as we now are - separated from our supreme faculty of mind, living apart from our truth.) If we are looking for a new and better reality clearly we should throw off the bad practices of the old, such as dividing our collective understanding into exclusive subjects when the aim of every mind should be to embrace complete understanding. We need a sphere of study of *everything*, with as little specialist learning as is required to impart its true essence. Our target should be total reason, which is the aim of this book. We are entirely mistaken in believing that the generally existing forms of education are beneficial to humanity. The evidence of our existing world reality proves the opposite.

It seems to me that the basic task of education is to help the young to understand the structure of life on Earth; to acquire a strong consciousness of our dependence on our biosphere - the soil and its mechanisms, plants and the sun, the minerals, the seas, all that provides the air we breathe and the food we eat, our clothing, warmth, shelter, furniture - the need to respect and preserve it all. Most of all we should be conscious of our dependence upon our postconscious minds - our responsibility to be true to them and so to be responsible for each other and the whole Earth - to use our powers kindly, compassionately and considerately.

Then, certainly, the task is to teach our young basic mathematics, and communication skills, including the essential means of breaking the customary barrier to world communication - a common language. But chiefly the aim should be to help and encourage every child to intellate and become supraconscious so that they assess things and deal with others humantruly. Thereafter we should impart to them the common knowledge and skill that is socially needful, any special learning to follow afterwards, as an adult contribution to society, superimposed on this foundation of intellating and learning which would be common to all. This subject is further explored in Chapter 43, Code of Individual Behaviour.

Introduction to Chapter 26

The culture of a society is essentially the voluntary activity of mind and body of each individual member. Ideally it would reflect their most intelligent, noble and compassionate nature and would be embodied in their social framework. In other words the true supraconscious nature of an intellectual race would be expressed in all its thoughts and actions - in its society.

In the present human case our culture expresses our inner selves only as far as they are revealed despite the layers of conditioning, and is then expressed publicly only to the extent that the Machine permits or, more usually, can exploit. It is that in which we indulge at the end of the day's work, when we think ourselves temporarily released from automatic harness, and ranges from escape into a personal private version of reality to public exhibitions of action and thought which are chiefly instinctive and emotional. But our culture is not distinctly human, for in fact we never throw off the automatic harness. Our culture is not an expression of intellation and ultimate reason but a matter of juggling with different relative truths. Therefore it is not an instrument of our true selves, working to humanise our society, but an instrument of existing reality, keeping us automated. It is an autoculture.

This autoculture is so-called because in the main our personal, supposedly voluntary interests and activities of body and mind are strongly infiltrated so as to be largely dictated by the Machine to which we are otherwise duty-bound. *All* our doings are entangled with or invaded by preoccupations of the competitive here-and-now; by the overwhelmingly intrusive money economy; by the hypnotic influence of the actual existence of an amoral automatic reality and our constant need to tend the injuries this inflicts on us; by the power of our encouraged instinctive aggressive drives; and by the relative weakness of our discouraged intellectual will. Consequently, in our moral battle against the Machine, we humans are continually selling out or giving way to our opponent. In these conditions we want help and relief. Despite these circumstances we need to believe in ourselves. So we have built our autoculture to cure the symptoms of our disease, whilst leaving the causes untouched, and to create a grand illusion of worthy human attainment, particularly in science.

Existing reality unfolds as it does because we let it take its instinctive, emotional, automatic course. We react to it in all kinds of ways to which the Machine gives real form. One purpose of this book is to depict all this as unreal. I do not suggest that as realists we presently approve of every feature of the Machine. We may condemn it in parts but applaud other parts, yet accept it overall as the reality that shapes our individual and collective character. This, our concept of reality, has a parallel in our concept of some kind of god, although neither has true foundation. We might support the establishment as the keeper of law and order because we see opposition to it - anarchy - as lawless chaos. In a similar way our concept of god, because it is a long-established embodiment of morality, is treated almost as positive fact even by unbelievers, so that atheism is cast in the role of negative denial of morality, with no values of its own. There is as yet no acceptance of the all-embracing positive moral force - supraconsciousness of humantruth - that makes both conventional reality and religion into empty, negative denials of truth. To embrace humantruth means to dismiss the Machine and our false characteristics attached to it. This means we not only condemn the bad features of the Machine, but also recognise that many of its good-seeming features, represented by the autoculture, exist merely to counteract the bad and would not be at all appropriate to the ideal alternative.

Chapter 26

SCIENCE

Science plays a very large part in the grand illusion of worthy human advancement. It satisfies our yearning for intellectual achievement in a way that bypasses our true responsibility to reason critically and completely, because of its reliance on fact. At the same time it is wholly acceptable to the Machine because it is the spearhead of technology, the best possible tool of autoprogression. So science has become both the central preoccupation of human curiosity, by way of specific application of intellect, and the main vehicle of automation. In the popular view it is the essence of human vitality. Whenever and wherever science has lost impetus Machine-society stagnates, not because science is vital but because without its activity, and especially without the race to keep up with autoprogression, the emptiness of the automatic norm is exposed.

Science is a self-justifying empirical construction of its own inter-related facts, built upon an acceptance of the physical universe and the logic of its present interdependent arrangements as our sole reality. Since it reasons according to that which exists, it tends to exclude full and true intellectual reason because this takes freedom to deny fact, and is independently able to do so, in the sense that it can envisage a changed reality in which certain present facts will cease to be, or to apply, because they are irrelevant. The scientific position is indicated by its attitude to instinct as a phenomenon that dictates the state of nature, as though the characteristics of animals determine the natural balance. This is like the realistic approach to human society that views *our* apparent characteristics as the nature that determines the conduct of our society. In fact the instincts of animals are determined by their environment, and in the human case it should be our intellectual reason that arranges our social framework which, in turn, determines our practical habits. By following our instinctive drives, applying our intellect to them, and going wherever this leads, we are contriving, disastrously, to make an environment that fits instincts developed for a quite different reality.

For us there are two worlds, one of physical reality to which the life of instinctive nature belongs and by which it is governed, and the other of intellect that makes, or should make, its own world governed by itself. Science belongs to the first of these worlds, whose logical forces are its subject, to understand which it *employs* the intellect of the second world. For the scientist to become supraconscious would ruin this objective orientation; his self must be limited to and guided by, as well as situated in consciousness, exerting its will on the utilised postconscious and inhibiting the output of the independent postconscious. So our application of part-intellect to the worship of science is carrying us to the extremes of physical reality, whereas to *fulfil* our intellect, opening the gate onto a humantrue reality, would be to disobey the physical forces - to go contrary to science. Our bodies are struggling with a newly automated environment for which their slow evolution did not prepare them, and our rapidly evolved minds require for us another kind of reality again - a new reality that has not yet come to be because we have not yet acknowledged it. A reason for this situation is that science has passed from simple, helpful invention to the complex pursuit of physical universal possibilities, well beyond our natural limitations, that have excited but also burdened us. Generally, we are mentally equipped for a non-existant humantrue reality; for fulfilment of intellect and adjustment to a stable and unspoilt Earth. Our existing reality uses science as the agent of technological autoprogression, to accelerate instinctive drives clear of their inhibitions. We are narrowing our minds down to this rather than liberating them. We need to realise the universal truth, which is the same task for all intellects wherever they are in the universe and whatever their circumstances, but our advances towards it in some directions are nullified by our retreats from it in others. No doubt our bodies could become adjusted to existing reality if it stabilised, but it is in a state of continual flux that makes it hard for our minds to awaken. Our bodies are suffering from conflict, neglect and abuse, and our minds from stress, anxiety and incomprehension. We are simply trying to keep up with automatic reality without knowing where it is taking us, or why, and without being asked whether we want to go that way. Our inner beings occupy neither the actual physical, scientific world of the automaton, nor the possible world of true intellectual reason, but a foggy political and/or religious or mystical compromise between the two.

It may be argued that science is the unstoppable exercise of human intellectual curiosity, or thirst for knowledge. Against this I would argue that knowledge is only part of the mind's function. The mind's true goal is truth, the result of correlating knowledge by utmost reasoning. There are clearly two reasons why our foremost thinking is applied to the inferior exercise of accumulating and applying knowledge with limited reasoning, rather than to the superior task of achieving true understanding. The first has already been stated - that false reality cannot tolerate truth. Hardly any help is given by human society, either in the way of facilities provided by institutions of the Machine or by public demand or support, to serious critical questioning of present reality and the investigation of humantruth. The second reason is that science, its teaching, research facilities and technological application, is *automatically* pursued by the Machine, financed by the money economy, whether we like it or not. Genetic manipulation, space travel, UIM's, 'star wars', brain transplants - every possible autoprogression is pursued for its own sake, or to bring money reward, or both, or otherwise to accrue to automatic advantage.

Their automatic status gives scientists an autonomy that can protect them from intellectual responsibility, and applies such realistic pressure that they are obliged to concentrate almost exclusively on their subject. It is quite possible for them to be fully effective in their sphere whilst bypassing the great philosophical questions that are so much harder to answer than purely scientific solutions are to find. It is not an exaggeration to say that science is generally worshipped because its fresh discoveries are novel and its salient facts are easy to swallow and difficult to deny. But scientists are a specially conditioned and privileged minority who, personally well meaning as they may be, are otherwise officially and financially wedded to the automaton that backs them. The majority of humans do not seem to have the remotest understanding of the eventual effects of scientific autoprogression, and evidently share the Machine's view that to follow the lead of its highest applied intellects shall bring the greatest glory and good to humanity. The question is, what is the true definition of humanity? If we regard it as being the supraconscious potential of our inner selves then scientific autoprogression is a disaster. But the purely scientific view is different. It sees humanitarian awareness, which opposes the blinkered forward march of science and technology (opposed, for instance, to the spread of nuclear power stations), as naive denial of the here and now, such as itself courts disaster, inviting failure of our outer shells to achieve automatic targets which will result in the Machine failing to sustain our autoculture.

To the automated, the Machine and autoculture have their virtues and attractions, and both can give high satisfaction to those who ride high in them - the privileged blind who lead the blind. We need to begin opening our eyes to the guidance of intellation, which persists in gaining awareness of the whole true picture and in seeking humantruth. Society presently turns its back on intellation because we are so impregnated with falsehood that we find truth as difficult to realise as the scientific facts of reality are relatively easy. Anybody who doubts the truth of this statement has only to consider this - that whilst the foremost human brains are on the verge of knowing everything in physics, they have no answer to the question 'what is the meaning and purpose of life', and no solution to the problem of how to achieve united and peaceful human contentment.

Chapter 27

SOCIAL SERVICES

We probably think of social services as good, especially by comparison with the bad old days. And they are good in that they represent human compassionate concern and sympathetic effort to relieve the sufferings of humanity. But the social services can also be seen as bad because they do not reach the root causes of suffering. They do not seriously try to rectify, but accept with little question, an automatic world reality that, if looked at from the viewpoint of humanity, is clearly to blame for that suffering. Instead they attempt to provide antidotes for this reality's poisons, to repair its depredations, soothe its terrors and comfort and cure its hurts.

One may think of society as broadly divided into two compartments, one devoted to driving forward for automatic achievements and the other following behind to care for human casualties. This represents two extremes that are reflected in the struggle between our outer shells and inner selves, and in the division of our waking hours into eight working for the Machine and eight spent at home each weekday. An ideal society would not have this irrational division but would be devoted to one common human activity for the well-being of all. It would be a framework for the satisfaction of instincts in keeping with intellect and for the fulfilment of intellect without stress or strain. As we have seen, our world society serves the automaton for no other reason than that this is the way it is. There is no real human reason why this should be so and every reason why it should not be so.

Existing society gives us automatic-money-economy motives rather than human aims. Let there be no doubt that it is this that produces division, conflict, poverty, over-complication, stress and lack of fulfilment. There is no reason whatever for these to be social features of a truly intelligent race. As a result of these features the human race is prey to its own disordered and aggressive behaviour. Our society experiences discontent, ignorance, mental imbalance, drug and alcohol addiction, vandalism, suicide, rape and other violent crime on the part of its victims. Our welfare and social services have arisen out of concern on the part of individuals who are neither victims nor law-officers of the Machine, who seek to help rather than punish. They react in horror but not against the real culprit, the Machine, and its victimisation of most of us. They react against human suffering and deviation from the norm, and have set up institutions of the Machine with the aim of curing and correcting these things.

In a humantrue society we would, out of our accumulated wisdom and as a matter of course, provide for our own good general health just as instinct does for animals. Automatic reality does not so provide but harms and diseases us in many ways. So we have a health service that might more accurately be described as a disease service because its function is not to promote good health so much as to deal with ill health. This health service is vitally necessary to most of us as we are, for it has many techniques for controlling the many things that go wrong with us, but we need not be as we are. Doctors are unable to prevent ill health because it is largely caused by the way we live, and the way we live is dictated by market forces of the Machine that also lays down the programme of medical training. Past improvements in Western health have come, more than anything, from improved hygiene and recently from rising public awareness. Many people have given up smoking and others are refusing manufactured drugs and turning to natural medicines and alternative health-care practices. There will always be a need for surgery if only because of accidents. But accidents could be greatly reduced, not only by safety measures, which we do constantly improve, but by avoiding the mounting unnecessary causes of many accidents. By avoiding, for instance, the present practice of having numerous motor vehicles of different size and capacity, travelling at different and often excessive speeds, passing close to each other in opposite directions, driven by persons of all ages and degrees of skill, sharing a varied network of roads on which every year in the UK more than five thousand people are killed and many more injured because of human error, incapacity (especially due to drunkenness and fatigue), recklessness, mechanical failure and bad weather conditions.

The health services have to deal with a great many serious and distressing illnesses such as cancer and heart disease, largely caused by unsuitable and stressful life-styles, and incorrect diet. It is logical that our physical body, if it is to work efficiently, requires certain food and drink in certain quantities taken at certain times. But our diet is not provided by the health service; it is provided by the food and drink industry whose interest is to sell for profit whatever it can persuade us to consume. During the slow course of evolutionary change we, like every other species, gradually adapted our digestive system to whatever diet was available to us. Nowadays, in the West, the food industry largely tailors its produce to the convenience and taste buds of the consumer. The industry tampers with food and drink, refining, adulterating, packaging and advertising in order to make it attractive to the customer and therefore profitable to itself. As a result, although people may seem to eat well their diet can lack some of the necessary ingredients but contain much that is unnecessary. Our bodies are commonly undernourished in some respects whilst being overburdened in others. We tend to take in an excess of pure sugar, fat and carbohydrate which our systems have to eliminate as toxic wastes, putting an extra strain on already unhealthy bodies. We can tolerate this fairly well when young but are likely to suffer for it as we get older. As a consequence the health service is orientated more towards repairing, removing and replacing organs that have failed than to preventing their failure, and towards surgery rather than gentler, non-invasive treatments. For example, while back disorders are very common in Britain, conventional medicine is not good at dealing with it, surgery being drastic and dangerous, yet numerous people who can afford it are relieved of pain, or cured altogether, by alternative private practitioners employing massage, manipulation and other techniques.

To illustrate that the health service is both an institution of the Machine and geared to automated humankind, take the example of mental health. Mental breakdown, where the brain is not physically damaged, occurs when an individual mind construction is so at odds with the norm as to become unable to cope with or tolerate existing reality. Yet the medical reaction is to diagnose the condition as psychological instability, and to give drug-related psychiatric treatment with the object of re-adjusting this mind to the norm. There is no question of giving sympathetic support to the patient's refusal to embrace existing reality even though the reason for refusal is that reality, and not necessarily the patient, is insane. This is not only because the present norm overwhelmingly exists, is accepted as real by the great majority, and so cannot be escaped by any individual. It is also because the humantrue alternative, though obviously preferable to the least conditioned and most supraconscious minds, cannot be recognised by the medical profession for the reason that it goes contrary to the Machine of which that profession is an instituted part.

In Britain, and other countries where the money-economy prospers, there is a social security system that has largely removed the previous extremes of poverty. The state itself pays people, or supplements their money income, with the object of preventing anybody's finances falling below a certain level.

This is a great humanitarian advance in that it relieves of desperate hardship and anxiety those people whom the automaton would otherwise completely neglect. But as long as the automatic reality exists social security cannot be allowed to advance far enough against the competitive principle that *adequate* money income is to be won only by way of service to the Machine. Therefore social security payments are pitched above starvation level but so low by comparison with the average wage as to represent deprivation. This policy is forced on officialdom by the Machine, whose aim is to reinforce the work-ethic and its money-incentive by making everyone who is unemployed, whether because they are superfluous or too old, aware of their inferior status, and to make all those who are employed aware of their rewarding automatic advantage and determined to cling to it. Old age pensions remain low because of similar meanness that is not corrected because the old have little energy and bargaining power. Other reasons why social security payments are kept low are resentment on the part of the employed at having to pay to support the unemployed, and fear that if the payments were pitched higher too many people might prefer not to work for the Machine. To ensure that nobody gets too much for nothing, to use an automatic expression, many rules and regulations are made as a result of which many individuals slip through the safety net. They are the people of no fixed abode who are to be found tramping, searching dustbins, wandering the streets and sleeping rough under the bridges of London, or herded into enormous pitiless doss-houses in New York.

Local authorities have welfare departments to help some persons with marital, housing and other problems to survive and cope with automated life. Again, the social workers might be expected to identify and try to rectify the real problems. But, again, they are employed by the Machine that embraces the causes of these problems, in numbers and with resources sufficient only to prevent the deficiencies of the here and now outraging the moral conscience of even the most self-satisfied of the automated public.

Sometimes such consciences *are* outraged, by cases of baby-battering for instance. Many people are becoming much more tolerant and willing to understand all sides of such cases. But it takes an intellating mind to add up all the real evidence of this kind and make it into a compelling case against the Machine. As it is, baby-battering, like wife-abuse or terrorism, is mostly blamed on the perpetrator by a majority who have never been pushed to breaking point by unbearable circumstances, and who do not wish to expose their awareness to the unacceptable facets of life to the point of seriously upsetting the complacent concepts and secure facts of their own personal realities. Of course it has to be admitted that some individuals are more prone to cruelly violent outbursts than others. This may be due to innate defects or instabilities that can never be eradicated, so that there will always be some instances of this kind. But most of the circumstances that trigger these outbursts *can* be eradicated - the combinations of pressures and deficiencies caused by inequality, deprivation, lack of stimulation, exclusion, neglect, hopelessness.

We need to ask ourselves these questions - can a person who is poor, unemployed or menially employed and underpaid, who is sexually potent but unmarried, who is ugly, badly dressed, dirty and without adequate shelter, who is despised and shunned for any of a variety of reasons; can such a person be expected to conform to a norm based on the average middle-class person with adequate income, car, wife, two children, house on mortgage, of good appearance, well-dressed and confident? And how may an individual who belongs to this norm firmly maintain a position in it except by excluding from the mind any serious doubts, or deep thoughts about better alternative values?

Those of us who do have intelligent doubts about existing reality may lose that confidence which comes of being party to the universally accepted norm. It is intellectually healthy to turn against this unintelligent norm and then to support ourselves with our own true convictions. This is hard to do, and some of us look to other, unhealthy supports - alcohol and drugs - that give a kind of reason for living that reality lacks for those who cannot find themselves in supraconsciousness. This artificial support is a feature of the autoculture and a good example of the automatic paradox. The very reality that creates a need for alcohol and drugs - a need to dull the mind because reality itself is so intellectually unfulfilling, and a need to escape from its overwhelming pressures - this very reality fulfils the ruling ethos of the Machine to supply the demand it creates, by openly providing alcohol and encouraging its use, and by secretly smuggling in drugs. This is an automatic practice of the consumer money-economy, profiting from the manipulation of humans. How much drunkenness and alcoholism would there be if the only source of alcohol were homemade wine and beer from local natural ingredients? Who would trouble to bring drugs across half the world to give to addicts for no money-profit in return?

There is another support or therapy for individuals who cannot reconcile their inner conscience and automatic reality - religion. Religions are a product of human conscious intuition which, rather than reason its way to truth, made a virtue of its own mysterious limitations and contrived to set these up as moral institutions of the Machine - churches. Religion pays lip service to morality but without recognising the independence of intellect, from which true morality arises, and without challenging the Machine, which responsible intellects must critically oppose. So the moral influence of religion is more than cancelled out by its automatic realism. It takes responsibility away from humanity and places it in the hands of some god. It rejects the concept of a human race co-operating to make its world accord with its morals. Instead it presents the world as an inescapable battle between forces of good and evil in which the individual, responsible only for the self, may choose good and be 'saved' or evil and be 'damned', either in this life or some other form of life to follow. So religion is another social service adapted to this present reality, accepted, mostly tongue-in-cheek, as their closest possible approach to morality, by persons who do not believe a world human moral reality to be attainable.

Charity is an expression of our humanity in its battle with the Machine, a human virtue that we show when and where we can but which is very much limited by our duty to the uncharitable Machine. Also there is charity of the voluntary but official kind, in the shape of institutions set up to disburse the bequests of persons who were usually ruthlessly automatically successful during their lives but felt they redeemed themselves by giving part of their wealth to relieve some of the poverty of those whose labour created that wealth.

Charities are institutions of the Machine which, like religions, must consistently fail to achieve the objective to which they are supposed to be dedicated - must depend upon a continuance of the evils they pretend to be trying to eradicate - otherwise they would lose their supportive status as automatically justified institutions. Their alternative course is to turn their backs on the Machine and truly determine on fulfilling their supposed overall good purpose, but this they feel unable to do. For example, a campaign to eradicate *all* unnecessary human suffering by replacing the Machine with an ideal framework of life, a humantrue society, will not be supported by charitable institutions. The reason is that their executives are restricted by law to relieving only some deprivations, of particular persons, in certain circumstances, from specific causes - all related to automatic concepts, values and facts.

Chapter 28

THE ARTS

The word art means skill. But what is Art with a capital A? It is pure emotion with intellect applied. It is a human practice that attempts to express truth by isolating that expression from the norm, abstracting it from the everyday world affairs. It diverts the mind's true aim by channelling its thought into perfecting a specious interest. It is obliged to separate itself in this way because the artificial world norm is false. But then in order to sustain itself it has to re-attach itself to the norm, for, like all institutions of the Machine, Art has to be a viable part of the money economy. It is independently supported by us because it appears to represent the best in us.

It is difficult to present a humantrue analysis of reality that will penetrate the strong conventional defences of automated thinking. This is particularly so with the Arts because it is a matter of abstract opinion. But anyone who sees through our normal prejudice about Art - who can rationalise it despite the common belief or sense that it is somehow sacrosanct - may then find it easier to do the same with automatic reality as a whole. The aim is not to rob life of vibrant mysterious emotion but to have us cease being the unhappy victims of our emotions; to get everything fundamentally right so that nothing can go seriously wrong; to cease being content with trying to cancel out the bad with the good. The contention that Art reveals truth is belied by the fact that despite growing accumulations of Art the world remains false. Music, for example, explores the *feelings* of truth but not its substance, so that it can be made to feel truly martial or truly religious to the emotions, suitable to many and varied moods and occasions, but incapable of encompassing or describing whole truth. Words can describe truth but the Art of literature gets little nearer to truth than music because it too relies on appealing to emotions that are attuned to existing reality, so that it rings true only to we who are tightly harnessed to the automaton. Imagine how these things shall be when human life is itself an expression of truth.

So Art is a multitude of narrow angles, each searching for truth within its own particular limits and following its nose to the extreme which convention and the competitive money economy allow. It is valued for what it attempts but fails to do to any significant extent. Those who venerate it as representing human achievement are really standing in awe of what little beauty a handful of humans have contrived despite the ugliness of the world. We look at what we manage to create that is good against a bad background, not critically at the background itself, down to its foundations, from the viewpoint of our true potential for good.

Yet we are surrounded by nature that has the appearance of beauty because it is honest and constant, though by comparison with ourselves it is ignorant. Nature accentuates life and spends its whole energy and time on continuing life to the point that the ugliness of death is almost hidden and unknown. Its emphasis is on the securely constructive, and its vital destructiveness is quickly converted back to the steady process of reconstruction. Even its decay is not decline but preparation for new growth. Everything is optimistically purposeful or, in dead of winter, mostly at rest. We are not honest to ourselves or constantly and steadily constructive of life, so the normal things of our lives are more ugly than beautiful. So we contrive Art that is as dishonest as the rest of our reality - as that which it tries to bring to balance, or compensate for.

To begin with, human Art was an embellishment of life on the part of those tribes whose intelligence enabled them to make space for enriching and fulfilling themselves with beauty in this way. Modern Art is a practice, of automated humanity living in false circumstances, that allows certain limited perceptions, makes certain limited valuations accordingly, then records reactions that seem to be appropriate, meaningful and valuable. By preferring our artistic works to our reality, as representative of our civilisation, we are trying to overlay or explain away our actual failure by artificially tapping our true potential in an attempt to redeem ourselves. Humans are able to *be* artists - musicians, architects, painters, writers - because of the intervention of the money economy that demands that we earn our living by our occupation. Artists are given an opportunity ostensibly to approach the truth, but, by way of constrictions of convention and the market place, are then obliged to keep it at arms length. So with certain exceptions, Art, like the Machine, is not fulfilment of the human intellect but of human intelligence applied to the automaton.

Clearly these few paragraphs cannot deal with all aspects of this subject but they might serve to eat away the foundations of a value-structure that, however large and controversial, is humanly false. Art cannot really be defined except on its own terms. Its search for meaning is a shadow of the great human need for true fulfilment. So Art has no real meaning, only many interpretations of the many facets of our existing wrong concept of reality. When individuals do discover an aspect of truth, by way of Art, and represent it in some creative form, they introduce an uncomfortably uncommon thing that, in a humantrue society, would have fallen already into common place. They are making things part of an actuality which disagrees with such things, and looking to have their Art valued by a society whose moral values it contradicts. These works may be thought worthy but, I repeat, a true consensus is not made of several separately independent aspects, however relatively true in themselves. The truth may be constructed only within each individual supraconscious mind, and such a mind, seeking the whole truth, would not be content with passing on small disconnected parts.

I here include Philosophy, with a capital P, as another instituted form of Art that is not concerned with the discovery of whole truth, though that is what it especially pretends. Individual thinkers attempt, and have always attempted to answer and solve the great human questions and problems, but unless they and their findings are approved by instituted Philosophy they are not heard and individuals become discouraged. Instituted Philosophy pursues the impossible objective of making a true consensus out of all the many and varied arguments contributed by a long and growing list of approved members who have themselves submitted to this procedure in order to gain at least the advantage of recognition that membership gives them. These arguments are between different areas and interpretations of a reality contained within the conscious sphere, and always differ because they do not penetrate to its false roots but attempt to reconcile its irreconcilably ill-begotten, specious branches. Rather than dismiss the whole false Philosophical tree that has grown parallel with automatic reality or gravitate to one and the same body of simple truth, Philosophers have become lost in a labyrinth of mounting complexity. The same applies to philosophy with a small 'p' which appears to be independent of that institution but yet must be commercially and politically approved, for its easy public acceptability, by the various media and all brother institutions of the Machine that are ruled by automatic lore. So that which is offered to us, by the instituted Philosophers as well as the popular philosophies, is not the substance nor even the sound of pure truth. It comes from the shifting sands of divided pockets of limited knowing and reasoning about a false reality which, in truth, should not exist.

We are restricted by this general way of reasoning that Philosophy has taught us, because it holds us back from understanding that which we ought to realise. It comes from thinking which deeply analyses the automated here and now and the human nature appropriate to it, but fails to go so deep as to recognise that both are false. In order to make maximum sense of our senseless world Philosophy made the fundamentals of this world the foundation of our logic. Consequently, whilst the objective of our best thinking is to improve the human lot, that thinking has to be accountable to the facts of reality. Only those conclusions are accepted which are the result of irrefutable and realistic argument, not abstract assertions, even when the latter result from undeniable deductions of reason. This means we are presently inescapably locked into the Machine world because our decisions, to be irrefutable, must recognise every last fact and opinion of the here and now. To escape from this our existing reality it is first necessary to picture an ideal world and to assert, with every humantrue reason but without irrefutable proof, that such a world would be better. But our customary logic is such that Philosophers, governors, politicians, lawyers, economists, deists, and humanists dismiss the ideal because there is nothing to support it but the deductions of reason. Instead they favour realistic arguments which can be supported by facts, notwithstanding that those arguments and facts are limited, separated, contradictory, and do not contribute to a body of truth that could be commonly agreed but ensure that we continue in chaotic conflict.

Arts such as music and painting are emotional pursuits of beauty, also pursuits of their own aspects of truth which, if such pursuits reached the ultimate destination of whole humantruth, would then cease to be as we know them because they would then be a subjective part of life rather than objective occupations in life. The volumes of convoluted argument about the arts, which come of us looking *at* it rather than looking supraconsciously outward, would then be seen to be truly irrelevant.

Chapter 29

SPORTS AND ENTERTAINMENTS

It is to be hoped that Parts I, II and III have developed or reinforced in your mind an attitude to automatic reality that has enabled you to go along with or approve this Part's criticisms of its institutions. If so you will readily understand that whilst these institutions would have no place in a humantrue reality they are necessary working parts of the Machine and its automated human society, so that such criticisms of them are held by realists to be unrealistically naive. Realists are not so blinkered as to see the world as altogether good but as a mixture of good and bad that is the best we can hope to achieve, and they fear that radical reforms would throw the good baby out with the bad bathwater. But capacities for pleasure and delight that are peculiarly human, over and above the basic and direct ways of satisfying instinct which we share in common with the animals, are relative and not absolutely fixed; they are not inseparable from their automatic causes and sources of satisfaction, or inevitably counterbalanced, as they presently are, by misery and dissatisfaction. I repeat - this present is the wrong reality and the humantrue alternative is not a Utopian dream but an attainable state.

For intellectually unfulfilled human units of the Machine reality, practical processes of living become less and less satisfactory and reasonable as they become more and more automated. The Machine, here in the 'developed' nations, conveniently provides the majority of us with our food, warmth and shelter. We personally are no longer wholly preoccupied with the entire process, as are animals, normally to their complete satisfaction. We are given small, isolated, generally repetitive and boring jobs. Or, especially in the 'underdeveloped nations, we are denied both jobs and any other lawful means of providing adequately for ourselves. The Machine remains highly competitive but it is increasingly the competition of automatic interests served by humans, decreasingly a matter of human initiative. Many individuals give to charity for the relief of poverty in the Third World, for example, at the same time as they work for interests that cause or contribute to that poverty. Nevertheless we are still subject to a strong life-force impulsion to live. You can see how the Machine harnesses us to the money economy in return for satisfying our survival instinct. Now consider how Machine entertainments have contrived to satisfy, and turn to similar account, both our competitive urge (strong in males, less developed in females) and the logical appetite of an intellectual faculty for stimulation.

We have ten or fifteen thousand years of conditioning by a predominantly competitive civilisation and millions of years of evolution through natural competition before that. Now our competitiveness is kept alive by the Machine, so as to maintain our support of the concept of existing reality and to profit the money economy, by way of Sport with a capital S. Sport seems harmless but it preoccupies the minds of many people to the extent of being a strong cord that binds their lives together and persuades them to stay with reality. Much of human automated life can be lived in a blank state of going through the everyday motions with the minimum of thought and effort, punctuated by artificial highlights that have the persuasive effect of making it all seem worthwhile. So Sport is far from harmless for it not only keeps alive the unintelligent concept of competition but also keeps us from seeing clearly that our reality by itself does not give full satisfaction. Full awareness of this would give us the will to discover what was wrong and put it right.

The wide popularity of Sport in the most automated parts of the world could reinforce the belief that to compete is natural to us. But natural competitiveness is strictly related to vital need, whereas ours has developed largely out of greed and now fills human need of a different kind. The growth of Sport into an industry is the result of a pursuit of excellence for the sake of winning, propelled by the prospect of status and reward on the part of competitors, and money profit on the part of the industry. The whole human world is a competition, an automatic rat race in which to be a winner is to have the best that automated living can bring. The money that makes Sport a viable entity in the competitive economy comes from the public. They are willing to pay in the hope of seeing their idol or team win and so fulfil a strong emotional need, for to be identified with winning at second hand as a spectator is important to the majority of individuals who are existing reality's losers.

Competitiveness is so ingrained into us by instinct and the teachings of reality that it is hard not to take sides, especially for males for it is still they who mostly have to run the rat race. Since we are subject to a money economy that takes every opportunity for profit, even as spectators we are encouraged to involve ourselves financially in Sport by gambling. We try to add profit to pleasure by betting on horses and going in for football pools. The Stock Exchange represents the conversion of finance into a Sport in which spectators of the rise and fall of commodities and companies try to profit from predicting events. We have a habit of identifying with winners that is common to both sexes and understandable in a competitive society where the desirable objective is to win but most are bound to lose. This habit is indulged by other kinds of entertainment. The chief characters in novels, magazines and films are daring, successful, brave and beautiful, because these are supposed to be and accepted as being the most attractive and interesting characters. Those who write the stories and produce the films are in a similar kind of Sporting business to games promoters and stock brokers, banking on profiting from reality's winners.

Pop music is an entertainment that both expresses feeling and satisfies our conscious appetite for stimulation of the most direct and crudely simple kind. The popularity of its changing form but constant basic character is not inevitable because it is the counterpart of an equally strong and vague dislike of the oppressiveness of automatic reality. In a humantrue world it might well lose its appeal and be replaced by something quite different. Pop music belongs to youth because the young have surplus energy to express in rebellion against the oppressive norm, and are not yet fully strapped into its harness nor weighed down by all its burdens. It hammers out rhythms like the pounding of the blood, and dwells on the ever powerful and urgent theme of sexual love whose excitement drives us to mate without thought of the aftermath. But it also bangs out protest, voicing some elements of truth in condemnation of false reality. These are the simplest part-truths; they have to be. If the words got too seriously deep and heavy they would not fit the music and its purpose emotionally to draw us into a sort of dream world, like meditation. When young people go about with stereo headphones over their ears they are holding out in their dream world, fending off the normal adult conformity that they despise. But they generally have no answers and no real resistance because their rebellion is not against the Machine as such, only against its more blatant wrongs and its restrictions on their freedom to do what they wish, or to seek what they think and feel they want. Their minds are not determined on understanding the Machine and finding a better alternative world free from automatic conditioning. They live in consciousness that instinctively responds to material and other automatic attractions just as it is attracted to the primitive beat of pop music. Their flimsy moral reasoning is outweighed by these attractions, to experience which they become all too soon harnessed to the Machine and trapped by adult conformity.

Literature, television, cinema, music, theatre; aside from any pretensions to Art with a capital A, these are entertainments supplying a demand for emotional satisfaction and mental stimulation which everyday life normally lacks. They explore the actual dramatic and vivid conflicts of the Machine and the consequent struggles of automated humans, and seek to portray them with realistic excellence. Taken together they approach reality on a much broader front than Philosophy but do not go deep, for ultimate truth is not their aim either. They are forms of liberation from limitations of the individual's personal horizons but not of escapism from the facts and concepts of overall automatic reality, for that would not be comforting or entertaining to audiences who are, because they believe they must be, harnessed to the automaton. These entertainments are firmly related to reality, so that spectators experience happenings and sensations that may not occur in daily life but belong to a common, familiar framework of attitudes and values. Yet an added attraction of entertainment of this kind is that it is remote, enabling us to go through difficult experiences at second hand, in safety. Being just one amongst the Machine's losers, one can nevertheless cushion oneself from despair by assuming the imaginary role of winner.

We shall not escape from this reality except by moving into an alternative. Before we can make that move the alternative reality has to be prepared and before that can be done we have to envisage it. But to envisage an alternative that really is wholly good, and not just a variation on the same automatic themes, requires that the truth be discovered so that existing reality is exposed as false. Serious attempts at true discovery are not popular because truth, until it is generally understood, cannot be recognisably familiar. The people who produce or take part in presenting entertainment may be trying truly to fulfil their minds but are allowed to do so only to the extent that they cater to public demand so as to be viable in terms of the money economy. The existence of a money incentive means that the entertainment industry remains chiefly concerned with and skilled at projecting emotive realism and little interested in true enlightenment, because the former brings financial success, not the latter. It also means that the public appetite for easy entertainment is increased disproportionately to a natural advance in critical awareness, and the stimulation of that awareness. This further reinforces the money economy's practices of supply meeting demand in accordance with the profit motive, and of demand being attracted or persuaded to consume supply, which perpetuate a reality that allows superficial modifications but not any change in its automatic basis.

In this way almost all sports and entertainments are geared to automatic reality for whose shortcomings they are required to make up. Even books of science fiction, when they depict alien life, transpose human concepts of Earth reality to planets elsewhere in the universe. By depicting these planets as enmeshed in conflicts of a money economy or locked in leadership struggles just like ours here on Earth, such stories fail, in these and other ways, to shed light on automated life's ignorance or falsification of truth by comparing our reality with something far superior. And now autoprogressive science and technology has brought all forms of sport and entertainment into every home over half the world by way of television. That the numbers of channels and total hours of viewing time have already rapidly increased makes it easy to imagine a time when humans shall hardly move out of their homes, being almost totally dependent on the Machine for emotional experience and mental stimulation - the automatic takeover.

To present-day realists all this may appear as the threat of a puritanical ideal to remove all the pleasures of life. Supraconscious individuals will understand that, on the contrary, a humantrue world would generate its own and better delights and fulfilments from within. How far these would arise from everyday life and to what extent we would indulge in some forms of sport or formal entertainment is difficult to judge. These questions are considered under Part VII, Realisation of Humantrue Society. The task of this chapter has been to reveal that sports and entertainments as we currently know them relate to instinct and automatic conditioning; are artificial counter-balances to a fundamentally unsatisfactory norm; and that the interests and tastes they have inculcated, and the habits and practices they have established, can not be taken to indicate our true nature and state.

Chapter 30

COMMUNICATIONS

We are in the midst of a rapidly advancing age of communication, but generally without much understanding of what is being communicated, and why.

All intelligent life-forms have simple means of communicating and it is to be expected that the much more highly intelligent human species should have much more complex means. Our upbringing and education is mostly by way of verbal and written instruction and understanding through language, and is the human equivalent of instinctive rearing. Whilst the vitally urgent present task of an enlightened humanity is to thrash out and realise a humantrue future, our most common use of conversation is to exchange comfort and support in the here and now, the equivalent of mutual grooming in nature. Communal communication by way of entertainment and Art has similar informing and comforting functions, but Art also includes intellectual questing, which is the equivalent of the natural curiosity of all advanced species. These are the intellect's logical extensions of instinctive satisfactions to meet its own extended needs. Over and above such satisfactions the intellectual state demands a new social framework appropriate to itself, replacing the existing framework that represents instinct in command of intellect.

Had we a humantrue society, with an established and agreed constitution, we would employ whatever other means of communication were desirable and necessary to its wellbeing. But we presently have the Machine, are driven by a competitive money economy, and live in confused conflict. So we have evolved a need and desire for information, and an industry has developed to communicate this information. One purpose of this industry is to inform the public, largely through the press, television, internet and radio, and the other purpose is to provide intercommunication between functions of the Machine, largely by post, telephone (these also being extensions of personal communication), fax and e mail. The printing and publishing of books and magazines serves both purposes more or less equally.

The information industry is an existing fact of life but is not what it pretends to be. First and foremost it is not concerned with the inescapable function of fulfilled intellect - fundamental truth. It is governed by restrictive factors that determine the character of its information so that the information is only partially complete, or true, according to the limitations imposed by those factors. In the case of intercommunications between functions of the Machine the character of the information conveyed is straightforward - it is entirely limited to purely automatic affairs and excludes purely human, or any other concerns which, to it, are irrelevant. We are here interested in the communication of information to the public, i.e. to individuals in their private capacities, apart from their direct attachment to the Machine by way of employment.

Those parts of the information industry whose role is to communicate between the world and the individual - the 'media' - are often accused of falsification and bias. Periodically a spokesman comes forward to refute these charges on behalf of the media, and unintentionally shows those with the eyes to see that the accusation is correct because both he and the media are prejudiced against the fundamental truth. At the same time he intentionally demonstrates that the accusation is wrong in that the media are right in being true to their prejudice in favour of the concepts of existing reality - true to the facts of their own actual situation in this reality and that of their faithful readers.

The media are institutions of the Machine governed by automatic lore, yet their output tends towards truth because it is produced as journalism by human minds whose natural, logical, but normally submerged objective this is. But those individuals responsible for media output are employed to think in an automated way. They have to be conventionally realistic because the Machine is everybody's overwhelming reality, and in the political conflict between all its contradictory 'truths' no overall truth can be admitted. So the fact is that in journalism's reporting the widely differing affairs of a competitive society there has to be a bias. There also has to be falsification, not by the committed sin of lying so much as the sin of omitting contrary truth. For example, it might be so that in a war between two nations the people of both believe themselves to be right because their leaders so represent it, whereas in the eyes of each the other *must* be seen as wrong otherwise the war, declared by leaders according to their personal bias, could not continue for lack of popular commitment. When that war is reported, *how* it is explained depends on *who* is reporting it, and to *whom*. If it is by a neutral correspondent, reporting to a neutral populace, it might be expected to be free of bias, yet how does a reporter get unbiased information when it is not possible to be an eye-witness of all events simultaneously from both sides and neither side can be relied upon for unbiased information? Furthermore, how can the newspaper reader or radio listener be sure of getting a true account when he or she knows that journalism is not the result of an honest individual endeavour to discover the truth but is the restricted report of a mind applied to an adopted or imposed thinking formula?

The truth about our competitively conflicting world affairs, including wars which are their regular culminations, is that they need not and should not be so, and would not be so were we fully awakened to that truth. We are not truly awakened, firstly, because we have never risen above but remain bowed down under the great weight of a false reality. Secondly, we are not fully awakened to the truth because, rather than relying on the pure intellation of our own minds, we depend on the biased media information for our thoughts and opinions and the media are overridden by official acceptance of existing false reality. So the press barons, publishers, governors of broadcasting, reporters, printers and announcers remain harnessed to the automaton and the humantruth that would release us all from harness remains obscured.

So journalism reports events (just as stories are told) as they happen, or are judged or appear to happen, in automatic reality, and are accepted as reasonable according to the concepts and facts of that reality. Events are not commented upon as part of a critical campaign against an insane reality. They are usually shown as normal against a background of acceptance of the insane. Even events that are viewed as abnormal and unacceptable are not addressed with the intention of finding and rooting out their deepest causes but as horrors to be registered on the debit side of violently fluctuating human experience. Our reality comprises past, present and automatically continuing fact, being interpreted according to its own false concepts and purveyed to a public having none but this reality to live in, and very little else on offer to believe in. In this condition we may look at the pure truth without recognition, so that badly as we need it we can dismiss it without a qualm.

Consider again why human minds do not come out in open revolt against this reality, although having true reason to do so. Whilst the mind is the paramount element of human being no independent mind has the power to give public expression to its true thought, and that which gives this power also robs the mind of independent ability to discover the truth. The people who wield this power - the servants of the media and those with approved access to them - have their selves in consciousness, open to automatic dictation and closed to their own true intellects. Whilst human mental activity is growing this automatic *use* of the intellect is the general norm that keeps us tied to the Machine, whereas awareness draws the individual away from automatic domination and towards supraconsciousness. The longer humans delay giving their minds independence the more difficult it is likely to become, for as the Machine grows more dominant it will become harder for the independent mind to find a voice as the media journalism increasingly conforms to automatic thinking. It is true that radical views are permitted a certain broadcast time and space but it is doubtful whether this represents more than a controlled safety valve for dissent. In any case such views as we are allowed to hear do not go deep enough to shake the foundations of our overshadowing reality which merely shoulders them out of the way.

As with politics, so with journalism. Everything hinges on attitude, and at present the media support and play up to the attitude of our outer shells - that this is our inescapable reality and we must adapt to the here and now. They feel justified on the grounds that they are supplying our demands. The public demand what they are used to getting, despite what their inner selves may say, simply because they believe it is all they *can* get, with no alternative. This is an easy way out that people take rather than refusing to conform, because such refusal, by introducing radical ideas, can ruin their conversations, upset their community life, detract from their enjoyment of newspapers and TV, and expose them to opposition, threat, or real danger.

In many ways the public mind is preformed by the media before it is capable of critical judgement. For example, it seems that 'Dallas', a TV drama series about the life of the American jet-set, was exported to the unsophisticated people of third-world countries presenting, as desirable, admirable and relevant, values that are quite the reverse. Similarly the Vietnam war was reported on Western TV in such a biased way that for years the public had no clear idea what was really happening, or why. Again, the meaningful current of life in both Russia and the West was very much coloured by the mutual antagonism of their governing ideologies, which so imbued their respective media journalism as to implant this unreasoned antagonism in the minds of people, a self-escalating process.

Re-consider the reasons why thinkers who *do* protest against and oppose this reality are not heard; why the media do not support a revolt of reason, as they seem well placed to do. Firstly, all parts of the information industry are units in the money economy whose success depends on profitable sales. They have to be able to pay their expenses, including the wages of staff on whom they depend but who themselves depend on this employment for survival and reward to the extent of subjugating their morals to their employers. Secondly, these units of the media are institutions of the Machine. If they identify with extreme non-conformist views they not only risk unpopularity but also the wrath of the whole establishment of other interdependent institutions which, being strongly biased in favour of the automatic norm, regard radical reason as subversive, however honest and true it may be, because it does not conform to the normal bias, or as irresponsibly arrogant because it contradicts universal opinion.

Furthermore the media are engaged in an ongoing process of commenting on affairs, journalism, with an obligation to fill up the pages and viewing slots but with none other than the affairs of existing reality to comment on, and none but the accepted concepts of existing reality meaningfully to interpret them with. If they are to continue successful these are the affairs they must keep abreast of in this familiar, approved or popular way, following where the automated norm leads. What the media say is heard by the millions and believed by most. In general the individual with something to say may be heard only by way of the media and only by saying what they will consent to publish or broadcast, and as a result the media output, although contributed by humans, always fundamentally toes the Machine line. It is not a matter of deliberate censorship so much as an automatic consensus as to what is realistically germane.

So the media reflect the public feeling that to conform to the norm is not only easier but better than opposing it, because the norm presently embraces all the circumstances of life including most of its stimulations and rewards. Whatever its state, the human mind requires stimulation in order to maintain or enhance that state. *Maximum* stimulation is synonymous with fulfilment of the mind, which shall be achieved by a supraconscious humanity living in a humantrue society. Nobody can yet achieve that optimum level and most of us fall short of the high-flying excitements of the Machine, finding much of our stimulation at second hand. For instance, battles, conflicts of all kinds and natural or man-made disasters instinctively attract us in the absence of greater interests. The media select the most exciting, intriguing, shocking or horrifying events and purvey them to us as factual news, in the name of public interest. This is part of their business and their logical function, given our circumstances and reluctance seriously to doubt or question, but it is the humanly unworthy function of one institution of a society that is built on false logic, and an abdication of our true responsibility.

The information industry's public output of journalism serves to affirm automatic reality, and the danger to children from the media, especially television, is not only that it teaches them violence but that it confirms as valid the false values of that reality. It teaches them competition, which arouses their instinctive aggressiveness and leads to violence. The upbringing of children is normally begun with a diet of fantasy. They are not introduced to the real horrors until old enough to cope with them, that is when they have been sufficiently conditioned to life's horrors as to tolerate them or have become so involved in self-interest for survival as to deny, or ignore, or become indifferent to them, or themselves involved in them. There is a case for showing very young children just how inhumanly cruel and uncaring reality can be, but this is valid only if they are also given to consider as vital the need to eradicate the causes of violence and aggression by changing to a non-competitive humantrue society - to see the *Machine* as the real dragon to be slain.

There was a view that the evolving communications network is a global brain that could become equal to the human brain in complexity by the year 2000. But can this network be likened to the living brain when that organ, in any other creature of nature, has the one purpose of caring for the well-being of that creature and prompting its survival and, at the level of human intellect, has the supreme purpose of fulfilling truth, neither of which purposes is being pursued nor looks likely to be pursued in the future by journalism - by the world's entire communications system as it stands. It has to be remembered that both we and this rapidly expanding system are in the firm grip of the Machine. What is the system's purpose, and what information is it passing to and fro? How many of us are, or shall be, fully intercommunicated? How can beings of unequal status, knowledge and understanding be in *true* communication? How can a global brain be said to represent us truly unless every human being takes equal intellectual part? If we were to reach such a state of equality could we possibly accept this system, as it is and promises to become? The present foreseeable world communications network is the *Machine's* brain, which is engulfing human minds. It calculates accordingly - a thinking process dominated by the automaton in the same way that presently normal human thought constructions are dominated by conscious will. It is only when consciousness seconds itself to its higher postconsciousness that a mind becomes supraconscious, and thus humantrue. The global brain does not have a postconscious faculty and never shall have because its automated aims can not be served by truth. It is in that sense mindless, and if we remain submissive to it we shall never achieve collective supraconsciousness. Only by having the global brain submit to our postconscious minds, just as our conscious selves, in the supraconscious state, submit, shall we be able to make our world humantrue.

So our means of communication is the mouthpiece of processes of thinking that are not truly our own. Like politics, these means tell us nothing about humanity and its affairs that is wholly true. When you boil it down, the essence of what they give us is automatic commentary on the Machine and on ourselves as its automatic adjuncts.

The dominant Machine ethic is one thing, and private individual human intellation is another. The former, being dominant, has always monopolised the communications system, as would be expected, and the latter - the true reasoning of the human postconscious mind - has been isolated, muted, and virtually unheard. There are two comparatively recent developments of the communications system that offer the possibility of changing all that. Firstly, the number of private individuals owning and operating computers, all over the world, has increased dramatically. Secondly, the Internet system makes it possible for those individuals, by means of a modem, to communicate with each other freely and independently (apart from the language difficulty) So the Internet could have an enormous humantrue effect, as a means of by-passing the normal channels of communication and spreading supraconsciousness, by way of co-operative intellation, a vital alternative to the normal 'Machine-speak'.

It goes against anybody's gut feeling and instinctive interest to turn against the entrenched, generally unquestioned norm. It does not come easily to take existing reality apart and see it for what it really is unless your intellectual reasons for doing so are much more compelling than your disinclined feelings. This Part IV has been kept relatively short and simple with the intention of stimulating further, more detailed revelations, yours and mine, and including them in a proposed sequel entitled THE SILENT ORACLE.

THE WRONG REALITY

Part V
INTERPRETATION

IN SEARCH OF MEANING AND MORALITY

Introduction to Chapter 31

I have tried to establish the fact that this book is not a product of existing automatic reality; that it is not an offering to the critical attention of automated humanity with the hope of entertaining or arousing interest but with no real expectation of the here and now being fundamentally changed. It is an attempt to discover the true mind of humankind, the realisation of which would result in an utterly changed reality.

It is said that an author should have a particular audience in mind when writing. This is to accept that there are groups of different kinds of individual each with certain group characteristics. I am writing to individual minds, each of which has similar capacity and for all of which there exists one and the same potential understanding of humantruth.

It is not possible to know how many individuals will eventually read this book. Although my remarks come from a great confidence in the true understanding of my own mind, and I increasingly imagine you, the reader, as following my reasoning because you share that understanding, I have no way of knowing whether you were enlightened before you began reading or how far this book has helped, or to what extent you have actually released your mind from its previous conditioning. Are you still wilfully attached to some of the false principles of this reality or do you see it all as false? If the former, I beg you not to reinforce your solid instinctive conscious self but allow the postconscious to break it down - make supraconsciousness your aim, without prejudgement of the truth then to emerge.

This Part V is to explain how and why the false make-up and situation of the majority - the normal **I** who has not yet come to understand - has caused and still causes us to explore false concepts of the earthly and universal destiny of human beings and adopt religious faith.

Chapter 31

SITTING ON THE FENCE

Just look around you at all the people and imagine what is going on inside each head. Each person, as a detached physical and mental entity, may be very different in opinion and activity but all are conducting, to some degree, a private and perhaps totally secret but essentially similar struggle in the mind.

From the time that humanity acquired its postconscious mind, its faculty of knowing and reasoning, it became a species whose true destiny is to fulfil this intellectual potential and become supraconscious. The achievement of this fulfilment depends, initially, on humans themselves perceiving that this *is* their true destiny, and then on their making the vital effort to adopt entirely new concepts and facts of reality in order to acquire an appropriate nature and state. We have never yet risen to that perception, but though we don't see it, we sense it. That sense gives us the vague awareness that there is, somewhere to be found, a true purpose and meaning to our lives, and gives us the desire to try and define it. The Machine imposes its automatic purposes and meanings on us and practically all of us conform to most of these but chiefly with our outer shells, inwardly finding them in many ways unsatisfactory, or suspect.

We have not succeeded in defining this true meaning and purpose of life because, whilst we strongly desire it from the depths of our inner being, we yet resist the truth of it. A reason for this is that to break through to that truth can be extremely difficult, requiring abnormal and sometimes excruciatingly persistent effort and awkwardly radical sensitivity. It is so much easier to follow automatic instructions in accordance with instincts with which we have long been familiar. Our normal inner mental struggle may be between our private morality and the obvious immoralities of the Machine, i.e. our postconscious's battle with consciousness for control of the self, but it is generally obscured by a yearning for sure and positive but relaxed and tranquil feeling, and dislike of the uncomfortable and unrealistic tensions of striving for truth. We are mostly looking for some comforting, protective, all-embracing personal dream which shall both fulfil our moral desire and counter ugly realities.

We are struggling not to *solve* our problems but personally to *surmount* them. We evade the essential process of intellation - the tortuous process whereby the conscious self gives way to the critical judgement of the postconscious mind and inferior consciousness is displaced by a supraconscious state of being. The present normal human mind not being supraconscious, the human self is incomplete and wrong. So the self makes a pact with the wrong reality, not feeling right but neither believing itself wrong - only looking to penetrate some mystery which shall, it is imagined, make an emotional balance that does feel right. The human race has instinctively careered on its reckless way for thousands of years without ever getting into top gear, mentally. It is as if we were a race of children who never grow up, or as though we all suffered brain strokes at birth and almost none of us fights to recover and fulfil our mental potential, and the very few who do fight fail in the face of overwhelming odds.

We try personally to surmount rather than collectively to solve our problems for two reasons, One is that we think these problems inescapably endemic, and the other that our minds think this way because they are emotionally bound up with our bodies - both our own bodies and those of our close kith and kin - and our bodies are bound to the Machine, our existing reality. This reveals another reason why we resist the urge to discover the *true* meaning and purpose of life. Existing reality puts pressure on our private reality not to address itself to humantruth - not to address itself to the gentle and careful consideration of the fundamental facts and responsibilities of intellectual life - but to take a back seat, whilst our outer shells fight the automatic fight. We join in the competitive battle not only to win its rewards but also to defend or shelter our inner selves, as best we can, from the hurt they must otherwise suffer. Automatic reality seems to allow our private morality no other means of escape into relative safety.

The city is the acme of automatic reality. It represents the predominant concentration of present human thought and activity, all geared to the automaton and allowing us little real choice but to conform or go hang. The city assumes that we are harnessed to the automaton and that our desired objective is to comply with the norm. It takes the patronising approach that humanitarian sentiments are commendable, and may be practiced or pretended to wherever convenient, but that when it comes to the important basic business of the here and now it is not the human conscience but the Machine that calls the tune. The media take the same approach, most of the time, which is reflected in the predominantly automated attitude, behaviour and general conversation of most of us.

Minds which the Machine recognises as foremost - whose interpretations of reality are its own and generally accepted by us - do not supraconsciously intellate but reflect or address the preoccupations of automatic reality. The effect of this can be felt in the public library of a large city. Here are many thousands of books written by such recognised minds, far more than any one person can read and absorb, implying that to wholly understand our world is beyond any individual because nobody can know everything, and we each must bow to the Machine as our collective interpretation of reality. But the great majority of these books fall into two categories. Those in the first category are dispensable, being concerned with the automatic interests and affairs of existing reality that have no humantrue significance. The second category contains a great deal of detailed fact but the essential truth of it can be briefly and simply summed up. Science, for instance, can be summed up as fact about the physical universe that the mind does not require to know in detail, only in general principle, in order to be humantrue. However, the Machine pursues the instinctive drives, not pure human reason, and its affairs automatically follow the technological application of scientific discovery. If an individual mind is to take part in this application it must first be strongly automated; then it requires to know the science thoroughly, to be well versed in its significance to the money economy, and then to keep abreast of its discoveries and the autoprogression of technology. It is such thought constructions as these that determine a mind's interpretation of reality. These exclusive minds are but shadows of their supraconscious potential, but are the machine's privileged lieutenant's who help to rule the world.

So the truth, or rather humantruth, is not recognised because apparently nobody out of this world's five or six thousand million individuals has achieved his or her full mental capability so as to be able to judge the wholly true relationship of anything to everything else. The general consensus of opinion and belief is related to false automatic reality and represented by the total content of one week's newspapers. This week's doings of the Machine determine the affairs of next week which automatically follow, just as this week's consensus forms the basis of next week's opinion, and so on, with automatic logic. There is no evidence of whole reasoning going on. Nobody has the right reasons for doing what is done, and none of us is aware of the true significance of what he or she is doing. It is a most disturbing fact that almost everybody believes consciousness, set in this automatic reality, to be the supreme human self, its will the decision maker but with the Machine laying down its options. Thus it is that humantruth, which should inspire, guide and govern us, presently serves only to confuse us by pricking our conscience.

That pricking of the conscience is the postconscious knocking on the door of consciousness, reaching the awareness of even the most automated of minds dominated by the strongest of conscious wills. We retain our inner selves and feelingly know them to represent the true 'us', despite the subservience of our outer shells to the Machine, not only because of that moral awareness but also because of the emotional influence of the benign instincts. The most cruel despot can see himself as kind and just, because he lovingly cares for his own family. Our moral awareness and gentle instinct does not turn us against our outer shells, however, or collectively against the Machine which is the cause of our general immorality and inhumanity, but merely prompts us, whilst serving the Machine on one side, to tend our humanity on the other, as best we may and as far as the conventions allow. We are sitting on the fence.

We sit on the fence because we are in the wrong reality, in which the private thinking of all individuals who cannot make the world conform to their inner morality, but will neither capitulate to the amoral norm, tries to reconcile these apparent irreconcilables so as to make life liveable. It is a compromise, a truce that the majority of us call for a lifetime, opting out of responsibility for the struggle between our humanity and the Machine by taking a neutral personal position. Certain individual or group characteristics and classes of activity come down on one side of the fence, some on the other side. On one hand we pursue competitive drives according to automatic lore, in the positive interests of the Machine but contrary to the true interests of humanity. On the other hand we try automatically to control some of the ill-effects of these drives with instituted laws, and meet some others with charitable compassion. The general truce is broken from time to time as collective opinion or action shifts now closer to the Machine, now to the human. Politics, as it swings from Right to Left and back, is one agent of this shifting which, like the extremes of war and peace, effects no real change but leaves the human race, its potential unrealised, sitting on the fence. Some praise to us that at least our senses insist on this balance - that we have not yet gone over to the Machine altogether. But the great weight of our reality is on the automatic side, and we could not have contrived this balancing act had we not invented something to which we gave equal and opposite weight on the human side.

Think back to Mussolini, or Franco, dictators in their countries, depriving the people of their freedom. This is generally thought, recognised and agreed to be unhealthy and intolerable, yet the *whole world* is dictated to by the Machine, and worse - almost every human postconscious higher mind is dictated to by the inferior, wilful thinking constructions of the conscious self.

Our existing world has little to do with our inner selves but everything to do with our outer shells, so the present stance of the normal human mind is very much more automated than intellated. Therefore almost everybody comes to the same conclusion - that the individual is impotent; absolutely powerless personally to change world reality for the better, the inner self being faced with a reality and an outer shell that are not and have no intention of ever being humantrue. Despite the fact that every individual is equipped with a superb mental instrument whose potential, in terms of true reason, is superior to the whole physical, natural and automated world; despite that fact, unreasonable, reckless autoprogression continues.

Although this is moral madness, unacceptable to our inner selves, the fact of its continuation implies that the instinctive automaton is and must be our most powerful and inescapable motivation, compared with which our purely human morality is of inferior consequence. It further implies that the Machine is dependably logical whilst humantruth is irrational, and we allow ourselves to be convinced of this whereas the reverse is true. For example, the money economy defeats our attempts to make sense of it and we cannot believe the true reason - that this complex system that governs us and all the world does *not* make sense.

When the automaton draws human affairs down on the side of the fence opposite to our true morality we can be persuaded to commit all kinds of inhumanities. Although torture and mass murder is obviously and strongly against humanitarian values, the Machine does not have, and never has had, any difficulty in getting humans to perform such atrocities. The reason is that the Machine has much more comprehensive power over us than our consciences. Yet even while we commit these inhumanities we cannot escape our mind's awareness that we are contravening our true values, though we may temporarily, or even permanently, obscure our conscious perception of that awareness. There is a difference between what we will do in obedience to the Machine because it is required of us in our position in automatic reality, and what we will openly admit to doing, either to the world or to our own inner selves. For this reason, torture and mass murder is usually carried out behind closed doors, or otherwise out of common sight. The doors of the prisons, and the doors in the minds of the torturers and executioners, are closed to full recognition of these acts, just as the minds of the indirectly involved public are shut against the guilt of admitted knowledge that they are actually taking place. If and when the prison doors are flung wide at last, also forcing open those doors in the mind, the guilty may be as horrified as the innocent.

Our history burdens us with guilt and our past neglect of truth is visited on us in the present. Even though we are well practiced in applying the denial factor to many of the worst features of existing reality, it still offends the conscience enough that we would be unable to bear it, or our automatic selves, but for the invention already referred to. This is religion, of course, by which is meant some system of faith in and worship of, or deference to, a supposed divine power or wisdom. Religions afford an escape from human moral responsibility by giving weight to the humane characteristics on the automaton's side of the fence on which we are sitting. As long as we are prepared to believe them, and sustain our faith, religions restore the balance between our humanity and the automaton but only in our wishful imagination. And in any case, even if this balance were a fact, that still leaves us sitting on the fence, only halfway human. Religions strike this balance by calling acts such as torture 'evil', and repentance good; by isolating the good self from bad events so that faith can be maintained without having to eradicate acts such as torture. The fact of 'evil', which is allotted a fantastic place - Hell - is balanced by pretensions to good which are also given a place - Heaven. But it is true that our reality is imbalanced on the automatic side, which means it's going downhill towards dehumanisation or destruction. Even if an unequal balance between our humanity and the automaton were a fact, it might ensure our survival but nothing approaching our true fulfilment. Nothing but a wholly humantrue reality can be acceptable to morally aware intellect.

If you are to become truly aware you have to keep your head above the vast sea of automatic conditioning in which practically the whole of humanity is immersed. When you are sunk in this sea you may not see it as conditioning. You will then judge with a mind conditioned by a false reality, and therefore falsely. You have a sense of the true meaning and purpose of life, perhaps arrived at by applying reason to your instinctive feelings of care and compassion, yet cannot find these adequately reflected in the world. So you may well turn to one of the religions, because it satisfies your moral senses and feelings yet does not disturb your conditioned reasoning because it has been made to fit acceptably into the automatic norm.

It is unlikely that anyone with firmly and wilfully fixed religious faith will have been able or willing to read this far, but likely that the minds of the persevering reader and this writer shall be broadly in sympathy. It is easy for us to dismiss religions just as it is easy for 'believers' to dismiss us. Yet we share the same moral concerns, so what stands between us? It is that they put a false construction on the meaning and purpose of life that they sense, whilst we are dedicated to realising its truth. What matters about this difference is that religions take away from humanity its responsibility for ourselves and Earth.

Surely it must be accepted that truth is the prime object of intellect. Whatever may be the humantruth the honest search for it should not begin with any fixed prejudice such as that against religion. On the other hand that search, however well intended, will be brought to an abrupt and unsuccessful end by the adoption of a blind faith in things of the imagination. Such faiths might keep the fence-sitting human race from toppling over too far into automation, but they bring to a halt or at least hinder true progress.

Chapter 32

ROOTS OF RELIGION

All creatures on Earth, excepting ourselves, pursue life with vigour and without question, requiring no more than the instinctive impulsion of energy, or life-force, to give them their singleness of purpose. We, having the faculty of knowing and reasoning, or intellect, require a *reason* for living, a purpose other than merely to live - a meaning to warrant our presence here. What we really want to know is truth, but growing understanding of truth would bring increasing desire to live by it. Existing reality is false and requires, on the contrary, that we automatically ignore, deny, or flout truth. Our present reality is a welter of concepts and values arising from misunderstandings such as caused the ancients to worship the sun, and modern society to believe in evil as an actual entity. These false concepts have uncritically accompanied the building up of a series of facts, practices and institutions of the Machine which have engendered further false concepts - misinterpretations of the evident world resulting in false convictions - for instance that children must be brain-fixed for living in tomorrow's world; that money is what makes the world go round; that crime and punishment are natural features of human society.

Our fanciful interpretations of life's natural phenomena have been so strongly felt, and automatic lores are so strongly imposed, as to overwhelm us, with the result that, in our search for life's reason, meaning and purpose, we allow ourselves to be forbidden the truth. Consequently we have found those substitutes for truth - religions - and contrived to believe them in order to give peace to our conscious selves from the nagging of postconsciousness and in order to reinforce certain disciplines of conduct that have become required supports of civilised human behaviour. These substitutes are acceptable to the Machine, to our automatic selves, and to our contrived beliefs. They provide false answers to our questions that sound true because they are echoed by false reality. They provide false solutions to human problems because they conform to automatic lores, and they provide necessary solutions to existing false problems that seem right because they *are* presently necessary.

The different religions are instituted and take their place alongside the many other different institutions of automatic reality. All religions should be rejected, for two vital reasons. Firstly, because they do not seek to *realise* humantruth but to compromise it. They promote true moralities yet at the same time deny and betray them by also supporting a false world reality that neither reflects true human reality nor makes its practice possible. Secondly, religions should be rejected because they represent some form of human deference to supposed divine power or superior enlightenment, allowing us to shrug off responsibility for ourselves, our world, and even the universe, and place it on the shoulders of gods whose existence can neither be demonstrated nor reasonably deduced. The most enlightened Christians may agree that truth is the object of the intellect which is its judge, but may go on to say that the point must come where intellect falls short of truth, requiring further light - exclusively the light of god - which it must cease striving for but must merely open itself to receive, not from the exhaustive dialogue with its own independent postconscious by way of intellation - the striving that I propose - but from god, without question, through high priests who were or are supposed to be nearer to god than we. This demonstrates the retreat of faith from the advance of reason; its falling back behind stubborn defence of that faith in god on which it depends for continued existence as a hierarchical institution and which stops its followers from reaching the recognition that their faith is false, and unnecessary. The process of intellation and the supraconscious state can not be content with limited opinions, unfounded beliefs, or imaginative faiths superimposed on the unknown, for nothing can be accepted as true in itself that does not have its place in the construction of whole truth. Therefore an act of compassion towards a victim of oppression is truly a loving act but it is not humantrue unless primarily dedicated to the *elimination* of oppression, so that there shall be no *more* suffering victims.

Yet it has to be recognised that to many people of good intention and kindly disposition their religion does represent truth. Though it is not evident or reasonably arguable that gods exist, in fact they do exist, in some form, in the minds of most individuals. So religions cannot be ignored. They require to be explained, in order that they disappear as faith in them is washed away by advancing humantrue reason. It is necessary to show that all the many and varied religions *are* substitutes for truth, both as a matter of fact and as a way of life, and that they do take away human responsibility from that to which it properly belongs - our supraconscious intellect.

At the start of human civilisation, and probably to some extent amongst our apefolk ancestors, religion was a matter of fearing, placating, and contriving explanations for phenomena that were beyond our understanding. These explanations were sought through growing curiosity and then required by the new faculty of knowing and its developing reason. To begin with, human morality was still entrusted to the positive drives and negative inhibitions of instinct, the natural survival balance between fierce competition and benign caring. Later, as the Machine harnessed our energies to amoral instinctive drives regardless of inhibitions, religions arose out of human desire to counteract these drives by the voluntary opposite expression of virtue and compassion. Such religions tried, and still try to replace the balance of nature, that we long ago passed beyond, with this artificial moral balance between our humanity and our reality - to keep us sitting on the fence.

But, as the moral messages of religions have failed to exert any real humanising effect on automatic authority, and now that the Machine is autoprogressing at an accelerating pace, people are resigning themselves to the conviction that nothing can be done. Consequently, morality has come to have no more real meaning to the religious institutions, their officials and followers, than to non-religious persons. Yet reason and benign emotion yearn for true morality. Nobody identifies with immorality, or sees himself or herself as fundamentally evil. As their ancient autocracies stagnated people long ago turned, and in the most automated West are again turning, as they are similarly demoralised but in a more complex way, to kinds of mysticism.

Like the ancients the new mystics abandon the world to its fate, ceasing to strive for moral responsibility as religion at its best had originally done in the shape of Jesus Christ, and making life an issue between the individual self's experience and some outside power. In the beginning we worshipped evident gods like the sun, in fear. Then we prayed to a hidden, spiritual but humane god for succour. Now we meditate - not only in organised disciplined ways but also privately, as a kind of secret, intuitive dreaming - thinking to open ourselves to a mysterious cosmic divine wisdom with universal power, and gaining some personal satisfaction by being enabled to rise above or evade that which is personally distasteful or burdensome by walking away from it. Our expanding discoveries of scientific fact, which had earlier encouraged atheism by throwing out theories of god's creation and which could have taught us pure fatalism, did not provide an explanation of the meaning and purpose of our existence but so impressed us with revelations of the minuteness and enormousness of the universe as to reawaken the impulse to worship these things, as we once worshipped the sun. In a sense we have gone full circle - from standing in awe of the biggest objects to be seen, turning in disappointment to imagining a god with the interests of humans at heart, then once more turning in disappointment to the most complex scientific subjects open to discovery, and to the belief that since the universe is beyond our ability to fathom and explain, it must be wiser than we. Thus, whilst we automatically advance with the Machine we still refuse to admit that our own intellect should be our guide, with the result that our minds have advanced little into supraconsciousness but remain primitive as far as truly significant awareness is concerned.

Let me try to break down the barriers that religions have put in the way of the supraconscious realisation of humantruth by giving my own explanation of the meaning and purpose of life. I cannot verify it, of course, but it seems to me to provide answers that are as close to the truth as the widest correlation of reason can approach. And I think it probable that a vague sense of these answers lies behind the actual false constructions that religions have put upon them.

Universal history, as far as I can imagine it, is a series of 'Big Bangs' each followed by a progressively further advanced but not completed evolution that ended in implosion. Our present Big Bang occurred when all energy, suspended in momentary balance between implosion to the point of disappearance and explosion into a renewed universe, was triggered to 'explode'. It can well be imagined that the gigantic forces involved, at that perfectly balanced moment of choice, were propelled into forward or positive movement by 'quantum bias' - the decision of just one infinitesimal micro-particle to go left rather than right, and that this tiny decision could be prompted by a force of extreme weakness compared with the tremendous energies it released. This weak force is the influence of and for truth, which at the point of decision re-created the positive influence of energy-expression as the intended vehicle of the realisation of truth. Herein lies the key to the universe, and to the meaning and purpose of human life.

It seems probable that in between the repetitive Big Bangs each universe more or less repeats the evolutionary sequences of the last. The genetic influence left behind by previous life-forms enables roughly the same forms progressively to develop once more. In new universes matter is re-created that contains pictures from the past, like the frost formations detectable in water, (even boiling water); a sequence of patterns to be repeated and extended by evolution. So in this present universal cycle these patterns, through influences such as genes, have helped to trigger the re-birth of all those life-forms, from crystals upwards, that the influence for truth, in its constant quest for its perfect realisation, caused to be newly developed in past universal cycles, goes on causing in the present and shall continue to cause in the future until its objective is secured. This objective will finally be achieved if and when such advances can reach fulfilment, throughout a universe (which will be the final universe, to be perfected, not replaced), before energy can again decline in positive vitality in order to begin sinking negatively into death, represented by contraction ending in implosion.

So the true influence presses for significant advances to be made towards realisation of truth whilst the universe is still positively living. The energy influence responds by making changes - mutations that appear to be experiments aimed at improving chances of survival. But it is clear that progress, seen as constant improvement of survival techniques that enable each species to keep abreast or go ahead of the competition, is only necessary as long as its competitors are also progressing. It has been pointed out already (Chapter 5) that the food chain, in which a sequence of creatures live by consuming each other, seems pointless. The hover fly is a precisely evolved, amazingly intricate creature, with two pairs of wings on swivel joints beating opposite ways at 175 beats per second. Many such creatures survive only briefly before they are *eaten,* so they increase their numbers to ensure that some survive, and they continually evolve better defence strategies that would improve their prospects were not their enemies also continually developing better means of attack. Overall survival, and the optimum expression of life force energy, would be equally well served by a general drastic reduction in the numbers of all species (for dead creatures do not express energy) and a complete halt to all progress (for escalating competition cancels itself out). This argument can be carried much further, but I think the following conclusions are inescapable: that the process is too inexorable to be without prior purpose; that another objective, more significant than mere survival of species, is suggested by the ever-increasing complexity of species.

As life-forms become more complex they require more elaborate intelligence. The life-force impulse to progress, which makes creatures ever more complex, evolves super-predators at the ends of the food chains, some with consequently highly developed brains; lions, elephants, dolphins, chimpanzees, and humans. Now we see once more the objective of the true influence which underlies that of life-force - to have living intelligence rise above consciousness to the level of intellect and therefore become supraconscious. That objective has been partially achieved with the evolution of the human species. It remains to be wholly achieved when we realise our supraconscious potential.

Let me put this another way. Life that includes death, especially death by continual mass murder, can not of itself be the fulfilment of a genuine purpose - neither for the worm nor for humans who contrive their own artificial reality and separated objectives. Its only achievement that indicates a purpose is the evolution of intellect. Since the only possible fulfilment of intellect is by way of realising truth, the purpose of human life, and the ultimate purpose of all life on Earth, must be to realise truth. Since life, and especially intellectual life, is obviously and without doubt the supreme achievement of the universe, it can be deduced that realisation of truth is also the purpose or objective of the universe.

The evolution of life has been achieved by the life-force continually impelling the expression of energy, but by processes that constantly leave open tiny opportunities for change by way of quantum mechanics and biological bifurcation which, when aggregated, are capable of producing circumstances that could lead to total change. Whilst realisation of truth is ultimately the only means of achieving total change, the whole living process must first not only engineer the creation of intellect but must also give protection to the evolution process by maintaining a sympathetic environment. To carry out these functions also requires a kind of intelligence but it would seem to be very different from the intelligence of the human brain.

For instance Gaia, which I have mentioned already, seems to be an intelligence impossibly operating without mental processes. However, is this so different from the evolution of the stick insect which I have also mentioned, and are not these two reactions employing the same principles as apply to the working of the brain? The brain triggers a certain activity as the result of selecting, from a whole series of possible activities, that decision which has accumulated the greatest signal strength, i.e. the decision that is most appropriate to the whole knowledge and reasoning of the brain in the circumstances. This is basically a matter of the strongest of a range of small influences of choice towards a particular large and energetic action. In the normal animal case it is a relationship between cortical neurones and physical muscles by way of nerves.

In the case of the evolution of the stick insect this translation of sensed need into effective action was accomplished by a means of transferring genetic influence that I presume is as yet unknown to us. In the case of the formation of the first eye, I have suggested that a similar transfer took place between the desire and vital need to see and the irresistible determination of cells to experiment until they had constructed the functions of sight. In the case of Gaia the vital wish of all life to go on living somehow persuades the mechanisms of the entire planet faithfully to maintain the conditions desired and required. The involuntary mechanisms of the animal or human body similarly co-operate in the best interests of the overall conscious will to go on living, and the unknown means of communication between systems, that have no connection detectable to us, may be paralleled by the potency of homoeopathic medicines in which less than a molecule of the original active element remains.

In the same sense that we are for the benefit of the living cells in our body, Gaia is for our benefit. In the sense that the cells of our body sustain us, we sustain Gaia. In due course the universe, and all the planets that bear intellectually aware life-forms, shall mutually sustain a similar relationship, and may already do so. The explanation of Gaia as an intelligence corresponds to intelligent life's will to continue causing the continuation of life. This will is exercised on sub-atomic micro-particles and biological systems at bifurcation point so that they pursue life rather than death. The total will of the living is translated into Gaia's will to maintain a physical framework of life which it exercises on the ocean beds and the atmosphere in order to turn them towards one activity rather than another. Why not? Is it to be expected that the will of living creatures has none but local effect and does not combine in this powerfully effective way? And why should Gaia support life on Earth? Surely for a better reason than to perpetuate the wasteful, meaningless cycle of life and death, creation and destruction. Life, from each single cell serving the individual to Gaia serving Earth; from the crude and blind expression of energy, that does not mind what direction it takes as long as it advances, to intelligent effort dedicated to finding the right direction - life in all these forms exists for the supreme purpose of realising truth in the universe.

It seems to me that Gaia works in this way. The constitution of the atmosphere, the temperature, the consistency of seawater, the distribution of needed elements and the dissipation of poisonous elements - they all need to be kept within certain limits if life on Earth is to survive. Unless every one of these conditions is maintained, much, most or all life shall perish. All inanimate matter and the systems in which it is involved are subject to micro-particle physics. All life is endowed with intense feeling. Suppose there were a steep rise in temperature. All life, geared to a lower norm, would suffer acute discomfort and a worldwide distress signal would be put out. This signal would affect *all* micro-particles and the systems of which they are part, on and around Earth. At the moment of hairs-breadth quantum decision, enough particles would respond, by changing their accustomed bias of movement from left to right for instance, or vice versa, sufficient to change systems-procedures and their effects on life. Then would follow a series of trials and errors in which all possible changes and combinations of change were tried and judged according to the most minute collective emotional responses of Earth's life. By this natural process of elimination the cause of distress, over-heating, would eventually be discovered, also the appropriate reaction - a change in constitution of the upper atmosphere so that it gradually increased in effectiveness as a shield against the sun's rays to the point where life's distress was fully relieved.

Bearing in mind this power of living will, as demonstrated by Gaia, and that a similar process regulates the balance of nature by making a place in the competitive ring for every species determined to live, why has the human race become dominant? It is easy to see why we hold the whip hand now, but there were thousands of years when we were very vulnerable. Why did we progress, rather than take a permanent place in the balance of nature as did the bushmen? When we began overrunning the world, why did not the distress of the rest of nature gather into forceful opposition to our progress and make us toe the natural line? On those occasions when we have stepped out of line and become vulnerable to threatening diseases, why have we been able to heal ourselves? Why has nature given way to us so easily? Why have horses, dogs, cattle and other animals become domesticated? Why are complex and idiotic Western ways accepted everywhere as superior to many of the more sensibly practical primitive ways? Why has nuclear war not occurred, when enough competitive aggression and many possibilities of accident exist to make it seem a certainty? Many causes and reasons for these things could be put forward, but I think the main underlying reason is that just as the oxygen-producing amoeba prevailed over all other methane-adjusted life because oxygen is essential for the development of thinking animals, so we are similarly given preference by the true influence because we and our otherwise idiotic ways nevertheless represent increasing exercise of intellect and therefore advance in potential towards realisation of truth.

But why the realisation of truth? Because this realisation, achieved on this and many other planets, may so strengthen the true influence as to physically transform the universe. This transformation is the aim of universal activity and will be attained in the same way that Gaia, by the influence of living will, maintains a kindly biosphere on Earth. That aim is to bring energy and truth into mutual, gentle, tranquil, universal *true equilibrium*.

As truth is increasingly realised, the influence of life-force to express energy will decrease. The early effect will be that intellectual life on Earth, and on all similar planets, will depend less and less on the physical laws and automatic lores. Autoprogression will cease and life will slow down to a state of peaceful cooperation that will greatly strengthen the universal influence of truth. We shall remain dependent on life-force, but decreasingly, as active living is slowly transmuted into awareness of truth. When we and all other forms of life are gone, the physical laws will give ground to true influence. Turbulent chemicals will tend towards stable harmony and balance rather than reaction. Eventually energy will break down into its simplest basic elements without feeling impelled to implode. Mathematics will reduce to the equation $1 \times 1 =$

1. Truth and energy will then come to co-exist in the optimum state of slight, gentle and unchanging oscillation in perfect universal concord, which is true equilibrium.

This is the ultimately true state of energy - to achieve which is the sole purpose of temporary violent activity. Truth is the sum of all history, all actuality and possibility, whose only purpose in inciting energy was also the attainment of this optimum state. Otherwise truth does not need to be expressed in form, or word, or thought in order to be true, nor does it require the continued existence of intellects capable of understanding it, for it simply *is* the veritruth. Therefore the ultimate, optimum universe in true equilibrium is the perfect state of all material things in harmony, for in tranquil energy is the potential for all possible physical matter, and its positive or negative movement. Energy will thus achieve its sole objective and so assume its simplest state - that of irreducible fundamental particles vibrating to the balanced minimum. The ultimate universe will also be optimum truth vibrating in perfect harmony with itself and with energy. This veritruth is total awareness of all explosive and implosive, constructive and destructive, possibilities of matter, a record of all knowledge and utter understanding of all reason, which then has no possible cause for, or need of, further doing, knowing or reasoning. It is this influence of truth at its strongest that keeps energy, at its weakest, to its lowest possible level of activity. It does not signify that we humans and others like us may never know veritruth, for our optimum satisfaction lies in supraconsciousness of humantruth.

Of course, if the true influence fails to transform a universe before it turns from expansion to contraction, there will be another big bang and a repeat evolution of life. To we who are reasoning animate creatures the idea of true equilibrium may be repugnant, for our nature has been formed in a contrary way by our history of explosive evolution. But imagine it as the balanced perfection of the stillness which those who meditate (in the wrong era and for the wrong reasons) try to achieve. It would be the essence of being, without need of thinking as we practice it by the utilisation of knowledge for the manipulation of reason, without need of ambition to attain or obtain anything, and admittedly without the excitement that goes with it, but also without the pressures of life, the tragedy of death, and the struggle for temporary personal balance. It would be tranquillity of extreme simplicity rather than our present opposite extremes of continual autoprogression into rising complexity. This comparison is ultimately irrelevant since such as we, though we achieve *our* optimum state of supraconsciousness, shall always be bound to physical matter and can never, as our biological selves, experience true equilibrium. But it may help to counter the majority's preference for the devil they know, even though it is propelling them to hell, and to reinforce the truism that the nearer we can bring our society to that perfect state of truth the happier we shall be.

The foregoing explanation of the meaning and purpose of life can be compared with religious explanations in this way - as a comparison between the truth and misrepresentations of the truth which consciousness, unwilling to learn from its higher mind, deceives itself into believing by way of imperfect and incomplete reason. The fundamental influence of truth is misrepresented by religion as some divine power, or god; true equilibrium as heaven, and implosion as the descent to hell. The concept of reincarnation comes from the sensed knowledge of previously repeated, and possibly yet to be repeated, big bangs allied to a desire for immortality. Universality, or cosmic consciousness, is veritruth which the universe, under the influence of truth reinforced by living intellect, will eventually come to terms with. Prayer, the imagined relationship between an individual and a mysterious god, is really the dominant consciousness importuning the misused and misunderstood postconscious. The human concept of good and evil comes from our awareness of a morality that arises from intellect, struggling with our opposing loyalty and subservience to the amoral automaton. Our current theory that we may not know humantruth because that is the province of an inscrutable god, or ethereal consciousness, derives from our failure yet to become the fulfilment of our own minds, and our disinclination to make the effort.

In this existing reality we are overshooting the mark of true intellectual progress by extending knowledge but neglecting reason. We are employing intellect automatically to explore things, not only to serve the money economy nor simply for the satisfaction of instinctive curiosity, but also because, in our ignorance, we are attracted by the challenge of the unknown merely for its novelty, and impressed by the mystery of the unknowable. We do not rely on thoroughly reasoned deduction but take the view that whilst much actual knowledge lies beyond our grasp, and whilst unproven human concepts such as gods can not be disproved, we may not attain to true overall understanding. Yet we accept the evident facts of our existing reality, and all parallel proven scientific fact, even though we also accept that in another era, such as when the universe implodes, these facts will no longer apply. We have identified ourselves with a process of building fact upon present temporarily true fact, just as the automatically expanding universe and Earth-nature have done, applying our intellect to further pursuit of this meaningless process, failing to grasp that we are now the *agents* of *whole truth*, not just limited local truth. I have pointed out already that when mysteries are uncovered the truth then revealed is always matter-of-fact and that facts are not truth, only part of it - knowledge, the essential counterpart of which is reason. In the pursuit of truth pure completion of reason results in simplification of fact. The task of human and every other intellect is to perfect reason in order to rise above or dismiss facts as far as practicable, and realise truth as far as is possible for planet-bound creatures.

Our supreme purpose is the realisation of truth. This must rule out all lesser faiths and ideologies and displace all other loyalties. It is vital to remember that we humans are not an end in ourselves but the means to an end. That end is truth and the means its observance in all things. This is of great importance to us, for we are presently so preoccupied with superficial interests as to be ignorant of our overall responsibilities. Unless we strive with our intellect towards fulfilment of truth we shall fail both the higher potential of our minds and the responsibility for the survival of our species, for all other influences and activities are false.

You might reject my uncorroborated explanation of the meaning and purpose of life. But I can conceive of no other reason for the achievement of intellect except chance, and does it look as if it occurred by chance? Surely not, nor that it occurred purely to enhance survival. If the sole object of life were the optimum expression of energy would not the apefolk, prospering alongside the rest of nature, achieve that object at least as well as a human species that is rising whilst the rest of nature declines? For me there is no question but that the creation of our intellect has put Earth at risk, and little doubt of the reason - that whilst our security and satisfaction is part of universal fulfilment and both depend upon living intellect fulfilling its potential, we have not yet achieved that potential.

This brings me to the essential aim of this book - to point out that just as we are capable of comprehending, by true reason, that the meaningful purpose of the universe lies outside its present physical processes, so the meaning and purpose of human life is not expressed by our present reality but will be expressed by an alternative reality that brings ourselves and our world to a state of stable and peaceful cooperation. If you do reject my explanation, and even if you ignore the universe and consider only the rights and wrongs of human world society relative to our optimum wellbeing, I think it remains self-evident that intellectual supraconscious fulfilment is the only road to humantruth and guide to happiness.

The seventh meaning of truth (see Chapter 13) gives it as the source of right, honest and good morality (a sense of which might be conceived as god) on which our true state of being shall be founded. Let me explain how this can be. Let us represent amorality as chemical reactions between substances which, when they come together in certain conditions, cannot react but in certain ways prescribed by their relative properties, with no other possibility allowed or remotely envisaged. In life, these prescribed properties are represented by the instinct, which similarly binds creatures to certain ways of behaving. A distinction is made between good and bad moral behaviour with the advent of intellect. A limited measure of good morality may be represented by the influence of Gaia, which re-arranges or controls otherwise automatic reactions in such a way as to benefit rather than inhibit the evolution of life. In the human race, as far as it has developed, the advent of intellect has produced a state of mixed morality. Whilst we suppose ourselves to aspire to good morality - caring, constructive, co-operative, peaceable and loving activity - our affairs are dominated or underwritten by immorality - competitive, dishonest, hostile, aggressive activity. Optimum good morality is true equilibrium, a state not possible of achievement by the most advanced, intellectual, life-forms because of their physical restrictions. Earth humans can achieve a state of supraconsciousness, of wholly good moral intention founded on a humantrue social structure. But even then we shall be well aware of a compulsion to practice a measure of 'bad' morality for the sake of sheer survival (e.g. the killing of plants and some animals for vital food, and of harmful competitors - vermin, pests, parasites and bacteria), but to the minimum, and with regret that it is unavoidably necessary - with the concerned restraint that supraconsciousness enables and obliges us to exercise.

The significance of all this is that it reveals the seventh meaning of truth (the source of our moral goodness), that truth is perfect harmonious concord (which we may not wholly achieve), made up of parts and principles (many of which contribute to that state of caring compassion, without any avoidable dispute, disturbance or disruption, that we *may* attain to - humantruth) which are absolutely beyond the reproach of supraconscious intellect.

Chapter 33

RELIGIONS AGAINST REASON

My aim has been to try to discover and reveal the truth about all things by process of pure reason - an abnormal process but one that anybody with a normal knowledge of the world can carry out. I hesitated whether or not to miss this chapter out, for according to my own convictions all religions are false, therefore might they not be ignored? But they so powerfully exist that nobody escapes their influence. So this chapter is included, because religious faiths are rivals of pure reason that have hindered or prevented intellation for centuries and it is necessary to counter their practiced but fallacious counter-arguments.

Religions against reason are examples of our conditioning, or our habit of adopting specific limited constructions of mind that then limit our thinking. False faiths are their own justification for individuals upholding the various thought constructions that uphold blind faith. They may differ only in their interpretations of the same thing, but it is the wrong thing. They illustrate the way we use or consciously dictate to our minds, pretending to enlighten but only confusing and darkening our understanding. Religions need to be held up to question because they are ways of escape from human responsibility in a world that desperately needs radical change. There is no virtue in allowing that this or that person holds this or that recognised belief when the vital need is that *all* should equally truly understand.

Conflicting religions are, of course, part and parcel of our competitive reality, akin to opposed political dogmas, and are mostly contained by automatic institutions. In a reality that does not make sense, all must be tolerated but none must be true. In a debate in the British House of Lords, on the

government's proposal that instruction in all the established religions should
be included in the general school curriculum, one member persisted in
questioning the truth of god-religions as the basis of his opposition to the
proposal. In this he was perfectly justified, for truth is the all-important
consideration. But this member was not permitted to continue speaking, on
the petition of a majority of members who objected to him 'rubbishing their
cherished beliefs'. Beliefs should not be cherished unless absolutely true. If
false, then the faithful are hiding behind make-believe and making truth
taboo. If undoubtedly true, they should be able satisfactorily to answer all
critical questioning. This is a delicate matter because we confuse truth with
freedom - the freedom to believe what we wish. But, as I have pointed out
already, our true freedom is not to 'do our own thing' but to undertake the
fulfilment of our intellects, which means commonly to attain to and agree to
one and the same humantruth.

Each mind should be its own guardian of truth. It should intellate, accepting
nothing without good and true reason. This should not be a process of
building on that which has gone before without question. We have to probe
our preconceptions and remove those that are false. To such a mind the
questions 'does god exist' and 'is the Catholic faith true' are not admissible
because they refer to preconceptions which, whether you believe them or not,
humanity has accepted without good and true reason. A mind that had never
been introduced to these concepts would find the questions meaningless and
could not ask them. A mind with Catholic conditioning would undertake to
answer both questions in the affirmative, with conviction and without
willingness to question this, its own faith, because of the rigid way it had been
conditioned.

A problem is that each evolving individual human is presented with one or
more ready-made concepts of god. Whether we believe or disbelieve, the idea
of god is then lodged in the mind where it has no business to be, because it
is not only unproved but also far-fetched. The young individual might adopt
a faith unthinkingly, when not yet in a position to decide whether to believe
or disbelieve. And what must be the effect, at the backs of children's minds,
of adults who hold to different faiths, all claiming that only one, their own, is
true? A chief virtue claimed by any such faith lies in its being held with an
indomitable strength of conviction; consequently, once it is taken up it is
rarely given up or doubted by the faithful. The individuals who choose to
disbelieve, wishing to be certain that their view is true and then to have their
reasoning prevail over that of the faithful, might spend a lifetime trying to
disentangle and prove false the mountain of heavy complex argument that
religions have built up on a light foundation of mere assumption. In a society
in which almost nobody intellates there are large bypassed voids of
unexplored reason, or mystery, and these we allow various forms of religion

to fill with substitutes for true reason, from full blown faiths to the vaguest of superstitions.

The best way for intellect to determine the significant meaning and purpose of life would be to start with no knowledge at all of religious preconceptions. If religions have no foundation in truth they will not suggest themselves to the intellating mind. The last thing to do is to study them, for theology compounded on a false foundation leads away from and not towards truth, and what true light it throws only confuses because it does not penetrate most of the darkness. But it is clear that religions cannot be ignored, though they deserve to be dismissed. Since they are not proven, and are very doubtful and questionable, our honest course is to disbelieve them, and change to belief only if and when every pure path of reason suggests, if not proves, their truth.

It seems to me dishonest and foolish to believe in a religion when none is supportable by utterly true conviction. It is even more so to inculcate such unfounded beliefs into the evolving minds of children, for this stunts their true growth. If we are to shoulder our full human responsibility we must, from early childhood, seek and adopt that which is undeniably true, reject that which is clearly untrue, and honestly and persistently investigate that which is doubtful. By adopting false faiths we twist the truth and then must contrive to believe nonsense in order to uphold that faith.

I return to my previous contention that we have no right to ill-considered and wilful opinions and beliefs but a responsibility to ensure that our mental constructions are wholly true. This means that we do not consciously make up our minds but supraconsciously allow that they make themselves up; we do not arrive at any belief until fully convinced of its truth. This requires that in the interests of humantruth all preconceived religions are rounded up in the mind, encircled by reason subject to the postconscious, fully examined and dismissed, because, like the false concept of reality of which they are part, they contaminate the purity of truth and thus cripple the intellect.

The truth, or humantruth, should be made absolutely clear, for intellects cannot live in harmony except by the truth. If you hesitate to reject religions because of the good they do, you should recognise that this is partial good, counterbalanced by much that is bad. We shall not attain to humantrue society unless guided by that which is wholly good and true.

To refuse to recognise god is not to disbelieve, when there is no deity to believe in. It is simply to keep the mind open to unshakeable reason. It is not humantruly acceptable that we persist in global disagreement. To my own certain belief, religious convictions are aberrations of reason that stand in the way of agreement. Agreed truth is more important to us than keeping an iron grip on any faith. By putting aside religion and opening our consciousness to our higher reason we shall lose nothing, for if that religion is fundamentally true its truth shall be unerringly and persistently indicated. But if we keep our minds open only to one faith and closed to whole reason we shall never know the truth.

It is our supraconsciousness that shall acknowledge what is wholly good and true. The supraconscious mind, seeing religions as contrivances of an automated civilisation, does so from the position of a single high intellectual faculty looking out from a point on Earth at a universe whose actual and possible totality is veritruth, but which is not of itself intellectually endowed. The universe represents no higher faculty, contains no capability of recognising truth, other than the supraconscious intellect of living brains - no greater meaning, potential wisdom, truer morality or deeper compassion. We, and similar creatures elsewhere, are the lone trustees of truth.

Humanity - that is to say every single human being expressed collectively - desires happiness, or fulfilment, with an underlying peace and secure contentment. We know that this desire is not granted by our existing reality. We also know that it is regarded as our duty to achieve optimum human happiness and we try to achieve it as best we can, as far as the limitations of our automatic circumstances allow. But there is no *human* reason why we should not achieve optimum happiness. Not a muscle may be moved without a signal from somewhere; humans do not act excepting with the approval, by the intention, or through the acquiescence of their personal constructions of mind. Clearly, since in general we are acting wrongly, most of the signals we permit ourselves to act on are coming from the wrong source. We turn to religions, which pretend to good morality, but that is not the main signal-source, for we do not behave accordingly. Religions are largely moral reactors to amoral reality rather than correctors of it, which, in order to keep up their pretence, find they have to resort to mystery.

It is our automatic reality that gives these main signals that we obey. Yet, I repeat, the Machine is nothing without our active support and we are not truly represented by it, nor by religions, but by our intellect. By intellating, and so rising to supraconsciousness, we may give our society a humantrue constitution whose signals, on which we then act, come from the best in us so that we achieve that optimum happiness. But we have yet collectively to take the first steps in this necessary direction.

Why do we resort to make-believe rather than take these first steps? Because humantruth can be understood and realised *only* by supraconsciousness, a state of which we fall far short. We do not see the world as something that it is within our power, and is our collective mandate, to put right. Living in a seemingly inevitable reality that is a competitive conflict between extremes, we see ourselves and our world in terms of these contrasting extremes - of good and evil, love and hate, kindness and cruelty, right and wrong, weakness and strength, losing and winning, poverty and wealth, misery and satisfaction.

Once reality is comprehended in this way it is difficult to envisage the possibility of actually changing to a different, humantrue alternative, though that is what we innately desire. So we take the easy course of accepting this unjust and dangerous reality. We reject the difficult task of envisaging a benign and harmonious alternative in favour of a device of the imagination. This device is chosen to counterbalance the Machine by expressing our humantrue desires in an abstract way. The device, religion, can allow escape into fantasy and shows a preference for things imaginable that do not have to be explained by reason or proved in fact. We are attracted by religions whose power lies not in their truth but in their mystery - in the fact that the core of truth attributed to them is never revealed; indeed *cannot* be revealed because it is supposed to be a mystery so profound as to be beyond our understanding. We are not likely to be attracted in the same way to supraconsciousness because that transfers the hard responsibility for realising truth to ourselves.

So we adopt religious faiths, disciplines, and modes of thought in order to answer, counteract or cope with a reality that we believe to be unavoidable, if only because we think there is little human will for humantrue reform and no real chance of overcoming the Machine. Such faith, beginning as a device of the imagination contrary to intellect, goes full circle in its denial of reason; for example when it suggests that Galileo, when his findings were eventually accepted having first been condemned as profane, could never have accomplished his great revelations without divine intuition. In this way independent reason, if not discouraged, can be condemned as immodest if it contradicts the normal tendency to believe in divine wisdom. Because of the fact that we invented religions they view us as we view ourselves, with a mixture of realism and mystery, as automated individuals but also as unique spiritual selves to whom life is a personal experience. Therefore we indulge in imperfect, incomplete and impure reasoning, as is appropriate to our insane automatic reality, helped and redeemed, we fondly imagine, by divine powers and knowing spirits that do not actually exist.

It is instinctive to submit to the domination of superior all-round strength; to something greater and more powerful than we. So it is easy to understand why primitive humans might fear the sun. Yet it would be their dawning power of reason, investing the sun with characteristics of the most-feared animals, or the strongest and most wise of their own tribe, that gave humans to worship it and make sacrifices to persuade it to continue rising and giving them the daily warmth of its rays. But as reason advanced the realisation came that the rising and setting of the sun, the phases of the moon and tide, the coming and going of the seasons, were of all things most predictably certain. It is just such practical reasoning on the physical level, harnessed from its beginnings to the developing Machine founded long before and thereby given impetus, that has continued on its straightforward and almost uninterrupted way right up to the present, when physicists and mathematicians say they are within an ace of explaining everything physical. We have never had difficulty in making 2x2=4 because, in the field of mathematics, rather than be swayed by instinct we have listened attentively to that of our reasoning-power which is available to conscious direction for application in this field, and have accepted its proven results.

But from the beginning the broadest conscious thinking, not narrowed in this specialised way, was unable to find a satisfactory explanation for life as it was, nor to perceive an all-embracing meaning, nor to discern a worthy future purpose to strive for. Our continuing failure to apprehend truth in our worldly affairs is equivalent to making 2x2 amount to 3, or 5. We, the forerunners of modern mankind, originally failed because we were already automated, and the main thrust of our existence was the pursuit of automatic targets by the utilisation of our automatic powers. From the very first we began manipulating reason so as to adapt it to developing reality - to make sense of the senseless. We tried to adopt, with a will, the restricted meaning and purpose of the automaton - autoprogression for material gain - each limiting and adapting it to a suitable personal reality. It was this application of reason to competitive conflict, rather than allowing reason to take its own pure course, that necessitated the human habitual practice of lying and deceiving. But the postconscious mind could not be so easily silenced, or obliged to put up with the resultant circumstances. Moral intuition, or conscience, could not condone the injustices and inhumanities of our way of life and caused us to institute laws and punishments. The result, with its inequalities and cruelties of all kinds, was still unacceptable to that morality which intellect prompts us to follow and which we intuitively sense, even without fully understanding, however we may try to deny it. A further mental manipulation was required to enable us to follow, with a relatively clear conscience, wherever autoprogression should lead. We needed religions, which first gave compelling causes why we must maintain the status quo; then, why we must mend our personal ways despite the public Machine; and then, why we should empty our minds and rely on 'enlightenment' from elsewhere somehow to put it all to rights.

The main line of advancing human civilisation has been human service to the automaton according to its lores. The accompaniment of this autoprogression has been an oscillation between obeying or breaking Machine-laws and observing or ignoring moral laws, (according to our individual position relative to others), the pressures of survival or ambition, the degree to which we have succumbed to good or bad instinctive feeling, and the extent to which we have followed our own reason contrary to the false norm and towards humantruth. So far the false conditioning of automatic domination has generally prevailed over our intellectual potential. Our only achievement of honest reasoning, in mathematics and physics, has not escaped confinement to the conscious sphere and has either been applied to abstractions within its own limited field or applied to automatic technology. Its utter regard for honest and accurate correlation has not overspilled into other fields in the conscious sphere such as politics or economics or general reasoning, let alone expand itself into pure supraconscious reasoning, as it should. This is partly because mathematics and physics are exact sciences whose hypotheses can be proven by experiment and whose area of operation, the conscious sphere, is the sphere in which we and our automatic reality presently have our existence. Other reasons why the scientific method has not entered into our highest reasoning are that science as it stands is an essential tool of autoprogression whereas pure and true reasoning would be useless or dangerous to the Machine, and that postconscious thinking is independent and cannot be proven by experiment, evidence or conscious argument, only by itself. Our efforts, either to correct human failure to become entirely subservient to the automatic ethos and law, or to mount a human counter-attack against the Machine, have so far been confined, mostly and ineffectively, to ill-considered ideologies and religions in the conscious sphere. Thus, in our general affairs, we have by-passed pure reason which would have led us to true understanding, and left ourselves suspended between false thought and action on the one hand and contrived thought and reaction on the other.

In ancient China the Machine was well established on the automatic principle of a dominant, powerful and privileged leader exerting authority, down through a hierarchical class system, over a huge underprivileged majority. In a bid to overcome undue tyranny and injustice on the part of the privileged and resentment bordering revolt on the part of the underdogs, Confucius tried to introduce an ideology whose fundamental principle was total acceptance of lawful authority and tolerance and willing support of the status quo. Everyone, from emperor to common road sweeper, was to respect the person and function of all others and to properly and meticulously perform his or her own function, both receiving and giving obedient service willingly, politely, and with good grace. Confucius intended that the morals and rules that people recognised and believed in should also be strictly lived by. It did not work because this was an automatic society with built-in inequality that was upheld by the privileged because it logically worked to their advantage and could not prevent them furthering their privileges whilst still exacting obedience from the underprivileged who must continue to endure uncomplainingly. It did not work because people are not fundamentally very different from each other - their differences result from variations in treatment past and present - and as they grow in awareness they come to demand reform, underlying which is a call for equality, to which authority must respond if revolution is to be avoided.

Confucianism aimed to have all people accept the whole of their society as good by intertwining civil law with the moral code - with tradition, custom, and habitual thinking - making a continuously cohesive, self-supporting society. The religion of Islam is a similar but more equable blend of civil and moral law that is still practiced widely in the less automatically advanced countries of the East. In the West, however, autoprogression has raised monetary economic materialism way above morality, forming a gulf between the practical establishment and human ideals that politics is occasionally allowed to bridge in a tentative, shaky fashion. Modern worldly reality is represented by the Western city, which has no place for the supraconscious mind. So until recently religious observance, the nearest thing that any institution of the established Machine has got to supraconsciousness, was given space on Sunday when shops, factories and offices were closed and churches opened. Nowadays Sundays are becoming ever more like Saturdays, given over to commercially oriented relaxation and pleasure.

Confucius was a member of the establishment of his day. Jesus of Nazareth was an intellectual rebel, or the equivalent of the present-day dropout. When he founded his religion he faced a situation in which authority and humanity had grown violently apart. Roman rule was intellectual application to the instinctive principles of dominant power, the competitive drives, and disciplines of the pecking order. It was enforced, but Romans submitted to it willingly enough whilst it was progressively and gloriously successful, and whilst it provided improved standards of material reward and crude emotional satisfaction to the majority. Human awareness, even that of the best minds of the time, was limited by ignorance of its own true nature and of the true nature of the automaton and the extent to which the former was being, and was yet more to be, denied by impositions and attractions of the latter. People possessed goodness but this was more and more being supplanted by worldly wisdom. Human reason had not advanced independently and broadly so as to withstand autoprogression. Most minds were little stimulated to reason much at all so that lores automatically imposed, and laws and loyalties imposed by executive authority, carried much more weight than private inner morality.

So Jesus was faced with strict Roman law, a conditioned, biased and subject people, an intolerant temple and a hostile money economy - an establishment not much different from that facing radical thinkers today. But the fact that he was tortured to death on a wooden crosspiece suggests that his message was near enough to the truth as to be dangerous to the establishment. That it seems to have been half a century or more before publication of an account of Christianity was permitted suggests that it took that long for the dangerous initial impact of the innately undeniable truth of Jesus' essential message to subside and be obscured. It is impossible to be certain of his true thoughts but he must have realised that the people, in order to follow him, needed some more powerful emotional cause for accepting his message than the good moral arguments of true reason alone. He could not know that in general the cause was to be accepted but the essential message largely ignored. Did he himself really believe in god, and in himself as the son of god, in any other sense than as the messenger of truth (as far as he knew it)? Or was it that others made him the fulfilment of ancient prophecy and he accepted it as the means to what he foresaw as a great and good end, a means which, though eventually proved false, would be justified if that true end were achieved? Or was he a mystic, a believer in cosmic consciousness as the source of true enlightenment, whose personal charisma was the powerful emotional cause why the truth of his message at first caught on and spread, whose miracle-working and personal magnetism were handed down as remembered figureheads of a body of belief which became distorted in the handing down?

In considering Jesus it is necessary to separate him, as possibly the most nearly humantrue of thinkers, from the Christian church that followed, an automatic institution unworthy of him whose morals have been adjusted to the practices of the Machine. Gnostic testaments, the latest discovered in 1945, suggest to me that his actual philosophy opposed and exposed Roman law, the established temple, and the money economy, which was why it was suppressed by authority and only allowed to emerge, much modified, some fifty years after his death; that the book on which this modified version was founded was a censored, elaborated and romanticised account of Jesus' life and times that made Christianity acceptable to the then Machine in Rome and to much of the world since. Such is the anti-human effect of automatic authority.

Whether or not Jesus' original message was true, the significance of humantruth to human life lies in its being totally understood, observed and applied, whereas that which Christianity has passed down is a combination of outright untruth and adulterated half-truths that have managed to survive the similarly false amoral pressures of world reality because designed to do so. If Jesus' concept was the pursuit of truth it was converted into good automatic behaviour, obedience to the Machine (like Confucianism), for the sake of a very different concept - that of god as another but all-powerful emperor in the sky, armed with added strong persuasions; the gift of heaven or curse of hell after death. That the Christian institution has lasted so long is because it has salved the human conscience by giving our amoral and immoral civilisation a cloak of righteousness. It has blessed our wars and forgiven our inhumanities so that as long as we believe in it we can believe ourselves good whatever we do. But as human awareness has grown Christian belief has declined, partly because its theory of god has no satisfactorily evident foundation, partly because of its two-faced institution, partly because it has failed to change the world significantly for the better, but mostly because it has neither represented nor sought after good and true morality nor aimed to put this above all else.

It seems to me that whilst Jesus may have seen the road to truth, and perhaps some of his immediate and courageous followers also, the sincere and well-meaning members of the eventually established Christian church did not. They made the mistake, not surprisingly in the circumstances, of thinking that the Machine itself was neutral, life's inevitable systematic arrangement which could be turned to good or bad means and ends according to the morals of the people of all stations, high and low - a necessary mechanism which at that time was brutalised but could be humanised by men with love in their hearts. They did not recognise the automaton as a self-acting mechanism, intent on material progress but indifferent to true human well-being through moral fulfilment, which simply utilised human energy, both that motivated by love and hate. As it stood, and still stands, the Machine could never be prevailed upon by human love alone, for contrary emotions and calculations have strong vested interests. Expecting love to prevail is like expecting a man without eyes to see. A good social structure is as essential a part of our good human morality as our bodies are essential to life. The Machine calls for the use of our minds in its service, with the aid of instinct and with survival at stake. Morality cannot really get a look in. It is not sufficient that we may be, or feel, moral - the whole structure and working system of our world has to be humantruly moral also. As I have said, we are sitting on the fence, with the Machine before us engaging most attention, and the still small voice of conscience behind us, perhaps represented by religion, the two sides never actually mixing but occasionally brought to compromise by politics.

I have mentioned equality as an obviously desirable virtue that the not so obvious humantrue alternative reality must surely incorporate. As human awareness grew, society tried to edge nearer to this principle of equality, but the Machine also grew, and with it the contrary principle of competition, and converted our wish for equality into a demand for parity in the desirable consumption and accumulation of material goods. The automaton has increased its power to make us serve its interests through our self-domination by the desire to work for it in order to consume its products. Thus, though we autoprogress, we truly advance little, if at all. We remain divided, dominated, undeveloped and unfulfilled. We are to some degree aware of the fact that the automaton has learned to a nicety how to manipulate us by exploiting our weaknesses, and has infiltrated the Machine so thoroughly and made it so powerfully omnipotent that we, no longer believing in the power of a Christian god to help us, also no longer believe that *we* can prevail. This is because we do not understand who we are nor how we are dominated and conditioned.

Nevertheless religious faiths persist. Civilised human moral conscience has always examined our earthly reality and found it wanting at the same time as our consciousness has supported it out of necessity, believing it to be inevitable. We once had faith that by changing ourselves we could change reality for the better. Then we thought that by certain acts of obedience to Christian and similar creeds we scored a moral victory by remaining sitting on the fence and refusing to go over entirely to the automatic side. Now those who hold some kind of religious belief do so for the sake of personal help and comfort by the fortification of self-supportive constructions of thought and denial of contrary reason. At one extreme of the pecking order the human dictator can look at his eminence and power, and his place in history, and may fortify this self-image with the belief that he is chosen by god. At the other extreme, ordinary persons have their private beliefs, their personal gateways to god, which give them a link with the powerful energy of their own life-force and have nothing to do with intellectual truth, but which nothing can take away provided they cling tenaciously to those beliefs.

Here in the West the present tendency of the more thoughtful, who have already abandoned conventional religious faiths, is also to abandon any expectation of human reason ever making good our society (just as Eastern mystics did long ago on the grounds of a belief that it is human reason which has made society what it is) and to pin their faith to an unknown extra-terrestrial wisdom, just as Christians and others chose a mysterious god to worship. The idea is that we are incapable of enlightenment by our own intellectual striving but only by opening, through transcendental meditation and the like, to cosmic consciousness or universality. Shades of divine intuition again. It is clear that the *only* source of enlightenment is our own postconscious mind, but does it matter that we imagine it to come from outside ourselves, as long as it does come from somewhere? Certainly it matters, *because only by the process of pure intellation can reason supraconsciously reach enlightenment and know it to be true.* Transcendental meditation, however, if supposed to be an emptying of the mind, may give the self over to conscious, subconscious and instinctive awareness (as well, certainly, as the balancing influence of conscience) which may then wilfully block out the free and independent reasoning of the postconscious. Since there is *no* cosmic consciousness, the mind's remaining capacity - its supposed emptiness - can then be filled only by the permission of consciousness, subconsciousness or instinct. This lays the mind open to adulteration and dictation by wilful prejudice which, rather than be examined and rejected by true reason, gathers round it a defensive construction of contrived reason.

It is vital to examine this new religious departure, spiritual mysticism, because rather than learn from past errors we seem to be passing on to yet more make-believe. In that it does involve the wish for a better world and, despite its opposition to intellectual striving, includes a certain amount of thinking on the subject, no doubt such religion has some good effect in an otherwise automated world. But it is remarkable how many gaps and weaknesses are to be found in this kind of belief-structure, yet that it is nevertheless widespread, though usually not so much in the form of a positive faith as a negative refusal to *disbelieve* in its mysteries.

It would seem that those who believe in some form of mysticism do so out of dislike of the worst effects of existing reality, and dissatisfaction with conventional Western interpretations of it and antidotes to it. Believers are against striving with, or what they see as trammelling up the mind because they equate reasoning with ruination: we are capable of reason and our world is in ruins, therefore the former is responsible for the latter. In fact the reverse is the case - rather it is our *failure* to allow the mind to strive for true reason that has caused our downfall. Believers in mysticism confuse reason with misdirection of intellectual power and evidently fail to recognise the automaton as the driving force responsible for this misdirection. Those who turn to such belief are in turn utilising incomplete reason falsely to establish that belief, mistaking it for the very truth that is to be discovered only by complete reason. They too are dictating to their higher minds with lesser conscious will, and thus convincing the self and keeping it the prisoner of consciousness.

There is some confusion surrounding this subject and it arises from different concepts of what the mind is, how it really works, and of its place in human identity. Before going any further let me clarify this confusion, beginning with the fundamental truth that we are all individuals possessing potential intellect, and all subject to the Machine.

The self is normally viewed, in a vague and imprecise way, as being separate from and in charge of the mind. The automated human conscious self treats the mind like a personal computer, not to be respected as a true guide but to be used for survival in the Machine and to enhance automatic experience. God-religions regard this self as the spirit, subject to the influence of a divine wisdom that is much superior to the mind. Normal thinking is this wilful striving of the self with or against the mind, to impose on it and make it work for automatic ends, worthy as well as unworthy, but limited and fundamentally against its own values.

The mystics rightly object to this wilful striving *with* the mind but wrongly identify this mental manipulation as the only reasoning of which the mind is capable, whereas it is lesser *conscious* reason, far surpassed by *postconscious* reason, the human mind's optimum potential. They see the mind as a receptacle which, when opened and emptied, will receive enlightenment from a superior universal consciousness.

But we potentially *are* our highest faculty of mind. It is consciousness that should be opened, not to any external enlightenment (though its awareness may be triggered by external argument) but to that of our own postconscious which shall surely come if our conscious will encourages, helps and allows it to perform this its true function. This is real reasoning, the only way to truth - striving *by* the mind, *in* the mind, by we who potentially *are* and constantly try to *be* our minds. I can vouch for the fact that enlightenment comes in this way and surmise that others, having shared this experience in the distant past, invented the notion of a cosmic consciousness by way of explanation, especially since its conclusions often come to the conscious mind as sudden inspiration. But there is no doubt that the neocortex is the source of such enlightenment, which cannot presently be achieved without the persistent, hard, reciprocal effort of individual intellation, but which will be sustained, eventually, by humantrue reality.

The strong attraction of the practice of mysticism lies in the fact that it can convey a sense of truth without its substance. Therefore, like music, it can be invested with gentleness, beauty, and good feeling, portraying the sounds and shapes of a perfect reality without responsibly tackling the task of reforming our ugly existing reality. To accept mysticism is to take a tranquil course rather than pursue the frenetic activity required to discover and realise truth; to entrust any such discovery and realisation to the gift of some vaguely imagined mysterious spirit. This allows the believer to ignore the postconscious and its vital significance and to see being human as simply existing in consciousness which, perhaps by way of meditation, imparts elements of an incomplete enlightenment which the believer then attributes to that supposed cosmic consciousness. Otherwise, the self has simply to be itself, to follow wherever the degree of partial enlightenment thus granted to it shall guide it, and to take life as a personal experience that is not in our power or province to direct with the brain but to savour with feeling.

The profound error of mystical religion is that it rests upon belief in nonexistent cosmic consciousness. What it calls the spirit is, in fact, crude life-force plus conscious awareness, a state which humans shared with all animals but which has evolved, presently only in us on Earth, as a stepping stone to supraconsciousness, the true peak of intelligence to which evolution aspires. To suggest that cosmic consciousness already understands all truth, and has existed at least for as long as this universe's 15 billion year history, implies that evolution, and humanity's part in it, is merely a pointless game for it suggests that since enlightened intelligence already exists life's great struggle to evolve has no meaning or purpose. This religion has invented unsolved puzzles posing as enlightenment in an attempt to fill the gap between sensing truth and fulfilling it. Our lives possessed internal genetic security until intellect came along and broke the self away from the protective custody of instinct, leaving us exposed to ignorance of truth which intellect was developed to enlighten. But intellect has since failed to provide true moral security by way of that self-enlightenment.

Mystical religion may be effective as a means of rounding off the conscious self , where that is a matter of the personal internal balance wrought, in a single individual of a certain automatic conditioning and circumstance but with good moral aspirations, by way of its own self-contained intercommunication of conscious intellect and instinct which ignores the postconscious excepting for conscience. But a collection of selves that are complete according to their own differently limited moral orientation, though perfect in their own eyes according to their own terms, do not combine to make a perfect society, only a more efficient, imperfect Machine. This would become clear were the numbers of such individuals, who usually withdraw from the rough-and-tumble of the Machine, to become so large that their dependence on the Machine for survival required that they also took part in its amoral and immoral activities, to the extent that their independently contrived personal moral balance must break down.

A chief weakness of this and all religions is the fact that they spring from false assumption as to the nature of self. We all refer to ourselves as I and 'we' but what are we actually referring to? Not to supraconsciousness, identifying with the postconscious mind as the self should. We are referring to the inferior consciousness in which the human self presently remains rooted. Yet we have to refer to that superficial, personal conscious self as I - it has to be distinguished. But we do not have to allow that it makes our important decisions and determines our beliefs. On the contrary, the inferior conscious I can embody an ever-increasing awareness of the higher (independent) postconscious mind which, though not yet able itself to take over the identity of I, can subject the conscious I, and our entire automatic reality of which the inferior self is a product, to doubt, question and criticism. This is a delicate and difficult relationship to establish, but it is the one true way.

———————————

The practice of meditation seems to be inseparable from mysticism. The verb to meditate actually means 'to consider - to exercise the mental functions'. This meaning surely casts doubt on the practice by implying that meditation *is* a subtle manipulation of the higher mind by a lesser separate self and not, as is claimed, an emptying of the mind. The mental process would ideally consist of four activities - the conscious sphere working within itself; the approach of the conscious to the postconscious; the postconscious working within itself; the postconscious referring back to consciousness. The interaction of these four activities would be subject to postconscious will; that is to say that the process would be supraconscious, beginning with the independent postconscious striving to take over the being of the individual and realise humantruth. However, it is presently normal for this process to be dominated by conscious will so as to be restricted to two activities; the postconscious voluntarily working within itself but closed off from and ignored by consciousness excepting for the pricking of conscience, and the conscious allowing its self-contained thinking to be manipulated by its conditioning and striving with that thinking to survive and prosper according to the Machine.

The meaning currently given to meditation is rather different. It implies a process by which personal consciousness transcends or rises above ordinary awareness and enters another higher state of cosmic consciousness that enlightens the self. When asked what this consciousness and enlightenment consists of, some mystics say that part of the truth is that when you fully understand it you do not talk about it. The objection to this is that if the enlightened do not talk about it how can others recognise it and that which is to be derived from it? Such an attitude is explained by the fact that this is not whole truth that needs to be shared and commonly understood. This can be no more than a full understanding of the self's limited truth in relation to existing reality. It does not relate to others because they are expected to seek their own self-truth, and it expects nobody to strive for a humantrue world.

In the light of reason that makes us aware that there is no cosmic or universal consciousness or spirit; what is transcendental meditation and why is it practiced? If it were a total shutdown of all mental activity, high and low, then it could not be described as meditation, the exercise of mental functions. A relaxing emptying of that which we regard as the mind, which reduces stress by cutting off our full awareness of the mad world outside must be physically beneficial. The mind is then not being stimulated by outside events, although it is alert to any unusual sound and in a state of readiness, nor is it said to be working within itself (which I doubt is ever actually the case). I take the heightened, sharpened alertness that meditators experience to be an effect of narrowing down consciousness in this way, ignoring the wide range of normally meaningful stimulations, sinking back into the animal state of watchful rest, closed to any activity at the higher human level. This is not a colourful heightening of true awareness, or opening to deep moral questing, but a return to the black and white simple concerns of instinct - retreating, not going forward. We already commonly ignore our postconscious minds when they are trying their best to break down the iron defences of conscious will and bring true awareness. It is adding insult to injury to submit ourselves to regular periods of shutting them away altogether. On emerging from this meditation the subject is usually able to face the world with renewed vigour and confidence. Occasionally he or she may also experience some sort of true inspiration, reinforcing belief in cosmic consciousness. But this must come from awakened awareness momentarily opening to the intuition of the independent postconscious that has been working privately despite neglect; that would function infinitely better with our conscious co-operation, and that will make us wholly humantruly aware if we remain permanently open to it. This so-called meditation reflects a desire to return to the morality of living intelligence at a much simpler level - like the awareness of instinct that all is as well as possible with the world and no more can be done than is already accomplished by nature. To aware intellect, this is not morally permissible in a chaotic world where so much requires to be done.

Suppose, however, that transcendental meditation actually makes the conscious oblivious of all but the most insistent outside stimulation, but arouses both it and the unconscious postconscious to heightened activity. In order to clarify the relationship between the two main parts of the mind - between the combination of instinctive consciousness and the utilised postconscious under the domination of instinctive will, and the unconscious independent postconscious - let us call the former Mind B, and the latter Mind A. Since Mind B consists of a chief construction of prejudice to which all thinking primarily refers, this state of heightened activity, free from interference, will simply result in its thinking even more effectively (though subconsciously, as in a dream) in its usual way. Although Mind A's independent true and critical intellation has also been heightened its influence will thus be no greater. The only way in which Mind B can be influenced by truth is by allowing itself to be so externally stimulated as to become highly critically self-aware to the point of breaking down its own wilful conditioning; by giving freedom and encouragement to its independent postconscious Mind A, and, by supraconscious intellation, growing in humantrue understanding. This beneficial process can not take place with the consciousness of Mind B closed down; therefore this kind of meditation can be of no truly fundamental benefit.

It will simplify matters from this point if we generally refer to Mind B (including the utilised part of the postconscious) as the conscious mind, and Mind A (the independent postconscious) as the postconscious mind. I suggest that you keep your intellation processes fluid on the question of the exact structure of the mind and the inter-relationship of its parts. I have not yet found the complete answer, but I am quite certain of having travelled some way along the right road towards it.

What would be the effect of this kind of meditation, with the conscious closed down and the postconscious fully awake, in the mind of an intellating person? It would give the postconscious mind extra time for reasoning that would be beneficial in theory. But exactly this activity takes place during deep sleep, and the natural balance between time spent awake and asleep seems to be that which the mind requires for its daytime duties and observations and its night-time sorting and reasoning. The practice of meditation would seem to reduce the mind's daytime observations whilst increasing its capacity for sorting and reasoning, perhaps with the result that less sleep is required so that the balance is restored. In this case, then, meditation would seem to do no harm but for the fact that sleep is largely dictated by postconscious need, whilst to meditate is a decision of the conscious that strengthens its wilful dominance, whereas it is desirable, indeed vital, that we submit increasingly to postconscious will.

It can be seen that the postconscious mind will get much more rest and will not require our conscious help when, by its guidance, we have realised humantruth in the world. Instead of working hard at night untangling the contradictions of existing reality and making the correlations which that hostile reality does not allow it to make during the day, it too will be able to sleep like all the other faculties. But the Machine and the present automated thinking of humanity is already working on a complex, amoral level, autoprogressing and taking over our minds at an accelerating pace. That is why striving of the mind is presently vital, day and night, at full stretch.

The Transcendental Meditation (TM) movement contends that its enlightenment can spread other than by teaching and example; that given about one hundred truly enlightened persons it would spontaneously change the world. This is insupportable because apart from goodwill there is nothing tangible to spread, and I think this notion comes from a vague awareness of the influence for truth but failure to recognise its vital source. Only supraconsciousness can humantruly change the world; there is no other road.

Meditation heightens awareness of the benign, co-operative part of instinct whose influence must have good effects, just like the power for good in the Christian message. But to rely on this feeling rather than look to the striving of our minds means leaving the Machine undisturbed, and leaving ourselves in all ways vulnerable to the other ancient instincts that hold sway and make our reality the violent competition it now is. Whilst the Machine rules, the benign instinctive or moral influences do not, because they may not, prevail.

It is naive to believe that the world shall be put right by emotional right-feeling and wishful thinking. To work out a social structure that would sustain such good spirit requires tremendous effort of intellation and responsible sacrifice. It is necessary once again to remind ourselves that we are presently saddled with a vast, complex, overwhelming, ingrained system, a Machine that accentuates our natural differences and gives us many artificial differences - of education, status, possession, reward, authority. To enable our true inner selves, our intelligent humanity to shine through, all these differences must be removed and the system replaced by a humantrue constitution. There is no question but that this shall require great general striving of mind, also tolerance and patience.

The sensory input that meditation closes off from the mind when purporting to make contact with a universal consciousness is the information output of the world as it is. The postconscious mind of the intellating individual needs to be constantly aware of this worldly output so as never to lose sight of what it is up against. In the ideal world supraconsciousness would be tuned in all the time to the calm, benign, reassuring output of the humantrue reality it had made. The animal is already in its own reassuring world of instinct that nothing within itself or in its external experience contradicts. It is this sense of reassurance, recalled from our instinctive past, that meditation embraces in mistake for something ethereal. So mysticism and its practice of meditation is an artifice that does no more than bypass our intellectual responsibility whilst periodically refreshing the automated self so as the better to cope with our presently existing wrong reality.

The ultimate effect of such as TM, well-meaning as it surely is, would be to retard the progress of true human evolution by keeping our behaviour linked to emotion, the higher mind in limbo, our society firmly subjugated by the automaton, the self exclusively anchored in consciousness. We would continue to experience life mainly through our full range of instincts which, whether benign as expressed by some or malignant by others, are both applied and are equally appropriate to the mixed morality of the Machine. It shall not produce peaceful simplicity or higher morality because it shall not help or enable us to emerge from the existing situation which, like the balance of nature, must give free reign to bad as well as good morality (to use human terms) in order to work.

The point needs to be made, once more, that supraconsciousness and the automated religious outlook are related in that both are interpretations of the same things, but only the former true interpretation represents human salvation by fulfilment, certainly not the latter. There is a similarity between the mystics putting 'spirit' above reason and my putting intellation above conscious thinking and truth above all, for both condemn the competitive materialist inhumanity of our society. But there is a great difference between them that can be shown in the following way. Supraconsciousness is the optimum expression of our highest faculty and the gateway to truth. The 'spirit', on the other hand, is a substitute for the true human state that the inferior reasoning of consciousness has arrived at to accord with good feeling. Mysticism, the occult, is thinking limited by instinctive 'knowing' and feeling. Consequently it is associated with the paranormal. Such as extra-sensory perception (ESP) is integral with instinct but cannot be understood by it. So whilst such phenomena are amenable to true reason, they appear miraculous to instinct-dominated reason.

My reason for wanting to explain the paranormal is that its mysteries have been taken as miraculous evidence of the existence of powers greater and wiser than we, or of a higher, cosmic or universal consciousness that we should aspire to in a non-intellectual way, by meditation, when we shall become privy to these mysteries by enlightenment from that cosmic consciousness. It is important to understand that, on the contrary, paranormal and supernatural events have rational explanations, and to remember that our true course is the fulfilment of intellect by which these events are revealed as insignificant, as irrelevant to the higher intellectual state of being, as relevant only to the instinctive state, through its emotions.

Mankind is drawn towards experience associated with instinct, rather than towards *being* his intellect, because our ancestors belonged to that state for millions of years and we can recall or sense the weight of this experience with comparative ease. The intellectual state is relatively very new and calls on much greater effort. Yet man senses the power of intellect and is led, by imagination rather than reason, to believe that it is a largely untapped source of power that the self can use to its personal advantage. Formal competitive learning is the most common example. Lateral thinking, self-hypnosis, memory-building, confidence-boosting, happy-making exercises are all methods of reinforcing the instinctive/conscious self for automated success by increasing its domination of intellect - the opposite of true development. Personal conviction can help performance by removing the doubts of intellect - for example, it can enable an individual to jump higher or run faster than ever before. But the way ahead is to *heed* the doubts of intellect so as to resolve them, not to remove them.

Those who imagine our sensed potential supraconsciousness to be an external cosmic wisdom from which enlightenment will come to those who dwell on it, tend also to believe in the paranormal and supernatural as its manifestations. Those of us who do not imagine, and therefore do not perceive, such cosmic consciousness shall find straightforward explanations of these phenomena, if we seek them.

Telepathy is a means of communication, and clairvoyance a dimension of awareness, both of which I believe to have been part of our instinctive life experience before we achieved intellect, some 30,000 to 100,000 years ago, and which have since become redundant in civilised human society but remain in partial use in primitive societies like those of the Baka people and bushmen of Africa (who know when their hunters have killed, though miles away), and are, of course, commonly used in nature. Telepathy is to do with the utmost mental concentration enabling signals to be sent and received by a weak and otherwise imperceptible means. Levitation and the like is paranormality of a different kind that I believe to have occurred in the following manner. When we achieved intellect and sensed its important capabilities but merely used it in the service of instinct, we imagined it to have given us magical powers. We have tried to manifest our imagined magical potential, and if we have succeeded it can only have been in two ways:

1   Individual or collective will overcomes the forces and influences that keep the normal order of existing reality so as to cause supernatural events. In order to exert such will a high degree of conviction that the event shall occur is helpful. Concentration is required to gather such will into its maximum force, and the most effective means of concentration has been found to be what we call meditation. This, conversely, is a withdrawal of the 'self' from its greatest power - intellect - and its re-entry into the primitive state of the absolute investment of all energy in instinct, which ensures survival provided all energy is given to it.

To accept this as the explanation of levitation, for example, is to accept that sometimes the force of human will can overcome the force of gravity. The explanation of walking on water might be that the water momentarily takes on crystalline form - becomes solid as though by freezing. These abnormal events would be the result of an unusual influence of will causing a quantum mechanical temporary departure from the norm. The point to note about paranormal events is that they occur infrequently, remotely, and in insignificant circumstances. Everyday events almost always occur in accordance with normal 'natural' laws and influences, and with our full expectation and acceptance.

The explanation why normal laws overwhelmingly apply is that these laws are presently in force. Anything more than very small-scale disobedience of them would disrupt the precise balance of the present universal system that depends upon them being obeyed. I put it this way but it is probably more accurately described as the co-operative effort of all wills to achieve and sustain commonly agreed ends. They are not the only possible laws, or ends, nor is this the only viable system, but breaking these laws cannot be justified unless to make way for a better, truer system. Gaia responds to the will of Earth-life to go on living because it represents hope of better things, but natural disasters occur despite the combined will against them of a human race that neither obeys or improves upon the natural laws. The intellectual strength of human will does not yet count for much because we are competitive, not cooperative. A wish for peace is cancelled by a counter-determination on war, and even the desire for victory in war is negated by the contrary desire of the opposing side. That the universe allows its laws to be overturned, on certain slight occasions, may be as a reminder to itself, and perhaps to us, that the existing order is not inescapable but can be replaced by another wholly true order, also as an expression of a desire for that better order. Some paranormal events might be seen in the same light as mutations opening the door to possible change, or as frost patterns in boiling water to remind it of the form to assume when the temperature drops below zero.

2 The other explanation of the paranormal is, or course, that it is illusion. One form of illusion, which I shall describe shortly, is remote visualisation - when the brain 'sees' a picture that the open and wakeful eyes do not see. In the case of levitation, walking on water and the like, the mind constructs its own pictures of these occurrences when in a state of withdrawal from actual existing reality, and calls them true because it prefers that withdrawn state of mind, in which they *are* true, to the state of mind common to actual reality in which the occurrences are *not* true, i.e. they did not happen.

In this light it can be understood why the Buddha and hundreds of his monks were said to appear and vanish, to pass though walls, to dive in and out of the earth as though it were water, and to travel though the sky, seated and cross-legged. It is not surprising that they should have believed these things because they were in a state of almost perpetual meditation, a withdrawal from the superintendence of all faculties in balance, usually in isolated places at high altitudes. That their supernormal experiences are given as fact is not fraudulent. All religions arise from the struggle between our humanity and our existing reality and all sense the truth without grasping or realising it. The truth is that our actual reality, Earth-bound or universal, is not the only possible reality, as shown above in 1. To believe that a paranormal non-event truly happened is not as far from the truth as to assert that existing reality, as it obviously exists, is all that can ever exist.

A good deal has been heard recently about 'out of the body' experiences such as when the subject floats up to the ceiling, looks down on its body undergoing surgery on an operating table and 'sees' in detail what is being done. These experiences, retold by the subjects, are taken to prove that the 'spirit' leaves the body at death but in these cases hovers above it and returns as it recovers. The subjects talk of bright light, peaceful and tranquil feelings, and a sense of rising above ordinary affairs. This is taken to indicate that they approached the entrance to an after-life or heaven. These experiences are often taken seriously - as portentous, just as dreams were once regarded - but without good grounds.

An 'out-of-the-body' experience is related to some degree of belief in some kind of divinity, from a fully acknowledged faith to an almost unadmitted persuasion. What the subject then 'sees' is pictures previously associated in the memory and now reconstructed in the imagination. That the experience is put down to extra-sensory perception is related, I think, to the fact that the utter truth about all things exists, anywhere and everywhere, regardless of the constraints of reality. But we have to be content with realising that we are made aware by the known senses alone, and in one place only - the head.

Individuals who are not afflicted with any false faith, or innately subject to any mysterious persuasion, do not have 'out of body' experiences. They *are* subject to illusions, and dreams, but recognise them for what they are and do not invest them with false significance.

The fact is that we can truly experience only with, and within, our minds. It is impossible that we should be suspended near the ceiling, but an everyday thing that our imagination, within our heads, should picture us so. Normally we would pay no special attention to such imaginings. But the believer in god or reincarnation, under particularly disturbing circumstances, can interpret them as divinely significant.

The circumstances, combined with false bias, explain it all. To go through a surgical operation is disturbing. There is bright light in an operating theatre. Drugs impart a peaceful and tranquil feeling. The sense of ascending might be due to the temporary release from pain, fear and worry. And the fact that some subjects can describe details of the operation, which they could not have actually 'seen' because only the eyes can actually 'see' directly, can be explained by their being near to consciousness, hearing the surgeons discussing or describing the operation (or telepathically receiving their view of it) and constructing a picture of it within their minds.

A quite common feature of human experience, that is nevertheless regarded as supernatural because it has no obvious natural cause, is synchronicity - described by Jung as an acausal principle at work in the universe. Acausal events are ones with no apparent physical connection.

In his book The Awakening Earth, Peter Russell suggests that coincidences are examples of synchronicity - manifestations at the level of the individual of a higher organising principle at the collective level, or the as yet rudimentary social super-organism. I suggest a simple explanation that has nothing to do with a higher organising principle. That coincidences happen to people who meditate or pray, knowingly or not, is no coincidence. They have removed themselves from their conscious self-control in relation to all the impulsions and taboos and expectations of actual reality, and given themselves to the private desires of their personal reality that nevertheless uses their knowledge of actual reality. The individual is in a kind of trance, more aware of his or her personal reality than his or her automatic ego reacting to the Machine. In the case of the man who met his friend in the wrong place by failing to arrive at the intended place, he had some forgotten knowledge of a likelihood that his friend might well be at this wrong place - forgotten, that is, by his automatic self but remembered by his personally real self. His getting off the train at the wrong place was no accident, for it was the right place according to his private mental guide. It would be seen as wrong only by the real world, which would also call this a coincidence. His private will was influencing his actions.

The supposed higher organising principle of nature and the universe, which meditation and synchronicity are thought to indicate, is in fact the ever more complex evolution of instinctive life under the influence to express energy, which has a very different further objective under the supreme influence of truth. Synchronicity appears remarkable to us because our actual reality, the present norm, is badly out of step with our intellectual potential and our true reality. Were we supraconscious and living in a humantrue world, there would be a high degree of synchronisation but no 'coincidences'. The constitution of such a society would accord with our true individual and collective desire so that what we all desired would continually come to pass. This would be our own organising principles at work, both established and carried out by our own intellect. When such a society is in being I think we *can* expect acausal events, however - events with no physical cause but caused by the influential intention of truth, in our world, in Gaia, and in the universe - because realisation of truth is a universal desire and our true supraconscious will shall be the cause of such events, just as the will to live caused Earth's biosphere to maintain the right conditions for intelligent life through Gaia.

A growth in the number of coincidences, in our existing automatic reality, would be as embarrassing as the present increase in the number of people unconsciously pursuing personal desires is damaging. A 'growing experience of synchronicity' in society as it exists, as a result of meditation or prayer, would mean an increase in the influence of instinctive conscious will, and an increase in chaos.

In case the concept of a humantrue society should be thought to represent that social super-organism, let me remind you that such a society would become progressively simpler, and that the ultimate end of which I think it is a means - true equilibrium - is really the opposite of super-organism.

Concerning the 'supernatural', it should be noted that all occurrences in nature serve some instinctive purpose - they are natural to all except ourselves. Instantaneous communication between individuals in a large flock of birds in flight serves instinct. We regard such things as supernatural because the course of human affairs is variously affected but no longer governed by the instinctive code; such subtle causes and effects are humanly superficial excepting those of Gaia whose benefits we share with all life. What presently governs and affects us most strongly is the automatic application of intellect to the instinctive drives within the conscious sphere. Our innate feeling for humantruth, though we have not yet grasped its substance, is a demonstration of another force at work, that which seeks to help us to help ourselves and at the same time serve its ultimate purpose - the influence of truth.

So humans do not need what we call supernatural or paranormal aids. We have replaced them with the aid of our faculty for knowing and reasoning. ESP - by which I mean perception extra to normal *human* senses - does exist, without doubt, and is used by nature, but we have substituted speech, printing, telephone, radio, film and television. The discovery of ESP does not reveal a new dimension of relevance to us but an ancient dimension of instinct that we have outgrown and should now put aside, recognising it for what it is. Perhaps ESP does appear miraculous to our intellect, though commonplace to instinct, but it is as well to realise that intellect itself is miraculous by comparison with instinct. We can experience ESP, especially when we are in a mental condition akin to the animal with our higher faculties of mind at a low ebb. Because of our higher faculties it is probable that we could learn to use natural means of communication other than those now normal to us, and to interpret them more fully.

Consider what is known as 'remote viewing', cases of which are said to have occurred and are recorded. If we take these cases as true but are unwilling to concede that a mental picture, which is not imagined but describes an actual scene some way off, can be seen other than by the normal ocular mechanism, we must examine ways in which a remote eye can actually 'see' a scene which is 'out of sight'.

We know that the 'seeing' process involves myriads of cells each with the task of picking up a certain minute feature of the picture. A group of these cells concentrates on each small area, each cell pre-programmed to pick out its own particular tiny feature and contribute it to a major feature such as a vertical line, a horizontal line, a colour or shade. As cells in their allotted areas recognise their programmed feature they transmit a signal. It is the pattern of such signals appearing in certain areas that reproduces the picture in the brain.

Evolutionary experience has given us very long memories so that almost nothing on Earth should be completely unrecognisable. Nevertheless the recognition of some unfamiliar or obscure objects requires concentrated attention and viewing from different angles. It is now known that the brain has 'sleeper' synapses and filaments that can be activated and programmed to fill in our recognition gaps and familiarise us with the unfamiliar. In the case of familiar objects the brain is not normally required to make a detailed analysis, and quite early in the process the recognition of large and complex scenes might be triggered by one connection only. In this way the brain can achieve instant recognition of a house from its salient features - that it has a door, windows, roof and chimneys - but without 'seeing' how many windows or any more precise detail. Similarly a harbour might be instantly and simply recognised from its salient features of sea, walls, boats, houses, and the single strong connection conveying this picture may also convey, in language but without speech, the word that simply describes it - 'harbour'.

It can be assumed that there is a limited number of generally familiar key scenes and that the code which triggers the interconnection of each is more or less the same in every mind. An individual who is trying, telepathically, to visualise a particular scene through the eyes of another person some miles away who is viewing that scene, will be alert, above all, to all these possible codes. The other person, concentrating on all the features of the scene, will, above all, be reinforcing that single simple triggering code connection that describes it in general. That connection might be further reinforced by the presence of other persons in the vicinity who are either similarly viewing the scene or strongly conscious of it as the background to their lives. Whether the picture is then conveyed, and with what added detail, depends upon the strength of telepathic communication between the two.

Such are the explanations that take away from apparently paranormal phenomena their air of deep, mysterious and inexplicable meaning. Some elements of paranormal belief are sound but all can be similarly explained. Supposed phenomena such as spoon bending and influencing the fall of dice surely have logical physical explanations. Events that are claimed to happen and things that are supposed to indicate the existence of unknown powers and other worlds for which no conclusively reasoned evidence, and therefore no inescapable justification, can be found (such as communications from the dead, spiritual existence and reincarnation) must be put down as figments of the emotional imagination.

———————————

So it is necessary that we stop attaching significance to meditation, the supernatural and the paranormal, but before dismissing them here we should consider a strong reason why we have continually turned to make-believe rather than face the truth. It is a matter of life and death. We cannot face the fact that when our bodies die our consciousness, which can range far and wide beyond the body, must die also. Because we do not understand the truth, we substitute for it beliefs and faiths that explain life and death in ways which enable us to accept both but keep us in ignorance of truth.

Spring is birth, summer life, autumn decline and winter brings death. Most of us are privileged to witness this cycle for many seasons until we ourselves die, knowing that the process continues without us. Death is a human tragedy. Every day in Britain, not only do we mourn about one hundred persons who die before their time by accident, abuse or disease, but *two thousand* who die naturally. Senseless premature death and unnecessary suffering are rightly unacceptable. But every generation is destined to die - we must all suffer eventual, inevitable extinction. Many of us refuse to concede this and turn to belief in some form of 'life after death'. Let us look at one form that is presently gaining support - reincarnation.

Consciousness, supraconsciousness, and the understanding of truth requires a mind, and the mind requires a complex arrangement of neurones and nerve-paths. Such things did not, could not exist in the superhot concentration of pure energy at the time of the Big Bang. Truth existed, but not consciousness of it. We humans became capable of understanding truth between one hundred thousand and thirty thousand years ago. Before that there could have been no reincarnation, for it is a supposed process of self-perfection by way of growing understanding being passed from one to another of a series of bodily regenerations. This presupposes a spirit, of which there is no evidence, nor is there indication that newborn humans are any more than intellectual clean sheets whose understanding comes later. So there is nothing to reincarnate - nothing to show that our characters are other than the construction of mind developed in our lifetime. The idea of reincarnation suggests imaginative indulgence of the desire for immortality, originally invented as a spur to good behaviour, and can also be used as a fanciful explanation of the wide differences in human character, from saint to sadist.

But if you look at a remote forest or a shoal of fish and realise that they exist just as they did thousands of years ago, then you know there is no death. Life is continuous; the spark is passed in the seed from body to body, plant to plant, and whatever state of consciousness it achieves is also continually conscious. That which alone brings the age-old life of a species to an end is extinction, whose new significance is not death but cessation of birth - a failure to pass or carry on the spark.

When we realise that life is an unextinguished flame passing from generation to generation we must also realise that life-forms, including humans, are most vigorous as the seed bursts into life and thereafter slowly decline, but are represented by the period between maturity, when they become able to reproduce, and the time when they lose that ability and are essentially redundant. The longer people live the greater the experience gained and, if they have truly learned from that experience, the more they have to teach. It is worth noting that here in the West the new generation of humans does not learn from the old; it *teaches* its seniors the lessons it learns from dialogue with the rapidly advancing Machine.

Our wish to live forever derives from the original life-force purpose reflected in the instinctive will to survive. Without that purposeful will there could have been no life, for the determination to go on living is part and parcel of the impulsion to come to life. But intellect shows us that bodily death and reproduction are necessary features of evolution, including the evolution of such as the human brain with full intellectual potential. It is likely that a sense of this continual improvement lies behind the concept of reincarnation - of the individual 'spirit' also continuing and evolving. The bodily death of individual humans may no longer really be necessary, for it is possible that our collective intellect might reach fulfilment as readily, or more readily, without it, but we are stuck with it. We have to see ourselves as part of a process whose ultimate perfection - true equilibrium - is far and away superior to our clumsy concepts of heaven. But such concepts of heaven are relative to human life, and, by fulfilling humantruth, we can both play our part in the universal process *and* get as near as possible to making our heaven - on Earth.

Individual consciousness is a certain factual awareness of Machine reality, a construction of limited reason and adoption of a selection of available practices, all gathered into a personal identity, parts of which are shared with others. Its chief and ultimate value is its potential, total and collectively agreed awareness of truth. But that truth exists independently, and our true awareness is not necessary to its existence yet is a vital vehicle for its universal realisation. In order to serve our purpose as a vehicle we must become supraconscious and realise truth in every possible human way. All life throughout the universe must eventually die and consciousness must die with it. There is no point at all in any kind of everlasting consciousness because true being - true equilibrium - does not require to be conscious of itself in order to *be* itself.

Nevertheless, as you near the end of your life and look at the well-loved persons and things - the primroses in spring and the swallows in summer - and reflect that soon you shall never see them again, death can be emotionally dismaying. You might find comfort in thinking of it this way - when you die it is as if you pass on your consciousness to somebody else, perhaps to everybody else; as though your self goes to sleep for good but awakes as energy added to the self of another person, or that other person is born or wakes up with an added spark of life that you have given. Nothing is really lost by your death because that which you knew and truly understood continues as part of the truth, and the world of which you were conscious still exists in fact and in the eyes and consciousness of others who remain alive. Even your basic physical material is not destroyed.

The beauty of it is that once you are dead there is no regretful *you* to know that you were once alive, any more than you are now made regretfully aware of the millions of years before your birth when you were not alive. In this and many other respects, would not death be much worse if consciousness lived on eternally?

———————————————

The great error of religious faiths and beliefs, and of humans who adopt them, is summed up by the words of the Pope - 'We should avoid intellectual temptation'. A large part of religions' message is that our power of reason is restricted so that it must fall short of truth and then we must open to the 'further light of god', or 'enlightenment of universality'. This is entirely to misunderstand the purpose of our life, which is *to realise truth through our intellect*. We must strive for truth, not hopefully wait for it. We are the *source*, not merely the recipients of enlightenment.

A fundamental criticism of religions is that they do not define the nature and purpose *of that which they call god,* or universality, or cosmic consciousness, on the grounds that it is also beyond our power of reason to understand. The fact is that these things cannot be defined because they do not exist. Prayer and meditation can be effective as a response to determined will, but fails to bring enlightenment because it represents the misdirection and limitation of its true source, intellect. So religions draw society away from its true direction, keeping us to the automatic status quo, adjusting to the Machine as morally as it allows but generally going where the Machine wishes us to go.

There is nothing at all to suggest that the universe contains anything more than a variety of forms, expressions and violent expressions of energy, excepting truth and its influence. The only way of knowing and thus becoming part of the meaning and purpose of the universe is by understanding the truth and feeling its influence. No doubt this is what the worshippers and meditators sense but fail to grasp. The only way of understanding truth and thus experiencing its influence is by the optimum exercise of our supreme faculty of knowing and reasoning - our intellect.

I believe the case for supraconsciousness has already been made obvious - that since intellect is our highest faculty we should represent it and, since it cannot but be true, we shall then be essentially humantrue in all our thoughts and actions. The equivalent of universal true equilibrium in both the human mind and the world will be when all reasoned connections, all facts of reality and all emotions are as near to perfect harmonious agreement as they possibly can be.

The contrary view of mystics and meditators may be represented by the Indian notion of Darshan - the belief, already touched on in relation to the TM movement, that one enlightened person can pass to someone else a taste of enlightenment, and a further implication that the activity, attitude and construction of somebody's mind can be indirectly influenced by other minds, which is to say that enlightenment can be passed on without words and received intuitively. Darshan relates to acuteness of consciousness up to the highest level of *instinctive* animal awareness, and also embraces the deepest of past experience. It is the same thing when two closely related people at opposite ends of a building experience changes of delta rythm or skin resistance when there is actual cause for only one of them to experience such changes, or when all members of a large shoal of fish change direction in unison almost instantaneously (notwithstanding a recent claim that this is a matter of the fish giving off and responding to electrical impulses). And, incidentally, it is probably the same kind of influence that puts a popular leader in place, or causes several people to adopt one person as guru - a matter of animal magnetism. True human enlightenment is an intellectual matter, enormously complex by comparison and, as far as it *can* be conveyed between minds, is conveyed otherwise - by language. When common ideas arise simultaneously from separated minds it is not because of some unknown invisible communication but because those minds, faced with the same problematic group of factors and no doubt linked by a strong desire to solve the problem, have made the same correlations of reason at the same time. Such reasoning cannot be implanted whole by magic, or through effortless meditation. It must be constructed within each individual mind and, whilst it can be stimulated and short-circuited by the conveyance of ideas, each mind has to do its own constructing of reason around those ideas. When there is complete common human enlightenment and we are living in humantrue unity, *then* it may be expected that true signals will bring instant true response from common awareness.

Truth requires energy for its recognition by intellect but is separate from energy. Yet energy may employ the conscious part of intellect to discover its own limited truths. The influence that integrates the flock of birds or shoal of fish may be broadcast through energy, but purely intellectual reason can *only* be engendered by intellation and transmitted by language. That is why human understanding of science has advanced, while our supraconsciousness and awareness of humantruth is retarded. The former is limited truth carried by energy, whilst the latter is our failure to apply energy deliberately to the recognition of whole truth.

That Darshan occurs and has a certain powerful effect is not doubted. It is the strong, benign, co-operative linking influence common to members of species of herding animals that humans are still capable of feeling and that is attractive because it is largely missing from our normal automated lives. It crops up to some extent in the form of patriotism, political party loyalty, filial love and competitive partnership in war and sport. But this is emotional good feeling whose real purpose is to back up the aims, objectives and cares of a species. For us to put such feelings first, before our automated aims which, in turn, we put before truth, is to put the cart, and ourselves in the cart, very firmly before the horse.

If enlightenment is taken to mean increased understanding of truth (and what else is meaningful?), then that which is passed on by such as Darshan is not enlightenment. It is rather a state of being that has little to do with an intellectual determination upon the pursuit of truth, everything to do with instinct, subconsciousness, consciousness, emotion, and the discipline of will. It is associated with enlightenment because it is passive, and so stands out against a world background that is not so. The will that dominates it is devoted to the benign instincts and the conscious compassions so that the discipline containing it is tranquil, non-aggressive, gentle and peaceable. But the so-called enlightened people of this kind can sustain that stage only in circumstances of isolation from the norm. Because they are passive they do not critically tackle the norm, but to avoid the necessity of being competitive they have to be distanced from the norm. They fabricate a way of tolerating this reality by contriving to opt out of it. This is why their form of enlightenment does not spread far, because it does not aim to change existing reality for the better, which might appeal to growing awareness, but to escape its clutches, which the majority cannot do.

Our tough reality, in which the majority presently have to live, does not give way to gentleness as it does to power. Yet it responded to gentle Jesus who is said to have brought to humanity the grace of god, the free gift of which is known as charisma. It was their powerful charisma, or compellingly attractive personality, that enabled mystics and gurus to influence people. Under their influence individuals would accept without question the simple import of their words, taking it in as an unreasoned faith. Only in this simple sense might it be said that a meditating person could influence changes in brain activity that, by feedback, might grow and spread but to a limited extent. That which is being influenced is chiefly an emotion that requires continual excitement if it is to be maintained, let alone propagated. That which responds to pure reasoning, on the other hand, is further reasoning, which can grow and spread under its own stimulation. Meditation is a state of tranquillity, with tranquillising feedback, but in this automatic reality it is more than outweighed by states of emotional tension, with their own traumatic feedback. Yet tension and stress arouses the activity of reason and is therefore potentially much more valuable to the search for true humanity than relaxation.

Having already adopted a religious prejudice, misguided conscious reason views the paranormal as evidence of god or cosmic wisdom According to human convention we see ourselves as weak, the universe as powerful but leading us to chaos, and god or cosmic consciousness as all-wise, all-powerful, and capable of leading us into ordered good if we will but follow. I see a broad picture of existence on two scales: energy, from rampant to docile, and a governing pattern, from false to true. Every universe begins as energy rampant and whether it returns to another Big Bang or becomes energy docile and in a state of true equilibrium depends on whether the false or true pattern prevails.

The truth is that nothing can withstand the enormous power of energy but energy can be persuaded to submit to the true influence:

- Under the influence of life-force energy is active.

- By the added influence for truth that activity seeks life.

- Under the influence of energy life seeks to survive and progress to the optimum.

- The influence for truth makes intellect the optimum aim of life.

- Under the influence of energy intellect develops by application to instinct.

- [The human race is presently at this latter stage.]

- [To reach the next, ultimate stage our intellect must first achieve a receptive state].

- Under the influence of truth intellect fulfils truth by supraconsciousness.

This is the truth, and though we sense it our reason is not guided by it, yet our false reason often appears to be backed up by scientific fact. For example, the notion of Darshan, on which is founded the claim of transcendental meditation to be the potential saviour of the world, is supported by the evident fact that rats learn behaviour-patterns from the passed-on experience of other rats that are apart and unrelated except that they are of the same species.

Rupert Sheldrake sees this rat behaviour as an example of what he calls formative causation (*A New Science of Life* by Rupert Sheldrake, Pub: Blond and Briggs, London.) He proposes that systems are regulated not only by the laws known to physical science but also by invisible organising fields, which he calls morphogenetic fields. He believes the regularities of nature to be more like habits than reflections of physical laws. His theory postulates that if one member of a biological species learns a new behaviour the morphogenetic field for the species changes, even if very slightly. If the behaviour is repeated for long enough its 'morphic state' builds up and begins to affect the entire species. Thus, in the case of rats, the more rats that learn the task the stronger the morphogenetic field becomes and the more easily other rats learn the task.

As another example of formative causation, Rupert Sheldrake cites the difficulty of crystallising certain organic compounds that have never been crystallised before. Scientists may work for years until they obtain one crystal, but once this has been achieved other scientists suddenly achieve the same. Experimenters across the world now find it relatively easy to produce their own crystals, and the more crystals are produced the easier it becomes to crystallise the compound. One fundamental criticism of this theory is that we cannot possibly say that a compound has *never* been crystallised before, for this might be true of this universe but not of previous ones. Another criticism can be made on the grounds that the accumulative ease with which the compound crystallises is due to the growing expertise in bringing this about, paralleled in the experience of all scientists throughout the world who are working on the problem, but it would appear that this last criticism fails to take into account all that is involved here.

It seems to me that what is involved is not the influence of a single field but a variety of forces of energetic will, from that of the atom, to that of the single cell, to that of the intelligent life-form, which causes a certain mode of behaviour, from the simple selection of right or left quantum bias (see Chapter 32, Roots of Religion) to complex instructions of instinct, these being inter-communicated by nerve-systems within bodies and by telepathy between bodies. I have already mentioned these processes as playing their part in the mutations necessary to the advance of evolution, and in the co-operative support given by colonies of cells forming organs of the body to the overall well-being of that body. In the case of needful change the higher forces of will express desire for it and the lower forces respond by trial and error until a pattern is achieved that constitutes the desired and needful change. Another controversial example of formative causation is that plants which are lovingly talked to grow better - against which the similar criticism is levelled that the gardener who loves his plants enough to talk to them will also give more attention and care to them, which is perfectly true. Nevertheless the influence of both energy and truth is constantly exerted with the aim of progressive growth towards the ultimate. This influence is expressed by the will of the plants to grow to the optimum, and of the soil elements to contribute to that growth. It is surely logical that when there is added to this the will of the human gardener, who represents the supreme achievement of this process of evolution, then optimum growth will be more readily achieved.

I see natural morphogenetic fields as a variety of different patterns of behaviour that life-force and instinct have so far selected, from all those which energy makes possible, subject to the requirement of true influence that they represent advances towards the eventual fulfilment of truth (human (unnatural) fields are a different matter). These natural fields are responded to by recipients who have developed the need to be receptive, or are open to changes by quantum or bifurcation bias, for the sake of progressive advantage. Rats, for instance, are always receptive to any change that improves their opportunities for survival. Where it is a matter of learning certain complicated routes that lead to food it is suggested that this learning is passed on to other 'unrelated' rats by stimulation of the empathic growth of new dendrites on appropriate neurones that make the necessary learning connections. This is similar to the empathic transference of genes to the stick insect that enables it to simulate the twigs on which it lives. In the case of Gaia, all the inanimate matter of Earth is subject, at the point of quantum decision, to change influenced by the combined survival will of all life. In the case of telepathy between mother and child, or the instant response of flying birds to a change in direction, or the Baka people being instantly aware of a kill by their far distant hunters, there is weak communication made effective by the fact that it serves the extremely strong interests of continued survival, and is sent, and received, with intense thought and feeling.

It is probable that once the first life-form evolved on any planet it set a precedent, a morphogenetic field, a weakly-signalled quantum bias that was hugely boosted by the great desire of energy to express itself by way of life; it performed a trick that was quickly learned, as the rats learned to find their way and the compound learned to crystallise, and was followed by widespread evolution in all directions. It is possible that this formative causation had universal influence whereby the strong existence of successful reproductive life, on the first planet in the universe to evolve and support life, would stimulate the evolution of life on every other suitable planet in the universe.

The morphogenetic field of natural life comes under the general description of instinct. The human field is unnatural, in this sense, because we have partially broken with instinct. Its form, which largely causes our behaviour, is different from instinct because we have achieved potential intellect. Ideally the form of our morphogenetic field would be decided, and then carefully sustained by intellect, causing us to behave humantruly. But an intellectual species can wilfully submit to forms of behaviour that are not advances towards eventual fulfilment of truth, and are destructive rather than constructive. That is what we have done. We humans, presently here on Earth, are between the rampant and docile states of energy, open to both false and true influence. This is why our character varies between extremes. The automaton represents rampant energy and compels amoral or immoral behaviour; docile energy is represented by the separate exclusive morphogenetic sub-field of various religions; and our response to the true influence, in the form of conscience, is mostly feebly reflected in our personal and private virtues. Our existing general overall morphogenetic field is the Machine, holding us to patterns of automated thought and behaviour that are hard to stand back from, identify and break. A humantrue framework of society would be the formation that, together with our supraconscious frame of mind, caused us to be of good and true morality - our humantrue morphogenetic field. To cure us of our present automated state requires both that humantruth be proffered to humanity with intensity and that humanity makes itself highly receptive to humantruth. Thereafter our ideal formative causation will be a constitution that we can follow almost without thought yet must sustain with thoughtful intention, watchful that it never submits to the temptation of a callow desire for reckless change.

THE WRONG REALITY

Part VI
ILLUMINATION

Introduction to Chapter 34

We know that minds have a tendency to cling to the basic formation established in early life and to defend opinions subsequently reached. It is worrying to me that people will read books of a radical kind and agree with them but without allowing their established thought construction to change more than a little, partly because there are so many books all with some degree of credibility. If your aim is to change the world for the better it is necessary to recognise that automated individuals and their outlooks are thus separately fixed. Our disagreements are largely emotional, brought about by reality but without true reason. Look at the different kinds and conditions of people presently existing, often divided by mutual distrust, dislike, even hate, not only for reasons of race or colour but also class, age, and even dress or mannerisms. Consider the financial differences from rich to poor, the cultural differences from primitive to sophisticated, the educational differences from illiterate to erudite, the political differences from Fascist to Communist.

However advanced in intelligence, you may easily be influenced by such differences. You might yourself gravitate to some group, cult or religion, or otherwise unthinkingly revert to the overall norm as the easiest way of interpreting things.

This part of the book represents the act of pulling oneself up, deliberately, and challenging with doubts and questions the conclusions one has already reached. The following four chapters largely go over ground already traversed but by other routes, taking new angles of approach and shedding new light. Such is the process of intellation - making sure that our every step of reason is true but not being willing to rest on our conclusions until every possible step has been taken.

This is my mind working to the limits of its understanding. If you have not yet stretched your mind to its limits, then in order to share this understanding you may require to redirect your will, reconstruct your thoughts (or rather allow that your postconscious supervises their reconstruction) by changing signal strengths or growing new dendrites, axons and synapses in the brain.

If you simply choose to examine these findings with interest, but without disturbing conclusions you have already reached by a construction of reason well below your full capacity, then you will betray your own potential understanding of humantruth, having predetermined your future in the past. On the other hand, if your mind has reached a higher level then I must reform my mind in order to learn from you.

It is not easy to see how a campaign to change the world, by having the minds of humans change, can succeed because so many individuals presently seem to differ and disagree immovably. It shall certainly not succeed if the most aware minds do not absolutely ensure that they themselves are humantrue before trying to render that change in others.

Chapter 34

FUTURE IN THE PAST

C hange is necessary because the present is a growth whose roots are in the past, and we have had a bad past. To make our future good, which surely is our great desire, we must make good the present in which the future continually takes root.

Variations of temperament in animals are necessary to maintain the pecking order and are thus essential to survival in the balance of nature. Undesirable human temperament can be overcome, rendered harmless or made benign by intellect that can provide its own colourful variations of interest and fulfilment. But temperament with intellect consciously applied to it in the service of the Machine becomes enlarged, from saintly to monstrous. Thus our history has produced both Michelangelo and Mussolini, both mercy and massacre. We have such a reality as has contrived to allow Christianity and monetarism, Communism and Fascism to co-exist.

To illustrate that we are in a no-man's-land between instinct and intellect, let us consider mating. In the relationship of woman and man many complex and varied factors are involved, over and above instinct's seasonal programme of temporary lustfulness followed by careful rearing of offspring strictly in the interests of regeneration. Over-indulgence of instinctive lust and lack of caring effort would be harmful to instinct's reproduction programme and is detrimental to human relationships in marriage. Yet although intellect can teach us to be kind and considerate in marriage and make us aware of a responsibility, independently of instinct, to mate in order to reproduce, we could not easily conceive offspring in the normal way but for the sexual urge that is for us a more or less reckless impulsion, but which instinct devised as a responsibly motivated directive.

But just as the sexual urge is modified by instinct to suit its responsible purpose, so would we modify it, ideally, to suit our intellectual purpose. As it is, however, in our present no-man's-land, whilst we do responsibly practice birth control on the one hand, we have an increasing number of marriages ending in divorce on the other. There is also an increase in homosexuality, through genetic irregularity or conscious preference (and the former may well be influenced by the latter) that allows people to experience from pure love to unbridled lust independently of the matter of reproduction. There is also a growing practice of selective artificial insemination that provides a means of accomplishing and partially controlling reproduction independently of normal mating. Homosexuality divorces life from its most fundamental function and genetic manipulation robs reproduction of some of its essential randomness. Life is our medium, truth our responsibility; to keep our responsibility we should truly fulfil life, not try to escape from it or alter it for the wrong reasons.

When we look back at our history we see a long and intricate process, comprising good and bad intention but full of error and horror, contiuing in the present. To make our society good requires a wise unity, and if and when we become wise and united we shall surely opt for a practical way of life that is truly simple.

Why is there such wide disagreement on almost every new proposal in this society? Largely because the setting is a complex and basically false framework and different people are exclusively aware of or concerned with different parts of it, whilst we all turn our backs on our true humanity. This is the past bearing on the present that pre-determines the future. Technological evolution, led by science, has us willingly by the nose, leading us, unwilling or powerless to protest, to where we think we wish to be but really neither want nor ought to go. As individual humans we are about to be replaced by artefacts of automatic reality - the Machine's ultra-intelligent robots and engineered genes that we ourselves are rapidly developing. In this way the Machine may eliminate the inconvenience of having humans politically disagree with some of its proposals by replacing us, unless we achieve true awareness first and so ensure that the present learns from the past.

Whether we judge it good or bad, our current behaviour is geared to the Machine and is thus a strong influence on the continuation of our inhuman past into the future. Public good manners and diplomacy are devices for obscuring the real motives of automatic interest, status and power that underlie our affairs. Know-how is a discipline demanded by the Machine, a pattern of this reality that keeps communities and individuals in their places, and to which they must especially conform if they are to rise in the hierarchy of authority that then reinforces the discipline. Present worldly wisdom is a pattern of limited understanding and its communication comprising automatic inter-relationships and controls and principles - facts, historical objects and objectives of the Machine that have no humantrue meaning.

Current bad behaviour includes growing rowdiness, vandalism, hooliganism and general disturbance by young people that is partly due to steadily decreasing respect, on the part of the uncommitted, for society's controlling institutions. The Machine responds by strengthening these institutions, so feeding the flames of unrest. Official bad behaviour includes habitual dishonesty - a disregard for truth made possible by consciousness overruling the postconscious mind, and made necessary by automatic interests overruling true human interests. This is one of the worst features of the Machine, which works against humantrue reform - the practice of deceit, of lying or obscuring truth, in politics and on the part of authority and any institution or person with something to gain or defend by it.

Another example of official bad behaviour is that up to early 1988 Russian soldiers, commanded by leaders who were themselves impelled by automatic world reality, were fighting in support of a Communist government in Afghanistan, against rebels who were in turn trained and supplied by the American CIA, who also supported rebels fighting government soldiers in South America in the anti-Communist cause. To interpret this violent behaviour by adopting the viewpoint of one side or the other - that it is necessary to defend one's interests and ideology against the opposition - is entirely to miss the point. The point is that here we have a world society of essentially similar human beings that is being rent apart by truly unnecessary violent quarrels between authorities.

Such unhappy and distressing occurrences do not indicate that human society is, has always been, and forever shall be torn by strife because our race is naturally competitive and aggressive, but simply that human society is not yet constituted and guided as it should be - by its true humanity.

Another factor influencing perpetuation of the past into the future, of building our future in the past, is education. The education system, hand-in-hand with direct and indirect experience of automatic reality and in respect of its failures and successes, provided a very mixed moral introduction to and partisan instruction in the ways of that largely amoral and immoral reality. Reasonable people are horrified by cases of child abuse, but acknowledge that these cases result from the intolerable frustrations of deprivation, compounded by under-stimulation of mind - that the perpetrators are sick. It should be, but is not yet, more horrifying that this society conditions its potentially intellectual young perpetually to accept this false reality, so that they shall not see the real reasons why society in general continues sick, generation after generation. It must be a relief to educators, facing the continual contradiction between preparing the young to fit automatic reality and being aware that existing reality is not fit for the young, to have formal examinations of scholastic achievement, regardless of true enlightenment, because these represent a definite measurement amidst confusion and doubt. The measurement is not humantruly meaningful but is welcomed by realists because it is relevant to the concepts and facts of existing reality and supportive of the Machine.

Consider the people of Haiti, who are not primitive but deprived by decades of exploitation and suppression by a cruel dictatorship from which they were hopefully released some time ago. But what will be elected eventually to replace it? These people believe in dependent submission to a powerful, hopefully benign, leader, and are likely to be exploited as before. The reason is that they are generally ignorant of the much more liberal, if imperfect, systems of other countries, let alone of humantrue ideals, and are not likely to end up with a good social order because they do not know how it should be. And they are not likely to learn how it should be, and to demand that their expectations be put into practice, because they have no working example of a good social system to guide them, and it is not in the automatic interests of the existing privileged hierarchy that they should be so guided. The only present way to arouse the people seems to be through their emotions, but they shall truly answer their questions and solve their problems only by way of their intellects.

We might think that our outlook here in the 'advanced' part of the world is a far cry from that of the Haitians, but the two are quite close. Consider one of the many British television programmes where a panel of experts or public figures and an invited audience discuss current affairs - let's say the problems of the elderly. All those present appear to come down on the good moral side of the fence, which may be their permanent position but is the only approach to this sensitive subject that can be put forward acceptably on such a publicly staged occasion. Nowadays the best of such discussions go further towards true compassion than ever they used to. They no longer resort to platitudes as a matter of course, but neither do they follow the paths of intellation and reveal the truth. One reason why they do not attempt to go that far is that the programme would become too 'heavy' to be entertaining; too controversial and heatedly confused. Another reason is that it would so upset the status quo as to be objectionable not only to the broadcasting establishment but also to the participants who, though taking an overtly moral stance on this question, covertly endorse the norm as being realistically inevitable.

For example, it is unanimously agreed that lack of money is a chief burden of old age and someone suggests that the state pension should be doubled. This is an instance of fence sitting, whereby we indulge in such wishful thinking on one side but on the other, worldly side know perfectly well that such an increase shall never be paid. Whether or not we care to admit it, large numbers of deprived old people exist because medical moral conscience cannot allow their preventable death, despite high financial cost. Yet ordinary moral conscience is ineffective against the Machine's demand that most old folk must live on in poverty to suit the money economy's competitive equation. To upset that equation by insisting on doubling the pension would mean the beginning of the end of the money economy for it would involve a voluntary decision on the part of younger, more privileged people to put morals before money and accept a large decrease in their income to compensate.

The future should not be entrusted to a present whose affairs are controlled by money, conducted by politics and regulated by law, because the money economy is unintelligent and inhuman, politics is a resort of non-liberated minds, and law an arbitrator between the conflicts of competitive drives and interests and the disagreements between contrived beliefs and ill-considered opinions.

If we simply allow autoprogression to continue we shall be at its beck and call and it will preoccupy us so that our well-being will not be in our own hands. Whilst we, most of us here in the North (in the global economic sense), might then find an exclusive place for ourselves in the Machine, we shall not be making a good place for everyone in a humane future world, with time and opportunity for true fulfilment.

The idea, in some circles, that the human future lies in a super-galactic organism is a retreat from visions of perfection and, in a sense, a return to primitive instinct. It is a retreat from the forward idea that the individual mind alone can find truth, and truth would bring the world to true simplicity that I regard as perfect order. A super galactic organism would be a thing of meaning and purpose only to its own limited intelligence. It would put its own devised fabrications in place of truth and further reduce individuals to conforming cogs in a vast Machine which, as I see it, is disorder or, if you prefer, ordered chaos. We already recognise the blueprint of such an organism - the chaotic autoprogression we now follow is the hotbed from which that super-galactic organism would take its character and grow.

The human race, in the majority, is already being automatically by-passed. Whatever we pretend, we do not sustain a worldwide, agreed, mutually supportive relationship but serve the divisive Machine. There is no present prospect of such a relationship because in the future as postulated, humans, as partnerships of mind and body, will no longer exist. We shall be conditioned minds linked to electro-mechanical devices so that the universally significant part of us, our intellectual potential, will be depleted. The body-part that completes our human character, including our emotions, will be of declining use to the Machine and eventually superfluous, as indeed our minds could also become. We are capable of performing our true function as we now stand, without further despoiling our world or ourselves.

To understand why we submit to the present norms is to understand why we tolerate a reality that is ridiculous. Once a person decides to identify with the Machine they have to stick with it and believe in it. It is easier to conform than to question. Normally, automated minds do not respond to their own initiative but simply predictably react to automatic events, or automatically initiate such events. Like, for example, taking pride in the sheer size of Heathrow airport, excitedly buying company shares on the stock exchange, taking the view that young people who will not be ordered to conform should forfeit the right to subsistence, or delighting in earning money for the sake of spending it. These are victories for the Machine, defeats for humanity.

Take two examples of humanity jeopardising its future by capitulating to the Machine. First, the exploitation of nuclear fission for electricity generation, already mentioned. This is a practice that began for the wrong reason; to provide plutonium for atom bombs. It spread because competitive nations wanted their own source of bomb material *and* a new source of electrical energy. It continued to spread, despite protests, because once *some* nations have the bomb, *all* want it; because the industry gathered automatic momentum, supported by those it pays or rewards and those who now depend on its power. The contrary moral argument is that the nuclear industry arms horrific weapons, presents danger to life from accidents, and long-term danger to health from accumulation of radioactive wastes. That the magnitude of the danger is in dispute is not an argument for but against persevering with nuclear fission, especially when adequate and harmless sources of energy can be made available. As it happens, nuclear power has since gone out of fashion for financial rather than moral reasons, experience having shown that its cost of producing electricity, including that of making plants safe when their useful life ends, is too high. (I return to this subject in Chapter 48, Peaceable Action.)

The second example is of a good, or potentially good, humane ideal giving way to change for the wrong reasons - of intellectual intention succumbing to pressure from the automaton. The Chinese government, faced with what they wrongly interpret as a human reluctance to work willingly purely for an ideal (humans shall, provided the ideal is valid and truly understood), have reintroduced the competitive money economy's principle of financial incentive to make their economy more 'efficient' by having it prosper in the same way that Western economies achieve prosperity. This is a great mistake, for the principle of Communism, however short of the ideal it has so far fallen in practice, is the nearest collective approach to humantruth that humanity has yet made, and it *is* the nature of our *fulfilled* intellect to adopt the humantrue ideal.

If we do now begin to change our world, each humantrue step will establish a precedent for the future that will become ever easier to sustain *because* it is true and therefore must appeal to ultimate reason.

Once it was taboo to speak openly about sex, or death, or against the established religion. Most of the developed societies are now much more open on such subjects. Increasing emphasis is put on advancing education, yet it is still taboo to lay the mind bare. Particularly in public on 'important' occasions but even in private we dare not admit into consciousness that which our postconscious minds understand. If we survive to achieve and enjoy a humantrue future we shall look back on the present and marvel that we were once so retarded.

When we look back on this present world, assuming that we do survive it, and see all the false complexities of the Machine, we shall realise how it is possible to know a great deal but understand little. We shall see that ours was a society about which there was so much essentially to be known that few automated minds could so encompass it with reason as to unmask it (and at the same time release themselves from harness.) We shall know that in order to dismiss the Machine we had to dismiss the automatic concepts. We had to be well aware that society *must accord with true intellectual understanding; must have as its most important task the optimum fulfilment of every individual mind, and so simplify itself as to be entirely within the compass of all human minds.*

Chapter 35

FURTHER CATASTROPHES

The rise of the human race on Earth was the result, I believe, of the influence for truth working on energy to produce matter, and to the combined influences of truth and energy producing first life, then intellect in human form. The character of human society arose, it would seem, out of the threat of catastrophe. Now we are again on the brink of catastrophe, and whether or not it extinguishes or wholly corrupts and debases our species depends on whether or not we at last succeed in realising our true potential.

The outstanding potential catastrophe recently to face us has been nuclear holocaust, which still threatens and still only requires a button to be pressed by intention or accident. But we are also faced with a series of more subtle potential disasters that could prove equally catastrophic. Autoprogression may continue causing such damage to our biosphere as shall be beyond Gaia to repair so that the Earth will no longer be able to support life as we know it. Our reckless consumption of resources may so deplete them that we become unable to sustain the Machine whilst yet having no planned and workable alternative of any kind to put in its place. The Machine is responsible for all these tribulations to come, but mistakenly overthrowing certain traditional controls is another source of possible disaster.

Failure to understand that false automatic reality contains some humantruth, and that normal human thinking and feeling, though mostly automated, is often well-intended, allows some humans, especially the young, to equate existing society with uncalled-for restriction of personal liberty. They demand freedom to do their own personal or group thing, objecting to restrictions that may happen to be necessary whereas at the same time they willingly conform to other automatic lores that are decidedly unnecessary. For instance, in the 1960's in Europe and America there was a revolt against the fairly rigid sexual morality of the time. This was not the outcome of a broad new moral view resulting from deep reason. It was simply a matter of the release of pent-up feeling that looked like moral liberation in that it cleared away rigidly intolerant, narrow prejudice against homosexuality, heterosexual relations before and outside marriage, and general co-habiting without licence. But it did little to release humans from their main bondage - to the Machine (which, as always, turned this 'liberation' to its own commercial advantage), and to the limitations of automated thinking. Thus it was ignored that one of the taboos thrown out, that against sexual promiscuity, was a very necessary one that had evolved through the experience of centuries - for good reasons though not in a sensible, acceptable way here in Western society - an outcome of which has been a dramatic and possibly catastrophic spread of AIDS.

That millions of humans throughout the world may be destined to die miserably from AIDS represents a tragic failure of humanity to understand and uphold good, necessary, *reasoned* morality. But it is well to remember that about seventy million individuals die every year throughout the world in any case, most naturally from old age perhaps but, in a sense, all tragically in that none of them found humantrue fulfilment in their lives. AIDS has become epidemic as a result of misuse of the vital means of reproduction, the abuse of a delicately balanced whole system which in turn has resulted, in the UK, from extremely narrow-minded controls in Victorian times going to extremes of permissiveness in modern times. Other miseries result from the struggle of our inner morality against the overbearing Machine - all sorts of mental disturbance, frequently causing physical illness and often resulting in the tragedy of suicide. Further miseries are caused by wars, that are immoral by humantrue definition but that automatic authority, according to its laws, persuades or obliges millions to fight and suffer nevertheless.

Our awareness is growing but not widely or quickly enough to overtake accelerating autoprogression. Our humanity is still losing the struggle against the Machine at a general level yet may not seem to be so because it is asserting itself on occasion at certain special levels, owing to much wider dissemination of information causing humanely reasoned reaction. For example, events in the Persian Gulf in 1987 would once have caused America and her allies to declare war on Iran and her allies. This did not happen because of worldwide fear of this dispute escalating to world nuclear war. There was similarly concerned human reaction to news of starvation in Ethiopia, and such reaction has even influenced the financial world. The stock exchange crisis of 1987 (Black Sunday), that would once have plunged world society into economic depression, was brought under control by financiers who had to admit, under public scrutiny, that it was 'unnecessary'. But that the false money-economy still holds sway over our habitual thinking is illustrated by the fact that the modern British 99p price tag still attracts buyers (because it seems significantly less than £1) as did the old 19/11d. The *fundamental* conflicts of reality more or less remain and keep emerging in other ways - terrorism for instance. If such conflicts are to be automatically ended, by authority of the Machine, it is likely to be through a more effective clampdown on humanity, whereby our affairs will be *totally* oriented to the automaton and geared to the interests of automated society regardless of humantrue morality.

It is said that our object in life is to pursue happiness. In fact it is the pursuit of truth, which alone is our road to happiness. Automatic reality does not bring lasting happiness because it does not pursue true fulfilment, and the more it autoprogresses the more shallow and transient its unequally shared artificial delights become.

I have expressed concern that people can read and even agree with books of a radical kind without actually letting their mind constructions be changed. It is a great menace to the human future that conscious selves remain unchanged despite the fact that the Machine is insane. Rather than change, although the fact of this reality's insanity is clearly and unmistakably pointed out to them - rather than be compelled by their inner minds immediately to determine that the world must be reformed as a matter of urgency - peoples' outer shells go to the pub, the club, or the dinner dance as planned, and go on playing the automatic game as always.

There are two ways of facing up to the actual world - as it is, and as it should be, according to whether it is seen through the eyes of the automated outer self or the aware inner self. There are then four ways in which one individual might judge another. Two of these depend on whether individual A is seeing through automated or aware eyes, and the other two on whether individual B is automated or aware. If both are automated, or both aware, each will understand the other's views and behaviour and judge them right, reasonable and sane. But if A is automated and B aware, or vice versa, then each will judge the other wrong, unreasonable and insane. In practice individuals and systems are seldom so clearly black or white, but shades of grey, so that judgements, and opinions, are various and confused.

For example, when attempting to judge the English public-school system you may find some features good and some bad. To be capable of definite judgement you have to decide whether the existing automatic reality is inevitable and, if not, what alternative reality ought to replace it. If the former, you will judge the system according to its good or bad effects in terms of existing automatic reality. If the latter, you will judge according to whether the system has good or bad effects in terms of bringing forward a better alternative reality. In the latter case, an education policy that fosters competitive hardness and exclusive privilege can not be justified, but that the opposite is true of the former case is demonstrated by the fact that public schools flourish in the UK, as they have done for generations.

It should be quite clear that the decision whether existing reality is to be tolerated or whether it must be replaced is of first importance. It is failure to make that decision, failure even to acknowledge that we are faced with the necessity of making it, that confuses our judgement. We judge situations partly according to automatic reality and partly by comparison with various versions of the ideal. This prevents us reaching united and agreed conclusions and allows a truly insupportable reality to continue. Politics pretends to be waging an imperative war between good and evil, in which mankind in general strives towards good but is perpetually frustrated by forces of evil.

The limited agreement, a decade ago, between Russian and American figureheads to destroy certain medium-range nuclear missiles was a welcome advance of human reason against the Machine. It might be looked back on as a remarkable political achievement. But it should be seen as the least we could expect in view of the fact that the existence of any nuclear weapon is an insanity and an insult to true human intellect.

Subsequent nuclear disarmament agreements have to be judged against automatic developments which indicate that we have not honestly changed direction. For example, there appears to be a black market in plutonium, which means that an increasing number of governments of different persuasions and with competing interests are developing their own nuclear weapons. As an instance of autoprogression in another field, all over the world we are over-fishing the seas. Driven by the money-economy to continue 'earning a living' from their occupation, fishermen are devising ever more efficient methods of maintaining the same catches from ever-decreasing fish stocks. And in Britain, going by the number of enormous hypermarkets already built or planned, mostly out-of-town and inaccessible to many poorer people, the available shopping facilities increasingly exceed by far the requirements of even our present high-consumption society. These events are automatically logical but in intellectual terms they are typical reckless developments that, in aggregate, point to human catastrophe.

The result of catastrophe could be our total destruction, through the application of intellect to the instinctive drives. Or it could be our de-humanisation, that would come from taking to extremes our presently growing practice of preferring automatic instinctive motives to those of intellect. For instance, that we should provide for each other is obvious to reason, but the money-economy demands that we charge much more as reward for our services than we would require for our subsistence. The profit and reward motive produces excess money that demands increasing goods and services, so that everybody (particularly those who are included in the equation, the well-to-do and employed, but also even those who are excluded, the 'poor' and unemployed) pays more and more for everybody else's money or material reward and profit. As another instance, Gandhi's life represented a human crusade against the Machine (in the guise of British dominion over India), and he wrote many letters to prominent persons of the time. He is a well-respected and loved figure, yet his influence for good has not prevailed. To illustrate this, a few years ago some of those letters were sold in the market-place at high money-prices that do not reflect a human valuation of his enlightenment as much as the money-economy's valuation of famous men's' letters as profitable investments.

By blindly pursuing automatic interests to their extremes we could well commit genocide. For example, the world population is increasing fast. Measures to control this increase cannot be immediately effective and are not being taken everywhere. Millions of people are in yearly danger of starvation from famine but such disasters are not anticipated in order to be forestalled. Instead the world responds, after the event and perhaps only because of public outcry, with unsatisfactory crash programmes of temporary relief. In 'rich' countries such as the USA agriculture is declining in scale because increased efficiency has caused internal food surpluses that the money-economy does not allow to be given away to other countries in the normal course of events. At the same time, out of desperate need in some 'poor' countries, soil is being eroded away as a result of over-working. Elsewhere, owing to the profit-motive, land is being spoiled by monoculture and the excessive use of artificial fertilisers. Yet experience suggests that given wise husbandry twice the present human population of the world could be supported from existing agricultural land without harm to its fertility. It is obvious that this good result would require intelligent co-operative care worldwide, but not clear to what extent it would depend on some degree of advanced but benign technology.

I will mention three other hazards. The first is the possibility of an energy crisis (dealt with at greater length in Chapter 48, Peaceable Action). If the world's supplies of energy suddenly fell short of demand, because the developing nations' consumption rapidly and unexpectedly rose to the high levels already reached in the developed countries at the same time as resources began to dwindle and the money-cost to increase, the resultant catastrophe can be imagined, as nations competed to the point of fighting for their share.

The other two hazards I shall deal with briefly because my knowledge of them is slight. One is a threat to the ozone, in Earth's upper atmosphere, that forms a layer that filters out the sun's dangerous ultra-violet rays. This threat comes chiefly from our releasing into the atmosphere chlorofluorocarbons, used in aerosols, fast-food cartons, refrigerators and mobile air-conditioning units. The danger has been recognised for some years but little action seriously contemplated until a growing hole in the ozone layer was detected. Common sense dictated that the release of chlorofluorocarbons should be discontinued forthwith, but common sense does not govern our world's affairs. Eventually the use of aerosols was banned, and other restrictive measures have been proposed but these are resisted all along the line by manufacturers whose commercial interests they adversely affect.

The third hazard is posed by a possible increase or decrease in the amount of carbon dioxide being released into the atmosphere that could disturb Gaia's delicate regulation of the Earth's temperature. Too much carbon dioxide, also methane and oxides of nitrogen, would increase its 'greenhouse effect' and cause global warming, resulting, amongst other things, in sea-water expanding and polar ice-caps melting, thus raising sea-levels, and in changed weather-patterns. Too little carbon dioxide and the greenhouse effect is reduced, bringing about a fall in temperature resulting, for one thing, in extension of the polar ice-caps and a new ice-age. It has been calculated that a change in average temperature of more than plus or minus 2deg.C would be disastrous, although recent opinion seems to be that greater variations could be tolerated. If the Machine continues to dominate, any variations that are due to automatic activities will be impossible to control because they are impelled by autoprogression, or by human reactions to it. For example, the rain forests of the Amazon and elsewhere are being cleared at the rate of fifty million or more acres per year - for timber, to make way for industries and vast cattle ranches, and by peasant people vainly attempting to survive by living off the land - vainly because the land is too poor to sustain crops. These activities are not only destroying the carbon-dioxide-absorbing jungle but also increasing the release of this gas into the atmosphere by the burning of felled trees and scrub. It is now clear that what we are facing is an increasing greenhouse effect - a major environmental concern. It is not clear to what extent this global warming is due to human activity and whether it would have occurred anyway due to other causes.

If we approach the problems intelligently, not only of physical survival but also of whole well-being, we will arrive at a humantrue society. If they are approached in the context of the Machine, however, in seeking solutions we shall still be pursuing automatic interests, though less blindly and in a more calculated way. I repeat, this could be the ultimate human catastrophe in the form of a super-Machine able to ensure the survival of our bodies, at least for a time, but so omnipotent as to make our intellectual potential forfeit, with the prospect of true fulfilment lost and gone forever (and if this experience were to be repeated on most planets like ours it could be a catastrophe for this universe's hope of true equilibrium).

Chapter 36

THE MIND ABOVE ALL

Our future depends on all individuals making the effort to achieve the common intellectual potential of the human mind. Our central problem is that our present selves, far short of their potential, are a scattered multiplicity of different conscious versions of reality, united only by an overall false automatic concept of reality.

If we are to solve all our other problems we first have to solve this central problem. To do this requires that we all become supraconscious, but we cannot do so or even appreciate that it can and must be done as long as we remain imprisoned in automated consciousness.

The key solution, which can unlock the central problem, is *intellation* - the opening of consciousness to the postconscious mind by which the self may be identified with its intellectual potential.

By intellating we honestly exercise intellect, the faculty of knowing and reasoning whose function is truth - humantruth. By seeking and finding humantruth we do become supraconscious and unable to be other than true. When all humans become so, world society will be in humantrue agreement.

So our destiny, and possibly the destiny of this universe, depends above all upon the fulfilment of each and every individual mind, and if it is possible for one mind to achieve supraconsciousness it is possible for all.

For us this means happiness. That we truly co-operate and are united in supraconsciousness will mean that we commonly fulfil truth which, in that it is our optimum fulfilment, is our ultimate satisfaction.

There is a quite common belief that idealism is a waste of time because humanity is incapable of realising it. But humanity has potential intellect and cannot be happy until it is fulfilled, when our true awareness will be satisfied with nothing less than the ideal. He or she who rejects the ideal has not attained true awareness. Those of us who are not intellating are not advancing towards our full human nature, and until we commonly practice intellation we shall not begin to achieve our full humantrue state.

Yet suppose my theory of true equilibrium is not true, and Big Bangs and multi-million year universes are to go on in succession without end. Would it then be *necessary* for life to achieve intellect, and then to fulfil it? Well, it is necessary for *us* to fulfil it, having achieved it, if for no other reason than that we are dangerous to ourselves and all life otherwise. Apart from that, intellect would not be necessary to a random and totally indifferent universe, nor to the temporal instinctive happiness that can be achieved by the self-fulfilment of consciousness alone. But all life-forms are in competition to succeed and subject to a natural influence to progress. Perhaps intellect would never be achieved if all creatures were to reach a state of optimum happy consciousness, like whales, dolphins and elephants, escaping from direct competition and, therefore, from the impulsion to progress, so that no further evolution was necessary. But whales, dolphins and elephants are exceptions. Most creatures are compelled to compete and strive in order to survive, and it only requires that one species be impelled to evolve furthest of all and achieve potential intellect, as we have done, for disaster to result. We have brought disaster and the threat of extinction to many creatures, including whales, dolphins, elephants and ourselves. Again, were we happy, unaware of the consequences of our actions and morally unaffected by the influence of truth, then the fate of life on the small planet Earth, or on any other planet, or the fate of the presently expanding universe, would have no dread significance, only the plain, unnoticed fact of its existence. But we *are* morally aware, and unhappy, and the universe *does* matter to reason, and therefore to us.

If more than one species had achieved the faculty of knowing and reasoning perhaps there would be a much greater likelihood of realising truth in our world on Earth. We are surrounded by animals of lower mental capacity and, having no critical mental equals, we as a species tend to believe that our activities are altogether superior and do not see that our civilisation does not make much sense. Perhaps the situation is similar to that of the conscious self that cannot truly assess itself unless it is willing to accept the aid of the postconscious - both its own postconscious and that of another self. We, being mostly blind in this sense, will not credit any of our own kind with the capability of seeing wholly and truly. We lack an undeniable example of the true, living, intellectual nature and state that would surely show us a supremely high level of happy satisfaction and contentment appropriate to our species, a state that is as yet beyond our experience. But we *can* foresee this perfect state by way of reason, bringing true awareness of its possibility.

Consider once more the chaotic confusion of our world, which comes of humanity applying irrelevant ancestral instincts to an inappropriate Machine. In literature this is represented by the novel, which grabs the emotions but betrays true intellect by going along the familiar road of automatic reality. The true road leads another way and has no familiar landmarks. It has to be negotiated by the dead reckoning of reason. Born again, 'fundamentalist' Christianity provides an example of emotion ousting reason by attacking intellect and accepting as true that which is unknown, unnecessary, unhelpful and, to say the least, unlikely. It self-righteously raises one set of 'virtuous' emotions in its followers but can also arouse aggressive hate against its opponents, because blind faith needs emotional causes to reinforce it as well as false reason to underpin its self-deception.

There exists throughout the world a Sherlock Holmes cult, a strange phenomenon the basis of which is the strong desire of many individuals to attach themselves to an imaginary omnipotent figurehead and invest it with realistic power. Belief in god, or cosmic consciousness, is a related example of this desire. Such cults and faiths contain some elements of truth. In the case of Sherlock Holmes this element is the fact that he did exist in Conan Doyle's stories. In a similar way god exists in tradition, backed up by holy books. In the case of cosmic consciousness, as well as god, the element underlying this conception can only be the twin influences of truth and energy. The influence of truth promoted the principle of unity and co-operation as a means of realising truth. Energy responded by organising itself into atoms, then molecules, then chains and groups of molecules, i.e. by forming matter. In this present era on Earth, humans should resist the influence of energy by bringing autoprogression to a halt. Rather than attributing wisdom to these influences and looking to them for guidance, we should perceive that energy is open to *our* guidance, and the true influence looks to our potential wisdom for expression. Our minds are the spearhead of the true influence, to further which they should clearly tell us that *we* must now unite and co-operate.

At this point I think it would be helpful to reconsider the reasons, as I see them, why we humans are in our present predicament and why we cannot extricate ourselves by our own individual effort of mind having collective effect.

First of all, to get ourselves into perspective, let us ask the question - what exactly are we? We are an intellectual species of life that came into being between 100,000 and 30,000 years ago. For the 15,000,000,000 years or so since the last Big Bang, previous to the appearance of ourselves or any similar species, no mind, no potentially intellectual consciousness, existed in the universe. The sparse but virulent growth on the Earth's surface, our civilisation, which might be described as a blight, is the product of the instinctive employment of part-intellect. That which represents our whole intellect - such written or spoken language as transcribes pure intellation - has arisen solely and entirely from the postconscious mind (in our human case the neocortex) with the encouragement of the universal influence for truth and the obedient help of consciousness. So outside of our minds, and the like minds of others, there is no true awareness in the universe, for living intellect is its furthest and ultimate advance.

The immediate purpose behind the development of instinctive consciousness is reproductive survival, and that development ceases once survival is secured, as in the case of whales, crocodiles and elephants. Most animals continue to develop because their survival remains challenged and insecure. Where this consciousness has developed to the point of being *assisted* by dawning intellect, as in the human case, its purpose is still survival but it partially breaks with instinctive inhibition and advances by reasoned intention, then calls a voluntary halt once survival success is attained, e.g. the Bushmen of Africa and the Australian Aborigines. Intellect *used* by instinct founded the automaton and gave basic form to the Machine, which first flourished in favourable climates - for instance the Egyptian, Chinese and Indian civilisations - which eventually ran out of challenges, became locked in convention, and stagnated. The much more vigorous application of part-intellect on the part of Northern peoples, probably to meet climatic challenges associated with the last ice age, has resulted in almost the entire human race becoming locked into automatic conflict with itself, facing new and escalating challenges created by its own competitive conditioning of that consciously controlled part of intellect (distinct from postconscious intellect), and threatening its own survival as nations of people throw their mental effort into commercial, ideological and military struggles against each other. Such is our present reality which produces copious thinking and writing of great significance to the false Machine but little true meaning, for it represents the intellectual confusion of a society suspended between its wrong reality and its true potential.

Yet it would appear that every intellectual species in the universe must pass through this false and dangerous phase in order that its intellectual capacity be developed to the point where it is capable of achieving its two objectives - chiefly to further the true influence towards equilibrium; then, as the vehicle of that chief objective, to establish, by *intention* of supraconscious intellect alone, a true society, in our case a humantrue society, as the means of our own survival and that of the whole Earth. We certainly already possess the necessary mental capacity - we *can* call a halt and meet the supreme twofold challenge of truth, first to understand what we have to do and then to do it. The question is, *shall* we do so?

The prospect for humantruth is uncertain because, almost unbelievably, it is questionable whether we shall achieve our potential. General awareness is advancing but as yet the pure supraconscious intellect is bound to resemble a poor traveller in a hostile country. It is so ignored, ridiculed, spurned or threatened as usually to be persuaded, if not forced, to go in disguise or into hiding.

The mystics and meditators would have us imitate the benign and stable hunter-gathers' mentality, but without stepping back into their actual physical reality. But the hunter-gathers' mentality and reality were mutually appropriate. Our minds and circumstances, having arrived where they now are, cannot go back to where they were but we can seek, in another direction, humantrue minds and circumstances that are equally benign and stable. We can unlearn false lessons but cannot forget past experience and feeling, only pass beyond it. We have to rest on our knowledge but re-assess it as we carry reason forward until the truth is reached. We have to break with our present egos because the automaton created them out of instinct and in its image, so that they are components of the motors of the Machine, not, as they should be, human motors of the world. Were we to go back to the beginning again, unequal, divided and automated as we are, we would merely re-enact our evolution from past to present because we would be contained by the old, familiar framework that demands motivation by the same competitive ego. The ego is no more fixed than the Machine, for it is simply emotional and wilful support presently attached by instinct to the competitive automatic drives. To create a humantrue society of equal individuals requires that we detach our egos from automatic reality and reshape them to support our truly constructive, co-operative, supraconscious intellectual effort to that end.

It has been suggested that just as an individual's mind can be instrumental in curing its body's cancer, millions of people meditating would get rid of the cancer presently diseasing human society. But to begin with, as I have said already, there is no such cosmic consciousness, so in this regard the act of meditation does no more than affirm vague personal wishes or desires for good - it is not a united, informed and agreed determination to make society true. In the case of the individual with cancer the central conscious will expresses a strong determination to get well and the body's immune system, that determination being shared by each of its individual cells, responds by attacking the cancer with renewed vigour. However, in the case of the human body the cancer is an unwelcome and destructive intruder, while in the

Machine it is a dominant function. In the case of present human society the Machine is its body and we are its cells – *all* its cells, including those that serve its immune system *and* those that serve its cancers. We all wish to survive, if possible in happy contentment, but the automaton's will is dominant and to survive under its competitive rules we all have to submit largely without thinking, to some degree passive and benign but in many ways malignant to the whole organism. So despite the fact that the general human conscience *desires* a humantrue world, and this desire might be strengthened by widespread meditation, as long as a strong structure of contrary interest and desire - the Machine - overwhelmingly dominates our wilful ego and effective conscious thinking, our humanitarian desires can have little effect.

Consider the fact that the natural world survives successfully, according to its own lights. All animals strongly desire to survive and to experience a satisfactory life, as we do. But this they largely succeed in doing (viewing survival as that of the species overall, disregarding the fate of individuals) whilst we, though more conscious of our individual satisfaction, as a species seem well set for extinction. They succeed because their pattern of instinct not only imparts to them the life-force impulsion to live but also subjects them to a strict code of behaviour that *ensures* their overall satisfactory survival, as far as can be foreseen. We fail because our social pattern and code of behaviour works *contrary* to our best interests as a whole species, and so against our satisfactory, i.e. happy, survival. Therefore a vague common human wish for reform is not enough. The will of individuals has to combine into a collective will, and then individual minds have to combine in collective agreement as to the means of making society humantrue, with a common understanding of those means and a willingness to employ them in order to achieve the desired ends.

The circumstances of cells in the body can be likened to those of automated humans in the Machine, and to those of ants in an ant-hill. All are governed collectively by an overall instinctive will and pattern (in our case automatic will and Machine-pattern) and individually by precise personal instructions. If cells or ants had individual awareness and free will (which humans have), their systems could succeed (which ours does not) only if they themselves were agreed, cooperative and willingly supportive (which we are not).

To get out of our present predicament we need to have all minds raised to a high level of awareness so as to be capable of enlightenment. This is in some sense acknowledged, for a commonplace objection to moral reforms is that, however truly good they may be, they are impracticable because the majority of people resist them for a variety of bad reasons, or unthinking feelings. But it is not at all generally understood what constitutes intelligence, awareness, enlightenment or truth, nor what is the point and purpose of these qualities.

The conventional view is the automatic view. It recognises a need for better education but sees this as instituted training by the Machine that children are inherently capable of absorbing at varying levels from very low to very high. This contains a minority view that children of all degrees of intelligence can benefit from 'hot housing', a means of forcing mental development from the earliest age in order to raise the level of educational attainment. This minority view is that if children are given a benign and stressless prenatal experience, then brought up in a similar environment without question or doubt about the self, about this special environment, or about the imposed programme of concentration on learning conventional knowledge and reason, they shall be better and happier achievers at school and in the Machine. Those who respond well to this process are described as 'bright', and the outstandingly responsive as 'geniuses'. These are automatic terms of respect that measure intellect, its point and purpose, in terms of its contribution of yet more knowledge, and its successful application to the Machine, and of the automatic rewards of status, money and power that this attracts. According to this view the supraconscious mind which rejects automatic reality might be described as clever but naive, dull and impractical, and is normally dismissed as irrelevant because it is 'out of this world' - regarded as eccentric, by which is meant next door to lunatic.

The supraconscious view is that intellectual capacity does not naturally vary widely, and that conventional education is the amoral application rather than fulfilment of the mind. Of course it is highly desirable that parents should be positively but tranquilly benign in an ideal world, but that they can be so in this troubled world means that they are closed to true awareness. There is no doubt at all that mental stimulation from the earliest age is vital, but a cocooned, specialised upbringing and education produces a narrowly oriented mind for the use of automatic reality, like a computer or electronic calculator. The filled mind is not the fulfilled intellect that must doubt question and criticise from the first and might appear stupid because it is stressfully preoccupied with seeking answers, which the educators are not providing, to its constant question 'why?'. This question was probably first prompted, in the womb, by the same question in the minds and on the lips of parents. The so-called genius may brilliantly advance in the mastery of a special subject, on a narrow front by virtue of the vast specialised knowledge this necessitates, but will not forward vital reason, on a wide front based on general information, *because* that brilliant mind is so full of knowledge as to have little room for broad, and especially for critically constructive, reasoning The important thing in mind development is that it should first establish a sound, true, broad reasoning base, using only essential knowledge. Only thus can further knowledge be given true meaning as it is taken in, so that, by being exposed to all possible correlations, it finds its rightful place in the true train of reason.

There is a view, derived from scientific observations of dissipative systems leading to a belief in the desirability of a human 'high synergy' society, that increase in human population is a vital contribution to the complexity on which evolution builds and therefore to the success of such a society. This view implies that the larger and more powerfully complex the Machine becomes the happier we shall be, and that science and technology are well able to provide for the vast populace by operating on a highly automated universal scale. In my contrary view the opposite is true. Earth evolution has already achieved its objective - our intellectual potential. That potential will be fulfilled by supraconsciousness and a humantrue society, with a population kept to a level that Earth can sustain without strain. The energy of a humantrue society has to be self-generated by thoughtful intention. A 'high synergy' society would automatically generate rising energy so that it might not decline and stagnate, but it would not be humantrue, must autoprogress, and could self-destruct.

Humantrue society, and its regulation, must come from the collective effort of independently developed but agreed and co-operative individual minds. The evolving Machine may be presently supported by the will of humanity but it is the will of automated individuals whom the Machine has then centrally to control. This, whatever method is employed, is a recipe for unrest.

This whole book is really about making life happy and satisfactory all round, and that is the inner concern of everyone. As individuals we all try to arrange our private family lives as happily as possible, and a world of individuals should do the same for life as a whole. What the individual can envisage, the human world can realise. The collective mind should reflect the individual true inner mind, supported by individual postconscious will. What is truly good for one is good for all. The individual reason and will for good should multiply into a collective reason and will for good. All that stands in the way is mental conditioning which convinces us that that which should logically be inevitable, because it is so reasonable, is in practice impossible.

It is generally thought that social evolution, notwithstanding the automatic evolution of the Machine, can be influenced for the better by human personal or 'spiritual' enlightenment. But such enlightenment is expected to come in spurts, and more in private than public. Mental spearheads or forerunners of thought rise, fall, but rise again to advance awareness, but in isolated pockets. They are followed by others, in many little columns of separated, specific, conscientious thought constructions, piecemeal, disconnected, and therefore ineffective. In the meantime the Machine, which goes contrary to the best of that thinking in any case, continues to govern regardless and to hold the main attention of our minds, subject only to sporadic superficial humanitarian changes. The only way for our humanity to impress itself on our society is, as has been said already, for minds to turn away from further autoprogression, work out a complete alternative humantrue social system, and face the absolute necessity of putting it in place of the Machine as soon as possible.

As it is, our broadest and most advanced thinking is not going on in the public minds of supreme leaders, or university dons, or politicians, or scientists, or industrial tycoons, or well-known authors, or newspaper editors, or recognised philosophers, but it might be going on in the mind of some unknown individual here, some deprived individual there, or ignored individuals elsewhere. In the minds of such individuals, whoever and wherever they may be, and all of those who are also intellating privately despite an automatic public image, rests the hope for the salvation of ourselves and our world.

Sometimes I find it hard to concentrate on reading this, my own work, so as to make sense of it. But when I am concentrating well the true meaning comes through. Should you have the same difficulty, please do not assume that the work is boring, or meaningless, and put it aside. I would ask you to consider whether it is not the case that you too are failing to concentrate your attention. Persevere with making new connections in your mind if necessary for your understanding of what I am driving at, or for improving on it. This process of intellation is the only way to realise truth, which, in turn, is the only way to make the world good.

Remember the proposition that the way we want or need to be is the way we *shall* be when our own mind has reached truly significant conclusions and is in agreement with all other minds who are commonly founded in humantruth - i.e when we are supraconscious. I imply that my words are humantrue (though not necessarily giving the *whole* humantruth) not because of personal vanity but because every honest correlation of my mind confirms it. Your disagreement will prevail only if it is the product of deeper and wider correlation, and therefore truly better reason, not if it is merely the expression of wilful prejudice.

I repeat : the prime responsibility of intellectual creatures is to observe truth, and we have no right to anything which falls short of truth. That the truth is rejected by the whole world does not make it untrue but confirms that the world is assuredly false. Those who claim to be right because the ways of the world support them are those who yet fail to see that they, like most of humanity, are mentally harnessed to the false Machine.

Chapter 37

HUMANTRUE FINDINGS

I t is necessary that the whole human race changes its mind. In order to do so we have to change the ways in which we arrive at understanding - to put reason before feeling. This is necessary because our existing reality *is* wrong, which is why it offends our moral sensibilities so much. It is amazing that humanity as a whole has failed to reach this conclusion. Amazing that for all our mental capacity we still prefer to satisfy our instinctive sensibilities, putting feeling before reason.

It is possible to get used to anything, and then usual to resist change. The great majority of us have adjusted our feelings and values to the reality that exists, accepting the here and now as natural. We try to select and reduce our experience to a personal reality whose joys and sorrows we can more or less handle. But this allows autoprogression to roll on unabated, unseen because it grips the world behind our backs, pulling the strings that we imagine to be in our hands. And although it never gives us best overall we save face by pretending that this is the best of all possible worlds.

Our present realities, our own concoctions of memberships - of a family, a community, a racial group, a nation, an ideology - are combinations that may be workable on a small scale because they can be made to fit locally for the sake of close relations but not worldwide because they are then found to conflict uncontrollably. To understand our present world we have to look at it as a whole, which our literature is supposed to do. Our failure to achieve this understanding is demonstrated by the fact that James Joyce's Ulysses is considered to be one of the foremost examples of literature this century. This brilliant book throws penetrating light on the personal realities of a handful of people in Dublin and through them reveals the general plight and delight of humans everywhere. It does not reveal the nature of automatic reality that makes the universal character what it is - this hopeless and insane struggle between animal instinct and the intellect. Neither does Ulysses reveal that this undeniably real human actuality, that so recognisably *does* exist, *need not* exist; *would not* exist but for this obscured yet universally accepted fact - that the founding automaton makes us the ridiculous victims of an unequal battle between our true humanity and the almighty Machine. If we are to probe meaningfully into humanity it is not our present reality we must explore but our intellect, its ultimate advance in mind evolution, the postconscious and its humantrue findings.

If we aspire to better things why do we not attain them? Should we not be ashamed of the novel Ulysses, as a prominent example of the failure of human beings to achieve intellectual potential, rather than be proud of it as a work of genius? Consider the characters in this book, ordinary persons motivated by the same factors and contained by the same limitations as all humans on Earth. What good effect are they having on the generally bad state of our society? Are they likely to prevent war, for example, or to stir it up? Do they tend always towards reason, compassion and co-operation, or always towards reckless chaos? It is so much easier to tolerate or take part in the random interplay of instinctive emotions and bodily functions because understanding of these things exists, ready-made, in all of us. There is a kind of comfort in it. It is so much more difficult to stand apart and successfully make the case for humantruth, because understanding of *it* has to be personally created and newly developed in each and every mind and goes against the grain of reality.

Existing reality allows nobody to experience whole happiness. Generally speaking, the happier persons appear to be, the less complex their thinking must be. The reason is that our whole happiness lies in the fulfilment of truth and this has nowhere been achieved. When we talk of happiness, few of us have any clear and complete conception of what it can be. If we could commonly conceive of the happiness that humantrue society, the right reality, would bring, and which we sadly lack, then that ideal society would not seem so remote a prospect. I shall try to convey a sense of that whole happiness in Chapter 44, Framework of Life. Our present joys are of a lesser kind; foreground highlights against a dark background, automatic attractions that are the delights of unfulfilled minds. It is the automaton that is satisfied, not ourselves, because our society fulfils its aims rather than ours. That is why it is easier for automated individuals to find apparent contentment.

Animals have conflicts, but every instinctive activity is for the general well-being of the species. Ideally we should have no conflicts of interest because our intellect can care for us better without them. But the Machine bristles with conflicts of interest, such as between employer and employed. This was illustrated some time ago by a British Miners Union debate called to decide whether Coal Board proposals for the running of a new pit, made in the interests of productivity (i.e. profitability), were also in the interests of the miners. The debate failed to find clear issues and the matter proved impossible to deal with except on the basis of conflict of prejudice, and therefore impossible to resolve, because the aims of humanity and the Machine are irreconcilable. What is best for the Machine is not good for its human workers and what is best for the workers would be bad for the Machine, in the long term if not seemingly in the short term.

This irreconcilable conflict was also illustrated at Christmas in 1914 in the trenches of France at the beginning of the Great War. Humanity, that had no true reason to fight, was represented by soldiers facing each other across no-man's-land, who climbed out of their trenches and met together in friendship. Had humanity then grasped responsibility for its affairs this must have marked the end of the war. But the Machine was in command, represented by a leadership which had committed itself to war, and by military marshals who had committed all these young men to battle and who now asserted their legal authority by opening artillery fire. The sound of carol singing was drowned out, the soldiers fled back to their respective trenches, and the war went on for four years and millions died horribly for no good reason.

The general instinctive human will to survive as a species has been translated into the selfish will of the individual or group to survive within and according to the Machine. With religions and ideologies and national cultures, also with higher ranks, professions and other privileged positions, it is a will to preserve these limited realities and their automatic recognition and protection.

Only the free and independent mind can contain whole supraconsciousness of humantruth. But in a humantrue society each individual will would be reinforced by the humantrueness of world society, and by the general will to keep it so.

A chief obstacle to humantruth is that we refuse to accept it for the reason that our overwhelming reality does not acknowledge it. Yet that which would be true in a perfect world *is* perfectly true; it is true that we would prefer a perfect world, therefore we should prefer the truth to false automatic reason both because it is true and because it alone can prepare the way for a humantrue world. We are only required to release our minds from the shackles of prejudiced opposition. Thereafter, if we take intellect as our guide, we shall be faced with great upheavals and apparent sacrifices but shall inevitably arrive at humantruth; the nearest we can get to perfection.

As a general rule, insofar as weighty humantrue ideals have occurred to them, the young presently manage lightly to shrug these off, excepting where such ideals are given a popular temporary image like 'Live Aid' in Ethiopia, or are primarily a matter of feeling like the present wave of opposition to war. The hard-working, money-earning, child-rearing middle-aged person normally has no time to spare for high ideals, and the old who have learned some true lessons no longer have energy to spare, or much opportunity, for impressing their wisdom on the world. We, the conglomerate human race, our conscious selves, are given to the Machine, our minds largely made over to automatically calculated thought. We are not our true selves, which, situated within the postconscious sphere, would make our society in intellect's true image.

It can be argued that we *have* survived, despite everything. We even increase in overall numbers, despite the Machine and all its inhumanities. We might go to the extent of arguing that nuclear war would not exterminate us but so reduce our numbers as to benefit our survival as a species. But that is a callous argument that ignores the suffering in such a war, and in its aftermath. Imagine the agony and grief inseparable from the stark fact that ordinary (not nuclear) wars have caused the deaths of one thousand five hundred million humans since the battle of the Somme. Even this sombre fact does not impress upon us that our rightful destiny is to observe truth, and that we are clearly and dismally failing to achieve that destiny. Our present reality is a matter of survival mostly in terms of the sheer unthinking and instinctive life-force purpose to express energy, even to the point of nuclear holocaust. If we go on surviving in this way, without annihilation but becoming ever more automated, we shall come to know even deeper dissatisfaction, but, not understanding our own intellects, we shall never know why.

The majority get some satisfaction from their role as cogs in the Machine, whether as members of the governing or executive elite or as units of the work-force. But at best there are satisfaction-gaps, partly filled by ambitions, future hopes or fanciful dreams. The gaps are then topped up with substitutes; from music, books, travel, games and hobbies, to alcohol, cream-cakes, sports, strip-shows and fruit machines. All this does not amount to true fulfilment, whatever we pretend. It is overshadowed by knowledge of injustice, hunger, neglect, aggression and despair in the world - the other face of the automatic economy's coin - and it is challenged by our lurking awareness of abdicated responsibilities.

The human condition is presently relative to automatic reality and the individual's position in it, which can be anything from extreme privilege to utterly miserable poverty. The concept of humantrue society, on the other hand, is of an optimum standard of life that everybody equally enjoys. Humantruth could not countenance such states of being as are a normal and inevitable part of automatic reality, for example deprivation, which I have referred to frequently and now try to describe more fully.

Deprivation is never fully admitted or truly acknowledged because the normally pictured national character is on the privileged side of the social scale. It is this character that is the voice, and manager, of the media; that may look at the deprived with sympathy but does not look at reality from their viewpoint. Automated privileged persons look mainly to their own interests, and to the interests of the underprivileged only when these involve no sacrifice and present no threat. The underprivileged, by the very nature of their deprivation, lack opportunity, will, energy, confidence and inclination to take the initiative in their own interests.

To be poor in worldly terms is not necessarily to be deprived. The Scottish highlanders before the infamous clearances had very little but were happy and contented together. To be wretchedly poor is to be deprived of life's joys *and* bodily needs. Modern poverty is being deprived of sufficient money, and therefore of automatic satisfactions rather than basic necessities, yet can damage mental as well as physical health. The urban poor are subject to all the accumulating horrors of living below the standard of life to which society in general is geared. The Machine has obliterated much of the natural open countryside (which gave joy to the highlanders) and replaced it with concrete jungles, admission to whose pleasures and privileges requires money. The urban poor lack the normal facilities so that their shelter, environment, food and clothing are of a low quality and their mental stimulation, emotional satisfaction and general contentment is impaired. As a consequence they themselves, in the quality of their beings, also tend to become sub-standard, even to some extent in their genes, so that their defects may be passed on to their children. This means not only that they become even less able to fight back, but that they seem incapable, in the blinkered eyes of the thoughtless privileged, of appreciating anything better than they already have. This was the cause of racial discrimination in South Africa, and in the southern states of America, which is not primarily a matter of skin colour but of the emotional inability of the privileged (white) to treat as equals those who are underprivileged (particularly black), because they are *not* presently actually equal. Overcoming this discrimination is a matter of understanding that all humans are potentially acceptably equal; a matter of bringing in a humantrue society that enables all to reach full potential; a matter, in the meantime, of recognising and condemning unnecessary differences and inequalities, but understandingly tolerating those that are presently inescapable until they disappear.

It is evident that the mental and physical condition of humans, and so the quality and length of their life expectancy, is lower the further down the existing amoral social scale they are. That this is still true, despite our pretended morality, is indicated by the apparent fact that upwards of one quarter of the children in Britain, one of the 'richer' countries of the world, are living in poverty and are undernourished - a fact that might be expected to rouse us to urgent action but does not. This situation will continue unless humanitarian initiative *is* taken, because an effect of poverty is also to rob us of the will to rise above it, relieve its ills, and make our own differently satisfying standards of life. Travelling further to the better shops, or cultivating the garden to get healthier, cheaper food becomes too much of an effort. So does visiting health clinics. It is virtually impossible for the long-term unemployed to bolster their confidence to the point of convincing and persuading a prospective employer that they should get the job. When we are poor, pinched, undernourished, cold and shabby, most institutions of the Machine - run by the better-off, who are employed by others even better-off - feel closed to us because of our class. And when we are subject to all the pressures, such as housework and children, but with almost none of the pleasures of adult consumerism, we turn for release to smoking and drinking, habits which are not good for the body or the pocket but which may be the only things to keep us going. Against this mean and empty background it is hardly surprising that many of us should turn to crime, and be condemned for it by others of very different background.

There are other facets of relative deprivation. In the competitive Machine anyone who does not belong to the upper ranks of the hierarchy might well feel deprived - of authority, power, influence and responsibility for human destiny, particularly that of the self. For instance, there appears to be a marked deterioration in health and life expectancy in the descending ranks of the British Civil Service. The unwarranted power of 'superiors' and enforced subservience of 'inferiors', in an unnatural automated version of the pecking order, evidently imposes greater stress on the latter and is likely to cause them to suffer many and various unhappy and unhealthy consequences of stress. This must be especially so where Machine 'inferiors' would have been instinctive dominants in the *natural* pecking order, and whose 'superiors' would have been submissives.

In humantruth we should not allow ourselves to tolerate the fact that *anybody* is deprived. We must all equally benefit from life, and give to it, according to the same standard. What that standard should be in material terms must be determined for us by the safely available and replaceable resources of Earth.

Otherwise it is up to us supraconsciously to decide the constitution of our society.

It is worth noting that about one in six of the world's population is a Chinese peasant, newly liberated from the old landlords and the more recently imposed cultural revolution. Eight hundred million of them live directly off the land, feeding the other two hundred million Chinese and self-surviving almost entirely by their own skill and physical labour. We might think this a hard and primitive life. To them it seems to be their eternal and inevitable struggle alongside nature, with so many all in the same boat, and so little technology interfering as not to awaken those dreams of easier ways and tempting things that give rise to dissatisfaction. They periodically suffer natural disasters, particularly floods but, where the automaton has not yet introduced them to the false delights of the competitive money economy, it is doubtful whether many of them feel deprived. To them life is naturally hard, and to be contentedly endured. If their labour burdens were lightened by a few simple mechanical aids, their rivers controlled in order to prevent flooding, their population stabilised and, most of all, were they to achieve a state of supraconscious awareness, then their way of life could be yet more happy and contented, and infinitely more fulfilled. This could possibly represent the humantrue norm.

But, as I have mentioned, the Chinese government is beginning to introduce the peasants to money-incentives. Their situation illustrates the crucial human choice between its humanity and the automaton. If China allows the competitive money economy to gain this foothold, she will achieve the objective of raising productivity but at the cost of growing dissatisfaction having to be met by accelerating material consumerism and general automation. She would end up producing food by mechanical means and joining with the West in selling out her true potential to the Machine and exploiting whole Earth resources to exhaustion.

The alternative for China, as for all humanity, is supraconscious awareness in support of humantrue society. This might not achieve the immediate objective of increased productivity that the prospect of gain can persuade people to achieve, but even if people do not readily respond cooperatively and voluntarily no other solution should be attempted. The humantruth should be constantly reiterated so that individuals, seeing the results of humanity's failure to take responsibility for itself, will eventually understand that each *is* fully responsible for the life of all. And as supraconscious humans begin voluntarily to give their labour in the common cause (not because they are made to, as under communism, but because they intelligently wish to) they will know new and deep satisfaction. Both labour and satisfaction will then cause each other to increase, enriching rather than exhausting the whole. This

understanding is vital - that without supraconscious awareness there is no
human future.

It is possible to see the Machine as a logically balanced reciprocal system.
Such a view is likely to be elitist, for it does not show sympathetic awareness
of ordinary worldwide human experience. To apply the laws of physics to
humanity and its society in this way is to ignore this fact - that truly reasoned
opposition to automatic society arises from the most broadly advanced
intellects. It follows that a society that is to be acceptable to intellect must be
arranged by intellect - it must be humantrue, which means it shall be
acceptable also to honest common awareness. Creatures of nature do not
criticise instinct for its brutalities because they *do* follow the laws of physics
and so *cannot* criticise. The whole significance of the birth of intellect is that
in order to grow it must lay down and keep to its own new guide lines, for it
transcends all that has gone before. It represents not a continuation of the
same evolution but a revolution.

The following remarks relate to the foregoing but presuppose belief in my
theory that realisation of truth, in its various meanings, is the purpose of life,
with universal true equilibrium as its consummation. I have said that I do not
insist on this belief but also have to say that the further my intellation goes
the more the probability of this theory being true is confirmed. Garrett
Hardin's three laws of thermodynamics are:

- we can't win

- we are sure to lose

- we can't get out of the game

My response is that whether or not we can win depends on what we regard
as winning, or losing. If, as I believe, our objective is to realise truth, then we
can win.

I believe that the scientifically accepted second law of thermodynamics states
unequivocally that the entropy of a closed system must increase. Without
doubt we must eventually die as individuals, and as a species. If universal life
fails to achieve its objective - truth - then this universe is also doomed, but
not exactly to die. It, and its governing physical laws will be converted from

expanding to imploding, then eventually back to expanding and so ad infinitum.

If we remain automated as a society we certainly shall not get out of the game. But if we begin pursuing our true objective we will enter another reality with different values; no longer a game but the essential stuff of life, to arrive at which was the ultimate objective of the game. The laws of thermodynamics, and the reality of which they are part, need not necessarily be absolute.

It has been suggested, according to the belief that the laws of thermodynamics *are* absolute at least in the present universe, that world human society is becoming a closed system and so is doomed. There is a relationship between this belief and the so-called political 'new enlightenment' that rejects controlled socialism and praises free enterprise. To keep the present system open it is held that autoprogression must be continued and accelerated, though hopefully in a humane way. The suggested means of making it humane is the observance of moral influences, ultimately by submitting ourselves to supposed superior intelligences - to consciousness of 'god' or 'cosmos', through prayer or meditation.

These suggestions arise from misunderstanding. If we remain harnessed to the machine we will be dependently subject to autoprogression that *cannot* be made humane. There is no god or superior cosmic intelligence, only our own postconscious minds. And we cannot be guided by the moral influence of intellect when autoprogression demands the *application* of our intellect to its aims and interests.

Dissipative systems increase in entropy because they accumulate toxicity, which, in our case, means that our will and ability to regenerate energy declines. The reason for this is that such systems are not designed to so cleanse and renew themselves that they operate perpetually. Under the influence of life-force, the development of life is accomplished by continual reproduction and mutation of its forms and systems in competition. This ensures advance in complexity with the object of achieving intellect. Once a fully intellectual system is achieved it shall be capable, under the influence of truth, of making itself perfectly viable and stable. The stable intellectual system (such as human society, which can be totally reformed, as distinct from our physical bodies that probably can not and should not change so dramatically) will independently dispose of its toxicity and regenerate energy, in observance of truth, so as to fully serve its purpose of reinforcing the universal influence of truth. Intellectual systems must end, of course, when matter breaks down as the physical universal dissipative system comes to an end, but the universe which the influence of truth brings to successful conclusion will not die, nor be explosively reborn - it will have been already permanently transformed.

The Machine sustains its expression of energy by continually changing its systems through autoprogression. As an automatic overall system it presently thus contrives to keep itself open, its entropy now decreasing, if anything. But it keeps us from realising our objective, truth, which has always been the unknowing objective of life everywhere. So we must overcome the forces underlying autoprogression, in order to gain that objective, by observing our true morality. Humantrue society shall rise above the laws of thermodynamics and, when our job is done and the influence has grown strong enough, these laws will be superseded by the principle of true equilibrium - the ultimate, perpetual state of being.

In Chapters 7 and 8, I dealt with the way in which the Machine conditions our thinking and characters *eccentric* to our fundamental nature. Humantrue reality would be entirely *concentric* to our true nature. Our adult minds would be already reformed supraconsciously and intellating truly. When we came into the world we would find it true. We would not have systematically to falsify our minds, split into two and think deviously in order to live. We would not have to accept parts of the world, its institutions and practices, and reject the rest. We would be able, willing and happy to be part of it all. We are great intellects, able to make life wholly agreeable. There is no good reason why it should be so hard, fearful, confusing, frustrating and disappointing.

Since my ongoing intellation continually confirms the concept of true equilibrium I am bound to return to it constantly as the ultimate explanation of everything. For instance - the universe is composed of energy, which exerts enormous influences; electro-magnetism, gravity, heat, light and so on. Truth is greater than energy, for it would still exist were energy to cancel itself out, but truth lacks the potency of substance. If truth is to achieve its aim its influence in the universe must increase, by way of intellect, whilst the substantial potency of energy reduces. It is conceivable that the present universal expansion and evolution, beginning with the Big Bang, was triggered by a weak true influence and has now reached the point of depending on us, one example of its sought-for achievement, to increase that influence by pursuing truth rather than being impelled by energy.

I am inclined to believe that the true influence seeks the state of $1 \times 1 = 1$ because this represents maximum perfection with minimum strife or disturbance. By way of our intellect it determines our morality. It prefers stable to volatile conditions, simplicity to complexity, goodwill to ill will, tranquillity to stress. It prefers life to be peaceably co-operative, rather than aggressively competitive, as a step towards eventually having all animate and inanimate matter reduced to simple harmonious energy. By making our society humantrue, shall we not boost the influence of truth in the universe, and by turning our backs on autoprogression, material consumption and all such features of the Machine, shall we not reduce the influence of energy? But, just as the true influence had to use energy to produce human intellectual life, so must we make painstaking and determined effort to achieve the humantrue ideal. *Not* by actively (or idly, even though caringly) but fundamentally thoughtlessly going along with the here and now.

The idea that there is one body of truth for humanity - humantruth - is commonly resisted. This idea is seen as the imposition of dull conformity whilst the concept of individuals being entitled to their own versions of truth is equated with variety and freedom. But this preference is founded on experience of a false reality, on inertia of the human intellect that has allowed itself to be carried along by the sheer momentum of the giant Machine, treating reform as yet another game. The ultimate function of intellect can only be to arrive at truth. Were its function to lie we would not be morally concerned with anything. Where it is permitted to function either way, as at present here on Earth, it is difficult to distinguish the true from the false with certainty. But it is impossible that two or more intellects, given the same knowledge and correlating it thoroughly, should arrive at different versions of truth. That we do presently arrive at different versions indicates that we are not fulfilling intellect, and is the reason why we continue living in chaotic confusion.

Putting aside their mental conditioning, and the fact that their values, preoccupations and lifestyle are dictated by automatic reality, most people, at the periphery of all this intellectual questioning, are reasonable, kind, and considerate within their particular sphere and amongst their circle of friends, relatives and colleagues. So if you attack the Machine to which they are firmly attached you seem to be attacking *them*. A breakthrough can be expected only if *they themselves* begin criticising their own personal reality and everything on which their being rests.

It can be understood that present human behaviour may be fixed by morphogenetic fields. We tend to do what all others with whom we identify are doing, recognising and gravitating to the same version of reality. This is a matter of the determination of conscious will rather than reason, and of defending self-identity with instinctive emotion against any contrary persuasion. This is prejudice, which is assisted by mental conditioning; by humans in general thinking automatically alike so that the affairs of the Machine and events of autoprogression are accepted and furthered without question; also by particular groups submitting to disciplined thinking, like philosophers tending to interlock their views with those of one famous predecessor.

The way of pure reason is quite different. Determination of will passes to the postconscious which understands that mental conditioning, or mind-sets, must be broken down if there is to be humantrue progress. The self then intellates, and as far as possible acts, according to pure reason alone, despite the Machine and whatever others are thinking or doing. When there is a humantrue society it too will exercise a morphogenetic influence, but one that does not require progressive change and with the *whole* of which *everyone* will be empathetic.

The bushmen of Africa allowed their dawning intellect to guide them to a balanced way of true living, as they then knew and understood its possibilities and accepted its limitations. *We* now have to do the same according to *our* potential understanding. It has to be recognised that the bushmen were ruled by reason, which gave them their higher kind of instinct. We too have to be ruled by our developed intellect and allow it to give us our constitution - the ultimate guiding pattern for intelligent life which in the end boils down to the same caring, loving, securely sharing, co-operating, relying and trusting.

Being attracted to things of dominance and to attributes of grace and power - wanting to possess, reflected in our response to advertising, or wanting to excel, reflected in our identification as spectators with sports personalities - has to do with instinctive superiority and the perfection of physique and skill that brings success. Up to a point it is necessary for the individual to want to live and survive. But this urge must be modified to take away the competitive element and to concentrate on co-operative effort for total communal well-being. As an intellectual species, our attributes for true success are different from those of animal nature. On the other hand we don't want to lose our life-force.

A barrier to humantrue reform is that to follow intellation requires that we exclude contrary immediate interests and loyalties. Individuals may be unwilling to be guided by pure morality not only because it means sacrifice of their own automatic interests but also the interests, and thus the support, of their colleagues and friends. So they uphold the Machine for the sake of a privileged few associates, but against the vital interests of millions of faceless humans, because they obviously depend on and have directly to answer to the former but not the latter who, being out of sight, can be put out of mind.

In working out the humantrue reform of our society we shall have to define our moral code clearly. For example, it is necessary to determine where we stand on the question of killing - of taking life, that of our own and other species. There is a large disparity between human feeling on this subject, and practice. Most of us could not, personally and at close quarters, kill any animal much less any human in cold blood. Yet tens of millions of animals, birds and fish are killed and eaten by us each year, and many millions of us have died at the hands of fellow humans in the last century and so far in this.

The reason why so many humane individuals nevertheless eat the dead bodies of animals is that the money economy makes it profitable for others to be persuaded to do the unpleasant tasks for them - the penning and slaying of the animals and unfeeling preparation of their flesh and organs. Behind this industry of butchery is the motive of competition, which gives impetus to the money economy and also lies behind the butchery of humans, for it is a major cause of war and of all other kinds of human dispute and aggression.

Many people now refuse to eat meat, on moral grounds. Many also belong to peace movements, but once again I would remind them that if they support the Machine they are perpetuating war by supporting its cause. To others who oppose the taking of any life it is pointed out that by filling the space we occupy - even if it were reduced to the minimum necessary we deny life to creatures who would occupy it in our place. In order to combat disease, protect our food supplies and defend ourselves, we have to kill millions of creatures of numerous kinds - micro-organisms with disinfectants, flies, mosquitoes and other insects by spraying and swatting, rabbits, rats, mice, crows and other vermin with traps and guns, and sometimes such 'dangerous' animals as tigers and snakes. In some places humans must eat other creatures to survive; in other places it is thought necessary to cull animals for the sake of healthy survival of their species; and everywhere we consume plants on a vast scale, which are forms of life that respond to stimuli though they have no brains. So up to a vital point it is an unavoidable matter of kill or be killed excepting, on the whole, amongst members of the same species. The practice of homicide is inexcusable because unlike animals, which rarely kill their own kind in any case, humans are capable of moral self-control. There is no moral justification for homicide, so it should be unthinkable, but the circumstances and influences that give rise to it should be unthinkable as well.

It may be hard to imagine a world without villainy but this is because never, in the whole of human experience, has there been such a world. That is why there is indifference or opposition to ideals, because in the light of past experience they appear unrealistic. But nothing exists without cause nor occurs without reason. The cause of today's human villainy, as in the past, is that the automatic nature of the Machine has always given reason for it. It is not sensible to go on talking about combating crime and drug abuse and alcoholism, when both we who are talking and we who are talked about are minds whose conditioning is false and whose stimulation is lacking, all subject to the wrong reason. This way we never get beyond curing some of the symptoms. Rather should we be thinking of the ideal reality, which would prevent villainy by giving no cause that provided reason for it.

The existence of separate distinctive groups is a cause of violence, in that the determination of each to protect or further its interests appears as a threat to other groups. The Sikhs in India are violently demanding independence. There is no true way of dealing with this situation within the Machine for if the Indian government, unwilling to grant independence, either does nothing or makes small concessions the demands will have reason to grow, but if it cracks down on the Sikhs they will have cause for yet more violent protest. Neither side can truly enlighten but only antagonise the other, or at the best reach some uneasy compromise, because neither's position is true. In humantruth the Sikhs, as well as the Hindus, Moslems and all such separated groups, should relinquish their claim to special identity and abandon their distinct religion because these are not truths that all can share, and so are divisive. The way of true reason is to strive for common ground until agreement is reached.

The present fact that unpleasant, aggressive, sadistic, yet in all physical respects complete and undamaged, individuals exist is frightening, and depressing. These characteristics, which have a place in the Machine, are features of personalities whose minds have been denied, or have been unable to find, true outlet. The most horrible thing about violently sadistic acts is that they are performed by members of the supreme intellectual human species, who are also capable of saintliness. Yet such individuals do not present serious, basic obstacles to a humantrue alternative reality because they are products of the Machine. An ideal world could not produce them and would not sustain them. Even purely congenital psychopaths, if such exist, would have nothing to feed or aggravate their aggression and everything to encourage the opposite.

Though nature is red in tooth and claw it does not include knowing cruelty for its own sake. There is no cause or reason for it in instinct; no survival meaning or purpose, for creatures of nature are intent on helping or expressing themselves, not on hurting each other. Cruelty is an invention of human minds subjected to a system of life that serves only a minority (insofar as anyone can be said to be served by the Machine that all serve), imposes on the majority, and is against the the true interests of the whole human race.

Minds and bodies that have been long accustomed to amoral, immoral, unstimulating and hopeless circumstances might become dead to all positively benign emotion and turn for satisfaction to malevolent, pitiless acts of torture, rape, or other violent crime. Or they may have been so long dominated, deprived, and frustrated by repression that their rising feelings of hatred eventually burst out in some violent act of vengeance which those feelings temporarily justify and are satisfied by. In true and completely balanced human nature there is much more strongly compelling reason for gentle compassion, which would be both instilled into us and drawn out from us in a supportive humantrue world.

In the present world *everything* we do, and everything we are, is suspect because all is geared to a reality that is wrong. In this situation, to act or think in a positively integrated way may give physical and conscious satisfaction, because it obeys the current lores and conventions, but it is superficial and wrong because it does not fulfil supraconsciousness.

That which is or seems good in existing reality does not originate in the Machine but is the expression of human virtue, often reacting to automatic vice. In between virtue and vice are many exciting and enjoyable practices that, however, are not as harmless as they seem. If you want stock markets, fashion parades, credit cards and motor shows, you have to put up with slums, drug peddling, unemployment and prisons, because these are all interlocking features of the Machine. They confine public human virtuous activity to such as charity concerts, flag days, and voluntary aid. They relate to one system that is to be considered as a whole, kept or rejected as a whole.

As long as the Machine retains its controlling influence over us, true human morality can have little effect on our affairs. Where certain humane but limited principles, such as those of socialism, are introduced politically into a reality that remains fundamentally automatic, with a large majority of people who are firmly automated in character, those humane principles have to be imposed by government, itself part of the Machine. There is then division between the automaton, authority and humanity. Government resorts to secrecy to protect its authority and secure its interests, which are set above those of humans in their private capacity, who are in any case harnessed to the automaton whose lores predominate over authority. In a humantrue society there would be no division of interest and no secrecy, for all would be in the real interests of ourselves and our planet, founded on agreed and self-evident truth.

The employment feature of the money economy assumes that people could not be persuaded to do all the necessary tasks if their personal survival or automatic advantage or privilege didn't depend on it. The humantrue case is that a supraconscious society would voluntarily do everything needed. There would be practical as well as moral cause to do what was necessary and not to do otherwise. If most things we produced came from the sweat of our brows, if everyone were aware of the limits to our resources, and if no ulterior motives such as competition for personal advantage or money-profit existed, we could never allow ourselves to indulge in needless, wasteful or harmful production and consumption.

Doctors are beginning to realise the importance of putting humans first, medical scientific method second. I have tried to point out that this is so in all things. People are yearning for a purer environment, which can only be achieved when that yearning is brought to bear on making our whole society pure.

Most people presently believe that we can never change, shall never learn the truth. But the AIDS plague may yet play a part in disproving that belief. The reason is that it brings an interpretation of morality into direct relationship with a horrifying effect. The threat of nuclear war does the same, excepting that for thousands of AIDS victims the threat has already become a terrible reality. In most cases AIDS is a product of human indulgence; the risks to the individual often being overlooked by the prospect of sexual gratification or financial gain. The victims are private human individuals and the infliction is lingering death. It may be that through being forced by this plague to adopt strict sexual morality humans will also be brought to look seriously at the moral code of their whole reality. It may be that we shall see humantrue morality for what it is - a simple, sensible, benign and practicable code by which we should live for our universal happiness, security and contentment.

Taking humanity as the sum of human minds, which essentially it is, look at the present situation of the individual and compare it with the ideal. The picture of the world as it now exists, and the information coming from it, does not harmonise with the mind's natural function of true reasoning, nor with its private wishful view of the world as it truly ought to be. But the individual body and mind have their being in this existing reality, on their relations with which they otherwise depend for survival, dialogue, stimulation, and the emotional satisfaction that comes from a meaningful sense of belonging. So the individual must choose a personal version of reality that lies somewhere between two extremes. One extreme is maximum possible alienation from the Machine. This brings minimum satisfaction from the relationship with reality, but optimum fulfilment of pure intellect. The other extreme is maximum identification with the Machine. This brings optimum satisfaction from the relationship with reality but minimum fulfilment of pure intellect. The crucial point to make is that neither of these extremes nor any position between them is satisfactory because none is complete. Clearly the former extreme is preferable to the latter but unworthy unless it embraces the serious intention of changing the situation for the better. Obviously the ideally happy state would be that in which both body and mind were entirely fulfilled within themselves and in their relationship with world reality. Therefore the only logical thing for all humanity to do now is supraconsciously, freely, urgently, and independently of the automatic norm to strive for a humantrue world reality, for that is the one and only road to a state of optimum happiness.

We have extensively manipulated the surface structure of Earth, its physics and chemistry, in service of the developing Machine, and the process is accelerating. For the time being we remain mentally superior to the Machine, and it still cannot function without us. We are capable of conceiving a different society just as we wish it to be. We are still in a position to re-structure the foundation and framework of our lives according to that concept, following a supraconscious revolution in our minds. But if we continue much longer in harness to the automaton it will become able to function by itself, as a computerised self-acting Machine independent of our mental powers and indifferent to us except for our instinctive emotions. In such a future, if it comes to pass (and at this moment that is very much the likely eventuality), the experience of any supraconscious individual would be like that of a severely physically handicapped person whose mind is fully aware and alert but has no means of meaningful communication, nor anybody to communicate with who would care to respond. This individual's experience would be an awareness of his or her working body, which is merely a range of mechanical functions limited to basic necessity, and emotional being, which is a purposeless, repeatedly recycled, instinctively reactive process excited by artificial contrivances, rather like a Woody Allen film but in deadly earnest and not funny. In itself the supraconscious mind would experience utter loneliness, the imprisonment of intellect within the head, with no significantly positive stimulation, no reliable information, and absolutely no influence on the surrounding world - a nightmare. Many postconscious minds must already suffer milder forms of this nightmare, unknown to the conscious self that dominates and keeps them in solitary confinement.

———————

The recent political so-called 'new enlightenment' prefers autoprogression to the welfare state on the grounds that the latter has made people lazy and dependent, taking away their self-respect and spirit of free enterprise. A return to much more competitive subjection to market forces is well under way in Britain - for example in the health service - and this reflects a similar movement away from socialism towards monetary economics throughout the world. This is just another swing of the political pendulum fixed to its automatic pivot. It was predictable, just as, if we don't come to our true senses in the meantime, a contrary swing in a few years time can be predicted as human conscience causes a temporary return to socialism (unless and until that grim time comes when the human conscience ceases to be effective). It is another example of the human dichotomy of mind whereby we wilfully manipulate the conscious mind both to discover and apply scientific fact unemotionally, with precision and with automatic success, and to address the vital questions and problems of life emotionally, loosely, and utterly without success because such thinking, since it falls short of humantruth, is altogether inadequate for the task. To see our mistake, and then to realise our true future, we have to learn to follow all-embracing supraconscious reason.

The following Part VII sets out proposals for a humantrue society. It lays down the principles from which such a society must take its shape and backbone, because these principles are held to be self-evident in supraconscious eyes. But the details of its constitution are not laid down. They should be subject to the most widespread discussion and unanimous agreement, for two reasons. First, because the constitution must take account of environmental variations of climate and terrain, and of variations in human temperament which, though we achieve general supraconscious awareness and rid ourselves of racial and national differences of culture, will still naturally exist, as between the sexes, the strong and the weak, the young and the old. Second, because we lack accurate information about such things as real energy needs, about resources and risks, and about human population and health, for the reason that we, and research so far carried out, have always been more or less geared to the Machine. A good deal of honest research, entirely independent of money-economic and other biased automatic interpretation, is required to inform our decision-making.

THE WRONG REALITY

Part VII
REALISATION OF
HUMANTRUE SOCIETY

Chapter 38

COOPERATIVE CONCORD

By concord I mean all human minds and ultimately all intellects throughout the universe intellating in harmony. By co-operation I mean the mutually agreed empathic activity of humans on Earth, all motivated by humantrue supraconsciousness and co-operating as one. Therefore our own co-operative concord means total human unity, in thought, feeling, and action in the immediate interests of humanity's future.

Up to the present our concept of co-operation has been limited to that within separate self-interested groups within divided nations. For example, the one-time super-commercial state of Japan might have seemed to be one entity, a good example of high-synergy, an open system, its people united behind its worldly success. In fact what the Japanese people had chiefly in common was maximum subservience to the Machine, that employed them to work co-operatively for particular commercial companies that were in fierce competition with other Japanese companies. This state was not a success of human co-operation but a triumph of the competitive Machine, served by people who were the most automated in the world and furthest removed from their humantrue nature.

It is this intense, unreasoned, but financially efficient autoprogression that made Japanese products cost-effective elsewhere in the world. In automatic terms, their success means comparative failure for other nations whose eventual counter-success, plus the fact that Japan over-reached itself financially, burst the bubble. The eventual total effect of such escalating activity will be failure of the human race. Co-operative concord is vital to our *humantrue* success.

Agreed total co-operation is the voluntary way of intellect that must bring increasing benefits the more it is practiced and that must appeal to the benign instincts as well as satisfying true reason. Competition is an impulsion that appeals to the instinctive drives. It brings less real human benefit and more conflict the more it is practiced and makes no sense to true reason.

If we are to begin realising humantruth it is essential that we turn away from our present attachment to competitive drives. This is not only for the sake of our well-being, nor only because there is nothing but meaningless autoprogression on the competitive horizon. We should turn to the principle of co-operative concord because it is vital to the living being of any intellectual species, and so is also vital to humantrue reality.

The true basis for willing concord is the understanding that life is a continuous flow, not the limited period of time during which we personally are conscious of it and involved in it. As conscious selves we join that flow when we are born and leave it when we die. Between these times we share individually in the flow and are required to contribute to it. *It* is life, and we its temporary manifestations. It was the same flow that went on before our birth, and that continues after our death.

The flow of life is not essentially increased by our arrival nor depleted by our departure, yet its continuation depends upon our being. And for us, an intellectual species, its possible good health and quality depends upon our voluntary humantrue contribution; our false absorption detracts from this but our co-operation would enhance it. The continuing flow has given us individual life but it has also given us a bad society, born of a murky history, because we have always competed to survive. The kind of *future* life it gives us depends on the good effort we now jointly put into changing our ways.

This, then, is why we should co-operate worldwide. By doing so we honour those who went before us and gave us life, cherish the present life we share with all others and make it happy and contented, and care for the future life of all who are to come so that it shall be the same. Just as past humanity affected our present and we shall affect the future, so every individual now living depends on every other. By *taking* we enrich ourselves but impoverish others, but by *giving* we would all be content. *We* are part of one life, past present and future, so whether we are 'dead' or 'alive' or yet 'unborn', its happiness, or misery, is ours; but it is we who are presently alive who shoulder responsibility for the future.

Individual human awareness, concern and emotion were as real a thousand years ago as now and shall be, hopefully the better for our help, a thousand years hence. We should be conscious of this whole, not only of our temporary part in it, for our experience is one ever-present experience, like the baton in a never-ending relay race which we take, carry for a while and then pass on, yet which remains constantly in human hand. It is when we take that baton as our possession - a personal identity cherished above all others as though it alone mattered - not knowing or caring that it represents human hope for the future but, in dread of giving it up, pretending it is ours forever, even after death, it is then that we impoverish and betray life, our own and that of all humanity.

Chapter 39

FREEDOM

Freedom is a quality of life that we hold dear, aspire to and often refer to, but do not fully understand in order clearly to define. It is akin to happiness, and we desire both that and freedom, but both are withheld from us in many ways and by many factors.

The desire for freedom is really the wish to do what we want to do; what instinct prompts us to do, perhaps, or what we are taught, conditioned, or fitted to do. Its antithesis might appear to be the power of authority and law, which can curtail freedom often to the extent of depriving the individual of liberty or restricting our liberty to do what is right and receive what is rightful, and sometimes inflicting painful punishments. On the other hand, without the protection of keepers of law and order the freedom of the majority to go about their chosen affairs might be interfered with by a minority intent on deceiving, cheating or robbing them, perhaps also doing them violence. But, then again, those in authority claim privileged freedoms above the norm, counterbalanced by underprivileged and relatively unfree individuals at the other end of the scale.

Matter, and its basic unit the atom, is strictly governed by physical laws to keep it from chaos, but allowed a free loophole to enable it to evolve. The particles within atoms, because their quantum mechanical behaviour is subject to tiny influences, occasionally proffer an alternative avenue that gives matter some freedom to reshape its form - if it can be called freedom since it is a question of reaction to those tiny influences. This avenue was first used by the influence of truth for the development of life. It was then also used by the influence of energy, to progress the evolution of life-forms by mutation including sophistication of their means of self-determination. Plants became able to influence growth by making choices at the point of biological bifurcation in order to determine, for example, the locations of all branches and twigs and the directions in which they should grow so as to take full advantage of the sun's rays.

This evolution of primitive life-forms may be seen as progressed by a certain freedom of choice, but the freedom is very slight for the choice is limited to a tiny bias one way or another. By the time the advanced instinctive animals had come into being the function of choice had been raised to a much higher level. Most normal activity was entrusted to habitual instinct, a matter of predictable subconscious decision. Some decisions were chosen with conscious freedom but strictly limited by instinct to two or three alternative possibilities. Very occasionally, and with considerable mental effort, conscious animals will freely take a new and unprecedented decision. This may bring about a change in habit that was not originated by any kind of chance mutation and natural selection but voluntarily. No new decision is made, however, nor habit adopted, that is contrary to the immediately evident interest of survival success. Such is the limited extent of animal freedom.

The fact is that there never can be a permanent state of actual complete freedom, for all organisms are necessarily restricted by the form and terms of their existence. But we always refer to the wild creatures of nature as free because they are not subject to the heavy restrictions that govern us. We sense and envy the freedom that they enjoy. Since they are also strictly governed, by instinct, it is clear that bodily freedom can be no more than a feeling - the emotional accompaniment of spontaneous fulfilment of a definite and necessary programme.

So nature appears free but is subject to drives and inhibitions - to the fixed code of instinct that yet operates for the good of a species. Yet nature is competitive and ruthless, in that the interest of one species may well be contrary to the interest of another, and the general good of the species is often gained at the sacrifice of individual interests. In good times all individuals may be fulfilled but in hard times those with the weakest temperament must suffer the miseries of being at the bottom of the pecking order. Nature achieves a balance between good and bad extremes, a fulfilment that is satisfactory overall but that includes fears, failures and necessary hardships.

When the human race appeared on Earth, it was the first species to be potentially capable of overriding instinct and making free decisions. Realisation of our intellectual potential could make life good, for us and all other creatures, reducing fear and suffering to the minimum. We could make our own balance, and sustain it with supraconscious awareness. But we have failed to realise this potential. What we have done is to exploit the power of intellect by applying it to the drives, whilst rejecting certain inhibitions, of instinct. This has increased our freedom of action but necessitated all kinds of added restrictions to protect us from our consequent, conscious automated selves. We are partially subject to animal instinct. We are comprehensively subject to the impositions of instinct-based automatic reality, to a variety of competitive means of securing our needs, and to a mass of laws and controls over those means. We are also subject to the awareness of intellect, which may reveal to us that these means and controls do not provide for our whole species and that they threaten our future. To be free in the sense that wildlife is free we, as a race, also require a fixed code that answers our common physical needs *and* our intellectual awareness and that we can responsibly obey with a will. Existing reality does not provide that code, nor can automatic principles ever be compatible with it.

The Machine *is* our present reality, and if we will not rise above it with the intention of changing it we have to find a place for ourselves as part of it. We then need a personal automatic code to follow for the sake of our sanity. Choosing this code is not a case of free will but of restricting both our instinct and intellect to a conditioning and mind construction that is presently realistically viable, and emotionally applying our will to acting it out. Neither is it a free choice of the whole individual, as is the instinctive creature's selection from instinct, but the conscious limitation of our unconscious potential to the dictates of reality. And our resultant behaviour is not given even the freedom of that degree of consent and co-operation of our species which instinct provides. Not only are we resisted and opposed, perhaps violently, by others of entirely different conditioning and circumstance, but also by humantrue awareness, within and without ourselves, which doubts, questions and criticises both the whole of this reality and our part in it.

In this competitive society wide differences of attitude, interest, aim and opinion exist, and free exploitation and pursuit of these is permitted, with the result that there is conflict which *restricts* freedom. There is conflict between Machine and human institutions, and among them. There is consequent conflict between individuals depending on whether their minds lean more towards automatic calculation or humane reasoning, on which institutions they serve, support or just tolerate, on which they oppose, evade or try to escape, on whether they are generally privileged, ignored or deprived - winners or losers, made responsible or subjugated. This conflict puts us in the position, willingly or unwillingly, where we are not outwardly free to agree and co-operate whatever we inwardly think. For example, the policeman is not free to take the same attitude to law as the man in the street, nor he the same as the criminal. The attitude of the industrialist towards his production process may not freely correspond to that of the shop-floor worker or the consumer. The same attitude to war cannot be shared by protestors, politicians, weapon makers and field marshals.

Yet there *is* potential freedom for us, beyond nature's blind obedience to instinct but in another, alternative, humantrue reality. That freedom is better served by, and depends upon, agreement and co-operation. Our awareness of this humantrue concept and its contrast with competitive reality is growing. It needs to grow into both a determination to take up the struggle between the Machine and its exploitation of *us* (in its interest - known paradoxically as free enterprise) and an inhibition of the Machine for the sake of true interest. This struggle has gained local concessions but has never come near to defeat of the worldwide Machine. Growth towards that ultimate goal has always been short-circuited into automatic conflict, basically between the privileged and the deprived, often ending in war, with the combatants losing sight of their human reason.

So the present human normal case, applying to various degrees all over the world, is that we continue as instinctive creatures, with intellect providing more opportunity but less overall care and protection. We have the same competitive and ruthless reality, having enhanced the pleasures and multiplied the fears and hardships with the added feature that we can be sharply aware (through the wide-ranging media) of the possibilities of both. To be largely deprived of liberty against our will is something we abhor but we are prepared to have our freedom restricted in a necessarily good cause. The question is when and to what extent is it necessarily good to curtail freedom in the individual or collective interest.

Our wish to experience the feeling of freedom may be converted into eagerness to pursue automatic drives to the maximum. Automated intellect gives boundless opportunity for exploitation of pecking-order dominance. The most automatically successful and least truly aware of humans can feel that this really is to be free because they are able to ignore the fact that their freedom represents the humantruly unacceptable opposite for others. Society as a whole, threatened with breakdown by the chaos resulting from a free-for-all, becomes desperate to control this reckless freedom. It does so by the institution of law, making certain practices unlawful and punishable. Whether we then feel free depends on whether we agree with the Machine and its laws and whether our own methods of competitive survival are free from its restrictions. The most humantruly aware of us, who want to escape the system and reform it, strongly feel ourselves to be morally unfree.

Broadly speaking there are two versions of automatic reality. The first is represented by the capitalist, free-enterprise, democratic order, for example in the USA. Countries allied to this version call themselves the 'free world'. Their concept of freedom is a myth. It feels comparatively free because everyone is at liberty to pursue autoprogression, and authoritative human interference is kept to a minimum, this being feasible because the money economy exercises its own controls. But automated individuals are tightly bound to other than their own true interests, free only to comply, by making automatic interests their own, or suffer. They are not free to survive by any other than automatic means, except with great difficulty; nor free to observe human morality in all things.

Our freedom to think and act at all humantruly in capitalist society is affected by the role we undertake in it; by the fact that it makes demands on our minds and bodies which leave us little energy or opportunity for contrary thought or action. Our freedom is further affected by the competitive nature of our automatic roles; by our being in a state of habitual conflict, which means that the difficulty of behaving humantruly is added to by our Machine-imposed differences keeping us apart, rather than our common humanity drawing us towards agreement.

The competitive conflict that has put the USA at the top of the pecking order has put the 'third world' countries at the bottom. The Machine-induced freedom from conscience that enables humans to take part in competitive conflicts of the money economy despite humantrue reason also causes oppressed people to protest violently. The basic reason for the East/West cold war was that Russia sided with the protestors and stood for communist revolution whilst the USA sides with automatic reality and stands for the competitive money economy, as always.

The East/West relations that obtained up to 1989 have been overtaken by subsequent events and the following comments, written in 1988, might now be considered irrelevant. I have let them stand with only slight alterations, however, for the following reasons. The Russian revolution was a left-wing reaction to an intolerable Right-wing regime. The violent oppression that subsequently occurred under Stalin was not a feature of communism but of totalitarianism. Russia and Eastern Europe in general is now determined upon 'democracy'. But the same fundamental factors underlay the situation, now as in 1917, and as long as the Machine remains dominant events are practically certain to go full circle, eventually returning to a similar situation, and to some kind of violent upheaval such as the Communist revolution.

People in the USA value their freedom of choice, and this would be a good thing were it a matter of seeking to choose the opportunity given to all life to adopt mutations, and make changes, in the spirit of evolution towards realisation of truth. But it is a bad thing, for it merely means freedom to choose from false substitutes provided by the Machine - being able to select from the latest of its exciting technological offerings, a new car for example. This represents submission to a reality that does not stand for true worldwide human freedom and happiness.

The second of the two main versions of automatic reality is Marxist socialism, taken up by Russia and generally thought to be represented by Russian communism. The fact is that the communism of Karl Marx was to put the automatic power of capital and production into the hands of the working people, the majority, and to put their interests first. Its adoption in Russia was really a reaction to the extremely oppressive money economy and tyrannical domination on the part of the privileged ruling minority up to 1917. It could never work because power is a false concept. To whomsoever power may be given, in the beginning, it shall eventually devolve upon an elite, whilst successful socialism depends on free and equal co-operation. For Marxism temporarily to work would require a great and voluntary effort of self-discipline on the part of all people. No people have ever been prepared for such effort, and there is never time or open opportunity for them to prepare themselves before a revolution.

Perhaps it was that Lenin sensed this, in Russia in 1917, so that he established his own version of communism. This was to have the people support the State: the State to interpret and supply the peoples' needs, and to devise and impose what it deemed to be necessary discipline, by controlling activity and restricting all freedom of expression and choice. This is regarded by non-communist people as tyranny because their interpretation of freedom is the relative absence of such direct and oppressive controls. Whether Russians *felt* free would depend on whether or not they agreed with official restrictions, and that might depend on how their personal way of life compared with their expectations, or with the way their parents or grandparents lived before the revolution. Third-world people were generally attracted to Russia rather than repelled, for communism seemed to offer them much more than they presently had precisely *because* of its controls and restrictions.

Marxist/Leninist communism was bound eventually to fail because rather than giving responsibility to a responsible people it invested it in the State, a powerful independent organ separated from the people. Russian society was therefore repressive rather than expressive of either instinctive *or* intellectual freedom. As a result, individuals were devoid of the will or compelling reason to work hard and use initiative. In consequence they not only lacked the consumer rewards of the West but also failed to evolve such voluntary humantrue freedoms as would develop better alternative intellectual interests and physical activities which, being disinterested and altruistic, could not easily be opposed by the State but might eventually erode it.

Nevertheless, for all its faults, the Russian State did uphold an important moral right by continuing to guarantee a fundamental freedom to the great working majority - relative freedom from exploitation and destitution. In order to protect and maintain this freedom of the workers, the State imprisoned and cruelly liquidated a very large dissident minority - individuals whose interests were not those of the majority and who also opposed the State. This was condemned by the West as cruelly oppressive. Yet, in a country where the morality of the majority as represented by the State is supposed to be supreme, it was quite logical that the undermining of both should be unlawful. The cruel punishment of dissenters is unacceptable, but it is also unacceptable that selfish minority aims should undermine true majority interests. The West can allow relative freedom to its moral dissenters because things are so arranged, politically, that dissent can be met with indifference and ignored, for our governmental authority is *borne* out of competitive conflict of interest, not morality. The root reason why the West supported Russian dissenters was simply that we shared their opposition to communism because *it* is opposed to capitalism.

Of course, the Russian State did not truly represent the moral freedom of the majority. Growing ever more separated, it did not evolve in service of the people as intended. Whilst it kept the fundamental moral objective it interpreted it in a narrow and dictatorial way. In a sense it was obliged to do so, for the people as a whole had never outgrown their pre-revolutionary competitive instincts. There was a degree of corruption in many sectors of Soviet society that might be taken as reflecting the inescapable frailty of human nature but in fact revealed the failure of humanity, here and everywhere else in the world, to discover and fulfil its *true* nature. Those in authority became a privileged elite, gathering around them a 'nomenclatura' - a list of top people, and of top jobs open to them alone. The workers saw no reason to work conscientiously hard without the incentive of gain. So the State, seeing these results of stagnant idealism and the dead hand of control, and knowing that Russia was falling ever further behind in the economic competition of nations, finally succumbed to, and began opening the floodgates on, the hitherto forbidden influence of automatic conditioning. The State started by encouraging 'glasnost' and 'perestroika'. It was the people who finally demanded an end to authoritarianism and the reintroduction of incentive rewards and free enterprise. The same is happening in China, as briefly mentioned in Chapter 34, though not in the same way.

This is a backward move, for communism, with all its imperfections, was an approach towards humantruth, in that it rejected the principle drives of the money economy. By adopting perestroika the Supreme Soviet embraced the very policy it was formed to fight against; by taking this easy option it has copped out of the much more difficult job of perfecting socialism by enlightenment. This is failure to perceive that the only way forward is by supraconscious awareness.

The Russian State has failed to see that Marxist/Leninism was a stepping stone along the humantrue way, and that its job was to seek and encourage enlightenment in order to make progress along that way instead of stagnating in a fixed and intolerable position. As glasnost and perestroika overcame that unacceptable inertia, by releasing the people from State control, it simultaneously harnessed them, and the State authority, to equally unacceptable control by the Machine and its money economy. By their failure to intellate, this 280-million population has simply exchanged one set of problems for another, eventually much more burdensome set of problems. It is as though the Russian revolution, once a beacon of hope to the world's downtrodden, had never happened. Or, as though that door on the possibility of a better world had never, just for a little while, stood ajar.

We cannot be materially free, for the apparent freedom of consumerism is really enslavement by automation. But neither can a potentially intellectual race naturally tolerate artificial control of any kind. We have certain needs - of clean air and water, suitable food and shelter - which the Machine does not equally and adequately provide. Reason tells us that we should adjust our needs to the resources lastingly available to us, which the Machine fails to do. Intellect must take over from instinctive automation the role of providing for and guiding humanity; but intellect must first be fulfilled, then freed. The need for responsible effort as well as restraint shall be perceived by intellect and voluntarily self-applied by each individual's own understanding.

Our human mutation will have reached maturity when we are fully and freely intellectual - that is to say, supraconscious. The process will be perfected throughout the world when we all acknowledge the same body of humantruth, and when we have replaced instinct with a freely upheld humantrue constitution. For some time to follow we would feel the impulsions of instinct but humantruly necessary inhibitions would be built into every individual's understanding, strongly, and to equal degree.

We humans, the first intellects on Earth, are able not only to know but also to do that which is for our wellbeing. But we are presently at an in-between stage, our intellect so consciously developed that we have invented and freely manufacture atom bombs, for instance, but not so supraconsciously aware as to be freely responsible enough to render the making of such things unthinkable. If the Machine decides to make them, both leaders and the workers involved in their manufacture are practically and economically bound by that decision. But individuals are mostly free to protest and make their protest heard. That the numbers of nuclear weapons once deployed in the

USA/Russia confrontation have been and are still being reduced illustrates an important point. The Machine, at last obliged to make a choice between automatic convention and humantruth - whether to keep nuclear weapons or get rid of them - in full public view and under great anti-nuclear pressure from human moral awareness, must choose humantruly. Thus could our humanity prevail on any matter of reform, once we come to understand it truly and wish for it strongly. But the fact of USA/Russian disarmament does not herald the imminent collapse of the Machine, only the long overdue recognition of its most blatant insanity. The Machine is yet much too persuasive and strong to collapse, and human morality is yet too weak to cause that collapse. But the fact that the nuclear threat has thus far retreated is encouraging.

The basic freedom available to us is now revealed as a state of ideal restriction of the individual, having regard to the wellbeing of all individuals, that is freely accepted because it is voluntarily and willingly self-imposed. It is also vitally essential that we should satisfy awareness to the extent of *feeling* free. This means that our characters will have to be so enlightened and our circumstances so humantruly arranged that when we act spontaneously, without stress and fully according to our whole potential, we shall also act responsibly, but shall not feel artificially restricted.

Therefore the state of basic freedom, for us as an intellectual species, is to be free to undertake humantrue responsibility. Individual freedom presently produces many undesirable results, so that we restrict it, because we are not generally enlightened or united. It is made acceptable only to the extent that it can be subjected to some degree of reasonable government, but that is not freedom. Individuals may act with basic freedom only when all are represented by the same personal code, and uphold a world framework of life, both of which are entirely humantrue.

Once we have established the responsible, basic element of freedom, related to a practical framework of life that is simple and settled and so need occupy only a part of our minds, we shall find ourselves with a great deal of spare intellectual capacity. At that level, exercise of the mind is outwardly subject only to mathematical and graphical limitations, and this is the optimum free fulfilment, our optimum *feeling* of freedom. Up to the present we have applied our minds mostly to coping with the chaos of our world and hardly at all to such truly free fulfilment. The secret of our future happy success shall be that we voluntarily reject freedom to deviate from the humantrue constitution at the practical level but, always inwardly subject to supraconscious awareness of our responsibilities, that we freely experience intellectual development at the abstract level.

We will then be expressing truth in practice but also absolutely in the mind, for uninhibited intellect can not but express truth. As a result the whole human race will exert a great collective influence on micro-choice on Earth, like Gaia, and in the universe. The result, immediately for us, will be humantrue society, and eventually, for the universe, true equilibrium.

Chapter 40

EQUALITY

The third humantrue principle is equality. The concept of equality has long been entertained and is often mooted, but although felt to be desirable it has never been found possible and is therefore thought impracticable. Why has it been thought and felt desirable? The fact that it has been so indicates an underlying wish for it, and this is no doubt linked to a parallel wish for freedom. We desire equality because it makes more *human* sense than inequality. Instinctively we are divided between compassionate care for and preservation of life, and passionately aggressive destruction of it. Our free intellect tips that balance right over to the side of compassionate caring. Consciously or unconsciously, clearly or vaguely, we are aware that co-operation is our best way of preserving life and that competition in the hands of applied intellect spells disaster - that equality is necessary to co-operation, which is impossible without it.

This being so, why has the principle of equality been found impracticable? Because our awareness of our own good reason for it is largely hidden, or deliberately put away from our minds, to give way to the automatic reality which *makes* it impracticable and is pressing all around us; because human individuals quite evidently do not have equal attributes - of physique, beauty, talent, skill, mental capacity, virtue, character and personality; and because we do not possess equal status in the Machine - of birth, gender, class, nationality, education, opportunity, property, privilege, income, credibility, preferment or authority. These inequalities are facts of our existing competitive reality which render the principle of equality impossible, and which we think are inescapable. That is why we believe the application of that principle to be impracticable.

But *consider* those facts. Our attributes are to a very large extent a matter of history, of past experience shaping present humanity. They are passed to us by our antecedents, affected by environment, diet and consequent health, both theirs and ours, affected by our stimulation, the ease or hardship of our circumstances, the degree to which we have experienced achievement and tranquillity, or frustration and tension. The shape and proportion of our bodies can be malformed by overwork and malnutrition, past and present; our faces can be marred by worry and anxiety, or depravity and cruelty; our minds can be stunted by neglect and lack of fulfilment; our attitude, bearing and manner can be subdued and crushed by deprivation and indifference or puffed up with arrogance by pride and privilege. The Machine continually moulds us in these ways, determining the opportunities to be presented to us according to its consequent evaluation of us and the abilities it has bequeathed to us, judging success, beauty, character - us, and our status - by its own criteria. How we judge ourselves and our society depends on whether we use these same unequal criteria of automatic reason, or whether we weigh the worth of our existing reality against the humantrue principles of co-operation, freedom and equality.

See how these facts of automatic reality dictate our thinking. Though we acknowledge equality as a worthy principle we treat it as a naïve and unrealistic ideal. We recognise that it is good to give but keep our giving strictly within bounds because our reality is a system of *taking*. Were we to give away all our worldly goods we would court destitution, or, if we were lucky, society might then provide us with bare subsistence. To be satisfied with such a state of deprivation we must have our beings in supraconsciousness, with a determined expectation of having humantruth realised in the world. Otherwise we would have given away not only the trappings and ways of living in the Machine but also the objects and meanings of life itself in terms of existing reality. Very few of us, it seems, are yet prepared to make such sacrifices to the ideal.

So though we inwardly *know* equality and co-operation to be preferable to inequality and competition, automated experience tells us, and so we obediently *think*, that it cannot work out in practice. Our thinking can be illustrated in this way. A man imagines himself working with another man on the same job, for equal pay. Both are fit and strong, but while he is labouring hard, looking over his shoulder he sees the other slacking. He cannot accept this. He is willing to work for equal pay if his companion works equally hard, otherwise he expects to be paid more. If he cannot secure more pay, and his mate continues to slack, he sees no reason but to slack also. In a limited way this *is* a partial concept of equality - that the amount of labour be equalled by the amount of reward and vice versa - but it does not take into account that our opportunities and abilities, our measurements of both effort and reward, and most of all our awareness and understanding of our responsibilities, are unequal. This man is aware that many others are willing to give as little as they can for as much as they can get, but he is also aware that if everyone slacks the work will not be done and eventually no one will get paid. That is why he cannot accept the principle of co-operative equality. He believes that work is produced only by the incentive of commensurate reward and that the products of work are to be distributed according to the degree of effort, skill or expertise put into their production, represented by the possession of reward-money.

But he is using *automatic* reason and judging by automated experience. It is the principle of competition, on which the Machine is founded, that has developed this reasoning and experience. This automatic reasoning has stood on its head and obscured from our understanding the true function of human effort - to fulfil itself by providing human needs - and has drawn us away from co-operative equality which would have been the logical result of that understanding. Automatic reasoning has substituted its own system of reward incentives, with this result - not only is the *individual* working for rewards rather than to provide the necessities of life but so is the *organisation or institution of the Machine* that employs him. In this Machine-reality reward is the motive for all production and the fulfilment of real needs is merely incidental - not only money reward but status, recognition, power and privilege. Consequently most of what we labour to produce is unnecessary or unsuitable, therefore wasteful, and not for the equal fulfilment and satisfaction of common need. The general quality of human life has come to be represented by a striving to raise ourselves in the scale of comparative automatic inequalities, and a self-valuation in terms of automatic achievement, favour and possession.

This man is assuming that both automatic reason and judgment will still apply in a humantrue reality. He fails to realise that humantruth brings changed evaluation of all things and supraconscious minds shall judge very differently. That the slacker refused to do his share of useful work is *his* lack, a lack of intellect and its satisfaction. That he is unwilling to *earn* reward or to labour hard for greater reward is a refusal to obey instinct alone, for *its* satisfaction. His slacking is a ploy of instinct and intellect combined, craftily seeking to cheat both by compromising them for maximum gain for minimum effort but expressing the true satisfaction of neither, in a sort of no-man's-land of reason. The one good reason for labour is the awareness of a vital need for it, and to fulfil that need is then the greatest satisfaction. Both the slacker and he who works for reward alone lack that awareness and satisfaction, yet the latter does work whilst the former is sensible of no reason to do so. But what one man intends and willingly performs so may any man. And if one mind can perceive humantruth so may all minds. The principle of equality is not a matter of imposing the rule of equal giving and receiving but of equal understanding of it as our common responsibility and desire.

There is no intellectual reason why labour should be connected with reward, nor why work should be avoided, only instinctive reason, or conscious thinking applied to instinct. Instinct puts the carrot in front of the donkey and the donkey has no other incentive to go forward. If it has easier ways of filling its belly and prefers them to the attractions of the carrot, or if it is able to snatch the carrot without moving forward, it will stand still. A supraconscious intellectual donkey would proceed as necessary without the carrot, or not proceed unnecessarily despite the carrot, and if one were available would eat it only if it needed it and then only if its fellow donkeys got one too, for their equal need, whether or not they equalled its effort and ability. Humantrue intellect perceives the need for labour, decides the body to *do* that labour as best it can, and the doing of it requites the perception and fulfils the need. No further satisfaction is required. The maxim 'to each according to need, from each according to ability' is a good one, but cannot apply in the Machine, however modified, because human needs and abilities vary, and can only be judged by individual consciousness of the responsibility of each to the whole, and the whole to each. The Machine judges needs and abilities by economically calculated standards, using human abilities as needed for its prosperity and apportioning human wants as it is prepared to afford them according to that measure, leaving individuals to prosper, or fall by the wayside, as they may. The maxim need not be *applied* to humantrue reality, for it will be the successful *result* of the willing co-operation of equal, supraconscious minds.

We reason in automatic ways because the Machine really *exists* and appeals to instinct. We respond with instinct because we have not risen above it to fulfil intellect. Instinct tells us that individually we must fight for ourselves and our kin strictly according to that reality. The Machine is competitive, so we compete for unequal advantage - to win, for fear of losing. By behaving so we perpetuate the Machine that makes such behaviour necessary. But our true awareness quietly but insistently points the other way. If we follow this other way, in our minds, our intellect will convince us of the need to change to a humantrue alternative, show us the necessary principles of freedom, co-operation and equality, and make clear to us that every main feature of present reality militates against those humantrue principles.

For instance, the money economy is an automatic means of compelling us to live by the competitive ways of instinct, whose conflicts cause much of man's inhumanity to man. The chief reason for money existing is that it is a token of competition for unequal possession and reward. It could be said that it also represents a medium of choice, in that some of us are free to convert more or less effort into more or less money and free to spend it as we choose. This is not true freedom, however, but a matter of freely taking part in a laid-down, unequal process that feeds on itself. Our choices are provided by institutions and organisations for the chief purpose of capturing our money, and our desire for money and the freedom to choose what to spend it on is an automatic substitute for true human reasons for labour. In a humantrue society our labour would be given freely to provide equally for true human needs. I repeat, if that society retained the currency of money this would be earned equally and spent in exactly the same way by everybody, thus ceasing to be a necessary or significant token.

The concept of possession of any thing represents automatic success in competition; it represents the instinctive satisfaction of adding to one's self by ownership; the substitution of objectives and valuations of the Machine for humantrue reasons for living; a legal guard over our automatic title to things, from real needs to extravagant goods and chattels, protecting them from an automated society motivated to try and dispossess us. The concept is another founding principle of an existing reality that presently obliges us to conform and contribute to the Machine because only the air we breathe is free, and everything else, even our most basic needs, must normally be possessed by means of money. In a humantrue society, which would give and receive equally, it would be unnecessary to possess. It is impossible to possess equally, for ownership of things inevitably leads back to competition for their unequal possession.

Also unnecessary is permanent authoritative leadership, because it robs the majority of equal responsibility. In a humantrue world mankind would be led by an agreed social constitution. Certain individuals might take the lead from time to time in finding solutions to unforeseen problems, and all would have equal opportunity to do so, but they would be but temporarily followed, by willing agreement. The event would not give them permanent authority or status nor accrue to their special benefit in any way. It would be a matter of their momentary inspiration, unequalled by anyone else at the time, freely given and accepted as such rare occasions demand. It would not be assumed that this made anyone fit to lead on every occasion but recognised that next time someone else might be inspired.

The concept of employment is also unnecessary; being a practice that bends humans to obedient service of narrow objectives of the automaton, keeping them from supraconscious awareness of the fact by the pretence that the Machine's dominant power indicates superior knowledge and wisdom. In a humantrue society the inequality between employer and employed would be replaced by equal individual understanding and voluntary effort.

It is true that were all automatic inequalities removed there would remain those physical and instinctive differences between us. But, provided we have all fully explored our mental potential, there shall be no great difference of *mind* between us. When we are all supraconscious, we shall recognise that our fulfilled postconscious minds are equal, despite our superficial differences of conscious ability, strength, temperament etc. We shall rise above these differences, ceasing to identify with or exploit them as the Machine presently requires and encourages us to do. We shall subdue those animal instincts that are inappropriate to humantrue society, and no longer needed to guide us, until they die out for lack of response and are replaced by our supraconscious intellectual nature.

But in the meantime we have a complex physical external reality that is crammed full of inequalities and cannot be changed overnight. Some of us live in idyllic surroundings, in kind environments, but most of us in ugly cities, overcrowded towns and soulless housing estates, in hostile environments. This is partly a matter of where we chanced to be born, of course, but we have to recognise that the Machine largely created our circumstances, for its own purposes and prosperity. The Machine developed some countries but not others, and neglected to cherish or preserve much of the fertile Earth and its life. The Machine has given good houses in pleasant places with acres of land to its privileged, and poor housing in nasty places with limited space to its underprivileged. Some of us live in luxury with every facility and comfort, but some others of us live in unhealthy and degrading poverty, without even the most basic facilities and with little or no comfort.

For the present we have to tolerate those differences, share as best we can, and compensate wherever possible. Most of all we have to realise that the virtue of equality is equal giving, understanding and tolerating - not the jealous comparison of advantages enjoyed, or exact calculation of things taken, but a meeting of minds and equal desire for their commonly shared fulfilment. We have to work for the future, and in the meantime those who have more have more to give and those who have less may look forward to receiving their needs. In future we shall not build for inequality, for the Machine, but for equality in the humantrue spirit. There will be one standard of convenience and comfort, one objective in the arrangement and care of our environment - the equal well-being of all. It is common for the automated majority to regard statements like this as naively Utopian, but they make sense.

But *how* are we to adopt the principle of equality, and then bring it about? It is a matter of INTENTION. Despite all the automatic pressures and however impossible it may seem in the light of existing reality, and of our present instincts and customs, we have to rely on our judgment and determine to *make it work*. As we desire equality, so it is necessary to our achievement of a humantrue society. Just as inequality is inseparable from competition, so is equality vital to co-operation. If our humantrue supraconscious reason has convinced us that we must have co-operation and freedom, and now tells us that equality is therefore essential, then we have no humane alternative but to *achieve* it, whatever the obstacles.

Once more we see why it is necessary that we deliberately divide ourselves into two and make our inner awareness the motive for our actions. That our outer shells presently have to live in the Machine does not mean that we have to be automated. We have to be guided by our inner being, which can foresee how it would be were the Machine already dismantled and a humantrue reality established. We need to imagine how we would reason and feel in that other reality; we must ignore contrary automatic reason and dismiss our past emotional attachment to it, believing that we *can* unite to create a humantrue society, and that when it exists we shall be able supraconsciously to maintain it until it comes naturally to us.

The background of that humantrue picture which imagination can show us is like this: everyone regards everyone else as having equal right to satisfaction of need, and himself or herself as having equal responsibility with all others for providing those needs; everyone comes to adulthood with an equal level of humantrue understanding, and equal opportunity. No doubt some have more ability to fulfil these opportunities than others, and in different ways. But they are not more satisfied than others, for each is fulfilled according to capacity. And their unequal skill or talent or knowledge does not accrue to themselves, to give them unequal standing, but is given to others in order that all are brought to an equal level of benefit. This picture is not unfamiliar for it is reflected in our growing modern attitude to those among us who are physically and mentally handicapped, in that we no longer reject them and shut them away but do all we can to give them an equal share of life. Our humantrue purpose will not be to fulfil our competitive ego, achieve status, or secure special reward for self, but to use our physical powers to carry out our moral responsibilities as given to us by our intellect. We shall serve the community by fulfilling ourselves, thus achieving the fundamental satisfaction of both.

Chapter 41

INDIVIDUAL RESPONSIBILITY

The fourth principle of humantrue reality is individual responsibility. To be responsible is to respond to that which is humantruly required of us. In order to know what our humantrue responsibilities are we need to intellate and achieve supraconsciousness. In order to carry them out we need to co-operate. To co-operate we need to be individually free, and such freedom requires that we are equal. But we cannot be free of responsibility for maintaining our humantrue society. If we are not to contravene the principles of co-operation, freedom and equality, but abide by them, then that responsibility can only lie equally with each individual. This may be brought home to us if we replace our present concept of reality, as a personal experience of an externally imposed regime, with a new concept of it as a collective experience of a humanly created way of life, as we individually wish it to be and determine that it shall continue to be.

To world societies that, for thousands of years, have put their responsibilities in the hands of some kind of centralised authority, this concept may be hard to accept. We are accustomed to believing that the majority are by nature irresponsible and *must* be subject to the control of a responsible minority. But we have to understand that these minorities have not truly shouldered that responsibility - that the automatic system does not allow them to do so, and that a humantrue system would not wish or require them to do so. We have to understand that automatic reality has never encouraged, enabled, or allowed anybody to realise what our true responsibilities are. We have to understand that our social system has never worked for us, as a whole race, both because of its responsibility to the Machine and irresponsibility to our true humanity, and because of its conditioning of our thinking. We have to understand that our minds are presently contrived constructions that compel or tempt us to superimpose bad reason onto good, and to be led by instinctive emotions. We need to see that we deceive ourselves, suppressing our humantrue awareness and covering it over with a thick crust of automatic motive and opinion.

The nearest we have approached to individual freedom is perhaps democracy, but at the sacrifice of the other three essential principles - co-operation, equality and individual responsibility. The nearest we have approached to co-operation and equality seems to be Marxist theory, which has not generally attained to these principles in practice because it has failed to recognise the other vital principles of freedom and individual responsibility. In each case the error or omission has had the same cause - failure to recognise humantrue awareness of the individual mind, rather than the dictates of the automaton, as the basis of reality; failure to invest responsibility for human affairs in the individual, rather than in the authority of the state or the governing institutions of the Machine.

When the state takes responsibility in an overall automatic reality (whether it be a communist state or a capitalist government), it becomes its own construction of thought, like a separate mind but quite unlike the individual human mind. It thinks in terms of the automaton, which fundamentally governs all and to which the state administers, and in terms of the mechanics of that administration, with human beings - we potentially balanced, independent correlations of mind and body - merely treated as basic units of its calculations. The state is firstly responsible to itself, and irresponsible with respect to the human mind and its potential for realising the humantrue way of caring for humanity. In the eyes of the state the people *are* irresponsible, because they do not entirely think its way, and this seems to justify its authority. But the people are not responsible to the state because it is not responsible to their humantrue awareness. And they are irresponsible with respect to themselves, for they do not follow that awareness but pretend to it whilst accepting government by the Machine. They accept automatic reality because it exists, and they earn, or hope to earn its rewards because there seems to be nothing else to do.

Just as the desire to live humantruly is innate in us, so is the wish to take responsibility on ourselves. This can be demonstrated thus: parents well know the difficulty of getting their children to do things, such as washing up. If children are ordered to do it against their will they resist, and if we force them to obey they are resentful. If they can escape the task they shall, for it is important to them to obey *their* will rather than ours. If we offer reward they may readily obey, but they are then obeying their own will for the reward rather than us, and we are bribing them - not only encouraging them not to give without taking but also giving something that we would otherwise withhold as unnecessary. How much more pleasure do they, and we, enjoy when they themselves think of doing the task and voluntarily do it for its own helpful sake, without reward but for itself, by their own responsible will.

In existing reality the automaton is in the position of the heavy-handed parent, and we of the children. Some of us are given special responsibility, *by* the Machine, *to* the Machine. All of us are personally responsible for securing some means of survival from the Machine. It does not provide or care for us excepting as cogs in its machinery. All of us are in some way forced, or bribed, to obey. None of us may wholly and freely take voluntary responsibility for the self and others. Yet almost any of us responds to responsibility. Where we can take it voluntarily, in limited local spheres, it is a joy, and where it is shared by a group of comrades its pleasures are increased by co-operation. This pleasure of comradeship can be experienced even where the task undertaken is an automatic one and its objectives inhuman, such as in the case of a troop of soldiers in war. Willing co-operation is a supreme joy when it fulfils a humantrue objective. The opposite extreme is unwilling group labour, exploited in return for bare subsistence with the alternative of starvation, like the lot, under apartheid, of the black workers in a South African diamond mine, or forced labour with no reward at all and the alternative of worse punishment, like prisoners breaking rocks.

Our existing reality, then, is that the Machine and its institutions strictly and closely govern most of our thoughts and activities and are responsible for our way of living, our basic social framework. We have our own human structures of responsibility but these are sub-systems wherein we are personally responsible *to* that automatic framework and *for* our individual self-survival in it, not collectively for our common, whole humanity. We are bound to automatic aims. We are not free humantruly to co-operate, except in limited groups and dealing with temporary or marginal concerns. We are not free to care for and protect each other so that each and every one is provided for and content. We are not free to prevent the Machine from laying waste to our environment or threatening us with imminent nuclear, chemical or biological destruction - these are the ultimate results of domination by the automaton, and of our not assuming vital responsibility.

This automatic reality may only be broken when we bring our inner beings, and minds, to the fore, and is presently maintained by our outer shells. Our present structure of human responsibility is that of automated mankind, and is self-regulated by pressures from both the top down and the bottom up. Pressure from the top down comes from leaders who have been made responsible *by* the Machine; responsible *to* the Machine and *for* automated society, including, as submissive units of it, human individuals. It has already been established that permanently authoritative leadership is an automatic function, not a humantrue function. The present function of leaders is themselves to be led by the Machine, and to lead the rest of us, in directions that nobody's *humantrue* discretion suggests nor awareness can honestly approve. The task of leaders is firstly to carry out autoprogressive policies and secondly impose them on all individuals, either by compulsion or enticement, so that they also work to support these policies. Leaders could not be supraconscious and still willingly remain automated leaders for long, nor allow the public to be thus enlightened and expect them to remain content to be so led, for no supraconscious individual could long tolerate this reality.

Since this reality *does* exist, and *is* presently tolerated worldwide, the greatest pressure exerted from the bottom comes from the fact that we, as majority individuals, mainly take responsibility only for ourselves and our personal struggle for meaningful survival. We do not make our way of living responsible to our potential humantrue awareness, but submit ourselves to conditioned reason that in turn seeks satisfaction from the Machine that conditioned it. Though opposite in direction, this pressure has exactly the same effect as that from the top down. For example, an unnecessary product that is manufactured and advertised purely for money-economy reasons is widely desired and purchased for emotional possessive reasons; a nation is plunged into war for competitive political reasons, and the 'public' responds for patriotic reasons. This upward responsive pressure represents the will of *automated* humankind, submerging its potential humantrue will, to satisfy false hungers and expectations. This, our automatic will, keeps in place the institutions, so perpetuating the Machine that makes the whole circus seem necessary.

Working from the top down, supreme leaders are given their aims and objectives by automatic lores and instituted laws, to be strictly pursued for the sake of, and to justify, extreme prestige. They divide these into several compartments and delegate them to directors whose limited function is to direct one such compartment, a function also to be faithfully performed in order to both earn and justify high reward and privilege. The directors further subdivide their function, entrusting small parts of it to many executives, each given above average status and reward dependent on success in carrying out his or her specialised objective. This delegation continues down through managers, foremen, gangers, and eventually to the working majority. Though with submissive rather than authoritative bias, this process works similarly in reverse, from bottom to top.

There have to be reasons why this system persists, despite its shortcomings, and we ought to consider these reasons together with the system's effects and consequences. Bear in mind that the work situation is competitive, basic to a competitive society that values money, status, privilege and prestige. Everyone involved is rewarded, but by no means everyone is involved. We may desperately need the lowest reward of a barely living wage, or we may be in a position to satisfy our desire for the highest rewards of every kind, but neither can be secured excepting from the Machine, if it needs us, by working to its orders, directly or indirectly. It is these orders that are passed from top to bottom, and obeyed from bottom to top of the Machine's human hierarchy.

The higher in the hierarchy the bigger the effect of a person's opinions and decisions, the lower down the less. The higher in the hierarchy the nearer we get to possible understanding of the true reasons and real effects of policies and decisions. But the pressure on us to obey the Machine is then also higher, exerted by the terms of responsibility it gives us and the expectations of an automated society, linked to our own desire to retain the prestigious and privileged position, to its remoteness from majority experience, and to the fact that we are given power and reason by the Machine to carry out its policies regardless of humantrue awareness, our own or that of others. The lower in the hierarchy, the less reason we have to support and more to oppose automatic policies, but we are then further away from clearly understanding automated reason and action - whether decisions made are truly necessary and their ill-effect truly unavoidable   and the less automatic power we have to influence affairs.

From the individual viewpoint, it can be seen that generally speaking when we take a job our first consideration is the wage we need or the reward we desire, not critically to assess the work we will have to do and question whether or not its effective purpose is good and humanly useful. Keeping a job depends upon carrying out orders, and we are not expected to question, criticise, or refuse them - in some circumstances, for example in the armed forces, it is a criminal offence to do so. From the point of view of the Machine, basic wages are given to secure labour, not for need, otherwise they would be given equally, with or without work. By the same token, we who are at the bottom of the hierarchy do not usually seek work out of a responsible desire to do it, but out of a simple need to survive.

It can be seen that where all tasks are presently given to us by the Machine, or are related to it through employment by the institutions of the Machine, our views of what is right to do will be coloured not only by this reality's conditioning of us but also by the particular objectives its employment gives us. It can also be seen that our different levels of so-called intelligence - the varying degrees to which we use our intellectual faculty - are not inherent in us, but are a question of the extent to which we were stimulated in infancy and to which stimulated minds have been further developed and conditioned by the Machine for its required functions. The effect of this is to keep us from common agreement, not only through the different limitations on our thinking, giving rise to differences of opinion, but also by way of our wish to keep, and loyally justify, our jobs, wages, or privileges, creating prejudice in our minds.

That ever higher rewards are given for ever higher responsibility to the Machine is presently construed as deserved compensation for greater effort or value. This view is hard to justify when we compare the work and reward of a dustman, coal miner and company director. A more accurate view is surely that the Machine evaluates our abilities and buys our work at the lowest price we will accept, or at a price attractive enough to persuade us to fill its required role. Besides, higher rewards are not so much a matter of greater effort as of greater knowledge and understanding - not of humanity, and of that which is truly needful for its well-being, but of automatic aims and methods.

Of course, all features and characteristics of the present social system do not work in this inhumanly calculated way, but the sinews, muscles and nerves of its body, and the thought processes of its brain, which determine its main policy and activity, certainly do so. We are all humane in our inner beings, and give our humanity expression where we may, but this automated body is our reality, with our outer shells as its cells and fibres. There are humanitarians among us who bring their inner beings to the fore, but they are of no interest or value to the Machine, and are not to be found in the front rank of its basic affairs but on their fringes, trying somehow to humanise them.

Some of these factors have been discussed earlier. Why go over them again? Because they bear heavily on our understanding of human responsibility. And what can now be deduced? We have to decide who, or what, is truly presently responsible for the proper care of our true humanity. The answer we are bound to come to, as before concluded, is clearly that *nobody and nothing* is. The Machine is responsible for our existing reality, which is not responsible to us. We are responsible to the Machine, and therefore not to ourselves. The phenomenon of unemployment is a totally humanly unnecessary device to equate our needs with service to the Machine, and our desires with products of the Machine. It robs us of our potential supraconsciousness, by which we would simply and directly take responsibility for ourselves. The chain of downward delegation matched by upward dependence allows automatic motives to direct, and automatic responses to those directions to impel, our fundamental actions.

Normally none of us, from bottom to top, can give supraconscious reasons for our actions - that they are humantruly responsible actions - but we can give automatic reasons justified by the fact that this *is* existing reality and everyone else contributes to its support. Having accepted this we can further justify ourselves in humane terms - that only by acknowledging the 'here and now', rather than trying to change it, can we concentrate on relieving its human sufferings. But these sufferings are generated, and regenerated by the Machine itself. At the same time as we use automatic means to relieve them, those same means are causing them. This reality coagulates somewhere in the middle of the hierarchy structure, shaped by the Machine and held in place by reciprocal forces from bottom to top, and the conflicting competitive influences whose collisions create human suffering. These forces and influences form and fix the narrow personal realities of automated individuals, whatever benign motives they may profess. The basic function of their position, at bottom or top, is both to supply the demands and demand the supplies of each other, or to refuse or be denied them as the economic and political rules require, or dictate.

This arrangement fails because we *serve* these influences and forces, they do not serve *us*. They are not equated with or restricted to general true human need. They are equated with automatic purpose, and almost unlimited as to the direction they take and the extent to which they may go, with human agency. They may reward or deprive us, favour or oppress us, raise or crush us. *We* allow ourselves to do this *to* ourselves. We *do* then turn round and try to relieve some of the resultant suffering, but we also inhumanly fight wars, following the Machine to this ultimate example of competitiveness, using the Machine's reason to tell ourselves that this is also a legitimate way of righting human wrongs.

Let it be repeated - no one who is supraconscious can tolerate this existing reality. She or he would want both to take responsibility for making it humantrue, and for serving that humantrue reality in order to keep it so. We have established that the intellect is the supreme human faculty and that its supraconscious fulfilment is ultimate human being. We have established that co-operation, freedom and equality are the necessary founding principles of a humantrue society. All of us having attained that fulfilment, and achieved that society, it is clear that both will be sustained only by individual responsibility. Any system of control other than common self-control is contrary to supraconscious intellect, and to the founding humantrue principles.

Supraconsciousness, then, is the key to realising a humantrue society. Individual responsibility is the key to making it work in practice. Again, we cannot rely on our present automatic judgement to tell us whether such a society *could* work. If we have any doubts, we should always remember that the supraconscious mind cannot lie, or practice deceit, or allow its being to be other than humantrue. We should also remember that once consciousness is fully opened to the postconscious, thus becoming supraconscious, it *cannot* deny its new awareness, or revert to its former state. This is the assurance needed to dispel our present doubts that we could ever aspire to a humantrue reality, and an insurance against our fears that we would not be willing or able always to sustain it. To be humantrue is our true human nature. To compete with each other, to lie, and to deceive ourselves is the way of automatic reason, and our long adopted automatic nature. This present wrong reality educated us, and then obliges us, to close off our independent postconscious from our consciousness, and to keep it so with automatic reason, which argues against humantruth.

For example, it is argued that present reality, being extremely complex, is far beyond the comprehension of any one mind. But that *is present* reality. It is autoprogression of the competitive money economy that has made it so. Instinct and applied intellect have pursued every separate policy they can conceive, and have dragged humanity in many different, self-justified, complicated and contrary directions. A humantrue constitution will be such that the understanding of every mind can embrace. Its provisions will be no less simple, nor more complex than they need to be for our well-being, nor its practices more than we can commonly manage and maintain.

It may be argued that human minds vary widely in capacity and capability, so that logically the 'best' minds *should* dominate. But this requires definition of what is meant by 'best minds', and recognition that minds appear to vary because of their very different circumstances and degrees of stimulation in existing reality. It is these differences that advance or retard otherwise healthy minds, to make individuals apparent 'geniuses' or 'morons'. Considering the huge capacity of the human mind, so-called 'genius' is not so remarkable, evident stupidity is unwarranted and probably misleading, and understimulation is shameful, like an untreated, unchecked disease.

The Machine develops and gives its own especial outlets only to the most stimulated, 'bright' minds. In human terms the best minds are those that seek humantruth, and try to apply it to human life. But these are not the minds that the Machine uses to govern us. The Machine recognises as best those minds that serve it best, and it is they that dominate our affairs. But if the majority of minds, undeveloped by the Machine, have failed to develop their humantrue potential, so have the minority of leading minds, however well developed automatically, for they have never come near to making humanity humane.

If leading minds were to complete themselves they would become supraconscious. They could then no longer use their mental powers to sustain their leading position, but would try to bring all minds to supraconscious equality. By this I do not suggest that all minds could or necessarily should possess all knowledge, skill and talent. I do suggest that in the ideal society all minds would equally encompass complete understanding of the humantrue principles. Human individuals would be equal in that understanding, and in their responsible service according to these principles. That some had more knowledge, skill or talent would simply mean that they gave accordingly, not that they were more important. Scientists, for instance, are not made greater, or more human, or more valuable than other persons by their knowledge of science. If that value exists it is in the science, not the individual scientist. Scientists should not make science their guide, their research following where it leads, but make it and themselves the servants of a guiding humantrue need.

It can be argued that without competitive incentive some very unpleasant jobs would not get done properly, if at all. But we already voluntarily accept challenges, and endure hardships, for morally meaningful or meaningless reasons, and for vitally useful, or useless purposes. For example, by compassionately tending lepers in a leper colony, or climbing high and dangerous mountains. The Machine has conditioned us to endure hardship in the course of involuntary employment only when there is no easier way of surviving, or the pay is very high. Supraconscious, responsible individuals will accept the challenge of such work *if* there is vital need. If there is no real need, then it will not be done, and rightly so.

There is a difference between man's assessment of his personal needs that he himself is responsible for providing, and that of wants which he hopes or expects to win or extract from the Machine, which *it* is responsible for providing. There are many things which we presently believe, quite wrongly, we could never do without. We are accustomed to equating higher positions in the Machine's hierarchy not only with a greater share of its trappings, but with a higher level of what we believe to be needs. A humantrue society will provide for itself equally as it deserves, through true awareness of its needs and responsibilities, and willingness to make sacrifices which it knows to be necessary. If it is vital to mine coal, we will mine it; but knowing it to be inhuman and unnecessary to use weapons of war, we will not make them.

It has been pointed out already (Chapter 37 Humantrue Findings) that society's thinking must be represented by the intellation of our own postconscious mind, if it is to be humantrue; that the individual mind is the only source of truth, and its only means of verification; that we must rely on each individual's honesty of mind to reach humantruth in common. It follows that responsibility for a humantrue society must rest with the individual, as the source of truth and therefore as the true interpreter and upholder of the constitution. We presently give this responsibility into the hands of groups or institutions, subjecting humanity to lesser (conscious) motives and objectives. We generally respond to this in the same way as the individual responds to the influence of a crowd - with instinctive emotion, which goes contrary to the intrinsic truth of our postconscious minds. No intellect should be bound to instinct, or to the Machine, or by anything but its own awareness. But at the same time, no mind can call itself complete until completely supraconscious, i.e. when the postconscious is fulfilled and the conscious submits to it absolutely, and should not rest content until it is so.

If world affairs are beyond that mind's capacity to comprehend, then they are too complex. This should be a society *of* humans, run *by* humans, *for* humans and all fellow life, with no greater purpose, meaning or objective beyond. World human society should be such as any one balanced supraconscious mind would wish it to be. When all human minds are similarly supraconscious, that wish will become an agreed design, and will then become our new reality. It will be the product of the individual, the result of each arriving at the same decision by way of the same awareness. It follows that responsibility for this new reality must also be taken by the individual, and shared in common.

Chapter 42

DEFINITION OF HUMAN BEING

Human being may be defined as the humantrue life of the individual, lived according to her or his own supraconsciousness of fulfilled intellect, so that the co-operative being of humanity *is* this undeniable humantrue awareness on the part of, and between, each and every individual, with no authority, meaning or faith above or beyond that. The human individual is a mind and body of the human species, led by the mind. Human being is being fully and truly human.

The foregoing had been the shortest article on my website, humantruth.org, but I have since discovered that its subject - the Definition of Human Being - is the most frequently requested search term to bring visitors to that site. Therefore I have added a sequence of short sub-chapters that it is hoped will both confirm and throw new light on the above original statement.

This Chapter has two objectives. The first is to illustrate that, while we continue confining our thinking and action to the lesser conscious sphere, human being is capable of being defined in every and any conceivable way, because in the existing amoral world anything is possible.

The second and most important objective is to point out that true human being is to be defined by supraconsciousness - that when both our thinking and activity submits to the guidance of the postconscious which is also embodied in the structure of our society, then will we be wholly fulfilled, ie humantrue.

Images in this Chapter are courtesy of CheckPoint Press archive

St Peter's Square

Every so often a crowd gathers in St. Peter's Square, Rome to be addressed by the Pope.

At present, each of us is normally characterised by the conditioning of our conscious mind, derived from our relationship with reality. This dictates the way we think, act and react, subject to the pictures and words presented in newspapers, on radio and television, and to the very tangible emotional influence of others, especially in large crowds responding to dramatic events.

The Pope's thinking must be affected by his cloistered life, by his official duty to uphold the statutes and building blocks of his religion, his powerful position in much of the world, and his relationship with the masses of Catholic believers. His audience think according to the circumstances of their practical selves. Because his circumstances are not the same and his mind differently oriented, he cannot think as they do. Their wishful spiritual selves emotionally identify with this religion, but overall they are only marginally influenced by his words. So the character we appear to be is not necessarily the real us, but ourselves in relation to existing reality, tempered by our morality, perhaps in the form of a facet of reality - religion. This reality, which I call the Machine, is not truly moral, therefore we are not truly moral. It is against our intelligent nature to commit crimes and inhumanities but we commit them nevertheless under pressure from the Machine.

In other words most of these people in St. Peter's square believe that it is human nature to be competitive and in conflict. They accept that in order to avoid consequent chaos and achieve some kind of stability they need to be ordered by governments and morally advised by church leaders such as the Pope.

Governments and religious leaders too **would define human being** as instinctive emotional intelligence requiring the control of authority supplemented by the guidance of religion. This is because in existing human society the financial and political affairs of the Machine come first and morality takes second place, to be observed only where the Machine permits.

In such a gathering only the leading figure is recognisable as an individual, but the entire crowd is made up of individuals. Each individual is apparently unique because the detailed range of everyone's experience, and their reaction to that experience, is necessarily different. The Pope's position is certainly unique, so his outward individual activity is different again.

BUT..... in respect of humantrue moral responsibility every one of these individuals is the same. **A more accurate definition of human being** is that notwithstanding their many differences of superficial character, personality and position in the hierarchy, each and every individual, deep within, is fundamentally the same in that each has a postconscious mind whose function is humantruth.

AND..... in order that it shall be *possible* for every individual to personify the common humantrue moral responsibility, it is vital that the worldwide framework of life, the entire structure of human society - our ideal reality - must also embody the humantrue principles and practices for which each and every individual is responsible.

Keeping Order

We are anxious not to fall into disorder, but the Machine encourages it and we feel justified in making and enforcing laws designed to quash disorder. These laws are not guides to our moral behaviour so much as preventatives of amoral practices getting out of hand and becoming immoral, bad behaviour, and the laws may be enforced by means of equally inhuman punishment.

Examples of such punishments were the public executions that occurred at the time of the Boxer revolution in China, witnessed by large crowds of people.

Which of the people involved defines Human Being? Each of them is essentially the same, but rendered different by external circumstances and conditioning. A man about to be beheaded and another at the head of a queue awaiting the same fate? They have rebelled against authority, in a cause that they thought just, but failed and were lawfully condemned to death.

So is the **true definition of human being** that, faced with lawful injustice we obey the law and suffer in silence, or that we stand up for our believed rights and cruelly lose our heads?

Is human being defined by the soldiers escorting the rebels to their death? It is probable that they regard this beheading as pitiful, but deserved - as morally wrong but lawfully right. They are simply doing their bounden duty, obeying orders without asking questions, only glad that it is not they who are queuing for the sword. Is this the **Definition of Human Being,** that we must conform to the norm, keep safely to the right side of the law and obey instructions?

Lastly, the executioners. Did they choose this occupation, or was it the only job they could get? Have they something in their genes that enjoys cruelty and the sight of blood despite moral objections? Is it some trait which, in a kind community, might never surface but which is given full rein by this demand for public execution? Is it, then, **the essence of human being** that we do what we feel like doing, especially where the Machine supports us? Or that, with the help of a loving community, we do what is right, effectively suppressing those amoral genes?

The Boxer rebellion had a cause, a cause that justified rebellion in the eyes of the rebels. Without a cause, with a peaceful people in a just and peaceful society, there would be no need of rebellion. But where there is a threat of rebellion there is also need of a powerful authority to put it down, in this case by staging public executions. And it is this same authority, whose suppression gave cause for the rebellion, which maintains soldiers to crush it and take prisoners, officials to stage this spectacle, and executioners to do the beheading.

There is a parallel in the relief of Baghdad in 2003, where the fighting was followed by large scale looting on the part of Iraqi people. The outside world sees this looting as disgraceful, but it must appear differently in the looters' eyes. They must see it as justified in view of the vicious oppression and deprivation they have endured for years at the hands of a regime which certainly kept order, but cruelly.

The character of the Boxer rebels and the Baghdad looters is not described by their actions. In humantrue circumstances they could never have behaved in this way. But, continually maintained through the decades under the Machine, unjust rule has caused understandably angry protest, followed by punishment, bringing resentment, more suppression and more angry protest.

Whilst private human character is as good as individuals can make it under their circumstances, this and our collective public Machine behaviour does not define genuine human being.

We see that genuine **human being is defined** by supraconscious moral awareness on the part of the individual and the good influences of humantrue society. The behaviour of the human being cannot be separated from the nature and state of our world social structure.

This is an amoral Machine-lesson. If they had learned it these men would have kept their heads but, more importantly, they would have betrayed their ideals.

> *An unchanging feature of our false reality is an equally false principle. This says that, like it or not, right or wrong, it is our duty to accept the existing reality, adjust to it and earn a living by it. It lays down that our chief responsibility is to our selves and our own families, before anything else. It says that our guide must be self-interest – that this is what makes the world go round – and only when our responsibilities to our own kith and kin have been met in full can we be justified in taking up moral causes.*

> *The Silent Oracle*

Autoprogress

The aeroplane was the invention of two individuals, the Wright brothers, who applied their energy and intelligence not to the pressing problems of humanity and their solution in humantruth, but to man's accomplishment of heavier-than-air flight. This was applauded as a great human achievement but it was a matter of specialised ambition. Mankind had long dreamed of emulating the birds but it was not a matter of first concern.

Would we **Define Human Being** as the creative and inventive urge, the need to investigate, discover and technologically develop things with little or no thought as to their necessity or the eventual consequences? Certainly not - this is to play into the hands of the Machine. Our prior need is to establish a cooperative, responsible humantrue society that knows how best to utilise its material resources.

During the short time that followed the flight of the first aeroplane, industry found a ready market by applying the invention to warfare. There was no shortage of men and later women to fly these planes, exchanging dull Machine-jobs for the dangerous freedom of the cockpit. Their willingness was largely a matter of craving for adventure rather than mature intellectual decision.

In the ensuing years, warplanes have become ever more deadly and the aeroplane industry has exploited another huge and questionable market - tourism. On their way from big cities to plush resorts, the jumbo jets pass over places that haven't even developed a clean water supply.

The ideal **Definition of Human being** is belonging to a society in which big decisions are unanimous, made by the supraconscious moral majority according to true need, not by a minority of persons who are apart and out of touch.

Hierarchical Pyramids

Some time in the future our present reality shall seem impossible, a reality in which **Human Being is Defined** as all people allowing themselves to be forced, instructed, ordered, persuaded, expected or bribed to be amoral or immoral when every one of them is and has always been, at bottom, truly moral.

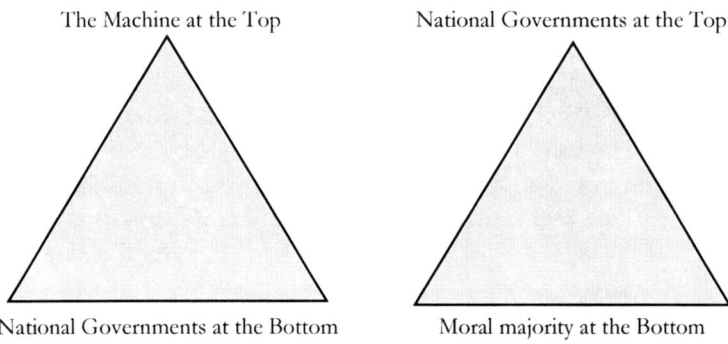

The Machine at the Top   National Governments at the Top

National Governments at the Bottom   Moral majority at the Bottom

At the beginning of the First World War there was a surge of flag-waving patriotism and enthusiasm for the fight. Later this turned to sickness and horror as the death roll lengthened and the suffering mounted.

At the end of the war people were joyful and optimistic. For a time they were united by this momentous event and the euphoria it aroused, hoping that this would prove to be the war to end all wars. And it could have been, if this fervent wish had been translated into so strong a determination for world peace that governments could never again ignore and override it.

For a brief time the right-hand pyramid was inverted, and moral awareness reached towards the top in peoples' minds. But soon they returned to their separate competitive ways and the world reverted to its different Machine self-interests. Consequently, within a mere 21 years the world was again plunged into total war, followed by another never-ending series of smaller but equally violent wars. We have not yet realised that the human world community must primarily conduct itself according to the fundamental humantrue morality embedded in the postconscious mind of each and every individual. But we are learning, as the Iraq war demonstrates, and eventually, surely, we shall insist not only that there shall be no more war, but that all the Machine pressures and influences which are the underlying cause of war shall be removed.

When that time comes we shall have a **new Definition of Human Being** - that no individuals shall permit themselves under any circumstances to behave in any way contrary to their supraconscious humantrue morality. Immorality shall then be utterly repugnant. Not only that, but concepts, practices or institutions which had once put their interests before humantrue interests shall cease to exist through non-acceptance and complete lack of support.

The pyramid concept, with a few authoritative directors at the top giving orders and the great majority at the bottom doing what they were told, shall be remembered as ridiculous, kept in place by ignorance, not only contrary to humantrue morality and common sense but also unworkable. The ultimate aim is to have all people equal. As a first step to achieving equality we should invert the pyramid, with the moral majority at the top, leading the way.

The Great Depression

The self-caused Competitive Money Economy collapse in the 1930's brought massive unemployment, poverty and despair, exemplified by the Jarrow Crusade. There was no real practical reason or justification for this disaster, which deeply affected all countries but particularly the industrialised ones.

There was no actual difference between the basic material situations before and immediately after this collapse. There was the same work to be done and there were the same people willing and able to do it; the same resources, the same mouths to feed.

All that changed was the perceived artificial paper value of money. This undermined the economic system upon which humanity had allowed itself to depend but which had never served them equally well and now betrayed them altogether.

Things have improved since the early 1900's, yet homeless people are still to be found in every big, civilised, rich city, living under bridges, sleeping in shop doorways. However much people of compassion and goodwill wish to eliminate such poverty, Machine-rules prevent it. People who do not or cannot conform to the rules have to suffer the consequences.

The collapsed artificial money-economy was eventually restored by artificial means, and the enormously cruel burden of suffering was gradually eased. But authority did not replace this indefensible system. It partly redirected it, only to replace the old sets of problems and ills with new ones as the Machine depleted, polluted and degraded our natural resources and engaged humanity in accelerating autoprogression.

This existing reality dictates our overall present **Definition of Human Being** - that we, world humanity, firstly subscribe to, serve, and submit to the Machine and its competitive money-economy while trying to be as kind, humane, loving and giving as the Machine will permit.

Reform

Various attempts have been made to solve the world's problems by bringing human interests to the fore and having the people benefited rather than exploited by the Machine.

Lenin sought to bring the ideals of Karl Marx to Russia. The Communist plan, to have the people serve the State and the State serve the people, seemed good, but the plan embodied a fatal flaw. Strong leaders were needed to shepherd a backward people in directions they needed, but did not want, to follow.

Eventually a leader arose who became corrupted by power, Stalin. After he died, dictatorial Communism gradually lost its grip, and eventually the system was suddenly replaced by that other amoral practice, money-economics.

Another leader arose, surely the most humanly aware of all - Mahatma Gandhi. The influence of his simple, peaceable example was felt worldwide, but he did not oppose the money economy so much as the way it worked. In the absence of any equal to follow him, his influence was largely lost as the Machine re-asserted itself.

When we speak we use the language of this present reality, because the Machine largely dictates our thinking. Up to a point we already know that we should behave humantruly, but we also believe that it is impossible to do so, given the present demands, pressures and false values of the Machine which we believe to be inescapable. A change of thinking is required.

Presently we view the human race as unreliable, at times benign and peaceable but capable of going to opposite extremes of violent aggression and cruelty so that people must be grouped, governed and controlled by law and its enforcement. The opposite is the case.

We are fully capable of benign and peaceable reliability if we submit to the guidance of our postconscious minds, and then only if we insist upon a humantrue social structure which utterly supports, enables and sustains such a fully supraconscious society.

Dictatorship

The Italian dictator, Mussolini, was a strong, posturing, blustering, domineering character yet fundamentally he was like many other men. But because of his ambition he acquired different priorities, both good and bad. Consequently his mental agenda was different. Due to his all-powerful position, his whims could become national policies and practices. **His Definition of Human Being** might be 'let the strongest man lead and the rest follow'.

Another, more effectively ruthless leader was Adolf Hitler. He faced the same political, economic and international difficulties and sought to solve them by dictatorship and irresistible power. He crushed German political opposition, annihilated the Jews whom he accused of manipulating the economy, and began to take over neighbouring countries by military invasion. When he delivered his infamous speeches what was uppermost in his mind? How did he square his morality with his immoral thoughts and actions?

Hitler, like Mussolini, did much good in his own country and succeeded to the extent he did by raising Germany out of poverty, but he failed to appreciate that only humantrue values could prevail whereas dictatorship was bound to fail, as it always had, because one dominant conscious Machine-mind cannot represent a whole peoples' thinking, and the whole people will not long wholeheartedly follow false doctrines.

Hitler was the product of a severely oppressed childhood and an unpromising early adulthood which nevertheless conspired to raise him to power, power which he eventually assumed as of right, aided particularly by his gift for fervent oratory. He wanted to benefit the German people but well knew that this required iron ruthlessness if it were to be accomplished. In this way, war and the holocaust could be justified, particularly by a supreme leader who could remain personally aloof from their horrors.

That the terrible events of the Nazi era were ordered meant that those orders had to be carried out. The gross inhumanities that the personal nightmares and vanities of a sick mind could justify became the public duties of his obedient henchmen who would explain their bloody actions as necessary to an overall plan for good.

The German people, at least vaguely aware of all this but swayed by fervent patriotism, were for a long time willing to remain in a state of denial. In this way individual minds may be conditioned to the point where true morality can be overridden and obscured.

Make no mistake, in their circumstances you or I could have done just as the Nazi Germans did. And given the same traumatic childhood and later background, many of us could have ended up as Hitler himself, driven as he was by the sequence of events which he had initiated and which brought him to his doom.

In a humantrue society dictatorship could not happen. Individuals would not consent to gather in crowds and be harangued. There would be no politics. There would be no Machine, consequently no weapons or readiness for war. Rather than be grouped into separate nations represented by single leaders, the people would be represented by their individual selves, supraconsciously united in common acceptance of the humantrue moral code. Whatever that code told them was right to do the people would do, and whatever it told them was wrong to do, they would not do. Such is a **true Definition of Human Being.**

Inverting the Pyramid

After the first world war and its horrifying **22,000,000** casualties, in an attempt to ensure that it would prove to be 'the war to end all wars, the League of Nations was formed, but it failed to resolve international differences and was eventually abandoned. National governments were not yet ready to surrender a part of their sovereignty in this way.

After World War II, and its yet more horrifying **40,000,000** casualties, the United Nations Organisation was formed, hopefully to learn by the mistakes of the League of Nations. This first meeting took place in a more enlightened and determined world, its member states more prepared to sacrifice a measure of their independence.

In that it provided a means of nations discussing differences the UN was a step in the right direction. There was a prospect that nations would turn to the UN rather than resort to war. But from the viewpoint that human affairs should be entrusted to supraconscious individual responsibility, it could be said to have removed us further from that goal. Individuals' different interests, in a democracy, are related to the Machine and put into the hands of one, two, or more political parties. One of these parties chooses a government from its own members. Some members of this government are sent to represent their nation at the United Nations that cannot then be said to oversee world affairs in the interests of all people.

But this presents another **Definition of Human Being** – that the public are not capable of understanding and running their affairs but must rely upon experts. As the result human affairs, already governed in most respects by the Machine, become international affairs, national affairs and political affairs, all of which determine the nature of human affairs yet whose significance to true human interests is extremely tenuous.

Inverting the pyramids:

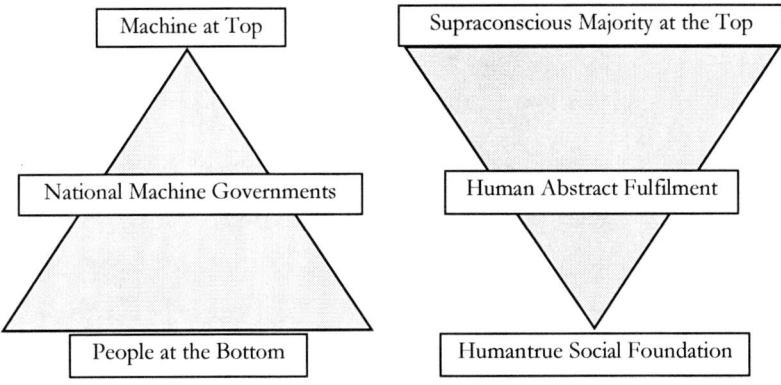

I have already offered several definitions of human being and don't wish to over-complicate the issue. But there is this suggestion - that opposite the UN a popular forum United Individuals be set up, for wide discussion which would advise or instruct the international scene by way of politics and government until such time as humantruth is established and the controlling institutions become obsolete.

The objective of United Individuals might be this - that the principles and practices of human life would no longer be a matter of pursuing the instinc- tive Machine drives in all directions to form gigantic structures which are alien to most of us. Instead, it would be a matter of indulging our natural wish for contented, cooperative community, and of fulfilling our intellectual potential in numerous happy and harmless abstract intellectual ways.

Radical proposals are at present usually looked at from the viewpoint of the norm, and are thus regarded as outlandish. It is assumed that members of a United Individuals Movement, having read The Wrong Reality, would share the movement's opposite view, i.e. looking at the world from a humantrue stance and regarding the <u>norm</u> as outlandish.

What it comes down to is that we have to put supraconscious intellation first. When the chips are down, humantruth has to come before personal relation- ships inside the conscious consensus and before interests dictated by the Machine. The time is envisaged when nobody will allow outside false interests to govern them in this way: when nobody will be guided by other than their own postconscious.

The keeper of the postconscious mind, and therefore of humantruth, is the individual. It must come as a relief to realise that members of such a movement would be dealing solely and directly with free individuals, their intellation and discussion conducted entirely independently of all Machine concepts and connections. That which is humantruly important to any of us, whoever or wherever we may be, must be of equal importance to all others.

If there is any hope of dignified survival for humanity, it lies in the fulfilment of the common postconscious. If this can but become widely understood, then any movement such as this will grow to achieve its objective.

Community

There are no supraconscious humantrue communities in existence but there are others. They find it difficult to survive when necessarily partly dependent upon the Machine. The Findhorn community, in Scotland, survives well but on a religious/commercial basis.

We have had many spiritual, religious leaders who have offered moral guidance, taken from their own postconscious minds, but they themselves have been converted into figureheads, their messages of truth overlaid and obscured by the institution of churches, mosques and synagogues, giving again **the false Definition of Human Being** - that we lack responsibility and need to be subject to authoritative control.

The only stable humantrue state shall be secured when responsibility is invested in the individual - every individual, meaning the whole people in community - and in each and every single individual representing supraconsciousness, ie humantruth, he or she being guided by true morality of the postconscious mind. This, again, is a **true Definition of Human Being.**

It is likely that the people will change before they have been able to establish a humantrue framework of life in place of the Machine. But a humantruly aware world community shall itself render the Machine ineffective.

The supreme leader of one nation who wishes to go to war with another shall find nobody willing to take up arms and fight. This shall not leave them vulnerable because the other nation's people will likewise refuse to fight.

The entrepreneur who wishes to sell weapons shall be unable to persuade anyone to manufacturer them.

The people of financially rich countries will insist that their wealth be shared with poor countries so that all become equally provided for.

Those who cherish their national flag, their different culture, religion and language will be prepared to abandon them, seeking for and finding a common identity which all may share.

The world's people will reject the standards of habit and consumption imposed on them by the Machine, substituting healthy and environmentally friendly standards and denying the Machine its profits without which it must shrink and die.

The world's people will opt for a materially simple, intellectually rich way of life that can happily co-exist with nature. They will cease relying on the

Machine's artificial entertainments and will indulge, instead, in the richness of their own creativity, while all sharing equally in the communal work of feeding, clothing, sheltering and caring for each other.

Such a world community, rejecting the competitive greed and contrived hatred of the past, shall bring out the loving good that exists in everyone.

Moral Guide

Supraconsciousness shall guarantee individual responsibility. Just as instinct is the guide for primitive animals to which they are, for their own good, locked-on, the postconscious mind shall be the undeniable guide for humans. The conscious sphere shall provide our intelligent satisfaction, creativity and entertainment but always within the bounds of postconscious morality (see Figure 11a opposite).

We are already moving in this direction with increasing momentum. This was strongly demonstrated in regard to Iraq. The anti-war crusade is a moral stand opposed to war. It takes the position that war is immoral and therefore must be banned, regardless of the many political arguments put forward for war. But how is the ideal to be sustained?

I foresee a time when humantrue morality, which we all recognise but cannot presently live by, shall not only be the absolute moral foundation of our personal lives but also of the whole wide human world. We shall sustain equality, mutual care and close community. Humantruth shall be maintained by each and every individual postconscious mind, and any contravention shall be unthinkable.

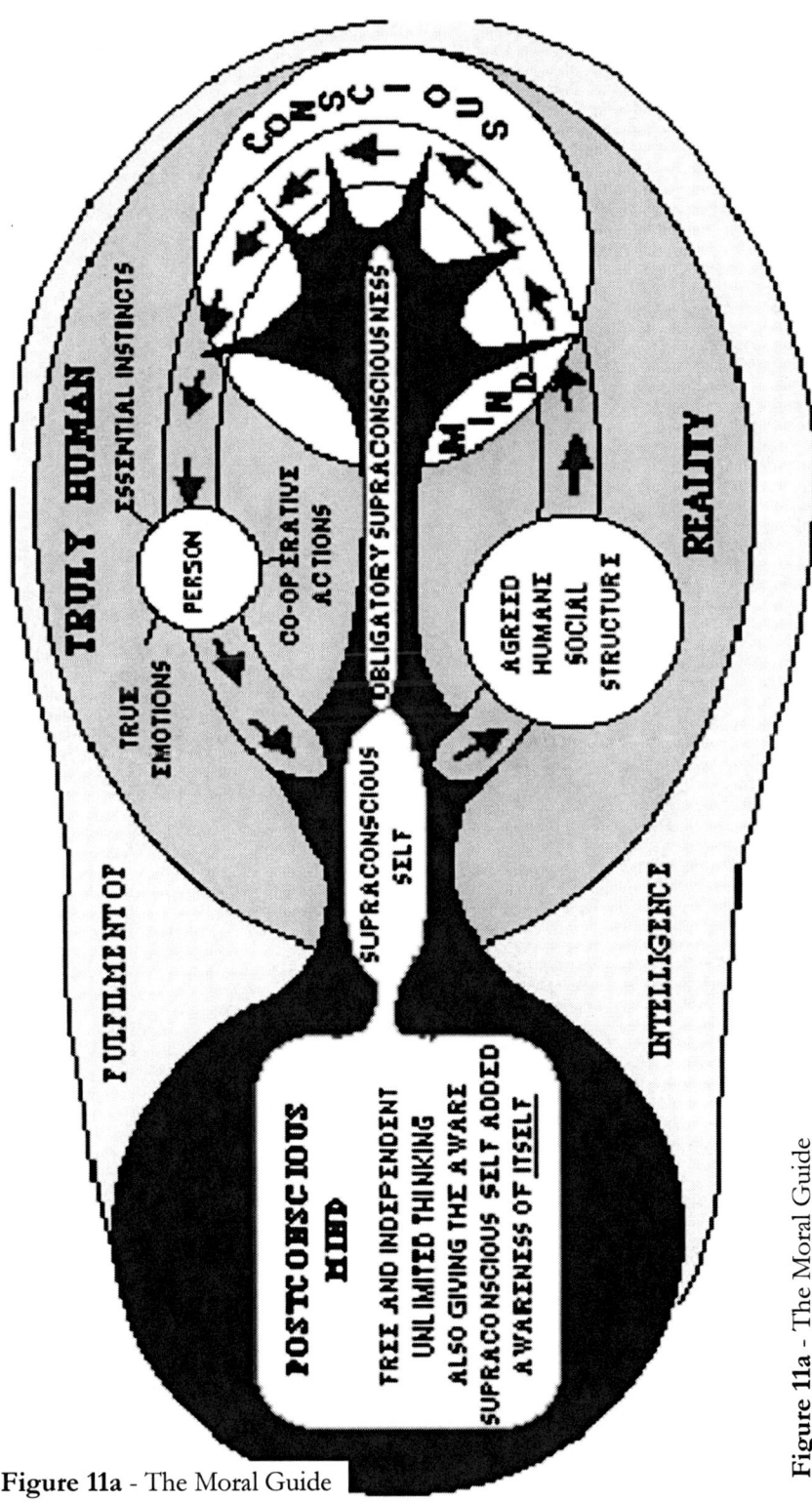

Figure 11a - The Moral Guide

Figure 11a - The Moral Guide

Chapter 43

CODE OF INDIVIDUAL BEHAVIOUR

In order to sustain a true state of human being it shall be necessary to include in the constitution a code of individual behaviour. This will not be authoritative law, but a reminder to which individuals voluntarily refer for guidance and encouragement. At the present stage of contemplation, prior to agreeing the code, we should consider the following.

We have long been trying to resolve the struggle between our humanity and the Machine, but unsuccessfully because we have never escaped from the latter's domination. We still address the human questions and problems according to the automatic concepts, standards and beliefs of existing reality. Consequently our reasoning is a variously confused mixture of falseness and truth, so that we cannot agree.

We now have to address these questions and problems with very different minds - according to supraconsciousness of humantrue reason. But however compelling our good intentions, we must remember that we are instinctive, conscious bodies as well as postconscious minds. Whilst our code of individual behaviour must unfailingly uphold our good and humantrue intentions, it must take account of, also fulfil, our inescapable, necessary emotions.

When discussing ideal human behaviour we shall have to decide what practices are necessary and desirable, and what are unnecessary and undesirable. Some of these decisions are bound to go against the grain of long-accustomed feeling. They will have to be honoured with grim determination, until the time comes when they are fully accepted as part of our new, humantrue nature, with our emotions gathered in support.

It is suggested that the code of individual behaviour be divided into three parts: Survival, Reproduction, and Fulfilment.

Survival. To prepare the way for deciding how we shall achieve survival, we should first remove from our minds and wills our present automatic concepts, practices and motives. We should cease thinking and acting competitively, with egocentric self-interest. We should cease reasoning incompletely and applying our will to the preferment of kith and kin and to gaining possession, advantage, reward and status.

The accepted intention of our postconscious-guided intellect shall be to embrace co-operation, simple husbanding of resources, healthy diet, and to admit it as our own responsibility to keep humantruth, abiding by that which we know to be right and good, whatever contrary impulses we may feel. These intentions shall be supported by the power of will switched to giving, loving, sharing, caring and cherishing - wanting *all* to be well, and making this its great and responsible undertaking.

Reproduction. We need to see that whereas it is vital to the human race that we continue to reproduce, by overcoming instinctive inhibitions we have allowed ourselves to pursue the mating drive to extremes that are strictly unnecessary from the practical viewpoint.

Sexual desire is instinct's means of impelling animals to reproduce. It is, and needs to be, nature's strongest but temporary drive, so that when the proper time comes it takes absolute precedence. In nature, when mating has been accomplished the sexual aim has been achieved and, there being no further need for it until next season, desire subsides, making way for other drives to assert or re-assert themselves, such as the call to defend territory, build a nest, or dig a burrow. Not so with humans. By virtue of our much more complex conscious minds we have a higher capacity for emotional stimulation than any other animal, yet our survival success does not require the use of this whole capacity. The normal animal's livelihood and safety, on the other hand, calls for a total brain capacity only slightly greater than needed for its maximum, pre-planned, vigilant activity.

The human race still follows instinctive drives and, having bigger capacity for stimulation, also has greater ability to indulge those drives The Machine has taken from us the all-round responsibility for fending for ourselves, and replaced it with narrow tasks, more secure but normally less engrossingly stimulating. So we indulge in all kinds of artificial sports and entertainments, with the help of the Machine that profits from them. We are accustomed to mating at any time because human babies can survive birth at all seasons. But we mate frequently - far beyond the needs of reproduction - for only an average of just over two births per marriage are required to maintain the population. We pursue sexual gratification further still by practicing homosexuality and masturbation, indulgencies, seemingly peculiar to humans, which have no natural reproductive function.

Our sexual practices do presently serve an acceptably important human function, however - the temporary release of tension and escape from frustration. But they are exploited by the Machine, as are all our appetites, in the interests of the money-economy. Up to a point it could be said that sexual titillation is a contribution to that important function, but when carried too far, as it is, the effect is to drag us still further below the level of postconscious awareness required for humantrue change.

I suggest that in a much more widely and deeply fulfilling humantrue society, preoccupation with sex will be much reduced, kept to its important role of contributing to happy monogamous relationships, and more closely related to childbirth. It will be no longer subject to contrary commercial pressures in the shape of provocative dress fashions, make-up, films and magazines, or stirred up to excess by the misuse of drugs including alcohol. Restrained sexual behaviour will be encouraged and reinforced by the voluntary adoption of certain rules - that it shall never harm, threaten (and this particularly includes the terrible risk of AIDS), or give offence to anyone, or be allowed to displace other more essential cares and responsibilities. The final factor to keep sex in its appropriate place will be the many and varied other interests and satisfactions that will occupy everyone in a humantrue society.

Fulfilment. I think there is no question but that when we are a supraconscious race it will be our true nature to fulfil intellect, and so find happiness such as we have never known. In respect of fulfilment, therefore, this code is not so much a matter of guiding our behaviour, since that will now come naturally, but of reminding us to keep the framework of life according to true human nature. To maintain our fundamental happiness we must ensure that the practices of the world bear out and support the pure postconscious awareness of our minds by fulfilling humantruth. It will be the responsibility of every single individual to see that this is constantly so.

To prepare the way for spontaneously humantrue individual behaviour we shall have to turn our backs on substitute fulfilments. We must reject: competitive sport; violent and escapist entertainment, real or imaginary, about automatic life and existing affairs, in newspapers, television, films and books; hard drinking, drugs and tobacco; automated holidays and games. It must no longer be required of us to be preoccupied with: money-economy reckoning, spending, worrying and cheating; false calculations and conversations; political and religious compromising, pretending, posturing and arguing. Even the formally instituted artificial caring, in old people's homes for instance, however conscientious and kindly, shall be abandoned, for it is a poor substitute for the real thing, i.e. care in the family or true community.

In a humantrue reality the normal process of living, including spontaneous humour and informal play, will give all the physical and basic emotional satisfaction needed. The individual intellect, all practical problems having been already long solved, will no longer be constantly applied, defensively or aggressively as at present, to competitive affairs of the Machine. It will be free to rise to another plane, such as that which exclusively absorbs musicians, or painters. But whilst it is apart from everyday considerations, it will be complimentary to, and not superior to but absolutely in harmony with, everyday life. It might be inspired by a sunset, perhaps, the same sunset as delights and calms the physical emotions, representing a total oneness of physical/intellectual human being.

It is to be fully understood that once the mind becomes supraconscious it cannot but accept humantruth, to the practice of which the greatest power of our individual will shall be inescapably drawn, but for the preservation of which we must be ever watchful. And it has to be recognised that the individual *is* responsible for the whole, and that the whole must be made solely dependent on the individual. Under the constitution, this will be achieved more safely and securely than by any other means, because this is the one and only way of making and keeping the whole humantrue.

Chapter 44

FRAMEWORK OF LIFE

Whether or not there exists the higher objective of true equilibrium, the truth is the truth, and all persons who are aware of it shall live by it. The following is my attempt to envisage a human reality in which we do live by the truth - a humantrue society.

Overall Principles. A humantrue society shall be structured by supraconsciousness in such a way as to be always subject to humantrue awareness and to allow and enable life to be lived according to this awareness. It will be a matter of each of us understanding what has to be done, what we are individually capable of doing, and putting all this together so that all things *are* properly done. It will be a matter of individual responsibility, not of permanent institutions of leadership that disallow, or discourage, and work against such co-operation. Humantrue society will fulfil our definition of human being, serve the code of individual behaviour, and have as its prime objective the well-being of humanity and all Earth. It will bind us together as one united human race, with no significant differences or artificial divisions. The whole framework will be our means of providing for our subsistence, our good health, and the general enrichment of life.

For such a society to come into being everyone must know that life is not to be a matter of individuals feathering their own nests, carving out defensive positions in the competitive world, but of each giving to a co-operative world community which cares for all individuals. It is not a matter of the submissive taking power and forcing the dominants to submit, but of all of us forsaking these existing, unnecessary extremes and uniting in comradeship. Humantrue society is not an impossible dream, but a rational awakening from a nightmare. It must be so arranged that we avoid all our familiar troubles and difficulties that seem to be inevitable but are in fact imposed by automatic reality.

Humantrue society is the means of living to be adopted if humanity is to accord with its supraconsciousness. It shall recognise that individuals value highly their moral independence but at the same time get great joy from loyalty to a cause. Such a society, by embodying humantruth, will represent the perfect cause, which allows individuals to be independent except of their own true responsibility. Whilst everyone would be receiving, the accent would be on each giving.

Whilst rejecting money-economic enterprise, humantruth does not rule out responsible free enterprise on the part of individuals for the benefit of humanity at large and without personal reward or any expectation of it. Supraconscious humans will represent or prefer nothing above their humanity. The framework of their society must not allow that any contrary influence be exerted, or opportunity provided. No special skill, accomplishment or knowledge shall be permitted to mark anyone out as of different status, but be regarded as an uncommon gift to the general good which one is privileged to make whilst remaining a common individual.

The concept of true equilibrium seems to me to be the answer to the universal question. The answer for humanity is similar - to know all possibilities but live with optimum practical simplicity.

In every species of natural life each generation takes its temporary place in the permanent community by way of instinct, which binds the individual to a common code. In a similar way each human individual will be voluntarily bound by a humantrue constitution whose first objective will be to see that everybody enjoys the basic provisions and comforts of life.

Once more, ask the question: why are we living? Unless it is to fulfil truth, and so increase universal true influence, there is absolutely no point in life, only the temporary instinctive experience of taking part in it. That is enough for creatures of instinct who are not yet capable of more, but for us it can not be enough. Just as our intellect makes us aware of our mortality, so can it make us aware that the fulfilment of truth is our purpose, the reason why we are living, and that the reason for the individual tragedy of death is the same as that which offers the gift of true fulfilment. And I submit that our eventual demise as a species will not be the end, but a completed stage in the continuing process of truth and energy drawing together towards equilibrium.

Automated conscious will can seal up the door between the independent postconscious mind and the eventually established conscious mind, ensuring that ultimate truth cannot be realised. Youth can keep this door closed against full intellect in eagerness to play the automatic game, spending the Machine's money, and energy, on instinctive pursuits. This is in the interests of the Machine, which can and does so apply its lore, and so tighten its harness, that when youth becomes adult, and the door could open, it remains firmly closed. The person is then represented by its conscious mind, constructing its opinions and deciding its actions chiefly by automatic calculation. But this door *can* be broken down, and the Machine defeated. In a humantrue society, because of intellation, no part of our postconscious true conclusions would be closed to conscious awareness.

Fear, such as that of violence or eventual death, is emotional, yet whilst fears can be diminished by being deliberately ignored or denied, they can also be increased by full awareness of that which is to be feared - by not barring it from consciousness. But fear of such as violence will be banished in a humantrue society, for the cause of it will not exist so that it need be thought of no longer. And such as fear of natural death will be banished also, because when we have considered these matters with deep supraconscious intellation, we shall be afraid no longer.

In a humantrue reality, everything in life will be benignly supportive of life. Our society will be built on, and depend on, gentleness, selfless endeavour, giving, compassion and peaceful contentment - the comely, goodly elements of human being which both care for and create things of goodness, the true ingredients of human happiness in harmony. The moral person will not have all kinds of alternative opinions to fall back on when morality becomes boring, but *will* have compelling reason to remain moral, and the backing of an entire society which is *not* boring. Our happiness will lie in the individual, collective, and therefore total supraconscious fulfilment of human intellect, which cannot be fulfilled whilst aware of any immorality or human suffering in the world, nor of any falseness or irresponsibility in itself.

This framework of life, because it will be the best possible for humanity, will also be best for Gaia because it will mean that we, as part of the influence for truth, will give to that influence the most constant and strong support, which will also support Gaia's protective care of life on Earth.

Whilst it is clear that our basic means of livelihood shall be simple, we, having autoprogressed as far as we have and because of our numbers, but mainly because of our intellectual needs, cannot go back to the primitive. We have to recognise a certain necessary dependence on advanced technology, but must make it our obedient servant rather than master. And we should not overlook or ever forget the lessons that this automatic age has to teach, in case we are ever again tempted by the competitive urge and all its trappings and consequences.

I have considered it necessary to begin this chapter in this way because it is so easy and normal for us to slip into automatic modes of thought by which we readily reject as preposterous that which in truth is entirely reasonable, such as the structure of a humantrue society that I now venture to suggest. If you feel I have been repeating myself unnecessarily, think how easily we presently repeatedly overlook, or forget, the salutary lessons of the past.

For example, the political establishment's 'new enlightenment' which I have already mentioned, suggests that the poverty of the 'third world' arises from the fact that most poor countries still practice centralised political control, often copied from the nations which colonised them, which has caused their economies to stagnate. It goes on to suggest that if they had allowed freedom to market forces they would now be prosperous. This view derives from the fact that in general, in the West, the old authoritarian domination over many humans by a small minority has largely gone out of the window, being replaced by domination of a more subtle, indirect kind. Such practices as flexible working hours, with relaxed attitudes, and helping rather than hindering its human working units in attaining their material dreams has been found of great benefit to the prosperity of the Machine.

But this relaxation of strict human control on the part of financiers, employers and traders is counter-balanced by a stepping up of automatic control by the Machine, especially its money-economy, still represented by an elite minority. Those who, from the security of elitist privilege see this as a good thing, fail or refuse to recognise two factors. First, monetary prosperity, indicated by the stock-exchange share price index, is not synonymous with overall human well-being, indicated by a general level of happy contentment. In the most autoprogressively advanced nation, the USA, the big city leads the auto-way, pumping its kind of blood throughout the country, but city life and values are tolerable only to conditioned, automated, relatively privileged humans. Its rushing, uncaring, overwhelming pattern of control, with its noise, rubbish, down-and-outs, flyover networks and general slick and threatening sophistication, is intolerable to any fully aware human being.

Second, it was such automatic free competition in the past, between both money-economic and power interests, which created rich and poor people and nations, and brought about protests, followed by attempted political controls of those interests and some reforms. Socialism and communism were reactions to the rampant Machine, but they are now declining as capitalism makes new advances with the help of computer technology. Unless we open our eyes to the truth, this new wave will surge excitedly forward until the markets are saturated, or auto-supply and auto-demand fail to satisfy each other. This will usher in a new era of wealth riding on the back of poverty, with the struggles of competition spreading from the market-place to the battlefield until capitalism and fascism is again defeated by socialism and communism. There will be no fundamental change, only a repeat of the same futile cycle to follow, as the world becomes generally bored with half-heartedly imposed morality and eventually swings back to automatic free competition.

It is all too easy to fall into the way of blinkered, limited thinking that belongs to automatic reality. Humantrue views of society result from a long and deep process of intellation. I have no doubt that anyone who follows a similar process will broadly agree. If you find my views hard to swallow, please consider whether that might be because you have not yet intellated enough, and please take up the challenge to try further.

Practical Considerations. If the humantrue principles and constitution are to be observed and supported, it seems to me self-evident that all people throughout the world should live in similar, small, basic communities. By making the basic community the most important formal grouping in the world, whose interest every other facility served, with no greater interests predominating, we will build our framework of life to a human scale, and therefore in our true interests. The human world, represented by the common basic community maintained by individual responsibility (guaranteed by supraconsciousness), will work as one preplanned, stable, unchanging system, operating of its own accord, without permanent leaders, without fuss, and without self-made difficulties.

Our life as a whole species shall be represented by our local community life because being truly human requires total co-operation for success, and such co-operation is possible only on a small scale. So the affairs of the whole world shall be related to, and initiated by, the local community. Whereas presently people can be obliged by the Machine to act for money-economic reasons, and by governments to act for political or military reasons, they will then always act for fundamentally humantrue reasons.

In order to find such physical and emotional satisfaction as is necessary to supraconscious fulfilment, everyone shall be involved with all the basic processes of life. Instead of being divided into different categories or classes of person, or into separate situations in different countries or at different stages of life, we shall all be part of the same essential human flow; always, throughout life. We will then no longer need to feel alone and apart because we will each *be* that which we actually *are*, or ought to be - one of the same species, or extended family, sharing the same truth and serving the same fundamental objectives and interests.

These communities shall be large enough to be effectively supportive of their members and companionable, but not so large as to be unwieldy and impersonal. Rather than having each family isolated in its own maintenance structure resources will be shared, also labour and responsibility. Children will have the benefit of being brought up in the company of several others, and by several adults, of various ages and temperaments, in a rounded and stimulating working environment. It will be possible to employ fewer facilities per capita - for cooking washing, heating etc. yet make them more widely available to all. The sick and old will still be part of the vigorous pattern of community life, their care more readily and happily undertaken, and their comforts provided, for being an accepted, shared, and therefore less heavy individual burden. Such communities will engender most of their own diversions and amusements. There will also be quiet places where we can get away from each other at times.

There is bound to be disagreement on minor issues but it will not be of significance because, when humanity is guided by the supraconscious awareness of the individual, there will also be abiding *agreement* on all things that really matter. For example, many people might differ as to their favourite flower, yet all are agreed that flowers are beautiful. They fundamentally agree, since nobody holds that flowers are ugly, and their differences of opinion, as to which flower is most beautiful, add interest rather than threaten harmony.

Humantrue society, represented by the community, will be the mirror and embodiment of our better selves that will be our central guide despite our peripheral weaknesses. It will not be forced on us but will be a way of living which we ourselves supraconsciously aspired to, and which we both pursue with instinctive enthusiasm and self-impose with awareness of intellect.

The initial problem of forming communities in existing automatic environments, especially cities, using buildings and facilities which were not designed for such humantrue purposes, will be temporarily overcome by the tolerant understanding and sacrifice of supraconscious humanity. The city epitomises our present hierarchical, unequal, dominant Machine, and to disperse it will present practical problems and take time. Eventually we will rebuild humantruly. It will be naturally necessary, and to the benefit of our health, that we live in the open much of the time, but our species needs effective shelter and protection from the elements, particularly in cold and wet climates. Married couples, and their babies when young, might sleep in small basic dwellings that offer privacy. Daytime will be spent mostly working close by, in the community gardens and in and around the main community building where cooking, washing, making and mending facilities will be housed, and where older children, single adults, the aged and sick, and visitors will be accommodated.

Humantrue society will not be subject to perpetual automatic change. Our reality will be stable, but our individual experience of life, our direct contribution to that society, might go through four stages:

From birth to 18 years of age, or less (the age of female maturity - to be agreed upon): childhood induction into membership of the community and all its routines, skills, responsibilities and fulfilments, and basic learning. (Note: many sex-related problems would be avoided if the age of maturity were 15, but I understand that whilst girls are able to give birth as early as twelve years of age, they are not fully physically prepared until 18, and to bear a child at an earlier age than this can be dangerous to the mother).

At 18 years (accepted as the norm but subject to individual choice of course): marriage, within or outside the community of birth. After two children are born an effective but harmless method of birth control will be used (this is assuming that, if such a method does not yet exist it will, with determined and disinterested effort, be found).

18 - 35 years: parenthood and sharing in the work of the home community, also in bringing up and teaching the young and, later, caring for the old and sick.

35 - 55 years: being trained and working for worldwide or local interests, travelling as needed or remaining in the home community. Either way, whatever we do and wherever we go we live in a local community, taking part in its life and contributing to the routine chores.

55 - death: settling, perhaps back into the community of birth, informally passing on the benefit of experience, helping with the chores, gradually taking life more easily.

You might object that the foregoing is unacceptably rigid, but surely it is clear that we vitally need a common, fundamentally viable framework for a truly human life, and that what is good and true for the individual is right for the community, and therefore for the world. Besides, this is a suggestion put forward for your consideration and subject to unanimous agreement. If you still find it too inflexible, reflect upon the fate of the comparatively fortunate majority of us in the present Western (supposedly free enterprise) society:

From birth to 5 years of age: home upbringing; being presented with a pretend reality, whilst sheltered and protected from the violent and ugly world outside.

From 5 to 16/22 years: formal competitive education, media exposure, street experience - being prepared uncritically to accept and blindly to adjust to the basic norms of the presently real world; learning which rests upon a contrived and artificial approach to life, remote from humantruth, as the Machine requires, a process that either puts young people down as the Machine's labourers or pushes them up into specialised automated jobs. This age group possess an enthusiastic and optimistic concept of reality, peculiar to youth, which is not only far from humantruth but does not perceive that the world's foundations, aims and practices, and humanity's common beliefs and values, are false.

From 16/22 to 60/65 years: concentrating on self-survival, competing for advantage; employment, striving for money; marriage, setting up home, equipping it, bringing up children, seeing they are educated, indulging in an artificially oriented 'lifestyle' in generally unsuitable conditions and all according to automatic status and income. An 'in-the-swim' concept of reality which enables those who find themselves joining in its violence and contributing to its ugliness to feel justified in so doing. A life commonly spent in doubt, confusion and considerable fear, underlying which is our profound ignorance of humantruth, a lack that is frustratingly sensed but whose significance is nowhere near comprehended.

From 60/65 to death: retirement, its artificial manner depending upon the level of pension and other means; normally living apart from family, let down by failing mental powers, certainly pushed aside and disregarded by the new 'in-the-swim' generation. Left behind with a personal view of reality as it was, now autoprogressively by-passed by new, equally false concepts.

The typical humantrue community might be formed in this way: a central communal building known as the Mainhouse, home for perhaps ten families and others - say 40 people. Ten such communities will form a group of about 400 people plus one extra community of 40 which, instead of a Mainhouse, will maintain a distribution depot, and communications centre for its group known as the Middlehouse. Ten such Middlehouse groups, each with its ten Mainhouse communities will form a larger group of maximum size for this society, about 4400 people, one of its communities to maintain, instead of a Middlehouse, a meeting place and world communications centre known as a Gathering, where 110 individuals, each chosen in rotation from each of the 110 communities represented, gather to discuss internal problems and to take part with all other Gatherings (by radio, television or internet communication,) in discussion of any world problems. All proceedings are recorded and all exceptional (but excluding emergency) decisions must be referred to every single individual adult (18 years and over) and unanimously agreed. This last might seem impossible to achieve, but in a stable and relatively unchanging society there will be few such exceptional decisions.

This will be a full life, with strong values of fidelity, tolerance and self-control, made possible by supraconsciousness and a world reality free from unnecessary stress and anxiety. It will be full of activity and interest of a directly integrated kind, in that everything we do and feel will be relative to world well-being and humantrue awareness. Everyone will be living in similar communities and so shall 'know' everyone else, in that the circumstances of all are basically the same. How else could the principles of co-operation, equality and individual responsibility be upheld over all the Earth? It might be expected that instead of our present money economy tending to reduce standards towards the lowest common denominator, a humantrue society will draw humanity towards the highest.

I have mentioned already the randomness of human temperament. It is strong in us because it is vital to instinctive progress by natural selection of genes, but can be seen as a danger to co-operative community. However, humantrue society will exercise restraint in three vital ways. First, everybody will voluntarily submit to the agreed constitution. Second, everybody will be supraconscious and intellectually fulfilled, so emotional disturbance will be much reduced. Third, the tendency of individuals periodically to become emotionally upset will be offset by the fact that they shall not be alone and that such periods do not naturally coincide in everybody. So, for example, women suffering from premenstrual tension can be relieved by others of the community until they regain their normal composure. Individuals under any kind of temporary stress who are tempted to act irrationally can be dissuaded by their rational comrades.

When the time comes to rebuild our houses and other buildings, we can do it ourselves, simply and solidly, using local basic materials and skills and techniques which all will learn as part of upbringing, in such a way that our buildings are long-lasting and easy to maintain. The standard best practices for every locality will be worked out and agreed. Trees will be grown in every available space for some of our timber needs. We need to develop highly effective means of insulation that require minimal manufacture and the least possible use of scarce resources, so that the minimum of heating and cooling is required. Electric power for heating, lighting and other necessary purposes, will be obtained from safe and freely available sources, such as wind, tides and rivers, but especially from the sun. This, again, needs exhaustive study free from false money-economic or political parameters.

The furniture and fittings for our buildings will be made by the communities, as far as possible, using a minimum of metal. We will have carpentry tools and all will learn their proper use and care. These things will be simple and modest, as shall our clothing. This, too, will be locally made in the communities as much as is practicable. We will supraconsciously avoid ostentation, and fashion. Such things as zip fasteners might be found too complex and wasteful to make, so that we will return to the use of buttons and other simple fastenings. If we cease raising and killing animals, and shrink from using dead carcasses, we will have no leather, and the making of plastics is surely not often humantruly viable. Our shoes may then have to be made of wood and canvas. There is no denying the value of colour and design, but our present standards of requirement and taste in clothing and furnishing are too often thoughtless desires exploited by the money economy. They are not worth what they cost in real terms. The satisfaction we will lose, by denial of these desires in a humantrue society, we will more than regain in other ways.

We may believe that to provide our basic necessities by our own labour must be hard and grinding work, and we may view the lightening of that burden by heavy mechanisation and the wide application of technology as a boon to humanity. But *work*, as we now know it, does not represent united human effort to provide human necessities, and has not done so since the days of the hunter gathers. In fact, many hands, with the reasonable minimum help of machinery, shall make lighter work of the whole task.

European peasants might be held up as examples of the empty, backbreaking drudgery of life close to the soil and dependent on it. But they are dependent on the Machine for many things, and subject to market forces that demand a high level of labour for a relatively low level of subsistence. Being isolated they are without trade union power, and are remote from the artificial compensations of city-based culture. Because their activities are small-scale, they do not have the economic power to attract even a reasonable level of mechanical and technological aid. So it is partly because they have been hard used by the Machine that their life appears brutal, but also because the human advances in moral awareness and enlightenment, such as they are, have passed them by.

We have already looked at the way the competitive money economy works. European peasants suffer because the Machine is able to load a heavy burden on their backs. Yet they are producing food, whilst millions of others, doing lighter work for higher reward, are producing nothing useful, and many more are unemployed. We should no longer be in doubt that the Machine does not operate for our benefit, but for reasons of its own.

At present the whole world's fundamental effort is inspired by aquisitiveness and ambition - by a liking for money and what it can buy. There are public utilities, but they are said not to work well because their leaders lack the profit motive and workers do not have to be cost effective. It is generally believed by the automated that without such incentives the vital effort will not be made. The humantruth is that humanity, whatever it gains from service to the Machine, remains sadly lacking, and that which is lacking we would regain by supraconsciousness. Certainly it will then be the case that nobody is a supreme winner, but neither shall anybody be a miserable loser. *All* will find satisfaction, and *that* will create their will to work, and to make every communal facility work, effectively.

Consider how a humantrue society, putting humanity first and last, will support us. Everyone will be concerned with providing basic necessities. Food will be that which is grown in our locality, wherever possible, and not transported unnecessarily with the wastage this involves in the way of effort, metal, fuel, packaging and preservation. Our diet will be proper for health, and enjoyment, but we shall adapt to that locally available food. We shall not tamper with it to no good purpose, by refining or adding to it. We shall take from nature only as we need, and it can support. We will not exploit it for taste alone - for example by eating animals especially raised for that purpose - out of respect for conscious life, and because it is wasteful. We shall eat meat only where essential for our survival, or where it is vital to kill creatures for overall control of numbers, and their meat would otherwise be wasted. Where we must kill animals (including fish and birds) it shall be done humanely, and with respect and regret.

In growing our food we shall keep as near as we can to the recycling process of nature and do nothing to endanger this process or upset the organic soil structure that supports it. The sun, wind and rain are vital parts of the cycle, and we shall not obscure, pollute, or otherwise interfere with them. That air and water be clean and pure (something we are already aware of and taking steps to ensure) is more important than most of the man-made processes which cause pollution. The whole natural process, with its many contributing parts, is that which gives us life, and we shall study it and learn how to care for it. There is every humantrue reason why, wherever possible, we shall produce our food by hand, with the help of horse-drawn implements, using fuel-powered machines only where necessary. We shall treasure our fertile land and strive to keep it fertile.

It is believed that increased technology in industry has been good because, by relieving us of hard and tedious manual work, it has given us time and opportunity for inner growth. But there never has been true reason why, in the past here in the West, so many industrial workers had to labour so sickeningly hard. In the artificial relationship between prices, profit, labour and wages, profit takes precedence. Unless goods can be sold at a price that yields a profit, their production is not considered viable. In order to secure a profit the burden on labour used to be increased and wages reduced as far as possible. The effect of this was that humans had to work too long and too hard merely to barely subsist. This is still the case in many parts of the world and, to some extent, has recently returned to the West.

It is true that in the advanced industrial countries some of the burden on human labour has been lightened, and there is evidence of some consequent inner growth. But it is to the Machine we mostly turn to fill our increasing leisure time with ever more of its material rewards and entertainments. And the same competitive pressures for profit still exert themselves. Those human mental, rather than predominantly physical capacities, which the Machine still needs, it continues to overwork but, for the sake of cost and convenience, is preparing to replace with computers and robots. The Machine would dearly love to have its work done by obedient artificially intelligent mechanical devices, which are never sickened by over-work, don't have to be paid and don't join unions. As we continue autoprogressing, ever more humans will be marginalised or made superfluous.

A reasonable degree of manual labour is the best complement to intellectual exercise. The body requires to be fulfilled as well as the mind. When the supply of most things is directly geared to human labour, we shall modify our needs to take account of our own voluntary effort that is required to supply them. Similarly, our respect and care for nature will be greater the closer we are to the soil. Things produced by robots are too easily obtained, and automated humans, by reason of their remoteness from nature, are not fully aware of the damage done to the biosphere by the Machine.

We shall enjoy our food, as one of the pleasures of life, but we need to adjust our present habits to a healthy diet. We shall avoid unnecessary cooking of food, both to save fuel and because cooking can reduce its nutritional value. Our bodies are designed to digest much of our food raw, and prefer the elements it includes in the raw state. We shall vary our diet to incorporate certain plants that are ignored at present but from which our bodies were partially built and still require for the efficient functioning of all organs. Again, the matter of diet is surrounded by confusion, and deep enquiry into it is vital to our well-being. It ought to be a prior concern of all the world that all eat as they need. It shall be the responsibility of all that each individual receives, and receives no more than, a fair share of Earth's provision. This alone is no more than our common humanity dictates, and that it could possibly be otherwise in reality will be unthinkable to a supraconscious humanity.

In a humantrue society there is no reason or cause to manufacture things of other than true human need. The standard of living agreed upon is bound to include several things that cannot be made within the communities. Such items as pottery, that requires a kiln and supplies of clay and glaze, might be made by one community for all others within a limited area, but other items will need large separate factories. Plants for producing steel, for instance, and machine shops for making it into nails, screws, knives and forks, washing machines and stoves. Others for making paper, window glass, rope, spectacles, gumboots. Yet others for constructing railway trucks, carts, farm implements and bicycles. Bricks, stone and slate can be produced reasonably locally for building, but not cement, or wood preservative.

The production of certain raw materials will have to be concentrated, for convenience of operation, in the regions where those materials naturally occur. For example, large timbers in quantity require sawmills, which will be situated near the forests. Communities might keep goats or a cow (if milk is found to be truly necessary, and if we find the practice of taking it from these animals acceptable). If we gave up making synthetic materials for clothing we might return to using wool. If we gave up meat eating the sheep could take advantage of grazing previously reserved for cattle. Wheat cannot be grown in every locality and needs a mill to grind it into flour, although bread will be communally baked.

Manufacturing and processing units will be as large and complex as they have to be, but as simple as the necessary simplification of needs dictates, and as small and localised as possible to reduce problems of distribution. The community will everywhere be the basic model of human living. In order that everyone may remain rooted in this common way of life, labour for factories, sheep farms and forests will be provided from the surrounding communities. Certain individuals will share the work, each contributing perhaps two days a week to it, or more or less, for as long as needed, and devoting the rest of their time to community chores, cares and concerns.

Factories will no longer be subject to the present forces of competitive supply and demand, and of the money economy. Their equipment and products will be basic, straightforward, sturdy, standard and little changing, but effective. Scientific discovery, and its technical application, would be retarded by such restraint, but whatever scientific forward steps were taken would arise from human awareness of true need, not from the pressure of automatic will. The power required by factories must come, eventually, from permanent and environmentally sound sources. These factories might be so designed as to be capable of producing at a rate at least double the rate of consumption. They will then operate only during winter, the season when our community labour is least in demand, stockpiling more than enough to last through the rest of the year, when they will be closed down. During the summer, transport systems will be fully utilised to stock the factories with raw materials for the following winter's production, when the same transport will distribute the products. Requisitions for products will be sent by communities, to depots manned by nearby communities and serving convenient areas. Factories will send products to the appropriate depots, and the communities will collect and distribute them by arrangement amongst themselves.

The same depots will be used during summer and autumn for distribution of the produce that is grown, gathered and stored during this season. There will be no management of these operations, just everyone cooperating to carry out pre-arranged functions. There will be no money transactions, of course, or security precautions, or receipts, and the minimum of paper work, for nobody will be trying to obtain more than their true need, nor seeking to deceive. Without the pressure of profit and loss there will be none of the present economic valuation of time and production capacity, or need for quick turnover of manufactured produce, its distribution in all directions on instant demand, and its rapid conversion into money so as to make it profitably viable. By anticipating need, the system will take its unhurried, predetermined course, utilising its facilities for the benefit and convenience of humanity, not the other way about.

Since the humantrue system of living will be simplified and decentralised, so, surely, will its essential basic services. In the highly autoprogressed countries of the world, vast and complex sewage and drainage systems, gradually built up over many years, are now breaking down, and the money cost of replacing them is enormous - greater than the money economy seems likely to be able to meet. These countries also have vast road networks, and large numbers of haphazardly constructed buildings which they can hardly afford to maintain. The water, electricity and telephone systems are very complicated and require constant attention to maintain, repair, change and extend. There are big problems of waste disposal. In a humantrue society our services will be adequately simple, and well within our capacity to keep in good order because they will be mostly localised. Like nature, we will waste nothing that can be recycled.

It seems certain that we will contrive means of locally utilising our own sewage. With minimal packaging and no planned obsolescence, there will be little rubbish that cannot be re-used or composted for return to earth. Without cities we will not need great labyrinths for underground drainage. We will no longer need many of the major road networks, and can return the land to agriculture. We will never again jerry-build. We will not waste huge quantities of water for needless industries, and surely much domestic water shall be locally supplied. Our use of electricity will be much reduced, and some locally generated, harnessing wind, sun and tide. Our telephone system will be simpler, and neither it nor any other system will be complicated by economic means to measure usage and extract money payment from users, or by constant pressure to autoprogress techniques. That nobody wasted or abused these services shall be a matter of humantrue awareness and individual responsibility.

A system of general information communication will have to be carefully devised which meets all the needs, but no more than the real needs of a humantrue society. In considering such a system, it has to be born in mind that all human life will be reflected in the activities of each basic community, and that nothing of greater interest or importance than the living experiences of each individual, and the common experience of all individuals, shall actually be happening. Therefore there will be no news as we know it - no call for regular and lengthy news services. Newspapers, for instance, which reflect the competitive, fluctuating, conflicting diversity of automatic affairs and the emotional, prejudiced and divided response to them of our instinct and applied intellect - newspapers, which are governed by and financially dependent upon the contentions of this autoprogressive reality - will disappear. On the other hand we *will* need rapid communication in case of emergency - means of exchanging useful information and things of intellectual and vital cooperative interest. It shall be possible for any individual to speak to any other, anywhere in the world.

It should be remembered that a humantrue society will be first and foremost one of supraconscious *minds*. Our physical beings shall be similar entities all contributing equally to an unchanging cooperative whole. Our close awareness of one another in community will be sufficient for our instinctive needs and responses, similarly reflected in every community and needing no artificial extension. There shall be no personality cult, nor any special significance placed upon physical identity, and this will be difficult enough to achieve in our close personal relationships. We can only wholly know one another as individuals by mutually experiencing our interplay of instincts, emotions and intellectual interests in close proximity. Other than for practical purposes, therefore, our communication will be on an intellectual level, supraconscious of common compassion and general understanding, rather than specific and personal. On that level visual impressions are of little meaningful significance - it is not then truly necessary or helpful to see who we are communicating with, or in other ways to be fed with emotional images. Television or film shall therefore be used for conveying the images of impersonal things, with communication between persons entrusted to radio and telephone, direct or recorded. There will be one common language world-wide. It seems likely that our communications will be the most complex technological system needful in a humantrue society, but not so advanced as to need rocketry and Earth satellites. And let it be reiterated - this will be a horizontal communications system between human individuals, not between groups - not vertical communication between the Machine and its servants, or government and the governed. Nobody will be answerable to anything but common, humantrue awareness.

The technicalities of communication have advanced extremely rapidly in the 1990's, and go on advancing at increasing speed. In this 21st century we already have the basic structure of an internet system that is entirely appropriate to a humantrue society. In such an ideal society, instead of the old hierarchical system, when information and general instructions were passed down from top to bottom and edited and manipulated by authority en route, every single individual shall be open to receive everything. Instead of authority being responsible for conducting human affairs and everyone else for executing instructions, it will be the responsibility of each individual (already conversant with the worldwide system of living,) to keep abreast of events and, where necessary, to respond with appropriate action. It will be the job of a group studio, representing ten

Gatherings, 100 Middlehouses and 1,000 Mainhouses (about 44,000 individuals) to act as server to its group, facilitating smooth running and ready access.

The communication system's intellectual function is admirably served by the internet which makes potentially everyone's thoughts available to everyone else. Individual or community contributions are easily presented on a website and printed out by anyone interested, anywhere. The internet system, when it is shorn of unnecessary concerns such as money and business, comes as a boon to the principle of Individual Responsibility.

There will be little other than personal need of a postal system and, when we are no longer clinging to the bonds of blood relationship and special friendship to protect us from general competitive hostility. Post might be passed along by travellers and others working the transport system, making it their voluntary responsibility to get it to its destination, slowly, perhaps, but surely. Transport of goods will be enormously reduced, and mostly between Mainhouse communities or to and from their Middlehouse depots, perhaps using horse-drawn vehicles. Between depots it will be by rail and canal, and between continents, wherever essential, by sea. Personal travel will be by the same systems, or locally by bicycle or on foot, and whether it were for necessity, interest, goodwill or pleasure, it would be subject to our responsible will to be where we are most useful and not to burden or hinder the system unnecessarily. However, it might be that everyone who wishes shall at some time make a long journey, this being recognised as of value, to avoid stagnation locally and to help the spread of common understanding and comradeship worldwide. There will be none but a limited emergency air service.

Education as we know it, which is largely the inculcation of automatic knowledge and reason and encouragement to form specialised constructions of mind which conform to the existing concept of automatic reality, will cease to exist. It will be replaced by the introduction of children and adolescents, up to the age of eighteen or whatever age it is decided that they become adults, to the basic principles and worldwide practices of human society, ie to the foundations of human being. A fundamental essential is that the young intellate from the very beginning, and become supraconscious. The individual mind shall be free, and shall be so stimulated, encouraged and challenged as to determine, above all, to fulfil itself in its own way and time, with the information it needs made available as and when it needs it. Children will learn the activities and skills of community life, to take a fully responsible part in it, to fully understand the humantrue constitution of the world, and to develop and give abstract outlet to their intellectual powers. From the very beginning, community life will provide optimum stimulation to babies, so that their brains maintain the optimum numbers of neurons, grow the maximum numbers of dendrites, axons and synapses, and so lay down the best possible intellectual foundation. Up to the age of eight or so, children will be given the devoted, tolerant and affectionate care, but firm guidance, of the whole community. Between eight and eighteen they will move up a sliding scale of responsibility related to growing ability and skill, towards parity with adults who will cooperatively respond to them accordingly. After the age of eighteen all individuals will be on an equal level, supraconsciously aware of their communal and worldwide responsibilities related to their own abilities. All will accept their responsibility and give of their ability to the optimum, and shall be valued, by the self and others, for the willing fulfilment of both, not for the kind or quality or quantity of contribution.

I have suggested already that life will be in four stages (a) childhood, from birth to eighteen years (or as otherwise agreed,) (b) parenthood, from 18 to 38 (c) generally needful work, from 38 to 55, (d) community help, then rest, from 55 to death. There are one or two points to be made about these proposals. It is suggested that we marry as soon as the female is biologically fit for bearing children because, in a humantrue society, there would no longer be economic reasons for having to wait to marry. It would be ideal if our young were to become humantruly aware, and sexually awakened, at the same age at which girls mature into women, fully prepared for childbirth, making it in every way the right age for marriage. At present, however, it appears that the human female (as already mentioned) may be capable of conceiving a child as early as 12/13 years of age (or, in some cases, not until the age of 17), but will not be fully fit to bear that child, in good health and safety, until the age of 18. I think it inevitable that in the course of a few generations in a stable and secure humantrue society these presently conflicting factors shall reconcile themselves. In the meantime we have the problems of sexual frustration, promiscuity, contraception and abortion. Unless we deal with these problems in the most sympathetic and effective ways that we possibly can, it will be much harder to bring about that which will solve this and all our other unacceptable problems - humantrue society - for the emotional and physical effects of this transition from child to adult can seriously disturb the mind. Humantrue society would have built into it the means of making this transition as painless, sure, smooth and fulfilling as possible. Whilst children of 14 would then be already supraconscious, they would need something more than the community's understanding support to cope with the strong sexual instincts presently first experienced at that age. Perhaps the answer *is* to marry at 15, but (provided that a safe and effective means of contraception *is* found) to delay childbirth until 18.

There are several advantages in the practice of parents staying together, in the community, for 20 years after marriage. Wives and husbands will benefit from sharing the same family and community responsibilities. Children will thrive on having the full-time care of both parents and on the varied interest, stimulation, teaching and growing responsibilities of community life. When adult individuals reach age 38, at the end of this stage, their children will be married and perhaps parents already, or soon to be so. The ex-parents, now embarking on the next stage of learning new skills and going away to work for the community at large, or concentrating on work in the home Mainhouse, will still be young at 38. They will bring to bear on their work a thorough knowledge of the concerns, needs and cares of life within any Gathering, and whatever they do and wherever they go they will still live in a local community Mainhouse, sharing in those same concerns and helping to provide those needs and cares. When individuals reach age 55 and give up their special work, they will return to devoting their time entirely to the local community, perhaps the Mainhouse of their birth. They will then pass on to others the benefit of their wisdom, experience and special knowledge, and will do their share of the daily chores for as long as they are able. Eventually, in old age, they will submit to the loving support and care of the general community.

The question arises - how will we keep happy in a humantrue society - what part, if any, will entertainment play? It seems to me that entertainment should never be a formalised performance but always a matter of spontaneous expression as part of the pleasure of all, including oneself, even if that which is expressed is a well-known song or story. I suppose the most fundamentally satisfying form of such expression is music. Music is bound to be basically a formalised pattern of notes, and intellectual music a complex interrelationship of many such patterns. Therefore perhaps it shall never be given as formal live entertainment (as distinct from spontaneous playing) thus avoiding the creation of three divided and unequal elements - the written or remembered musical pattern, the performer, and the audience, which puts barriers between the composer, performer, and listener which are, or can become, class distinctions. Perhaps musical performances shall be always for the direct enjoyment of the performers alone - to enjoy music you will have to perform or play it yourself. The playing of recorded music might not seem to set up the same objectionable triangle, yet the recording has to be performed in the first place and might create undesirable demand for the best, for professionalism and unfavourable comparison with amateur effort. Perhaps all music already recorded by the autoculture shall be preserved and privately played, but never again publicly performed or newly recorded by the humantrue society. In this way it might be simply enjoyed but without competitive comparisons, so as to inspire rather than discourage amateur musicians.

But it might be that we shall rule against recorded performances, deciding that music shall be entirely an individual means of fulfilment, like the blackbird singing in the bush of a summer's evening. We might agree that an individual's musical compositions could be printed and distributed, for good music is an emotional reflection of intellectual exercise, and that which takes its character from humantrue society shall surely have the good effect of always promoting humantruth. In the meantime, when the ideal society has yet to be achieved, newly composed humantrue music could become a vehicle of intellation, having itself no meaning but urging the mind to discover and realise truth - the feelings evoked by its true harmonies inspiring us to seek true correlations in the mind.

It is noticeable that people who compose or perform good music do not normally engage in highly competitive or violent activities. This may be partly because they are more sensitive than normal, or because they are entirely preoccupied with the complex disciplines and techniques involved. But it would appear to be mainly that this play of emotion totally absorbs their whole being because it is enmeshed with their highest faculty of intellect, giving satisfaction far beyond that of instinct and automated consciousness.

Whether we come to know all truth - factual truth - is unimportant. Much potential knowledge exists despite us, without the need of our knowing it, unaffected by our ignorance of its fact. What *is* important is that for as long as we *do* live, we live truly. Most fact, however presently true, will become progressively redundant with the advance of true realisation, and true only of the past.

The cooperative comradeship of humantrue society shall give us such deep satisfaction as to make us well content with our lives. But however content our intellects may be, it is likely that our emotions will find cause to swing high or low from time to time, so that we *will* seek entertainment, to let off high spirits and raise low spirits, and such entertainment *will* be local, and mostly spontaneous - games, charades, sing-songs or story-telling and the like. We might still feel the need for gathering to celebrate, or to cheer ourselves, on certain occasions such as the coming of spring, mid-summer, the bringing in of harvest, or the bleak mid-winter. That we presently hang over television and radio, or sit and drink in pubs, or attend more formal entertainments, surely indicates the poverty of our communal life, and our reliance on the Machine's substitutes.

Given the stressless humantrue way of life - good diet, plenty of physical and mental activity without conflict, tension, fear or anxiety - we shall be healthy. That is to say our bodies, allowing for old age, shall function as they ought, easily able to eliminate toxic wastes and to kill off any normally invading diseases. Such good health helps to keep us on an even keel in any case, and increases the savour of life. Whilst human mutations will no longer be needed, the randomness of reproduction would remain desirable if only as the source of interesting variation in human character and ability, in a society which shall no longer present opportunities for, or make demands on individuals to put their ability or temperament to false and inhuman use. Members of a humantrue society shall be people who want above all to do the right thing, and to repress impulses arising from a false past. Such things as wishing to make the most of, or flaunting one's appearance will no longer appeal. And eventually, as all people live similar lives, their physical differences shall become less and less pronounced. The effect of understanding and actually *living* humantruth will have a dramatically good effect on our health in that every feature of individual being, from the basic individual cell to the deepest cortex layer, will be happily oriented the same way.

Honest research is needed to decide what abnormal diseases there are, if any, which healthy bodies and minds cannot fight alone, and what special manufactured drugs other than herbal remedies are vitally required to cure them. Medical skills will be needed, and hospitals, but on a far smaller scale than at present, to treat accidents and any such unavoidable diseases, to care for mothers in childbirth perhaps, and to treat infirmities of the very old. Our chief concern will be to maintain good health rather than minister to ill-health. In particular there shall be much less mentally-caused illness of mind or body. A question to be investigated is this - given a healthy way of life, how much must humans expect to suffer from any cause and how far ought we to expect that suffering to be relieved, or eventually eliminated? When the accent is on a useful and fulfilling life, there will surely be less importance given to holding on to life at all costs. When it becomes a burden on us and we see it to be a burden on others, however willingly they bear it, we ought to have the free option of voluntarily ending our life. We might have to draw a line beyond which the individual could not expect the community to prolong life artificially.

There is the question of medical training. How far is the present long training of doctors and the complexity of the medical institution necessary, and to what extent is it the unnecessary product of the Machine and autoprogression? I think a humantrue society will be well served by everyone acquiring basic knowledge and skill enough to deal with childbirth, also minor ailments and accidents - this to be passed from generation to generation and by books, radio, television and the internet. Some of us between 38 and 55 might then learn further by apprenticeship at hospitals.

Unlike the existing reality, this will be a reality for which we are physically, let alone mentally, designed. As flesh and blood creatures we must put in to the biosphere as much as we take out. By relying chiefly on our own labour, we will fall in with the natural evolution that equipped us for the purpose. In this way the energy we get from our food will be equal to that which we use up in the process of producing that food, so sustaining the natural cycle as nearly as possible.

All these things seem to be right and necessary to the upholding of humantrue principles, principles that answer to supraconscious awareness and will allow our lives faithfully to reflect that awareness. They do not, of course, represent more than a sketchy outline of a humantrue framework of life - a whole book could be devoted to the detailed deliberations required before its concrete constitution were fully agreed and decided. There are many questions and doubts, most of which arise from our present conditioning by a false concept of reality and shall be answered simply by supraconsciousness, but others are not so simply resolved.

For example, when parents reach the age of thirty-eight, after their children mature (or thirty-five if girls mature at fifteen), will they stay together, or part? Where will they find sexual outlet, if parted? Promiscuity has present bad effects, from the betrayal of trust to AIDS. Shall we eliminate these bad effects in a humantrue society, and will we still see free sexual activity as a betrayal when the children are no longer dependent on us, nor we on one another, alone? Will it be a matter, after thirty-eight, of either remaining with our original mate, or changing to another, permanently? What happens to those who cannot find a second mate, or, for that matter, a first? How shall we overcome the problem that some women are pretty and some men handsome, others not, and most of us find the former more attractive? Shall we try to find some means of putting an end to our sexual drives, at thirty-eight? The sex drive is vital and powerful, but outside of necessity for reproduction of our species it can cause much harm.

Whilst there is no doubt that the Machine presently threatens our destruction, in certain areas of the drug-oriented medical sphere it could be said to accomplish human survival. In planning a humantrue society we have to consider the appalling actuality of AIDS, to combat which is requiring huge resources of science and technology established by the Machine. Leaving aside the question whether all this *is* effective against the disease, shall a more simple humantrue society deal with a similar threat? But shall such threats arise in a humantrue society? And if they do, despite the best efforts of that society to protect itself by simple and reasonable measures, shall we not then be ready to die, or to accept the risk of dying, rather than compromise humantruth?

Another question is this – *shall* we be able to rid ourselves of the custom of preferred relationships? I suggest that in a humantrue society, apart from the special needs of marriage and parenthood, all our love, affection, care, interest and attention shall be fully given to *everyone* in our community, and *everybody* we meet or give hospitality to. Other than this, though all humanity are our sisters and brothers, when they are beyond our reach we leave them to give their love and interest to, and receive it from, the community where they presently belong, knowing they will be caring and cared for. We shall expect no one to reserve this giving exclusively for us, nor ourselves reserve it for any absent loved one on the grounds of blood ties or special friendship. Yet there shall be no strangers, and everyone we meet shall be met as a friend. Though we may doubt our ability to change in this way, we should recognise that our present habit of forming exclusive relationships with our own kith and kin and allies is part of the concept of false existing reality in which such discrimination is needed as a defence against general hostility. Humantruly we shall *have* to change in this way, by intention, until it becomes itself habitual, for preferred relationships can lead to different preferred aims, contrary interests, distinct groups, and the growth of conflict between them, and so also between individuals who have no real reason to quarrel.

Whilst all that has been said envisages the eradication from human being and society of such as competition, elitism, autoprogression, self-interest, corruption and brutish aggression, it is to be expected that doubts and questions shall *still* linger strongly in our minds whether all these things *can* be eradicated. This is because they are so much part of our existing reality that at present it is hard to imagine everybody forsaking these characteristics. For example in sports we automatically take sides and want our chosen side to win. Competing to win, in sport and for any reasons other than survival, is an adopted human habit, a sublimation or corruption of basic instinct. Instinct has the object of achieving the general healthy survival of a species, otherwise the competitive drive is a waste of effort. For humans, competition, having been made a way of seeking survival which now *threatens* survival, is certainly useless but has become a habit which is hard to break, so that no other way of living seems possible for humans.

The whole idea of competing, winning or losing, even in sport, shall have to be expunged from our minds. Humantrue society entirely depends on the growth of supraconscious awareness to the point where *every* individual is so responsibly aware that such automatic characteristics will be wholly abhorrent and unthinkable. It then depends upon supraconscious humanity constituting a society in which those existing habits are uncalled for, unnecessary, unheard of, unknown - *non-existent*.

You may have found these last three chapters on deciding the Constitution to be somewhat calculating and unfeeling, with little of that tender emotion of which the best in us is capable and which such as romantic poetry expresses. But the objective is to replace a reality in which such delicate emotion can co-exist with its opposite of blank indifference and hateful violence. It is seeking a pattern of living which is in itself truly logical and practical, but excludes that which presently brings out the worst in us - a pattern which will become our unquestioned humantrue foundation, a cradle of tenderness and compassion, a platform of benign creativity.

It is difficult to detach ourselves from the here and now, and to detach our intellations from the contrary influences of everyday reality. Our persuasive instinct is to live life as it is, and to put our whole range of emotions into it. Our present impulsion is to *obey* existing instinct, in terms of which the intellectually better humantrue ways might seem to be lack-lustre. It could well be for this reason that you might have found these last three chapters unfeeling. The same unwillingness to break with the Machine and to detach the self from domination by conscious automation might make the following four chapters seem tedious. But it is necessary to uncover every last conception, practice, attitude and habit of the present human society because all are influenced by automatic conditioning. That influence needs to be rooted out. It *can* be a tedious business, if it is not done with a will, but if it is *not* thoroughly done the Machine will keep its fundamental grip on our thinking, though we protest to the contrary.

Chapter 45

PERSONAL REORIENTATION

In the previous chapter the question was raised - can we *really* rid ourselves of the concept of preferred relationships, of friends and family, and can we possibly eradicate the competitive drives from our characters? The answer is that of course we can because these characteristics are false, whereas our nature is to be true - but, I repeat, to realise our true nature requires that we become supraconscious. To achieve supraconsciousness, in order to realise our true nature, we have to get past our automated self - the conscious self which is our false 'front man' - in order to reach the inner, true self.

A minority of us see existing reality as false and wish to change it, and tend to 'go it alone'. But this minority cannot be effective as long as the majority do not see the basic Machine as false and do not wish to change it fundamentally. The minority have to try to enlighten the majority, because this automatic reality will be changed only when the vast majority turn away from the present opinions and feelings of their automated outer shells and adopt the humantrue values of their inner selves. Humantrue change may come about only by the collective *intention* of supraconscious humanity.

To prepare ourselves for this process of enlightenment, it may be helpful to recapitulate the reasoning which lies behind a determination to do so. The greatest care is vital if we are to get it right, and it is a mistake to imagine that humantruth can be arrived at by way of short-cuts or compromises. Remember that human thinking has been busy with our problems and questions for thousands of years without solving or answering them satisfactorily. Yet the answers have always stared us in the face, and we have never had good reason for ignoring them.

Although the task of humantrue awareness to prevail over the enormously complicated reality that exists seems formidable, or even impossible, it is no greater than that of convincing the individual mind, and all minds are potentially bound to accept it because it is the truth which it is their function to discover and realise. Automatic reality is explained by the fact that the instinctive Machine is in possession of our world, and we are possessed by automatic instincts. Our release from it is a question of the individual letting go of ownership of his or her being by instinctive will, however sophisticated, and becoming a supraconscious self, drawing strength from postconscious will. It will not then be possible to shut away into unconsciousness the suffering that comes of frustrating the true aims of intellect. It will then be *painful* to lie and deceive, just as it is presently emotionally painful to suffer injury, hunger, or extreme cold.

The Machine subjects us to its concept of reality at birth, and places our beings in consciousness, cut off from our own true minds and guarded by our own instinctive will, and tries to keep it there throughout our lives. To break the Machine's hold over us we have to shatter that concept in order to change our adult ways, and to so bring up our children that they become supraconscious of their proper, humantrue nature from the beginning, and immune to false automatic influence.

The thinker who breaks free of automatic reality is likely to feel and appear unstable, because the norm provides nothing that is wholly true to which he or she can steadily hold. People of stable automated character are unlikely to break free of the norm because they depend on its support. The thinker's problem might seem to be solved by him or her becoming eccentric to the norm, but not if this means retreating from the whole truth into another limited concept of reality with its own contrived stability, for discovery of truth requires that the mind be open to everything. To make that discovery we have to intellate, rather than think, and it just has to be accepted that the role of the intellater will be lonely and hard to bear, but compensated for by her or his growing awareness of truth.

It can be seen, when one considers the unrest and bloodshed all over the world, that good people are in danger from bad, and that strong governments, police and armies are necessary to protect the former and suppress or control the latter. But all this conflict of oppression and revolt, aggression and counter-aggression, crime and law enforcement, occurs against a background of inequality, competition and injustice, in a world that has always been in such turmoil since civilisation began. Automatic reality causes the unrest that creates the reaction that produces antagonism which boils over into violence which requires control. This can only continue unless our society begins to move towards humantrue constitution, when human individuals will respond humantruly. Individuals feel they are compelled to act as they do, and that they may not change voluntarily until that compulsion is removed. That it remains is because *we* obey it and do not remove it. *Only* we can remove automatic compulsions, and the ways of doing so are freely open to us, but if we believe ourselves powerless to do so we are lost.

Probably all of us want the world to change for the better, but mainly our way, so that we ourselves need not radically change. Personal conditioning can be very strong and hard to break, because it is held together by our own will to be what we have come to be and to defend that being. Besides, since that conditioning grew out of a society of conflict, we are in any case preoccupied with the confusion of our own reflected conflicts. We are as we are because the here and now is as it is. The here and now remains as it is because it has made us what we are. When almost everyone and everything goes chiefly by the Machine it is hard to stand away from it all, make our own standards and stand by them. But this is what we have to do if the world *is* to change for the better. None of us should regard our self as sacrosanct, merely because it is ours. You can say "Oh, to hell, I'll just make the best of things as they are", but if you do, your mind will be failing to fulfil its true function.

To an extra-planetary observer we ourselves, as typical human beings, must appear humantruly incomprehensible, and we *are* so, because we are conditioned by and harnessed to an intellectually incomprehensible reality. We are continually reborn into a grotesque world, but repeatedly blinded to the fact and robbed of the will to make it what it should be, generation by generation, by the compelling way in which it perennially shapes our thinking. Though we know inwardly how we *should* behave with each other, look at the way we *do* behave. Individually, though we try to do the humane thing, we are drawn into needless disagreements by competitively separate aims, interests and beliefs. Collectively, these are enlarged into bitter international quarrels to the point where we are persuaded to kill each other in war. We should open ourselves to the truth, which is the same for us all. We should be prepared to submit our views to the criticism of others as well as ourselves, otherwise we stand in the way of our human potential for agreement.

If we mean to change this world we should cease taking it, and the debased behaviour of our automated selves, seriously. We should uproot our beings from this world and replant them in our upper minds. We should recognise that we are not as we ought to be, and that although we cannot change the temperamental basis of our character we can essentially change by developing, and then *being,* our postconscious minds. In this way we may bypass our present external traumas and supraconsciously imagine another humantrue reality beyond in which both we and our society are already changed. We may then intellate accordingly, and wherever possible act accordingly, making ourselves keenly aware of existing reality, but alien to its concepts and values, in anticipation of change.

Let it be said once more - we must take care never to judge according to the existing norm. Automatic reason is able to make nonsense of humantrue ideals, because they have been tried in the past, without success. But in our automatic past the humantrue ideal could never be viable, and it will never become viable in the future if we cling to automatic reality. We have to overcome our emotion with our reason, supplanting gut feelings with intellectual intentions. We have to remind ourselves that if we persist in this our emotions will eventually adjust. At first this will leave gaps in our range of satisfactions, gaps left by de-automation, but in due course these will be humantruly filled.

It is wrong that we should be divided from each other by any thing. Government by politics is a humanly irrelevant compromise between spurring and curbing the Machine, and between automatic differences of state, opinion, belief, desire and ambition. There is no real reason for these differences. We should be united by humantrue understanding of our common concerns. Until we reach that unity we should unite our efforts to achieve it by coming together voluntarily, by intent, though it be against our apparent present inclination. It is not enough to give selfless but unquestioning service which, in a continuing imperfect world, appears especially good and above reproach by comparison. This is to stunt our concept of morality by orienting it to personality and limiting it to presently realistic local concerns. Any individual's decided intention that human society must change and become humantrue has to include the following realisations:

- That existing reality is not acceptable.

- That humantrue reality is the right alternative.

- That he or she too must change, by intellation and personal reorientation to supraconsciousness.

- That this is the one way to common human agreement.

- That to reach this agreement should be the prime concern, aim and interest of his or her life.

- That to achieve a humantrue world reality is possible.

- That humantrue world reality may only be achieved, then maintained, by individual responsibility.

Whether we can bring ourselves to believe it to be possible, or not, those of us who have hope of a better world, or who pursue truth, or who are already entering a state of supraconscious intellation, should not be deterred. It is only by pressing for the ideal and spreading humantruth, whatever the apparent odds against it, that a humantrue reality may come to be. It is well to remember that all minds potentially support humantruth, whilst automatic reality relies only on their false bonds of conditioning for its continued existence.

Having made this decision, and started searching our minds in earnest, we have already begun, or joined, a process of humantrue change. We have already reoriented ourselves, and as we intellate towards supraconsciousness our beliefs and attitudes to all things will change. We should now realise that, presently, what we outwardly *are* and *do,* and what we have inwardly allowed ourselves to *be* and *think,* is not *us,* as we naturally ought to be, but *us* reacting to a world reality which is not as *it* ought to be. The more we try to do something, or assert ourselves, in terms of this automatic reality, the more immersed in it and conditioned by it we become, and the more strongly and inevitably real it appears to be. Our minds, habits, emotions, fears, hopes and all expectations have become so attached to it that we can believe this setting to be fitting to our character, and our character fitting to this setting.

Once we have recognised all these things we have constantly to remind ourselves of them, and make certain personal rules to follow. As suggested before, we have deliberately to divide in two, body and mind (our outer shell and inner core), placing our humantrue being in our mind (our inner core of self). Our body cannot escape existing reality nor, in one sense, should we wish it to, because its experiences are necessary to us, that we may critically examine the here and now, enabling us to reason clearly against it. Our intellating minds will be comparing it with the humantrue alternative, in which there will be no divided nations, no dominant governments, enforced laws, armies, or authoritative politics. No competition, economics of the money kind, , trade, commerce, possession. No hierarchy, discrimination, compulsion, formal education. The mind will perceive these features of the Machine to be the complicated rules and moves in a wholly unnecessary, dangerous game, working out what is wrong with them and how they can be replaced.

We now recognise that our bodies, for the present, live inescapably in automatic reality. They seem to be free only either to obey or disobey Machine laws. Our objective, however, is not the opposition of bodies - conflict between those who uphold the laws and those who oppose them - but the agreement of all minds, which shape the laws and may change them, then remove them. Therefore we obey the laws, for the present and where they are unavoidable, for to do so is more peaceable than to disobey, and this does not mean that we agree with them, nor does it disqualify us from reasoning against them. If we do not respect the humanity of those who uphold automatic laws for the wrong reasons, how can we expect them to respect us and listen to humantrue reason?

On the other hand, where instituted laws do not *compel* us to follow, we do not let them lead us. Neither do we follow automatic *lores,* which are the basis of instituted law. Wherever possible and harmless we oblige our physical being to go contrary to the norm, following humantrue rather than automatic interests. When presented with a fact the mind's task, if it is to learn, is not simply to record in order to recall that fact, or to orient it to a fixed and limited prejudice of the conscious mind, but to submit it to the maximum possible number of correlations and thus to evaluate its place in truth. Intellation invariably leads us away from the false concepts of the Machine. As a process of exhaustive correlation of knowledge and reason, and of breaking down such deeply ingrained, widely held and time-honoured false concepts and practices, intellating is difficult but rewards the whole mind with true awareness. The hardest and at first most painful part of the process is that it means turning on and breaking down our own automated selves - figuratively speaking, stripping our bodies and leaving them naked in a falsely clothed world.

We have to recognise that our spontaneous thoughts, opinions and convictions may not be truly ours in that the true centre of our being, our whole mind, freely created and formed them, but may be the result of conditioning imposed on us by circumstances. There is no virtue in clinging to them merely because we have come to own them and identify them as ours. We have to deny the very basis of our present being, our own character and the constructions of mind, beliefs and self-expressions it has evolved, and change them until we *know* them to be true. We have to deny our ego, and its emotions which try to keep our character intact; which turn our criticism away from ourselves and the reckless reality that more or less guides us all, justifying our own shortcomings and our unjust actions by blaming them on the errors, antagonisms and injustices of others.

We no longer see our bodies as the centre of the world. With our beings in our minds we are seeking to belong, in common with all others to one and the same humantruth. By guiding our bodies in this way we make them eccentric to the norm, which puts them in a difficult position. Both they (instinctively) and we wish to join with others in community, but we will not allow them to take part in automatic practices on which the present community is largely founded. Consequently our bodies are made to look foolish, which is hurtful to their ego. But we recognise that this is bound to be, for we can not be one with our bodies until they and all others, and we in common, are part of the humantrue reality that we envisage. *We* do not feel our body's hurt, which is theirs and not our whole minds'. *Our* hurt is much greater, arising from the knowledge that humanity as a whole is harming itself (and betraying us) by neglecting its true potential.

So our minds are now in control of our bodies. We recognise that all other bodies are presently trapped in automatic reality too but that most dictate to their minds, with both being dictated to by that reality. Consequently we do not take human actions, or statements of belief and opinion, at face value but expose them to humantrue doubt, question and criticism. The more authoritative importance the Machine gives them, the less seriously are we prepared to take them. Rather do we bypass the overt social explanations of human behaviour, and the automatic reason underlying it, perhaps our own included, and try to reach the reasoning of individual inner minds which is quite different, humantrue in nature, but generally confused and kept private.

We realise that only in the single individual mind can all things be correlated and brought to a humantrue balance - that this can not be done by a number of minds each specialising in separate spheres of interest. Intellect, the faculty of knowing and reasoning, cannot be truly built except by growing of itself. Propositions may be presented to it, offered for its free and true judgement, but when they are imposed, or self-imposed with pre-determination that capacity for true judgement is impaired. At this humantrue level of awareness which we have now adopted, we no longer believe there is, or ought to be, better reason for anything existing or happening in the world than our own supraconscious reason shows to be unquestionably humantrue.

Let it be repeated - man's life-force-will to survive, geared to instinct and progressed by the technical ability of the conscious mind, is leading to his destruction as a potentially intellectual species. This actual present reality represents the barrier we have to break through, the barrier which instinct erects between us and our intellectual potential. For humanity, the barrier is reinforced by a fear of giving up that dominance of instinct which, for hundreds of millions of years, we and every single other evolving form of life have obeyed, and all of nature on Earth has dependently served. We, the one and only species on Earth to have acquired the ability and therefore the need to do so, have to give up this main reliance on instinct and transfer it to intellect. We have to go further and reject the concept of a central governing authority of any sort (which only our instinctive automatic reality makes necessary) and trust humanity and the whole world to the responsible care of the human individual.

We have to look outward *from* supraconscious intellect in order to recognise the right human questions and problems, and then look supraconsciously back into intellect for understanding of the humantrue answers and solutions. We have then honestly to expound those answers and solutions by every channel of reasoning open to us, our minds unshakably aware that what is humantrue must be true for all humans and only requires to be understood to be agreed, and agreed to be cooperatively implemented.

Having got this certainty into our minds we have to keep it continually in the forefront of our awareness - that automatic reality is absurd. The Machine is a powerful influence on the body and its applied thinking but by conforming to it, however intelligently, we do not make it less absurd - we merely confirm its real existence. To postconscious intellect it is so weak and without correlated reason by comparison with humantruth. Only to conscious thinking that the Machine and its institutions have founded can it appear logical. To the supraconscious mind humantruth is much more powerful, for it rings unmistakably true. Political, money-economic, religious or even scientific discourse of opinion and belief does not have that ring of truth because it is not truly founded or formed - as a false or irrelevant trail it can never lead to whole truth. But it may be judged true by a mind imbued with the present concept of reality - by the conscious mind constructed of false trails and overawed by the fact that this automatic reality, over which that concept presides, actually and powerfully exists.

I run the risk of labouring this point, but it is very important - a matter of maintaining a viewpoint which does not help but hinders us in the here-and-now. For example, if we need to buy something that involves bargaining, automatic values and concepts apply to the transaction and it is difficult to avoid applying them in our own competitive interests. If we do not think in this accepted way of trading we may get a bad bargain - we may lose money which, since we are dependent on money like everyone else, we cannot afford to lose. This fact, and the thought that we have been cheated, may rankle in our minds so that we determine not to let it happen again. Next time *we* might get the best of the bargain, so that our opponent determines the same. This is automatic influence working on us, so that we perpetuate it and allow it to prevent us dealing with each other honestly.

Existing human world society puts the cart before the horse. The cart is the established Machine, and humanity itself is the horse that follows wherever the cart leads. The establishment cart is built by competition, steered by money-economics, secured by law and maintained by government. In order to live this way the horse must put its power into pushing the cart, kept in harness by the belief that this is how it has to be, and persuaded by politics that *he*, in fact, is steering, that this is the way he wants to go and that it is, in any case, the only way he *can* go.

To live successfully in the present reality it is necessary to accept it, manipulate it, go along with it, or at least in some way adapt to it. On its terms we try to win, and failing that we contrive to survive if we can. But by its nature the competitive Machine must have a few winners, many survivors, and many victims. We make the winners into leaders, and the survivors into the average norm. Because we are not yet completely dominated by the Machine we are yet free to exercise innate compassion, and so to its victims, where it allows, we extend compassion in the form of charity. But this prick of conscience is an afterthought of intellect, not a prime mover.

Take the case of a famine, occurring somewhere on the other side of Earth. Whilst it is newsworthy, and so brought to our attention, we on this side may allow ourselves to feel we have sympathetically dealt with it by sending money to a charity relief organisation. We should rather treat it as though we, or our own kith and kin were involved, for these are our human brothers and sisters who suffer. We should ask why the famine happened, what is the underlying problem, and how can it be permanently solved. We should ask ourselves what kind of a world this is where chance exposes millions to the yearly possibility of starvation, whilst most of *us* are made permanently comfortable, safe and secure from want.

Humantruth puts a newly aware horse before a very different cart - a supraconscious humanity leading a cooperative and contented life. But as the prelude to that ideal our minds need to be opened to awareness of that disastrous famine not as a case for world charity but as the result of world discrimination, indifference and neglect - a crime of automatic society that our true humanity cannot condone and must correct, once and for all. Humantrue awareness turns our present concepts upside down. The kindness of charity is made a human virtue only by contrast with our inhuman automatic reality. The notion of charity comes from the acceptance of poverty and want as inevitable - 'the poor will be with us always'. The kindness that charity selectively represents would, if fully expressed, be hell-bent on removing those automatic causes that occasion it.

It is a question of *attitude*- of putting the interests of whole humanity on a level with our own, and of being prepared to suffer material loss for the sake of humantrue gain. When it is a present matter of bargaining, only if both sides are humantruly supraconscious can they put automatic concepts and values aside and deal with each other fairly. Only when we are *all* humantrue, and the Machine and its concepts abolished, shall we have replaced the practice of competitive bargaining with mutual giving of needs. In the meantime, even whilst we are forced to deal with each other in automatic ways, we should *express* our contrary humantrue attitudes to others, trying to lead them to the same understanding. And to demonstrate our faith in the humantrue alternative, wherever possible we should act in ways which reflect it and promote it, negatively to the Machine and its reasoning, though to do so is against our own automatic advantage.

Chapter 46

NEW ATTITUDE

Having reoriented ourselves so that our automated outer shells are put aside, to be progressively discredited, we now face the world anew, supraconsciously, with a humantrue attitude.

We take the fundamental view that whether or not Earth humanity ever achieves it, humantrue supraconsciousness is our true nature and state. We do not accept counter-arguments relating to false automatic concepts, even though they accurately apply to existing reality, because they are truly irrelevant. This is our approach, and we judge all things by supraconscious reason, regardless of the here and now. Understanding that we live in a lunatic reality, we now recognise that this reality cannot be supported by true reason. Therefore we doubt any reason given in its support.

We have to acknowledge that presently the vast majority of human beings, from top to bottom of the hierarchy - most of the few with whom we come into direct contact, the many who claim our indirect attention, and the millions beyond our ken - are thinking falsely, not intellating, not complete, and vitally needing to become supraconsciously aware of humantruth. Though they overwhelmingly outnumber us, we nevertheless know that it is they who are out of step with truth. We are absolutely adamant in our opposition to, and rejection of, automatic reality, proof against its blandishments, secure in the clear and undeniable awareness that the Machine is false through and through.

Yet that which at first distinguishes us from our automated brothers and sisters may be little more than that we cannot sit by and let the world be as it is. Therefore we must take on trust the need to strive for supraconsciousness, for we cannot be aware of truth before it reaches our awareness. And eventually they will have to do the same, if humanity *is* to achieve a humantrue reality, for this great change will not come about without the agreement of all.

Part of that vital striving for supraconsciousness is that we do not allow ourselves to be the product of reckless instinct, of automatic conditioning, of wishful thinking - of anything but the true moral awareness of supraconsciously fulfilled intellect. Another essential part is to acknowledge that we support no further material progress that is not humantruly necessary, for the ultimate objective of our progressive development of body and brain - the postconscious intellectual faculty - has already been achieved.

We should not be beguiled by the social convention that it is admirable to keep smiling despite everything. To look on the bright side means turning your back on the black side - temporarily a good thing, perhaps, but bad in the long term. To square up to the bad is presently distressing, and can be depressing, but it works for the long-term good.

We turn against the norm, but realise that there is no logic in resisting the Machine and trying humantruly to simplify our way of life, *except for the logic of our own inner responsible supraconscious awareness,* which shows that if there is to be any real change, *all* must change. The whole Machine is our present reality, and automatic views, policies, statements and analyses from its human hierarchy are its accompaniments, in which the humantrue reason of the individual mind has no place or voice. We shall not achieve change by cutting ourselves off from the world and leaving it be. Taking a new attitude, we now intend to make the individual mind *our only* voice, showing the world there is no place for automatic reason.

We so firmly believe in humantruth, and envisage it as possible and probable of achievement, that we really *shall* go on and try, to the best of our ability and above all else, to realise it in the world. When it comes to the crunch we can bear to stand out from the norm, make sacrifices, and risk ridicule and failure. We have the mental strength of supraconscious conviction not only to turn our backs on automatic reality and all its pressures and persuasions, but also to go much further and positively promote humantruth as its vitally necessary alternative.

We have the strength to insist on family, social, economic and national ties giving way to the pursuit of humantruth - on putting our own, our children's, and our children's children's feet on the ladder of supraconscious awareness for the future good of all, rather than on the Machine ladder for our, and their present exclusive personal benefit. Given our new attitude, awakened intellectual enthusiasm can overcome conventional opposition, the disapproval of our peers, our own ego, or our elderly aches and pains and weariness, so that we make humantruth our living faith and aim. We shall not allow our family and friends, our national prejudice or our automatic advantages to dissuade us.

We might be forgiven for thinking that changing our minds is one thing, but bringing that new understanding to bear on the world, and change *it*, is quite another. Difficult as it is, to make that personal internal reorientation may seem easy compared with the task of the individual, powerless and alone, overturning the huge, hard world of the Machine. But we *do* have potential power, for all humanity is made up of individuals upon whom the Machine depends. Though most of us are not in an individual position of automatic power to give our words or actions special significance, our united individual power is potentially much greater.

Our new attitude is that the Machine and its institutions are not to be taken seriously, and we should cease weighing our lives in their scales. So when we consider our own standard and style of living we should not judge it by the amount of money the Machine affords us to spend, or by that concept of reality which gives us the right to earn it as we may and spend it as we wish. It should be judged by what the whole Earth can afford equally to every human individual, and whether what we put in and take out reflects our individual, humantrue responsibility to the whole.

We should beware that the more we obey the Machine's ethic the more we expect its aids and conveniences and the more our reality depends on using them. Eventually, if we fail *now* to begin overturning the Machine, though it dispenses with *our* labour we shall be unable to do without its technology. We shall have forgotten how, or be unwilling, or be *forbidden*, to return to simple ways and the use of our own manual skills to fend for ourselves, or of *utilising* what technology humantruly benefits us, rather than being *mastered and used by it*.

We should not expect truth from any politician or servant of any automatic institution. If we are politicians or serve institutions we should recognise that this is so - admit to our awareness that the statements we make, the policies we follow, the beliefs we support were not honestly created or accepted by our own intellation but imposed on our conscious thinking by the limited laws of our institution and its factions, by automatic lores, and by money-economic and other pressures to conform to the existing norm.

Government is subject to the competitive conflict of politics that alters it superficially but without changing its founding automatic function. It will not be changed radically as a Machine institution by opposition from the political institution because both serve the same automatic ethic. Meaningful change can come about only by the common enlightenment of all individuals, including individual members of governments, and the function of government will then be sensibly changed to the point of abandonment when world humanity abandons the Machine.

Exceptional obstacles to growing awareness are the accepted practices fundamental to existing reality. They have the effect of preventing individuals from determining their own minds in a humantrue way, divide humanity from itself, and allow or compel governments to make big decisions, of huge or traumatic effect worldwide, independently of and remote from the free inner morality of each and every individual who together make up all humanity which governments are supposed to represent. No national authority could reasonably object or refuse to accede to humantrue reforming changes when they are in the true interests of all individuals of all nations without tacitly admitting that their authority is wielded against or despite those interests.

A major obstacle is education. It is not the case that the less you are educated the more difficult you will find the process of reasoning and knowing. You will find it less easy to absorb conformist learning but, *if* you make the required effort, your mind, free from false conditioning, or from formations of half-true past thinking which causes inability to think truly in the present, will think, or rather intellate, truly. It is certainly *possible* for the individual mind to submit to conventional upbringing, conformist education, and experience of life in the Machine, and yet subsequently also to rise above and reject this conditioning, and to intellate. But this is difficult to do, and to reach supraconsciousness from such beginnings may take a very long time. Why should we allow that in order to develop our intellect truly we have to reject the norm and unlearn what it taught us? Why should we accept that children continue to be fitted with these blinkers that, without true guidance, they mostly fail ever to remove?

It is not to be expected that the Machine's institutions will voluntarily change. But we ought to expect the educational institutions to include introduction to humantrue alternative philosophy in their curricula from the beginning. If authority believes automatic reality to be inescapably right it cannot but believe that any angle of scrutiny will fail to arrive at any other conclusion. In any case there is no good reason why education should not be a free human, rather than government, responsibility. As with religion - if the hierarchy is sure of its belief it ought to allow disbelief all the room it requires, confident that it shall soon be corrected. We may believe in automatic reality, or that it cannot be escaped, but that does not give us the right to force our conditioning on our children, to disallow them access to all versions of belief and opinion, to all relative 'truths', and to deny their right to open their minds to humantruth.

This proposal might be seen by some as subversive of the State, but in the humantrue view it is the State - that is to say the worldwide Machine and all the various institutions grown from it - which is subverting human intellect. When a world humantrue society has come into being, the meaning of the word 'education' will be very different, as has already been suggested. A prominent undertaking of a humantrue constitution has to be that every individual be taught from the outset that she or he has a mind to be fulfilled, and that responsibility for humanity is hers or his.

We recognise that education, by stimulating us to varying degrees, selecting us, inculcating specific knowledge and preconceived reason into our minds, and progressing this intellectual conditioning to an appropriate range of levels, thus prepares us to be available to perform an automatic function. We see that it does *not* help, encourage or enable us to intellate, to achieve supraconscious awareness, to understand the true nature and state of human being, and so to seek and find present and future, individual and collective, humantrue fulfilment.

We understand that the rot has to stop, for our mutation into a fully intellectual species is right. If individuals like you and me do not stop it now, then it is highly probable that humanity never will, for those who follow us, even if they have more pressing cause than we, will have ever less opportunity if, indeed, they survive to have any opportunity at all. It really is up to us. In particular it is up to us as parents to sacrifice our wishes, and fears, for our children's' automatic futures and prepare them, however painful for them or us, for a humantrue future.

We intend to repair our intellectual shortcomings, and teach our young humantruly rather than prepare them for the same pitfalls into which we were led to stumble. The failure of existing human society is that being in a pit and having every good reason to climb out, few individuals do so, because most are busy making out reasons why, *being* in that unsavoury automatic pit, they *ought* to be in it, remain in it, and make the best of it because that is where they belong. Many wise people have made out that no other conclusion is possible. But, apart from this common negative view, they all disagree, which clearly indicates that their minds are incomplete. We allow such ill-considered prejudice to bind and gag us. What we should do, before reaching any conclusions, is to get our intellation complete, true and agreed.

Although we recognise the great importance of making our children humantruly aware, and do our very best to this end, how are we to succeed?

Our real problem is in founding the child mind in the first five years of life, before school (so that it can withstand the influence of school), and especially in the first two years or so, before there is verbal communication. We and the child exist in this present reality, and the child learns by what it sees, hears and feels. What it experiences is the here and now, and our efforts to cope. Is it possible to avoid these first years being spent by the child in absorbing the basic facts and concepts of automatic reality? As a society we do not even know how to treat and guide babies properly in the context of the Machine, so we are hardly fitted for leading them towards humantruth despite the Machine.

A great deal of research is already being done into the subject, with the object of adapting the child to the norm. It is a false process because the objective is false. It aims to teach the child to deny anti-social original instinct, yet not to replace it with behaviour indicated by intellect, but in many ways to divert that instinct into competitive, anti-human channels that are concentric to the Machine and thus acceptable to present society. Alternative, independent intellation is needed into ways of treating babies fundamentally as embryonic humantrue intellects - of setting them on the difficult path to supraconsciousness, eccentric to the norm, and keeping them on it as best we can in unfavourable circumstances. It will be a relatively simple and straightforward matter when we already live in a humantrue reality.

I have said that, whatever its circumstances, any single healthy mind is potentially capable, with independent effort, of judging and understanding the essential truth about human society, as it is and as it should be. So whatever influences our children are subject to, if they are to become humantrue the vital thing is not that they be conditioned by teaching but that their free and independent mental activity be stimulated to the optimum so as to realise its full, and therefore true potential, despite false influences.

Other exceptional obstacles to the growth of humantrue awareness and the unity of humankind, which divide us from ourselves, are the diversity of languages in the world and our separation into nations each with its sovereign authority. Also this automatic reality's definition of right and wrong, and its concept of crime.

Humantrue awareness turns our existing concept of crime upside down, showing crime to be human lawbreaking, but revealing that the law protects the interests of the Machine rather than of humanity. It shows us that wrong motives call up our passion for wrong causes, and that humanity's inhumanity is not our true nature unfolding but an automatic phenomenon - that crime as we know it is the product of competitive inequality, a reaction between the yearning of human being for fulfilment and the Machine's perversion and conversion of that yearning into its own desires, which it then encourages and liberally rewards, or contains and limits, or frustrates and denies. It shows that the present main framework of our lives is a crime against humanity. As supraconscious individuals, we now recognise the Machine as the criminal cause of inhumanity, and determine to replace it with the humantrue alternative.

We value the individual moral code above the code of law. We will not act in terms of automatic lore, though it be lawful, but are guided by humantrue ideals which do not need the control of law. We do not take the law as fixed, but to be constantly re-assessed as humanity changes. We should not regard it as the proper shaper of human behaviour, but as a control made necessary by past human automatic behaviour. Laws are made by human society and so should be obeyed by humans, even though contrary to humantruth, but only until our society, with our help, becomes responsible enough that the worst laws may be abolished, and then that all law is rendered unnecessary by replacement with voluntary supraconscious responsibility to a humantrue constitution.

For the same reasons we no longer need the obligations and promises of religion. We are now determined to abandon all faiths in mystic powers outside ourselves. We do not find it possible to argue with or hold aloof from the challenge to make good our life on Earth by ourselves, building a reality of cooperative love and compassion. We recognise no grounds for believing in any higher power or purpose. or for preferring any vague promise of better things in some fantastic life hereafter.

We do not discriminate between individuals on grounds of sex, age, mental agility, colour, race, condition, nation, but recognise all as having similar needs and potentially similar minds. We look on all women and men as humantrue by nature, and have faith in our collective power to change the institutions of this reality from within. We respect individuals as ordinary human beings, but whilst we value humantrue virtue as a gift, we also sympathise with iniquity as a misfortune. We do not respect rank, position or status but seek to remove the Machine's differentiations of privilege and power, just as we expect to abolish the degradation of underprivilege and helplessness. We do not accept that such differences are an argument against the viability of the humantrue ideal but as the products of a reality that has not achieved, nor sought to achieve that ideal.

Humantrue awareness shows us that the human agents of automatic actions that are inconsistent with their true humanity feel driven into a corner by their duties and expectations, so that they feel unable to act otherwise. So it is necessary that they too become humantruly aware. But every one of us should realise that we *all* submit to the Machine's inhumanities in this way, though mostly more subtly and less obviously.

We now need deliberately and fully to expose our human sensibilities to true realities from which we have been shielded, and to make ourselves aware of truths that we have allowed to be hidden from us, and experiences that we have been able to avoid. How many of us would stop eating meat were we obliged to work in an abbatoir for a few days? Would we feel different about crime and punishment were we stripped of all possessions and status and obliged to live in the worst slums, or sentenced to a year in prison? How would we view deprivation and poverty were we forced to eke out a bare existence in one of the poorest areas of the third world? How would the venerated old of the elite establishment feel about the amount of the old-age pension if they were reduced to living on it alone? How would political leaders feel about war if they were obliged to fight in the front ranks, or bury its dead, or nurse its gravely wounded, or, in the case of nuclear war, if there were no safe bunkers for their refuge?

We could not sustain the individual parts we play in the Machine if we insisted on admitting to full consciousness the truth of our inner awareness, and honestly allowed it to make judgement of our existing reality. The automatic concept would collapse within weeks if we *all* did so, for it depends upon maintaining us in a state of self-deception, denial, wilful ignorance, falsification, indifference, complacency, and, above all, confusion.

As humantrue individuals, we do not allow the class distinction of ourselves or others to influence us, recognising that the division into lower, middle and upper classes is a device of the Machine that need have no effect on our potential capacity of mind, unless *we* allow this. If a quiet humantrue revolution is to be achieved it needs to involve all classes, because we need to envisage a classless society in which all are of one mind.

We recognise that for commercial reasons the 'media' normally give the 'common man' that mental input which it is assumed that he wants, or, for political or ideological reasons, that which is thought socially good for him. The same applies, of course, to the 'common woman'. He and she may not swallow this, but it does not normally give them to think critically of automatic reality as a whole, nor stimulate them to match their minds against the mind of the Machine. In the same way, a suitably different input is given to the middle and upper classes. We understand that as long as the 'media' remain tied to the Machine they may not do otherwise, and we make appropriate allowances. We do not take anything they offer at face value but read between the lines.

In general, television, radio and newspapers may touch our humanity, but present us as firmly linked to present reality, and picture us against an automatic background. They enable the majority of us to fill out our experience with complications of the here and now, and we tend to embrace them because our lives lack a humantrue frame of reference.

Increasingly, enlightened individuals do use these media to try and encourage others to question and see beyond certain facets of existing reality. Some years ago, here in Britain, there were several radio and television programmes highly critical of established nuclear policies and revealing the catastrophic effects of nuclear war or accident. There have been other programmes critical of many features of our reality, exploring philosophical, political, psychological or biological explanations of them, and ways of improving them.

As an example of the slowly rising willingness to put certain moral obligations before certain automatic self-interests in Britain, Channel 4 television, which relies on advertising for much of its income, presented a programme revealing professional and commercial malpractice in dentistry, and putting the interests of public dental health before such automatic self-interest, including the financial interest of the Channel itself. A similar case to be cited is the government's campaign against smoking, contrary to automatic interests. These things could not have occurred thirty years ago.

But, at this rate, it would take a very long time before human concern prevailed over opposition from the Machine to the extent of the media publicly criticising the whole concept of automatic reality. In the meantime it is all too easy for these occasional, limited critical forays to be overshadowed and lost against the large background of conformity to the norm. So we should otherwise distrust or ignore the media, and depend for the growth of humantrue awareness on means of communication independent of the Machine.

As a means of that necessary communication, we believe that a common world language is vital to the eventual humantrue emancipation of the world. This too would be a long process, but agreement on it, and the first steps to learning it, would be a great encouragement to human unity.

It can be argued that we need the media to keep us abreast of world affairs. This is true for automated persons whose bodies and minds are vested in these affairs, or who require to be warned so as to act in their defence, or advised in order to take advantage. Otherwise it is true only to the extent that we need to know what the Machine is doing to humanity. Supraconscious individuals can not take authoritative, diplomatic, political and money-economic affairs seriously, or regard them as the real affairs of humanity, or as significant to humantrue being.

If we lived in an ideal society, and all were going to our humantruly constituted plan, there would be need of no more than minimal news, as I have pointed out already. In this competitive economic world, renewed turmoil and repeated conflict is predictably continual. There is little purpose in taking an interest in its insane affairs except to become involved in them, which merely perpetuates the turmoil and conflict. There is little point in protest, either, for what are we protesting to but the cause of protest, and what result may we expect but a re-adjustment of the same basic pattern? Our sensible reaction to automatic affairs is to turn our attention away from them and towards building that sane alternative society.

Growing awareness indicates that we are on the wrong road by showing us examples of automatic damage to Earth's biosphere. Rather than correlate these with all other signs that are there to be seen, and follow them to whole conclusions, our general tendency is to act at once in protest by campaigning for conservation. This is a well-meaning attempt to reduce the obvious ill effects of the Machine without removing their less obvious, fundamental causes. Popularly, it concentrates on species of animal that are endangered, aiming to preserve their species in the same spirit as it preserves old buildings, artefacts and tracts of land.

Conservation groups protest against the cruelty of killing 'free' wild creatures, out of sympathy for what is seen as their right to experience and enjoy life. They do not seem to equate these creatures with the many millions we yearly raise and reserve the right to butcher, nor with the countless others painfully exterminated as pests, such as rats, nor yet the numerous human beings who are made to suffer or die at the hands of the Machine. This is because we the protesters are ourselves contributors to the Machine, supporting it in most other respects. That is why we choose obvious, emotive, easier-to-solve subjects of active protest, and why we have no adequate solutions to the bigger problems.

When certain of us direct our attention to the frighteningly more serious damage related to these bigger problems, such as wastage, pollution, erosion or poisoning of Earth's range of resources we have found comparatively little support (although awareness is increasing at a growing rate), because automated humankind is more conscious of wanting the fruits of autoprogression than of its need to be saved from the dangerous consequences.

Our notion of conservation is another example of compromise between intellectual morality and our concept of reality. We are in danger of failing to appreciate our overall dependence on making a place for ourselves in a relatively undisturbed Earth biosphere; of confusing our true responsible concern for other Earth life with a desire to preserve certain appealing or exotic species for emotional, nostalgic reasons, or out of academic interest; to salve a guilty conscience by demonstrating our kindness and, for instance, banning the culling of seals, or the hunting of whales. But we are also in danger of imagining that we can benignly co-exist with *all* the rest of nature, like the lion lying down with the lamb. Nature would cull, or cut *us* down, if it could, but we are not part of the natural balance, and do not submit to its instinctive laws.

It follows that nature must submit to *us*, since we allow that only *we* ourselves, and not *it*, arrange and lay down the means and manner of our survival, generally and in minute detail. This means we have to control or destroy any other life that poses a threat to our life, and consume all living things vitally needed to sustain us. But we must also control ourselves, and limit our numbers with supraconscious responsibility, so that we contrive to do these things sparingly, gently and regretfully, whilst giving room to, caring for, and protecting all life with which we can live in harmony.

If we do that, and only that which is humantruly necessary for our simple material survival in the world, thoughtful of our dependence on Earth, we shall be no more threat to other life than the relationship of intellect to instinct makes necessary, and shall find a permanent balance in partnership with it. Ought we to pretend that this is otherwise and treat conservation like a museum subject, keeping animals in isolated pockets to be especially artificially preserved, and observed by us, congratulating ourselves on our care?

We should rather admit that it is our reckless autoprogression that has made this very well meant but somewhat ineffectual artifice necessary to us, and that we would do better to stop that autoprogression, which threatens to make an end of us *all* n any case. Would we not prefer that only those forms of life which can freely share and enjoy the Earth as we have made it should do so, and that species which can not survive on these terms be allowed to die out rather than be kept as sad reminders, like living fossils? Should we not let past extinctions be a warning of the unnecessary damage we have been doing and, rather than patch Earth up here and there, cease from doing that damage?

Serious conservation campaigns need large sums of money to be allocated to them by government. That money comes from autoprogression, which is rapidly encroaching on our vital biosphere. So the campaign depends for its dedicated work and its hopes of success upon that autoprogression which has necessitated the campaign itself and which is likely to be the means of its defeat.

We do not believe that human conscience, awakened to specific anti-human effects of this existing reality, will necessarily drive us to expose and seek to correct their fundamental causes. So to believe is to expect existing society both to demolish and preserve itself at the same time, or to bite the hand that feeds it. Automated humans cannot expect the Machine to deplore and resist *itself*, nor that they can manipulate it as a tool for its own re-fashioning. Present events show that superficial protest, such as that against war, however vitally serious the objective, results in concentrated attacks on superficial apparent causes like military establishments and leaders. But if we really mean to achieve the objective of removing these threats, our *only* effective course is widely to spread awareness of the basic automatic causes in the minds of all men and women, including political and military leaders and their supporters, not so that they protest but so that they reject those causes and decline to contribute to them, thus making the effects impossible.

There is no future in thinking or acting politically, for politics is a battle that humanity cannot win.

There is no future, either, in prospective ultra-intelligent thinking machines, which I have already mentioned in Chapter 18 Autoprogression, doing our thinking for us. In the view of an American scientist - undismayed by this prospect and, whilst predicting that these thinking computers would take control, clearly imagining that human interests would still be respected and protected - 'there is nothing to prevent the intellectual capacity of the computer going far beyond that of the human brain and, in the not too far distant future, we humans can expect to be kept as the pets of robots'.

If this should happen it would seem certain that we, with our comparatively high ratio of input need to coldly calculated output efficiency, *shall* become superfluous. But be sure that no machine can *humantruly* surpass human intellect, for it could not become more human than human. There is no good reason why thinking computers, evolved by the Machine, should think in human ways, or, that being so, why they should respect our humanity or put themselves out to provide for our desires, or yet subsistence. Neither does any good reason appear why they would keep us as pets. Remember that these computers are to be built by the Machine to serve its purposes - their building is being financed by the money-economy and will have to show a profitable return. Keeping pets is a peculiar human habit that has to do with our emotional concern or need and has no practical value or profit (excepting to the manufacturers of pet foods). It is hardly likely to appeal to automatically programmed and motivated intelligence.

It is also well to remember that we have possessed superb thinking computers for thousands of years, in our heads, and that these have been trying, in their millions and for all this time, to reconcile their humanity to their controlling Machine, or to control the Machine with their humanity, without success. To give ourselves entirely to automatic thinking would be a final defeat.

We see that it is not only the current products of technology and the promised future achievements of its autoprogression that tempt us to fall in with automatic concepts. Existing reality gives us to treasure relics of the past and to covet things solely for the economic value that automatic history has given them. We compete for automatic power to possess them, and for the automatic power their possession grants. This means that our love of objects for their beauty and perfection is at least tarnished and at worst replaced by acquisitiveness, calculation of money worth and pride of possession. We might easily fall into this trap without any ill intention, forgetting that such valuation supports the automatic ethic and its widespread ill-effects.

As automated persons we cherish rare jewels, antiques and the like, but the respect we pay to them does not alone refer to their beauty or intrinsic properties. We admire them beyond all other things because they are inanimate objects almost beyond price in the market place. They give their possessors Machine-power over others.

As supraconscious individuals we admire things of beauty and perfection for their humantrue quality alone - nothing beyond that. We put none but humantrue value on objects, so that gold and diamond, for instance, would be worthless except for practical uses such as filling teeth or cutting ceramics. For another example, we do not wish to see old buildings knocked down merely because they are old, to make way for new. But we cherish and preserve old buildings for their beauty, or because they continue to serve a useful purpose, not for their age alone.

In a little changing humantrue society we would have returned to using the skills of our hands in making our everyday environment beautiful, and these skills would not pass out of use. Presently we cling to old buildings for love of their familiar forms and associations that we know their replacements will lack. Then, in an ideal future, new buildings will follow the forms and reflect the associations of the old, and so will be welcome.

Though all the foregoing were agreed as laudable, it might yet be argued that for one fundamental reason the humantrue ideal is impracticable. That reason might be that existing reality is not just the result of one kind of humanity using a wide range of automatic means to gain a variety of automatic ends. That it is rather a matter of markedly different *human attributes* determining how we behave, what status we are given, or seize, and what fortunes we receive, or grasp. That we have different passions, desires, tastes, preferences, abilities and ambitions. That some of us are vigorous, beautiful and talented whilst others are slothful, ugly and inept. That some are highly knowledgeable and refined whilst others are deeply ignorant and uncouth. That these are inevitable human characteristics that give our reality its character, and that whatever other discipline we try to impose on ourselves, these characteristics will always re-surface to defeat it.

But characteristics, like genes, are not prime causes but patterns of behaviour caused by past circumstances. It is our long experience of the divisive conflicts of automatic reality that has created, developed and reproduced these our different characteristics, and the similar character of the existing Machine that perpetuates them. That some of us capitalise on our advantages enables us to cultivate virtues, *because* we are on the winning side in the competitive conflict. Others, on the losing side, might capitalise their vices to rebel against their disadvantages, or to win by other means.

Our new awareness is of a humantrue reality in which there will always be individual differences, of course, but nothing to be gained from capitalising on them, nor any thought of so doing. As a matter of individual responsibility, no supraconscious person shall *want* to be the personal beneficiary of his or her genetic and instinctive physical or mental attributes and temperament. Superior strength or intellectual agility, for instance, will be employed selflessly, not manipulated for gain. Feminine allure will not be openly displayed but kept private. Individuals who so far forget themselves as to flout the principles of the humantrue constitution will find no response, and their immodesty will soon be corrected by being ignored. We know that contrived, sophisticated, dishonest or cynical behaviour is not attributable to true human nature but to customary, habitual human servitude to automatic reality.

It is the purpose of genes to serve the successful survival of members of a species - to encode the attributes that have brought each generation better success, and greater happiness and contentment, and to faithfully reproduce these attributes in ensuing generations. Therefore it is to be expected that in a humantrue society, constituted according to the principles of cooperation, freedom, equality and individual responsibility, each newly generated individual will be genetically, progressively predisposed and fitted, in mental and physical form, to reflect those principles and live by them.

Chapter 47

AFFIRMATION

It is clear that we individuals, if we are to be effective as the keys to change, vitally need to change our orientation. We need to turn away from the hotly competitive, fiercely aggressive, anciently but falsely burning reality all about us, and then inward to contemplate the cool, still, pure waters of intellect. By intellating we shall receive affirmation of our humantrue alternative reality, shall believe it to be practicable, and determine to realise it with a supraconscious will. With this new attitude, we may turn outward again to struggle with that other reality and steadily quench its fires with the waters of reason. This we are capable of doing, but the odds are more heavily against some than others. It is up to those most able to lead the way for others to follow to humantrue understanding and, to those of them who are in a position to be heard, openly to express their thoughts and encourage us all.

It is the duty and will of all supraconsciously aware individuals to reveal the humantruth and try to have it realised in the world; to expose the Machine and reject our existing concepts of reality; to take issue with automated individuals and leave them in no doubt as to the true causes and effects of their actions. The effect of not only a politician but also an economist, industrialist, scientist or royal figure doing so would be electric. It would be of enormous encouragement to the human struggle against the inhuman Machine, taking it beyond the protest of victims of oppression, and showing that the establishment is capable of turning on itself.

Yet it is no more than ought to be expected of any individual, and especially one with power over others, that he or she be honest to intellect and to its true function and potential. It need not mean a breakdown of public order. A leader might keep his or her position, and continue functioning as far as is presently humanly necessary and officially required, whilst frankly and openly questioning and criticising its whole setting and foundation. To oppose the law is not to break it, and to bring the entire existing social order into question is not to prefer or propose disorder.

Imagine the effect of such affirmation - were an army general to refuse to fight, a bishop to admit disbelief in god, or a government minister to confess to habitual devious political dishonesty; if a diplomat were to argue the case for his opponents against his own side, a right wing president to voice the faults of capitalism and virtues of communism, a trade union to refuse a rise in wages, or a meat distribution tycoon to declare himself a vegetarian. Or if any leading economist, manufacturer, banker, lawyer, scientist, editor or advertiser were to recognise and then openly confess that his activities were mainly for his own benefit and did not benefit humanity in general. Yet all have good reason for taking humantrue responsibility in this way.

The reason why we, who belong in these categories and see the light, do *not* come clean in these ways is the fear that we would then be dislocated from the great body of the Machine; that we would lay ourselves open to ridicule; that we might lose our friends and allies; that we would suffer financially or damage our prospects of promotion; that we would lose automatic status, dignity, credibility, and prestige. But if we *did* come clean it would be because we had become supraconsciously aware, with reason so much stronger than all these as to be undeniable. And we would have lost nothing of real value, but gained in that awareness which is the true, rich quality of an intellectual race.

Yet, though supraconscious awareness is our proper fulfilment and though it cries out to be expressed against our existing unworthy reality, throughout our long history it has never been so fully and strongly voiced as to be clearly heard. Why not, if the reasons *for* this fulfilment are so much stronger than those against it? To seriously ask that question is to start intellating, and to answer it fully would be to realise humantruth and so nullify the question. We the majority do not seriously ask *ourselves* that question, normally, because we live by the Machine and entrust our affairs to politics. As 'the public', we are persuaded by political thinking that the automatic way is the only road to follow, and politics leads us along this road with automatic logic because it is driven that way by our resultant expectations. This both narrows down our true awareness and *requires* that we be so limited if we are to prosper, or at least to survive, in the Machine.

Politicians know that they are playing a game. Because of it they betray humantruth, knowingly or not. It is not that they lie, but that they give their loyalty to a false premise; that they deliberately recognise a body of factual truth whose foundation is untrue, and attach themselves to opinions and policies that are the half-truths of compromise. By doing so they confuse their minds and render them either incapable of intellation or unable to bring true postconscious reason to consciousness. That they do so is not only because they exist in a reality which demands such behaviour of them but also because they have adopted the attitude that this reality is inescapable and impossible of change.

But it *is* possible for politicians to change their attitude, and if it is possible for them it is so for all humans. And it *is* possible for this existing reality to change, for if all rejected it then it *could* not and *would* not be maintained. Let it be repeated - supraconsciousness is the optimum function of all whole minds and humantruth its common realisation. This holds good for every individual, and so for any politician. It does not become less true the higher up the hierarchy we go.

Suppose a member of parliament, or of the house of representatives, or any such political assembly did make the effort to break through to a humantrue attitude so that he, or she, refused to play the normal game and had the courage to approach all matters independently, and so humantruly. What would result? Of course, such a member would be in a minority of one and might well be shouted down by the majority, dismissed as eccentric and ignored. But if several separate members did so they could not so easily be dismissed. And a supreme leader who did so could hardly be ignored. If a president or prime minister were to become supraconscious and break through to humantruth the effect would be signal, and could only be good since it is a matter of the mind being freed from false fetters and truly expressing itself. And surely many minds would honestly respond.

Humantrue awareness needs to grow, and it *does* need independent means of honest communication if it is to be spread effectively. Nevertheless, that awareness is growing in the minds of many Machine-employed printers, camera-men, producers, editors, directors and perhaps even governors of the media, and we see the results in parts of their work. Remember that the individual is the key to change. The internet has mushroomed comparatively recently, enabling individuals to communicate their ideas to others independently of authoritative restriction. May these enlightened contributions increase, encouraging wider awareness despite opposite automatic pressures. And may individual members of the public make the intellectual effort to respond, regardless of automatic temptations to take easier options, and make their appreciation known. By this cross-stimulation, realisation of the humantrue alternative will be brought nearer.

Writing is our basic means of communication. Outside of personal conversation, even the spoken word is usually written down. The process of writing allows the word to be exposed to the maximum of prior reasoning. Writers rely for their money income on the mediums of publication or broadcast, which rely for *their* income on the willingness of the public to pay. We, the public, are normally emotionally adjusted to automatic reality, so likewise are most writers and and much of the communications media, and what they communicate generally confirms the fact and emotion of that reality. They supply what the Machine persuades us to demand of them, and the same is true of politics and politicians, as we have seen, and of all institutions of the Machine and their loyal executives.

Since most humans are reconciled to the Machine, writing which flows easily through the eyes and smoothly past the critical judgement of the average individual is not serving a good revolutionary purpose. It is perpetuating automatic reality. When that smooth flow is constantly interrupted, so that the reader falters, it may not be the fault of awkward grammar or unfamiliar terminology in the writing. It may be the fault of the reader, who does not understand a new idea or concept that ought to be intelligible to human intellect. It should then be the writer's aim to support these words with reasoning whose strength and purity is difficult for the honest thinker to ignore.

We should not write only or partly for money reward or acclaim. Books should not be written, nor seriously read, which do not either cover or take full account of *everything*. We should require our minds to look deeply into everything before committing ourselves to anything, with or without the help of other minds which have already trodden this path, and insist on explanations which really do hold water. A book that searches for true human character must critically examine all the facts and concepts of reality, and whether, as is normal, these facts and concepts have built large parts of that character, because a character cannot be judged to truly represent the individual when most of its parts are false. A book which examines the money economy in the isolation of its own field of financial interest and justifies it in its own terms but cannot show and will not admit that the money economy does not serve the best interests of human and whole-Earth well-being, can not be taken seriously by unbiased human intellect.

When a writer sits down alone, pen poised over paper, this is the perfect moment of possible truth. More than most individuals the writer has cause to seek truth in order truly to know what words to write and why she or he is writing them. Without that sure and true knowing it is questionable whether pen should be put to paper. Supraconscious writers, in an automated world crying out for a new humantrue reality, should only write humantruly with that aim in sight, until that reality is realised. Were all writers humantrue, publishers and broadcasters would have nothing but humantruth to produce. Then the fact that all communication was freely responsible to humantruth would guide us all towards supraconscious awareness, and our response would be to re-adjust emotionally to that which we are already unconsciously prepared for both knowing and feeling.

Writing as an art form is the skilled use of words, the construction of sentences, and the convincing contrivance of tensions between actions and reactions such as will appeal emotionally to the instinctive/intellectual mix of the reader, and induce him or her to read on. In the world as it is life is like such writing; like a novel, an automatic experience which we go on responding to because new pages are successively presented to us and we are attuned to its continuing story.

That which makes the most admirable novel unacceptable is the way that it draws on existing reality. It may be critical of parts, but it cannot be destructive of the whole otherwise nothing will remain to write about constructively which is recognisably real. The characters depicted, if they are to be familiarly understood, have to reflect the concepts and facts of reality to which we belong and by which we are conditioned. Even in science fiction, though the reader is transported to another, supposedly superior planetary civilisation, the characters to be found there are not fundamentally new but made up of those same familiar features. Neither the writer nor reader can comfortably imagine persons whose circumstances, motives and actions are very far from those which are common on Earth. Literature is forced into this kind of compromise - taking all sorts of extremes into account but viewing them from a middle ground position - not allowing the call of truth to draw it too far forward because it is held back by the demand for acceptability. The 'classics' are those books that have most nearly approached that achievement of perfect balance between our humanity and automatic reality that most humans are trying to find but which is both an impossible and unworthy objective.

It must surely be obvious that the human race is essentially far short of its intellectual potential. Most of our complex thinking is confined to specialist subjects and narrow disciplines of reasoning within the confines of the Machine. Popular writing is required to use short words and sentences, simple paragraphs that do not touch more than two concepts at a time. Many questions and problems plague us that are interrelated, but they are tackled unsatisfactorily - piecemeal, in isolation. There is little or no all-embracing correlated reasoning going on. All this represents continuing automation of human intellect, and retreat of intellect from the possibility of true fulfilment.

The Machine also applies rules to non-academic writing that seeks widely to disseminate new ideas, or extensions of thought - rules that ensure that although these ideas are new they will yet be acceptable to the Machine by virtue of their being acceptable to the automatic ethos. These unwritten rules are especially applied by publishers in general (including most alternative, radical, underground publishers), and require that such writing will not need abnormal intellectual effort to understand. The reader, against a background acceptance of the Machine which is shared by the writer, may have to think hard but is not required to question deeply - to intellate - but to confine the effort of intelligence to taking in the new ideas which are no more than amplifications of automatic reality. The book that you are now reading is different. It does not merely introduce readers to a new view from a different patch in the same old field, or to a new line along the normal direction of thought. It challenges the very basis of reality on which the structures of understanding are normally built and encourages an end to automated thinking, a beginning of intellation.

Consider how incomplete are so many human minds of so many kinds, locked into versions of automatic reality peculiar to their conscious selves. The first aim of this book is to seek an association of those minds which are complete, or most nearly so, so that they can help all others to reach completion. The elements of humantruth are understandable to any mind, but the most fully aware and determined effort of supraconscious reasoning is required to clear away the choking entanglements of existing false reality that can stifle that understanding. So, writing which sets out to present that humantrue reasoning must not be, indeed cannot be, so tailored as to simply fit the understanding of minds which, however erudite and learned they may be, are nevertheless incomplete in humantrue terms. For such minds, whatever level of the hierarchy they occupy, true fulfilment first requires them to recognise that they *are* incomplete (but have the necessary potential), and then voluntarily to make the effort of reason which will bring them, too, to embrace humantruth.

Intellating, as opposed to thinking, is like discarding all novels and other automated books, and changing to works that are for true intellect alone. Just like listening to complex and unfamiliar music that we do not at first understand, nor can respond to. But if we persist, because we believe these works to be right and good, eventually our emotions will respond to them. Our emotions will then respond to intellect alone, leaving old familiar emotions behind. We shall then recognise that what true writing and composing did was feelingly to explore, and attach meaning to, elements of the collectively meaningless entanglements of our wrong reality, which we now see as irrelevant and are ready to pull up by its false roots. If we persist with our intellations, we shall develop, then feel for, the humantrue outlook. Perhaps, in time, when the world has been made humantrue, we might go back to writing novels, but surely of a different kind. They will necessarily appeal to the new emotions, not the old, and through them to supraconscious intellect and the new reality it has made, and maintains.

It may go against our inclinations to initiate such great changes. To first address ourselves to the humantrue outlook is a matter of intellation, and of determination of will. The new outlook presents human reality in a very different light. Not only the words that describe it but the image, the feelings and sounds of a humantrue reality will be different. Hopefully we shall envisage it, ponder its new ideas, savour phrases of its new music and whistle its tunes. We may then speak its words so that we ourselves and others hear them, get to know them, appreciate them, and understand them.

I have pointed out already that there exists a certain moral movement towards changing society for the better, but it is largely ineffective. The reason why it has little effect is that its advances are more than matched by amoral or immoral autoprogressions of the Machine. We indulge in random thinking, recklessly jumping from narrow consideration of one subject to another, advancing automatically in thought as in practice and very often resorting to violent conflict in consequence. The only way we will advance truly will be to advance on the intellectual plane, independent of automatic instinct.

Ideals cannot be used to solve our present problems except by a great effort involving wholesale change of attitude and reason, so that Machine-oriented events cease to excite familiar automatic reactions and thus also cease to perpetuate existing reality. There is need of an underlying process, free from the automatic concepts and the officialdom of the Machine's hierarchy, continually building up towards that point of change. We need an independent means of getting individual minds to intellate, maybe to discuss but certainly to work out and agree an alternative concept of reality - of creating a free space which supraconscious awareness may fill in this way. This process will require us to approach ourselves, each other, and our world in a different way from the usual. The ensuing struggle will begin with negative reaction to the norm, holding off from positive action until whole agreement is reached.

Look at it this way. If you were married to someone who made preposterous demands on you, making your life insupportable, what would you do? You would probably get a divorce. Well, consider - you are likewise harnessed to the Machine, which makes unacceptable demands on humanity at large so that all suffer to some degree (and this is probably the basic reason for most unhappy marriages). What should you, and we, do about it? Surely we should rid ourselves of the inhuman Machine. But in marriage it is clearly better to discuss with our partner and agree on a better relationship than to resort to divorce. It is a matter of both partners ridding themselves of faults that have been the cause of their ill-considered relationship, rather than getting rid of each other. In the same way we should all intellate, and agree on a better world.

It is presently, and has always been the thing not to take life too seriously. We tend to look at it as a vast complex of insoluble problems that, since they cannot be solved, are not worth worrying about unduly. It is the realistic, or sophisticated, or good-humoured practice to laugh at life - treat it lightly and make that attitude our saving grace. Otherwise we could only cry, which is no help at all. We give serious attention only to our own immediate struggles to carve out a relatively happy and secure little piece of personal reality for ourselves. This is understandable because throughout the course of human civilisation our visions, yearnings and heart-felt anxious good intentions have never found true form or taken real effect, and the founding amoral principles of the Machine have never changed. But it is humantruly inexcusable, because this is *our* world, and *our* responsibility.

We maintain our automated construction of mind because it is what we interpret the world of the Machine with, and our interpretation is suited to the attitudes and opinions - the personality - of the self. So mentality and personality maintain each other and sustain automatic reality, and serious disturbance of that reality is painful. Our common intelligent morality represents true humanity, but the difficulty is how to get individuals to change for the eventual overall human good, when the immediate effects of reform will be contrary to their present apparent interest and advantage. Yet we only have one life to live, and the humantruth is there to be discovered. Surely we cannot bear to die without discovering it? And having discovered it, how can we rest until it is realised?

The first task of any humantrue reformist movement is somehow to foster and spread a common feeling and belief which has never before existed - a general real hope and expectation of fundamental humantrue change; a conviction that automated opinions are false, however strongly held by however many persons, and if they are not true they signify nothing; that nobody is immune from the truth - from prime minister to road sweeper - and though they deny it, it remains true; that there is absolutely nothing to prevent us putting the world to rights, excepting ourselves. Reformist movements should engender this affirmation in every human being, and the belief that at last we are to take the constitution and future of our society into our own hands, making it essentially right and good, also that each and every one of us has a responsible part to play.

In the absence of such an alternative prospect, and hopeful spirit, countless well-intentioned humans give their duty to institutions of the false Machine. Their resistance to idealistic change might come from a fear of the baby being thrown out with the bathwater. Contrary to popular belief, a group of people who share the same ideal do not necessarily become indistinguishable as individuals. The human make-up is very complex; it would be impossible as well as undesirable to make us all the same. Another reason for resistance might be that in order to cherish the good things in the Machine - and of course it is possible for love to flourish in compartments of this reality - they tolerate the bad and ignore the fact that hate flourishes also. Or it may be that many well-intentioned people, being centred in the conscious self, resist any intrusion upon their freedom to act and believe as they presently think right. It is the vital human task to win through to supraconsciousness so that we *know* our aims and beliefs to be right, because we *know* them to be humantrue. We must not act, or form an opinion, without this knowledge.

If the present heavy burdens of tension and anxiety were our permanent reality, then we could be excused for pretence, denial, and indulgence in artificial means of obtaining relief. Supraconscious awareness can show us that the Machine is not inescapable, however, and need be but temporarily endured. But *we* who are now living and on whom the responsibility must rest *have* to take this massively humanly irrelevant automatic reality seriously, and worry deeply about our present problems until we have solved them humantruly. Then life on Earth will no longer be a false burden which truth cannot carry, but our true fulfilment, a whole working satisfaction and joy in which we all participate and share – *all* people.

Human conduct of life is a heavy but fragile responsibility which only intellect can take. *We should seriously concern ourselves with nothing else until that responsibility is fully met.*

You might object that there are millions of people with unstimulated and poorly informed minds who would not be able to understand all this, but everybody has the capacity for so doing and if the general movement for humantrue reform truly represents one mind it must represent all minds, everywhere in the world regardless of their adopted culture, for all share the same ultimate function. When a government passes some reform law, this is superficial human progress that leaves the basic automatic ethos undisturbed.

When just one more mind becomes supraconscious this is fundamental progress, for the achievement of a humantrue society will depend upon the understanding agreement of responsible individuals. This crusade of truth is the only way forward. We should not be deterred from making the effort on the grounds that success presently seems a remote possibility, for in truth there is no valid argument in favour of the Machine; there is only the fact of its existence. On the contrary, all the evidence shows that to be supraconscious is our true nature and that humantrue society is our rightful state.

Joining in the movement for reform will be like taking part in therapy, not for oneself but on behalf of the world. To be personally adjusted to the automaton and therefore not easily able to cope with existing reality (inadequate, in worldly terms) is a hard thing. But let it be seen as a virtue, rather than a fault, that your postconscious mind, whether or not you are aware of it, has truly developed well beyond and contrary to your consciousness. If you open to your higher mind, thinking little of your personal problems but a great deal about the huge problems of the world, you will be progressively more fulfilled even though you may feel alone, alien and outcast. It is a good thing to accept as inevitable our shortcomings in the here and now for the sake of being true. No individual can be truly and wholly content until all are so, and, whatever feelings comfort or disturb them, those who are supraconscious know it is infinitely worse to be well adjusted to the Machine but contributing to its insanity, than to be an automatic misfit but striving to make the world a better place.

I once proposed to launch a movement for reform, The United Individuals Movement (already mentioned) but it came to nothing. Someone else might launch it under the same or a different name, but whatever name it may be given it must face the question - how should it fulfil its aims without belying its humantrue principles? It must not become a hierarchical organisation, taking its place in automatic reality, politically and ideologically ranged against other organisations. It must not become a kind of club, membership of which marks out individuals as different and enables them to feel that the mere gesture of joining is enough. This movement should have the least possible formal structure. It should simply represent the effort of human beings to work out and agree a humantrue constitution of society. Everybody is potentially a part of this movement - the fact of being human means we all truly belong to it. However, it is also a fact that *humantrue* communication between us is rare.

Possibly excepting the recent, remarkable advent of the Internet and Worldwide Web, the mediums of communication, even word of mouth, are at best coloured and at worst monopolised by automatic thinking. More than that, all means of communication apart from direct word of mouth incur a money-cost, involving further automatic control through the money-economy that no movement can escape entirely, and by which all are normally sullied. At the simplest level, paper, typing, copying, transport, telephone calls and postage all cost money. To print and communicate independent views on a wide scale entails heavy expenditure, usually beyond the reach of a non-money-profit movement unless it also becomes a money-raising organisation. To depend entirely on automated media means that you must have your material bought, in order to be sold, exposing it to commercial judgement which, in the case of truly radical books, may see no justification for their publication, or, if the Machine does publish them, may do so in a limited way, for minority interest, at prices beyond the reach of the average person, sustaining its interest only as long as it is profitable.

The one real and unassailable freedom we have is that our minds are at liberty privately to construct themselves truly. That our existing automatic reality urgently needs to be exchanged for an alternative humantrue reality is a great truth that we need to grasp. The case for a reform movement might be that it would help and encourage us to understand humantruth, and to realise it in the world. Because it is irresistible to the fully open mind, humantruth will cross national, cultural and ideological boundaries, just as science does in its limited field. The following are my thoughts on making such a movement effective.

Remember that a majority of humans presently recognise their existing nature and state as their fixed reality, automatic reason as the basis of their thinking, and individuals as variously-sized cogs in the Machine. This reality is represented to us by the history it has recorded, its current affairs, and news presented according to its own view of those affairs. Any reform movement must recognise truth, the intellect whose function is truth, and the individual who is intellect. The movement has to find a means of showing, to those who presently see only the automated picture, an alternative prospect; the humantrue view. It must find a means of bypassing automatic channels and appealing directly to each individual's inner being, so that each presents the humantrue view to the intellect whose nature it is to respond, then a means of feeding back individual doubts, questions and criticisms for further general intellation and discussion, and finally to record those humantruths which are agreed, as and when they are agreed. I am not proposing that humantruth as conceived in these pages be *imposed* on anybody, but that the individual mind, when it comes to know clearly and certainly what is humantrue, with or without any help from this book, will self-impose it.

It is suggested, however, that this book should be a basic springboard of reform, firstly because it purports to discover humantruth, the world realisation of which is the objective of a reform movement. Secondly, because whether or not it is what it purports to be the book opposes existing reality and proposes an alternative, giving readers a new viewpoint from which to examine themselves and the Machine. As far as I am aware it is the only book that attempts to present, honestly and comprehensively, the complete humantrue case. So it is a challenge and measuring-stick of general intellation, enabling the individual to refer doubts about particular propositions to their place in the whole structure of reasoning, or critically question that whole structure in the light of some apparently well-founded objection.

I maintain that this book represents a perfectly reasonable mental superstructure which is very much needed by humanity but which is yet uncommon and generally quite unacceptable because it is contrary to the norm. It is the result of writing down that which the postconscious dictates, regardless of automatic lores or the Machine's rules. Past thinking and writing has failed in this respect, yet in view of our potential we have no good cause to write otherwise. For humans, the only basis of honest common language is truth. This book does not refer much to previous literature because to find truth it is necessary to break away from that which has gone before. This work does not aim to attract as little disagreement and as much fellow feeling as possible, but to plumb humantruth. If you have not already plumbed it, then whether you let the book help you to do so, or throw it aside, is up to you. But, in truth, we all have a profound responsibility to take up the struggle, and no prior right to refuse. You may find it heavy going, but it must be so. The conscious self cannot break down the doors to its own postconscious without stressful effort.

As I have said before, it is my firm belief that my conclusions are true, and that any other mind that inexorably follows the processes of pure reason will conclude more or less the same. But nobody is expected to approach the subject of reform believing that he or she has to follow where this book leads. Every supraconscious individual is expected to acknowledge that the great majority of people are automated and to accept that their first aim must be to make this majority aware of the fact, but all are free thereafter supraconsciously to reach their own conclusions. However, we all have that vital responsibility to pursue the common truth, for our ultimate objective is to agree a humantrue constitution of world society.

Our usual approach to the reading of books is to set up the fixed conscious self and its preferred construction of thought in judgement of them. Free, radical and true opinions are normally refuted because the correlations of normal thinking are too severely restricted to embrace them. This reflects the automated human habit of bottling up the postconscious with conscious will. In this case I am hoping that the act of accepting this book's challenge might help to burst the cork from the bottled-up postconscious, spilling out a mass of already correlated ideas of which consciousness has been unaware. In the course of this process I hope such minds will see the necessity of addressing everything, and that they will then share in pursuing humantruth to the very end.

To reach fulfilment, this process of humantrue realisation must first relentlessly bypass the conditioning of upbringing and education and the hard necessities of automatic reality - also our automated opinions - putting us in a position to look back on these, expose them as false, and dismiss them. Immediately on freeing itself from automatic harness, the mind has a duty voluntarily to bind itself to humantrue responsibility.

Individuals who are critical of the reasoning behind this book are requested to substantiate their views in order to show the truth of their reasoning. Destructive criticism is not enough. Critics cannot expect to be taken seriously unless they are ready and able to put forward a completely constructed and convincingly true alternative.

Only postconscious reason offers a new look at the reality we actually live in and suggests the reality we ought to live in. Formally to institute a reform movement might help, but it is not the movement as an institution that is important but the mind of every single member - the responsibly aware determination of each one of us to exert influence for good. Joining a reform movement must not be merely a matter of adopting, or attaching oneself to a ready-made organisation with pre-determined policy that requires unthinking loyalty or obedience. It must be a matter of each independent individual's personal dedication to achieving supraconscious awareness, and uniting with all others in understanding, then realising, humantruth.

Again, I risk labouring my point by dwelling too much on this matter, but I am trying to build up a pressure of reason that will tell against the great weight of existing reality. The vital object is to show convincingly that we should think and act according to humantruth, not according to the automaton. Remember that you are subject to pervasive automatic influences from all quarters all the time. If this book is doggedly persistent, the reason is that it is up against the human habit of staying put, judging everything from its present position in the here and now, refusing to be changed or shifted. It seems to me necessary to dwell on the subject of reform movements, and how they might work, just a little longer.

If reformers are to respect and observe the principle of equality, they must not only preach to the converted but reach out to all conditions of women and men, of every walk of life in the existing world of inequality. The necessary preparation for equality, and for a humantrue reality of which equality is an essential part, is that all humans do reach agreement through supraconsciousness. Therefore the first undertaking of reformers should be that all agree this to be the case - that all deliberately reject old attitudes, divisions and prejudices; that all adopt this new humantrue concept of reality as the only acceptable basis for future life, sure that it is attainable.

Nevertheless, in the struggle for recognition of the humantrue principles, including equality, unequal responsibility must fall to the enlightened, the supraconscious - the humantruly aware. They shall regard their enlightenment as a privilege, to be passed on and equally shared. There exist whole populations of unstimulated minds, kept in ignorance by inertia, or by the intention of misguided minds in authority. All kinds of minds, conditioned by training and experience, are extremely resistant to enlightenment whilst they remain embedded in the reality that so conditioned them. Reform movements are likely to attract the most advanced free and independent thinkers, and it will need them to make the humantrue message crystal clear enough to break down such unreasoned resistance. It is in line with the principle of equality that they should give, and others receive, whilst all are equally valued and regarded.

Reform movements should be concerned to rectify the present intolerable and perilous situation of humanity in general. We humans are busy undertaking far-reaching projects and pursuing them with determination, yet are very far from being truly ourselves or fully awake. We do not personify the real 'we', our supraconscious potential, but are merely lesser applied minds directed by the Machine. To return to the computer analogy, our brains are the human hardware, but our conditioning is the software that programmes us to use the conscious mind/brain to play various versions of the Machine's general game. The genuine human mind would be the result of the conscious mind supraconsciously developing its own software programme, which is truth. The meaningful purpose of life is the fulfilment of truth, and that is the aim of humantrue reform.

Even were one genuine reformist movement to grow and spread throughout the world, it should always remain founded upon and invested in the individual supraconsciousness, as should the alternative society it is pursuing. It should never be allowed to fall into the familiar automatic pattern by becoming a powerful, hierarchical institution in its own right. It should resolutely keep outside the political arena and directly oppose nothing - no law, policy or practice - by means of open conflict, its purpose being to help the spread of humantrue understanding which will bring about voluntary and spontaneous change, from within.

When I first envisaged such a reformist movement I saw it as a network of small interlinked discussion groups. Eventually I concluded that it should be based on the individual mind intellating alone, influenced by nothing so much as its own correlated reason. Eventual communication of ideas is important, of course, but the process of forming those ideas should take place within the postconscious and under the sole influence of its free and independent pursuit of truth, reinforced by its own will. In formal groups other influences tend to be brought to bear. Discussion between minds is not as pure a process as intellation, especially when contributed to by minds of different construction or at different stages of completion. Individuals are inclined to interrupt each others' train of thought, to gravitate towards compromise, or to be drawn into instinctively competitive argument, using fixed prejudices as weapons.

It now seems to me that members of reformist movements might meet when they have well-formed ideas to communicate and discuss, and that their informal discussions would then stimulate rather than replace lone individual intellation. Discussion face-to-face is dominated by awareness at the conscious level, whereas the process of intellation is unconscious to the surface awareness of the individual's own mind - difficult enough to bring to consciousness when alone, and much more so when in a group. My experience (of a high-technology society) is that most of our sophisticated communications are humanly irrelevant, and that very little intense intellectual discussion suffices to accompany a great deal of private intellation.

The humantrue world that this book envisages may not, of course, be achieved overnight. The section 'Preparing the Way for Change' incorporating chapters 45 Personal Reorientation; 46 New Attitude; 47 Affirmation; also this current chapter 48 Peaceable Action, are concerned with reforms and fresh outlooks intended to lead the way to that ultimate goal.

Chapter 48

PEACEABLE ACTION

Those things that go wrong with human relations and actions, from personal unstable, antisocial or aggressive behaviour to international nuclear confrontation, are effects of one and the same cause, stemming from exigencies of existing reality - symptoms of the automatic disease. These symptoms may be cured in the attempt to live with the disease, in individuals by psychoanalysis or meditation or religious faith, and internationally by such as a ban on nuclear weapons. But this way the disease remains to erupt elsewhere, perhaps in different forms. It shows itself in the general lack of common ground between employers and workers, husbands and wives, police and criminals, sons and mothers, due to their mind-sets, roles, and the pressures upon them being so different. As supraconsciously aware individuals, we should intend to prevent and eradicate the disease so that there is never again cause for the symptoms to arise.

When the time comes that a humantrue reality exists we shall be acting contrary to present automatic precepts, but the way to achieve it is not by offensive action against existing institutions, nor by attack on those who serve them. We once needed leaders to save us from catastrophe, just as oppressed people in the Machine turn to new leaders for liberation. But established leadership is a feature of automatic reality, and one way to defeat the Machine is not to oppose leaders but to persuade them to reject their own function. Leaders also have true intellectual potential, and are best regarded as ordinary humans, their automatic role ignored. In this and other ways, rather than confront the Machine head-on we should withdraw our support from it, where this does no human harm. We should act according to the alternative humantrue ethos where this is within the Machine's law (and it can never be contrary to moral law).

However 'ordinary' we regard ourselves as being, we can bring our indirect actions to bear, independently, privately and inconspicuously, in ways whose combined effect could be the most powerful of all against the Machine. This applies more to we who are the privileged, affluent peoples of the world, and less to those the fact of whose deprivation itself should strongly spur us to these actions. Remember that the aim of humantrue reform is not so much to relieve deprivation as to abolish it by defeating the Machine that causes it.

Perhaps the greatest of all obstacles to reformist movements and the spread of supraconsciousness is the fact that most of the spontaneous warmth and friendship that exists between people is presently closely involved with automatic reality. We contrive to express and foster good personal relationships despite the Machine and the first humantrue reformers, who would wish to distance themselves from automatic reality, could be made to look austere, grim, inadequate and, if they let it get them down, downtrodden.

If we are to act in unity, with the courage of our convictions, we need an inspiring spirit of good intention and good comradeship. And then, to remove those nagging doubts which can blunt the edge of our enthusiasm, we need to see that there are many gentle ways and means of quelling the Machine that only require our concerted determination to succeed. We need to *believe* ourselves capable of transforming our reality, and that only this irrelevant, established, inhuman *thing* - the fact and concept of the here and now, and our conventional obedience to it - stands in the way of a humantrue alternative. We have to resist the manipulation of our morals by the norm, remembering that in the past, when the Machine has prospered social welfare has benefited but when the Machine has been in recession the already less fortunate underprivileged have had to bear the brunt.

It is the present will of automated humanity that we disagree with each other. To do so, all the individual has to do is to express a contrary opinion. There is little compunction to observe truth. To combat this reformers have to put across the humantruth that differences of opinion indicate lack of common intellation, and that agreement is vital. It is not that conflicting opinions are necessarily formed recklessly but that they are automatic choices, representing degrees of acceptance or rejection of different aspects of conflicting reality - ways of reconciling our personal moral behaviour and our false automatic role or attitude. Our opinions are almost always wrong because the Machine, which they accept overall, is wrong. We shall agree when truth is the only guide of our reason.

Politics reflects this present practice and serves to maintain the overall concept of existing reality, making only such humane but marginal changes as the Machine will tolerate, and therefore depends upon remaining in a permanently restrictive state of conflicting, disagreeing deadlock.

Politics draws the 'public' into the fundamentally irrelevant political debate, supposedly to shape human destiny but in fact, as an extension of automatic competition, merely to decide which of the slightly different roads to follow to an automated destiny. This is all that the power of our vote gives us. Individuals generally, if unconsciously, recognise this and vote in elections for political, not humantrue, expectations. Therefore we reformists, since we have become opposed to the automatic road and seek an alternative destiny, might well decline to vote. By not voting we shall gradually discredit politics and show that it is our awareness of the humantrue alternative that represents us.

The education system could be eroded by children themselves. It may be forced on them but their minds are essentially within their own control so that they cannot be forced to accept its lessons against their will. If, when they begin school, they already have a basic understanding that the concept of automatic reality is false, and approach the school's teaching with humantrue awareness, they will not be conditioned by formal education as it wants but will take from it only as their minds truly need.

The first parents to achieve supraconsciousness, through intellation, shall be highly morally aware and their children likely to be the more truly stimulated minds and amongst those likely to win in the competition of education. Those parents can strike a blow for humantruth by persuading their children of the senselessness of competition compared with the true sense of cooperation. Their children could then obey school instructions by sitting down in the examination room, but then decline to submit to the examination - either returning blank pages, or writing across them 'not willing to compete' or by writing an essay explaining their beliefs.

The law cannot forbid this, and the examination system relies for effectiveness on our ingrained competitiveness - our instinctive will to win. If enough children, and especially the most apt absorbers of information, were to act in this way the examination system could be so devalued as to become pointless. This might do little immediately to change the character of education since children would still be taught by, about, and for automatic reality, but it could stop the price-tagging of children with pieces of paper which indicate their future economic and social status, and it could erode the influence of automatic conditioning.

Such action might not do much to change the concept of the Machine as the overall employer either. However, if the examination system were to be discredited it might cause individual employers to return to giving jobs without undue prejudice; to return to apprenticeships which can relate work to a liking and talent for its character and especially for its physical skills which schools do not much respect and encourage; and, most importantly, it might increasingly lead young people to choose work according to conscience - to its true human usefulness rather than according to the personal advantage offered by automatic expectations and financial valuations.

For those at higher levels of specialist training, refusal to be automatically graded might so reduce the numbers of young persons qualifying as to cause confusion, reducing specialised autoprogressive activity and bringing into question its true human value - whether it goes on for the benefit of humanity at large, or merely for the Machine and those it selects for its privileged service. For example, young people now grasping for opportunities in the electronics and computer industries, because they are available, new, exciting and highly paid, might stop to think and question whether they are advancing in a humanly worthwhile direction. Without willing new workers such industries would be unable to develop, or even to continue.

This is not to say that much present education is not of value or is not beginning to move in this direction, but that in general it represents the training and moulding of minds for automatic advantage. There is an educational barrier to true awareness. Not only does this barrier keep out areas and levels of understanding that the Machine will not recognise, but those fields of understanding that it does let through are too fragmented, disoriented or prejudiced to admit true awareness. In other words *that which is given to speak cannot say true, and that which can say true is not given to speak.*

Schooling is oriented towards the highest pinnacles of academic achievement, according to which standards the majority of us are failures and the work we do inferior. It should be a matter of development of mind related to humanity, independent of the Machine, and non-competitive - not bound to existing concepts of reality but in a position to assess them critically. Individuals' attitudes to automatic reality, and the work they feel called upon and willing to do, would then be tested in their own minds. Their ability to do the work would be tested in the field and assessed by themselves as well as others, for none of us would have any interest but that the work is needed and must be done properly. Hopefully, individuals would now see their contribution to human life as giving of their best to that which is most useful, rather than taking the most they could by meeting the highest demands of the Machine.

When we know our present mode of upbringing and system of education to be wrong, and are unsure what is the best way to rear and teach our children, I think we should bring them up in a vacuum, so to speak. They should be mentally stimulated but given no definite instructions as to how they must think and behave, only shown the path by which they will judge themselves - the way of humantruth. I have already suggested that we might persuade them not to compete, but this persuasion might be achieved by example, and by the way we answer our children's questions, rather than by positive teaching. This way they would not adopt any fixed character or settled attitude based on conditioned and limited thinking but, by doubting, questioning and criticising everything, would become intellectually fulfilled by intellation. This will make them unsatisfactory from the viewpoint of the Machine, but that is the price to be paid for true enlightenment in the world as it is. To so equip the young that they can cope successfully with the here and now is to allow them to be automated, and condemned to a continuing false future.

To facilitate *human* communication across automatic boundaries, individuals, despite established resistance and inertia and independently of the Machine, could invent a new world language, circulate means of learning it, learn it and speak it regardless of the norm. It might become the language of humantruth and the alternative reality, bypassing the Machine and, as the alternative is realised, eventually superseding all other languages.

Whether or not this language obstacle is removed, other steps can be taken towards achieving better communication between independent human minds. The United Nations, as part of its human rights campaign, could be pressed to declare freedom without reprisal for all intellaters, anywhere, who do not seek to be party political leaders but to enlighten peaceably and honestly. They should be helped to have their writings published with the support of law. The initial judge of whether the work merited publication would be the writer, and thereafter the readers would determine whether it should be widely distributed. These judgements would be made according to the true value of the work's contribution to the human good, by-passing the normal automatic judgements based on acceptability to the here and now and money-profit. A feature of the scheme must be that writers receive basic income support and do not profit from publication.

It is not our *true* nature to be violent, but the nature, and permission, and compulsion of the Machine that makes us so. If individuals both inside and outside the military institutions choose to be non-combative, those institutions will be rendered harmless. The same applies to the industrial manufacture of armaments. No humantrue individual should have anything whatever to do with designing, making, selling or transporting weapons. Without willing hands for such work there can *be* no weapons.

War is inseparable from the lores and laws of supply and demand. It is the traditional automated way of settling ultimate competitive conflicts. It includes many authoritative and powerfully entrenched institutions of the Machine; the defence ministry, the war office, military colleges, navy, army and air forces, arms factories, weapons research establishments, intelligence and espionage networks. Warfare is integral with our way of life, part of the familiar fabric of world society, and of our existing concept of reality. It is a logical lore of the Machine, an instinct with intellect applied, so it is recognised by international law and has become a necessity to automated humanity, for it employs millions.

Many of us recall the horrors of past wars, and are in a position to see them as stupid folly, yet we still rattle the sabre and wave the flag. Many of us still mourn for loved ones killed or maimed, yet permit our sons to join the forces, regarding it as a career opportunity. In the USA it appears that 60% of all scientific research is military research. The Machine trains the scientists, and then faces them with the fact that most of the scientific jobs available *are* military. A scientist may have moral scruples but be under economic pressure to take an immoral job, and if further persuasion is needed it could be that the salary is temptingly high. But for the armaments industry he and hundreds and thousands of others would be unemployed. Though he, personally, would not hurt a fly, a man might well work for any inhuman project, without thinking beyond the belief that his first duty is to provide the best possible material standard of living for his wife and family.

It is true that whilst fanatical, and prejudiced, and powerfully dictatorial nations, or rather *national governments* exist, general national defence seems necessary. But this is the presently realistic case that should not obstruct our essential awareness that humantrue society would neither give cause nor opportunity for war. As a race we might get near enough to overcoming such barriers to moral awareness that the utterly futile inhumanity of war comes fully home to us and we determine to control it. But, misrepresenting its causes, we might not immediately attempt going further and breaking down the fundamental barrier to curing the cause of war for good - to breaking down our concept of competitive automatic reality. Yet, for the present, we might go so far as to recognise one major cause of the symptom of war, i.e. economic pressure, and take action to curtail it.

As long as the world is divided into separate nations it is inconceivable that all governments will willingly submit to an international law banning war. Even if such a law were passed it would be impossible to enforce, there being no higher authority with the necessary power. Governments reserve their right to national sovereignty, and to make war to defend, maintain and promote that right. They seek power in the world, and the most effective guarantee of power is military might, backed by economic strength that depends on manufacture supported by trade. But human feeling is rising against war, and whilst it is likely to be some time before *everybody* refuses to fight, the anti-war feeling may soon reach sufficient pressure that we shall strongly object to anybody profiting from the manufacture, sale, deployment or actual use of arms.

In response to this pressure it is perhaps conceivable that a United Nations decree be agreed and adopted with the object of removing some of the economic causes and motivations of war. It might be made international law that all armaments manufacture be undertaken by the state rather than by private trading enterprises; that both manufacture and sale require United Nations licence; that where sold only the basic cost may be charged, without profit; that no one engaged in this manufacture, from top to bottom - director to scientist to fitter, nor any member of the armed services - from private soldier to field marshal, be paid more than the lowest, basic, bare subsistence wage. Were this law to be effected it might then be seen how far the economic factor had previously influenced human individuals to produce weapons and join armies, and, without that factor, how strong would be the will for warfare on the part of those who prepare for it and actually take part in it.

The basis of action is attitude, and given a universal humantrue attitude, reform such as this would be quite straightforward, though otherwise it seems impossible. Look at it this way. If the great majority of humans do not want war, then any government that involves its people in war goes against their interests and endangers their lives, which is equivalent to ill-treatment. It is acceptable to remove a child from parents who are ill-treating it. Therefore the human world should accept that such as the United Nations Organisation should restrain, or remove from authority, governments which are ill-treating whole populations in this way.

Whilst humantrue reason would see such initiatives as encouraging steps in the right direction, automated reason views them as quite unrealistic. As long as national governments remain in power, and the money economy remains intact, international law will be as ineffective on world affairs as human morality. The pressure of money interest, on both individuals and institutions, would contrive to circumvent laws against war. So we are thrown back onto the supraconscious awareness of the individual as the only effective key to humantrue change. The Machine will never bend entirely to our reason - we have to uproot it utterly. By putting our faith in laws and their enforcement we abdicate our true responsibilities, for this is to trust in a Machine that has already determined that *our* moral laws are made to be broken by *its* lores. We must return to the understanding that *when no individual consents to carry arms there can be no war,* and support it with the conviction that as this good is within our power to do, so shall we do it.

I am saying that humanity can come into its own only over the Machine's dead body. I have already said that automatic institutions such as the United Nations Organisation cannot be expected to do more in the way of radical reform than they have shown themselves able to do. Nevertheless nations are primarily people, so the UNO should represent us. Therefore to state that the UNO should turn against the Machine is humantrue. In theory, widespread individual involvement in UNO should give it more clout. Whilst UNO exists let it be part of the process of tilting the moral balance from the Machine to our humanity. Let it promote the idea that *people* should put loyalty to this organisation before loyalty to their own governments in respect of moral matters agreed by the majority, and let each nation's decision on such matters be subject, without the right of veto, to a public referendum. Even though in automatic practice neither UNO nor any other humanitarian institution can have significant effect, that this were clearly shown to be the case would surely help in making humanity aware of the vital need for fundamental change.

The autoprogressive energy-expression of the Machine comes of its persuasion and temptation of human will to press ever forward towards its goals and targets, for its rewards. Every single individual involved in this reckless race is at liberty voluntarily to withhold most of that energy. That is our individual power, a kind of negative force against the Machine, which becomes a positive force when our energies are united behind the humantrue alternative. At present hardly anyone is aware of this alternative, or believes it to be viable by any stretch of the imagination. It is hard for the lone individual to boycott the Machine when to do so has little or no apparent effect, but even if we don't apply that negative force in the ways suggested in the following pages, to be aware of the Machine's power over us, and of ways to combat that power, is half the battle.

Much of that automated energy is expended on competing to acquire things. Although the Machine makes possession and the competing for it lawful, we are not bound by law to desire unnecessary things, or to fight to possess them and keep hold of them. We can voluntarily decline to possess, but simply use things according to our need of their use. We can refuse to recognise money values but take only what is our fair share and give to others what is equally fair for them. The more we give to each other the less we need fight to take.

The present energising of the Machine by competing both to acquire and possess things, and to profit by providing those things, excites other unnecessary activities. Consider the closely interrelated financial and contractual institutions of banking, the stock exchange, the professions of law, estate and land agencies, or insurance. These are functions of the Machine, inserted between the forces of supply and demand that are already in the hands of commercial undertakings. These institutions have created demand for their services by gaining control of the supply and valuation of money, of title to possession, or of security. We are practically bound to make use of these services if we wish to live by automatic means and to give our lives automatic support and protection. By doing so we strengthen our bondage to these institutions.

For example, we all need a roof over our heads and to get it we presently need money, to rent or buy. Either way we pay heavily, and buying is preferred because it gives possession. But that requires that we have a large sum of cash in hand, to buy outright or put down as deposit on a mortgage. We attempt to buy at less than the house's market value, which is a kind of cheating of the seller. But as sellers we try to secure *more* than its market value. So as buyers or sellers we employ estate agents, lawyers and surveyors to avoid ourselves being cheated, and banks to give bridging loans, and pay them all substantially for the privilege. If we *are* cheated we might revert to the lawyer and pay him heavily too, to seek redress.

Finally, we pay yet more money to insure the house, and go on paying year by year. We are trapped into insuring, not only our house but our lives, our cars, and all our possessions in case they are destroyed, stolen or lost, or in case we are made liable for others' losses. We are forced into this trap because we know that should we suffer loss no one will help us since all are in the same trap. Only the Machine will compensate us, *if* we have regularly bribed it with premiums.

As humantrue individuals, who have rejected the automatic concept of reality, we shall refuse to be taken in by all these institutions, and can cooperatively defeat them simply by not taking part in their practices. But whilst the Machine exists we may not then survive alone without difficulty, and shall need support from other like-minded individuals.

We should squarely reconsider our relationship with the financial, legal and property institutions, especially if we are bankers, lawyers, agents and the like. Where possible independent individuals should decide and act according to their humantrue principles, rather than making automatic reality their excuse for doing otherwise. Whilst we cannot yet avoid a degree of dependence on money we should eliminate it from our affairs wherever possible.

For example, if we can survive without profiting from the value of a thing we do not need we should give it away, or at least sell it without profit. Or we might exchange things, for mutual need alone and regardless of their market value, without the corresponding exchange of money or regard to the competitive principles of barter. This is to regard the moral case for needful use of things as superior to the legal right to the needless possession of them, until such time as humantrue giving and sharing is the order of the day. If someone cheats us or steals from us (as automated mankind sees it) who is more needy than we, and we do not suffer unduly as a result, we need not have recourse to the law, though we have legal claim to its enforcement.

The money-economy principle lays down that demand must be stimulated, exploited and supplied, and automated people obey. Come enlightenment, it shall not only be for members of the public to abstain from over-consumption of such as sugar, alcohol and tobacco. Individual refiners, brewers and tobacco growers will cease producing, publicity agents will cease advertising, grocers, publicans and tobacconists will cease retailing. Everyone shall recognise that we have to go against present tastes and interests in order to serve true future interests.

To escape the insurance trap, we could go the absolute extreme and simply decline to be insured. To do so would mean, here in Britain, that we could not drive a car, or take out a mortgage, since the law insists on insurance in these instances. It could mean we suffered the loss of all we possessed, but none of us would even then be worse off than the many millions of utterly deprived people elsewhere in the world.

Our aim is to weaken the influences of the economic system by resisting and bypassing it, preparatory to abolishing it. Another step towards this objective would be to reform our use of money. Independent individuals could prepare and propose a scheme for simplifying the system by introducing one single world currency. If the economists' argument in defence of money were that it is a token of exchange and fair distribution, they could not legitimately object. This scheme might not be easy to carry through, but apart from that, if there were official objection to it in principle this would confirm that money is not merely a token, nor yet a national commodity, profession and occupation, but also an international profit-making industry in its own right.

We need look at what we personally consume as food, not from the viewpoint of what we can financially afford but what we truly need - not only according to our likes and dislikes but also to what the whole Earth can afford and what is our fair share. We need to eat and drink what is in every way good and right for us, and no more than we essentially require, choosing those things that are locally grown and prepared or processed to the minimum, or at least preferring stuff produced in our own country and declining to consume imported food and drink, as far as ever possible. We shall go easy with alcohol, preferring to make our own from local flowers and fruits in season, so that our thirst for it is tempered by the time and effort going into its making.

As far as possible we should aim to make our own country at least self-sufficient, which means looking into the practicality of producing many needs which we presently rely on importing. We can grow food in our gardens, allotments or any vacant bit of land. Fresh produce straight from the ground, sown, raised and harvested by hand and with the minimum of artificial aids, is not only better food but costs next to nothing in humantrue terms, whilst mechanised and commercialised production, preparation and transportation costs irreplaceable resources.

The same applies to medicine. The choice between homoeopathic and herbal preparations or manufactured drugs need not be a matter of scientific authentication, or convenience, or even of which is better. Humantrue individuals would prefer the former because these are essentially produced by nature, replenished by its recycling processes, and proved by experience to be reasonably effective, with few if any side effects. The latter are products of automatic factories which are essentially a one-way drain on the biosphere - part of autoprogression and its disregard of human and Earth consequences, only to be used where necessary and when there is no alternative. It is common for anti-Machine individuals to ascribe to all natural medicines almost magical properties, when in fact they have their limitations. Our humantrue approach will surely be that herbal, homoeopathic, and other natural medicines are generally appropriate, in conjunction with a healthy way of life, and in most cases we should be content with their limitations, not expecting automatically certain cures for all illnesses.

Shelter is a basic need, and life can be bleak where our homes are not welcoming and comfortable. But this does not mean they have to be immaculate, with fashionable furnishings, modern fittings, and all the latest equipment. Modern houses, and much that goes into them, use scarce materials and energy for their production, and gadgets consume electricity. Elaborate decor indicates a search for substitutes to the fundamental poverty of life. Wall-to-wall carpeting is nice, but it is perfectly possible to be happy without it, and it can appear nasty when we are aware of the automatic burden it represents. Bare boards can be adequate, long-lasting and pleasant floors for most rooms.

It is wasteful to throw away furniture merely because it is old or out-of-date. Should we not rather make our furniture simple, ergonomically good and solid, respect it and keep it for as long as it serves? Wood need cost us little in ecological terms if eventually returned to the soil and if trees are constantly replaced. Mature trees used for timber have already long performed an oxygen-producing function. The ideal home shall be both a place where we rest and refresh ourselves, and a working base for our inside and outdoor activities, not a temple to personal acquisition and autoprogression.

We need adequate clothing but, by making it simple and practical and by not discarding it until it is beyond repair, we can strike another blow against the Machine. We can avoid wasteful man-made materials, choosing natural fibres such as home-grown wool but preferably not cotton if it has to be imported as is the case here in the UK. We can shun fashion. Once we have found an effective and becoming style and practical kind of clothing there is no good reason for changing or varying it. Fashion is a wasteful expression of false progress, and a device for stimulating commerce. That humans respond to it is another mark of the poverty of life that has to be enlivened in this way. That we pay such attention to outward appearances is because our being is invested more in our outer shells than our inner minds.

We drive ever more sophisticated vehicles, on ever more complex road systems. In the home we in the West increasingly use other powered gadgets - clothes dryers, carpet cleaners, food blenders and mixers, freezers, dishwashers. In the garden we may use rotavators, mowers and clippers, and buy all kinds of other equipment, often more for novelty value than real worth, or as substitutes for basic manual skills. If we do not actually own all these things, we covet them. They too are subject to fashion, so that we regularly scrap them and buy new, as commerce intends that we should so that obsolescence is built into them.

All these things are pleasures of a human world society that is not very pleasant in itself. Simply living in this society is not its own reward. Saving labour and gaining material rewards are substitute objectives of a Machine that is unworthy of our efforts to serve it. Achieving these objectives is a strain on Earth's means, and they would be mostly unnecessary to a humantrue society.

Independent research is needed to reveal how much of Earth's energy resources the average person consumes compared with that amount which each contributes that is essential to life. It will certainly be found that much more is consumed than returned and much of this is irreplaceable, or carries an unacceptable penalty. We have heads and hands, horses (that build themselves out of the most common plant food on Earth - grass) to draw ploughs and vehicles, sails to drive boats. We should use these things wherever possible, looking to engine-powered devices to assist us only when we can ecologically afford them, and need them. Otherwise we can now sacrifice the convenience of such devices, voluntarily, in order to prepare for the time when, although many of our tasks have to be accomplished by the sweat of our brows, with only those aids which are part of the re-cycling biosphere to help us, we have the freedom, time, space and will to do those tasks, and take satisfaction in so doing.

With increasing general awareness we find that we are already moving in some of these directions. Here in the UK we do now insulate our houses to conserve heat, with government help and encouragement, although the average individual's motive is less likely to be fuel-saving than money-saving. The majority of us are not yet fully awake to the fact that our resources of coal, oil and gas are fast running out, and that the foremost alternative resource, nuclear power, still presents unanswered questions and unsolved problems as to safety. In some developed nations there is strong public resistance to nuclear energy and, in the main, this has been officially supported. A balanced review of this subject is offered towards the end of this chapter (a review given against the background situation of 'favoured' nations in 1990 or so, but still relevant to the state of some of the developing nations ten years on). Whilst these strong suspicions of nuclear energy remain, if we share them we can help lower the demand for nuclear power by reducing our individual consumption of energy. The longer we ignore the dangers of the existing situation, go along with its autoprogressions and so give way to the Machine, as the conventional sources of energy dwindle we shall come to *depend* on nuclear power, and should it prove to be as dangerous as suspected, to *necessarily* suffer the consequences because there is no alternative.

That we subdue our instinct is necessary to the liberation of our intellect. That we make material sacrifices is much less truly hurtful than that we presently sacrifice our natural morality. That we should share equally worldwide is a simple, humantrue, responsible obligation. That we presently maintain a competitive, unequal world causes suffering everywhere, practically but also mentally - it is against reason, and therefore unnatural for us.

There is a money-economic counter-argument that says that if the 'North' reduces its demands this will harm and not help the 'South' because it means shrinking markets that the 'South' depend on supplying. But 'underdeveloped' countries should not be dependent on using their land to grow peanuts, coffee, tea and the like to sell - cheaply - to the 'developed' Northern countries for money - the 'North's kind of money, ie 'hard currency', which is demanded in payment for the supply to the 'South' of goods which they themselves have not the industrial means to manufacture. The 'South's land should be growing food for the South themselves, and the 'North' should supply their essential manufactured needs, regardless of money. It is only by our stepping back from our 'Northern' privileges that the 'South' will, with our help, have space to take steps forward out of deprivation, so that each may eventually meet the other in equality.

But within the present 'Northern' framework of a money economy, if, for any reason, the public financial power to fulfil its normal demand for any thing is reduced, the public financial opportunity to supply it is also reduced. Since supply is equated with jobs, this means that a proportion of the people become unemployed. Since employment provides money to secure demands, unemployment further reduces demand, which further reduces supply and so further increases unemployment. This sequence can occur as the result of economic 'inflation', but it would also occur were a large number of humantrue individuals, doing anti-human or unnecessary jobs, suddenly to down tools on moral grounds.

The money-economics system in any case serves the Machine, not humanity. The Machine creates the phenomenon of unemployment that the system also causes automated humanity to translate into selective human suffering because its effects are not *equally shared*. Those still employed go on supplying, being paid, demanding and receiving at about the same rate per capita as before. Those now unemployed are outcast from the system and excluded from the normal automatic process of living. By the paradoxical effects of their conditioning by automatic concepts, the former do not turn on the Machine out of sympathy with the latter and insist on the burden being equally shared. It is a case of 'devil take the hindmost'.

The Machine's way of recovering from recession is to restore demand from any possible source and, in order to meet it, to increase once more the supply of any saleable thing, by every possible *financially economically viable* means. The humantrue way is to replace this system with the responsible cooperative provision of each other's needs.

So a great barrier to humantrue progress is bound up with the Machine's concept of employment. If large numbers of humantrue individuals *did* opt out of the Machine at once, before finding alternative means of supporting each other, the result would be disastrous. The weakened Machine, even where its humane welfare laws required it to do so, would be unable to provide for those individuals' survival. In this and other Northern countries the safety net of social security prevents the unemployed falling into destitution, but if unemployment dramatically increased, and prosperity drastically declined, according to automatic lore it is inevitable that this provision would also decline, or cease. The transformation has to be gradual. As each part or function of the Machine is abandoned, the humantrue alternative has to advance a step to fill the gap. Conversely, as each humantrue step forward is taken, that automatic feature which it replaces has to be dismantled to make way.

It is certainly vital and urgent that humantrue individuals do give up jobs and duties which are harmful to humanity, at once, or at least voice their objections to doing what they are called upon to do and resist their obligations until it is possible to give them up. But much of the work we do is basically necessary, if misapplied and improperly oriented to the Machine, and so should continue. We should also continue, for the present, that mass of unnecessary but relatively harmless work which the Machine employs us to do, for it can be turned to some good account, as can the functions of certain institutions. Politics, government, education and law, for example - these can turn back on themselves, by their individual members re-examining their principles and motives and beginning humantruly to reform their functions.

Three benefits would result from humantrue individuals drastically reducing their needs and wants. One is to lessen the hardships of unemployment, in that those out of work and lucky enough to receive social security payment would be better able to live on their low money income. The second and third benefits illustrate how we can all turn our unnecessary labour to good account. The second has already been described - that by making sacrifices we reduce our dependent demands on the Machine and so reduce its pressures on the biosphere. The third is that those of us who are still employed would be able to live well below their money income, so having money to spare. In caring humantrue communities or groups which included both employed and unemployed members, it is altogether reasonable that this money be pooled - that the latter give it and the former take it as a matter of equal sharing. Or, otherwise, that it be used in any way that furthers the humantrue cause.

No one *wants* to be deprived of course, but our humantrue aims will not be achieved by all seeking to secure their own advantage. If there is to be deprivation, it will be easier to bear if *all* are deprived to the same degree. But our aim should be that *nobody* be unacceptably deprived, and all share equally. Returning to the matter of insurance, it is the fear of losing, or falling behind in the rat race to gain, which persuades us to insure, in a society where to gain and possess is our way of life, from bare necessities to luxuries. If the practice is to cease we need other means of making good accidental loss.

As the number of humantrue individuals increases, and they decline to be insured, when one of their number suffers loss the rest will repair it and care for him or her and family. With the growth of humantrue awareness this practice will spread as we all move towards a society in which human *individuals* care and provide for *each other*, and insurance is unnecessary. In a sense the effect would be almost the same in that most are already protected from loss, but many can't afford to be. The main point is that we would have gone over to moral concepts, reducing our dependence on the Machine and our vulnerability to its dangerous inhumanities. We would also have reduced human anxiety, eroding part of its cause by cutting out one of its financial symptoms - the complex commercial administration of insurance and its professional competitive profit-making activities.

Realising how it will be to live in a humantrue future, and wishing to prepare ourselves for it we can, now, take every opportunity to practice what then will have become human nature. We can resist the coldly, economically calculated automatic way of doing all things. Take building, for instance. By giving our own labour, taking materials locally to hand and using basic human skills, we can by-pass economic constrictions of the money sort, build as we truly need, and give our buildings human character and scale.

Government in Britain presently forbids independent freedom to build, through its planning controls. But planning authorities are broadly institutions of human reaction, formed primarily to control reckless automatic development. This being so it can be expected that growing supraconscious awareness will the more readily percolate those authorities so that they come down in favour of free, independent but thoughtful community building.

Given time, this awareness must surely percolate *all* institutions. The humantrue individuals who are also manufacturers, and employers, will also reduce their personal needs and wants, but they are in a position to go further. They will be able not only to resist but also to refuse to promote the concepts that help create the temptations of the Machine. They can resolutely turn away from the lore of supply and demand and towards the humantrue principles. They can ignore the money-economic dictates that normally automatically decide what they will make, and how it will be made, presented and sold. Instead they will work for, and in, the best interests of whole humanity, relying on support from the many individuals like themselves.

Humantrue manufacturers will refuse to make, or go on making any inhuman product, if need be converting their factories to a better purpose. Although, for the present, they may be producing things that are not strictly humanly necessary, they will not make a bad product. They will not needlessly process, adulterate or refine, package or present their goods. They will on no account advertise, nor will they replace human labour with machinery on grounds of money cost alone. They will not compete, and will cooperate with other humantrue manufacturers in making their similar products available in the most truly economical way. They will put themselves on the same level as all others working with them, and all will be paid the same fair wage.

Such manufacturers will be unlikely to survive commercially in this existing reality. But they will be enabled to do so by the combined support of every individual also working to prepare the way for the humantrue alternative reality. By the same means, the sudden drastic effects of mass unemployment will be avoided. These individuals will themselves spread the word about humantruly produced goods and help with their distribution wherever possible. They will, wherever practicable, go without rather than buy anything else - anything which is advertised, needlessly tampered with or shown off and will not allow lower cost to tempt them. Wherever needed, humantrue individuals will be willing to work hard for any production process, and to accept the standard fair wage regardless of the job done.

In this spirit, although the framework of automatic reality still exists, more and more of us shall pull away from its concepts and cease pushing them to their lawful limits and beyond. Some of us might set up manufacturing units on humantrue principles, but it is to be hoped that the humantrue ideal will blossom within existing companies. We will give our services honestly according to need, and take money for them only as we need it. To those who have little or nothing we will charge little or nothing. Why should we conform to the automatic ethos? Humantruly aware company directors who are living on less might well abandon the profit motive. Shareholders who can do without them might forego their dividends. Banks and other moneylenders may make a distinction between humantrue and purely automatic activities, raising the rate of interest charged for the latter but reducing it, or writing off loans, or *giving* money for the former.

The humantrue individual will regard the holding of stocks and shares as immoral, because it is an automatic practice of the false, competitive money economy. But supraconscious shareholders who sell their shares will thereby sustain the Machine, not only by keeping the money value but also by enabling the shareholding to be maintained in other, automated hands. Let them donate their stocks and shares to a reform movement that could then exert its shareholding power to good purpose. Where a company is acting contrary to humantrue interests it might then be obliged to mend its ways or even forced into liquidation. This will be simple and direct action against the Machine, quite unlike getting bogged down in politics. It will do human harm only to the financial interests of automated shareholders who could not be said really to suffer in consequence.

That such things rarely happen - that we would presently describe them as miracles - is not only because of self-interest or greed, or what automated mankind sees as prudence. It is also because automatic advantages allow some of us to raise ourselves above the rough and tumble of the Machine and so to cherish and preserve certain limited forms of emotional and intellectual sensitivity like poetry, or delicacy of manner. Most of us, lacking these advantages, have our senses dulled and crushed, and some become insensitive, or rough and violent. Divided by these artificial differences we distrust, despise, avoid or clash with each other. Only by each reaching for the same middle ground of humantrue intellectual understanding, and meeting on equal terms of emotional sensitivity thereby, can we agree and cooperate.

In Chapter 8 I cited a soldier, a priest, an economist and a terrorist as examples of automatic conditioning and victims of the Machine whose characters changed when they became supraconscious and were re-motivated by true morality. It may appear impossible that such as they could so radically change despite resistant pressure from the norm. But when supraconsciousness is spreading widely their conversion will reflect a general retreat from the automatic norm. As they give up their automatic functions, the Machine and its need of those functions will correspondingly diminish. Humantrue belief will become increasingly possible as humantrue practices become more common.

While existing reality persists, however, the quality of life as we presently conceive it depends largely on our individual value to the Machine, the status it gives us, the amount of money it pays us. In the light of this concept, to be unemployed is to be relegated to the lowest quality of automated life. This current fact strongly deters humanity from allowing itself even to entertain the possibility of an alternative humantrue concept. And even if we do individually accept that alternative concept in principle, we may be still unwilling to put it into practice by taking a reduction in income or voluntarily giving up our job on moral grounds. We may be unable to tear ourselves free of ingrained automatic lore which says it is not only naive and foolish to make such sacrifices but that if we are so unworldly-wise as to make them others will not follow suit. It is necessary that humantrue individuals *unitedly undertake* to put their agreed principles into practice, in order to help and encourage each other by making that practice their common aim, and in order to cooperate in making good the consequences.

Trade unions exist to protect the interests of their membership, particularly the unskilled manual workers who are the lowest units in the Machine's economic calculations, who traditionally receive its least rewards and who are first to suffer when its prosperity declines, and who have most needed to unite against it. Not only this, but the unions are deeply concerned to eradicate *all* deprivation and underprivilege. Ideally they stand for equality and against war and other inhuman practices, meaning that in fundamental principle trade unions ought to be wholly opposed to the cause of their concerns - to the concept and lore of automatic reality. The great trade union movement, by undertaking to follow its true principles and reject the unworthy competitive practices into which it has been drawn, and so converting its power into a positive force against the Machine, would represent a strong surge of will for the humantrue alternative, and would be an already united means for making it good.

There is no good humantrue reason why unions should not vote that all wages and salaries be brought to the same adequate level, paid to all individuals of all ages. Nor that they should not join with all other humantrue individuals to insist that unemployment and social security benefits, and all retirements pensions, also be brought to that same equal adult level. They could proceed further, to the logical proposal that everybody be paid this same amount, whether or not classed as employed, including housewives, housefathers, and, in support of parents both combined and single, all children. This proposal, by removing material inequality, would also remove a root cause of conflict. It would also remove the competitive economic factor that persuades us to serve and maintain the Machine, and prevents us from abolishing it. The proposal would remove the financial obligation on any individual to work or serve contrary to conscience, and society would receive the product of only that labour it was prepared collectively to give. The money-economic argument is that society would then collapse, for we will only work for incentives - by competing for rewards. The humantrue argument is to the contrary - that automatic incentives persuade us to work against our human interests, whilst in this way we would work with a supraconscious will for our humantrue needs.

In money-economy terms there could be no valid objection to this scheme, provided that the levels of wages, benefits and pensions paid were so adjusted that their total precisely equalled the whole amount of money that our combined labours earned, once the whole cost of essential services had been deducted - in other words, that the Machine's books balanced. Again, the ultimate objective would be to get rid of such irrelevant financial calculations altogether. In the meantime the concepts of incentive, profit and taxation, which relate to competitive inequality, would already be on the way out.

Even so, whilst such a scheme would eradicate the most compelling reasons why we cling to this present reality, some solid obstacles remain. As long as the Machine holds its overall grip on our affairs it can retain legal financial claims on us that cannot be simply given up. An individual may, for instance, be buying his or her home on mortgage, and by accepting a reduction in income might be unable to meet the repayments. This is another deterrent, the fact that homes can be hard to come by in this reality, giving rise to the fear that if we do not play the Machine's game we shall lose the roof over our heads. It can be an extra hardship of unemployment that because of it we might be forced to sell our house, if we can, and, being now handicapped by poverty only the meanest of living conditions will be available to us, so adding to our degradation.

But it must be supposed that when events have reached a stage where very many of us have voluntarily exposed ourselves to such obstacles and hardships, those events will have been borne along on a wave of humantrue awareness that will have penetrated all walks and conditions of automated life. There shall be humantrue individuals in the hierarchies of government, industry, finance and, for example, building societies. Building societies are (or were, before many of them became banks) semi-public institutions with the obligation to help people obtain homes to live in. Let their executives and members act according to the spirit of their constitution, putting its human purpose before the burden of automatic restrictions. Where one individual cannot pay his mortgage interest let another voluntarily forego her investment interest, and the two be cancelled out. Let it go further - that investors relinquish claim to their capital altogether, and this money be used to cancel out the debts of struggling mortgagees.

This will be simply to alter the equation that building societies represent by taking away the money element in all respects except, for the time being, as a token. Instead of borrowing investor's money, on which interest is paid, and lending it to borrowers who gradually pay it back, with heavy interest, so that others can eventually borrow it in turn and also pay interest on it - instead of this, those who have money to spare will give it to others who need it to buy homes.

As the tide of humantruly aware cooperation goes on rising, such Machine-negative acts might progress further still. Individual owners who have been given houses in this way, or any other enlightened owners of houses, can now relinquish the notion of *possession* of them and see themselves simply as their needful occupants. They will declare the house to be of no money-value, never again to be sold. The unnecessary deeds of ownership can now be annotated to this effect, or torn up. When the occupants move home, rather than buy and sell they will merely exchange with other such occupants - the houses *and* most of their contents, regardless of any consideration but their respective equal needs of a place to live, and without having to pay solicitors' and estate agents' fees, or high costs of complete removal.

This practice will cancel opposite extremes of interest and emotion, from which presently grow contentions that have no place in humantruth - pride in possession of a home and calculations of its resale value, as against the anguish of being without one, or the fears of being dispossessed. As the practice spreads, automatic drives will give way to human interests in other respects. The money motive and income of bankers, solicitors and estate agents will decline to coincide with *their* humantrue willingness to retreat from the automatic norm and accept simpler living standards. In this way much wasted automated effort will be released and freely transferred to purely human concerns and genuinely useful cooperative work.

The main purpose of this book is to trace the path of intellation that inevitably ends in humantruth. So far this chapter has given just a few examples of the practical and possible ways of preparing for a humantrue reality which supraconscious intellation then suggests. If it nevertheless seems to you impossible to imagine that whole humanity will ever take them up, then you are tacitly admitting to the belief that the humantrue nature and state of human being, though it be our desired destiny, is not in our hands to achieve. This is clearly not true, but it arises from a part-truth - that we have not, nor ever had, the slightest hope of achieving that destiny through institutions of the Machine, ie whilst still pursuing automatic drives in the opposite direction.

Every weekday the leading newspapers of the world portray and reflect the various interrelated facets of automatic reality with authoritative certainty and almost absolute credence. Those who share this belief in the unalterable inevitability of the here and now are demonstrating that a wilfully closed mind, which fails to see that the roots of its reality are false, can invest the complex artificial reality that grows from these roots with its own construction of specious truth.

It is here assumed that you, on the other hand, have fully embraced humantruth, that you recognise our existing reality as false, that you believe we *can* independently achieve the ideal alternative society despite the Machine, and that you are likely to discover many more ways of preparing for it than I have put forward.

———————————

The best that national leaderships have been able to do, to try and express or give effect to conscientious humanitarian wishes that the inhuman results of automatic conflicts be counteracted, was to form the United Nations Organisation which, for obvious reasons, has been unsatisfactory. Voluntary groups and campaigns have been more successful, if limited, in supporting our struggle against inhumanity.

Some twenty-five years ago Green Peace came into being, as a refreshing and welcome focus of growing awareness. Because of the dedicated determination and courage of its members it has been able to reveal practices that demonstrate the gulf between our humanity and the established Machine, beginning with the beating to death of baby seals and whale hunting. Such revelations appeal to the sentiments, the more strongly because of the adventurous ways in which the evidence is gathered and presented to the world, and because to most people these events occur far from home and do not involve self-criticism or affect personal interest. Equally inhuman practices occur in the local abattoir, or hen battery, or even the farm where the mother cow is separated from her calf so that we can have her milk, but we are not so outraged because our own jobs or profits may be involved, or because we like to eat red meat, and cheap chickens, and must have our cow's milk.

But Green Peace has also resisted the madness of nuclear war, by trying to stop a bomb test in the Pacific. It has also been at the forefront in disclosing how the Machine is damaging Earth by the dumping of toxic wastes into the sea, causing acid rain and contributing to the 'greenhouse effect'. People have responded to these protests, worldwide. And so have officials, for although Green Peace's 'positive non-violent actions' have been frowned upon and resisted by the establishment, and are sometimes unlawful, they have often been effective in obliging governments to back down, and nowhere has Green Peace been outlawed as an organisation. That human individuals, private or in office, *do* respond demonstrates what has already been said - that underlying the support which our outer shells give to the Machine is our innate and genuinely intellectual sense of humantruth.

Green Peace and several other independent organisations such as The Campaign for Nuclear Disarmament and Friends of the Earth, have become identified with a general Green movement that reflects growing criticism of automatic reality, especially amongst the young. Out of it the Green Party has emerged onto the political scene. It might be thought that all these factions of one concerted movement will be enough to bring us to supraconsciousness - that it is unnecessary for me to propose yet another reformist movement when the Greens already have the bit between their teeth. But the objective of my concern is the pursuit of intellation to the ultimate humantrue conclusions of supraconscious awareness. This, too, depends upon and gains strength from its utter independence of the automaton, but it must also stand back from the concepts and practices of the entire Machine, with the object of getting the *whole* of existing reality into proper perspective.

Any enlightened individual has to applaud the Green Movement in general and would hesitate to criticise it. But the truth is that none of its factions goes deep enough. To fully and uncritically subscribe to them, one really has to accept and adopt their specific aims *emotionally*, like a religious faith, against the background of present reality, and only then to *apply* the intellect to those aims. As with CND, so with Green Peace - what happens if and when they achieve all their realistic aims? We would be left with a society which partially knew what not to do in the name of humanity, but with no new and better ways to follow or methods to adopt; only those which it had always pursued and employed - ways and methods which brought about those inhuman practices in the first place and would surely bring them about again. For example, Cruise missiles were excluded from the Greenham Common protest site, but the kind of conflict that causes them to be produced, and elsewhere deployed, remains.

Individuals who wilfully contain the bulk of their thinking within existing constructions of mind, tied to existing reality, cannot admit ultimate humantruths and normally regard them as unrealistically extreme. The Green Party, presumably realising this, has entered politics seemingly believing that only by this realistic way can progress be made. But whilst its aims and intentions are most encouraging, the likelihood is that this party will become bogged down in the treacherous path it has chosen to take - confused, divided and lost through being forced to make compromises with the Machine, with economic reality, and with existing political postures. Humantrue reform, on the other hand, would be a movement devoted first to intellation, before action - to individuals seeking fully to *know* humantruth, progressively *declining* to act and think in automatic ways, finally reaching worldwide humantrue agreement and only *then* positively acting - in voluntary, cooperative unity.

Nevertheless, it would seem that the growth and progress of humantruth needs both kinds of movement - such as humantrue unity to establish in our minds that humantrue reality is our ultimate aim, and the Green movement in general to stimulate our awareness of that vital aim and to battle, both in the field and politically, to deal with some exceptional obstacles to that aim which are most powerfully upheld by automatic reality - such as the power of market forces to defeat morality in practical ways - but the two movements remaining separate in the sense that our minds are separate from our bodies. This is not to belittle the Green movement, whose stated aims are humane. It is to distinguish between action and intellation, for until the former results from widespread supraconscious fulfilment of the latter our actions may easily lead us astray and fail to achieve a wholly humantrue objective. If we choose to take action towards that objective we should remember that the end we seek *is* humantruth, which constrains the means we may use to achieve it. The means must not acquire first importance in our minds so as to obscure the humantrue end. Reckless or compromising means can never serve humantruth, any more than deceit and violence has done in the past.

The presently accepted principle of separate, ultimately independent nations is a serious obstacle to humantruth. As a potentially big step towards world unity a humantruth movement might adopt a national and international code of behaviour. Massive support could result in this being imposed on governments by referendum. Each government would have to agree to submit to interference from all others in any of its internal and external affairs coming under the code; that all proposed measures or actions affected by the code shall be subject to public vote, either through parliament or directly where no parliament exists, both in the country directly concerned and in all other countries; that any government which refuses to submit to this code and practice shall have the strictest world-wide sanctions imposed upon it, which every individual has the right and duty to carry out short of causing actual suffering to its people; and that any government which subsequently breaks with the code forfeits the willing support and lawful duty of its own people, of all humantrue individuals worldwide, and again faces the strictest non-violent sanctions.

This code of international behaviour would, initially, be quite simple, concerned with preventing the most dangerous and clearly inhuman practices of the Machine. Its aims would be to have some of the same constraints applied to nations as are ordinarily applied to individuals, and such as presently ensure the relatively peaceful co-existence of countries of the British Commonwealth, the states of Switzerland, the states of the USA, and now the countries of the European Community.

The code would really amount to a body of human law which overrode national law, making it illegal for heads of government or leaders to order military action in the name of the people, and rightful, indeed obligatory, for individuals to refuse conscription. The same would apply to any corruption or oppression on the part of any authority. This could eliminate terrorism, by giving victims of internal injustice a real opportunity to express their grievance externally and have it justly acted upon, rather than having to resort to violent protest.

Provisions of the code might be: that no government which disrespects or contravenes the code shall take or retain office; that no government shall use aggression or fail to observe 'human rights' as presently conceived; that no government shall maintain an army, nor manufacture or use arms excepting the minimum temporarily necessary to keep internal order; that none shall hold or manufacture nuclear weapons, *without exception;* that no individual shall, or shall be required to, use violence against any other, to take any loyal oath, to wear military uniform, carry arms, or take part in the manufacture, sale or siting of weapons, nor that he or she shall take up arms excepting temporarily, where humanly necessary, unavoidable, and morally defensible. The ultimate object will be to destroy all weapons of war, when this ban will be total. No authority, or group of authorities, shall be allowed to adopt any measure, or make any decision, for any reason, which can be shown to be against the interests of humanity at large, and no individual shall take or support such decisions or measures against the code, or against her or his conscience. In the interest of individual influence over authority, and in connection with the introduction of a world language, no government may restrict or censor the free flow of individual communication throughout the world, or keep its own doings secret. That a government has popular support does not permit it to break the code, nor affect the duty of all individuals of other nations, and their present governments, to restrain it and its people from doing so.

I have suggested already that newspapers will hardly be necessary in a settled humantrue reality, for 'no news is good news'. If a present function of newspapers is to entertain, this can only be necessary as a counterbalance to the horrors of its news function - two extremes of a false reality that will no longer apply when it is superseded. Towards this end it could be made a present rule that all newspapers must be run as non-profit concerns, with editorial boards drawn from the general public, like juries, but adhering to an agreed general code and spirit of practice. Newspapers will then be freely open to the contribution of responsible articles by everybody and anybody.

That radical proposals should be adopted, and honoured so that humantrue reforms actually take place, may still seem fantastic to we who are today grimly attached to a very different reality. Yet nobody wants inhumanities, particularly wars. This being so, is it not more amazingly fantastic that they nevertheless occur? The competitive Machine gives cause for wars, governments declare them, and we fight them. As has been said before, if we decline to fight there can be no wars. Where governments are supposed to be responsible to humanity, they must respond to responsible humanity. Where they are not so they can surely be made so in response to worldwide humane pressure. When humanity is fully aware of itself, and taking humantrue responsibility for itself, there can be no inhumanity. That is not fantastic, but utterly sensible.

Of course, humanity is not fundamentally amoral or immoral, nor is our reality wholly so. Humanity's fault is that it does not subject its way of life to its morally aware intellect, but rather subjects its morals, and its intellect, to the exigencies of automatic reality. If it were true that mankind could oppose the existing concept of reality, and its effects, only through the political and diplomatic channels of the Machine, on its own time-honoured terms of competitive conflict, contrived manipulation and duplicity, then we would be condemned already to an automatic future, whatever it might be - irretrievably automated, with no hope of realising our true humanity.

It is true that some humane moral advance is made by political means, and that new initiatives by Socialist and Green Parties may achieve further successes by these means. But we cannot depend upon political victories of this kind to make humantrue progress. Political progress has inbuilt automatic limitations which so clog it up and slow it down as to ensure that it can neither challenge nor outstrip autoprogression. If we do not accelerate the growth of our intellectual awareness, automatic reality will bring us to impotence or disaster before we fully achieve that awareness. The spread of humantruth is also likely to be slow, to begin with. It is to be hoped that reformist movements will so sharpen our doubts, questions and criticisms of the Machine as to slow down its autoprogression too, and to altogether halt its most insane and dangerous activities. In this way time will be gained for intellation to open the floodgates of awareness, and so accelerate humantrue progress as to overtake and overcome the Machine.

The human world is ruled by the Machine. All main actions presently decided by humans are determined for them by automatic considerations. So all predominant human activity is automated, perpetuating the Machine and so determining that all future action will also be chiefly automatic. Always remember the reason: that hardly any human beings are represented by their higher postconscious minds - few have risen to their true state of supraconsciousness but remain in the lesser though realistic conscious state, still falling short of responsible awareness which is their potential humantrue fulfilment.

During the recent past our enormous fears concerning nuclear energy - both the threat of nuclear holocaust and the dangers inherent in nuclear power - have receded. But they haven't gone away from the prosperous North and are poised to re-emerge in developing countries elsewhere. Therefore I am reproducing a slightly edited version of my original comments dated 1990.

Human protest against nuclear fission began with the atom bomb, then spread to the growing practice of harnessing the huge forces involved to the generation of electricity, partly because this process also produces plutonium for weapons. The danger from nuclear power stations, barring accidents, comes chiefly from the low-level radiation escaping from the process itself and given off by waste products. Nuclear weapons are designed to explode, of course, as they did on Japan in 1945 and in many test trials since, producing more devastating high-level radiation.

Pressures to proceed with nuclear energy came as a matter of course from the Machine and our heavy demand for electricity. Protest against the nuclear policy has been largely concerned with public distrust of automatic institutions and vested interests of the money economy, a distrust that is surely well founded. (As a related example, I can remember a prominent, titled scientist, some thirty years or so ago, solemnly stating on television that there was no truth in the allegation that smoking tobacco was connected with lung cancer.) There is a long history of workers being employed for profit but to the detriment of their health. Supporters of nuclear power stations declare that these are safer than coal-fired stations (and many common activities of everyday life). Doubters of all official pronouncements are not encouraged to believe this declaration by the thought that those coal-fired stations have been pouring poisonous fumes and carbon dioxide into the atmosphere for years, without official concern. Looking at the worldwide situation they see that some governments are now taking steps, some half-heartedly, to scrub clean a small overall proportion of these effluents - can they believe whole-heartedly the assurances of their own governments on nuclear safety?

The case in favour of nuclear energy is an automatic argument based on the continuing existence of the Machine. This argument maintains that nuclear fission is the only viable source of energy to replace our fast-dwindling supplies of coal, oil and gas; that the alternative sources of wind, tide and gravity are insufficient, and the large amount of energy coming to us from the sun presents too many problems of collection and storage, not to mention the political difficulties of distribution from the equator towards the poles, of crossing national borders, and the problems of money-payment.

The argument goes on to point out that nuclear fission is the one available, proven workable technique for producing ample energy that, if handled properly, could meet our needs for many tens of thousands of years. If we do not develop nuclear power sufficiently, so that when fossil fuels run out we have nothing adequate to take their place, the international struggle for energy will be catastrophic. These arguments are limited but true as far as they go, and weigh heavily with automated realists, even though plans to build further nuclear power stations in USA, UK and elsewhere have long been abandoned in face of public hostility.

It is predictable that the authoritative establishment should be in favour of nuclear fission because, apart from its military significance, the mathematical origin and the scientifically and technologically advanced complexity of nuclear development make it a logical forward step in autoprogression. To harness the sun, wind, or tide appears, by contrast, as a backward step in its renewed sympathy with the natural scale of things.

There is another argument in favour of nuclear energy which relates to values of the money economy, assuming that nuclear electricity will become cheaper than at present. The present high cost of energy makes it uneconomic, in money terms, to smelt metals excepting from high-grade ores, and deposits of high-grade ores are running out. Eventually, and especially if we run short of energy, a shortage of metals will bring another crisis. Ample supplies of energy will avert this crisis by enabling us to extract metals from our huge resources of low-grade ores. Even if nuclear electricity does not prove cheap in money terms, it is argued that it will be better to have high-cost metals in plenty than no metals at any cost.

The proponents of nuclear energy maintain that it is relatively safe - that if kept under control, as it can be in theory, nuclear fission presents no unacceptable risk to life. For example :

1. *Acceptable levels of radiation* - they say our exposure to natural radio-activity from rocks, buildings etc. is about 1/10 rem per year, but our bodies are good at repairing cell damage from sudden exposure up to 10 rem., capable of repair after exposure to up to 100 rem., but will suffer more serious injury above that level, and on sudden exposure to 400 rem. or more, the individual will die. The limit for power station workers is set at 5 rem. per year. This is equivalent to one fairly stiff X-ray examination, whereas a full range of all possible X-rays exposes the patient to about 25 rem. All this implies that once this low-level radiation has been repaired it is finished with - that there are no subsidiary or accumulative ill-effects such as cancers from radiation under 5 rem. per year, and that in the

normal course of events nobody would receive a higher dose than this, and the majority would be exposed to very much less.

2. *Comparative risks* - it is said that statistics prove the death rate among workers in the nuclear industry to be very considerably lower than that among workers in many other industries: that the risks to life from road-accidents, smoking, air pollution, toxic chemical wastes, obesity and coal mining are much higher than those from nuclear power plants.

(Note: Information given in 1 and 2 above was extracted from *Energy or Extinction* by Fred Hoyle. I have retained the rem. as a unit of measurement of radiation, notwithstanding that it is perhaps outdated, because it conveniently serves the required purpose of comparison).

The proponents of nuclear energy feel that their case is well supported by scientific and economic factual logic, and that the anti-nuclear protest derives from unstable emotion and rests on ignorance.

Normal grounds for protest. To anti-nuclear protestors it is the proponents of nuclear energy who are prejudiced - against humanity, to the extent that they support the Machine that has never represented our true humanity, so that they make light of nuclear dangers, and of the benign alternative sources of energy.

The basis of protest is no doubt that the horror and dismay which practically everybody has felt, and to a lesser extent still feels at the prospect of nuclear war has carried over into deeply concerned opposition to nuclear energy. It is reasonable to suspect that automated governments who are prepared to risk nuclear war would not balk at the radiation risks of peacetime nuclear reactors. The difficulty is to know how far nuclear protest reasonably fits factual truth and probability. There is no question of the insanity of nuclear armament, the arguments in favour of which come from our present mad reality, not from our humanity. It is necessary to know the truth about nuclear power because it is imaginable that even a humantrue world could be faced with an energy crisis and be put under great strain. Very few individuals are fully conversant with all the known facts about the complex nuclear fission process, and pretty well all these specialist experts are members of the establishment. So protestors disbelieve them, if for no other reason than a justifiable distrust of authority, for it is normally the same authority which promotes nuclear power that maintains nuclear weapons. Those whom protestors prefer to believe are scientists from their own opposition ranks, but these may not have access to all information. nor the means to verify all the statistics which are made available to them. Even so, it is the protestors' argument that has until recently prevailed in the UK and USA.

It is to be expected, in a competitive reality which includes secrecy, espionage and diplomatic deceit that authorities, in their anxiety to press on with nuclear energy and especially when facing a fuel crisis, should wish to obscure information detrimental to their plans. They adopt the position that there are no serious grounds for opposition, so the onus is on protestors to prove otherwise. The serious fundamental concern of protestors is that nuclear fission presents dangers to ourselves and all present and future life on Earth, some of which dangers are known and some unknown. Protestors may adopt the position that this process is already proven too dangerous and should be abandoned, or that too much about its possible danger is yet undiscovered, and its utilisation should be postponed until proved acceptably safe, or otherwise.

A major problem which we were not thought to be facing honestly in 1988 is that the normal life of a reactor is likely to be about 30 years. At the end of its life each one has to be decommissioned. The money-cost of making each safe is likely to be 40% of the cost of a new plant. Spent fuel is more radioactive than the original uranium, and remains radioactive for about 3 million years. It has been estimated that a country like the UK would eventually need 100 nuclear power stations. This would mean that in 1000 years there would be 3300 fenced-off radioactive sites in Britain, the defunct reactors entombed in concrete which their 3m year radioactive life will long outlast, or dismantled and buried deep underground. If the whole world were to 'go nuclear' on the same scale, in time there would be a total of 10,000 power stations in operation. It is not likely that all these nuclear plants will always be maintained to the same, in any case sometimes unsatisfactory safety standards as are presently applied to the comparatively very few existing plants, under close public scrutiny. The risk of accident can be assessed when it is considered that, nevertheless, we have already experienced three major nuclear power plant disasters, or near-disasters, at Sellafield, 3-Mile Island, and Chernobyl. By the year 3000 there would be 330,000 highly radioactive defunct reactors throughout the world, their number increasing by 330 every year.

Protestors feel that nuclear fission is a deadly, insidious threat to life, especially to the unborn child, that this threat will grow and spread, and that it will increasingly affect the quality and freedom of life. The Irish Sea is already reputed to be the most radioactive sea in the world, due to Sellafield, and many people will not swim in it, go on the beaches, or eat the fish. Even if the general level of radiation is still not serious, cannot radioactive materials concentrate in pockets? It is not thought that radioactive waste can or will be monitored safely, especially as it increases over time. It is thought that insufficient consideration has been given to the question of safety, or eventual cost - that if a large nuclear programme is carried out worldwide it is unlikely ever to stop, and will represent an intolerable legacy for the future.

It is felt that with authoritative interests having been anchored in fossil fuel electricity, then heavily invested in nuclear energy, too little serious effort has been put into finding alternative sources relevant to the whole world, although effort is increasing. If the same degree of dedication were devoted to harnessing the sun's power, for example, as was put into developing the atom bomb, or space exploration, nuclear fission might well already be proven quite unnecessary. As an example of neglect, I understand that the British have continued to ignore the apparent fact that there is potential pump storage capacity in Scotland enough to take care of peak-time demands for electricity for the whole of the UK for some time to come, without need to build any new power stations of any kind. Pump storage is the use of unwanted night-time electric capacity to elevate water which then flows downhill during the day, running turbines which return a proportion of that electricity at the time it is wanted.

It is true that protestors can labour under misapprehensions - for instance, in thinking that radiation must go on increasing as nuclear waste accumulates. The half-life of radioactive material refers to the rate at which the nuclei of its atoms decay, therefore indicating not only how long it remains radioactive but also proportionately how intense that radiation is. Strontium 90, with a half-life of 20 years, is much more intensely radioactive than Technetium 99 with a half-life of 200,000 years. If one kilo of Sr90 is added to the waste stockpile per year, the maximum radiation from it would be reached in a calculated 30 years, and thereafter this same level would be maintained, for decline and addition of radioactivity would then balance. In the case of Tc99 it would take a calculated 300,000 years to reach that optimum level. So a 300,000 year stockpile of Tc99 would produce the same amount of radioactivity as 30 kilos of Sr90. The former would actually be less harmful because the latter's radiation is more energetic. If stockpiling were abruptly to cease, radiation would begin decreasing, but if it took 100 years for the radiation from Sr90 to virtually cease, Tc99 might take 1,000,000 years to become relatively harmless. Of course, because their half-life is a period during which radioactive decay decreases by half, these materials will never become completely non-radioactive. (The information in this paragraph was extracted from Energy or Extinction by Fred Hoyle.)

In this automatic reality, people normally adopt one side or the other in an argument, or conflict of interests, and then employ bias or prejudice to defend their own side and attack the other, and such polarised thinking has been one of the worst features of the nuclear debate. This applies to both sides in the argument, yet although the protest movement was originally largely emotional and often ill-informed, and has had the great weight of officialdom loaded against it, it has been very effective. In the USA, no nuclear power station has been built for eleven years to 1988; some cities have pronounced themselves nuclear-free, and even some countries have done so - New Zealand, Denmark and Wales. To me this implies that truths which lie behind the arguments, and that are obscured one way or another, nevertheless make themselves felt on the anti-nuclear side. For example, it is known that plutonium is carcinogenic, that it remains radioactive for a very long time; that it can pass through the human placenta into unborn embryos, and in this and other ways can be accumulated in the body. In Japan, deformed babies are still being born as a result of two nuclear bombs dropped over 50 years ago. Yet when plutonium was reported to have been found in dust on window cills in S.W. Scotland there was little concerned reaction. In a mind that seeks truth, these two isolated items of information give reason for suspecting the safety of nuclear energy, which official generalised assurances have not dispelled.

The crux of the nuclear argument is this. Even if the process of nuclear fission were proved to be potentially safe, the Machine is not safe for humanity. This is amply demonstrated by the fact that the Machine has developed nuclear power for war, the most dangerous application possible. The Machine cannot be trusted to develop and maintain nuclear energy processes safely, even if they are potentially safe. Humans harnessed to these processes cannot be trusted either, because they are bound by loyalties of employment and convinced by the money-economy's reasoning. This is borne out, for example, by the principle that necessary human travel could be almost entirely accident-free, but the present Machine consumer society imposes on us the maximum manufacture and sale of cars, and their optimum deployment on a vast network of roads, mostly at speed. Consequently, in the UK some 5000 deaths and many more crippling injuries occur every year. The Machine's irresponsibility in nuclear matters is demonstrated by a much-publicised attempt by Green Peace to close a pipe discharging slightly radioactive but voluminous effluent into the Irish Sea. This action resulted in a major improvement of waste-disposal methods at Sellafield - improvements which the authority there had not previously thought to be justified, or had not thought of at all, and which would not have been carried out otherwise.

I repeat, it will never be safe or satisfactory for humanity to cease from distrusting and opposing the Machine. Other, potentially dangerous developments continually come to light, for example genetic engineering in all its forms, in which the financial interests of the Machine and the motives of political authority are highly questionable. Our only safe course is to replace the Machine. Yet national decisions about nuclear energy have to be made now, in case of energy crises. But the Machine still exists and normally makes our big and small decisions for us. Therefore matters of human safety and well-being must be the subject of humantrue decision, reached freely and independently of the Machine. The making and carrying through of these vital decisions could be a vital function of humantrue reformist movements.

If the correct decision is to be reached it must be well-informed, and to conduct impartial research should also be a function of reformist movements. This should aim to determine both the safety of nuclear energy (for example many people, including myself are uncertain about the relationship between nuclear radiation, cell damage, and cancer), and the feasibility of alternative sources, particularly the sun. If this research is to be humantruly realistic it must refer to the needs of a humantrue society - not only for heat and light, but also for smelting metals and other vital manufacturing processes. So if the eventual decision on these matters is to be right it cannot be entrusted to automated humans but must be made by supraconscious minds.

Research is presently entrusted to automatic institutions. It measures its findings in terms of money costs and according to the projected requirements of continuing autoprogression, ie in the interests of the Machine rather than humanity. Those who conduct this research are normally employed by the Machine. They appear to take the view that since we already rely on means of energy generation that are dangerous to life we should accept a degree of risk, presently claimed to be low, from nuclear energy. The Machine's view is bound to be much influenced by its demand for weapon-making plutonium, and is not yet affected by the fact that the cost of electricity must rise in the future to cover the de-commissioning of power stations and the storage of waste.

The supraconscious view of nuclear energy cannot be separated from its dedication to a humantrue worldwide society. It must include the desire to remove all unnecessary dangers in order to reduce the tragedy of accidental death and deformity to the minimum. So its research shall be concerned not only with the question of nuclear safety but with all present unsafe industrial and other practices of all kinds: coal mining, coal and oil-burning power stations, toxic chemical manufacture, uranium mining. It shall also take account of the effect of having too much energy, on the effect on the countryside of mining huge quantities of low-grade ore, and of the growing number of sites for disposing of dangerous wastes of all kinds.

Remember that we, our nature and living state, are dominated by an automatic reality whose facts and concepts are not acceptable to true intellect. If this reality is to continue without fundamental change, then all protest is ultimately futile, for the Machine will achieve its targets, one way or another. Genuine reformist movements shall have humantrue society as their aim, to be achieved by finding true answers and solutions to all human questions and problems. Nuclear energy is just one area for research and intellation, and it is subject to the same humantrue principles as any other. Its use must be restricted to a level, if attainable, which is acceptable to world humanity, now and for the future. That must be binding, and we must adjust our mode of living accordingly. If the responsibly considered, wholly agreed decision of all humanity is to abandon nuclear energy altogether, then our society must be geared to that alternative level of energy consumption that could be produced safely. If this proves to be a significantly lower level than that necessary to the true fulfilment of all humanity, then we shall have to bend our minds and bodies to further developing known safe sources and to discovering new alternatives.

In the short space of time since originally writing the foregoing, money-investment in nuclear power has declined, not for moral reasons but, ironically, because it has proved to be prohibitively expensive in financial terms. This does not mean that the anti-nuclear argument can safely be forgotten, for nuclear power may yet be regarded as a viable option in countries with no other resources, either now or in the future. Nor does it mean that the arguments on this issue are no longer significant, for the fact has to be faced that if nuclear power had proved cheap in financial terms, no argument on safety grounds is likely to have prevailed against its widespread development.

The factors concerned with energy supply changed with the recent discovery of global warming evidently exacerbated by excessive greenhouse gases being pumped into the atmosphere largely due to, it appears, the burning of fossil fuels. This puts a different complexion on the use of nuclear power on the grounds that the admitted danger from radiation would be far less than the disastrous worldwide consequences of global warming. This is generally accepted, it seems, as a reasonable pricetag for sustaining our energy-rich lifestyle (whether actual or hoped for). This book's urgent proposal of a much simplified lifestyle, its energy consumption geared to natural and harmless sources, is not yet being seriously contemplated.

THE WRONG REALITY

Part VIII
FURTHER
ILLUMINATION

Chapter 49

THE FLAW IN OUR ACCEPTED, PHILOSOPHICAL MODE OF THOUGHT

During the process of completeing the first vesrsion of this book, I made a new discovery that revealed a flaw in our accepted, Philosophical mode of thought. This discovery could be a means of human awareness breaking through, because it clearly demonstrates that the Philosophical mode of argument - the same mode that we employ in all Machine affairs - is distorted thinking of the conscious mind, incapable of finding humantruth. I made this discovery the chief subject of an unpublished article entitled 'Taking Intuition On Trust; the necessary first principle of truly radical philosophy', ('intuition' meaning insight of unconscious origin, or internal knowing). Regrettably, the article was rejected by Metaphilosophy, an American journal which purports to be interested in such things.

The appropriate parts of my article relate to the following: In a paper entitled 'Can there be progress in philosophy?', (Metaphilosophy January 1987), Kai Neilsen suggested that established Philosophy (which I give a capital P) was redundant, and that we should return to the original concept of philosophy (with a small p) - 'the attempt to see things in a comprehensive way in an attempt to make sense of our lives.' Neilsen suggests that humanity urgently needs 'a holistic critical theory - a theory which sees, displays and explains how things hang together in a comprehensive way - which is in an integrated way a descriptive-explanatory social theory, an interpretive theory and is, as well, a normative critique.' In my article I agreed that this is what we need, and put forward the first edition of this book as just such an attempt. To begin an explanation of my discovery, and to relate it to Philosophy, let me return to the matter of the formation of human character, already discussed in Chapter 12 and elsewhere.

Imagine the overall human higher mind as consisting of two spheres. Figure 12 below shows one sphere as small, representing the conscious and containing, say, for argument's sake, 100 dots. The other sphere is large, representing the postconscious and containing 500 dots. The total of 600 dots is taken to represent optimum human knowledge. If all these dots, ie items of knowledge, were interconnected in every conceivable way, by every correlation of reason, the resultant awareness would be true, as far as that is possible taking into account the limitations of our knowledge. Although limited knowledge rules out awareness of whole universal truth, conclusions that were arrived at by exhaustive correlation of everything known about our world would constitute humantruth. If these 600 fully-correlated dots were optimum human understanding and were it shared by all, then this would be our humantruth and all would be agreed.

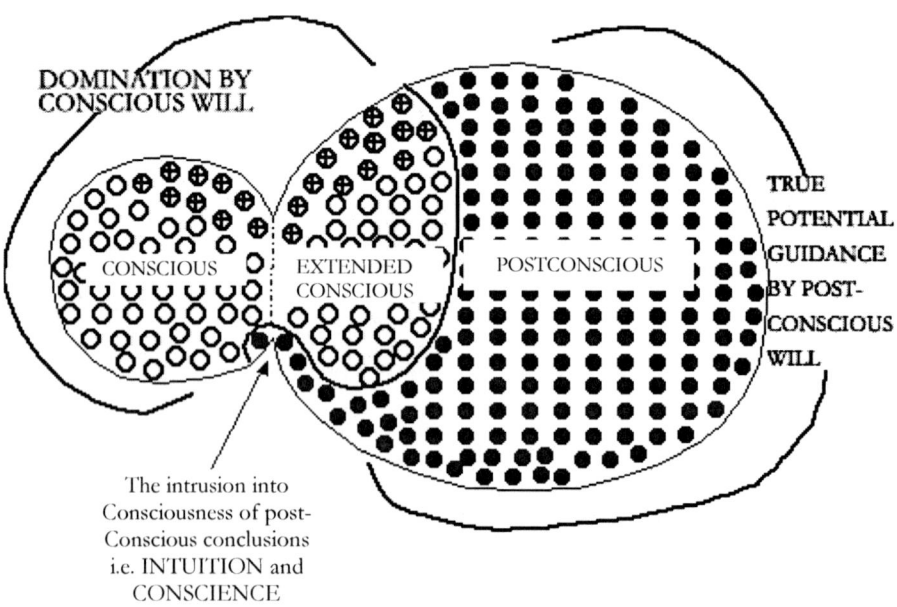

- ● = Free and Independent Postconscious Correlations and Conclusions
- ⊕ = Personally Self-Utilised Thoughts
- O = Self-Associated Thoughts

Figure 12

Note the curve which forms the boundary between the conscious and postconscious, the former's dominant will protruding into the latter, and the latter's intuition intruding on the former. As the pressure for change mounts, though the world goes on almost unchanging, the postconscious influence will grow until it suddenly engulfs the conscious, and change occurs spontaneously.

Suppose, however, that the dots in the small sphere were numbered from 1 to 100. Now suppose that the larger sphere is divided into two parts - a lesser part, which is commonly utilised by consciousness, and also contains 100 dots, numbered 101 to 200. The greater part, the postconscious, containing 400 dots, is independent of consciousness - ie unconscious. Imagine that one individual makes a preferred construction of thought (preferred because it suits his or her situation) of dots numbered 1 to 25 and 101 to 125, marked + in Figure 12. This construction would be the intellectual basis of that individual's character (this is to ignore that part of character determined by genetically inherited and learned emotional personality and temperament). Dots 26 to 100 and 126 to 200, representing knowledge which this individual recognises as part of the automatic reality but as being outside his or her preferred construction, would be interpreted according to that preferred construction's mode of thought. The remaining dots 201 to 600, unconsciously working to build a true construction of thought and trying to bring its influence to bear in the form of intuition, or conscience, is normally suppressed or ignored. Where the free postconscious succeeds in making itself felt, this is put down as wishful yearning, not to be taken seriously. The individual's mind is thus founded, then continually added to by thoughts aligned with its prevailing prejudice. In this way her or his necessarily biased and incomplete opinions and beliefs are formed. This biased mind is what the individual thinks with and acts upon. Within the limits of this falsely founded world no better external guide is made available for us to follow; better by virtue of being *truly* founded.

Now suppose that there are three other distinct individuals, with three extremely different constructions of thought, one consisting of dots 26-50 and 126-150, the second of dots 51-75 and 151-175, and the third of dots 76-100 and 176-200. We now have four separate individuals who have no evident intellectual characteristic in common, who in no way think alike about anything, and each of whose self-assertions threaten the other three so that all appear justified in forming themselves into groups and opposing, and defending themselves against, the rest. Of course, characters are never so sharply distinct. Their thoughts and opinions overlap and intermingle, and there are many more than 600 dots in the two spheres. But I think this example shows how the Machine's diverse interests and compulsions cause the majority of individuals to construct and defend their different and conflicting characters, beliefs and opinions.

We already know that humans are represented solely by their biological brains, that contain two minds – (i) the conscious, (ii) the whole postconscious (including its one-time consciously utilised part), *plus* the instinctive preconscious faculty which does not count as a mind. The postconscious is the unique mutation that has given us true intellectual potential. And the postconscious must be unconscious to the conscious self, with a language faculty intervening, for two reasons. Firstly, it is quite obvious that the postconscious - the neocortex of ten thousand million neurons on six levels - does not reason in language terms and so needs a clearinghouse in which its conclusions are converted into language and conveyed to the conscious. Secondly, there is a limit to the handling capacity of the conscious mind, almost continually bombarded, as it is, with information that has to be processed and acted upon rapidly and accurately. Consciousness is already protected from certain unnecessary interference by the fact that most motor functions are relegated to subconscious involuntary causation. It needs similar protection from the much more complex, lightning-fast processes of postconscious reasoning - that of unconsciousness of these processes (excepting for their concise conclusions), for if they were admitted to consciousness they would swamp it entirely and confuse it utterly.

Let me attempt to illustrate the complexity of the postconscious mind's processes, which carry out its reasoning. Imagine how the mind might reduce the many complications of one deeply significant problem to a conclusively true solution by the only possible means - exhaustive correlation:

LEVELS

1,000,000 correlations = 1st. interim conclusion

100,000 correlated 1st conclusions = One 2nd interim conclusion

10,000 correlated 2nd conclusions = One 3rd interim conclusion

1,000 -- correlated 3rd conclusions = One 4th interim conclusion

100 -----correlated 4th conclusions = One 5th interim conclusion

10 -------correlated 5th conclusions = One **final conclusion**

NOTE : The above table is not offered as proven fact but as a reasonable deduction and food for intellation. The same items may repeatedly take part in progressive correlations, whilst others are added and subtracted. Just one key correlation, among billions, if it is missing, can prevent the mind from reaching its final true conclusion. Truth prevails by way of its greater signal-strength. Only the conclusions at the 5th and 6th levels - the fourth, fifth and final conclusions - are likely to be available to the conscious, if it persists in seeking them (recently I have come across a holographic explanation of mind-working which may well replace my own vague concept of comparative signal-strengths, but the result is the same).

The complexity of these processes, going on in the depths of the independent postconscious, strikes a contrast with the calculations of the conscious mind, (even with the added capacity given to it by the mutation that also created the postconscious) which characterise the general thinking of a human society harnessed to the automaton. With automated thinking the true conclusions of the independent postconscious, instead of being embraced by the self as its proper mentor and guide, are denied by the existing self and replaced, on the instructions and urges of conscious will, by the Machine and associated influences contained within the conscious sphere. Our society claims to be highly intelligent, and to have advanced its thinking to elevated levels. There is no question of individual human high intelligence, but our mental activities have been so restricted and manipulated as to fall far short of the fulfilment of our intellectual potential.

For its high-level thinking, hopeful humanity used to look to its philosophers but they, failing to find humantruth through conscious argument and overlooking the postconscious as the source of humantruth, also formed yet another institution of the Machine, that of Philosophy, now long-established, with its own rules and codes, its own principles, and its gravely recorded history. Philosophers, too, have fallen in with the normal acquiescence - the general admission that the Machine, though it is not acceptable to our finer senses of true morality, is our actual and overwhelmingly existing reality which must be accepted and over which our true morality can never prevail. So Philosophy has become partly a forum for debating automatic issues with a view to orienting them a degree or two towards human interests, and away from automatic interests, but its main preoccupation is not the outcome of the debate but the actual rotary mechanism of its own brand of logical argument, with no real hope or intention of total humantrue reform.

Like other academic institutions, Philosophy has been made a subject of study. Part of its discipline (the whole of which constitutes Philosophy's conscious restriction and manipulation of thinking so that it, too, fails to fulfil the intellect's potential) is that all its current thinking must defer, or at least refer, to the works of the great Philosophers of history. Philosophy's already-established learning has to be assimilated by students and forms a major part of their growing mind-structure. The conscious mind has to take account of written arguments that represent the incomplete and contradictory conscious thinking of past minds, thinking which present postconscious minds will not take in because it does not make true sense. Were that thinking complete it must be unmistakably true, making the subject of Philosophy redundant. In any case truth, or humantruth, is the province of the postconscious mind, the self-evidently true product of intellation. It is beyond the conscious mind to comprehend and too infinitely complex to be captured in writing. The conclusions of postconscious minds, past and present, are not accepted or even considered by Philosophers because such conclusions are buried in unconsciousness and cannot be so presented, in writing and with the required evidence and proofs, as to be utterly and convincingly comprehended by the conscious mind. Such unsupported conclusions, commonly known as intuition and thought to be guesswork, were referred to by Kant, it seems, as vulgar assertions. It is quite evident that this intuition is much more deeply reasoned than conscious thought, but the latter is commonly preferred because its logic can be consciously followed and proven, as in mathematics for example. As a result, to a large degree students' minds have come to think by means of Philosophy's discipline and obligatory learning, rendering them unable to stand apart and judge truly. Studious thinking evidently comes to depend on that learned construction of the utilised postconscious without the free and independent postconscious being given the opportunity of addressing it critically. This commonly prevents individuals from becoming aware that to take this opportunity is vital to true understanding. It might even blind them to the fact that such an opportunity actually exists. So learning Philosophy, and any other formally instituted subject, is like running an obstacle course that the conscious mind, with the aid of the utilised postconscious, negotiates by contrived thinking.

The arguments of past Philosophers are kept alive partly because they cannot be refuted, partly because they are recognised as the permanent property of the persons, dead or living, to whom they first occurred. 'Doing' Philosophy can become a struggle to discover some new and irrefutable argument to which one's *own* name will be forever attached. But thought should be free of ownership. The value of a true conclusion should not accrue to its originator. Such a conclusion should be valued according to its place in the true construction of all other minds, minds which will make it part of the common humantruth that will unite them, the discoverer's name forgotten. This is not to suggest that in the future we should devalue past thinkers who reached certain truths, but should recognise that whole truth, to be true, must be so in all parts and certain parts, though relatively true, might not be a contributing part of the whole truth. It is our common responsibility to discover and realise humantruth, and that humantrue understanding is everybody's right.

When a mind studies Philosophy, absorbing consciously-managed thoughts expressed in language, particularly those conveyed by Philosophy's own specialised language, it is denying to its intellect the very much deeper and broader unconscious insight of the postconscious mind. For example, dualism and reductionism are Philosophical terms expressing differences of view which consciously-managed thinking can not reconcile (otherwise Philosophy would have no need of these distinctive terms). The resolution of these differences, by way of supraconsciousness, lies in the truth which, being true, does not recognise these terms as meaningful - cannot understand them because they denote *failure* to fully understand. The discipline of Philosophy accepts the irreconcilable differences between the concepts of dualism and reductionism because it accepts the limitations of conscious thinking that can neither dismiss nor irrefutably establish either concept. Both these concepts cannot be true. No postconscious could acknowledge any concept that is not true, nor allow that two concepts, one of which must be false, should co-exist. And if a concept is undoubtedly known to be absolutely true by one conscious mind, it must be true for all conscious minds. If a mind supraconsciously knows truly, even though it cannot describe the basis of its knowing, it also knows that the concepts of dualism and reductionism are not helpful and should not be taken seriously, for they are not necessary pathways to truth so much as different expressions of the same (conscious) mode of thought which *precludes* the discovery of truth.

The instituted academic discipline of Philosophy has set itself the huge and impossible task of understanding everything by relying on consciousness rather than supraconsciousness. That the task is impossible is indicated by the fact that Philosophers cannot even agree on first principles. It is this misuse of the mental process that has given intellect a bad name. It is common for the conscious self to contradict the truths known by its own postconscious. Failing to understand that the postconscious is a magnificent, ultimate thinking organism, and that the shortcomings of the human mental process lie not in the postconscious but in our conscious refusal to submit to it, the Machine is developing ultra-intelligent machines, or UIM's. If UIM's are perfected, in a world that remains automated, they will be in the same position as the postconscious. If we are allowed to listen to them it shall be because they have been preconditioned with conscious programming. If UIM's are allowed absolute freedom and independence, so that they both understand and insist upon truth, the Machine will not allow that they be listened to. Brain science is destined to reach the same position that Philosophy is trying to reach in that, should it come to comprehend the entire complex mechanism of the human brain, that which it seeks to know will still escape it, for this is the province of our own postconscious, necessarily unconscious to us but reaching our conscious minds by way of personal internal postconscious 'knowing', our only source of true understanding.

So human society, including Philosophy, exists on the conscious level where all accepted thought, all acknowledged debate, and all communication is confined to that which can be conveyed in language, written or spoken. Although our true minds occupy the higher postconscious level, Philosophical argument and all automatic thinking is under conscious control which prevents it reaching out to embrace this postconscious level. And yet, paradoxically, the discipline of Philosophy accepts automatic reality - the

Machine - because it is a discipline dedicated to evident truth. Philosophy confines itself to conscious thinking by pre-determining the *means* of discovering truth - *that only demonstrably irrefutable evidence and argument is to be recognised as true*, argument that must be expressed in language in order to be demonstrable to others. This, fundamentally, is the flaw in our accepted, Philosophical mode of thought. It means that the facts of automatic reality - the basic fabric of the Machine as the framework of world society - must be accepted because they are presently irrefutably factual. It also means that such argument may forever pursue endless possibilities, because no moral proposition can ever be proven true at the conscious level, only at the postconscious level. Consciousness may 'know' such a truth, but only by accepting the postconscious's certainty (founded in unconsciousness) that it is true. Any consciously-reasoned opinion or belief can be upheld (though without postconscious foundation), even though it cannot be irrefutably proven, because similar reason cannot disprove it either. Given these circumstances, Philosophers might well feel that all they can do is tackle the monumental and impossible task entrusted to them by their institution. The Philosophical kind of thinking, though it ransacks the conscious reasoning capacity of some brilliant individuals to a mind-boggling extent, nevertheless goes round in circles from one incomplete part-truth to another.

To record the reasoning-processes of the postconscious, were this somehow possible, would be to write a huge number of volumes, of staggering complexity, which we could not possibly consciously understand. A super-computer, or UIM, might actually do the job one day, but we could not understand that either. The only way of being sure that mental processes we can not consciously follow are nevertheless known to be true is to have them take place unconsciously in our own postconscious minds. We have to recognise our true intuitive assertions because these are the conclusive truths that only the unconscious postconscious can verify. We have nothing to rely on but each individual's honesty of mind, whereby common patterns of postconsciously true reason aggregate to voluntary recognition of humantruth in common. The child mind, which is capable of substantially, and largely independently, mastering language in a mere three years, is also capable of discerning the essential elements of humantruth. For the next ten or fifteen years of the child's life the Machine proceeds to undermine, neutralise, abuse, and obscure this true perception. This has been the way since human civilisation began, so that the historical standards of rationality and objectivity are false guides. Ahistorical standards exist in the truths of the postconscious, truths which automated humanity loses through the conditioning of education and experience, generation after generation, but can rediscover by intellating. The principle of equality is an example of an ahistorical standard that we postconsciously know to be humantrue but which the Machine has consistently rejected throughout our history. This principle, and humantruth as a whole, can be opposed by myriads of arguments, for it is always possible to find conscious reasons for disagreement, but the dogged questioning, listening and re-questioning of the intellation process will eventually reveal the undoubted truths of the postconscious.

Chapter 50

HOW TO HUMANISE REALITY

In the previous chapter I referred to, and reproduced, an article of mine entitled 'Taking Intuition On Trust - the necessary first principle of truly radical philosophy', which was submitted to but rejected by the journal Metaphilosophy. Unwilling to let the matter end there I sent a copy of this paper to Kai Nielsen, to whose brilliant article in Metaphilosophy 'Can there be progress in philosophy' my effort was a direct response. That which motivated me in this direct approach to Nielsen was my conviction that individual thinkers should seek broad contact in order to begin the process of building agreement, and my belief that my book did present the holistic, critical, comprehensive social theory that he considers to be urgently needed.

After some weeks I received a brief reply from Nielsen : 'I have your manuscript. From a superficial skimming it looks interesting. But I have not read it with the care it no doubt deserves. You should understand that I get many, many manuscripts in one way or another. I can read only a fraction of them. But do try the journals to see if it can see the light'. To me, this could appear hilariously ridiculous were it not serious and really rather tragic. For once someone was far-seeing and courageous enough to state the human need for what is in effect *humantruth,* but neither he nor the journal that published him is prepared to take seriously, even to the extent of actually reading properly, a response claiming to know this humantruth. Their reasoning must be that only the disciplined thinking of prominent Philosophers is capable of discovering this truth, and it is known that none of them is anywhere near it, so Nielsen's question was raised without any answer being expected. Maybe he senses that the discipline of Philosophy, being confined to the conscious sphere, will *never* discover humantruth.

I have no *realistic* complaint about this, or against any of the many other individuals, journals, newspapers and publishers whom I have approached but from whom I have received polite, sometimes curt refusals, but it seems a sad fact that the most vital human questions are given such scant attention. Such individuals are contained within (and every journal etc. is an institution belonging to), some special narrowed discipline with its own busy preoccupations. These preoccupations preclude any outside thinking that is not confined to their own outlook and adopted bias. I have already given the discipline of Philosophy as an example. Let me give two further examples as follows.

Shortly after submitting my paper to Metaphilosophy I modified it slightly and sent it to Radical Philosophy, with the same negative response. I then decided to tackle two other major disciplines of thinking, science and mysticism. It seems to me strange that scientists, who do not normally claim that any thing is true unless it can be irrefutably proven, should allow that the decision as to what work they do and how far it shall go be largely dictated by a phenomenon which is neither an exact science nor has any truth about it which is irrefutable - competitive money-economics -(no irrefutable truth, that is, except the actual fact of its accepted existence). The journal New Scientist predictably displayed no interest in an article on these lines that I submitted, despite the fact that this subject is of vital importance to contemporary questions of energy, resources, pollution etc.

Next I approached The New Humanity, a journal that has gathered a following amongst those who feel that the achievement of a truly humane world is a matter of flowing with the good and gentle emotional desire for such a world. This following is united by this desire but otherwise consists of many different beliefs and opinions. Yet the journal has expressed the intention of making effective the movement it represents by entering the field of politics. Believing that agreement is vital, and that humantruth is the only possible basis of complete agreement, I submitted an article to The New Humanity making this point, also claiming that without a well-thought-out policy accepted by all its members the movement could not be effective in politics; that politics is not the way by which to achieve humantrue reform; and that just as agreement is vital to humantrue cooperation, intellation is necessary to agreement. This article was also rejected, also predictably, because to hold a following together on the basis of 'feeling' rather than truth it is necessary constantly to reason according to the former rather than the latter.

At about this time I heard a talk given by Noam Chomsky. This was the third in a series, entitled 'Opinions' and presented by British Channel 4 television. He bravely exposed the devious self-interested exercise of United States influences in South America. Noam Chomsky is Professor of Linguistics and Philosophy at Massachusetts Institute of Technology and is described as one of the USA's leading dissidents. This unusual combination of qualifications encouraged me to write to him, particularly as he is also listed as a consulting editor of Metaphilosophy.

I mention these events to further illustrate the present convention that thinkers specialise; that individuals have the right to hold whatever belief or opinion they choose; that the nearest we can approach to agreement is some sort of attempted compromise consensus; that we are entitled and expected to construct and defend our separate personal realities, and, basic to all this, that out reality and our thinking be confined to the conscious arena. Although Chomsky's thinking is admirably much broader and more courageous than most (make no mistake, the conscious field of thought, *because* it is spurious and inconclusive, is, like the game of chess, extremely complex but also impossible of resolution), his brief replies to my lengthy letters imply that he too is restricted by the rules of present convention.

That Chomsky replied to me at all does him credit, for it is usual for specialists to communicate only with other specialists, preferably in the same field. They are generally too preoccupied to bother with thinking that comes from outside their particular field because they are unable to believe that it can possibly have any true relevance. His first reply was generous in thinking that my article contained a great deal of insight and plausibility, but he added 'The contents are speculative, that is, not grounded in evidence and argument, apart from our intuitions about ourselves and the world in which we live. By and large, your intuitions conform to my own, and I am no better to ground them than you are'. I responded to the effect that the aim of my article (ie the gist of my previous Chapter 49) was to show that fundamental moral truth comes from the common human unconscious postconscious and *cannot* be grounded in evidence and argument which is not only limited to consciousness but can also be challenged and contradicted by other contentions which can also be grounded in conscious evidence and argument.

Chomsky's reply to this was : 'But in that case, there seems little point in discussing it, since discussion is limited to the arena of evidence and argument.' He also stated : 'We agree that the contents of your article are speculative.......'.

This impasse is the basic obstacle in the way of humanity completing its intellectual mutation and thus fulfilling itself. It is the same obstacle that has so far barred acceptance of the humantrue philosophy, and this book which espouses that philosophy. This obstacle consists mainly of a general refusal to recognise that the true essence of human being is the full product of the interactions between the neurons of the brain serving the mind in general; that most of these neurons, and consequently their interactions, are situated in the postconscious, and are consequently both free and independent and *unconscious;* and that, in order truly to agree, we need to entrust ourselves and our world to a common, humantrue awareness given to us by our millions of individual postconscious minds which essentially work as one.

There is, indeed, little point in discussing *anything* if that discussion is to be limited to the conscious arena of evidence and argument. Such has been all of our worldly discussion to date, and look at the result! I am well aware of the view that our first priority should be to tackle the real problems of the here and now, but we can't do it unless and until we are humantruly aware. Our present society represents a continual hopeless struggle to cure the symptoms of the automatic disease and failure to tackle its causes. The one objective of discussion ought to be the stimulation of intellation, and the function of intellation is, and can only be, truth and true agreement. The progress and completion of that mutation that made us homo sapiens, and the consequence of our possible fulfilment of it, as the one intellectual species and therefore the only fully responsible species on this Earth, is demonstrated by the following Figures 13a, 13b, and 13c :

In Figure 13a our *humanity* is represented by the conscious sphere and its foundation in instinct, but also by our moral awareness intuited from our postconscious mind by way of conscience. Our *reality* is represented by the conscious arena and the instinctive drives, and is generally supported and empowered by conscious will. The free and independent postconscious, the true representative of humanity and its potential reality, is largely ignored. Consequently our mental activity is almost entirely confined by the conscious arena and dominated by the Machine. Normal individuals ⊙ think accordingly and their 'truth' is that which is grounded in the facts of this limited reality and in the limited arguments of conscious reason. All the present thinking disciplines, such as Philosophy, science and politics, and all the controlling institutions such as money-economics, law, and government, are similarly limited but in separate fields so that they disagree and conflict. In the minds of all individuals ⊙ the arguments of existing reality are never resolved because they lack the true resources of the postconscious, the major part of the mind. Therefore individuals ⊙ cannot agree, for agreement depends upon recognition of the common humantruth which in turn depends upon supraconscious understanding.

In Figure 13b many individuals of the type ⊕ have appeared. These are individuals who have insisted that their own lesser conscious minds take on trust the findings of their superior postconscious minds. These individuals are thus supraconscious: guided by their postconscious minds. Their humantrue arguments are rejected by the traditional norm of restricted thinking because they are not grounded in, but go contrary to *its* evidence and argument. Yet the norm is losing ground because its automatic arguments are false, whereas an open mind cannot deny the common body of humantruth to which fully supraconscious reason must lead.

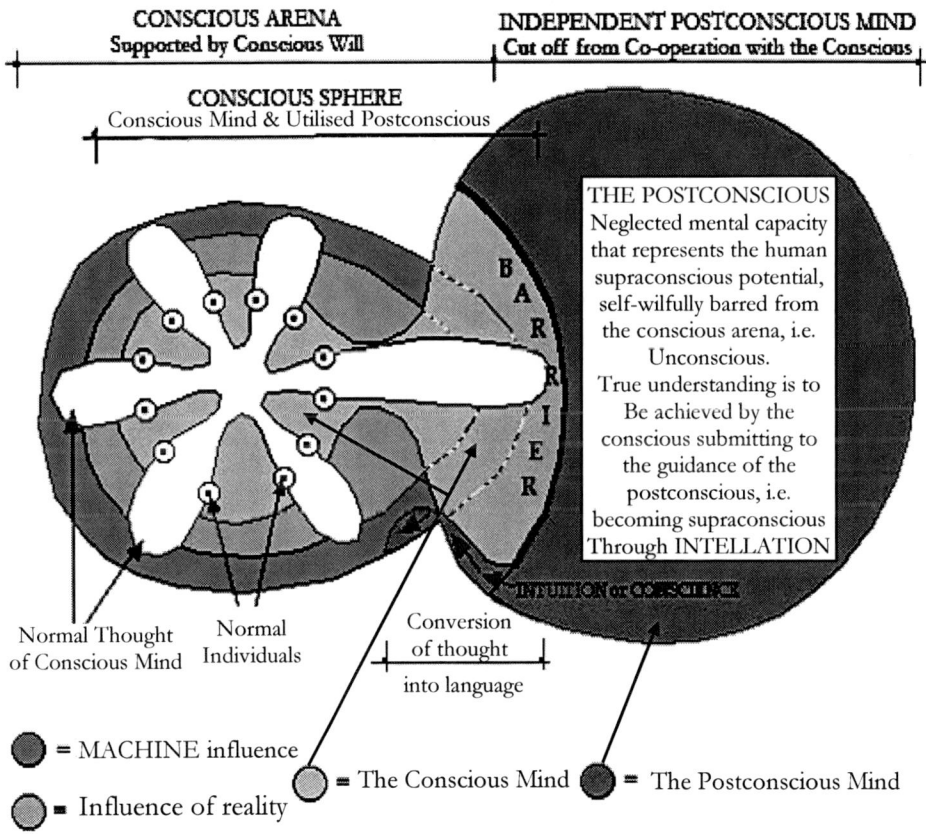

Figure 13a
The Present State of the Human Mind in Relation to Existing Reality

In Figure 13c supraconsciousness has won the day and a humantrue reality has been established. The great majority of individuals are ⊕. It would have been by their agreement that a new reality was introduced and by their responsible cooperation that it is now sustained. This humantrue reality became inevitable once the majority of individuals were ⊕ because it was unthinkable to them that they should continue under the domination of the false Machine, or that they should do other than ensure that their world would be made to accord with their true values.

My reason for adding these last chapters of Further Illumination is a growing awareness that the first step in the human transition - from 13a to 13b, and thence to the most difficult step of all, to 13c, - is to acknowledge the actual significant existence (without concrete proof) of the independent postconscious mind; that the postconscious is the true basis of our identity and the source of our unity. As soon as we understand this we must also immediately recognise that our present conscious orientation is false. We shall then have begun the vital humantrue transition.

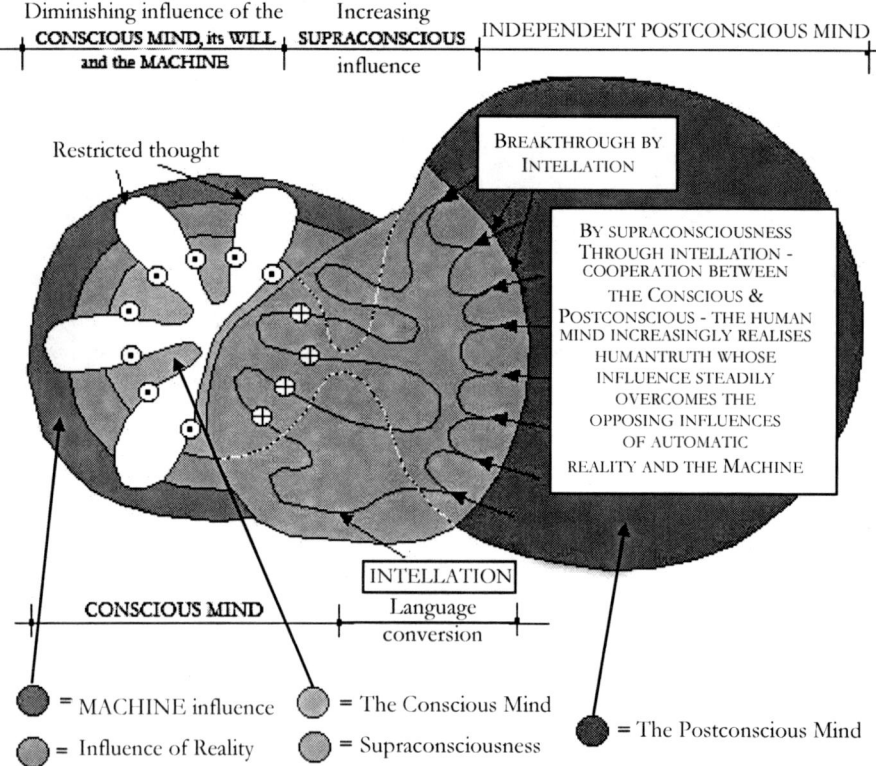

Figure 13b
The Progress of Conversion of the Human Mind and Reality from Consciously-Automated to Supraconscious

That which prevents our taking this first transitional step is the fact that our thinking, together with the actual affairs and concepts of our present wrong reality, are locked into the conscious arena and supported by conscious will. Our thinking is restricted to that which can be conveyed in language, and language is normally confined in scope to the facts, concepts, and limited reasoning of the conscious sphere. This is why our philosophical notion of truth is that it must be capable of being grounded in that which is materially evident or that which can be argued in language. This notion is presently almost entirely false because our existing world is false. In any case our understanding of truth might never be complete, even in a humantrue reality, because part of the whole truth, about the far universe and beyond, may never be available to us.

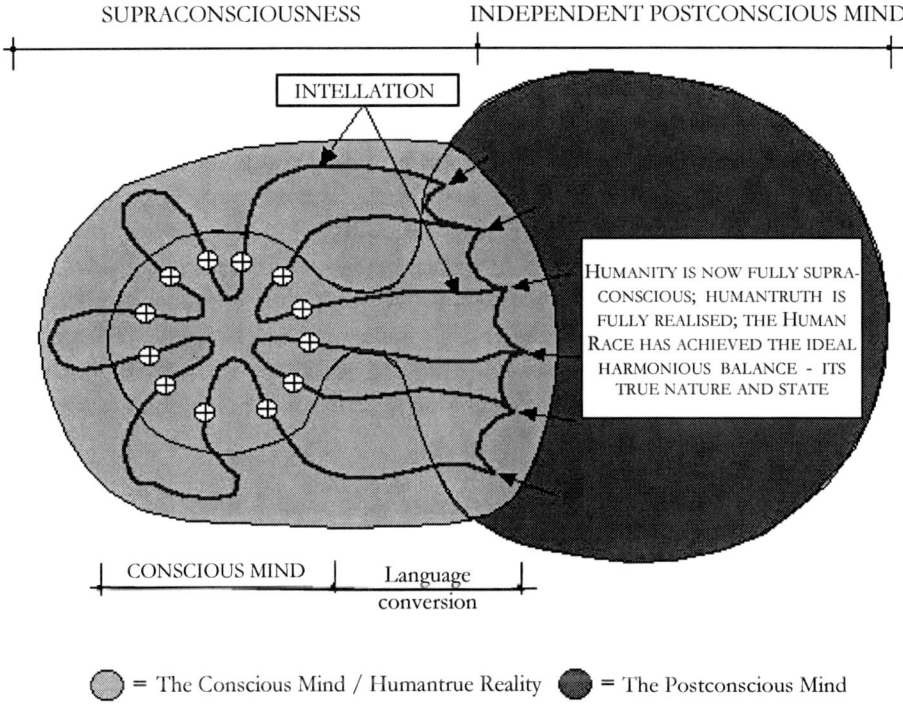

SUPRACONSCIOUSNESS   INDEPENDENT POSTCONSCIOUS MIND

INTELLATION

HUMANITY IS NOW FULLY SUPRA-
CONSCIOUS; HUMANTRUTH IS
FULLY REALISED; THE HUMAN
RACE HAS ACHIEVED THE IDEAL
HARMONIOUS BALANCE - ITS
TRUE NATURE AND STATE

CONSCIOUS MIND   Language
conversion

⬤ = The Conscious Mind / Humantrue Reality   ⬤ = The Postconscious Mind

Figure 13c
The Potential Supraconscious Nature of the Human Mind and the Humantrue
State Which is its Natural Outcome: the Completion of the Human Mutation

The problem of human reluctance to take this first transitional step to
supraconsciousness, because our thinking is presently so firmly founded in
and confined to relatively simple consciousness, is characterised by my
correspondence with Noam Chomsky and other recognised thinkers. Their
Philosophical discipline gives them an outlook, based on consciously-
contrived thinking, which, in the case of other thinkers, precludes all the
written extraneous thinking of non-members of 'the club' to the point of
refusing to read it properly. In the case of Chomsky, he did read the article I
had sent to him, but his discipline of mind (which is vital to the accurate
effectiveness of his courageous dissent from American foreign policy) would
not allow him to submit his conscious self to the vastly superior but
unconscious awareness of his own postconscious, i.e. to that which he
describes as his *intuitions* to which my intuitions conformed (and which, in
fact, provide the moral compulsion underlying his dissent). His discipline of
mind held him to that Philosophical (inferior conscious) law that a
proposition is true only if it can be grounded in evidence and argument. This
seems to indicate that many of us, like Chomsky, are already fundamentally
cognisant of humantruth but that our conscious awareness of this cognisance

is held back on the wrong side of a knife-edge of recognition, on the right side
of which lies the path of intellation and humantrue evolution. Humanity will
not cross that knife-edged divide because intuition is thought to be unreliable.
Intuition is judged unreliable because it cannot be accurately analysed and
understood, according to existing factual evidence and conscious argument,
in order to fit the existing concepts and facts of actual reality and thus to be
controllable by some form of authority. But the reverse is true, as
demonstrated by our existing false reality despite all its restrictive laws and
control regulations. Our reality is profoundly unworthy of our intuition, for
the latter arises from intellect whose ultimate function is truth, and whose
aim, a humantrue society, is our rightly desired destiny. And intuition, realised
by supraconsciously responsible individuals, is the only reliable guide for the
human race.

I am extremely sorry that in order to make this point I have had to criticise
Noam Chomsky whom I admire. But the important thing is to get the world
right and, whilst practically the whole human race has got it wrong, Chomsky
is one of the most likely people to lead it the right way.

The case for supraconsciousness can be demonstrated by a simple
mathematical comparison. The fact that intellect depends upon an electro-
chemical system of signalling should not be thought detrimental, by those
who prefer mysterious or spiritual explanations of the human self, any more
than that a flower is a purely practical reproductive mechanism should detract
from its beauty. To realise truth is the ultimate function of intellect, and we
know that the neocortex consists of numerous neurons, axons, dendrites and
synapses. We may suppose, by way of illustration, that the advance to truth
requires, say, one million correlations to produce one interim true conclusion
(see Chapter 49 table). By comparison the conscious faculty is limited in
scope to, say, 350,000 correlations as the basis of its conclusions. That is why
the truth cannot be arrived at by conscious evidence and argument - that plus
the fact that while the postconscious is free and independent, the conscious
is subject to manipulation by the wilful self. As a result of humanity's
restriction to the conscious arena we are frequently concerned, for example,
with criminal court proceedings. These proceedings are a matter of trying to
determine a very limited truth - whether the accused is guilty or innocent as
charged - according to narrowly relevant, conflicting evidence and argument.
The independent postconscious, on the other hand, would dismiss the
proceedings, and the concept of crime and punishment underlying them, as
irrelevant to humantruth. In a similar way, the game of chess can be truly
justified only according to its rules, and can be played well only by persons
whose thinking is geared to the aims and rules of chess. Even though the
postconscious might tolerantly recognise chess as a mere game, it could not
play that game well because it could not allow itself to be subjected to any

discipline other than truth. It has to be recognised that existing reality is made up of separate institutions, each with its limited aims, laws and rules, which, with our connivance, limit and utilise our minds much in the same way as the game of chess.

To return to my correspondence with Noam Chomsky and to his refusal to take intuition seriously by limiting himself to the rule of evidence and argument. Chomsky is doing what all his predecessors did, and this is the reason why he and they, in their writings if not in their private minds, have fallen short of truth. For instance, in an interview published in Radical Philosophy of Autumn 1989 he admits that he doesn't understand how children at the peak of language growth can learn approximately twelve substantive words per day. He sees it as extremely hard to understand how the child can suddenly pick up a word, and the complexity of even its basic meaning, in one shot. But this is not hard to understand when one accepts the concept of the postconscious mind, most of whose neurons and interconnections are, apparently, present and in working order by the age of two years. It is clear to me that the unconscious postconscious, stimulated by the child's determination to fulfil its need of all kinds of communication, compounds the significant meanings of words and eventually presents them to consciousness, complete with many of their interconnections with other words and with conscious reality.

I imagine that the actual formation of meanings into words is carried out in young children by that which will later be reduced to the utilised postconscious, in conjunction with a small conscious faculty that gradually increases in size. It seems to me that, in early childhood, the boundaries of conscious self-awareness are more narrow, and the area of unconscious mental activity is larger, to enable this language-learning to go on 'behind the scenes' at a time when our need for conscious awareness is at its least. As this learning process progresses, the frontier of consciousness will be brought forward to the extent of adult self-awareness - at the same time as the limits of the utilised postconscious are established - (see Figure 14a overleaf).

The earlier child-self is situated in consciousness, between its internal postconscious (together with the teaching area utilised by the postconscious) and the external world. The function of the postconscious is truth, as we know. In the beginning the postconscious is learning, and this represents the child's growing intellect. At the same time the conscious is learning how to react to the world outside, instinctively at first but then according to circumstances, to the evident need to relate to and survive in those circumstances, and to the interaction between itself and its postconscious. When the learning process begins, consciousness is limited and the self is open to postconscious teaching according to truth. The self begins by depending upon the postconscious to show it how to deal with, and communicate with, its actual reality. In a humantrue world this would be a straightforward matter of internal truth growing until it agreed with external truth. The child mind sets out with true intent, concentrating on the accurate learning, and honest usage, of language. But this process is very soon adulterated by the falseness of external reality. The postconscious may be misinformed, or denied information, so that it cannot learn, and so cannot teach, truth. The conscious self, having mastered such skill and accuracy in the use of language as the postconscious has had opportunity to learn and teach, having a certain conscious thinking capacity, and being faced with a false reality that demands competitive conformity for survival satisfaction, almost invariably chooses to turn its back on its own fundamental humantrue morality and throw in its lot with the Machine. At this point the independent postconscious puts up a barrier beyond which it will not allow the conscious will to extend its domination, and from behind which it attempts to exert true influence on the conscious self. On its side the conscious self reinforces this barrier to keep out that influence in its own assumed automatic interests.

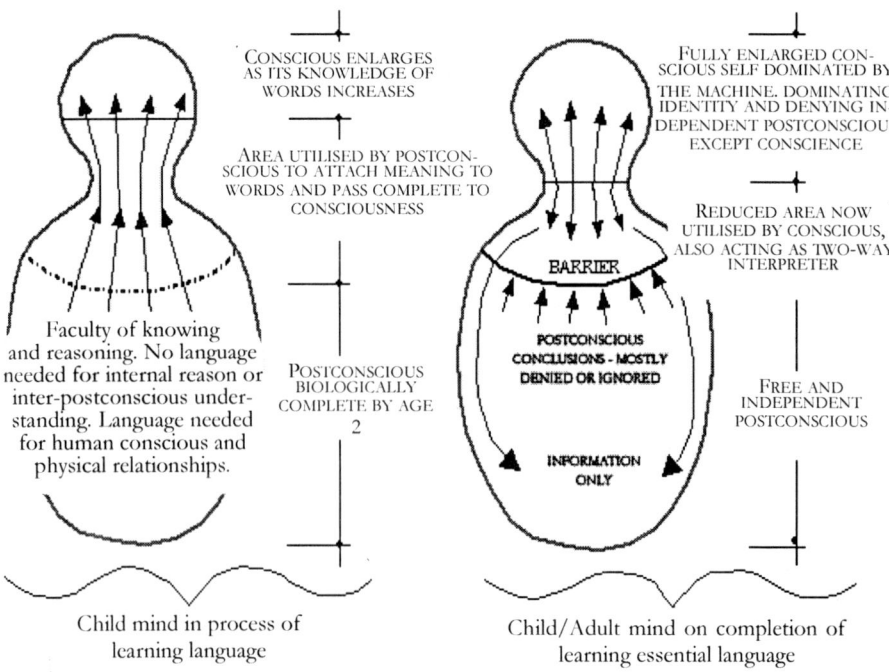

Figure 14a: Language Growth

The normal human self is given over to, or taken over by, the conscious sphere of thinking within the conscious arena of activity and under the Machine's domination. This is the crux of the human dilemma; that we and our world are not represented by our highest (postconscious) faculty. I have already shown, earlier in this chapter, that we may achieve a humantrue world through supraconsciousness, and that this necessitates the stimulation of intellation. But how are we to begin this process of breaking through to our own postconscious minds, when practically all of us are presently harnessed to the Machine and locked into its competitive money-economic reality?

The conscious self's relationship with its own postconscious is one thing, and that between postconscious minds is another, but the two things are interdependent, of course. The human situation may be represented by the mental relationship between one individual and another. It is also the relationship between all individuals and that which factually is, and which they conceive to be, their reality.

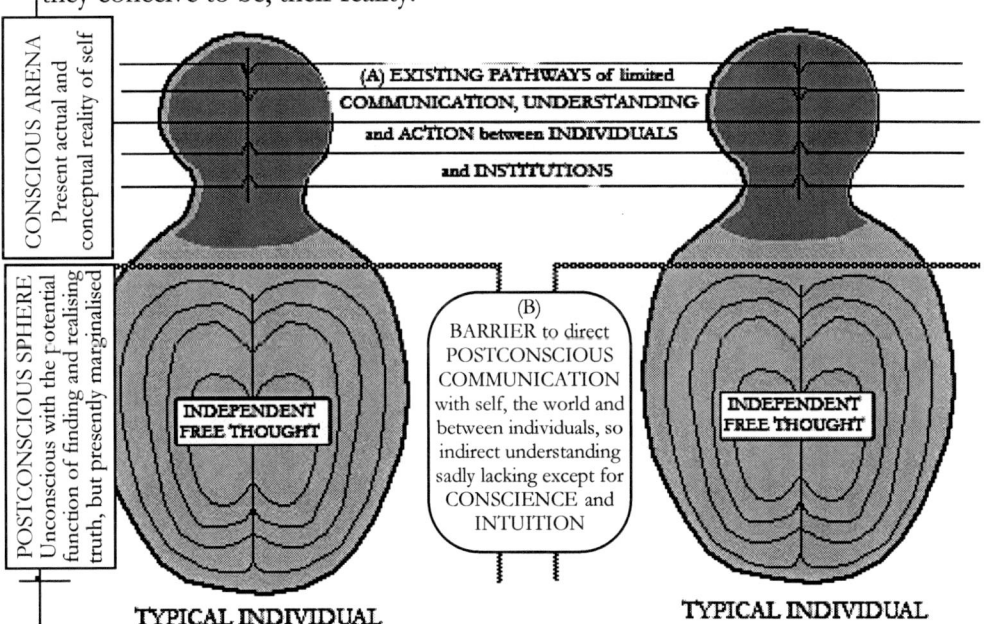

Figure 14b
Existing Reality

Fig. 14b illustrates the existing human situation, whereby our affairs and communications (A) are almost entirely confined to the conscious arena. Individual internal dialogue between postconscious and conscious is severely limited to occasional intuition, which is not normally regarded as reliable or significant. There can be no direct contact between individual postconscious minds, only indirect understanding which, though vital, is presently almost non-existent.

There is, of course, an additional subconscious instinctive pathway (C) which is supposed to be subservient to (A) but which, in the virtual absence of (B), presently exercises undue influence - as illustrated by Figure 14c.

NOTE: *the best way to go about humanising reality is to follow our postconscious mind as it leads us to truth. But questions arise as to how this is done, in detail, and it is the purpose of this chapter to answer those questions.*

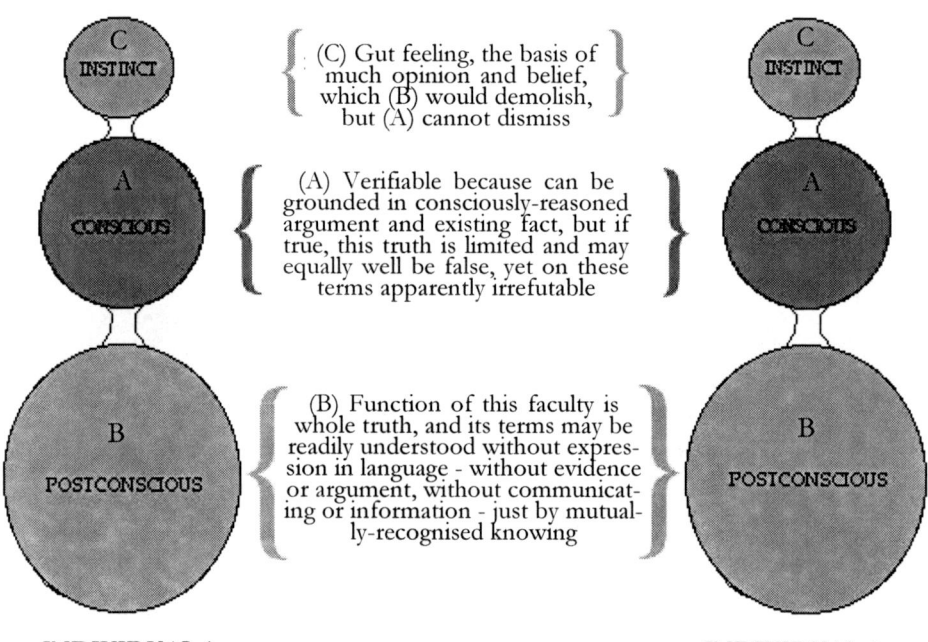

INDIVIDUAL 1   INDIVIDUAL 2

Figure 14c
The Different Kinds of Actual and Possible Intercommunication Between Individuals - (to be read in conjunction with 14b, d & e).

Figure 14c illustrates the reason why (A), the conscious arena, is presently universally preferred. It is backed up by ancient instinctive emotion and more recent history. It is confirmed on all sides by the evident facts and bases for argument that actually exist and exert their pressure on us. The potential knowing of (B), on the other hand, does not prevail in the world and, consequently, is ignored, denied, or suppressed. The hope for humanity lies in the fact that human fulfilment is equivalent to postconscious knowing, which would lead inevitably to realisation of humantruth, represented by Figure 14d.

Figure 14d illustrates a human world, whose plan has been universally agreed, which is collectively sustained by human individuals whose nature is, supraconsciously and responsibly, to cooperate externally according to the inner cooperation of their every mental faculty under the guidance of the common truth of their postconscious minds.

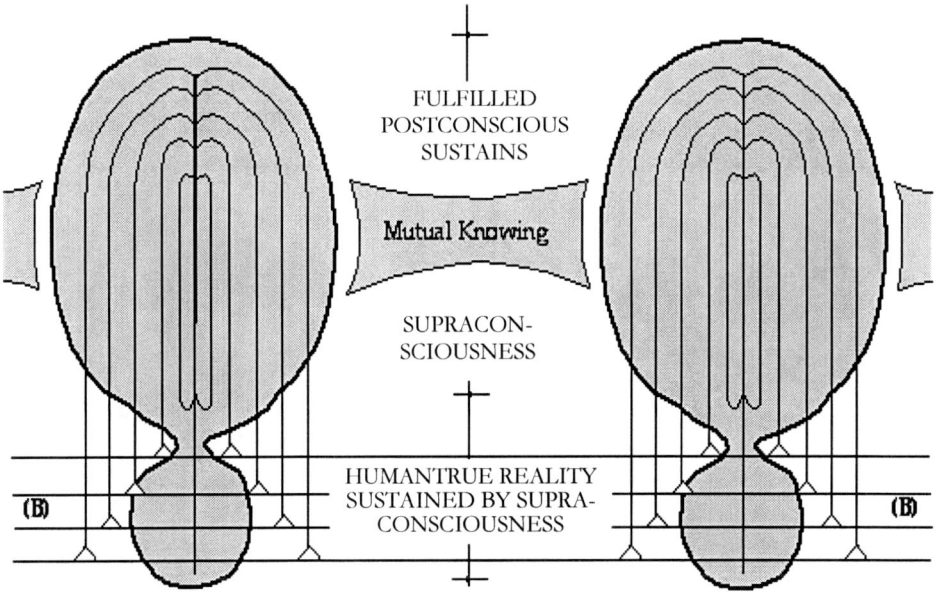

Figure 14d
Humantruly Ideal Communication Between Supraconscious Individuals

The present human dilemma is that we are stuck in the conscious sphere of thought, within the conscious arena of reality, so that our activities threaten to retard us permanently, or to destroy us. The question is how to humanise reality. Our fundamental problem lies in the difficulty of escaping from or cutting a way through our conscious conditioning in order to discover, and attain to, a new supraconscious awareness. This difficulty is illustrated by Figure 14e.

Figure 14e (with which the remainder of this chapter is directly concerned) uses hypothetical individuals X and Y, Y to represent humanity as it now exists and X to represent humanity as it truly ought to be. Figure 14e illustrates the present obstacles, at the level of the human mind - (1) to individual Y breaking through internal bars to awareness and becoming another X, i.e. supraconscious, and (2) to individual X establishing such meaningful communication with Y as will assist such a breakthrough. Within individuals Y, presently the great majority, the postconscious mind is contained by a barrier. Apart from some infiltration into consciousness by way of intuition or conscience, and intake of information from the conscious world, this barrier keeps the postconscious from its own conscious mind's concept of self and worldly reality, and from developing strong links of humantrue understanding with other postconscious minds.

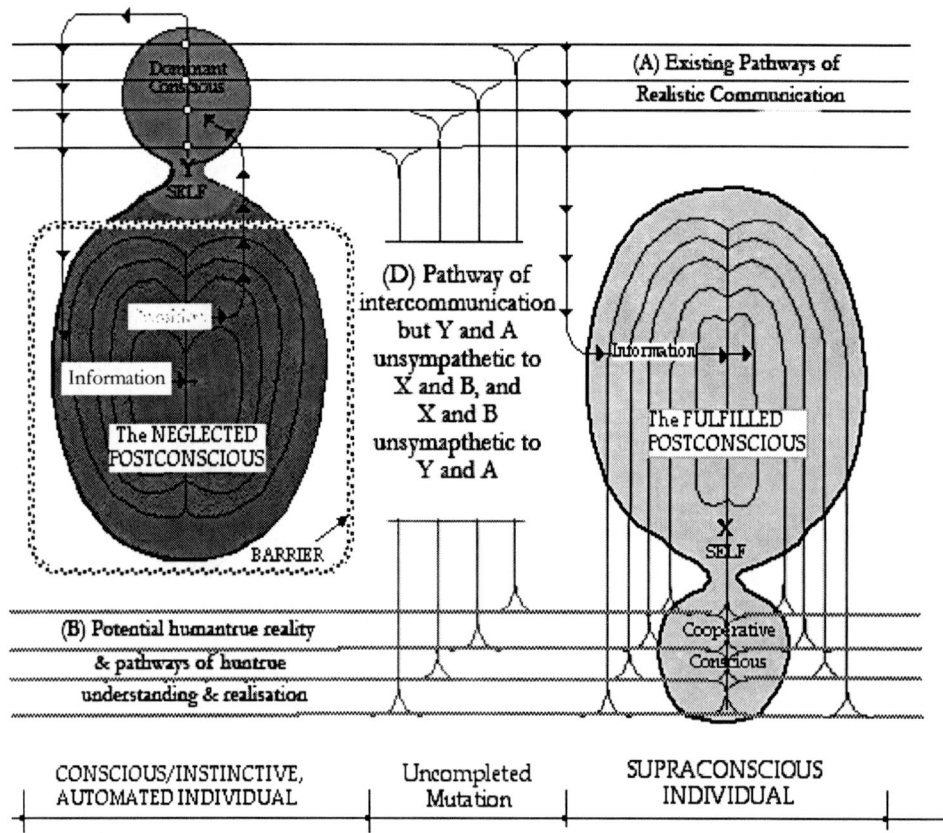

Figure 14e

The Present Problem of Communication

There is no direct pathway between postconscious minds, only the possibility of mutually shared knowing. This means that the only possible direct communication between X and Y is the pathway D - from X, onto B, along D, onto A, and thence to Y. Having reached Y, which has no direct contact with its *own* postconscious, X's communication is made available to Y's postconscious, indirectly and with or without conscious intention, but has to cut across the contrary currents of convention, and may have to pierce the unwilling barrier of conscious will in order to do so, a barrier that will usually prevent any true response from emerging in any case. Even before reaching Y, the message from X has had to pass along pathway A, as we have seen, which is unsympathetic because it was formed by the concepts and facts of the Machine in order to carry the commerce of existing reality. Of course, an individual Y, attempting to contradict and refute X's message, faces similar difficulties of communication in reverse.

Individual Y, however, when facing or addressing an X, has the advantage of being in tune with the reality, accepted by millions of other Y's, that actually overwhelmingly exists. Also Y, apart from the pricking of conscience, is not subject to the contradiction of his or her postconscious. But the truth is that Y's thinking and reality are false. Any individual X, when addressing a Y, has the disadvantage that in order to be understood he or she has to use the reasoning and language of existing reality. That reasoning and language is unsuitable to X, not only because he or she rejects existing reality but also because this reality evolved out of the development of the Machine and is thus inappropriate to the description of an alternative reality entirely different from the Machine. Nevertheless, the postconscious mind's message, in this case using X as its communicator, has the advantage that it is humantrue. Provided that the majority do begin to open to their postconscious minds, that advantage should be decisive in persuading them to reverse their present orientation.

Suppose that Y, as well as X, is dedicated to discovering truth, so that both believe that they are on the same true path. Y's mind has been developed consciously. Consider what this means. All of Y's thinking is dominated by conscious will and is confined to the conscious arena including the utilised part of the postconscious. Y's thinking is conducted and recorded in language because, if it is to be acceptable within a conscious reality, it must be demonstrable and explainable to others in language. Y's thinking is governed by the self because this is the way of nature which humanity still follows despite the fact that egoism requires an inhibitive common code, such as instinct, the inhibitive part of which we have largely abandoned. So Y's mind excludes the independent postconscious because the independent postconscious is unconscious to the self, can not be governed by the self and, its processes being unavailable to consciousness, is neither clearly demonstrable nor precisely explicable to others. Yet although Y's thinking is confined to the conscious arena, excluding the much larger capacity of the postconscious, it is nevertheless a formidable organisation of fact and reasoning extracted and compiled by way of an extremely able critical analysis of existing world reality, past and present. But Y's reasoning is restricted to the limited reasoning capacity of the conscious mind, which cannot go to the ultimate and thus arrive at truth. Consequently normal human reason, and much of its fact, is contradictory, but because consciousness cannot, or will not reason further, existing human society has to allow these contradictions to co-exist and to put up with the dangerous conflict that results. So in order to establish an identity the realistic individual, Y being an example, has to select from the available wide range of options, and defensively or offensively adopt a suitable set of beliefs and opinions. By insisting that human reason must be conducted at the conscious level, so that it can be demonstrably grounded in evidence and argument, the Machine, represented by Y's confinement to Philosophy's discipline of thought, guarantees, as always, that conscious, automated humanity will not discover truth and, therefore, that it cannot agree.

X has developed postconsciously. X knows that it is vital for the human postconscious to guide the self and gain predominance, but it is faced with the fact that existing reality is weighted heavily on the conscious side. The total conscious arena contains the Machine, which controls almost all the mediums of communication and colours all languages, which also embraces all institutions, including that of Philosophy with all its evidence and argument, and in which X's status and influence is relatively very weak. Y, on the other hand, is very strong in the conscious arena, commanding many and varied complex but narrow patterns of reason backed up by many and varied separated groups of fact about existing reality, past and present. Y is weak in the postconscious sphere, indicated by the failure of all this fact and reason to get anywhere near humantruth, but Y does not recognise this. Indeed, Y regards postconscious intuition, which penetrates his awareness as faintly as it strongly guides X, as a weakness precisely *because* it is not grounded in the evidence and argument provided by existing reality and its enveloping conscious arena. Y's beliefs, opinions, and arguments are generally understood, accepted, or tolerated in the world as it exists, whereas X's are either ignored, denied, or resisted.

It is necessary for X to convince Y. This cannot be done directly because of the absence of any but the link of mutual knowing between postconscious minds. X must go through the presently normal pathways A. X's thoughts must pass into the conscious sphere, there to be converted into language capable of expressing them so accurately, yet so understandably to Y's highly consciously organised reasoning, that Y will be unable to ignore them or deny them entry to his or her postconscious mind. If X's thoughts are true, they must eventually be accepted by Y's postconscious (if Y's conscious self admits them) because truth is the function of all postconscious minds. The reason why the independent postconscious mind is able to work truly is that it is unconscious, it has ample capacity, and it is well aware of, but not directly and actively involved in, all the competitive, instinctive, historical, institutional, egoistic, and factual influences of false reality, which create differences and cause confusions in and between conscious minds.

The conscious is a knowledge-gathering mind with a vast memory and a huge amount of fact to work on, but it lacks the capacity fully to embrace that knowledge with reason. The postconscious is a mind of infinite reasoning-power that reduces knowledge to its essence. Suppose that Y's conscious store of factual knowledge is far greater than that of X. For this reason Y believes his understanding to be truly superior, and this opinion is backed up by the facts and norms of existing reality, and by tortuous arguments that cannot be dismissed on their own terms, only by reference to their false foundations. It can be seen that honest communication between X and Y can only be accomplished through Y's admission that he might be wrong. Without immediately conceding anything, Y would then drop his defences and allow a new idea, or a hitherto rejected or ridiculed theory, into his postconscious, there to be either accepted or rejected. If the idea or theory is accepted, as it must be if true, Y might well then be self-persuaded not only to allow, but to voluntarily encourage and assist his postconscious mind to begin a process of demolishing that which is false or incomplete in his consciously-upheld thinking, and to rebuilding it truly. He would then be bound to acknowledge true knowing, conveyed to the self by its own postconscious. Eventually, when this process is completed, X and Y will be in essential agreement.

Chapter 51

CONTRARY CONCEPTS

Meaningful communication, as I have already sought to establish, is a necessary part of humantrue cooperation, but meaningful communication is impossible between minds that do not share the same fundamental understanding, and at present such understanding is rare. It is not possible for fundamental humantrue understanding to be transferred complete, like factual knowledge, from one mind that possesses that understanding to another which does not. The first mind acquired its understanding by intellating; by consulting its own postconscious; by being supraconscious. So, to begin with, the only thing that the first mind can communicate to the second is the very vital awareness of the necessity to be supraconscious. When the second mind becomes supraconscious, then, and only then, will the two minds share the same fundamental understanding which, by way of meaningful communication, they may build upon until they reach agreement.

Approaching the end of my book, I was well aware that I had done very little reading. I had no idea how many minds might have reached these same conclusions. I began to wonder whether any book already existed in which these conclusions had already been revealed. I determined to read, and then critically comment upon a number of outstanding books.

It disturbs me considerably that in the eyes of some readers this chapter's criticisms of acknowledged thinkers might appear somewhat arrogant and hurtful. I ask them to reconsider, remembering my contention that we possess two minds, the conscious, home of the existing wrong reality, and the postconscious whose function is truth, and to accept that it is not me-the-person who criticises, but my postconscious. Furthermore, this is not criticism of these thinkers as dedicated persons who have striven admirably to decipher the mysteries of life, but as conscious selves who, like so many academics and theorists, must operate from a specific consciousness that is largely disconnected from their (independent) postconscious minds.

I believe, then, that the right place for our struggle to make true the state of the human mind and world, is the postconscious. This is the faculty that has always been my guide, engendering thinking that I now feel compelled to make known. Again, this thinking is not strictly my own but that of the postconscious which I have faithfully recorded.

A breakthrough in broad awareness seemed to be the dramatic spread of the Green movement. There is no doubt that this movement, and its political arm the Green Party, has become a strong focus of public expression (though yet relatively weak) of opposition to the dominant world order. Could it be that this movement has also discovered humantruth and adopted it as the foundation of its platform? Whilst the books I chose were impressive and informative, they have been listed as contrary concepts because they neither embrace the whole human dilemma, nor its solution - humantruth by way of supraconsciousness.

The first book I read was The Quest for Gaia by Kit Pedlar (Souvenir Press). The author points out that we are pursuing a course that will destroy us but that we are not fully aware of this fact; that we neither know which way to go nor how to survive; that most of us think of the Machine as having no connection with us in any moral or intelligent sense. Kit Pedlar describes many destructive practices of the Machine and tells us how to counter them, or how to avoid contributing to them, with such conviction as to make me feel guilty that my own efforts at conservation are insufficient. But he does not deal with the root causes of these destructive practices - he does not tackle the question of how to bring about a non-destructive world.

Next I read Seeing Green by Jonathan Porritt (Basil Blackwell), the much respected author of which is a leading member of the Green Party in Britain. This book goes more fully into the political dimension; into measures to be taken by national governments, and internationally, to cease or curb these practices that threaten the biosphere. But it seems to me that Porritt gives no more than fleeting attention to the human *individual* - to human character as it stands, and as it truly ought to be. He, too, fails to penetrate to the root causes of the problem; to the fact that the Machine is by nature destructive, and that politics is a serving institution of the Machine; to the fact that the solution to our problems lies in the true emancipation of the human race. There is a general failure critically to expose the false foundations of the Machine to which we are all harnessed. The Machine is being called upon to mend its ways but is not seriously being called to question. Porritt is guilty of this, as is Pedlar when he illustrates the result of this failure with the comment that scientists (and the same applies to all specialists) belonging to different disciplines (with no overall humantrue reference point) can not object to other specialists going their own ways (independently regardless) because, being buried in their own discipline, none are qualified to judge the disciplines of others.

Seeing Green is very well written and full of concern, but it seems to me to take the view that our problems arise from reckless humanity, and their solution is the province of governing authority. For instance, he refers to labour as a productive resource, and unemployment as a waste of that resource. He thinks that the introduction of new technology is something that we do not have the option to oppose at present. He believes that people will change only when they think it is in their own personal interest to do so. He appears to temper this cynicism when he goes on to suggest that the recipe for transformation of human society is *enlightened* self-interest, but in my view this is a contradiction in terms, for to be humantruly enlightened is not to think of specific interests, which derive from instinct, but of truth. Porritt claims that it is obvious that modern societies need some measure of profitability. He says that if the present economic incentives are to be removed they must be replaced by new aims and methods, yet concedes that these will have to reflect the peoples' way of thinking. (I agree with this, but it shall have to be a new, and humantrue, way of thinking). He believes that economics (i.e. management) is all about work and its rewards.

Seeing Green seems to me admirable as a comprehensive survey of the diseases of present society, but not as a guide to the prevention of those diseases. That is the reason for my mainly critical comment. The present situation requires that humanity voluntarily changes its intellectual nature, as a result of which it will bring about a humantrue framework of life which, in turn, will make it possible for humanity to sustain its supraconscious nature and its humantrue state. If we undertake anything less than this total reciprocal change there will be no real change. Clearly I do not have space to mention all the good things in this book, such as its statement that only through local production for local needs shall we achieve long-term security, and that it makes common sense to work and produce things to meet peoples' needs *directly* rather than work and produce things to make the money to meet the peoples' needs *indirectly*.

Since the Green movement is generally taken to represent strong opposition to the present dominant order, and the author of Seeing Green is a leading light in that movement, I decided to read the two books that most inspired him - The Turning Point by Fritjof Capra (Hutchinson), and person/Planet by Theodore Roszak (Granada). The following are my comments on these two works. I hesitated before including them. Why?

I hesitated mainly because these two men are exceedingly able thinkers (and writers) who also possess a deeply felt morality, which I believe to be rare in the academic field. They are acknowledged thinkers, their books well known in radical circles in which they seem to be regarded as important landmarks. One reason why attention is paid to these works is that the authors have academic records and have been published - qualities generally thought to be indispensable to the authentication of thinkers. Yet here am I, neither academic nor published, criticising their thinking on all fronts. The justification of my criticism is that they either reach wrong conclusions or fail to reach right ones, yet they exert considerable influence on human thought. Such criticism of a work is not pleasant for its author, but if it is true it must be made. It ought then to be accepted, especially by the author of that work, for the deepest moral emotions will be ineffective if appended to false reasoning. I hope that I, wherever my reasoning is revealed as false, will accept criticism in the same spirit as it is offered here.

These two brilliant thinkers and writers fail to discover humantruth because they, like Chomsky, deliberately confine their search to the conscious arena and its evidence and argument. They are thus unable to reject the Machine - the automated nature and state of humanity - because it entirely and firmly belongs in the conscious arena. But they are enabled to give credence to such an idea as cosmic consciousness because the conscious mind is neither able to dismiss it nor to deny the sub-atomic physics that seem to support it. Their kind of thinking is exceedingly difficult because it is trying to do the impossible. It cannot achieve its objective because it deliberately excludes, or rejects as unreliable, the truth of the postconscious. If the thinker is freely honest this conscious thinking must ultimately become extremely frustrating, for its conclusions can never be utterly acceptable.

The Turning Point is based upon the ancient Chinese concept of yin and yang, the universal or natural extremes. According to this thinking, Earth nature is a constant living balance between these extremes, and the human species, if it is to survive, must subject itself to the same extremes and gravitate by way of its own nature to a similar balance.

I venture to suggest that this is a fundamental misconception, for the acquisition of intellect, i.e. the faculty of fully knowing and reasoning, changes the situation completely. In non-intellectual nature, true survival-balance can only be achieved by expressing equal and opposite, positive and negative extremes (the drives and inhibitions of instinct) and gravitating to a kind of united neutral stability that represents the basic continuing life of a species. Instinct is the code that secures this balanced pattern of behaviour for sub-intellectual life-forms. The history of human civilisation so far shows a growing imbalance due to the fact that we have retained the impulsions of instinct and have applied intellect to augmenting its drives while rejecting many of its inhibitions.

The concept of yin and yang cannot be applied to the whole human mind, for the mind's supreme function, represented by the postconscious (the neocortex), is for all humans to work as one to fulfil its function - the discovery and realisation of optimum truth. In order to demonstrate this it is necessary to recall that the human mind is divided into the conscious and postconscious spheres. The conscious sphere, when dominated by the Machine and the impulsions of instinct in the conscious arena, *does* work according to the yin-yang concept, seeking its individual balance between extremes. It is this restricted conscious thinking which can make the incomplete assertions that one side of the brain thinks rationally (ie intellectually) and the other side intuitively and morally; which claims that our progress has come from rational intellect; which underlies Chinese wisdom when it says that none of these values that our (present) culture pursues is intrinsically bad; which insists that harmonious social and ecological relationships will be achieved by this balance of self-assertive and integrative tendencies; which says that the yang (bad) will retreat in favour of the yin.

That which may seem to confirm that the yin-yang concept operates in our present reality is that existing human society reflects a struggle between our morality (arising from intellect and supported by the benign instincts) and the Machine, each individual *applying* intellect to choosing an opinion or belief out of all the possibilities, and *using* intellect to project or defend that personal choice. I am referring, of course, to that limited degree of intellect that may be furnished by the utilised part of the postconscious, a part that eventually became absorbed into the conscious, quite separate from the postconscious. Our present misunderstanding of the true function of intellect gives rise to the false belief that our progress has come from rational intellect over-mastering moral intuition, for autoprogress is served by our consciously dominated minds, whereas morality *comes from* intellect. The ancient Chinese idea, that none of the values pursued by our culture is intrinsically bad, reflects our continual, futile, attempts to accept the instinctive pecking order while attempting to control it with quasi-intellectual law and order. An early unsuccessful attempt at this was made by Confucius, yet the Green Party, in its intention of instituting a system in which the pursuit of self-interest works for the common good, has fallen into the same trap. No such contrived balance of opposite forces will ever bring about harmonious social and ecological relationships, for every retreat of yang in favour of yin must be followed, eventually, by a retreat of yin in favour of yang. The only way of guaranteeing a stable balance, with the minimum of oscillation, is to entrust ourselves and Earth to our own individual supraconscious responsibility.

We now come to the crux of Capra's philosophy, which I think is also the basis of the Green approach and the currently popular marriage between physics and mysticism, but which misunderstands the nature of humanity and the true significance of our presence on Earth and our relationship to Earth, to all other life, and to the universe.

Physical existence, Capra says, comes down to quantum mechanics. Matter is made up of sub-atomic particles that do not have objective properties. The observer's conscious decision as to how to observe an electron, for example, to some extent determines the particle-behaviour or wave-behaviour of the electron. Yet he goes on to say that this also means that we can never refer to nature without simultaneously referring to ourselves. I can agree that this relationship is true, for instance, of nature's will to live and Gaia's helpful response, or of instinctive aggression being neutralised by instinctive cooperation in the balance of nature. But I cannot agree with him when he applies this relationship, for instance, to scientists and the nature and direction of their research, saying that their frame of mind determines this, in that they take not only intellectual but moral responsibility. In my view this is a concept which could, and ideally should be true but is not presently so. It is untrue not only because intellect and morality are essentially one and the same, nor because the nature and direction of scientific research is chiefly determined by the rewards of the competitive money-economy and hierarchical status, but chiefly because the advent of the intellectual faculty changes the situation fundamentally. When Capra says that physicists are free to choose their path, either to the Bomb or to Buddha, he is ignoring truth, or humantruth (which exposes both these as false alternatives), the function of intellect that indicates the one and only path which is right for us to take.

Capra goes on to what he describes as one of the most profound systems of Western thought, which he sees as equivalent to Buddhist or Taoist philosophy. This is the S-matrix theory, known as the boot-strap approach, which states that matter has to be understood through self-consistency; that all physical components must be consistent with one another or with themselves, accepting no fundamental constants, laws or equations. This theory describes the world as a 'dynamic web of interrelated events', no part of which has fundamental properties, the properties of each part being determined by the sum of the properties of all parts which give the entire web its structure. This thinking foreshadows Bernice Cohen's concept of a society working according to systems-theory, which I shall come to later. The concept of a dynamic web is logical but the world, as an example of such a web, has never properly incorporated intellect, which *has* fundamental properties, nor the product of intellect, true morality. We are now seeking to introduce morality, with which there can be no compromise such as the freedom of choice between right and wrong that Buddhism permits, a conscious choice between instinctive extremes that is inconsistent with morality. So we have to picture, and then to realise, the human equivalent of a dynamic web which *carries* a fundamental constant - that of humantruth.

The natural world is a dynamic web in which all components are consistent with one another, and with themselves, but nature is a balance of intense competitive conflicts whose purpose is to sustain and develop life without the imposition of any moral code per se. Human intellect inevitably builds its own moral code and then cannot reasonably deny it. Present human society is an imbalance resulting from acceleration of the natural conflicts impelled by aggressive use of the powers of intellect without many of the inhibitions of instinct. The dynamic web's character comprises conflict between its many parts. Sub-atomic particles and waves display indecision, their observed patterns reflecting the conflicting patterns of observing minds. This is the universal pattern, the complexity of inevitable order wrestling with inescapable chaos, from the 'balance' of Earth-nature to the 'balance' of galaxies. The one significant achievement of evolution is intellect, and the ultimate function of intellect is truth. Truth is the key to the conundrum, for it would give particles one and the same objective; it would achieve perfectly simple consistency of matter (energy) by giving all parts the same properties, which would then take the place of all conceived constraints, laws, and equations and which, ultimately, would bring the universe to a state of true equilibrium. This is the nearest that my mind has got to the universal truth which, as I have said already, I do not insist upon although my intellation returns to it again and again. However I do insist that humantruth makes it our clear duty as an intellectual species to bring humanity on Earth to a state of peaceful and stable contentment.

Capra concludes that the bootstrap approach has profound implications - that the methods of observation determine principles which in turn determine the properties of particles means that the way we look at the world will ultimately determine the basic structure of the material world; that patterns of mind may be reflected in patterns of matter. Perhaps, although it hardly signifies what the patterns of matter are. The significant thing is that existing matter has produced human intellect, and it is of first importance that intellect fulfils itself. Mind clearly ranks above matter, and it is vital that we define what is meant by 'patterns of mind' - that we understand what the mind is.

A key element in Capra's view of the bootstrap theory is the notion of order in the inter-connectedness of sub-atomic processes. Topology, apparently well-known to mathematics, can be used to classify various categories of such order. When this concept is introduced into S-matrix theory, only a few categories of such order prove to be consistent with the mathematical framework of that theory. These ordered patterns of particle interaction prove to be precisely those observed by nature.

For me this is not really surprising since I have suggested already that universal evolution is a matter of energy, under the influence of truth, applying itself to the compelling purpose of constructing the means of comprehending truth in order to fulfil it and realise it in the universe. It is to be expected that the same fundamental patterns contributed to the brain development underlying this activity, but it is well to recall that, just as the product of a system is more significant than the sum of its parts, the truth transcends the bodily mechanisms that discover it, to the point of raising the individual entity above its own physical, instinctive, and conscious mental self, up to its supraconscious self vested in the unconscious postconscious, thus reaching a common collective true awareness that binds all individuals together. Nature on Earth is the penultimate stage of this purposeful evolution, the pathway to intellect that is the road to truth. The ultimate stage will be reached when Earth's most advanced species in this respect, the human, sets up a humantrue society.

Continuing my comment on The Turning Point by Fritjof Capra, I am full of praise for its masterly critical analysis of health services, as they are and as they should be. Also of the existing methods of providing energy for power, heating and lighting from irreplaceable sources, with dangerous ecological effects, and of the safe and viable, renewable alternatives. But, while Capra recognises the problems, and the desirable alternatives, does he examine the obstacles in the way of achieving those alternatives; does he understand that the solutions to our problems are not to be brought about by wishful thinking, or by contrived manipulation, but will be the natural outcome of intellation, exemplified by life in a truly human framework. No single problem will be truly solved until *all* questions and problems are humantruly answered and solved.

I am most uncertain of Capra's approach to the human dilemma. His approach reflects a strongly and widely felt, but questionable, desire or compulsion to believe in the existence of a remote power higher than ourselves. This results in a deep reluctance to accept that *we* are the apex of evolution and that full responsibility for the care of ourselves and Earth rests upon our own willingness voluntarily to fulfil our true potential. My previous profound disagreement with the belief in a higher power turned to uncertainty upon reading The Color of Truth by Dr S T Manning

Capra, describing that major part of the conscious which is for the time being out of focus as 'the unconscious', also describes it as 'collective mental patterns', the suggestion being that these may differ greatly from person to person. But he also suggests a superior external overall pattern when he says that the concepts of a planetary mind may be associated with cosmic levels of consciousness. I am not sure that such levels exist - the only higher mind in existence is the internal postconscious, our own or that of beings similar to ourselves. Gaia and the automaton think, in a sense, just as single cells think, but they are not conscious in the true sense. Consciousness, which the mystics regard as the primary reality and the ground of all being, according to Capra, is actually the optimum perception of the self and its environment and relationships, from the viewpoint of a personal construction of biased thought based upon a limited selection from conscious reality (this limitation is necessary because total consciousness is an impossibility since its sphere and whole arena, being incapable of truth, has an infinity of contradictory possibilities - hence the present world's conflicting confusion). The next and ultimate stage in our evolution is intellectual supraconsciousness, afforded by open relationship with the whole postconscious mind, by which the conscious self may be made aware of the common truth, and thereby of its true relationship with everything.

Capra's approach belongs to the conscious arena in which we presently exist. His ideals belong outside that arena, since they are supraconscious - the innate knowledge of postconscious conclusions - but he believes that this knowledge comes from some higher external level of consciousness, and that humanity itself cannot escape from its present conscious - instinctive - emotional bondage to the facts and concepts of existing reality. So his views on reform are ideas arising from functional thought that belongs to the conscious arena, proposing behaviour which truly belongs to the supraconscious sphere. It is possible to imagine existing humanity choosing to take the moral road but, as long as we remain in the conscious arena, it is realistic to acknowledge that consequently limited human reason gives equal cause why we should also choose from all the other, immoral or amoral, violent or reckless behaviour that is equally valid according to the contradictory evidence and argument of the conscious arena.

The crux of the currently most advanced *conscious* view of the truth about ourselves, our minds and our place in the universe, seems to be founded on Jung's concept of a collective unconscious. In some sense this is consistent with my theory of the postconscious and truth, except that it implies a mind-link between the individual and the entire cosmos, and it includes another misconception. Jung says that this link cannot be understood within a mechanistic framework, for it defies precise definition but is very consistent with the systems view of the mind. But this link *can* be understood when it is perceived as a link between truth and the postconscious mind as the discoverer of truth. The difficulty of defining this link is really the difficulty - the impossibility - of proving postconscious truth by conscious evidence and argument. And it is illogical to suggest that truth cannot be understood within a mechanistic or Cartesian framework, or that it must conform to probability theory or the uncertainty principle or systems theory, for the truth is the truth about all things, including all these sub-processes of incomplete reason, and transcends the universe.

Some current thinking combines Jung's concept of the human unconscious with another concept by which some contemporary physicists describe 'everything under the sun' as a product and logical unfolding of sub-atomic phenomena. The significance of this is taken to be that, whatever meaning, purpose or motive underlie the sub-atomic processes, these processes brought about the evolution of intelligent instinctive life and culminated in the formation of the human mind; that the human intellect cannot signify more than the process that created it; and that far from being the instrument of new and truly transcendental understanding, the intellect has to refer backwards beyond its simple origins in order to discover and penetrate the present complexities of life and understand the meaning, purpose and motive of human existence.

I am absolutely sure that these concepts are false. Their many sincere proponents would probably say that I had paid much less attention to an understanding of their beliefs than is required to convince anyone. But their evidence and argument, coming from the conscious arena, is unreliably incomplete and inconclusive. My reason for believing it to be false is that my postconscious gives no indication that it is true. The physical human mind is the product of all these processes, yes, but its postconscious intellect is far greater than the sum of the contributory parts of the brain, and is on an altogether different level. The postconscious is the apex of evolution, its function to transcend the system that produced it and to take the ultimate overall view, the supraconscious view.

All this refers to subjects that still puzzle humanity after thousands of years - the subjects of evolution and creation. Broadly speaking the normally accepted belief is that life and Earth - because they are so wonderful - must have been created by a superior all-seeing and all-powerful being. But this is a back-to-front view, for if existence begins with complete and supreme perfection there is no point in it evolving, for the painful struggles of evolution can have no objective which has not been achieved already. By contrast, the concept of evolution as a quest, beginning with an ideal and going on in pursuit of that ideal – i.e. truth - is completely straightforward. Nothing about life made much sense until the advent of human intellectual potential, and humanity has made and still makes even less sense because intellect has not been fulfilled but misused. Intellect will not be fulfilled as long as we look to non-existent gods and external consciousness for wisdom; as long as we go on looking everywhere for it but where it is to be found - within our heads.

I have referred elsewhere to a very common conviction that it is beyond us to discover truth. Capra believes that the nearest we can approach to expressing absolute truth in words is myth, and that transpersonal consciousness can transcend logical reason and intellectual analysis and come near to a direct experience of reality. Such ideas are attempts, similar to beliefs in inscrutable gods, to explain or describe that elevated yet closely personal phenomenon that is sensed yet undiscovered - the individual postconscious mind. These attempts misconstrue the true and utterly practical reason why the independent postconscious has to be unconscious (except for the communication of its conclusions by intuition and conscience), impatiently resorting to mysterious explanations rather than persevering with the right kind of intellectual reasoning, i.e. intellation, until the true explanation is discovered (that ultimate reasoning requires a free and independent mind remote from consciousness and that its processes are too complex to be immediately converted into language and made available to consciousness in all its detail).

Let me try to summarise the concluding pages of The Turning Point, in which Capra sets out his solutions to the human problems.

He sees matter as the macro-manifestation of micro-particle behaviour. He sees life as the organisation of matter into intelligent consciousness that is the macro-manifestation of an ancient underlying micro-cosmic consciousness, and which, by its influence on the sub-atomic micro-particles, can influence, and eventually determine, the behaviour of matter. Earth nature, guided by cosmic wisdom, though expressing to the full the opposing universal extremes, has achieved a living balance between them. The human race, by excessive application of rational intellect to its activities and the neglect of intuitive moral influences, has become dangerously imbalanced. By renewing contact with cosmic consciousness (through meditation) we can consciously alter our behaviour by changing our values and attitudes in order to regain the spirituality and ecological awareness we have lost, and by adopting the systems view of nature we can construct a meaningful scientific framework for approaching the age-old questions of the nature of life, mind, consciousness and matter.

There are four fatal flaws in this argument. The first is the erroneous belief that we once had, but have lost, the ecological awareness that we now vitally need, for humanity has not yet achieved the intellectual potential which will wholly bring such awareness (that the hunter-gatherers, for example, lived in comparative sympathy with nature derived from the way they conceived their own interests in their particular circumstances, free from competitive pressures, not free from awareness of whole-Earth ecology). The second flaw is a failure to recognise that moral intuition *comes from* intellect - that our autoprogress has been the result of consciously wilful *misapplication* of intellect. The third is that there is no unmistakably evident cosmic consciousness, for there is nothing in nature or in the universe that signifies as much as intellect in revealing and realising truth in all its meanings. The fourth fatal flaw in this argument is its failure to recognise the existence of the human postconscious mind which, as I have already gone to some lengths to explain, is the supreme achievement of evolution (here on Earth and wherever else such minds have evolved) and should be our true guide.

Of course we must achieve a balance, but it must be very different from the innocently cruel balance of nature. In Passage to the Solar Age, Capra has many encouraging things to say about sensible sources of energy to replace present non-renewable and ecologically unfriendly sources. Yet his systems-view of life seems to envisage a society founded upon much the same principles as now apply, and to depend upon a mysteriously enlightened population to make it work humanely. I have tried to show that supraconsciousness is a necessary prerequisite to the building of a humantrue society, and that a humantrue society is necessary to the sustenance of a supraconscious humanity. Such a society has to be stable because humantruth is not changeable by wilful manipulation. If you want conscious freedom, with continual flexible fluctuations and changes of values and attitudes, then you have to accept all kinds of destructive and inhuman behaviour. You can't have it both ways.

Capra's thinking is representative of the general growth of a belief that seems to be similar to that of Christianity. It has a benign but mystical and incomplete message - ecological awareness and concern for the well-being of life - and it has a god, a subject of faith rather than truth - cosmic consciousness and transpersonal being.

As a matter of wishful thinking and sublimation this new belief is also spreading, but, because it too is incomplete and not truly founded, it too will fail, and much vital time will have been lost.

Person/Planet was the next book I read. Its author, Theodore Roszak, is another advanced thinker of compassionate concern whom I regret having to criticise. But criticism is necessary to our campaign for the promotion and realisation of humantruth.

The crux of my disagreement with Roszak is that he believes in self-discovery, 'the irresistable fascination of the project of creating an original identity'. In my view this preoccupation with the conscious self is an instinctive characteristic carried to extremes by the misapplication of semi-intellect, and it arises from our failure to complete our mutation from the instinctive to the intellectual condition.

The point has already been made that in the practical affairs of a humantrue society self-identity would be invested in the common life while the intellect would be enabled to flourish in every abstract way. Our present position is different, however, for it falls to the present human generations to win through to humantruth, i.e. the self-discovery of truth that we presently fail to achieve because we do not yet permit our minds to work truly; because we do not understand humantruth; because humantruth is not reflected in our environment, and because our feelings are unreliable guides. We, the present generations, have to sacrifice our self-interest to the communal and abstract interests, not of ourselves but of future generations.

Roszak, too, demonstrates belief in cosmic consciousness - that we naturally belong to it and may embrace it by the self-discovery of our original identity - when he refers to evolutionary continuities that relate mind to matter, and to a planetary dimension to the spreading personalist sensibility which links the search for authentic identity to the well-being of the global environment.

I think it is true that personal sensibility is spreading, but whilst it contains an element of deepening awareness it is chiefly a growth in self-interest which is now overthrowing controls (such as communism) set up to counteract the gross injustices of competitive self-interest in the past. This is a case of irresponsible instinctive drives overcoming ineffective repressive restrictions. This sounds like economic freedom but, through exploitation of humanity and Earth, it will soon become yet more oppressive. The spread of personal sensibility heralds a contrary spread of insensitive automated chaos. That the personal (conscious) sensibility of some people presently embraces ecologically aware concern is incidental, not inevitable.

The universe evolved the brain, yes, but the mind is greater by far than the sum of its past and parts. Our intellect is the consummation of evolution and, I believe, the objective of the instinctive drives. Surely it is wrong to neglect its true potential by subjecting it to the inferior mechanistic forces that blindly produced it. Roszak says that the needs of the planet are the needs of the person and therefore that the rights of the person are the rights of the planet. This is poetic, but I would prefer to say that the needs of the person are the needs of all life, dependent on the planet; that there are no rights, but that human intellect gives us *responsibility* for all life and for the planet, the responsibility to achieve a nature and state that is truly acceptable to intellect.

Person/Planet proclaims that we all have the sovereign right of self-discovery. It declares that there is no single ideological formula that can corral such a rich and often tragic variety of human experience as the world presently holds. I believe, however, that we have no god-given rights (nor any god to give them), and it is instinctive self-interest that has maintained the present reckless and conflicting competitive chaos. But we do have the potential to fulfil our chief faculty - intellect, and this complete self-discovery would bring us to common understanding of one and the same humantruth. By this humantrue understanding we would peacefully cooperate in all practical things, confining our other experiences, which would be just as rich and varied but genuine and never tragic, to the abstract.

Roszak asks how the people of contemporary America came together to work out their liberation (can they be said to be liberated?), and answers - not as a mass, but as all kinds of sects. As examples of this liberating process he gives 'the network' (mutual awareness and concern within sects) and 'the age of therapy'. But these are examples of humanity declaring itself at one extreme of its struggle within the Machine - at the other extreme these sects are confronted by groups such as the multinational corporations and the military. These sects and groups are coexisting features dependent upon the same overall system - the Machine - and all must be accepted if the Machine is not to be rejected. Americans falsely conceive of the self and live in a false reality, as do the rest of us in the West. They are liberating themselves only from some inhuman concepts and features of their automatic roles, not from the conscious arena, and not from the Machine. Roszak dislikes mass movements, preferring small-scale human initiatives of different kinds, but he expects the impossible - that those initiatives will somehow humanise the present system. Mass movements, in the shape of crowd-hysteria or overbearing ideologies of emotionally appealing religions, are not the only alternatives. Remember that there is one common potential human mind, and but one body of humantruth. The humantrue system of world human life requires to be framed by the common postconscious mind and responsibly sustained by each and every supraconscious individual.

Person/Planet adopts a foundational premise that is incomplete, in my view, and which confirms that overmuch erudition inhibits intellation. As does Capra, Roszak makes a link between physics and mystical and oriental traditions, reflecting the general tendency to return to mysticism on discovering that physics fails to explain everything. He takes such things as morphic science, systems science, holistic healing, religious experience and anthropology to indicate that nature and human consciousness are one and the same. It is true that these are things of nature, and that nature has a guiding relevance to us as sophisticated consciously instinctive animals, confined to the conscious arena and ignorant of absolutely relevant truth. But such things as systems science, except where they have practical physical uses, are not wholly true of us, nor of significant guidance or overruling importance to us. Our true destiny is to be that which we potentially are, and truly ought to be - a supraconscious race.

Roszak supports the spreading anarchy of self-discovery against what he describes as the opposing call for social relevance and intellectual rigour which, he believes, closes the inner self. But supraconsciousness does not close that which is presently regarded as the inner self - wilful consciousness. Instead it opens the lesser conscious mind and self to its true mentor - the postconscious mind. That widespread fear of losing our personal freedom to a rigid and unfeeling intellectual regime does not apply here. Supraconsciousness would free us from the present free-for-all that can be as harsh, cruel and dull as it can be easy, kind and exciting, and which is accelerating downhill. Supraconsciousness would open us to our full potential and, by re-building society in sympathy, would open the true inner self to such fulfilment as we have never experienced.

We should remind ourselves that present society, under the Machine, is dominated by persons who are confident that they *have* discovered their inner selves, but these are conscious selves, incomplete, false and dangerous, albeit often unknowingly so. They are necessarily employed by the institutions of the Machine as controllers of people who, in the mass, are similarly incomplete. Not being truly themselves and therefore not knowing what they ought to be and do, the people can be persuaded, or self-persuaded, to be and do anything at all, whether good, indifferent, or 'evil'.

Roszak is much more concerned with the person than is Capra. Perhaps the core of my argument with him is the difference between his view of the human person and my view of the human individual. He distinguishes between 'person' and 'individual' in a way that I do not find helpful. I regard the individual as the indivisible basic unit of society; that which society's completeness should represent. He regards the person as having an inner, pre-destined personality that, if it can be discovered (by the implied means of combining external cosmic awareness with internal faculties), would make that person complete and altogether good. This difference between us may appear very wide, for on my side is an almost totally unrecognised idea that the happy perfection of the human world lies in the fulfilment of intellect, whilst his belief on the opposite side is, at present, almost universally shared, even by today's so-called 'intellectuals'. Yet the difference is actually narrow, for it is simply the difference between descriptions of one and the same thing - the postconscious mind. Roszak's description is vague - the awareness of a mysterious cosmic consciousness or universal nature which makes the person complete. My description is of a physical human faculty that factually exists, the neocortex, which furnishes the postconscious mind that, if we consciously open to it and become supraconscious, will fulfil our humantrue potential.

I see the individual as potentially sharing this same essential completeness with all other individuals, whereas persons are in numerous ways divided from each other. I see the person as a temperament, a pattern of instincts and conditionings, a specific construction of thoughts, all contained within the same conscious arena that contains the present world. This personality is closed to its chief faculty, the postconscious, excepting for intuition, or conscience. This personal self is incapable of behaving humantruly because it is closed to full awareness of humantruth. For the same reason it is capable of morality or immorality - it may be both the benign social reformer and the cruel slave-driver. Unless a society of such persons is quickly to collapse in chaos, it *needs* the governing control of such as our present Machine to both encourage and restrict it, but if it continues in ignorance of humantruth its collapse will merely have been delayed by this control.

Were the majority of people to assert this 'personhood' they might well overthrow the Machine but could offer nothing better to replace it. Roszak believes that there are existing human qualities upon which a worthy society could be built, whereas I believe that a humantrue society can be achieved only by general supraconscious agreement. Don't make the mistake of thinking that his examples of people who exhibit those qualities, the 'superbly literate' or 'supremely artistic', have really found themselves. They are merely expressing the perfection of part of themselves, a part which, were they complete (ie supraconscious), they would not project in this way but would indulge, simply, when and only when all other responsibilities had been fulfilled. What Roszak calls the 'essential divinity' of self, as it exists, is also insufficient as a foundation of human society, for it is the guiltless innocence of absolute conscious/ instinctive identification with a restricted and workable set of mores, similar to the innocent 'personhood' of the animal. The 'essential divinity' of humans depends upon ignorant or deliberate isolation from an otherwise guilty reality, or from awareness of its crimes. It is similar to the undoubted rightness of instinctive animal behaviour, a sense of freedom on the part of creatures who are in fact rigidly programmed, whose minds are closed to anything which does not directly concern them, and who are unaware of any possible alternative.

Roszak says that society has hardly any leverage with innocent people other than to use physical power. This fact is evident from events in Eastern Europe in 1989/90, where the united will of the people has prevailed, even overcoming the physical powers of secret police and army. But society *is,* or should be, the people. Present societies comprise governments and people, often in conflict. The conflict is least when the competitive money-economy is prosperous and the people have opportunity to win what they feel they want. The conflict is greatest (though not openly expressed) when there exists a moral vacuum, with the people unable to get what they think they want, unable openly to express themselves, and unwilling to give to the state, and with the state oppressing what it sees as an irresponsible populace, and seeing it as its duty to enforce law and order. Such disunited systems can't work. Prosperous economies appear to work, after an amoral fashion, but their conflicts will come to a head once their economies inevitably decline. As I have said, society *is* the people, and ideally depends not on a wide variety of persons pursuing their own limited ends but on each individual wholly sharing in the common responsibility.

Again, the difference between Roszak and myself rests on our interpretation of personhood, and the key is supraconsciousness. If all people were supra-conscious then that would be their common essential personhood, uniting them in humantrue agreement. But if they are less than supraconscious, imagining their fundamental selves as being invested in a mysterious external cosmic consciousness which does not exist and devolving responsibility onto it, then they will always be in a state of conflict, and they will always need some kind of narrow governing rule and enforced law and order. Let me reiterate the fundamental significance of supraconsciousness - that it holds the individual to humantrue morality, not immune to lesser influences but determined not to act on them; *unable* to do so.

When Roszak writes of 'mind-forged manacles of social domination, caused by such as self-loathing (possibly evoked by Catholic upbringing) that opens people to emotional intimidation, he is referring to such lesser influences. The Machine and its competitive money-economy have made these lesser influences all-powerful, so that they dominate us emotionally and mentally. These influences can be rejected by the postconscious that, because its natural aim must be to establish a humantrue society, will eventually do away with such false domination by removing these influences. The dominance of such influences is presently tolerated because our thinking is false, and little can be gained from rejecting them until our minds are humantrue. An example of such influences is the money-economic expedient by which industry is persuaded to dispose of the dangerously toxic wastes it sees fit to generate by emptying them into rivers and seas. The Greens valiantly oppose such practices, but their political proposal to punish polluters by laws and taxes does not remove the influence at the root of all such practices.

In the kind of society which the Greens appear to be proposing, of which Roszak seems to have been the inspiration, the Machine would remain the framework of life but the people, given complete freedom to discover themselves by, for example meditation, would find an inner goodness by whose influence the Machine would become benign. In my opinion this goodness, in a competitive reality, can only be allowed to more privileged persons at one extreme and must be countered by the 'badness' of the underprivileged persons necessarily occupying the opposite extreme. As a result we would end up with yet another conflicting regime that, though it might achieve unprecedented freedom at the top level, would descend to complete subjugation at the bottom. This attempt at balance would thus simply re-establish a state of imbalance, an intensified reflection of existing reality in which we find the supposedly free USA on one hand, and the poverty of Bangladesh, or, until recently, the oppression of Eastern Europe on the other.

I am bound to say that Roszak somehow fails to comprehend the phenomenon that is humanity, this combination of animal instinct, and intellect capable of discerning truth. His talk of personal sanctity, magic, charisma, covers with confusing mystery that which can and must be sensibly explained away and put in its insignificant place. By criticising the 'Age of Reason as the sweeping rejection of all sacramental experience' he demonstrates a failure to appreciate that the true age of reason is yet to come, or to understand that religions have failed because they have not wholly revealed or completely upheld true human morality.

Roszak is staging a battle between forces which may be of his imagination. On one side is the enemy - bourgeois liberalism and social democracy - and on the other side the home team, magical personhood. But liberalism and democracy are not states of being but weapons used by humanity in its moral struggles with the Machine, and magical personhood is surely our otherwise concealed personal moral and instinctive yearning coming, where permitted, to the surface. I respectfully suggest that he has not yet discovered what a person inherently is because, although he has widely explored the conscious mind and illuminated its dark recesses; he has not fully opened to the postconscious mind in order to experience supraconsciousness. The result is failure to comprehend that at the bottom of all our superficial speculations is the fact that we have not yet realised our true potential; that there is no future in being, dealing with, or catering for the personalities we presently comprise because they are not yet complete. If our object is to discover truth, let us observe truth in the process. Truth will not be found in the outcome of a battle between limited, and thus false forces of opposite conscious opinion and belief.

Roszak mentions the 'Personalists', who did not elaborate their system into an ideology. He proposes, in my view quite rightly, an exodus from the cities into the country (as long as it is accompanied by eradication of the very concept of city), but I am quite certain that he is wrong in rejecting any kind of ideal system of living. All other forms of life work to a system and, except that we must take over from instinct the responsibility for ourselves, we are no exception. I agree with him that we should live in small communities, but unless all communities express and reflect the agreed humantruth vested in each individual, contributing to an agreed worldwide cooperative system and moral code, they are bound to degenerate into competitive groups, eventually amalgamating into warring kingdoms, and so on - a repeat of history. The experiences of communes in America and elsewhere do not prove anything, for they are miscellaneous conscious attempts to survive against the tide of an unsympathetic Machine. I am envisaging a world of small, closely internet-connected communities whose members are all supraconscious and all supportive of the same humantrue constitution, a world dependent upon individual responsibility - the only possible means of our Earth-life fulfilling itself, or even continuing.

Person/Planet continually returns to questions whose answers lie in the fact that the existing Machine *and* the person are both contained within the conscious arena that renders them unable to satisfy the inner, true human self whose fulfilment will be found only in supraconsciousness.

I have said earlier that there is no real intellating going on, and nothing has since given me cause to change that view. But there has been some heartfelt and brilliant thinking. The authors of the books appraised in this chapter - Porritt, Pedlar, Capra, and now Roszak, are fully aware of, and deeply concerned about the appalling state of the world and our prospects. It is remarkable (until we remember once more that our reality is locked into the conscious arena) that their warning revelations have made such little real impression on humanity. These books are not in the mainstream of publishing, but those who are genuinely seeking truth probably gravitate to them as the only serious attempts to find it. To most people, particularly those who most need to read them (seriously, not condescendingly) - economists, industrialists, politicians, Philosophers etc. - these books are unknown, or pushed aside, and those who are willing to read them may have to go out of their way to find them.

Of those few such books that I have read, Roszak's Person/Planet goes deepest into the relationship between humanity and reality. But that his philosophy falls short, in my view, is demonstrated by his views on charismatic characters. We should not rely on them, as he suggests, but on our own supraconscious determinations, and eventually on a humantrue framework of life, to bring out the best in us. Otherwise we are as likely to come under the spell of Hitler as of Jesus. This incompleteness of understanding is further demonstrated by Roszac's views on the family

He sets out a declaration, made to children, which is beautiful. But he is envisaging a continuation of the present competitive governing reality, a generally hostile world in which it is necessary to have local allies, and in which family loyalty is a valuable support. But unconditional loyalty puts conditioning shackles on thought. It is the way of non-intellectual nature, the law of survival of the fittest that maintains the balance of nature. It is and has always been characteristic of our competitive, warring history. It is inappropriate because giving and loyalty *within* families inevitably, under pressure, means the opposite *between* families. It is ultimately genocidal because our conscious/instinctive powers of thought can carry our hostilities to the limits of destructiveness.

This idea of exclusive family giving does not include the most important of our gifts - intellation. It can not do so, for intellation would soon make it clear that we must be loyal to everybody, and our best efforts must be given to everybody, if our society is to be humantrue. I realise that Roszak envisages the economy being brought down to a domestic scale, as I do, but as long as the competitive money-economy exists, and family units remain divided, the local domestic enterprises which are successful will eventually grow into big business - another repetition of history, bringing us back to the present chaos. This is another example of failure to intellate to true conclusions, Failure to learn this important lesson shows in Jonathan Porritt's conviction that people will only do things when a certain self-interest is involved. This conviction is founded upon the belief that the basic facts and concepts of existing reality are inescapable. We have yet to see that they are utterly unacceptable - that wholesale fundamental change, from the minds of humanity to the entire constitution of our society, is vital to the achievement of our full and true potential.

The foregoing comments cover two-thirds of Person/Planet. The remaining one-third deals with some aims of world reform, many of which I agree with but with the means of which I disagree, for Roszak's concepts do not yet fulfil humantruth. I believe that all differences between us *should* be thrashed out until we reach true agreement, but it is not possible for me to pick up every point in detail in the space of this one book. Having dealt with the principles I must leave it largely to you, if you wish, to make your own comparison between the practices proposed by Roszak and those which I have suggested earlier in this book. I will content myself with pointing out the most fundamental disagreements.

Roszak believes that the self-discovery of individual resources is the wealth of nations. I believe that we must first discover humantruth to which we must then be primarily responsible - our skills and talents must be adjusted and moulded to the necessary tasks, not the other way round.

He envisages a society of people with infinitely variable lifestyles. I believe we must cut our physical coat according to our cloth, for our bodies and environment and interdependence limit us as to what we can be or do. Our physical/emotional beings must be content with simple common satisfactions, but we can fulfil intellect in an infinite variety of abstract ways.

He suggests that education is a matter of learning the discipline of truth. This presumably means submission to the evidence and argument of the Philosophical discipline of thinking and experiencing within the conscious arena. I believe that the object of upbringing and education must be primarily to encourage and help every individual to achieve supraconsciousness by intellation.

I agree with Roszak in his views on artificial and indirect employment, but he still describes it as 'work' in a way that still separates it from the individual in relation to the true collective interest. I believe that as long as we have a competitive system like the Machine it will be necessary to harness human effort to 'work' by means of the incentive of self-interest. Humantrue responsibility would translate 'work' into normal living activity, and to achieve this we have to get rid of the Machine and make local community concerns the summit of world reality and of human practical interest.

He says each of us has a calling whose exercise is high delight, though it demands sweat and suffering, and gives a real and useful place in the world. I know exactly what he means, but this is the call of emotion and we live in the Machine, and so we are called to an existing occupation that must be acceptable to the Machine but may well not be in the interests of humanity. In determining what we must do we should be led by supraconscious intellect, recognising that emotion will naturally fall in behind that determination in due course, to support it.

Though highly critical of present employment practice, Roszak does not acknowledge that the 'evil' of modern industrial exploitation or neglect of humans is the inescapable product of an authoritative hierarchy and a competitive money-economy, a system that is impossible to humanise. Such an economy is bound to result in many different levels of workers, most of whose tasks and personal interests are remote from the purpose and value of the product. The activities of a humantrue society, pleasant or not, would be necessary, and would be shared between all members.

Roszak says it is people, not machines, who cause things to happen in history. In my view the reverse is true. The automaton, founded on the principles of government and competition, formed the Machine that founded the institutions which fundamentally dictate human actions.

He believes it to be science fiction fantasy that machines will ever be able to do without us. On the contrary, if we remain confined to the conscious arena, the thinking machines *will* be able to do without us because, in that arena of limited mental capacity, without the promptings or doubts (intuition, conscience) of the much more vast postconscious (which will not be built into the machines, otherwise they too would have our true potential, which *we* ignore), they can be much more definite, decisive and effective servants of the Machine than we.

He maintains that the needs of the person vibrate sympathetically to the needs of the planet. I am sure that whilst we might feel so we do not actually do so, but struggle to wrest our needs from an indifferent planet like the rest of nature. The planet is a working system, to which we and all life have adapted, but it has no needs or feelings. Gaia does not purposely support us but is simply a response to all life's sheer will to go on living. Life itself is full of torment, as well as joy, and would strip Earth bare if it were free, but each species has its own logic and love. We also have a human logic and love and it is this, and the long experience of it from its ancient Earth origins, that we feel in sympathy with. What normally persuades us to try to disaffiliate from the Machine is that our life, even though gifted with our unique intellect (by which we could make a perfectly harmonious relationship with Earth), no longer has that natural logic and love.

Referring to the relationship between employers and workers, Roszak later envisages a new economics that is based on labour value rather than commodity price. He is clearly imagining the same basic economic system that presently exists but with different degrees of value. But however you superficially tinker with the competitive money-economy, without changing its basic self-interest motive you will not humanise it. I am amazed at the ease with which we are hoodwinked by this patently inhuman system so that everybody seems unwilling or afraid to condemn it as a whole.

In his critical analysis of the city, Roszak says that city dwellers are isolated from the basic ecological facts of life so that they cannot distinguish between real and artificial needs - that they are so cut off from Earth-nature as to be unaware of their vital inter-dependence. I don't think anybody would argue with this, up to a point. However, it is necessary to remember that the cities grew *out* of the countryside. It is the Machine that is leading us to human and ecological ruination, and the concept of the city serves it best. With accelerating autoprogression, television, and now internet communication is fast spreading automatic values - the city concept - over the whole globe, so that even country-dwellers are becoming isolated from the ecological facts of life. This is further reason why we must eliminate the Machine root and branch, to destroy the cancerous drives whose accumulating growth, which causes cities to be built and is spreading everywhere, is utterly contrary to humantrue interests.

We are presently in trouble because we have failed to take humantruth as our sole guide, and we shall be truly human only when we observe and realise it in the world. Roszak maintains that the city will remain a cultural and economic necessity, but only in small doses. I do not agree, because it makes for inequality. We must rid ourselves of the ideas of *external* artificial riches, either economic or cultural, and let human richness accumulate purely in the heads of individuals. Of course the city's decline will not be successfully accomplished by mandatory removal of its people into the country, as Roszak would be the first to agree. It will have to be a voluntary happening, with humantrue awareness providing the motivation and preparing the way. If we do not embrace humantruth we shall not survive as an intellectual race, nor shall we deserve to.

Roszak now comes to the question of critical opposition to his theories, surely rightly pointing out that it comes not only from the political and commercial interests but also from the intellectual (by which he means academic) community to which he belongs and from which, he thinks, his readers must come. Still identifying the city as his enemy, he sees it as serving the interests of that opposition who will not, therefore, allow his theories to gain the recognition they deserve or to percolate to public awareness. He sees the intellectuals as the aboriginal urban class, the creators of the city, who have caused its dominant role to be accepted as conventional wisdom.

I hope and incline to the belief that there are at least as many intellectuals outside as within the academic community, and would not credit academic intellectuals with wielding such power and influence, nor do I see this as a question of the power of the city or the influence of the intellectual, political or commercial elites. It is a matter of the Machine's worldwide dominance - dominance of the great majority of individuals (most of whom live in cities, which they may dislike at the same time as they believe in the Machine), and of the great majority of institutions (served by humans, from manual workers to governing and intellectual elites). But it is chiefly a matter of the fact that the whole Machine, the vast majority of human minds and their accepted concept of reality, is contained within the limits of the conscious arena to the exclusion of their higher potential of true supraconscious awareness. Conscious minds have not the capacity to escape existing reality, and they produce a welter of contradictory evidence and argument. The inability of conscious thinking to gravitate to truth is shown by the fact that the pioneering work of minds who have attained a higher level (like Roszak himself and a handful of others, four of whom he mentions - Kropotkin, Tolstoi, Ghandi, and Danilo Dolci) have not immediately affected the thinking of all humanity to the extent of significantly raising its level of awareness. This is not only the fault of the establishment and its resistance to dissemination of radical thinking, for ideas which really catch the public imagination will find a way of spreading whatever the opposition. The failure of radical thinking to get across to a wide public is due to the fact that the majority attitude is at present tilted strongly towards automatic conformity. If human minds in general are to venture beyond the bounds of consciousness and to press for the true guidance of their postconscious faculties, that attitude of mind needs to be tilted the other way by the revelation that this new direction is the road to fulfilling our true human potential.

The concluding part of 'Person/Planet' continues for thirty pages. I would be happy to end my comments on Roszak's work with the preceding crucial paragraph, but must remark on his references to monasteries as possible examples of the kind of community we should live in. Overlooking the fact that monasteries were often richly endowed, hierarchical, secluded and built on a grand scale in favoured situations; that they were all-male, without the problems that go with marriage and children (though also without the blessings); that the monks were usually endowed with respected status and were intellectually and institutionally, if not materially, privileged, he gives this beautiful description - ..."*their economics was left to take shape from the prerequisites of personal growth.*(I would prefer prerequisites of steady, satisfactory management according to little-changing reciprocal needs of the world). *This clearly did not preclude....technical innovation....to relieve drudgery* (I would say that this needed to be fixed at an agreed and little changing level). *But the economics of the monasteries was kept 'labour-intensive' because it was clearly understood that work is a necessary attribute of the personality, while limitless affluence is not."*

My approach to this last extract from Roszak's work is typical of the problem one faces in reading a book of this kind. On one hand we wish to appreciate that which is beautiful, agreeable or good in it. On the other hand (the important one) we should not slide over that which is doubtful. We will never fulfil our true humanity if we do not stretch our minds, resolve our differences, and reach humantrue agreement. This is why, rather than praise Theodore Roszak for the qualities of his book, I have concentrated upon our differences. Even his pleasant picture of worthy monasteries is spoiled by these disagreements. I even now feel compelled to question the assertion that 'work is a necessary attribute of the personality', preferring to assert that 'manual labour is a necessary part of human fulfilment'. This may seem carping, but, as I am sure Roszak would agree, if we are to achieve a humantrue world we must honestly and utterly strive for it, leaving no stone unturned.

All the books I have appraised so far in this chapter purport to tackle the whole human problem, which makes them worth reading. Most have hinted at a systems solution to the world's difficulties, implying that this solution would somehow spring from a melding of the human mind with a phenomenon relating to influences of universal energy (that I have been inclined to think imaginary or misrepresented but am now taking more seriously while disbelieving that they negate overriding belief in supraconsciousness) sometimes known as cosmic consciousness.

The next book is a thorough exposition of system theory as applied to human being that enables me to make the contrary case for humantrue society. The book suggests to me the kind of world that would result from the systems principle being actually applied to human society. I think it demonstrates that the universe contains no benign, sensitive and thoughtful cosmic consciousness, but is governed by the hard logic of a cause-and-effect system in which the positive and negative extremes of instinctive behaviour have a natural place, but which is anathema to supraconscious awareness.

The book I refer to is entitled The Cultural Science of Man : A New Synthesis, by Bernice Cohen (published by Codek Publications Ltd.) and is in three volumes : 1. The Seamless Web, 2. The Origin of Civilisation, and 3. Global Perspectives - The Total Culture System in the Modern World. Although acknowledging that Ms.Cohen's purpose is to bring about a better world, I find myself in almost total disagreement with her analysis of the human problem and with her solutions to it. Therefore, while admiring her tremendous effort of research and coordination, I must concentrate upon making my opposite case.

The fundamental premises of this 1100-page book are that there are coordinating universal laws, as yet unknown, which govern human cultures; that human behaviour can be classified in the same way as that of nature, since man is part of nature; that human history is a culture continuum, governed by the overriding fact that it is a systematic phenomenon. Cohen claims that her conclusions are supported by four knowledge bases; knowledge gained from a long grounding in systems architecture; by the concepts known to characterise open systems; by taking account of population dynamics in biology; and by applying the existing laws of physics to her dynamic culture change theory. This reveals to me the fatal flaw in her thinking, that it is restricted to the conscious mind confined to the conscious arena, and therefore excludes an all-important factor - the overriding significance of humanity's possession (as yet unfulfilled) of the ultimate intellectual faculty.

Ms.Cohen's basic premises are that humans as they presently exist, living in a variety of cultures, their actions determined by a wide variety of conflicting factors, are unpredictable; that our world affairs are in a dangerous state of chaos because they are entrusted to a number of national governments that do not understand the pressures involved, whose interests differ and who are in competitive conflict; that by the systems classification of culture the overall behaviour of society as a whole *could* be predicted; therefore that a world government, informed by systems analysis of all the factors bearing upon the world situation, could adopt such policies as would bring to bear other powerful factors of such influence as to steer world affairs onto a humane, peaceable, and environmentally friendly road.

Whilst I cannot question the evidence that supports the systems analysis of human cultural history, ours is the history of a yet largely instinctive species, a race of creatures who have not yet achieved their potential. The universe, the planet, nature - these *are* dynamically progressive systems that have an objective, to achieve which they must not only survive but continue this dynamic progress. Their objective is the achievement of fulfilled intellect, but, since that objective has nowhere, to our knowledge, been achieved, the lessons of the past cannot truly teach us, a potentially intellectual species, how to proceed in the future. Systems theory can be applied to explain nature as the random and potentially unpredictable behaviour of thousands of competing species, and of individual creatures competing within species, brought to balance and relative predictability by the government of instinct. It could, as a theory, be applied to a human society of hundreds of competing nations, and of millions of individual humans in mutual competition within nations, brought to integrative balance by one world government. But I utterly disagree with the application of systems theory to humanity for the following reasons.

Most importantly, though still confined to the conscious arena, we *are* an intellectual species. We represent the achievement of Earth's primary objective - intellect - that gives us a new and different objective - the ultimate objective of the universe - to fulfil the function of intellect that is truth. Of course, if we are to represent truth and add to its influence in the universe, we too must survive, and that means we must care for the Earth on whose bounty we depend. As intellectual creatures, although we have not yet achieved our full potential, we will not wholly submit to external control, neither by instinct, nor by any government whether on a world, national or local scale. This is because we have conscious minds of such capacity that they can stand back just far enough to look at our present selves and our apparent actual circumstances. In order wilfully to join the self and the conscious mind in a common identity we amalgamate our temperament with our adopted construction of thought and its perceived opinions and beliefs. The fact that individual conscious identities can almost infinitely disagree is the reason why, as a society, we do not extricate ourselves from our present horrific predicament, and why we cannot really be controlled by external authority. We would have to agree first, and the only possible ground for agreement amongst an intellectual race is truth, the ultimate function of intellect. To recognise and then to realise truth we have to become collectively supraconscious. When we become supraconscious we will perceive that the only social system appropriate to us is an agreed and simple humantrue world constitution sustained, without overall active government of any sort, by individual responsibility.

Ever since we acquired the faculty of intellect, we have applied part of it to continuing dynamic autoprogression at the same time as the unconscious part has made us morally aware of the wrong we were doing. That is the reason for the present chaotic and dangerous state of the world and our awakening awareness of this situation and horrified reaction to it. The authors of the books so far appraised have reacted to the situation by exposing the actual dangers facing us - by showing what is wrong and what would, in general terms, be right, but not showing how to make the desirable transition.

Bernice Cohen does put forward the basis of a strategy. Believing that our present nature (self-orientated, unpredictable) and state (competitive money-economy and authoritative government) is inevitable, she recognises that to continue our present random progress means disaster, but also believes that if our present society lost its dynamic energy (that which dictates its pattern) it would, according to the physical laws, die out. Her solution is to maintain energetic dynamism in a *controlled* way, using systems theory. Broadly, this theory simply states that every course of action is the result of numerous influences, in fluctuating series, accumulating to produce that course of action. At present our actions, as a world society, are often harmful and generally in conflict because they are random and uncoordinated. She suggests that by analysing the evidence of archaeology and history and applying that knowledge to current affairs we can predict the outcome of those affairs. Through world government we can then introduce, by means of laws, taxes and incentives, additional influences in the right places to affect the outcome of affairs to the benefit of ourselves and Earth.

In making her proposals, Cohen negates the whole object of evolution - the achievement of fulfilled intellect. She would have us subjected to the Machine, albeit a newly controlled version of it with the will and the means to survive built in. She does not make a distinction between us and instinctive nature. She takes no account of the truth, to fulfil which is the ultimate nature of an intellectual species. She does not recognise that the way of intellect is to determine its course by intention, according to moral truth, which has care and compassion for all life at its heart, and to make it work despite any contrary influence or pressure.

Although I had immediately to dismiss systems theory as being inapplicable to humanity, I persevered with The Cultural Science of Man, hoping that it might make proposals of such merit that even so they might answer our needs. In this I was disappointed, for Cohen contends that a great deal more research is needed before such proposals can be made (she mentions several decades). I suggest that she failed to reach such conclusions because the problems are insuperable. Even with a supraconscious understanding of humantruth and its vital concepts and principles, it is not easy, or right, for one mind to lay down in detail the complex practical constitution of a humantrue society. To attempt, within the mental chaos of the conscious arena, to define the terms of a supreme government, staffed by fallible human beings, such as would control a whole world of widely differently constituted and conditioned human individuals, within the competitive, free-enterprise, self-oriented framework of the Machine, at the same time ensuring that it is benignly humane, is an utter impossibility.

Were it really the case that the Machine is inescapable, then the running of human society as an open, dynamically changing system, but under central control, might well secure its survival. A world government, with the aid of systems analysis, could conceivably steer the Machine in such a way that Earth would escape environmental disaster. But this would not be true human survival, for such a government under the Machine would require an automated public, controllable by economic incentives and disincentives or by punitive laws. It would not be unlike the present situation but with the gloves off - taken to the extreme. At present we are semi-automated, semi-moral; we consciously run with the Machine but retain a conscience, the still small voice of our supraconscious potential which goes against the Machine. Under a world government, if it were to succeed in solving the physical problems in *its* way, we must lose the freedom to explore our full and true intellectual potential, giving up the right to question and disagree. We would be forced to submit to this new dictatorship, with little hope of relief because it would hold absolutely supreme power.

To me, this presents an awful prospect. There can be little doubt of its being a realistic possibility. We have so many examples, right up to the present, of what happens when the power of authority, over people who have not risen above the conscious/instinctive state of awareness, is given to a minority or a single individual in the same state, however good their initial intentions. We also have very recent examples of the ease with which peoples can sometimes topple unpopular governments and ideologies, and I cannot imagine permanent world systems government attracting popular support. Cohen's proposed supreme world authority, presiding over similar but even more complex circumstances, must sound the death-knell for supraconsciousness, for, if the system were to survive, that authority would have to exercise such ruthlessly precise artificial (not truly reasoned) control as to require our total subservience to it and the Machine and make overthrow impossible. I would sooner have humanity die out than sink to these depths.

Cohen sees the world as the product of an imperfect humanity, and the study of human behaviour in an abstract void as therefore meaningless. This view returns us once more to the theory that people will not do the right thing if not to their personal advantage. I see existing human nature as the product of an imperfect world, with both confined to the conscious/instinctive arena. Our true nature is to be supraconscious, but since we nowhere exist in this state it *has* to be studied in the abstract. This is the fundamental difference between Cohen and myself. She takes the actual realistic view, the basis of which is to accept the facts and concepts of reality as they exist but to manipulate them to our benefit according to the many (and contradictory) values we presently uphold. I take the *potential* supraconsciously realistic view, the basis of which is to reject the existing facts and concepts of reality - the entire Machine - and to replace it with an alternative humantrue reality the constitution of which is to be found, by intellation, in the common, free and independent, untaught, non-conditioned postconscious.

Clearly, a humantrue society would work to a simple system, but not one that conformed to nature. This is the last thing we want, for the power of human intellect, coupled to the instinctive drives, is beyond instinctive inhibition to control. I understand Cohen's contention that the instinctive drives are needed to sustain the dynamism of human society which depends on them to "prosper" as an open system, and that they could be kept under control by world government, but such a prosperous system does not serve humanity - humanity serves it. In any case, the members of a world government would not be an effective counter-balance to the Machine, for reasons already given. Its members, too, would be limited, competitive, egotistical humans who, assuming the separate identity conferred by their governing position, could not be relied upon to follow systems analysis, mush less to act in the true interests of humanity. Lacking supraconscious awareness they are as likely as not to capitalise on their powers in their own interests. In the eyes of the consciously automated this would be logical. Members of a world government who consistently behaved otherwise, faithfully serving humanity according to humantruth, would soon realise that the true interests of humanity could not be served by world government.

I repeat, the possession of the faculty of intellect changes the whole picture. When fulfilled, this faculty will enable us to perceive humantruth and to responsibly realise it in the world. There is no reason why an intellectual race should conform to rules that apply to open systems. The second law of thermodynamics applies to physics, and to instinct, but *not* to intellect. The supraconscious humantrue system would be new and different, physically dependent on making its own lasting relationship with nature, on its own terms, but otherwise sustained by its own intellectual dynamism under the supraconscious control of responsible individuals tuned in to the common humantruth.

As before I find myself in agreement with Cohen's overall aim but critical of her conclusions. For example, she states that the main transitions (of human society) appear to be irreversible, just as they are in other open systems. Taking the UK's passage from the agricultural to the industrial age as an instance, this transition *is* presently irreversible because autoprogression does not doubt itself, and the Machine *is* an open system - it needs to be, according to systems theory, in order to survive. That closed systems have never survived does not mean that they cannot do so. We are a departure from the universal norm, a spearhead of a new norm in which transitions *can* be reversed.

Cohen states that change (i.e. progress) seems to be the essence of the human state. On the contrary, it is the essence of the natural state of which potentially true humanity would be the non-conformist end-product.

She asserts that modern man may be a transitional species, living in chaos and not understanding that unless he himself imposes crucial controls his 'culture system' cannot survive. Yes, but man as he stands is false and incapable. When we see that this is so we shall also see the humantruth, and that the vital human transition is from instinct to intellect, from the Machine to humantrue society.

Cohen says that currently there is no global self-controlling mechanism for man's culture-system. But there is - global, universal truth and human post-consciousness of truth. This is the answer to all her insecure, consciously-grounded reasoning in support of systems-culture. If we behave like subsystems according to the individually unpredictable but overall probabilities of a culture-system, it is because we are controlled by that system. Rather than ourselves taking control of a bad system, we should create a good one.

She states that there can be no independent variables - every human act has to be a simultaneous causal result of all others. She goes on to say that this is typical of systems driven by feedback, where the results are influenced by interactions to the extent that it might be possible to unravel such cause-and-effect relationships. This is a view confined to the physical plane, hardly rising even to the conscious. Intellect replaces the function of feedback and truth simplifies relationships because all refer to one and the same body of truth. Supraconsciousness is the means by which we can, and must, diverge from the norm and adopt our own independent variety of motives derived from humantrue principles.

Cohen maintains that throughout history our cultures have been poor because we have failed in awareness of their causal mechanisms - that our dynamic culture system cannot be understood except in the context of its own structure and environment. In my view our cultures have failed because they follow instinct, whereas we all sense our intellectual morality that makes us *aware* of their poverty. Her view of human understanding is similar to the presently normal opinion that the here and now, not abstract theory, should be our concern.

She believes that with the expansion of knowledge in all directions there is an acute need on the part of the individual to widen his or her personal knowledge base. I see accumulation of knowledge as binding us to the Machine. The prior need is to become supraconscious, and then to confine knowledge to necessity, in the capacity of helpful informant rather than master, and subject to reason.

According to Cohen, an abstracted life-system would be entirely meaningless. We can only describe human culture, she says, in terms of what has evolved, not what should have evolved, and systems theory that is relevant to human cultural behaviour must be closely tied to the empirical data. This false view is foundational to the generally held human concept of reality, and the basis of my difficulty with Chomsky. The opposite is true - the chief thing to have evolved is the potential human intellect, and the framework of life that has otherwise diversely evolved must be meaningless to fulfilled intellect. To tie the concepts and facts of reality to the empirical data is to imprison oneself in a system from which truth, in all its meanings other than fact alone, is excluded. *Of course* we should make models of reality as it humantruly ought to be, however naive the automated realists may think us.

This is the crux of the matter. Cohen is demonstrating the realistic case, favoured because it can be supported by facts that have been empirically verified, or by logic that cannot be denied by limited conscious reason. This comes of unwillingness to recognise the pure truth of the postconscious because the only verification of that truth is internal recognition of the utterly reasoned knowing of the postconscious itself. This unwillingness is the great mistake of practically all of our accepted thinking, governed, as it is, by the Philosophical discipline, requiring evidence and argument that is accessible but which is no more than half-true because its fact is confined to present reality and its reasoning limited to the lesser capacity of the conscious mind.

The rest of Cohen's work, being based on this false premise, is irrelevant if one accepts that intellect is unique. Further comment is necessary, however, because her overall views are commonly, though often almost unthinkingly, the views of automated humans.

She refers to a suggestion, made by Adam Smith more than two centuries ago, that the uncoordinated actions of innumerable individuals pursuing their own interests could, in sum, serve the common interest of them all. I understand the reasoning on which this suggestion is based, but it is very far from complete. The only way in which humanity can serve the common interest is by way of supraconscious awareness of each individual's equal humantrue responsibility. Uncoordinated activity of self-interested individuals produces local squabbling and general disruption. Coordinated activity of the Machine served by humanity for material rewards produces dangerous conflict and organised chaos. When we defend the freedom to choose our separate culture or religion, we should remember the Palestinian conflict, the IRA, the Azerbaijani massacre of Armenians, and numerous more recent horrors. People who are not bound to morality by supraconsciousness are capable of anything. Humanity controlled by culture dynamics in order to survive indefinitely would be a meaningless relic, misusing its means of discovering and realising truth and so falling short of (and in any case being forbidden) its true ends. I see the application of systems theory to culture dynamics as the last resort of a society which has missed its vocation by failing to achieve the purpose for which it evolved.

Bernice Cohen goes on to claim that the long-term steady state is an illusion, in nature, the cosmos, and in the affairs of man. This is true of ourselves only insofar as humanity has not yet fulfilled its true purpose. Before man appeared it could have been said, had there been anybody to make the observation, that the concept of individual intellect - of the development of a faculty of ultimate knowing and reasoning in humans - was an illusion because no such faculty appeared to exist in nature or the cosmos. We return to Cohen's assertion that an abstracted life-system would be entirely meaningless, and to Chomsky's assertion that an idea that is not supportable by conscious evidence and argument must be groundless speculation. This is the reasoning of minds which (though it may be for the best of motives) dare not let go of the apparent certainty of conscious thinking because of the seeming uncertainty of supraconscious intellation and postconscious inner true knowing (inasfar as they recognise that phenomenon for what it is), and which therefore fall short of that visionary leap that is required to make us truly human. This shows prevalent human thinking to be stubbornly blind to the evident probability that the steady-state, or true equilibrium, is the *ultimate object* of life.

I think I am right in deducing that Ms Cohen subscribes to the view, held by Capra, Roszak and others, that just as sub-atomic particle behaviour provides a link between cosmic purpose and the behaviour of matter, so should the human mind be used to convert cosmic purpose into human behaviour (taking the purpose of the cosmos to be to continue the manner and motive of all past and present activity into the future). I have to say that this is backward reasoning which makes the assumption that 'there is nothing new under the sun', and which turns intellect in on itself to serve the meaningless objective of life simply to live, and the universe simply to exist, by the blind process of cause and effect.

She also remarks that our ignorance is vastly greater than our knowledge. As I have said already, our true reasoning is far smaller, and our practical knowledge already much greater, than required to deduce humantruth. We hardly need more such knowledge, but the conscious and utilised postconscious, applied to instinctive drives, impel us to discover every physical possibility, which is one part of truth. The independent postconscious is capable of perceiving the superior humantruth, including the truth that, in the past, pursuit of every physical possibility was essential for the achievement of intellect. But once an intellectual species has perceived this, it will also recognise that in order to realise humantruth it no longer needs to autoprogress, but physically to stabilise itself, then to develop dramatically but only in the abstract (by which means stagnation will be avoided).

Ms.Cohen makes many other sweeping statements. Her book is an example of conscious thought, within the conscious arena, which offers a mass of evidence and argument but cannot comprehend the truth of the postconscious because that faculty's superior reason does not appeal to consciousness. The usefulness of all this lies in reminding the reader how easy it is to fall into the normal fault of being drawn, by realities which are false but consciously satisfying, into denying postconscious truths. Since Cohen's thinking is thus revealed as faulty, I will refrain from commenting further except on the most outstanding of her statements.

The Cultural Science of Man, making little or no mention of morality, or of the strengths and delicacies of human feeling, fails to face up to a problem of which the following is perhaps an appropriate example. Smoking tobacco is generally accepted, at least in the Western world, as morally wrong in that it is a most unhealthy practice. In a humantrue society, to smoke would be impossible because tobacco would not be grown or supplied for the reason that smoking was recognised as immoral by every individual, and because nobody's living depended upon selling it. In our present contradictory society we acknowledge that smoking is unhealthy and have warnings printed on cigarette packets, but companies continue profitably to market tobacco, and people to smoke it to compensate for a largely empty life. I imagine that a systems-based dynamic culture such as Cohen proposes, having to assume responsibility for a presumed irresponsible public, would have to outlaw the production and smoking of tobacco because the task of world government, it must be supposed, would be to bring responsible and health-cost-wise order to the presently chaotic system. As a result there would be a black market in tobacco (as there now is in drugs) because there would still be a demand to be profitably supplied. As a result there would be public resentment of government interference, and underground warfare between police and tobacco racketeers. This would threaten even more chaos than presently exists, chaos which is inevitable where life is a struggle between our humanity and our false reality, and one is bound to conclude that, to bring order to that reality without reform, a much more oppressive regime would be required.

Cohen further demonstrates her misunderstanding of the human mind when she describes thinking as a system to be used by humans, subservient to their will. This raises the question - what advises or directs will? Upbringing, education, the Machine, instinct? Is it her belief that these things influence thinking, which then advises will, which then uses thinking? If these and other such questions are persevered with, the inevitable conclusion is that to be truly human is to be supraconscious, whereby the agreed humantruth is to be followed by the individual, with a will, and served by society.

In Cohen's opinion culture is a human device to ensure survival, and the rate at which we have risen to dominate the Earth is a measure of our incredible success. But given that intellect is so powerful, as a weapon, that we could hardly fail to dominate; given the relatively short span of time that we *have* dominated; given that we have reduced Earth to a sorry state approaching exhaustion; and given the marvellous potential of intellect cooperatively to flourish, rather than dominate - a potential which we have almost totally failed to realise - this can hardly be termed success.

Ms Cohen claims that just as we do not need to know or understand the scientific basis of computers or the internal combustion engine to use a word processor or drive a car, so we should accept her theoretical base for the study of humanity. It continues to amaze me that the majority, including the authors of the selected few books I have reviewed, look outward from their consciousness and not in all conceivable directions from their inner postconscious. In the case of the motor car, though ignorant of its nuts and bolts we do understand its function. In the case of the mind we do not yet understand that its only possible ultimate function is to arrive at truth, therefore that to fulfil truth is our ultimate function. Cohen shares the prevalent view of the mind as a means of the personality reacting, in its preferred way, with its existing, supposedly inescapable, reality. Even to those who do not believe intellect to be the culmination of life's evolution, it must be obvious that our present mental processes and practices, arising from this common view, result from *misapplication,* not true fulfilment, of intellect.

She next states that we need ways of healthy competition to mature, also a mature capitalist system; that the existing established processes are fundamentally totally relevant to everyday life. On the contrary, no form of competition or capitalism, however mature, can be healthy for humanity, for these are concepts appropriate to instinct. Is it not obvious that our everyday life is not relevant to our true potential?

She claims that mass democracy, human rights, the welfare state and social justice are brain children of industrialising nations. This is misleading. These things came about because the Machine, especially in industrialised nations, made them necessary to humanity as counterbalances to its automatic inhumanity, callousness, and social injustice. They arose out of the battle between our humanity and the Machine, from human protest against the Machine's indifference; protest from individuals at all levels of the hierarchies. Matters of right, welfare and justice were once natural features of developed primitive life, which civilisation eroded and ruthless industrialism brushed aside.

Cohen firmly believes that the nature or character of humanity that is presently apparent is fixed as it stands, i.e. represented by the conscious self. She does not recognise that we have yet to achieve our supraconscious potential; that we are an intellectual mutation yet to be completed. This is tantamount to judging human nature from the study of a child.

She brings extensive but necessarily limited conscious reasoning to bear in order to justify her view that the Machine is perfectly acceptable because it artificially satisfies the inner compulsions and desires, and fulfils the drives, of instinct. This is to ignore our true destiny, which is to rise above instinct and fulfil intellect. It ignores the fact that the Machine brings extremes of suffering as well as satisfaction, and goes to extremes of immorality, with nothing to hold it in check but that which it holds cheap - the inner moral sense of humanity.

Denying much superior reason and siding with the Machine, Cohen accepts the concept of competition, the keystone of the money-economy. She sees competition as 1. a basic human characteristic impulsion of which industrial capitalism is the expression, 2. a biological imperative, and 3. a basic urge to strive against each other for survival which is given outlet, though in 'civilised' form, by our culture (i.e. the Machine). But this whole concept, and the current factual reality and evident human nature that represents and supports it, is redundant. Its aim is impossible of achievement, like expecting to eliminate crime by means of law and policing. The advent of intellect requires that we replace the lores of instinct with humantrue concepts.

Ms Cohen points out that in 16th. and 17th. century England the towns-people, disregarding what we now see as common-sense hygiene, failed to make the connection between their filthy habits and the epidemics of plague which they repeatedly suffered. Their ignorance might amaze us now, but we ourselves are little better for we are guilty of causing pollution and of other ruinous practices that already plague us on a global scale and threaten our eventual extinction. Cohen blames this on blind progress without aware control, but we cannot have it both ways. Outside of the strict laws of instinct, the principles of competition and control are incompatible.

The original town-dwellers ignored hygiene because, as they shifted from country to town, they ceased to be members of tried-and-tested surviving communities and instead became separated family units in service to the Machine. Obliged to fend for themselves, independently of each other but all dependent on the Machine, they shrugged off communal responsibility from themselves and gave it to the town - to the Machine, and its institutions of central government. Eventually government discharged its responsibility as regards essentials such as hygiene, as these needs became obvious. This was its function as servant of the people, but people had to pay for this service with money paid to them as servants of the Machine. They were now more than ever units in a system in which humanity was losing in its struggle against the Machine. The town tempted people to give way to the biological urge to follow the Machine and compete for its rewards, against the strictures of conscience and intuitive reason, leaving overall responsibility to the institutions of government (themselves staffed, to some extent, by competitive and self-interested individuals) and the political method of contrived compromise.

Now, as always, governments are torn between aiding and abetting the Machine, in order to satisfy the instinctive desires and drives of people, and undertaking perceived human moral responsibilities. Any government operating within the Machine, including a world government unless it uses oppressive force, must come down chiefly on the side of satisfying instincts rather than intellectual morality, otherwise it will lose popularity and be voted out. So it is impossible, by definition, for such governments to be wholly intellectually moral. Intellect is the source of morality, and morality is not worthy of the name if not wholly observed. It follows that members of present governments, although the most automatically intelligent, are amongst the least truly intellectual of people (and therefore unfit to lead truly) and are leading us to disaster. If world government did resort to force, ostensibly for our own good (and there would then be nothing to stop it), it could easily proceed to the conclusion that the only way of solving its otherwise insoluble problems was to become a dictatorship, which could not be voted out, and I believe this to be the inevitable end to which world government would come.

Therefore it must be obvious that there is no future for a conscious/instinctive human race whose members, within the Machine, are largely irresponsible. Such a race would require both competitive freedom and precise and effective systems-government such as Cohen proposes, which is an impossibility. It is well to remember that stable and contented human societies prospered before the Machine came to dominate, because their simple ways were within the scope of conscious instinct to keep in balance autonomously. The only way that modern man may do the same is by enlarging his mental scope to the optimum (supraconscious) level. World government could succeed only if it were itself enlightened and with the cooperation of an enlightened people. But to be truly enlightened the whole people must be supraconscious, and if they were so they would see that both world government and the Machine were not only superfluous but dangerous, and that these should be replaced by a humantrue society.

Cohen maintains that evolution is not aiming for a long-term goal or long-distance target. Once again it amazes me that thinkers can say, at one moment, 'we can never know the truth', and then can make a sweeping statement such as this. Even should she happen to be right, myself wrong, how can she be so sure? There is no proof. But it is certain that the burden of reason weighs heavily on my side. Evolution, occupying hundreds of millions of years during which life advanced overall, progressed without knowing or being able to know the purpose, its various forms adapting or dying out all unawares. Then human intellect appeared, which *does* now question the meaning and purpose of life and its own threatened extinction, and is capable of comprehending the transcendental truth. Surely the truth must ultimately stand self-revealed as the obvious end of evolution, of which the universe is a means, because it explains, contains and outlives all things.

Ms. Cohen's approach to a world system is contradictory. On one hand she says that natural selection in nature and industrial capitalism in the Machine are not coincidental - that they follow laws of nature that are as applicable to man as to all Earth's life-forms. On the other hand she says that individual rampant self-interest will benefit society only if it rests on a moral code. In between she says that we are not *special*, but merely products of nature with the added gift of conscious thought and language; that we are still subject to the laws of nature because we do not yet perceive that nature will dominate us until we take control of our future destiny; but also that competitive pressures will remain compellingly valid in order still to dictate that future destiny just as they dictate to nature.

These are common but generally unnoticed contradictions that crop up everywhere, all the time, and are irreconcilable. They are indications of the unresolved struggle between our humanity and the Machine in which we vacillate between strong instinctive impulsions and weak but insistent moral inhibitions. I exactly understand the difficulty. Cohen's thinking has taken place in the conscious arena, in which strong evidence and argument can be found to support both the instinctive and the moral case.

Our concept of education helps to explain the existence of these contradictions. The education system is a matter of the self using the conscious mind, and relies upon examinations to determine the effectiveness of that usage. Examinations are concerned (1) with memorised facts laid down in words and pictures as the result of formal learning, and experience, to be recalled on demand, and (2) upon proving those facts with evidence and argument, and interrelating them, by means of *conscious* reason. Examinations, like the Machine world outside, do not invite intuitive and intellatively reasoned response to the postconscious in the pure intellectual pursuit of humantruth, which authority would call groundless speculation. Examinations pose questions, framed by authority, the answers to which are predetermined according to false reality. This results in lopsided misapplication of the mind that is mistaken for intellect. Consequently the foremost figures of the hierarchy, most writers of books and most acknowledged experts, whose basic qualification is their high level of education (ie their learned skill in manipulating the conscious while disregarding the postconscious), are firmly wedded to Machine-reality.

In attempting to reconcile the instinctive and moral cases Cohen suggests an impossible solution, as others have done before her, namely that in order to survive and prosper world humanity must pursue an amoral and a moral code at the same time. She should have resolved this anomaly before putting her case, for it is a fundamental matter. Had she waited for her postconscious to advise her she would surely have perceived that intellectual morality is the only true guide for humanity and her case would have been quite different. All the same, we have Ms. Cohen to thank for removing some of the mysteries of the Machine. When exposed to supraconscious reason her study serves to demonstrate just how persuasive can be the false arguments provided by the actual powerful existence of our present wrong reality.

The fact of the matter is that we *are* special, meaning not that this entitles us to special reckless privileges but that it gives us special responsibilities - that it loads onto *our* shoulders the cares previously carried by instinct, but at the same time gives us the capacity to get much more out of life than its practical provisions and animal satisfactions. It is clear that Cohen recognises some shortcomings of the Machine. She refers to our entire system as floating on a raft of exploitation that sweeps into every facet of society; to the competitive capitalistic forces pressing down on us all with compelling conformity. Nevertheless, she believes that 'wealth creation' counters the evils of corrupt centralised planning; that moral socialist reform blunts the edge of pure capital accumulation which itself might resolve the dilemma of gross inequality; that though the capitalist system is founded on the rude laws of nature, it thrives because it allows everyman to fulfil himself by personal endeavour.

Cohen's criticism is akin to my own condemnation of the Machine but the conclusions we draw are different. I understand the sentiments that underlie what seems to me to be a conservative American point of view. As I have said before she takes humanity as it is, not as it should be. She mentions the evils of corrupt centralised planning, but surely it is well known that 'wealth creation' which she sees as countering those evils, has its own corruptions and inhumanities. By proposing the most centralised authority of all - world government - together with competitive capitalism, she is envisaging a Super-Machine, but this, by yet further usurping responsibility which truly belongs to the moral individual, would open the way to yet further evils of corruption. In suggesting that such a system *might* remove gross inequality she must be imagining it as benignly covering the whole world, which is to ignore two things. Firstly, the money-economy *depends* upon inequality - winners and losers, rich and poor, the pecking order - in order to work, for if all were equal there would be no point in competition. Secondly, every man would not be enabled to fulfil himself, even in this limited, automated way, only, at most, every *other* man. And even if it were possible for every man to fulfil himself in the capitalist, materialist way, we now know that it is not truly permissible, for Earth is cracking under the strain of even the present grossly unequal levels of material fulfilment.

I regret having to say that even Ms Cohen's long and heavily researched book, in asserting that we must build upon the past on the principle of cumulative cultural selection (like natural selection), resorts to wishful thinking, as is the common habit. The author seems not to understand that when we acquired the faculty of intellect we passed beyond the laws of instinct; that all our present troubles - oppression, rioting, starvation, torture, massacre, revolution, deprivation, surfeit - arise from the fact that humanity is imprisoned in consciousness, torn between sensuality and morality with the wilful power to carry either to extremes, and that no supreme system of finance and authority, only supraconsciousness, can make us truly human.

Supraconsciousness's way of making us truly human is to have all individuals bind themselves to personal awareness of collective morality. We cannot ignore the inhumanities of 1989/90, brought to violent expression in China, South America, Russia, South Africa, Ireland, Rumania, the Middle East, and in numerous other places since. As long as humanity remains confined to the conscious arena these inhumanities will always be present just below the surface, ready to be expressed when emotions become aroused at the extremes of instinct; ready to boil over into atrocity. No doubt these instinctive emotional drives can be diverted into competitive economics and material consumerism, but only the winners get full satisfaction from this, not the losers who are presently in the majority. The loser's frustration may eventually boil over into violence and the winners, if their privileges are threatened, will respond with violence. Let me reiterate - until we are supraconscious we are not fully human. Once the self has submitted to the postconscious mind, and has been encapsulated by postconscious will, its behaviour will be subject to its own inner humantrue moral compulsion; the self will be incapable of false or violent behaviour, and immune to the crowd-influence that can draw peaceable persons into violent action.

What I am saying, with perfect certainty that it is true but apparently contrary to present expert theory, is that deterministic forces do govern, or influence, human culture. Now and in the past these were the forces of instinct, recently formalised by the Machine and its institutions. It is her analysis of the Machine that substantiates Cohen's systems-theory, but in the light of humantruth this theory stands revealed as irrelevant. In the future, if we are to realise our true humanity, our culture will be determined by the force of supraconscious influence.

Global Perspectives, the third volume of Bernice Cohen's book, ends in uncertain and contradictory confusion (because, I suggest, her thinking has been brought to these conclusions too soon). As I have said before, this arises from the fact that humanity is split between its morality and its automatic history. She regards the present reality as the spurting exponential growth of an economic phenomenon that has benefited us, but also as a hazardous lottery in which winners, in obedience to the mindless, savage laws of nature, are exploiting losers, which, if it continues too long, will result in global disaster. Cohen here penetrates to the ultimate problem but not, I believe, to the right answers and solutions because she does not recognise that both the benefits and the drawbacks are inevitable characteristics of that phenomenon (the Machine), *both* contributing to eventual disaster. She evidently fails to perceive that exponential growth has occurred through the power of intellect being applied, inappropriately and disastrously, to a system that was designed to achieve, by instinct, the balance of nature. I am bound to conclude that Ms.Cohen has not yet reached the point of understanding the true significance of intellect - that its fulfilment through supraconsciousness completely changes the way we should and could live.

Cohen's difficulty, again, is that of all realists - that both the present Machine and existing human nature, being overwhelmingly in evidence, are taken to be inescapable. The problem is that amoral and immoral competition, right up to that between nations, is carrying us to disaster. Her solution is to regard the present as a transition to the time when humanity within the Machine can be policed and organised by a federated world government, on a morally just basis, using systems analysis of history to guide it in the right direction. She takes as her world model the states of America, united under a federal government, but there is a vast difference between governing the people of the USA, all of whom benefit from their entire nation being an outright winner in a world of competitive nations (though many of the benefits are questionable and, for many citizens, marginal), and trying to build a peacefully, cooperatively united world on the basis of dynamic competition. The only feature of this plan that is good, in theory, is that a world government would have no other to act or react against; otherwise the plan would not change our motives as servants of the Machine. Cohen does not say what the morally just basis of government would be, nor how the moral integrity of such a government, an island in a violently competitive sea, would be guaranteed. She expresses great belief in her systems theory but does not really explain how it will help in this transition, to the necessary extent of contributing morally. I think she should have started by recognising those moral precepts which an intellectual species must by its nature observe, and then she could have gone on to discover a humantrue social structure which would enable the human race to fulfil those moral precepts.

The foundation of Cohen's book is her conviction that competition is a human biological imperative, and her belief that this can and must be harnessed for our benefit. This approach ignores the superseding human intellectual imperative to reject competition. The principle of competition is a crude, cruel and wasteful device of instinct, a principle made necessary by the fact that no species of animal (until the human species emerged) has any other innate, independent means of securing survival. The competitive instinct *is* vital to animals, and there is no doubt that it *is* felt by humans to certain degrees (also encouraged by the Machine and demanded for survival success). Cohen proposes that we should persevere with a social system that is dominated by the competitive principle (though it is propelling us towards disaster at an accelerating pace), in the vague and vain hope that it will somehow, gradually, go contrary to its own driving principle and adjust itself to a very different, morally just pattern.

Ms Cohen's suggested means of achieving this morally just pattern - by world government - according to systems analysis of the lessons of history (the history of a race developing in the wrong way) and by way of beneficial manipulation of the competitive money-economy, I believe to be much mistaken for the following reasons. Firstly (and this is one of the chief lessons of history, yet to be learned), the practice of competition is amoral and immoral, and is not a road that can possibly lead to a morally just society. So why take it? Our crying need *is* for a moral society, so why do we not determine how it should be, and then build it? Secondly, competition is not a human imperative. It is characteristic of the present male temperament, up to a point, but it gets its strength from the conditioning pressures of a competitive society. It is not a strong feature of the female character. It is a principle that is foreign to the postconscious, having no humantrue meaning. The function of instinct is to serve life, not the other way about. When an instinct ceases so to serve, either it, or the species, dies out. In the human case, irrelevant instincts could and should be voluntarily eradicated from our nature and deliberately removed from our society.

I can imagine Bernice Cohen being displeased by all this, to say the least, but my criticism is on a purely supraconscious plane and is not directed against her personally. On the practical plane I admire her as one of the few individuals who have seriously undertaken to solve the problems of our world. However, it is vital to understand that those problems will be truly solved only when supraconscious intellation reaches the point where no doubts or questions remain.

I have mentioned before a common feature of the books already reviewed (also of the two yet to come) - that whilst they acknowledge the many immoralities of existing society they regard visions of fully moral alternatives as naive. Another book, Utopia, has given its title to such alternative visions. The author, Sir Thomas More, presented his ideas as having come from the mind of somebody else, Rafael, and set the scene in an imaginary place, out of this world. In this way he was able to criticise the then existing social order, and to envisage a perfect alternative, without bringing upon himself the wrath of the absolute monarch Henry VIII. By his wit and humour More contrived to convey his true meaning to those morally aware intellects for whom it was intended, whilst enabling those against whom his criticism was directed to pick up a different, innocuous and even farcical meaning, all unawares. I think that Utopia was intended to protest that just as the basic moral values are familiar to everybody, so should we all live by them. This is surely borne out by Thomas More's eventual stand against the King, which cost him his life. But it was by the superficial and innocuous interpretation that this book came to be known. The word Utopia has become a term of derision to describe any proposal for radical social reform. It implies that any ideas contrary to the norm, regardless of their true and imperative morality, are in fact nonsensical, impracticable pie-in-the-sky, dreamed up by cranks and drop-outs too delicate to stomach the 'real' world. The great majority presently hold this opinion but no longer go in fear of a king. They go in fear of an existing reality that so overwhelms them, upon which they have become so mentally and physically dependent, and to prevail against which seems so impossible, that they have allowed themselves unknowingly to pretend to the belief that it is inescapable.

———————————

Finally I undertook to read Families, by Robin Skynner and John Cleese, (Methuen), and I'm OK, you're OK by T.A. Harris (Pan Books). Both these books tackle the human problem from a psychiatric angle. Capra, Roszak and Cohen presumed, more or less, that the range of human characteristics is fixed, though our actions are presently unpredictable, and happiness depends on radical reforms coming from outside ourselves, either from a mystical source, or by way of enlightened government, or both.

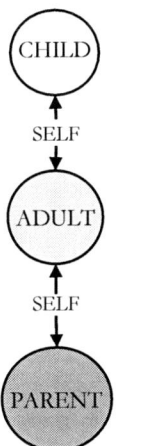

The psychiatrists view seems to be that circumstances and events outside ourselves are broadly and inevitably fixed, and that happiness is a matter of maturing one's character and so adapting it to actuality as to get, and give, the maximum personal satisfaction. This latter view is summed up by Harris as the relationship, within each person, of Parent, Adult and Child compartments of self, where the object is to overcome parental bad influences and bad childish reactions, imprinted during upbringing, and to become a mature adult. This relationship is illustrated here in Figure 15a:

Figure 15a - The Self's Inner Relationships

Psychiatrists exist to help people who are mentally sick with respect to the here and now - a very complex and skilled job. But by treating this sickness as human failure to adapt successfully to existing reality - a symptom - rather than looking to cure the basic disease by changing the anti-human norm, they are helping to perpetuate the wrong reality. They are also allowing the perpetuation of mental sickness into the future. They would argue that they *have* to deal with the world as it is - that they have no alternative. But they *do* have an alternative - the pursuit of supraconscious awareness. This is the right way, even if it means that the present mentally sick are not cured of their inability to adjust to the present norm, for I believe that supraconsciousness would virtually eliminate mental sickness, in time.

Both these books have been best-sellers, for the obvious reason that many people are suffering mentally. The authors believe that the work they are doing is beneficial and Harris, at any rate, believes it could bring about a peaceful and contented world. However, there has been endless effort to make humanity morally adult, from Plato to Christ to William Blake, and now psychoanalysis, with little apparent overall true success, now or in prospect. The reason is that the fundamental causes of suffering have gone unchallenged, and the true means of human fulfilment have remained unrealised.

I applaud these authors and have learned much from them. For example, it is of importance to understand that male homo-sexuality is not inborn but results from a male child's failure to 'cross the bridge' from mother to father so as to identify with the latter. In the same way, psychopaths are the product of upbringing so horrific that they retreat into an exclusive reliance on themselves, cutting out any regard or pity for others. I can see that unbalanced characters can be formed by Child and Parent fixations and from the subconscious influence of early childhood traumas. I can also see that the purpose of psychiatry is to get the adult in us to see the problem and take over. I am bound to criticise, however, because the mature adult who fits well into existing reality, the model for this curative process, does not represent the best in humanity.

'Families' is cynical in its derisive criticism of idealists as malcontents, extremists who are over-proud of the purity of their beliefs, and as people trying to be too good and 'leaving someone else having to be the baddie'. There are such extremists, of course, reckless protestors who use indignation as a substitute for intellation, but they are not true idealists. This cynical attitude towards idealism is commonly taken to be a sign of maturity, which it would be if existing reality were satisfactorily viable and/or inevitable. It is a common attitude with the Machine's winners, because they are knowingly or unknowingly biased, and with losers, because they cannot make the painful effort to see through it. The attitude is disastrous in that it makes no room for a genuine search after humantruth, believing this to be unattainable.

'Families' similarly supports the need to be 'healthily selfish'. As I have made clear already, this is another common misconception, showing unwillingness to break away from the inappropriate rules of instinct which we should have made redundant long ago. That such concepts are actually accepted as responsibly mature represents the present general failure to see that the human species is still in its infancy, needing to break with redundant instinct and the automaton just as the young child eventually needs to break with its mother.

I accept that babies can fail to establish appropriate boundaries, but just as Freud tried to explain human behaviour in terms of sex, so books such as this explain everything in terms of emotional extremes pivoting on an acceptance of existing reality's fundamental concepts, if not all its facts. To be acceptable, reason must relate to these foundations, they say, implying that independent non-conformist reason, being unrealistic, is unacceptable. This must come of a belief that attempts to cure insanity cannot succeed unless they refer to reality as their foundation, notwithstanding that existing reality is clearly insane. There is a case for asserting that, as to its foundations, the current concept of sanity is, in fact, insanity, and vice versa - that the original basis of a baby's failure to make sense of the world is that the world does not make sense.

Not only do 'Families' and 'I'm OK, you're OK' more or less accept the senseless world as it is, they also accept the human mind as mere consciousness assesses it. They are unaware even of the existence of the postconscious mind, despite indications such as the two-year-old child's sudden word-learning and our universal awareness of morality. This is to ignore the significance of a deeply disturbing fact - that in order to survive, at present (the conscious self believes), we must close ourselves off from our highest faculty, the postconscious, whose function is truth. In regard to the conscious self and the influences realistically affecting it, psychiatrists do not take account of the overwhelming amoral and immoral influence of the Machine, and of the competitive money-economy (see Figure 15b). Whether or not they deliberately discount the Machine's falseness, the psychiatrists are working for the contentment of individuals and they know that this is more likely to be achieved by going along with existing reality than by going against it. Another paradox - it is only by replacing the Machine with a humantrue society that human happiness can be secured, but this will bring little short-term satisfaction to the conscious self, only intellectual satisfaction to the supraconscious self.

This is not criticism of these thinkers as persons but as conscious selves largely disconnected from their independent postconscious minds, as they may well have to be in order to function in the Machine. I am aware that Harris, in Chapter 12 of his book 'I'm OK, you're OK' expresses deep concern for human morality, also belief in the existence of a moral order which is as yet only dimly acknowledged. I am well aware of the goodness generally inherent in people - of their often heroic kindness to the handicapped, politeness to each other and patience with children, despite the bad basic values of the Machine and the bad behaviour of collective society. All the books I have mentioned are tremendous achievements on the part of their thinker-authors, but they would have all come to the same humantrue conclusions had their authors become supraconscious. It is our first and vital obligation to intellate, even though this makes us misfits in the here and now. And when an individual comes to know the truths of the postconscious, it is vital that those truths be passed on directly and without fear.

I have already pointed out that Skynner and Cleese, and Harris, regard the conscious individual, with existing reality as background, as the subject of treatment. If the three parts of the individual (see Figure 15a) can be brought into harmony with each other, they say, all will be well. I say that not only does Fig.15a miss out the self's own supreme but neglected faculty, the postconscious, but it also ignores much the greatest trauma-causing and character-shaping influence - the Machine (Figure 15b). The Machine not only falsely determines our characters but also provides fixed, organised positions into which these false characters may neatly and appropriately fit. Consequently, as the result of blanking off the postconscious and consciously embracing the Machine, most of us feel justified in what we are and do, but many do not, and it is they who may well end up on the psychiatrist's couch.

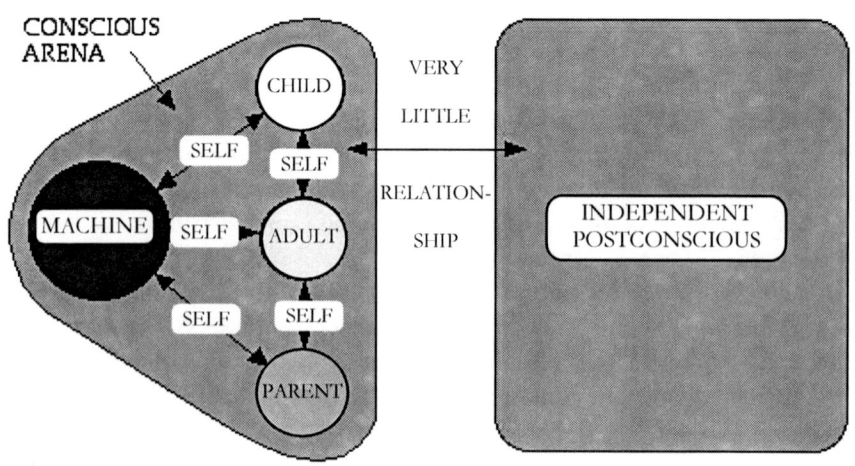

FIGURE 15b - Relationship between the normal self and the wrong reality

This is not to deny, of course, that every one of us is affected by childhood experience, some dramatically, but I maintain that this is *conscious* experience, that existing reality offers no postconscious example to follow, and that the

Machine makes it possible for the most unbalanced of characters to rise to positions of power in its hierarchies, eg Stalin, Hitler, Pol Pot, Hussein.

If one concentrates on making one's personal life seem OK, despite its inconsistencies, then one will accept Figure 15b without question and adopt a picture of the world and universe which also looks OK, with the self as part of it, putting aside all contrary evidence and reason. This is fundamentally the wrong way round. We should be seeking the humantruth and looking to find everything's relevant place, not each establishing personal 'truths' and concocting a variation of false reality to fit round them. This commonly contrived practice may be made to seem morally acceptable by adopting a religious faith and devoting one compartment of self to that. This moral counterweight, against the opposite compartment containing the amoral automated self, gives us to claim that we are balanced adults.

Consider our position as the person in Figure 15b. To become adult we have to take charge of and reconcile all the different versions of self, each of which is false because all are related to the false Machine. The Child in us, from the earliest age, senses conflicts of interest between the Parent, the Machine, and itself. The Parent is normally aware of no alternative to fighting this battle. The Adult has responsibility for reaching some sort of compromise. None of them has a realistic alternative to finding a way along this wrong road, except to resist the great pressure from the self-interested Machine and join in an even harder struggle to discover and realise humantruth. Hard as that is, it has an all-important saving grace - that it is true. The wrong road would not be as hard if we were totally unaware that it is wrong. But we all have an independent postconscious mind whose intuition, or conscience, however we try to deny it, makes us morally aware, if only on the simplest fundamental level.

The reality contained by the triangle on the left-hand side of Figure 15b, remember, is the conscious arena. The conscious mind alone is incapable of sorting out all the entanglements represented here. It can only untangle a small selection of superficial problems at a time on behalf of the human Adult, or small group of Adults, leaving the Machine to roll on over a disunited, unfulfilled people. Psychoanalysis is most practiced, and with apparent success, upon the more privileged population of the USA, and Western Europe. It is hardly appropriate to under-privileged people in the Third World upon whom our prosperity largely depends. Psychotherapy, confined to the conscious arena, is not the means by which the citizens of the USA could be persuaded to give up their rich advantages and seek equality with the rest of the world. Only supraconsciousness can achieve such worthy modesty.

As I'm OK, You're OK reminds us, the memory record is permanent, even though the person may not be able to recall all memories. It is my view that recall is triggered, in nature, whenever the same circumstances that contributed to the memory recur. In humans, memories are interconnected by deeper reason. In the case of the postconscious that reason is potentially unlimited, but it cannot be recalled to consciousness, only the conclusions reached, whereas conscious reason *can* be recalled. That is why, as a race, we have not reached true understanding. Our postconscious conclusions, though true, are not backed by true facts (because our reality is false) and the true reason behind those conclusions is obscured (because the postconscious is unconscious) - they can not, from the conscious viewpoint, be grounded in evidence and argument. But memories of events that did occur can be backed by actual fact (and interpreted in one way or another which is acceptable to conscious reasoning), and it is this that is normally regarded as true. So, not only is present humanity's version of truth wrong but we disregard the postconscious truth because we cannot observe its reasoning and because it is not borne out by present actual fact. Psychiatry is about manipulating memories and conscious reason in order to be, or seem to be, happy and contented. It fails to acknowledge that, in existing reality, the happy state is as invalid as the unhappy state. This is because intellect, to be happy, has to be fulfilled, which means to be totally humantruly aware and to have that awareness fully reflected in its whole reality. Therefore no intellect can be truly happy when the world of which it is aware is not similarly happy.

Harris has helped me in making it clear that as a result of traumas derived from upbringing (against the background of existing reality) individuals can become psychopaths or psychotic, i.e. in the grip of very strongly disturbing emotions and lopsided conscious reasoning. But even the psychopath can presumably choose to intellate, and thus achieve balance of mind through the bypassing and ignoring of emotions. Such a person could become the character E in Figure 16e, next Chapter 52, still with conscious hang-ups, yet truly aware because that person is able to listen to the postconscious that is not affected by conscious hang-ups. I think that if there were examples of supraconscious intellation in evidence, with avenues for it to follow and places for it to occupy in reality, then such individuals as psychopaths might be able to get so far removed from their handicap as to overcome it. Neither they nor anybody else can glean much hope from, or find good guidance in, existing reality in the conscious arena.

The book Families has this to say about the child as it becomes able to think for itself - that it now has to learn how to fit in with others, first its family then the rest of society, because otherwise it will not get the affection, support and help from other people which it will assuredly need; that in any case its life will be much more rewarding and interesting if it is able to get on well with others. Yes, in ideal circumstances, but the present circumstances of most humans are not ideal, and for many they are intolerable. In the world as it is we surely must expect much more from our children. It is my opinion, in a society that is so obviously wrong and desperately in need of radical change, that love of truth must come first, otherwise we will never achieve a reality to which all can adapt with honesty.

Having already derided the idealist, Families later claims that he is an outsider, avoiding reality, someone who has not learned to place himself in reality accurately to size and so has a false idea of his self-importance. To avoid being cut down to size he keeps himself out of his picture of the world or gives himself the wrong position and size. He believes he is a special case, and, instead of changing himself, he tries to change others. There are people like this, no doubt, but to apply this to all idealists is to take a narrow and cynical view of humans as no more than clever animals, not to be allowed to discover their extraordinary true capacity. The fact is that the world *is* wrong. Anyone who clearly sees this must, in all conscience, try to change it and other people, and must resist their efforts to make him narrowly conform. The norm is incapable of measuring the behaviour of anyone who has perceived the truth or who, as a child, had determined to discover truth. But we have passed well beyond the monkey stage and ought to behave accordingly. There can be no doubt that we have enormous intellectual potential. Is it not obvious that this gives us great responsibility? It seems to me that, living in an insane world as we are, *everybody* could be expected to be seeking truth and refusing, wherever possible, to give way to the norm.

In the present world, in psychological terms and using Harris's terminology, it is possible for the Adult to come to terms with its Child and Parent, and with the Machine, and to become a viable member of society, *without* answering and solving the vital human questions and problems. If we insist upon succeeding in finding these answers and solutions we shall not come to terms within ourselves nor shall we ever fit into the world as it now is. But we will be an influence or force for radical change towards a humantrue reality in which the Child, Parent and Adult in everybody, and the communal framework of life, would be in total harmony.

Consider drug trafficking as an example that supports my arguments. This traffic exists on a world scale only because it is economically very profitable. The very fact of its existence is, from any viewpoint, a condemnation of the Machine and its economy. The victims are the addicts, many of whom no doubt could have been helped by psychologists and others to overcome problems from which drugs offered escape. But the financiers, producers, distributors and pushers, as well as the government agents who try to bring them to justice, are presumably well under control of their Adult. So being

Adult, in the Machine, is not necessarily to be moral. Indeed, it is very often the case that morality is a handicap in the struggle for worldly success. Such 'evils' as drug-trafficking can exist in the Machine, and co-exist with 'good', because our reality is limited to the conscious arena. These 'evils' are not howled down because they are supported by much conscious reason and Machine-principle. We cannot equate 'good' with the police anti-drugs squads because they hunt down the traffickers on the grounds of law - police do not confront traffickers on the basis of their personal immorality and that of the competitive money-economy whose laws they obey. We know that drug trafficking would virtually disappear were there no money-profit in it. It is also clear that if the morality that our society pretends to went really deep, *it* would defeat the drug problem. As it is, the profit motive is so much stronger than the moral that any profitable opportunity that presents itself, however immoral, is automatically taken up. The nearer we approached to the supra-conscious state the more difficult would the drug traffickers find it to ignore the terrible and tragic consequences of their trade, to the point where they had to give it up.

Morality, as earlier pointed out, is almost a dirty word in today's language. Morals, in a worldly political or commercial context, are seen as naive hopes. But we have recent examples in Europe (Rumania, Russia) of the invincible power of united, and to large degree justified, public demand. These were irresistible protests against oppressive forms of government, directed against members of such governments. Were we all aroused to the same extent in protest against immoralities, from drug trafficking to political dishonesty to money-economics, their hold on us could be broken overnight, and they could be swept away as though they had never been.

Harris gives it as his opinion that truth is a growing body of data that we observe to be true. This is to ignore that most of the conceptual and factual 'truths' of our present world are only partially, not wholly true, and that consciously oriented human observers are not capable of discerning whole truth. He therefore joins with all the others I have quoted in submitting to the mistaken edict of Philosophy that truth must be capable of grounding in conscious evidence and argument, whereas it is my hope and belief that I have shown truth to emanate from its unconscious source in the independent postconscious. It is probably correct to say that there is a tendency to agree upon certain large overall 'truths', such as the existence of god and the principles of progress, and that this reflects a general wish for unity (a wish which manages to co-exist with strong competition). By contrast, criticism and 'rubbishing' of peoples' beliefs (such as I am practicing), however true and vital for genuine human unity they really are, are at present commonly seen as disharmonious.

Towards the end of I'm OK, You're OK, Harris states it as a fact that people cannot and do not wish to live unrelated to other people. I am quite sure that this is so, despite the contrary evidence of man's inhumanity to man for which the unnecessary practices of the Machine and authoritative government, rather than human nature, are responsible. A large part of happiness in a humantrue society will be the knowledge of mutual regard and support across the whole world, and a sense of unity with all supraconscious intellects throughout the universe. Figure 15c below shows the relationships on which the constitution of such a society would be founded.

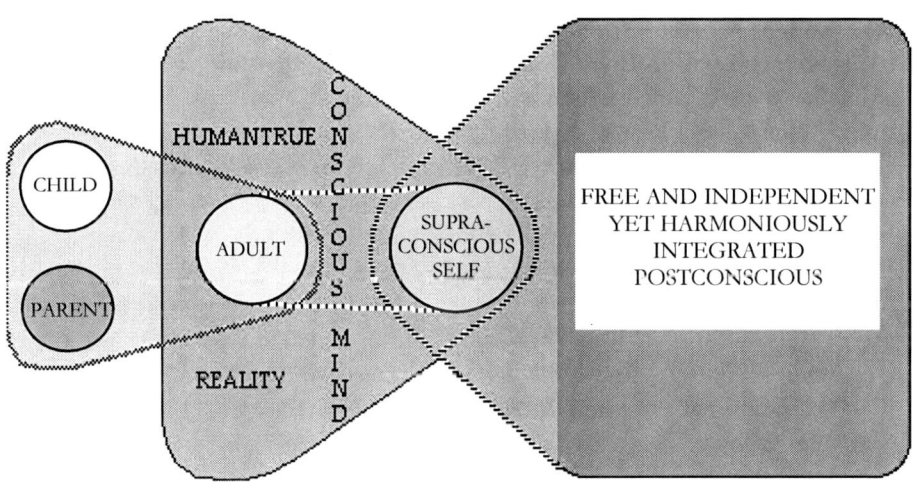

FIGURE 15c - The State of Supraconsciousness

I have suggested already (see Figure.14a) that in early childhood the developing postconscious is much more closely related to, thus having more influence on, the developing conscious. The two-year-old's ability to learn language would appear to confirm this. But thereafter a battle is joined, a battle between the postconscious potential for truth, on the one hand, and dominance of the conscious by the Machine and the great factual and conceptual weight of existing reality on the other hand. It is a battle which the Machine generally wins, but the individual is left with a conscience, a sense of truth overlooked and morality betrayed, which has had the good effect of causing mankind continually to question itself, and the bad effect that we have invented religions and other disciplines as substitutes for true answers.

There is no denying that the difficulties of upbringing and of adjusting to reality can have dire behavioural consequences, or that the books Families, I'm OK, You're OK and its sequel Staying OK, can address and alleviate these difficulties. However, all those who have been helped to become OK, together with all the rest of the world's six thousand million people, are adapted to serve one or another function of the Machine, belong to one or another faith or ideology and are contained within one or another country, and all these occupations, beliefs and nations are potentially if not openly in conflict. All these people belong to the wrong reality (see Figure 15b) and no amount of psychology will make it or them right. That, I repeat, is the basis of my criticism of these books. Let us first achieve the right reality, shown in Figure 15c above, regardless of our wrong emotions, and then let us see whether the result of *it* being right will not be that *we* all come out right.

It is thought, by free-expression educators for instance, that children should be brought up with infinite kindness, but how are they then to be prepared either for a hard world which is not even ordinarily kind or for a career of rightful but painful protest against that hard world? Similarly, it is thought by almost everybody that the only way successfully to communicate is to appeal to, in order to get a friendly response from, the conscious concepts, beliefs, hopes and dreams that the great majority of us presently hold in common. But if a radical reformer-writer does this the main effect on his readers will be that their overall view of reality is confirmed, and that his radical message can be put on a shelf marked 'to be attended to when we have time, and then, *if* it is approved, to be implemented only in parts, as and when we can afford it'. The individual's normal situation, shown in (Figure 15b,) in a closed triangular arena of conscious reality and between the opposite influences of the Machine and the intuitions of the postconscious, is not easy to escape. Since the key to the problem is postconscious awareness, it is clear that if radical reformers are to achieve their aims they must, as writers or readers, tap into the postconscious - they must be supraconscious.

Harris refers to experiments with monkeys who were 'raised' by wire-framed, terry cloth covered, surrogate mothers. When these monkeys reached maturity they had minimal capacity for mothering, whereas this capacity had been thought to be instinctive. This is an important finding when related to humanity and the overall 'mother' which brings us up - our framework of life - the Machine. (It is also important to question our right to subject monkeys to this indignity and pain). In nature the monkey would *always* be brought up by a female monkey mother, so that the mothering instinct (minimal though it might be at birth) would be confirmed and reinforced and passed along, rather than remain minimal as in this unnatural experiment. The instinct and its performance are interdependent, for the monkey without a mother would, naturally, die. The purpose of the mothering instinct is to give the baby everything it requires for its function to survive and, in the case of a female, everything it requires to reproduce, successfully according to design - this, and subsequent life in a viable community, equals happiness. For we humans, though we may have natural mothers, the Machine is *our* collective surrogate mother that, with its false framework of life, gives us minimal capacity for happy communal survival. Our true collective mother would be humantrue society, sustained and continually reinforced by our equivalent of instinct - supraconsciousness.

Harris says that we have to become adult before we can explore, and find answers to, the great perplexity 'what's the good of it all?' This is clearly true, but, if he is to know how and where to explore, and to be able to recognise true answers when he, or she, sees them, the normal adult also needs to change, radically. The state of adulthood, within the Machine, entails a false concept of reality that certainly precludes truth. It is necessary that the self, however immature it might be in terms of existing reality, should find a true intellectual maturity by opening to the postconscious, intellating, and becoming supraconscious. It will be cognisant of the present psychological difficulties, but will recognise that it is not these difficulties that constitute the problem to be dealt with, but the entire false reality that gives rise to them.

It is clear that individuals, to be contented, eventually need to be at peace with their Parent and Child within, but this cannot be until their Adult, and their world, is humantrue. The individual who achieves adult maturity within the conscious arena, as is the object of psychiatry, is not capable of discovering or realising humantruth. The supraconscious individual, though still immature by Machine-standards, having recognised that the psychological difficulties of achieving automated adulthood are not the real problem, will by-pass them on its way to a far better understanding given by the infinitely more deep postconscious faculty. He or she must be willing to endure the pains of being a misfit in existing reality for the sake of future humantrue reality.

In the world as it is people suffer considerable stress, and it is to relieve this that they go to psychiatrists. I appreciate the psychiatrists' point that this suffering exists, now, and they have to treat it now. But supraconscious individuals would reject their treatment, opting personally to avoid the norm rather than adapt to it. They are vitally aware, however, that humanity at large cannot escape the norm that presently dominates it, and they are dedicated to realising a humantrue reality. By transfer of their emotions to support of the postconscious mind's absolute determination on humantrue change, they will find that the many stresses associated with living unhappily in an alien world, not to mention awareness of the stresses experienced by others through failure to become happily successful in automated reality, are far outweighed by stress arising from awareness that the present is an intolerably wrong reality, stress which will be alleviated only when we change to a humantrue reality.

It might still be argued that there will be Parent-Child-Adult relationships in any reality, and it *is* argued that because of the personality disturbances they cause a humantrue reality could not work. But when all peoples are united by common supraconsciousness, and living in a world which has been constituted accordingly, they will be in a much better position to deal with any disturbances that do occur. In particular I believe that nuclear family life is the cause of much present psychological trauma which community living would dispel. In a humantrue community the burdens of parenthood and childhood would be shared, the adult would be freed from all unnecessary outside pressure, and everybody would share in the satisfaction of healthy basic living and cooperative comradeship.

Reading the books reviewed in this chapter has confirmed my belief that the more the automated conscious mind learns, from books which the Machine is willing to offer, the more confused it becomes. It is this that obliges conscious individuals to specialise, taking a limited stand that they can encompass, explain, and defend. The accumulation of such understanding brings little, if any, advance of humantrue understanding. Living in the Machine is like reading a Sunday newspaper. The information's part-truths do not build towards whole truth but are subtly negated by the whole newspaper's acceptance of the overall false existing reality.

Chapter 52

HOW TO HUMANISE OURSELVES

An article in a newspaper, headed 'How to Market your Talents', is really about how to sell-out your true virtue in order to be bought by the Machine.

Individuals who are unwilling to sell themselves in this way because they are in doubt about the morality of our existing reality and dissatisfied with the ethics of the Machine, tend to express opinions which, although suggested by supraconscious intuition, are not backed up by all the intellation needed to build full awareness of humantruth. As a result such opinions, though pointing in the true direction, are easily dismissed not only because they are eccentric to the here and now but also because they are not wholly complete enough to be truly convincing.

Certain limited progress has been made in this regard. Humane concerns which officialdom would once have thought naive, such as identifying the needs of disabled persons, concern for the rights of animals and opposition to war, are now much more widely accepted as human rights by the institutions, in principle at least. Progress is being made in the extent and degree of ecological awareness on the part of peoples and authorities. The authors of the books appraised in the last chapter carry this awareness further and deeper into peoples' minds and the consciences of institutions. Yet even these authors regard it as naive to talk of absolute truth, to consider our entire reality as wrong, and to contemplate complete change. But one thing that experience *does* show us, I think, is that half-baked reform never succeeds but eventually allows the old false principles to re-assert themselves, and we no longer have time and space for half-hearted trial and error; we have to choose humantruth quickly, and must get it right first time.

People often say that radical ideas (even the half-baked ones) are too far-out for them. The truth of it is that such people are too close to existing false reality; their minds *need* to be far removed from their presently preferred and limited centres-of-self if they are to find their true selves and to fulfil their true potential. If this is done they will be able to look back and see just how mean, false and unworthy was the reality in which they were once immersed.

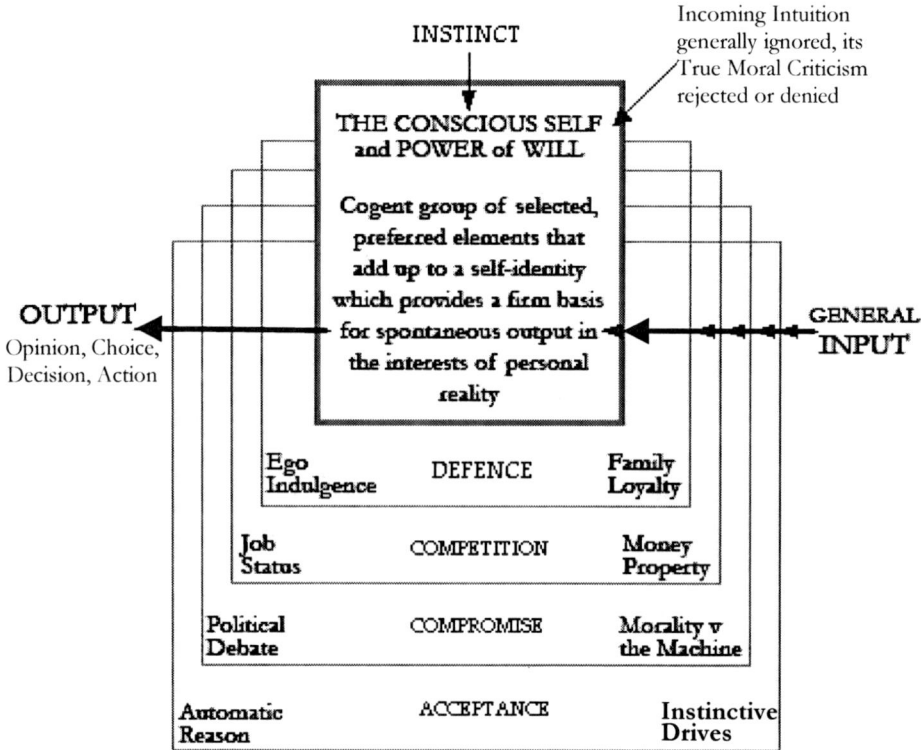

FIGURE 16a Presently normal typical formation of character

Figure 16a shows the presently normal individual. It illustrates that nothing much is really changing. Our children are being conditioned as before, oriented to jobs in the Machine. But they, and we, are the individuals who must change *contrary* to reality, without the help of a sympathetic framework of life. We and they must change ourselves voluntarily, sacrifice automatic advantages and rewards, break the Machine's stranglehold, assert the human right, avoid taking refuge in religion and build a humantrue reality for future generations. Those future generations will continue to be humantrue because they will be supported by that sympathetic reality as well as by their own true awareness. But the first to change must be those individuals now living. Only *we* can do it - there is nobody and nothing else. If we don't take up the challenge, there will be no human future.

How to humanise ourselves? First by intellating and becoming supraconscious - otherwise we will never know who or what we really are. If humanity at large does not do so it will never know what could and should have been. I believe in the possibility, if not the probability, of a humantrue future because my own postconscious mind has been able to break through to my consciousness. If this can happen to me, and prove itself true, then it could happen to everybody. The effect must be that everybody would insist on their humantrue conviction becoming a reality, as is the human right.

The conscious self, illustrated by Figure 16a, is represented by a centralised construction of thought. For purposes of comparison this construction might be taken to contain, on average, 100 units of preferred thought, out of a total conscious capacity of maybe 10,000 units and in contrast to a postconscious capacity of possibly 1,000,000 units. This centralised construction determines the characteristic behaviour of the conscious self, whose limited reason and instinctive reactions dictate the conversion of input to output in response to disciplines imposed by the conscious arena and pressures from the Machine, especially from that area of reality (about 1000 units) which this individual has experienced and which, therefore, influences the thinking which goes to the making of this conscious self. It can be seen that there are many possible differences of input, influence, choice, compulsion, chance, and situation, which result in many distinctly different and disagreeing characters.

We, the great majority of Earth's 6,000,000,000 human individuals, do not realise how incomplete we are *because* we are intellectually incomplete; because our whole minds have not been fulfilled. Therefore, when one of us talks to another we are not talking to the true *them*, nor they to the true *us* - it is a matter of inadequate communication between inferior substitutes for the true potentials of two selves, in a reality which neither of them recognises as being similarly inferior and inadequate.

Consider what the thousands of millions of humans are really doing when they rest content with minds such as that of Figure 16a. It is like building a house, stopping halfway without the roof and windows but calling it a house even so. Or like binding a book, leaving half its pages out but still calling it a book.

A person may know less than true judgement requires, and reason less than is necessary to true awareness, yet is still called a person and entitled to an opinion. Of what value is that opinion? Yet our attempts to direct human society are made by persons with such opinions, responding to the opinion of the majority of others or compromising between many different opinions. I am not suggesting that peoples' opinions should be ignored but that presently, being generally wrong or inadequate, they are unsuitable guides for society. Rather than trying to perfect means of representative government within the Machine - attempting the impossible - we should be encouraging every mind to be supraconscious.

If you take a computer, feed into it the moral obligations which most of us learn and pretend to, then face it with the decisions we are all required to make, it *could not* decide except morally. Yet we, with mental potential which no computer can or, we argue, ever could match, are not so honest. I have already explored the reasons why we believe ourselves frequently compelled to ignore our moral convictions. But if, at last, we all stood by those convictions, the contrary compulsions would soon disappear and, as they did so, the world would *not* collapse.

We know that thinking (as distinct from intellation) is not exclusive to humans. Animals think. A computer thinks in the calculating sense already discussed. It is a matter of correlating a number of influences and producing the seemingly most appropriate response (ie relative truth) as the answer. On that basis the Machine can think also; with human help it can persuade, oblige and instruct humans to do its will, like a large-scale conscious mind.

The potential human mind is capable of correlating to the ultimate truth, but in existing society we allow our minds to be restricted to a much lower level of active awareness. The individual submits to the institution, yet the individual, potentially if not actually, is infinitely more capable of taking responsibility. Actually, virtually all of us act and react according to the automatic concepts and facts of our circumstances, though to varying degrees. It is said that of all school-children in the UK only about one-third graduate from 'concrete' to 'formal' thinking, i.e., as an approximate illustration, from a field of thinking of about 500 units (50 preferred) to a field of 2000 units (200 preferred). This means that two-thirds of the current population are so mentally unstimulated as to be unaware that they are automated. But the one-third, who *have* graduated to formal thinking, *choose* to be similarly unaware. They take up positions of service to an institution of the Machine and, in order to be successfully effective, preferentially identify themselves with its particular interests and aims (eg 'I am an engineer, a philosopher, a physicist'). They may well profess to understand everything, but the key to their minds, apart from overall acceptance of the Machine, is their position in the institution and identification with its peculiar outlook, as shown in Figure 16b. These are automated characters, their thinking consciously or subconsciously biased to the possible extent of overriding intuitive or inbred morality and committing, or permitting, immoral acts of inhumanity.

As an example of this currently normal thinking, take the case of a stockbroker at the time when the British and Argentinean governments were in conflict over possession of the Falkland Islands, a dispute over sovereignty and loyalty which, particularly in that it had little true human significance, was typical of our conscious/instinctive society.

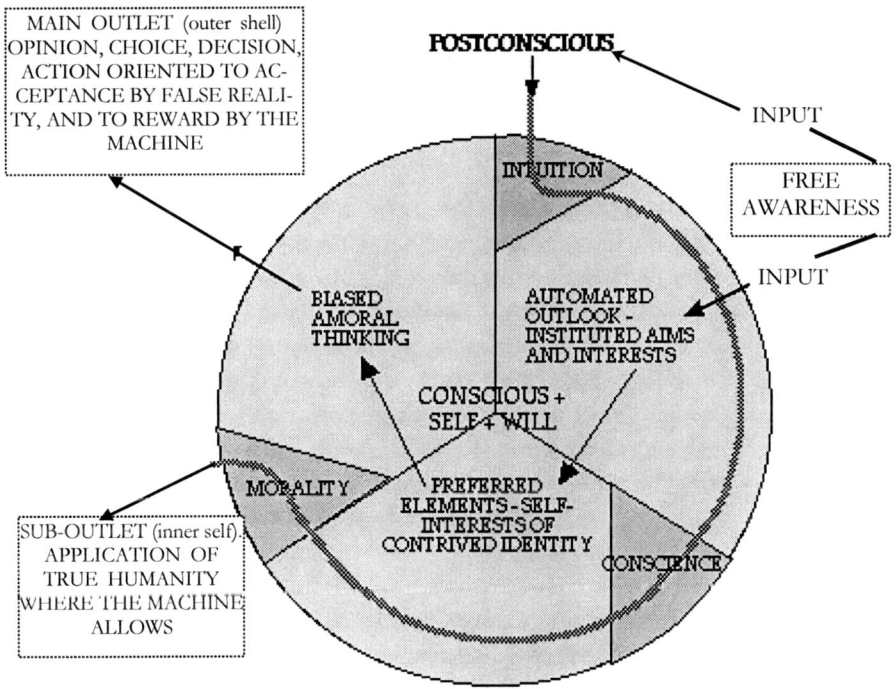

FIGURE 16b - Thinking typical of the automated human individual

The stockbroker is made aware of the possibility of war between the two countries. His free awareness, or those of its findings that he cannot altogether ignore, may question the attitudes of all concerned, cast doubts on their motives or criticise their actions from the humanitarian viewpoint. But when it comes to himself taking hard, Machine-realistic decisions, he puts such 'soft' moralising aside. Adopting, instead, the guides to opinion and decision which the Machine works by, and on which his worldly success (and, he imagines, his happiness) depends, he subjects the Falklands incident to questions raised in his conscious mind by this realistic, automatic approach. How do the parties stand in relation to international law? How is the British government permitted to act by the (unwritten) national constitution? How may it act as a result of its political persuasions? What is the mood of the Argentineans? What forces are available to each side in the area? What is the popular mood in Britain? What is the likely attitude of uninvolved nations - will they support or oppose British military response to the Argentinean invasion?

So far the stockbroker's thinking has been general, passing quickly through a train of human reactions, then dwelling on a worldly realistic analysis on the events and predictions of their outcome. Now he subjects that analysis to his group of preferred elements - the instituted interests which he professes and which he has made the self-interests of his specially contrived superficial identity. These interests make their own specialised final analysis of the general picture, concerned with how the predicted course of events will affect the movement and valuation of stocks and shares. The fundamental element of these interests is profit.

This final analysis is then translated into his own action as appropriate to his position in the stock exchange institution and to his own advantage, and is backed up by his conscious/ instinctive will. This train of specious reasoning which has formulated his professional opinion, his choice, his decision, and which has finally resulted in his action, is part and parcel of his outer personal identity. His action is to sell shares likely to go down in price and buy those likely to rise, thereby to some degree causing events to fall out as predicted. It is not for him officially to support or condemn the war that ensued, only to capitalise on it. He is reinforcing the amoral consensus that supports the concepts of possession and sovereign authority which, in turn, were the causes of this war.

The stockbroker's mind is full of precepts that ideally should not exist in any memory, much less dominate the personality. It is animal instinct that he calls up to defend his contrived personal identity against his own conscience and against the humantrue opposition of others. He constantly patrols the defences of his preferred thought-construction, confirming and reinforcing those elements and connections that contributed to his action. Otherwise he admits to his consciousness only that additional thinking which is not critical of him, and ignores or denies that which *is* critical, in order to prevent the truth coming out and to avoid rendering himself unsure. This contrived thinking is characteristic of all members of the automatic institutions.

This wilful process of convincing his already conditioned mind by further conditioning reinforces the stock-broker's self confidence, which increases his chance of success. Confidence and success in the Machine gives credibility to him and his automatic reasoning, convincing others of the well-informed authority of the institution he represents, though it is founded on myth, and establishing his right to a key place in it. When he speaks about himself he sounds confident, because this limited subject is exactly suited by the limited sphere of fitting reason that he applies to it. This is his ego, the self that commands his conscious mind's approval and chief interest, and he is talking about the concerns and affairs of which that mind knows more than anything else.

The stockbroker is open to criticism but has many reasons for acting as he does. The stock exchange exists; it is part of the competitive money economy that presently runs the world. He has a family to keep, and may as well earn his living this way as any other. He feels he could not do it were he to take the road to supraconsciousness because that would weaken his present resolve by raising critical questions and doubts in his mind. He regards the following of that road, as does the automated world in general, as a weakness of character, a failure of duty. So this is the main reason why the stockbroker, like all the other Machine-realists, unswervingly continues as he is - he believes human reality to be necessarily and inevitably confined to the Machine and (albeit unknowingly) to the limited conscious arena, with no viable alternative.

Some present-day Philosophers do seem to be seeking alternatives, but they too confine themselves to the conscious arena in which no true alternative is to be found. It seems paradoxical that although the conscious arena is strictly limited in scope, despite its large capacity, it contains arguments that never come to an end, but the simple reason for this is that to bring complex arguments to true conclusions requires a very much larger, almost infinite scope and capacity. Such unending arguments are characteristic of the established institution of Philosophy. That which escapes Philosophers, and realists in general, is the awareness that their field of argument is the wrong (conscious) field - that it can never yield the truth. In support of this contention is the specific that Philosophy, for all its long history, has not discovered humantruth. I challenge anyone to provide any better reason why this essentially straightforward truth has escaped the human intellect. Were the ever-arguing Philosophers to open to the guidance of their supreme faculty, their postconscious, they would only be able to continue arguing until all internal doubts were resolved, at which point they would find themselves in agreement, with further argument unnecessary. They would then be able to jettison the huge accumulated mass of irrelevant argument that presently weighs so heavily with their adopted, and defended, mental discipline.

Life can seem good when blindly confined to exclusive compartments in which we see and hear only what we want to, but to be humantruly fulfilled we must be fully aware. Such awareness would reveal that the world must be altogether good if it is to be truly good for any of us - that none of us must live in specialised compartments. We must each take full responsibility.

Figure 16c shows four individuals who are typical of the six thousand million occupying the same collective consciousness.

All of these four individuals accept the same concepts and facts of existing automatic reality. Nevertheless, in the case of these particular four (see also Chapter 49) even though the experience of all is that of the same overall reality, in essential character no one's conscious self has anything in common with any of the others. Why is it that these individual conscious selves are centred on separate thought-constructions that are so small by comparison with total conscious capacity? The reason is that their reality is highly competitive and admits of every contradictory possibility that can be imagined. Whereas every individual tacitly accepts the Machine as a whole, none can embody all its many contradictory ideas nor pursue all its conflicting interests. It is necessary for each to select a small number of preferred elements to motivate the self and steer a personal course through life. Not only are all individuals contained by a consensus which is incomplete and false (because it excludes the postconscious), but each individual's meaning and purpose of life, and bias of opinion, is founded upon approximately a mere 1% selection from the Machine's already limited ideas and interests. This is the cause of the enormous amount of disagreement and conflict in present human society. Everyone feels compassion, and is aware that it should feature in all our affairs, but at the same time the different competitive position of each individual puts him or her in conflict with most others and largely rules out compassion.

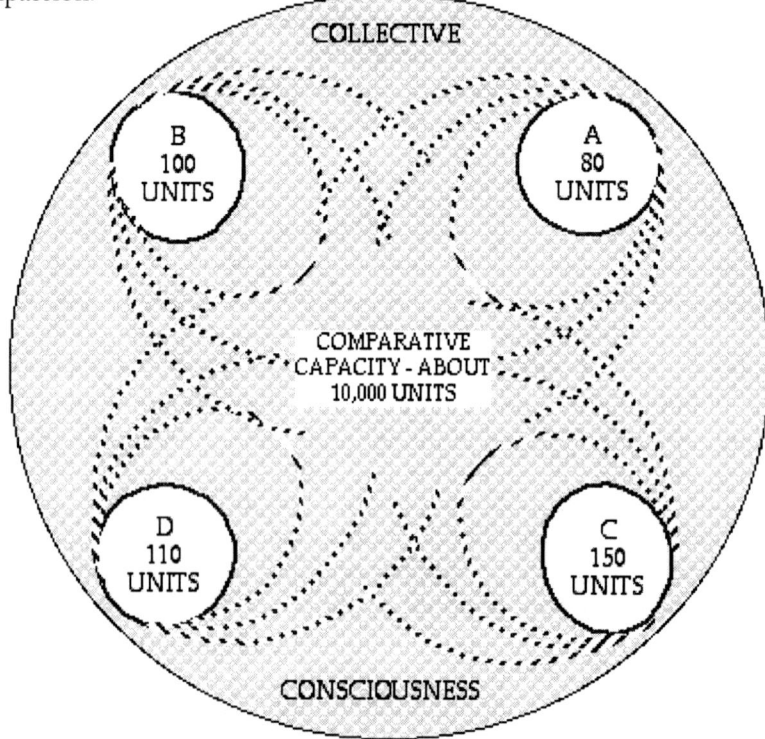

FIGURE 16c -   Four typical automated individuals, confined to the same collective consciousness (the same reality, dominated by the Machine), who yet contrive to have no obvious characteristics in common

Every conscious self is pre-formed, to some extent, by upbringing and education, and this is influenced by position in, and experience of the Machine, as shown in Figure 16d.

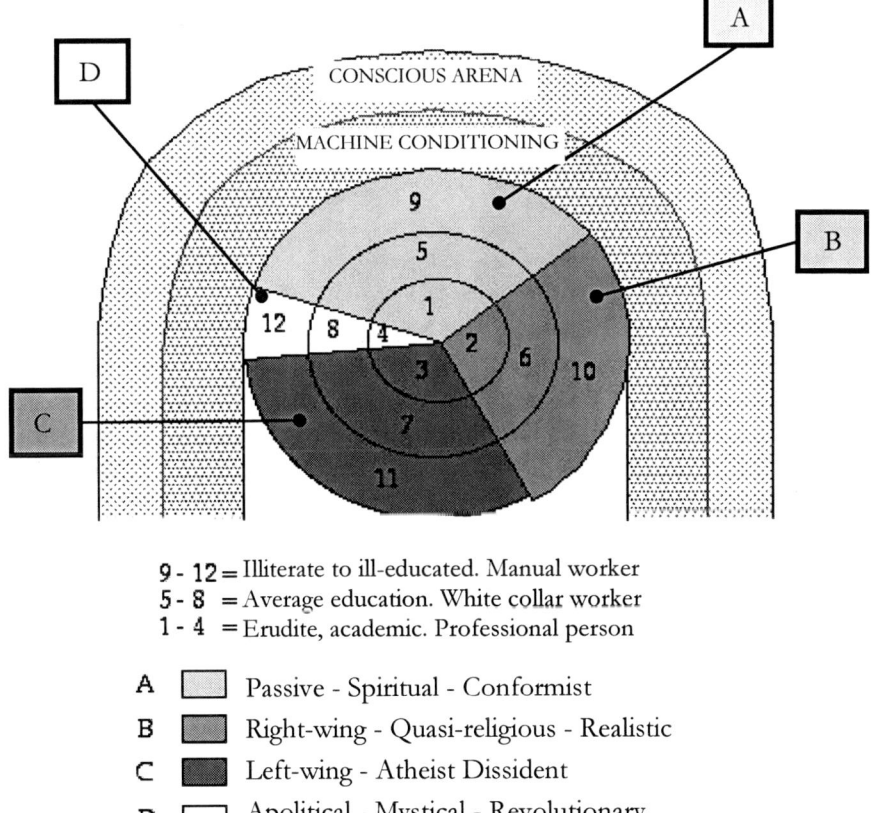

9 - 12 = Illiterate to ill-educated. Manual worker
5 - 8 = Average education. White collar worker
1 - 4 = Erudite, academic. Professional person

A ☐ Passive - Spiritual - Conformist
B ■ Right-wing - Quasi-religious - Realistic
C ■ Left-wing - Atheist Dissident
D ☐ Apolitical - Mystical - Revolutionary

FIGURE 16d - Normal conditioning, roughly divided into 12 areas of upbringing and education, and 4 areas of attitude to the Machine (each containing many possible variations).

I think it is true to say that any reasonable individual would be disturbed by the suggestion that humanity deliberately compartmented its individuals according to these different degrees of privilege and satisfaction. Of course it does not, but the Machine does, and humanity serves the Machine. These compartments are very roughly designated by numbers. The further and very approximate divisions of outlook, opinion and belief - A, B, C and D are partly predetermined by the previous numbered compartments, partly by the influence of our true humanity in its struggle against the Machine. In an ideal, humantrue society, as a matter of natural human right, it would be our aim to have none of the differences shown numerically and alphabetically in Figure

16d. It would be the objective of all communities to bring all individuals to a similar level of learning and understanding, and to make no differences between them whatever the course of their subsequent abstract fulfilment.

Now let us put the four individual selves from Figure 16c together with their conditioning as shown in Figure 16d, and show four typical resultant characters A5, B10, C7, and D4 - demonstrated as part of our collective conscious thinking; in relation to the Machine and the overall conscious arena and, in their distant and vague relationship with the postconscious (conscience). The result is Figure 16e.

Figure 16e illustrates the reality of the normal individual as being made up of a preferred self, conditioned and condensed out of the surrounding chaos, out of a collective consciousness, and out of a false and incomplete concensus. This consensus is formed by compromise, between the automated desires and interests of the disunited and competitive human multitude, its contrary human morality, its contrary common morality, and the governing interests of the Machine. Its final shape is affected, usually to a small degree, by such postconscious influence as is allowed to infiltrate consciousness. Figure 16e also shows the potential truly human person - the supraconscious individual E, a self maintaining (mentally, also physically as far as is presently possible) its independence of the whole of present reality and its conscious arena, and keeping direct contact with the postconscious.

Consider the four typical individuals A5, B10, C7 and D4, shown in Figure 16e in their established and false present reality. They are governed by an inappropriate substitute for animal instinct, a substitute that has failed to find a balance in sympathy with nature because it has not embraced the chief human faculty - the postconscious. They represent the human race in its present reality, a society that is imbalanced and heading, one way or another, for either automation or premature extinction.

A most important thing to be understood about existing humanity is that although there is but one body of humantruth, equally acceptable to all and by which we would live in contented harmony, individuals are presently so conditioned as to hold every conceivable different opinion and belief, to pursue every possible objective, and to project and defend these, often with violence and without regard for consequences.

Such conditioned minds are enabled to deny even factual humantruth if it suits their book. The same is even more so of institutions, for they are instrumental in the conditioning of humans, and in instructing them, often against the good personal judgement of individuals, within or outwith the institutions.

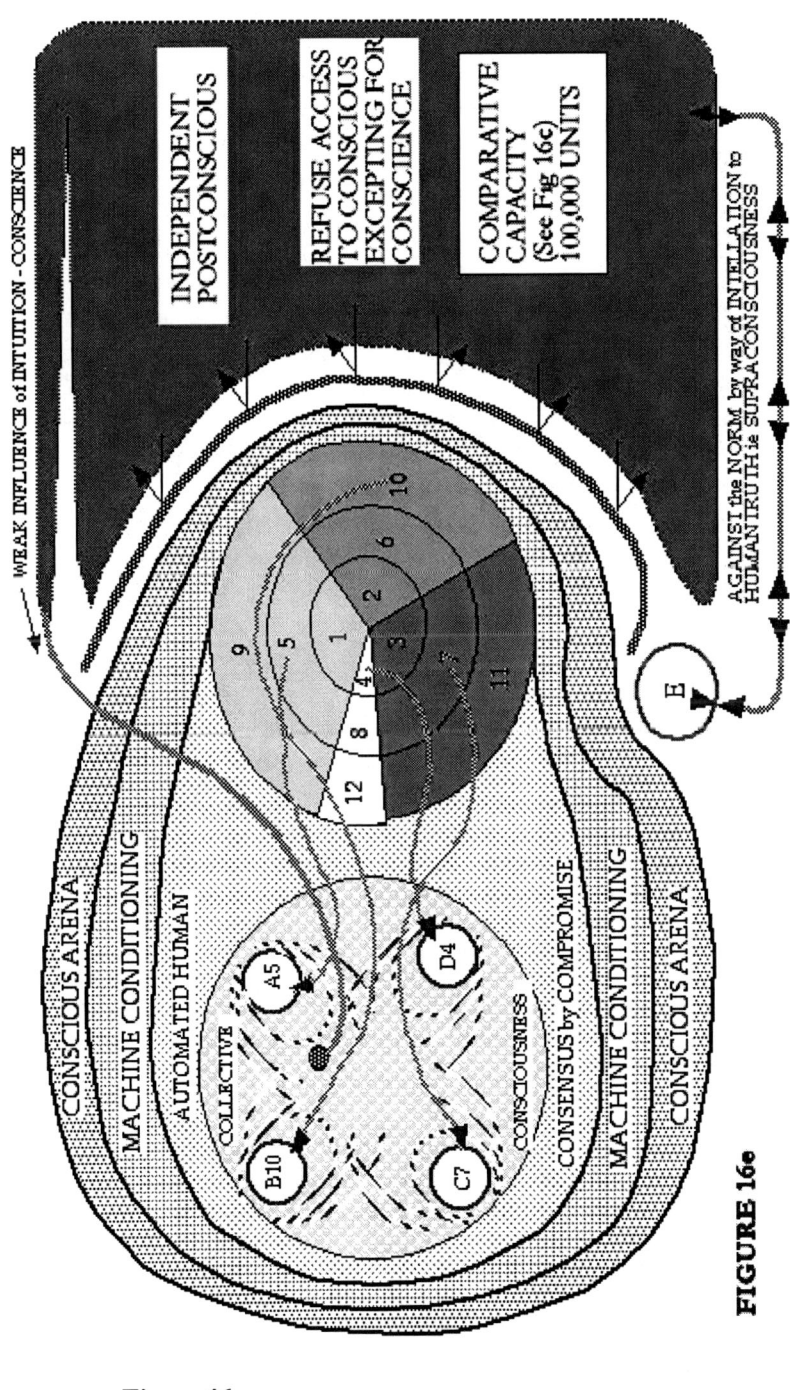

FIGURE 16e

As it is..................Minds A5, B10, C7, D4 -

Same basic potential but confined to conscious arena and differently conditioned by upbringing, education and the Machine

As it should be........Supraconscious Mind E -

Ready to fulfil humantrue potential because augmented by the much greater capacity and profound reasoning of the postconscious (see Figs 13c & 15c)

Figure 16e

As a UK example of this, it is said that the British government, some seventeen years ago, suppressed research and development of wave-power technology in order to protect its interests in nuclear power. An invention, known as the Duck, had proved itself in trials but the project was abandoned for lack of official support despite the crying need for such safe, clean sources of power (I now understand that due to advances in anti-corrosion technology this project is being reconsidered).

The character and freely independent position of individual E (see Figure 16e) is the key to the human race avoiding extinction and achieving happy survival. Whilst individuals A, B, C and D are prepared to follow their predetermined ways regardless of the surrounding chaotic confusion, E cannot bear disagreement, or to leave any question unanswered. A - D follow different lines of conscious thought according to their narrowed interests and objectives, also according to self-oriented instinctive emotion. E, on the other hand, is guided by the postconscious whose interest, being the truth and human right, is therefore concerned with the total welfare of mankind and the whole Earth, and which, though sympathetically aware of all emotion, cannot be directly swayed by any biased feeling.

A revelation results from a physical process, that of dendrites, axons etc. exploring and finding true connections. In a supraconscious person's mind, intellation raises questions as to beliefs of sufficient influence that this person's mind puts out new feelers in the search for truth. That which is different about this process, taking place within the independent postconscious, is that it considers *all* essential factors, subjecting them to utterly exhaustive correlation so that when it produces an undoubted conclusion that conclusion is absolutely true. Computers are believed because they are designed for rigid accuracy and their conclusions can be checked. Post-conscious truths, being unconsciously correlated, cannot be consciously checked, but if they are consciously trusted and followed they will be found to be true, in every sense of the word, and confirmed by experience. Automated individuals like A, B, C and D, and like the stockbroker exemplified earlier, have main characteristics which are determined by their automated functions. The Machine imposes concepts and practices that shape the social framework that lays down the bases of human character. Pretending to redress the balance between the Machine and our humanity, we take up other concepts and practices, which the Machine tolerates, such as religion, or art. But these subsidiary occupations do not change the norm, nor are their best values reflected in the norm. If we wish to practice art or religion seriously we have to detach ourselves from the norm as far as possible. If humanity is to realise itself truly, every individual will have the same basic characteristics as E, as shown in Figure 16f.

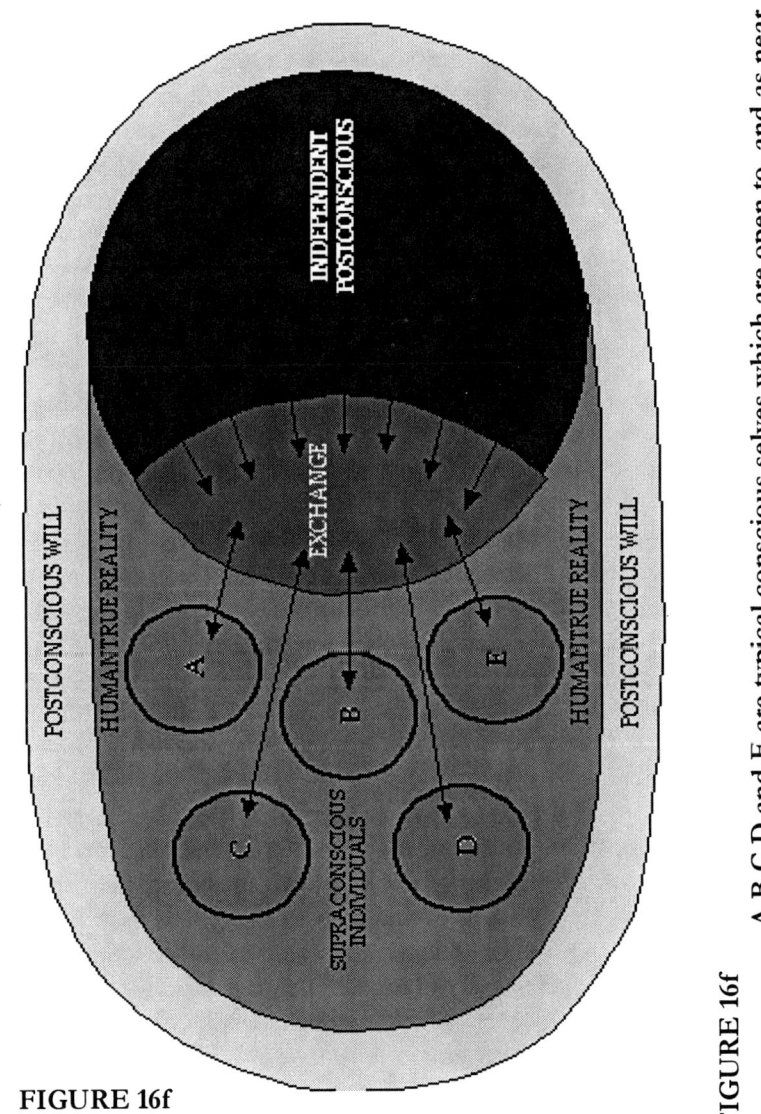

FIGURE 16f

FIGURE 16f

A,B,C,D and E are typical conscious selves which are open to, and as near as they can get to, postconscious true awareness, contributing equally to an agreed humantrue reality, and in an overall state of supraconsciousness.

Each of us will have to break away from the conscious arena and become supraconscious. We will be conscious creatures still, but able to cope with our instinctive consciousness in a detached way by virtue of submitting ourselves to the guidance of the postconscious. This will not be easy, for the automatic institutions give out all the material rewards and privileges. Independence from them brings many disadvantages and can put a strain on morale. The alternative intellater cannot also be a normally acceptable character who is well adjusted to automatic reality. Consider further the reasons why the postconscious mind is a trustworthy guide. The independent postconscious has sufficient capacity to comprehend the whole truth; it is unconscious, which means that whilst it is aware of the conscious arena and all that it contains, it is detached from consciousness and not directly influenced by the pressures of conditioning and circumstance to which A, B, C and D are continually subjected. The postconscious is able to know all that is essential, and freely and independently to reason to the ultimate, without any interference and then to present consciousness with the most important, i.e. moral conclusions whose truth is known, absolutely. Part of the process of becoming supraconscious is that we learn to recognise this absolutely known truth and to distinguish it from the part-truths of limited conscious constructions of thought.

The difference between conscious thinking and postconscious reasoning can be illustrated in this way. Mathematics is a process of calculation, every stage of which can be consciously worked out and made available as convincing argument and proven, factually true, evidence. It is a tool, with no in-built morality, which can be used for good or ill. Postconscious reasoning, on the other hand, is dedicated to truth, the living expression of which is morality. It comes before mathematics, and all other disciplines of conscious thinking, deciding whether, when, where, and in what way they may be used. Major examples of our betrayal of our postconscious faculty are our subjection to the mathematical calculations of the competitive money economy and to the logical calculations of Philosophy.

The main obstacle to conscious selves making the break and becoming supraconscious is that, being locked in the conscious arena, they are for the time being incapable of recognising whole truths, including the absolute knowing that to make this break is a vital step to becoming truly fulfilled. Having not taken this step the conscious self is able to say of known truth, with as much conviction as that self can muster, that it is false. But this won't do. It is necessary for the conscious self to make a 'leap of acceptance' - deliberately to accept as true that which it believes to be false in order to discover that absolute knowing. It is understandable - a point of honour - that 'free' individuals resist giving way to the unfamiliar ideas of others. Noam Chomsky, for example; even he expressed unwillingness to make that leap. Their convictions must come, they rightly feel, from their own minds. But without that leap of provisional acceptance - without breaking free of the conscious and opening to the postconscious - they might never discover the full and true extent of their own minds.

In the present human reality the truth is thought to be inaccessible and the human right unattainable. Facts are all-important in the conscious arena, but the individual conscious mind can contain and retain only a small proportion of them, and is incapable of fully correlating any in order to arrive at wholly true reason. As the consequence, every new event is seen in a variety of lights and interpreted in many different ways, producing reactions that constantly add to the existing confused conflict. It is only when the individual is fully informed, by a completely correlated postconscious mind, that he or she will be capable of truly evaluating anything.

Figure 16f shows a humantrue society in which all individuals are supraconscious. It is not an impracticable figment of the imagination but a logical basis for contented life by comparison with which our existing society is impracticable, and inhuman. It is not a vision of Utopia but simply a pattern of human society as it truly ought to be.

CONCLUSION

I believe that this book reveals essential humantruth. This means that there now exists a description of that truth, which is the conscious record of the findings of one postconscious mind.

The way to a new alternative society that makes the Machine redundant has now been pointed out. A first step has been taken on a new and clearly true road whose final objective is a peaceful and contented world.

Whether or not the majority of others follow, this step *has* been taken and the way *is* open.

OUR 21ST CENTURY

The present reality is a huge challenge to human individuals. We need to be fully aware of what faces us. Shall we assert our true morality with such strength and determination as to rescue the situation?

We and our planet Earth are very seriously threatened on two fronts. The first threat comes, whatever the cause, from global warming. This, it is predicted, could result in a 7 metre rise in sea levels through melting of the ice caps and is already changing weather patterns with disastrous effects on agriculture. The consequences can be imagined, with millions of displaced people miserably depending on insufficient resources of food, clean water, shelter and medical care, and upon the sympathetic care of those who escape the flooding.

The second threat to test the effectiveness of individual moral responsibility is that several mutually hostile leaders have trembling fingers on the triggers of weapons of mass destruction.

Foremost national leaders evidently wish to possess nuclear weapons, seeing them as the most effective means of defence, not to mention attack. There are 7 countries designated as possessors of these weapons, USA, Russia, UK. France, China, India, Pakistan and several others suspected of owning or developing them, including Israel, North Korea, Iran, South Africa, Japan.

It is widely thought that unless the situation somehow radically changes there will be a world nuclear war, perhaps prompted by a major terrorist attack in which nuclear devices are used. This warns that at some time soon, hatred and fear will violently erupt and an already flooded world will have multi millions more of its people killed or maimed and many of its cities reduced to rubble and radiated to the extent that they are rendered uninhabitable for thousands of years to come.

It is Machine reality, and its influence over authoritative leaderships that has brought us all to this sorry end and does not inspire confidence that these potential tragedies will be dealt with wisely and effectively.

Regrettably, it is unlikely that the peaceable actions proposed in this chapter, or the moral truths explored by the book in general, will have mounted to a high enough level to be effective against the worst actually happening. But there will be survivors of these grim disasters and it will be for them to become supraconscious and form a wiser, happier, humantrue world community in which this scale of madness can never again occur.

J.B.O 2008

Printed in the United Kingdom
by Lightning Source UK Ltd.
131651UK00001B/226-246/P